D122847

Iron Curtain

ANNE APPLEBAUM

Iron Curtain

The Crushing of Eastern Europe 1944–56

ALLEN LANE
an imprint of
PENGUIN BOOKS

ALLEN LANE

Published by the Penguin Group
Penguin Books Ltd, 80 Strand, London WC2R ORL, England
Penguin Group (USA) Inc., 375 Hudson Street, New York, New York 10014, USA
Penguin Group (Canada), 90 Eglinton Avenue East, Suite 700, Toronto, Ontario, Canada M4P 2Y3
(a division of Pearson Canada Inc.)
Penguin Ireland, 25 St Stephen's Green, Dublin 2, Ireland (a division of Penguin Books Ltd)
Penguin Group (Australia), 707 Collins Street, Melbourne, Victoria 3008, Australia
(a division of Pearson Australia Group Pty Ltd)
Penguin Books India Pvt Ltd, 11 Community Centre, Panchsheel Park, New Delhi – 110 017, India
Penguin Group (NZ), 67 Apollo Drive, Rosedale, Auckland 0632, New Zealand
(a division of Pearson New Zealand Ltd)
Penguin Books (South Africa) (Pty) Ltd, Block D, Rosebank Office Park,
181 Jan Smuts Avenue, Parktown North, Gauteng 2193, South Africa

Penguin Books Ltd, Registered Offices: 80 Strand, London WC2R ORL, England

www.penguin.com

First published 2012
004

Copyright © Anne Applebaum, 2012

The moral right of the author has been asserted

Set in 10.5/14 pt Sabon LT Std
Typeset by Jouve (UK), Milton Keynes
Printed in Great Britain by Clays Ltd, St Ives plc

HARDBACK ISBN: 978-0-713-99868-9
TRADE PAPERBACK ISBN: 978-1-846-14662-6

www.greenpenguin.co.uk

Penguin Books is committed to a sustainable
future for our business, our readers and our planet.
This book is made from Forest Stewardship
Council™ certified paper.

ALWAYS LEARNING   **PEARSON**

The loss of freedom, tyranny, abuse, hunger would all have been easier to bear if not for the compulsion to call them freedom, justice, the good of the people ... Lies, by their very nature partial and ephemeral, are revealed as lies when confronted with language's striving for truth. But here all the means of disclosure had been permanently confiscated by the police.

Aleksander Wat, My Century

Individuals need not believe all these mystifications, but they must behave as though they did, or they must at least tolerate them in silence, or get along well with those who work with them. For this reason, however, they must live within a lie.

Vaclav Havel, 'The Power of the Powerless'

This book is dedicated to those Eastern Europeans who refused to live within a lie.

Contents

PART ONE

False Dawn

PART TWO

High Stalinism

A *note about abbreviations and acronyms*

Abbreviations and acronyms were widely used to describe many different kinds of political organizations in the era described in this book – the Soviet Union had a kind of mania for them – but they can be very confusing for the general reader, particularly as they changed quite often. I have therefore avoided them as much as possible, often using 'communist party' in place of 'Polish United Workers' Party', for example, or 'communist youth group' instead of FDJ or ZMP. Still, it was impossible to avoid them altogether, and they are often used in other history books and memoirs. This is a list of the most important.

GERMAN

CDU   Christlich Demokratische Union – Christian Democratic Party

DDR   Deutsche Demokratische Republik – German Democratic Republic, also called GDR or East Germany

FDJ   Freie Deutsche Jugend – Free German Youth, the communist youth party, activated in 1946

FDP   Freie Demokratische Partei – Free Democratic Party, sometimes referred to as the Liberal Party

KPD   Kommunistische Partei Deutschlands – German communist party, founded in 1919, dissolved in the Soviet zone of Germany in 1946

SED   Sozialistische Einheitspartei Deutschlands – German Socialist Unity Party, the name of the German communist party after its unification with the Social Democratic Party in 1946

SMAD   Sowjetische Militäradministration in Deutschland –
        German name for the Soviet Administration in Germany,
        1945–9
SPD   Sozialdemokratische Partei Deutschlands – German Social
        Democratic Party, refounded in 1945, dissolved in the
        Soviet zone of Germany in 1946
SVAG   Sovietskaia Voennaia Administratsia v Germanii – Russian
        name for the Soviet Administration in Germany, 1945–9

HUNGARIAN

ÁVH   Államvédelmi Hatóság – State Protection Authority, the
        secret police from 1950 to 1956
ÁVO   Államvédelmi Osztály – State Security Agency, the secret
        police from 1945 to 1950
DISZ   Dolgozó Ifjúság Szövetsége – League of Working Youth,
        the communist youth movement, 1950–56
Kalot   Katolikus Agrárifjúsági Legényegyesületek Országos
        Testülete – National Secretariat of Catholic Agricultural
        Youth Clubs, Catholic youth organization, 1935–47
Madisz Magyar Demokratikus Ifjúsági Szövetség – Hungarian
        Democratic Youth Alliance, the communist-backed
        'umbrella' youth movement, 1944–50
MDP   Magyar Dolgozók Pártja – Hungarian Workers' Party,
        1948–56, the communist party after unification with the
        Hungarian social democrats
Mefesz Magyar Egyetemisták és Főiskolai Egyesületek Szövet-
        sége – League of Hungarian University and College
        Associations, university youth group in existence from
        1945 to 1950, revived briefly in 1956
MKP   Magyar Kommunista Párt – Hungarian communist party,
        1918–48
MSzMP   Magyar Szocialista Munkáspárt – Hungarian Socialist
        Workers' Party, the communist party, 1956–89
Nékosz Népi Kollégiumok Országos Szövetsége – National Associ-
        ation of People's Colleges, 1946–9

SZDP   Szociáldemokrata Párt – Hungarian Social Democratic Party, founded in 1890, dissolved into the MPD in 1948 after unification with the communists

POLISH

KPP   Komunistyczna Partia Polski – The Polish communist party, founded in 1918, dissolved by Stalin in 1938

KRN   Krajowa Rada Narodowa – National Council

PKWN   Polski Komitet Wyzwolenia Narodowego – Polish Committee of National Liberation

PPR   Polska Partia Robotnicza – Polish Workers' Party, the name of the resurrected Polish communist party between 1942 and 1948

PPS   Polska Partia Socjalistyczna – the Polish Socialist Party, founded in 1892, forcibly dissolved into the Polish United Workers' Party in 1948

PRL   Polska Rzeczpospolita Ludowa – People's Republic of Poland, communist Poland

PSL   Polskie Stronnictwo Ludowe – Polish Peasants' Party, founded in 1918, in opposition to the communists from 1944 to 1946, later part of the regime

PZPR   Polska Zjednoczona Partia Robotnicza – Polish United Workers' Party, the name of the Polish communist party after 1948

SB   Służba Bezpieczeństwa – Security Service, Polish secret police, 1956–90

UB   Urząd Bezpieczeństwa – Security Department, Polish secret police, 1944–56

WiN   Wolność i Niezawisłość – Freedom and Independence, the anti-communist underground from 1945 to about 1950

ZMP   Związek Młodzieży Polskiej – the Union of Polish Youth, the communist youth group from 1948 to 1957

ZWM   Związek Walki Młodych – the Union of Fighting Youth, the communist youth group from 1943 to 1948

OTHER

OUN   Orhanizatsiya Ukrayins'kykh Natsionalistiv – Organization of Ukrainian Nationalists

StB   Státní bezpečnost – State Security, Czechoslovak secret
police

UPA   Ukrayins'ka Povstans'ka Armiya – Ukrainian Insurgent
Army

Illustrations

Maps

North Sea

Baltic Sea

NETHERLANDS

BRITISH

SOVIET

Bydgoszcz •

Amsterdam ⊙

Berlin
⊙ Joint

• Poznań

G E R M A N Y

• Wittenberg

BELGIUM

Leipzig •

Brussels

Dresden •

Weimar

⊙ Prague

LUXEMBOURG

AMERICAN

CZECHOSLOVAKIA

• Brno

F R A N C E

FRENCH

Munich
•

Vienna

Bratislava

AMERICAN

SOVIET

FRENCH

A U S T R I A

Győr

Berne
⊙
SWITZERLAND

BRITISH

I T A L Y

Mediterranean Sea

Adriatic Sea

CORSICA

⊙ **Rome**

Eastern Europe, 1945

ESTONIA

SWEDEN

⊙ **Riga**

LATVIA

Baltic Sea

LITHUANIA

Kaunas

• Wilno

• Danzig

GERMANY
East Prussia

SOVIET
UNION

• Poznań

⊙ **Warsaw**

• Łódź

• Lublin

P O L A N D

G E R M A N Y

• Kraków

• Rzeszów

• Lwów

C Z E C H O S L O V A K I A

AUSTRIA

HUNGARY

ROMANIA

N
W   E
S

Poland, 1939

0   50   100   150 miles

0   100   200 km

Poland, 1945

SWEDEN

Baltic
Sea

Kaunas

Vilnius

Danzig

GERMANY

Berlin

POLAND

Poznań

Warsaw

Łódź

Lublin

SOVIET
UNION

CZECHOSLOVAKIA

Kraków

Rzeszów

L'viv

AUSTRIA

HUNGARY

ROMANIA

0   50   100   150 miles

0   100   200 km

Introduction

'From Stettin in the Baltic to Trieste in the Adriatic, an iron curtain has descended across the Continent. Behind that line lie all the capitals of the ancient states of Central and Eastern Europe. Warsaw, Berlin, Prague, Vienna, Budapest, Belgrade, Bucharest and Sofia, all these famous cities and the populations around them lie in what I must call the Soviet sphere, and all are subject in one form or another, not only to Soviet influence but to a very high and, in many cases, increasing measure of control from Moscow.'

Winston Churchill, Fulton, Missouri, 5 March 1946

Among many other things, the year 1945 marked one of the most extraordinary population movements in European history. All across the continent, hundreds of thousands of people were returning from Soviet exile, from forced labour in Germany, from concentration camps and prisoner of war camps, from hiding places and refuges of all kinds. The roads, footpaths, tracks and trains were crammed full of ragged, hungry, dirty people.

The scenes in the railway stations were particularly horrific to behold. Starving mothers, sick children and sometimes entire families camped on filthy cement floors for days on end, waiting for the next available train. Epidemics and starvation threatened to engulf them. But in the city of Łodz, in central Poland, a group of women determined to prevent further tragedy. Led by former members of the Liga Kobiet, the Polish Women's League, a charitable and patriotic organization founded in 1913, the women got to work. At the Łodz train station, Women's League activists set up a shelter for women and children, supplying them with hot food, medicine and blankets, as well as volunteers and nurses.

In the spring of 1945, the motives of these women were the same as they would have been in 1925 or 1935. They were witnesses to a social emergency. They organized themselves in order to help. No one asked them, ordered them, or paid them to do so. Janina Suska, in her late eighties when I met her, told me that she remembered these early efforts in Łodz as completely apolitical: 'No one received money for charitable work . . . everyone who had a free minute helped.'[1] Beyond aiding desperate travellers, the Łodz Women's League, in its initial incarnation, had no political agenda.

Five years passed. By 1950, the Polish Women's League had become something very different. It had a Warsaw headquarters. It had a centralized, national governing body, which could and did dissolve local branches that failed to follow orders. It had a General Secretary, Izolda Kowalska-Kiryluk, who described the League's primary tasks not in charitable, patriotic terms, but using political, ideological language: 'We must deepen our organizational work and mobilize a broad group of active women, educating and shaping them into conscious social activists. Every day we must raise the level of women's social consciousness and join the grand assignment of the social reconstruction of People's Poland into Socialist Poland.'

The Women's League also held national congresses, like the one in 1951 where Zofia Wasilkowska, then the organization's vice-president, openly laid out a political agenda: 'The League's main, statutory form of activism is educational, enlightening work . . . increasing women's consciousness to an incomparably higher level and mobilizing women to the most complete realization of the goals of the Six-Year Plan.'[2]

By 1950, in other words, the Polish Women's League had effectively become the women's section of the Polish communist party. In this capacity, the League encouraged women to follow the party's line in matters of politics and international relations. It encouraged women to march in May Day parades and to sign petitions denouncing Western imperialism. It employed teams of agitators, who attended courses and learned how to spread the party's message further. Anyone who objected to any of this – anyone who refused, for example, to march in the May Day parades or attend the celebrations for Stalin's birthday –

could be kicked out of the Women's League, and some were. Others resigned. Those who remained were no longer volunteers but bureaucrats, working in the service of the state and the communist party.

Five years had passed. In those five years, the Polish Women's League and countless organizations like it had undergone a total transformation. What had happened? Who had caused the changes? Why did anyone go along with them? The answers to those questions are the subject of this book.

Although it has been most often used to describe Nazi Germany and Stalin's Soviet Union, the word 'totalitarian' – *totalitarismo* – was first used in the context of Italian fascism. Invented by one of his critics, it was a term Benito Mussolini adopted with enthusiasm, and in one of his speeches offered what is still the best definition of the term: *Everything within the state, nothing outside the state, nothing against the state*.[3] Strictly defined, a totalitarian regime is one which bans all institutions apart from those it has officially approved. A totalitarian regime thus has one political party, one educational system, one artistic creed, one centrally planned economy, one unified media and one moral code. In a totalitarian state there are no independent schools, no private businesses, no grassroots organizations and no critical thought. Mussolini and his favourite philosopher, Giovanni Gentile, once wrote of a 'conception of the State' which is 'all-embracing; outside of it no human or spiritual values can exist, much less have value'.[4]

From Italian, the word 'totalitarianism' spread into all the languages of Europe and the world. After Mussolini's demise the concept had few open advocates, however, and the word eventually came to be defined by its critics, many of whom number among the twentieth century's greatest thinkers.[5] Friedrich Hayek's *Road to Serfdom* is a philosophical response to the challenge of totalitarianism, as is Karl Popper's *The Open Society and Its Enemies*. George Orwell's *Nineteen Eighty-Four* is a dystopian vision of a world entirely dominated by totalitarian regimes.

Probably the greatest student of totalitarian politics was Hannah Arendt, who defined totalitarianism in her 1949 book, *The Origins of Totalitarianism*, as a 'novel form of government' made possible by the onset of modernity. The destruction of traditional societies and ways of life had, she argued, created the conditions for the evolution of the 'totalitarian personality', men and women whose identities were entirely dependent on the state. Famously, Arendt argued that Nazi Germany and the Soviet Union were both totalitarian regimes, and as such were more similar than different.[6] Carl J. Friedrich and Zbigniew Brzezinski pushed that argument further in *Totalitarian Dictatorship and Autocracy*, published in 1956, and also sought a more operational definition. Totalitarian regimes, they declared, all had at least five things in common: a dominant ideology, a single ruling party, a secret police force prepared to use terror, a monopoly on information and a planned economy. By those criteria, the Soviet and Nazi regimes were not the only totalitarian states. Others – Mao's China, for example – qualified too.[7]

But in the late 1940s and early 1950s, 'totalitarianism' was more than just a theoretical concept. During the early years of the Cold War, the term acquired concrete political associations as well. In a pivotal speech in 1947, President Harry Truman declared that Americans must be 'willing to help free peoples to maintain their free institutions and their national integrity against aggressive movements that seek to impose upon them totalitarian regimes'.[8] This idea became known as 'the Truman Doctrine'. President Dwight Eisenhower also used the term during his 1952 presidential campaign, when he declared his intention to go to Korea and bring an end to the war there: 'I know something of this totalitarian mind. Through the years of World War II, I carried a heavy burden of decision in the free world's crusade against the tyranny then threatening us all.'[9]

Because American Cold Warriors openly positioned themselves as opponents of totalitarianism, Cold War sceptics naturally began to question the term, and to ask what it meant. Was 'totalitarianism' a real threat, or was it merely an exaggeration, a bogeyman, an invention of Senator Joseph McCarthy? Throughout the 1970s and 1980s, revisionist historians of the USSR argued that even Stalin's Soviet Union had never really been totalitarian at all. They claimed that not all decisions in the Soviet Union were really taken in Moscow; that local police were just as likely to initiate terror as those at the top of the hierarchy; that central planners were not always successful in their attempts to control the economy; that mass terror had created 'opportunities' for many in society.[10] Among some, the term 'totalitarian' came to be seen as crude, imprecise and overly ideological.

In fact, many of the 'orthodox' theorists of totalitarianism had made a number of the same points. Few had claimed that totalitarianism worked. On the contrary, 'because totalitarian rule strives for the impossible and wants to place at its disposal the personality of man and destiny, it can be realized only in a fragmentary manner,' wrote Friedrich: 'This is precisely why the consequences of the totalitarian claim to power are so dangerous and oppressive, because they are so hazy, so incalculable, and so difficult to demonstrate . . . This contortion follows from the unfulfillable aspiration to power: it characterizes life under such a regime and makes it so exceedingly difficult for all outsiders to grasp.'[11]

Political theorists in more recent years have taken this revisionist argument further. Some have argued that the term 'totalitarian' is truly useful only in theory, as a negative template against which liberal democrats can define themselves.[12] Others find the word altogether meaningless, explaining that it has become a term which means nothing more than 'the theoretical antithesis of Western society', or else simply 'people we don't like'. A more sinister interpretation holds that the word 'totalitarianism' is self-serving: we use it only in order to enhance the legitimacy of Western democracy.[13]

In popular speech, the word totalitarian isn't so much self-serving as overused. Democratically elected politicians are described as totalitarian (e.g. 'Rick Santorum's Totalitarian Instincts'), as are governments or even companies (one can read of 'The US's march towards totalitarianism' or learn that Apple has a 'totalitarian approach to its app store').[14] Libertarians, from Ayn Rand onwards, have used the word to describe progressive liberals. Progressive liberals (and indeed conservatives) have used the word to describe Ayn Rand.[15] The word is nowadays applied to so many people and institutions that it can sometimes seem meaningless.

Yet although the very idea of 'total control' may now seem ludicrous, ridiculous, exaggerated or silly, and although the word itself may have lost its capacity to shock, it is important to remember that 'totalitarianism' is more than an ill-defined insult. Historically, there were regimes which aspired to total control. If we are to understand them – if we are to understand the history of the twentieth century – we need to understand how totalitarianism worked, in theory and in practice. Nor is the notion of total control completely old-fashioned. The North Korean regions set up along Stalinist lines, has changed little in seventy years. Though new technology now seems to make the notion of total control harder to aim for, let alone achieve, we can't be certain that mobile phones, the internet and satellite photographs won't eventually become tools of control in the hands of regimes which also aspire to be 'all-embracing'.[16] 'Totalitarianism' remains a useful and necessary empirical description. It is long overdue for a revival.

One regime in particular understood the methods and techniques of totalitarian control so well that it successfully exported them: following the end of the Second World War and the Red Army's march to Berlin, the leadership of the Soviet Union did try very hard to impose a totalitarian system of government on the very different European countries it then occupied, just as they had already tried to impose a totalitarian system on the many different regions of the USSR itself. Their efforts were in lethal earnest. Stalin, his military officers and his secret policemen – known from 1934 to 1946 as the People's Commissariat for Internal Affairs (Narodnyi Komisssariat Vnutrenikh Del or NKVD) and only later as the KGB – and his local allies were not trying to make a point about Ayn Rand or progressive liberals when they created the totalitarian states of Eastern Europe. To paraphrase Mussolini, they wanted very much to create societies where everything was within the state, nothing was outside the state and nothing was against the state – and they wanted to do it quickly.

True, the eight European countries which the Red Army occupied in 1945, in whole or in part, had vastly different cultures, political traditions and economic structures. The new territories included formerly democratic Czechoslovakia, formerly fascist Germany, as well as monarchies, autocracies and semi-feudal states. The inhabitants of the region were Catholic, Orthodox, Protestant, Jewish and Muslim. They spoke Slavic languages, Romance languages, Finno-Ugric languages and German. They included Russophiles and Russophobes; industrialized Bohemia and rural Albania; cosmopolitan Berlin and tiny wooden villages in the Carpathian mountains. Among them were former subjects of the Austro-Hungarian, Prussian and Ottoman empires, as well as the Russian empire.

Nevertheless, Americans and West Europeans in this period came to see the nations of communist-dominated but non-Soviet Europe – Poland, Hungary, Czechoslovakia, eastern Germany, Romania, Bulgaria, Albania and Yugoslavia –as a 'bloc', which eventually became known as 'Eastern Europe'. This is a political and historical term, not a geographic one. It does not include 'eastern' countries such as Greece, which was never a communist country. Neither does it include the Baltic states or Moldova, which although historically and culturally similar to Eastern Europe were in this period actually incorporated into the Soviet Union. There are similarities between the experiences of the Baltic states and those of Poland in particular, but there were also important differences: Sovietization, for the Balts, meant the loss even of nominal sovereignty.

In the years following Stalin's death – since 1989 in particular – the eight nations of Eastern Europe took very different paths, and it has become routine to observe that they never really had much in common in the first place. This is absolutely true: before 1945, they had never previously been unified in any way, and they have startlingly little in common now, aside from a common historical memory of communism. Yet for a time, between 1945 and 1989, the eight nations of Eastern Europe did share a great deal. For the sake of simplicity, familiarity and historical accuracy I will therefore use the term 'Eastern Europe' to describe them throughout this book.[17]

Very briefly, between 1945 and 1953, it did seem as if the USSR would succeed in turning the widely varying nations of Eastern Europe into an ideologically and politically homogeneous region. From Hitler's enemies and Hitler's allies they did, during this period, create a clutch of apparently identical polities.[18] By the early 1950s, all the grey, war-damaged capitals of the 'ancient states' of the region, to use Churchill's phrase, were patrolled by the same kinds of unsmiling policemen, designed by the same socialist realist architects and draped with the same kinds of propaganda posters. The cult of Stalin, whose very name was venerated in the USSR as a 'symbol of the coming victory of communism', was observed across the region, along with very similar cults of local party leaders.[19] Millions of people took part in state-orchestrated parades and celebrations of communist power. At the time, the phrase 'Iron Curtain' seemed much more than a metaphor: walls, fences and barbed wire literally separated Eastern Europe from the West. By 1961, the year in which the Berlin Wall was built, it seemed as if these barriers could last for ever.

The speed with which this transformation took place was, in retrospect, nothing short of astonishing. In the Soviet Union itself, the evolution of a totalitarian state had taken two decades, and it had proceeded in fits and starts. The Bolsheviks did not begin with a blueprint. In the wake of the Russian Revolution, they pursued a zigzag course, sometimes harsher and sometimes more liberal, as one policy after another failed to deliver promised economic gains. The collectivist 'war communism' and 'red terror' policies of the Russian Civil War era were followed by Lenin's more liberal New Economic Policy, which permitted some private business and trade. The New Economic Policy was in turn abolished in 1928 and replaced by a Five Year Plan and a new set of policies which eventually became known as Stalinism: a push for faster industrialization, forced collectivization, centralized planning, draconian restrictions on speech, literature, the media and the arts, and the expansion of the Gulag, the system of mass forced labour camps. The phrases 'Stalinism' and 'totalitarianism' are often used interchangeably, and rightly so.

But by the late 1930s Stalinism was in crisis too. Standards of living were not improving as fast as the party had promised. Poorly planned investments were beginning to backfire. Mass starvation in Ukraine and southern Russia in the early 1930s, while of some political utility to the regime, had created fear rather than admiration. In 1937, the Soviet secret police launched a public campaign of arrests, imprisonments and executions, initially directed at the saboteurs, spies and 'wreckers' who were allegedly blocking society's progress, and eventually spreading to include the highest circles of the Soviet communist party. The Great Terror was neither the first wave of arrests in the Soviet Union nor the largest – earlier bouts of terror had been largely aimed at peasants and ethnic minorities, especially those living near the Soviet border. But it was the first to be directed at the highest party leadership, and it caused profound disquiet, at home and among communists abroad. In due course, the Great Terror might have led to real disillusion. But Stalinism – and Stalin – was fortuitously rescued by the Second World War. Despite the chaos and mistakes, despite mass deaths and vast destruction, victory bolstered the legitimacy of the system and its leader, 'proving' their worth. In the wake of the victory, the near-religious cult of Stalin reached new heights. Propaganda described the Soviet leader as 'the incarnation of their own heroism, their own patriotism, their own devotion to their socialist Motherland'.[20]

At the same time, the war gave Stalin an unprecedented opportunity to impose his particular vision of communist society on his neighbours. The first opportunity came at the very beginning, in 1939, after the Soviet Union and Nazi Germany signed the Molotov–Ribbentrop pact and agreed to divide Poland, Romania, Finland and the Baltic states into Soviet and German spheres of influence. On 1 September, Hitler invaded Poland from the west. On 17 September, Stalin invaded Poland from the east. Within a few months, Soviet troops had occupied the Baltic states, parts of Romania and eastern Finland as well. Although Nazi-occupied Europe was eventually liberated, Stalin never gave back the territories he occupied in this first phase of the war. Eastern Poland, eastern Finland, the Baltic nations, Bukovina and Bessarabia, now called Moldova, were incorporated into the Soviet Union. The eastern Polish territories remain part of Ukraine and Belarus today.

In their zone of occupation, Red Army officers and NKVD officers immediately began to impose their own system. From 1939 onwards, they used local collaborators, members of the international communist movement, mass violence and mass deportations to the concentration camps of the Gulag to 'Sovietize' the local population. Stalin learned valuable lessons from this experience, and gained valuable allies: the Soviet invasion of eastern Poland and the Baltic states in 1939 produced a cadre of NKVD officers ready and willing to repeat it. Immediately, even before the Nazi invasion of the USSR in 1941, Soviet authorities began to prepare the ground for a similar transformation of Eastern Europe.

This last point is controversial. For in the standard historiography, the region's postwar history is usually divided into phases.[21] First there was genuine democracy, in 1944-5; then bogus democracy, as Hugh Seton-Watson once wrote; and then, in 1947-8, an abrupt policy shift and a full-fledged takeover: political terror was stepped up, the media muzzled, elections manipulated. All pretence of national autonomy was abandoned.

Some historians and political scientists have since blamed this change in political atmosphere on the onset of the Cold War, with which it coincided. Sometimes, this onset of Stalinism in Eastern Europe is even blamed on Western Cold Warriors, whose aggressive rhetoric allegedly 'forced' the Soviet leader to tighten his grip on the region. In 1959, this general 'revisionist' argument was given its classic form by William Appleman Williams, who argued that the Cold War had been caused not by communist expansion but by the American drive for open international markets. More recently, a prominent German scholar has argued that the division of Germany was caused not by the Soviet pursuit of totalitarian policies in Eastern Germany after 1945, but by the Western powers' failure to take advantage of Stalin's peaceful overtures.[22]

Any close examination of what was happening on the ground across the region between 1944 and 1947 reveals the deep flaws of these arguments – and, thanks to the availability of Soviet as well as Eastern European archives, a close examination is now possible.[23] New sources have helped historians understand that this early 'liberal' period was, in reality, not quite so liberal as it sometimes appeared in retrospect. True, not every element of the Soviet political system was imported into the region as soon as the Red Army crossed the borders, and indeed there is no evidence that Stalin expected to create a communist 'bloc' very quickly. In 1944, his Foreign Minister, Ivan Maiskii, wrote a note predicting that the nations of Europe would eventually all become communist states, but only after three or perhaps four decades. (He also foresaw that in the Europe of the future there should be only one land power, the USSR, and one sea power, Great Britain.) In the meantime, Maiskii thought the Soviet Union should not try to foment 'proletarian revolutions' in Eastern Europe and should try to maintain good relations with the Western democracies.[24]

This long-term view was certainly in accordance with Marxist-Leninist ideology as Stalin understood it. Capitalists, he believed, would not be able to cooperate with one another for ever. Sooner or later their greedy imperialism would lead them into conflict, and the Soviet Union would benefit. 'The contradictions between England and America are still to be felt,' he told colleagues a few months after the war's end. 'The social conflicts in America are increasingly unfolding. The Labourites in England have promised the English workers so much concerning socialism that it is hard for them now to step back. They will soon have conflicts not only with their bourgeoisie, but also with the American imperialists.'[25]

If the USSR was not in a rush, neither were the Eastern European communist leaders, few of whom expected to take power immediately. In the 1930s, many had participated in 'national front' coalitions together with centrist and socialist parties – or had watched as national front coalitions were successful in a number of countries, most notably Spain and France. The historian Tony Judt has even described Spain as 'a dry run for the seizure of power in Eastern Europe after 1945'.[26] These original national front coalitions had been created to oppose Hitler. In the war's aftermath, many prepared to re-create them in order to oppose Western capitalism. Stalin took a long-term view: the protelarian revolution would take place in due course, but before that could happen, the region first had to have a bourgeois revolution. According to the schematic Soviet interpretation of history, the necessary bourgeois revolution had not yet taken place.

Yet as Part One of this book will explain, the Soviet Union did import certain key elements of the Soviet system into every nation occupied by the Red Army, from the very beginning. First and foremost, the Soviet NKVD, in collaboration with local communist parties, immediately created a secret police force in its own image, often using people whom they had already trained in Moscow. Everywhere the Red Army went – even in Czechoslovakia, from which Soviet troops eventually withdrew – these newly minted secret policemen immediately began to use selective violence, carefully targeting their political enemies according to previously composed lists and criteria. In some cases, they targeted enemy ethnic groups as well. They also took control of the region's Interior Ministries, and in some cases the Defence Ministries as well, and participated in the immediate confiscation and redistribution of land.

Secondly, in every occupied nation, Soviet authorities placed trusted local communists in charge of the era's most powerful form of mass media: the radio. Although it was possible, in most of Eastern Europe, to publish non-communist newspapers or magazines in the initial months after the war, and although non-communists were allowed to run other state monopolies, the national radio stations, which could reach everyone from illiterate peasants to sophisticated intellectuals, were kept under firm communist party control. In the long term, the authorities hoped that the radio, together with other propaganda and changes to the educational system, would help bring mass numbers of people into the communist camp.

Thirdly, everywhere the Red Army went, Soviet and local communists harassed, persecuted and eventually banned many of the independent organizations of what we would now call civil society: the Polish Women's League, the German 'anti-fascist' groupings, church groups and schools. In particular, they were fixated, from the very first days of the occupation, on youth groups: young social democrats, young Catholic or Protestant organizations, boy scouts and girl scouts. Even before they banned independent political parties for adults, and even before they outlawed church organizations and independent trade unions, they put young people's organizations under the strictest possible observation and restraint.

Finally, wherever it was possible, Soviet authorities, again in conjunction with local communist parties, carried out policies of mass ethnic cleansing, displacing millions of Germans, Poles, Ukrainians, Hungarians and others from towns and villages where they had lived for centuries. Trucks and trains moved people and a few scant possessions into refugee camps and new homes hundreds of miles away from where they had been born. Disoriented and displaced, the refugees were easier to manipulate and control than they might have been otherwise. To some degree, the United States and Britain were complicit in this policy – ethnic cleansing of the Germans would be written into the Potsdam treaty – but few in the West understood at the time how extensive and violent Soviet ethnic cleansing would turn out to be.

Other elements of capitalism and even liberalism did remain in place for a time. Private farming, private business and private trade persisted throughout 1945 and 1946, and sometimes longer. Some independent newspapers and journals kept publishing and some churches remained open. In some places, non-communist political parties were also allowed to function, along with selected non-communist politicians. But this is not because the Soviet communists and their Eastern European allies were liberal-minded democrats. This is because they thought that these things were less important, in the short term, than the secret police, the radio, ethnic cleansing, and the domination of youth groups and other civic organizations. It was not a coincidence that ambitious young communists invariably went to work in one of these areas. Upon joining the party in 1945, the communist writer Wiktor Woroszylski was offered three choices: the communist youth movement, the secret police and the propaganda department, which dealt with mass media.[27]

Free elections held in some countries in 1945 and 1946 were not a sign of communist tolerance either. The Soviet and Eastern European communist parties allowed these elections to happen because they thought that with control over the secret police and the radio, and with heavy influence over young people, they would win. Communists everywhere believed in the power of their own propaganda, and in the first years after the war's end they had some good reasons for that belief. People did join the party after the war, whether out of despair, disorientation, pragmatism, cynicism or ideology, not only in Eastern Europe but in France, Italy and Britain. In Yugoslavia, Tito's communist party was genuinely popular, thanks to its role in the resistance. In Czechoslovakia – occupied by Hitler in 1938, thanks to the appeasement of the West – real hopes were at first placed in the Soviet Union, which the Czechoslovaks hoped would be a more sympathetic power. Even in Poland and Germany, countries where suspicion of Soviet motives was strong, the psychological impact of the war also shaped many people's perceptions. Capitalism and liberal democracy had failed catastrophically in the 1930s. Many believed it was now time to try something different.

Hard though it is sometimes for us to understand, communists also believed their own doctrine. Just because communist ideology now seems wrongheaded in retrospect, that doesn't mean it didn't inspire fervent belief at the time. The majority of communist leaders in Eastern

Europe – and many of their followers – really did think that sooner or later the working-class majority would acquire class consciousness, understand its historical destiny, and vote for a communist regime.

They were wrong. Despite intimidation, despite propaganda and despite even the real attraction communism held for some people devastated by the war, communist parties lost early elections in Germany, Austria and Hungary by large margins. In Poland, the communists tested the ground with a referendum, and when that went badly its leaders abandoned free elections altogether. In Czechoslovakia, the communist party did well in an initial set of elections, in 1946, winning a third of the vote. But when it became clear that it would do much worse in subsequent elections in 1948, party leaders staged a coup. The harsher policies imposed upon the Eastern bloc in 1947 and 1948 were therefore not merely, and certainly not only, a reaction to the Cold War. They were also a reaction to failure. The Soviet Union and its local allies had failed to win power peacefully. They had failed to achieve absolute or even adequate control. Despite their influence over the radio and the secret police, they were not popular or universally admired. The number of their followers was shrinking rapidly, even in countries like Czechoslovakia and Bulgaria, where they had initially had some genuine support.[28]

As a result, the local communists, advised by their Soviet allies, resorted to harsher tactics which had been used previously – and successfully – in the USSR. The second part of this book describes those techniques: a new wave of arrests, the expansion of labour camps, much tighter control over the media, intellectuals and the arts. Certain patterns were followed almost everywhere: first the elimination of 'right-wing' or anti-communist parties, then the destruction of the non-communist left, then the elimination of opposition within the communist party itself. In some countries, communist authorities even conducted show trials very much along Soviet lines. Eventually the region's communist parties would attempt to eliminate all remaining independent organizations; to recruit followers into state-run mass organizations instead; to establish much harsher controls over education; to subvert the Catholic and Protestant churches. They created new, all-encompassing forms of educational propaganda, sponsored public parades and lectures, hung banners and posters, organized petition-signing campaigns and sporting events.

But they would fail again. Following Stalin's death in 1953, a series of minor and major rebellions broke out across the region. In 1953, East Berliners staged a protest which ended with Soviet tanks. Two major uprisings followed in 1956, in Poland and Hungary. In the wake of those uprisings the East European communists would moderate their tactics once again. They would continue to fail – and continue to change tactics – until they finally gave up power altogether in 1989.

Between 1945 and 1953, the Soviet Union radically transformed an entire region, from the Baltic to the Adriatic, from the heart of the European continent to its southern and eastern peripheries. But in this book, I will focus on Central Europe. Though referring to Czechoslovakia, Romania and Bulgaria as well as Yugoslavia, I will focus in particular on Hungary, Poland and Eastern Germany. I have chosen these three countries not because they were similar, but because they were so very different.

Above all, they had different experiences of war. Germany had, of course, been the main aggressor and then the biggest loser. Poland had fought hard against German occupation and was one of the Allies, although it did not share in the fruits of victory. Hungary had played a role somewhere in between, experimenting with authoritarianism, collaborating with Germany, trying to switch sides and then finding it was too late. These three countries also had very different historical experiences. Germany had been the dominant economic and political power in Central Europe for decades. Poland, although a continental empire through the seventeenth century, had been partitioned by three other empires in the eighteenth century and lost its sovereignty in 1795, regaining it only in 1918. Hungary's power and influence had meanwhile peaked in the early part of the twentieth century. After the First World War, Hungary lost two thirds of its territory, an experience so traumatic that it has echoes in Hungarian politics even today.

None of the three had been democratic, strictly speaking, in the period immediately preceding the war. But they all had experience of political liberalism, constitutional government and elections. All had stock markets, foreign investment, limited companies, and laws protecting property rights. All had civic institutions – churches, youth organizations, trade associations – dating back hundreds of years, as well as long traditions of press, printing and publication. Poland's first newspaper had appeared in 1661. Germans had produced an enormous array of competing media before Hitler's rise to power in 1933. All had elaborate economic and cultural ties to Western Europe, far stronger in the 1930s than their ties to Russia. Nothing in their history or their culture automatically destined them to become totalitarian dictatorships. Western Germany, although culturally identical to Eastern Germany, became a liberal democracy as did Austria, which had long been part of the Habsburg Empire alongside Czechoslovakia and Hungary.

History sometimes looks inevitable in retrospect, and in the decades following the imposition of communism some sought post-hoc rationales for the Eastern European communist regimes. The eastern half of the continent was said to be poorer than the western half (except, of course, that Germany wasn't); the nations of the region were said to be less developed (except that by comparison to Greece, Spain and Portugal, Hungary and Poland weren't) or less industrialized (except that the Czech lands were among the most industrialized in Europe). But from the perspective of 1945, no one looking forward foresaw that Hungary, with its long ties to the German-speaking lands in the West; Poland, with its fierce anti-Bolshevik tradition; or eastern Germany, with its Nazi past, would remain under Soviet political control for nearly half a century.

When they did fall under Soviet political control, few outside the region understood what happened and why. Even now, many continue to see Eastern Europe solely through the prism of the Cold War. With some exceptions, Western books about postwar Eastern Europe have most often focused on East–West conflict; on Germany's division ('The German Question'); and on the creation of NATO and the Warsaw Pact.[29] Hannah Arendt herself dismissed the region's postwar history as uninteresting: 'It was as though the Russian rulers repeated in great haste all the stages of the October revolution up to the emergence of totalitarian dictatorship; the story, therefore, while unspeakably terrible, is without much interest of its own and varies very little.'[30]

But Arendt was wrong: 'the Russian rulers' did not follow the convoluted stages of the October Revolution in Eastern Europe. They applied only those techniques which they knew had a chance of success, and they undermined only those institutions which they believed it absolutely necessary to destroy. This is why their story is so full of interest: it tells us more about the totalitarian mindset, Soviet priorities and Soviet thinking than would any study of Soviet history on its own. More importantly, a study of the region tells us more about the ways in which human beings react to the imposition of totalitarianism than would a study of any one country on its own.

In more recent years, a wide range of scholars have begun to acknowledge this. In the two decades since the collapse of communism and the opening of archives across Central Europe, Germany and Russia, an enormous amount of academic work has been devoted to the region. Particularly well covered, in the Anglophone world, are the physical and human consequences of the Second World War – notably in the work of Jan Gross, Timothy Snyder and Bradley Abrams – as well as the history of ethnic cleansing in the region.[31] The international politics of the region are even better understood. Whole institutes now devote themselves to the study of the origins of the Cold War and the US–Soviet conflict.[32] I have mostly relied on secondary sources when discussing these subjects.

The same is true of the political history of Eastern Europe, which has been very well told using archival sources in regional languages. I have not tried to replicate the work of excellent historians such as Andrzej Paczkowski and Krystyna Kersten, whose writings on the Polish communist leadership and secret police remain unsurpassed; Norman Naimark, whose book on the Soviet occupation of East Germany is the definitive work in English; Peter Kenez and László Borhi, who have written superb accounts of the political machinations in Hungary; Bradley Abrams, Mary Heimann and Karel Kaplan, who have described the period in Czechoslovakia.[33] Certain more defined topics have also been the focus of excellent articles and full-length books. Among the best, again in English, I would include John Connelly on the Stalinization of Eastern European universities; Catherine Epstein and Marci Shore on communists and left-wing intellectuals; Mária Schmidt on the show trials; Martin Mevius on national symbolism in Hungary; Mark Kramer on de-Stalinization and the events of 1956.[34]

General histories of the region as a whole are much rarer, if only because of the logistical difficulties. It's not easy to find a historian who reads three or four of the regional languages, let alone nine or ten. Anthologies are often the answer and there are at least two very good recent ones: *Stalinism Revisited: The Establishment of Communist Regimes in East-Central Europe and the Dynamic of the Soviet Bloc* (New York and Budapest, 2009), edited by Vladimir Tismaneau, and *The Establishment of Communist Regimes in Eastern Europe, 1944–1949*, edited by Norman Naimark and Leonid Gibianskii (Boulder, Colo., 1997). But though both volumes contain excellent essays, anthologies don't necessarily look for patterns or make comparisons. Since I wanted to do exactly that, I had the assistance of two superb researchers and translators, both writers in their own right, while working on this book, Regine Wosnitza in Berlin and Attila Mong in Budapest. I relied on my own knowledge of Polish and Russian.

Although much has been written about this period, there are still many, many untold stories. While preparing to write this book, I worked in former secret police archives – IPN in Warsaw, ÁBTL in Hungary, BStU (the Stasi archive) in Berlin – as well as the archives of government ministries, German art academies, the Hungarian film institute, East German and Polish radio, just to name a few. I also made use of several new, or relatively new, collections of Soviet documents on the period. These include the two volumes of *Vostochnaya Evropa v dokumentakh rossiskikh arkhivov, 1944–1953* (*Eastern Europe in Documents from the Russian Archives 1944–1953*), as well as the two volumes of *Sovetskii faktor v vostochnoi evrope, 1944–1953* (*The Soviet Factor in Eastern Europe 1944–1953*) and a three-volume series on Soviet occupation policy in Eastern Germany, all published in Moscow with Russian editors, as well as a seven-volume series published by the Russian state archive, on the same topic.[35] A joint commission of Polish and Ukrainian historians have now put together an imposing series of documents on their mutual history. In addition, the Polish Military Archive in Warsaw has a large collection of documents copied from Russian archives in the early 1990s. The Central

European University Press has also published two excellent document collections on the uprisings in Germany in 1953 and Hungary in 1956. A wide range of documents has been published in Polish, Hungarian and German as well.

In addition to consulting archives, I conducted a series of interviews in Poland, Hungary and Germany, in order to learn from people who actually lived through this period, and to hear them describe the events and the emotions of that time using their own language. I am very conscious that this may have been the last possible moment for such a project, and in the course of my writing this book several people whom I interviewed in the early stages passed away. I remain extremely grateful to them and to their families for allowing me to ask them extensive questions at that stage in their lives.

The goals of this research were varied. In the documents of the period, I sought evidence of the deliberate destruction of civil society and small business. I investigated the phenomena of social realism and communist education. I gathered as much information as possible on the founding and early development of the region's secret police. Through both reading and conversations, I sought to understand how ordinary people learned to cope with the new regimes; how they collaborated, willingly or reluctantly; how and why they joined the party and other state institutions; how they resisted, actively or passively; how they came to make terrible choices that most of us in the West, nowadays, never have to face. Above all, I sought to gain an understanding of real totalitarianism – not totalitarianism in theory, but totalitarianism in practice – and how it shaped the lives of millions of Europeans in the twentieth century.

PART ONE

False Dawn

I

Zero hour

The mad orgy of ruins, entangled wires, twisted corpses, dead horses, overturned parts of blown-up bridges, bloody hoofs which had been torn off horses, broken guns, scattered ammunition, chamber pots, rusted washbasins, pieces of straw and entrails of horses floating in muddy pools mixed with blood, cameras, wrecked cars and tank parts: They all bear witness to the awful suffering of a city ...

Tamás Lossonczy, Budapest, 1945[1]

How can one find words to convey truthfully and accurately the picture of a great capital destroyed almost beyond recognition; of a once almighty nation that ceased to exist; of a conquering people who were so brutally arrogant and so blindingly sure of their mission as a master race ... whom you now see poking about their ruins, broken, dazed, shivering, hungry human beings without will or purpose or direction.

William Shirer, Berlin, 1945[2]

It seemed to me that I was walking on corpses, that at any moment I would step into a pool of blood.

Janina Godycka-Cwirko, Warsaw, 1945[3]

Explosions echoed throughout the night, and artillery fire could be heard throughout the day. Across Eastern Europe, the noise of falling bombs, rattling machine guns, rolling tanks, churning engines and burning buildings heralded the approach of the Red Army. As the frontline drew closer, the ground shook, the walls shivered, the children screamed. And then it stopped.

The end of the war, wherever and whenever it came, brought with it an abrupt and eerie silence. 'The night was far too quiet,' wrote one anonymous chronicler of the war's end in Berlin.[4] On the morning of 27 April 1945, she went out of her front door, and saw no one: 'Not a civilian in sight. The Russians have the streets entirely to themselves. But under every building people are whispering, quaking. Who could ever imagine such a world, hidden here, so frightened, right in the middle of the big city?'

On the morning of 12 February 1945, the day the siege of the city came to an end, a Hungarian civil servant heard the same silence on the streets of Budapest. 'I got to the Castle District, not a soul anywhere. I walked along Werbőczy Street. Nothing but bodies and ruins, supply carts, and drays . . . I got to Szentháromság Square and decided to look in at the Council in case I found somebody there. Deserted. Everything turned upside down and not a soul . . .'[5]

Even Warsaw, a city already destroyed by the time the war ended – the Nazi occupiers had razed it to the ground following the uprising in the autumn – grew silent when the German army finally retreated on 16 January 1945. Władysław Szpilman, one of a tiny handful of people hiding in the ruins of the city, heard the change. 'Silence fell,' he wrote in his memoir, *The Pianist*, 'a silence such as even Warsaw, a dead city for the last three months, had not known before. I could not even hear the steps of the guards outside the building. I couldn't understand it.' The following morning, the silence was broken by a 'loud and resonant noise, the last sound I expected': the Red Army had arrived, and loudspeakers were broadcasting, in Polish, the news of the liberation of the city.[6]

This was the moment sometimes called zero hour, *Stunde Null*: the end of the war, the retreat of Germany, the arrival of the Soviet Union, the moment the fighting ended and life started up again. Most histories of the communist takeover of Eastern Europe begin at precisely this moment, and logically so.[7] To those who lived through this change of power, zero hour felt like a turning point: something very concrete came to an end, and something very new began. From now on, many people said to themselves, everything would be different. And it was.

Yet although it is logical to begin any history of the communist takeover in Eastern Europe with the end of the war, it is in some ways deeply misleading. The people of the region were not faced with a blank slate in 1944 or 1945, after all, and they were not themselves starting from scratch. Nor did they emerge from nowhere, with no previous experiences, ready to start afresh. Instead, they climbed out of the basements of their destroyed homes, or walked out of the forests where they had been living as partisans, or slipped away from the labour camp where they had been imprisoned, if they were healthy enough, and embarked upon long, complicated journeys back to their homelands. Not all of them even stopped fighting when the Germans surrendered.

As they crawled out of the ruins, they saw not virgin territory but destruction. 'The war ended the way a passage through a tunnel ends,' wrote the Czech memoirist Heda Kovály: 'From far away you could see the light ahead, a gleam that kept growing, and its brilliance seemed ever more dazzling to you huddled there in the dark the longer it took to reach it. But when at last the train burst out in the glorious sunshine, all you saw was a wasteland full of weeds and stones, and a heap of garbage.'[8]

Photographs from across Eastern Europe at that time show scenes from an apocalypse. Flattened cities, acres of rubble, burnt villages and smoking, charred ruins where houses used to be. Tangles of barbed wire, the remains of concentration camps, labour camps, POW camps; barren fields, pockmarked by tank tracks, with no sign of farming, husbandry or life of any kind. In the recently destroyed cities, the air was suffused with the smell of corpses. 'The descriptions I've read always use the phrase "sweetish odour", but that's far too vague, completely inadequate,' wrote one German survivor. 'The fumes are not so much an odour as something firmer, something thicker, a soupy vapour that collects in front of your face and nostrils, too mouldy and thick to breathe. It beats you back as if with fists.'[9]

Provisional burial sites were everywhere, and people walked through the streets gingerly, as if traversing a cemetery.[10] In due course exhumations began, as bodies were removed from courtyards and city parks to mass graves. Funerals and reburial ceremonies were frequent, though in Warsaw one was famously interrupted. In the summer of 1945, a funeral march was slowly wending its way through Warsaw when the black-clad mourners saw an extraordinary sight: 'A living, red Warsaw tram', the first to run through the city since the war's end: 'The pedestrians on the sidewalks stopped, others ran alongside the tram clapping and cheering loudly. Extraordinarily, the funeral march stopped too, the mourners accompanying the dead, captivated by the general mood, turned to the tram and began to clap too.'[11]

This too was typical. At times a weird euphoria seemed to grip the survivors. It was a relief to be alive; sorrow was mixed with joy, and commerce, trade and reconstruction began immediately, spontaneously. Warsaw in the summer of 1945 was a bustling hive of activity, Stefan Kisielewski wrote: 'in the ruins of the streets, there's commotion like never before. Trade – buzzing. Work – booming. Humour – everywhere. The mob, teeming life, flows through the streets, nobody would think that these are all victims of a massive disaster, people who have scarcely recovered from a catastrophe, or that they are living in extreme, inhuman conditions . . .'[12] Sándor Márai described Budapest in one of his novels at this same period:

> Whatever remained of the city, of society, sprang to life with such passion, fury and sheer willpower, with such strength and stamina and cunning, it seemed as if nothing had happened . . . out on the boulevard there were suddenly stalls in gateways, selling all kinds of nice food and luxury items: clothes, shoes, everything you could imagine, not to mention gold napoleons, morphine and pork lard. The Jews who remained staggered from their yellow star houses and within a week or two you could see them bargaining, surrounded as they were by the corpses of men and horses . . . People were quibbling over prices for warm British cloth, French perfumes, Dutch brandy and Swiss watches among the rubble . . .[13]

This enthusiasm for work and renewal would last for many years. The British sociologist Arthur Marwick once speculated that the experience of national failure might have given the West Germans an incentive to rebuild, to regain a sense of national pride. The very scale of the national collapse, he argued, might have helped contribute to the postwar boom: having experienced economic and personal catastrophe, Germans readily threw themselves into reconstruction.[14] But Germany, both East and West, was not alone in this drive to recover and to become 'normal' again. Over and over again, Poles and Hungarians in memoirs and conversations about the postwar period speak of how desperately they sought education, ordinary work, a life without constant violence and disruption. The communist parties were perfectly poised to take advantage of these yearnings for peace.

In any case, damage to property was easier to repair than the demographic damage in Eastern Europe, where the scale of violence had been higher than anything known on the western half of the continent. During the war, Eastern Europe had experienced the worst of both Stalin's and Hitler's ideological madness. By 1945, most of the territory between Poznań in the west and Smolensk in the east had been occupied not once but twice, or even three times. Following the Molotov–Ribbentrop pact of 1939, Hitler had invaded the region from the west, occupying western Poland. Stalin had invaded from the east, occupying eastern Poland, the Baltic states and Bessarabia. In 1941, Hitler once again invaded these same territories from the west. In 1943, the tide turned again and the Red Army marched back through the same region once more, coming from the east.

By 1945, in other words, the lethal armies and vicious secret policemen of not one but two totalitarian states had marched back and forth across the region, each time bringing about profound ethnic and political changes. To take one example, the city of Lwów was occupied twice by the Red Army and once by the Wehrmacht. After the war ended it was called L'viv, not Lwów, it was no longer in eastern Poland but in the western part of Soviet Ukraine, and its Polish and Jewish prewar population had been murdered or deported and replaced by ethnic Ukrainians from the surrounding countryside.

Eastern Europe, along with Ukraine and the Baltic states, was also the site of most of the politically motivated killing in Europe. 'Hitler and Stalin rose to power in Berlin and Moscow,' writes Timothy Snyder in *Bloodlands*, the definitive history of the mass killing of this period, 'but their visions of transformation concerned above all the lands between.'[15] Stalin and Hitler shared contempt for the very notion of national sovereignty for any of the nations of Eastern

Europe, and they jointly strove to eliminate their elites. The Germans considered Slavs to be subhumans, ranked not much higher than Jews, and in the lands between Sachsenhausen and Babi Yar they thought nothing of ordering arbitrary street killings, mass public executions or the burning of whole villages in revenge for one dead Nazi. The Soviet Union, meanwhile, considered its western neighbours to be capitalist and anti-Soviet strongholds whose very existence posed a challenge to the USSR. In 1939, and again in 1944 and 1945, the Red Army and the NKVD would arrest not only Nazis and collaborators in their newly conquered territories, but anyone who might theoretically oppose Soviet administration: social democrats, anti-fascists, businessmen, bankers and merchants – often the same people targeted by the Nazis. Although there were civilian casualties in Western Europe, as well as incidents of theft, misbehaviour and abuse perpetrated by the British and American armies, for the most part the Anglo-Saxon troops were trying to kill Nazis, not potential leaders of the liberated nations. And, for the most part, they treated the resistance leaders with respect and not suspicion.

The East is also where the Nazis had most vigorously pursued the Holocaust, where they set up the vast majority of ghettoes, concentration camps and killing fields. Snyder notes that Jews accounted for less than 1 per cent of the German population when Hitler came to power in 1933, and many of those managed to flee. Hitler's vision of a 'Jew-free' Europe could only be realized when the Wehrmacht invaded Poland, Czechoslovakia, Belarus, Ukraine and the Baltic states, and eventually Hungary and the Balkans, which is where most of the Jews of Europe actually lived. Of the 5.4 million Jews who died in the Holocaust, the vast majority were from Eastern Europe. Most of the rest were taken to the region to be murdered. The scorn the Nazis held for all Eastern Europeans was closely related to their decision to take the Jews from all over Europe to the East for execution. There, in a land of subhumans, it was possible to do inhuman things.[16]

Above all, Eastern Europe is where Nazism and Soviet communism clashed. Although they began the war as allies, Hitler had always wanted to fight a war of destruction against the USSR, and after Hitler's invasion Stalin promised the same. The battles between the Red Army and the Wehrmacht were therefore fiercer and bloodier in the east than those which took place further west. German soldiers truly feared the Bolshevik 'hordes', about whom they had heard many terrible stories, and towards the end of the war they fought them with particular desperation. Their scorn for civilians was especially profound, respect for local culture and infrastructure nonexistent. A German general defied Hitler's orders and left Paris standing out of sentimental respect for the city, but other German generals burned Warsaw to the ground and destroyed much of Budapest without thinking about it. Western air forces were not especially concerned about the ancient architecture of this region either: Allied bombers contributed to the toll of death and destruction too, conducting aerial bombardment not only of Berlin and Dresden but also of Danzig and Königsberg – Gdańsk and Kaliningrad – among many other places.

As the eastern front moved into Germany itself, fighting only intensified. The Red Army focused on its drive to Berlin with something approaching obsession. From early on in the war, Soviet soldiers bade farewell to one another with the cry, 'See you in Berlin.' Stalin was desperate to reach the city before the other Allies got there. His commanders understood this, and so did their American counterparts. General Eisenhower, knowing full well that the Germans would fight to the death in Berlin, wanted to save American lives and decided to let Stalin take the city. Churchill argued against this policy: 'If they [the Russians] . . . take Berlin, will not their impression that they have been the overwhelming contributor to our common victory be unduly imprinted in their minds, and may this not lead them into a mood which will raise grave and formidable difficulties in the future?'[17] But the American general's caution won out, and the Americans and British advanced slowly to the east – General George C. Marshall having once declared he would be 'loath to hazard American lives for purely political purposes', and Field Marshal Sir Alan Brooke arguing that 'the advance into the country really had to coincide to a certain extent with what our final boundaries would be'.[18] Meanwhile, the Red Army charged directly towards the German capital, leaving a trail of destruction in its wake.

When the numbers are added up, the result is stark. In Britain, the war took the lives of 360,000 people, and in France, 590,000. These are horrific casualties, but they still come to less than 1.5 per cent of those countries' populations. By contrast, the Polish Institute of National Memory estimates that there were some 5.5 million wartime deaths in the country, of which about 3 million were Jews. In total, some 20 per cent of the Polish population, one in five people, did not survive. Even in countries where the fighting was less bloody, the proportion of deaths was still higher than in the West. Yugoslavia lost 1.5 million people, or 10 per cent of the population. Some 6.2 per cent of Hungarians and 3.7 per cent of the prewar Czech population died too.[19] In Germany itself, casualties came to between 6 million and 9 million people – depending upon whom one considers to be 'German', given all of the border changes – or up to 10 per cent of the population.[20] It would have been difficult, in Eastern Europe in 1945, to find a single family that had not suffered a serious loss.

As the dust settled, it also became clear that even those who were not dead were often living somewhere else. In 1945, the demographics, population distribution and ethnic composition of many countries in the region were actually very different from what they had been in 1938. To a degree still not well understood in the West the Nazi occupation of Eastern Europe had brought about major population shifts, following waves of deportation and resettlement. German 'colonists' had been moved into occupied Poland and Czechoslovakia, with the deliberate goal of changing the ethnic composition of particular regions, while natives were expelled or murdered. Poles and Jews were both evicted from their homes in the better districts of Łódź to make way for German administrators as early as December 1939. In subsequent years some 200,000 Poles were sent out of the city to become forced labourers in Germany, while the Jews were herded into the Łódź Ghetto, where most died.[21] The German occupation regime installed Germans in their place, including ethnic Germans from the Baltic states and Romania, some of whom believed they were receiving abandoned or neglected property.[22]

Many of these changes would be reversed or revenged in the postwar period. The years 1945, 1946 and 1947 were years of refugees: Germans moved west, Poles and Czechs returned east from forced labour and concentration camps in Germany, deportees came back from the Soviet Union, soldiers of all kinds returned from other theatres, escapees came back from British or French or Moroccan exile.

Some of these refugees returned home but, upon discovering that home was no longer what it had been, struck out for new territories. Jan Gross reckons that between 1939 and 1943 some 30 million Europeans were dispersed, transplanted or deported. Between 1943 and 1948, a further 20 million were moved as well.[23] Krystyna Kersten notes that between 1939 and 1950 one Pole out of every four changed his place of residence.[24]

The vast majority of these people arrived home with nothing. Immediately, they were forced to seek help from others – from churches, charities or the state – in whatever form it took. Whole families, self-sufficient before the war, found themselves queuing in government offices, trying to be assigned a house or apartment. Men who had once had independent jobs and salaries were begging for ration cards, hoping to get a job in a state bureaucracy. The mentality of a refugee, forcibly expelled from his home, is not that of an emigrant who leaves to seek his fortune: his very circumstances fostered dependency, and a sense of helplessness he might never have known before.

To make matters worse, the extraordinary physical destruction in Eastern Europe was also matched by extraordinary economic destruction, and on an equally incomprehensible scale. Not every East European nation was wealthy before the war, but neither was the region as far behind the western half of the continent in 1939 as it was by 1945. Though some groups had profited during the war from the demand for guns and tanks – several economic historians have commented on the expansion of the industrial working class in those years, especially in Bohemia and Moravia – the second half of the war was a catastrophe for almost everybody.[25] In 1945 and 1946, Hungary's GNP was only half of what it had been in 1939. According to one calculation, the final months of the war had destroyed about 40 per cent of the country's economic infrastructure.[26] Budapest, the capital, suffered damage to three quarters of its buildings, of which 4 per cent were totally destroyed and 22 per cent inhabitable. The population was reduced by a third.[27] The Germans took much of the country's railway rolling stock with them when they left the country; the Soviet army, in the guise of reparations, would take much of the rest.[28]

In Poland, a figure close to 40 per cent is also used as a general estimate for damage, but certain areas were even more thoroughly devastated. The country's transportation infrastructure was especially hard-hit: more than half of the country's bridges were gone, along with ports, shipping facilities and two fifths of the railways. Most major Polish cities were heavily damaged, meaning that they had lost apartments and houses, ancient architectural monuments, works of art, universities and schools. In the city centre of Warsaw, some 90 per cent of the buildings were partly or completely destroyed, having been systematically blown up by the retreating Germans.[29]

Germany's cities were also badly destroyed, thanks both to the Allied aerial bombardment, which resulted in huge firestorms, and to Hitler's insistence that his soldiers fight until the very end, street by street. Even in Czechoslovakia, Bulgaria and Romania, where the devastation was not so broad and there had been no aerial bombing, the damage was still deep. Romania lost its oil fields, for example, which had contributed one third of the national income before 1938.[30]

The war had also altered the region's economies in other ways, harder to quantify. In two justly celebrated essays on the social conse-quences of the war, Jan Gross and Bradley Abrams point out that in much of the region – certainly in Hungary, Czechoslovakia, Poland and Romania, as well as Germany itself – the expropriation of private property on a large scale actually began *during* the war, under Nazi and fascist regimes, and not afterwards under communism. Mass con-fiscation of Jewish property and businesses in Central Europe, either by the state or by the German occupiers, was followed by a broader Germanization during the later years of occupation. Sometimes this happened by stealth: in the Czech lands, German banks controlled Czech banks, and thus could 'often dictate whether or not a Czech bank or firm was solvent or not, and, in cases of insolvency, rescue operations were put in hand by German banks or firms which thereby gained control'.[31] Sometimes control was imposed outright. In Poland, it often happened that German managers and directors were simply put in charge of factories and businesses which technically still belonged to Poles.

The occupation had also reoriented regional economics. Exports to Germany doubled and tripled between 1939 and 1945, as did German investment in local industry. Since the early 1930s, German economists had argued for the establishment of economic colonies in Eastern Europe; during the occupation German businesses began to create them, often by appropriating Jewish, or even non-Jewish, factories and businesses.[32] The region became an autonomous, closed market, which had never been the case in the past.[33] This meant that when Germany collapsed, the region's international trade links collapsed as well – a circumstance which eventually helped make it easier for the Soviet Union to take Germany's place.

For similar reasons, the collapse of Germany also created an ownership crisis. At the end of the war, German entrepreneurs, managers and investors fled or were killed. Many factories were simply abandoned, left ownerless. Sometimes they were taken over by workers' councils. Sometimes local authorities took control. Most of these abandoned properties were eventually nationalized – if they had not already been packed up and moved, lock, stock and barrel, to the Soviet Union, which considered all 'German' property legitimate war reparations – with surprisingly little opposition.[34] By 1945, the idea that the ruling authorities could simply confiscate private property without providing any compensation whatsoever was an established principle in Eastern Europe. When larger-scale nationalization began, nobody would be remotely surprised.

Of all the different kinds of damage wrought by the Second World War, the hardest to quantify is the psychological and emotional damage. The brutality of the First World War created a generation of fascist leaders, idealistic intellectuals and expressionist artists who twisted the human form into inhuman shapes and colours in an attempt to convey their disorientation. But because it involved occupation, deportation and the mass displacement of civilian populations as well as fighting, the Second World War entered far more deeply into everyday life. Constant, daily violence shaped the human psyche in countless ways, not all of which are easy to articulate.

This, too, was different from what happened in the West, particularly in the Anglo-Saxon countries. The Polish poet Czesław Miłosz, attempting to explain the mental differences between postwar Europe and postwar America, wrote of how war shatters a man's sense of the natural order of things: 'Once, had he stumbled upon a corpse on the street, he would have called the police. A crowd would have gathered, and much talk and comment would have ensued. Now he knows he must avoid the dark body lying in the gutter, and refrain from asking unnecessary questions . . .'

During the occupation, respectable citizens ceased to regard banditry as a crime, Miłosz wrote, at least if it was in the service of the Underground. Young boys, from respectable, law-abiding, middle-class families, became hardened criminals: 'the killing of a man presents no great moral problem to them.' During the occupation, it became normal to change one's name and profession, to travel on false papers, to memorize a fabricated biography, to watch all of one's money lose its value overnight, to see people rounded up in the street like cattle.[35]

Taboos about property broke down, and theft became routine, even patriotic. One stole to keep one's partisan band alive, or to feed the resistance, or to feed one's children. One watched with resentment as others stole – the Nazis, the criminals, the partisans. As the war drew to an end, the epidemic of theft grew even worse. In Sándor Márai's novel *Portraits of a Marriage*, one of the characters marvels at the entrepreneurship of the thieves who combed the ruins of bombed buildings: 'They thought there was time enough, if they hurried, to save whatever hadn't already been stolen by the Nazis, our local fascists, the Russians, or such Communists as had managed to make their way home from abroad. They felt it their patriotic duty to lay their hands on anything still possible to lay hands on, and so they set about their work of "salvaging".'[36]

In Poland, as Marcin Zaremba has written, the interval between the retreat of the Nazi occupiers and the arrival of the Red Army was marked by waves of plundering in Lublin, Radom, Kraków and Rzeszów, as Poles broke into empty German homes and shops, as one explained, 'not even to find something, or to get something, but just to rob the Germans themselves, to take German property after they had taken everything from us'.[37]

In the months following the war's end a more organized wave of looting swept the former territories of Germany, in Silesia and East Prussia, which had now become the property of Poland. Groups of looters in cars, trucks and other vehicles trawled half-empty cities looking for furniture, clothing, machinery and other valuables. 'Specialist' looters sought espresso machines and cooking equipment in Wrocław and Gdańsk on behalf of Warsaw restaurants and cafés. 'At the beginning, the looters weren't knowledgeable about rare books,' remembered one memoirist, 'but experts in that field soon appeared.' Former Jewish properties around the country were robbed as well, as were Jewish burial grounds, where peasants hoped to find 'buried treasure' or gold teeth. But most of the looters were utterly indiscriminate in their targets, attacking the property of Gentiles and Jews alike. Following the Warsaw Uprising, looting broke out in the smashed, broken Polish capital as everyone – 'neighbours, passers-by, soldiers' – plundered half-destroyed apartment blocks and empty shops in the wake of the tragic last stand of the Polish resistance. The fields around Treblinka were dug up by treasure-hunters in 1946, but in September of that same year bystanders also fell upon the casualties of a train crash near Łódź, not in order to help them but to search for valuables.[38]

Though the looting fever eventually subsided in Poland and elsewhere, it may well have helped build tolerance for the corruption and theft of public property that were so common later on. Violence had also become normal, and remained so for many years. Events which would have caused widespread outrage a few months earlier ceased to bother anyone at all. More than seventy years later, one Hungarian told me he still clearly remembered a terrible scene on a Budapest street: the sudden arrest of a man, out of the blue, from the side of his two small children. 'The father was pulling the children on a little cart in the street, the Soviet soldiers did not care, they took the father and left the children in the middle of the street.' None of the pedestrians on the street even treated this event as strange.[39] When more violence followed the official cessation of hostilities – the brutal expulsion of Germans and others, attacks on Jews returning home, arrests of men and women who had fought against Hitler, the continued partisan warfare in Poland and the Baltic states – no one found that to be strange either.

Not all of the violence was ethnic or political. 'No activity in the village ends without a fight,' one rural Polish teacher remembered.[40] Weapons were still available, murder rates were high. In many parts of Eastern Europe armed gangs roamed the countryside, sometimes calling themselves resistance fighters even when they had no connection to any organized structures of resistance, living by thieving and murder. Gangs of disoriented former soldiers operated in all of the cities of Eastern Europe and criminal violence bled into political violence, so much so that public records do not always make clear which was which. In two weeks in the late summer of 1945, police in a single Polish county recorded 20 murders, 86 robberies, 1084 cases of breaking and entering, 440 'political crimes' (not defined) as well as 125 cases of 'resistance to authority', 29 'other' crimes against authority, 92 arsons and 45 sex crimes. 'People's main problem is security,' the police report explained, 'it would be better if there was quiet here, and not attacks and thefts.'[41]

Institutional collapse accompanied the moral collapse. Poland's political and social institutions had ceased to function in 1939. Hungary's stopped working in 1944, Germany's in 1945. This catastrophe left people profoundly cynical about the societies in which they had grown up and the values into which they had been educated, and no wonder: those societies had been weak, and those values had been so easily overturned. The experience of national defeat – whether through Nazi invasion and occupation in 1939, through Allied invasion and occupation in 1945, or both – was extraordinarily difficult for those who lived through it.

Since then, many have tried to describe what it feels like to endure the disintegration of one's entire civilization, to watch the buildings and landscapes of one's childhood collapse, to understand that the moral world of one's parents and teachers no longer exists and that one's respected national leaders have failed. Yet it is still not easy to understand for those who have not experienced it. Words like 'vacuum' and 'emptiness' when used about a national catastrophe such as an alien occupation are simply insufficient: they cannot convey the anger people felt at their prewar and wartime leaders, their failed political systems, their own 'naive' patriotism and the wishful thinking of their parents and teachers. Widespread destruction – the loss of homes, families, schools – condemned millions of people to a kind of radical loneliness. Different parts of Eastern Europe experienced this collapse at different times and the experience was not everywhere identical. But whenever and however it came, national failure had profound effects, especially on young people, many of whom simply concluded that everything they had once thought true was false. Besides, the war had left them without a social network and without a context. Many really did resemble Hannah Arendt's 'totalitarian personality', the 'completely isolated human being who, without any other social ties to family, friends, comrades or even mere acquaintances, derives his sense of having a place in the world only from his belonging to a movement, his membership in the party'.[42]

Certainly that was what happened to Tadeusz Konwicki, a Polish novelist who spent the war as a partisan. Brought up in a patriotic family near Vilnius, in what was then eastern Poland, Konwicki eagerly joined the armed wing of the Polish resistance, the Home Army, during the war. First he fought the Nazis. Then, for a time, his unit fought the Red Army. At some point their struggle began to deteriorate into armed robberies and gratuitous violence, and he found himself wondering why he was still fighting. Eventually he left the forests and moved to Poland, a state whose new borders no longer included his family home. Upon arrival, he realized that he had nothing. At the age of nineteen, he was in possession of a coat, a small backpack and a handful of fake documents. He had no family, no friends and no higher education. This experience was quite common. Lucjan Grabowski, a young Home Army partisan fighting near Białystok, turned in his weapons at about the same time, and then realized he owned nothing as well: 'I didn't have a suit, those from before the war were too small . . . my wallet was empty, I had a single dollar bill which I got from someone and a few thousand zlotys which my father had borrowed from our neighbour. And that was all I had to show for my four years fighting against the occupiers.'[43]

Konwicki had also lost his faith in much of what he had believed to be true in the past. 'During the war,' he told me, 'I saw so much slaughter. I saw a whole world of ideas, humanism, morality collapse. I was alone in this ruined country. What should I do? Which way should I go?'[44] Konwicki drifted for many months, considered escaping to the West, tried to rediscover his 'proletarian' roots by working as a labourer. Eventually he fell, almost accidentally, into the communist literary world and into the communist party – something he would never have considered possible before 1939. For a very brief time, he even became a 'Stalinist' writer, adopting the style and mannerisms dicated by the party.

His was a dramatic fate, but not an unusual one. The Polish sociologist Hanna Świda-Ziemba has also tried to reconstruct the prewar morality of her generation – people born in the late 1920s and early 1930s – and has painted a very similar picture. Her generation grew up with a profound faith in the Polish state, a conviction in its special destiny. The very concept of 'Poland', she writes, was particularly important to her generation, because the modern Polish state had only come into existence in 1918, and theirs was the first group of schoolchildren to be educated within it. They learned to objectify the nation, to aspire to 'serve' it, to relate to it using other categories, such as faith and betrayal. When the nation collapsed, they had nothing left.[45] Many focused their disappointment on the prewar politicians, on the authoritarian Right and on the generals who had so catastrophically failed to prepare Poland for war. Another Polish writer, Tadeusz Borowski, satirized the saccharine patriotism of the prewar politicians: 'Your fatherland: a peaceful corner and a log burning obediently in the fire. My fatherland: a burnt house and an NKVD summons.'[46]

For young Nazis, the experience of failure was even more apocalyptic, since they had been taught not just patriotism, but a belief in German physical and mental superiority. Hans Modrow – later a leading East German communist – was about the same age as Konwicki in 1946, and equally disoriented. A loyal member of the Hitler Youth, he had joined the *Volkssturm*, the 'people's militia', which put up the final resistance to the Red Army in the last days of the war. At the time he was filled with intense hatred of the Bolsheviks, whom he thought of as subhumans, physically and morally inferior to Germans. But he was captured by the Red Army in May 1945, and immediately experienced a moment of profound disillusion. He and another group of German prisoners of war were put on a truck and transported to a farm to work:

'I was a young man, and I wanted to help. I stood on the truck and handed down the others' backpacks, and then gave my pack to somebody else, so that I could jump off the truck myself. By the time I landed on the ground, it was stolen. I never got it back. And it was not a Soviet soldier who had done it but one of us, the Germans. Not until the next day did the Red Army turn us all into equals: they collected all of our backpacks – nobody was left with one – and we were given a spoon and cup to eat with. Because of this episode I started thinking about the Germans' so-called camaraderie in a different way.'[47]

A few days later, he was appointed driver to a Soviet captain, who asked him about the German poet Heinrich Heine. Modrow had never heard of Heine, and felt embarrassed that the people he had thought of as 'subhuman' seemed to know more about German culture than he. Eventually Modrow was transported to a POW camp near Moscow, where he was selected to attend an 'antifascist' school, and to receive training in Marxism-Leninism – training which, by that point, he was more than eager to absorb. So profound was his experience of Germany's failure that he very quickly came to embrace an ideology which he had been taught to hate throughout his childhood. Over time, he also came to feel something like gratitude. The communist party offered him the chance to make up for the mistakes of the past – Germany's mistakes, as well as his own. The shame he felt at having been an ardent Nazi could at last be erased.

But memories of the war could not be erased. Nor could the past easily be explained to outsiders who had not experienced the same level of destruction, and who had not witnessed the indifference human beings could show to one another's suffering. 'The man of the East cannot take Americans [or other Westerners] seriously,' wrote Miłosz. Because they hadn't undergone such experiences, 'their resultant lack of imagination is appalling'.[48] Miłosz neglected to add that the reverse was also true: Eastern Europeans had deeply unrealistic expectations of their Western neighbours too.

Western Europeans and Americans were never indifferent to Soviet communism, either before the war or afterwards. Fierce debates about the nature of the new Bolshevik regime and about communism in general had raged in most Western capitals long before 1945. American newspapers wrote vividly about the 'Red Peril' as early as 1918. In Washington, London and Paris, much public debate in the

1920s and 1930s was devoted to the communist threat to liberal democracy.

Even during their wartime alliance with Stalin, the majority of British and American statesmen who dealt directly with Russia had plenty of doubts about his postwar intentions and a very clear understanding of the nature of his regime. 'Alas, the German revelations are probably true,' Winston Churchill told Polish exile leaders after the Nazis stumbled upon the remains of thousands of Polish officers buried in the Katyń forest, where they had been murdered by Soviet secret police: 'the Bolsheviks can be very cruel'.[49] George Kennan, the US diplomat who would shape America's postwar policy towards the USSR, spent the war years in Moscow, whence he 'bombarded the lower levels of Washington bureaucracy with analyses of communist evil'.[50] Dean Acheson, then Assistant Secretary of State, compared negotiations with Soviet delegates in the summer of 1944 to 'dealing with an old-fashioned penny slot machine ... One could sometimes expedite the process by shaking the machine, but it was useless to *talk* to it.'[51]

Not that it really mattered. In his memoirs, Acheson summed up his observations of those negotiations by observing that 'For us in State, however, this frustrating Russian interlude was soon forgotten amid the greater events then impending.'[52] In truth, wartime Washington and wartime London almost always had 'greater events' to worry about at least until 1945. Until the war's end, Russian behaviour in Eastern Europe was always a matter of secondary concern.

Nowhere is this clearer than in the official and unofficial accounts of the Tehran and Yalta conferences in November 1943 and February 1945, where Stalin, Roosevelt and Churchill decided the fate of whole swathes of Europe with amazing insouciance. When the subject of Poland's borders came up at the first meeting of the Big Three Allies in Tehran, Churchill told Stalin that he could keep the chunk of eastern Poland he had swallowed in 1939, and that Poland might 'move westwards, like soldiers taking two steps left close' in recompense. He then 'demonstrated with the help of three matches his idea of Poland moving westwards'. This, the minutes noted, 'pleased Marshal Stalin'.[53] At Yalta, Roosevelt half-heartedly suggested that the eastern border of Poland might be stretched to include the city of Lwów and the oil fields around it. Stalin seemed amenable but no one pushed him and the idea was dropped. Thus were the national identities of hundreds of thousands of people decided.

None of this reflected ill-will towards the region, just different priorities. Roosevelt's main concern at Yalta was the shape of the new United Nations, which he envisaged as the body that would prevent war in future, and he needed Soviet cooperation to construct this new international system. He also wanted Soviet help in the invasion of Manchuria as well as the use of Russian bases in the Far East. These concerns were simply more important to him than the fate of Poland or Czechoslovakia, and there were other issues at stake as well, from the future of the Italian monarchy to Middle Eastern oil. Although central to Stalin's postwar plans, Eastern Europe was only of marginal interest to the American president.[54]

Churchill, meanwhile, was acutely conscious of British weakness. Once the Red Army was actually in Poland, Hungary or Czechoslovakia he had no illusions about Britain's ability to force it to leave. In his memoirs, Churchill remembers telling Roosevelt just before the Yalta summit that 'we ought to occupy as much of Austria as possible, as it was "undesirable that more of Western Europe than necessary should be occupied by the Russians"'. It isn't clear by what criteria Austria was any more a part of 'Western' Europe at that point than Hungary or Czechoslovakia. But Churchill's fatalism comes through loud and clear: once the Red Army was in place, it wasn't going to move.[55]

Both leaders also knew that, as the war ended, their voters would be anxious for their husbands, brothers and sons to come home. It would be extremely difficult to 'sell' a new conflict with the USSR. Wartime propaganda had portrayed Stalin as jovial 'Uncle Joe', rough-edged friend of the working man, and Churchill and Roosevelt had both praised him in their public statements. In London, sympathizers had held fund-raising concerts for the Soviet Union, and erected a statue of Lenin outside one of the Bolshevik leader's former London garrets.[56] In the US, American businessmen already looked forward to profiting from this new friendship: 'Russia will be, if not our biggest, at least our most eager customer when the war ends,' declared the president of the US Chamber of Commerce.[57] To turn around and tell war-weary Britons or Americans that they had to stay in Europe to fight the Soviet Union would have been politically difficult, if not impossible.

The logistical difficulties were even worse. Churchill, who was never happy about the Russian occupation of Berlin, did, in the spring of 1945, actually order his military planners to investigate the possibility of an Allied attack on Soviet forces in Central Europe, possibly using Polish and even German troops. The result, a plan for 'Operation Unthinkable', was immediately dismissed as impractical. Its authors warned the British Prime Minister that the Red Army outnumbered British troops three to one, and that the result might be a 'long and costly' military campaign, even a 'total war'. Churchill himself wrote in the margins of the draft that an attack on the Red Army was 'highly improbable' – though some elements of Operation Unthinkable later formed part of the planning for a possible Soviet attack on Britain.[58]

There was also an element of *naivete* on the Western side, as Miłosz had complained: Roosevelt, particularly towards the end of his life, frequently expressed his faith in Stalin's good intentions. 'Don't worry,' he told the Polish exile leader Stanisław Mikołajczyk in 1944, 'Stalin doesn't intend to take freedom from Poland. He wouldn't dare do that because he knows that the United States government stands solidly behind you.'[59] A year or so later, American and British negotiators agreed to give the Soviet Union command of the Allied Control Commission in Budapest – the body set up to run Hungary after the war – on the strict condition that the USSR consult with the other Allies before giving any instructions to the Hungarian government. In the event, it never even pretended to do so.[60]

Some later contended that communist sympathizers in the American government and 'pro-Soviet elements' in Washington had also influenced American postwar policy.[61] But although Alger Hiss, probably the most notorious Soviet agent, was at Yalta as part of the US negotiating team, his influence – if any – would have been unnecessary. The transcripts show clearly that Churchill and Roosevelt had very definite interests, and that pushing the Soviet Union out of Eastern Europe was not one of them.[62] Those present were pragmatists. 'All that Yalta did was to recognize the facts of life as they existed and were being brought about,' remembered one American general: 'To me there was no choice to make.'[63]

Perhaps confusingly, this remained the case throughout the Cold War. Even when Western rhetoric became very aggressively anti-Soviet, great care was always taken not to launch a new European conflict. Neither the US nor Britain wanted a war with the Soviet Union, either then or later. In 1953, after Stalin's death, when strikes and riots broke out in East Berlin, the Allied authorities in West Berlin remained very restrained, even warning West Germans not to cross the border in support of the strikes.[64] At the time of the Hungarian Revolution in 1956, the US Secretary of State, John Foster Dulles, an avowed Cold Warrior, also went out of his way to deny any American involvement in the events, and to tell the Soviet Union that 'we do not look upon these nations as potential military allies'.[65]

In truth, the Eastern Europeans were often more naive than the Western Allies. In Hungary, pro-British politicians clung to the belief that their country would be liberated by the British. Many were 'fuelled by an irrational belief in Hungary's alleged geopolitical significance', in the words of the historian László Borhi,[66] and expected a British invasion of the Balkans well into 1944. Because their country had been a bastion of Western Christendom in the struggle against the Ottoman Empire, they thought they would continue to play this role in the twentieth century. 'Western powers could not afford Russian domination of [Hungary's] geographically important area,' declared one Hungarian diplomat with confidence. The Poles, whose political future really had been the subject of heated discussion among the Allied leaders, were equally convinced the British would not abandon the country in whose name they had originally declared war on Germany, and the Americans could not abandon them because the Polish-American lobby would prevent it: sooner or later there had to be a Third World War. Later, the East Germans found it hard to believe that the West would agree to the fortification of the German – German border. Surely the West could not afford a divided Germany?

But the West could afford it and could accept it, just as the West also came to accept a divided Europe. Although no one in the West – not in Washington, London or Paris – foresaw the extent of the physical, psychological and political changes which the Red Army would bring to every country it occupied, they exerted very little effort to prevent them from coming about.

2

Victors

During the last months under the Nazis nearly all of us were pro-Russian. We waited for the light from the East. But it has burned too many. Too much has happened that cannot be understood. The dark streets still resonate every night with the piercing screams of women in distress.

Ruth Andreas-Friedrich[1]

The Russians ... swept the native population clean in a manner that had no parallel since the days of the Asiatic hordes.

George Kennan[2]

In Budapest, John Lukacs saw 'an ocean of green-gray Russians, all coming in from the east'.[3] In an eastern Berlin suburb, Lutz Rackow saw 'tanks, tanks, tanks, tanks', and soldiers walking alongside, among them 'amazons with blonde braids'.[4] This was the Red Army: hungry, angry, exhausted, battle-hardened men and women, some dressed in the same uniforms they'd been wearing at Stalingrad or Kursk two years earlier, all of them carrying memories of terrible violence, all of them now brutalized by what they had seen, heard and done.

The final Soviet offensive began in January 1945, when the Red Army crossed the Vistula, the river which runs through the centre of Poland. Quickly marching through devastated western Poland and the Baltic states, the 'Ivans' had conquered Budapest after a terrible siege by the middle of February, Silesia in March. Their assault on Königsberg in East Prussia ended in April. By that time, two vast army groups, the First Belorussian Front and the First Ukrainian Front, were on the outskirts of Berlin, poised for the final assault. Hitler killed himself on 30 April. A week later, on 7 May, General Alfred Jodl unconditionally surrendered to the Allies in the name of the Wehrmacht High Command.

Even now, it is not easy to assess what happened in Eastern Europe during those final five months of war, because not everybody remembers the events of those bloody months in the same way. In Soviet historiography, the last phase of the war is always portrayed unambiguously as a series of liberations. According to the standard narrative, Warsaw, Budapest, Prague, Vienna and Berlin were freed from the yoke of Nazi Germany, triumph followed triumph, the fascists were destroyed, the population rejoiced and freedom was restored.

Others tell the story differently. For many decades Germans, and especially Berliners, spoke very little about the events of May 1945 and afterwards. Nowadays, however, they remember very well the looting, the arbitrary violence and above all the mass rape which followed the Soviet invasion. Elsewhere in Eastern Europe, the Red Army is also remembered for its attacks on local partisans who had been fighting the Germans but who happened not to be communists, and for the waves of both random and targeted violence which followed. In Poland, Hungary, Germany, Czechoslovakia, Romania and Bulgaria, the Red Army's arrival is rarely remembered as a pure liberation. Instead, it is remembered as the brutal beginning of a new occupation.

Yet for many people, neither of these opposing perspectives offers the complete story either. For the arrival of the Red Army really did herald freedom for millions of people. Soviet soldiers opened the gates of Auschwitz-Birkenau, Majdanek, Stuthoff, Sachsenhausen and Ravensbrück. They emptied the Gestapo prisons. They made it possible for Jews to leave their hiding places in barns and cellars, and to return, slowly, to something resembling ordinary life. Genia Zonabend, a Jewish internee, walked out of the gates of a small labour camp in eastern Germany and went into the first German houses she could find, asking for food. She was refused – until a Russian passing by heard her story and made sure she received food and, as she remembered, 'even warm water to wash'.[5]

Nor did Soviet assistance extend only to Jews. The arrival of the Red Army also made it possible for Poles in the western part of Poland to speak Polish after years of being forbidden to do so in public. *Nur für Deutsche* ('For Germans Only') signs disappeared from shops, trolley cars and restaurants in the Polish cities which had been rechristened with German names. In Germany itself, opponents of Hitler rejoiced when the Soviet soldiers arrived, as did millions of Czechs and Hungarians. 'I ran out in the courtyard and hugged the first Soviet soldier I saw,' one Hungarian told me, and she was not alone.[6] Another one of her countrymen described what the arrival of the Red Army meant to him and his wife: 'We felt that we were liberated. I know that this is a cliché, and these words do not have any real meaning any more but no matter how hard I think I cannot better describe the feeling we had, than to say that we were liberated. And not only did we feel like this, sitting there in the basement, weeping and holding one another's hands: everyone there had the same feeling, that the world would finally turn into a different one, and that it really had been worthwhile for us to be born.'[7]

One Pole told me the same: 'we had no mixed feelings about them. They liberated us.'[8] Yet even those who rejoiced the loudest didn't deny that the Red Army left extraordinary devastation in its wake. When describing what happened, many spoke of a 'new Mongol invasion', using language tinged with xenophobia to evoke the unprecedented scale of the violence. George Kennan was reminded of the 'Asiatic hordes'.[9] Sándor Márai, the Hungarian novelist, remembered them being 'like a completely different human race whose reflexes and responses didn't make any sense'.[10] John Lukacs recalled 'dark, round, Mongol faces, with narrow eyes, incurious and hostile'.[11]

In part, the Soviet soldiers seemed foreign to East Europeans because they seemed so suspicious of Eastern Europeans, and because they appeared so shocked by the material wealth of Eastern Europe. Since the time of the revolution, Russians had been told of the poverty, unemployment and misery of capitalism, and about the superiority of their own system. But even upon entering eastern Poland, at that time one of the poorest parts of Europe, they found ordinary peasants who owned several chickens, a couple of cows and more than one change of clothes. They found small country towns with stone churches, cobbled streets and people riding bicycles, which were then still unknown in most of Russia. They found farms equipped with solid barns, and crops planted in neat rows. These were scenes of abundance by comparison with the desperate poverty, the muddy roads and the tiny wooden cottages of rural Russia.

When they encountered Königsberg churches, Budapest apartments and Berlin homes filled with antique furniture, 'fascist' women living in what they perceived to be unimaginable luxury, the mysteries of flush toilets and electric gadgets, then they were truly shocked: 'Our soldiers have seen the two-storey suburban houses with electricity, gas, bathrooms and beautifully tended gardens. Our people have seen the villas of the rich bourgeoisie in Berlin, the unbelievable luxury of castles, estates and mansions. And thousands of soldiers repeat these angry questions when they look around them in Germany: but why did they come to us? What did they want?'[12]

They searched for explanations. One political officer wrote back to Moscow, explaining that 'this is a kulak agriculture based on the exploitation of labour. That is why everything looks nice and rich. And when our Red Army soldier, particularly one who is immature in the political sense with a petty bourgeois private ownership view, compares involuntarily a collective farm with a German farm, he praises the German farm. We even have some officers who admire German things . . .'[13] Or perhaps it was all stolen: 'It's obvious from everything we see that Hitler robbed the whole of Europe to please his blood-stained Fritzes,' one soldier wrote home: 'Their sheep are the best Russian merinos and their shops are piled with goods from all the shops and factories of Europe. In the near future, these goods will appear in Russian shops as our trophies.'[14]

And so they stole back. Liquor and ladies' lingerie, furniture and crockery, bicycles and linen were taken from Poland, Hungary, Czechoslovakia, the Baltic and the Balkan states as well as Germany. Wrist watches seemed to have almost mythical significance for Russian soldiers, who would walk around wearing half a dozen at once if they could. An iconic photograph of a Russian soldier raising the Soviet flag atop the Berlin Reichstag had to be touched up to remove the wrist watches from the arms of the young hero.[15] In Budapest, the obsession with them remained part of local folklore, and may have helped shape local perceptions of the Red Army. A few months after the war, a Budapest cinema showed a newsreel about the Yalta conference. When President Roosevelt raised his arm while speaking to Stalin, several members of the audience shouted: 'Mind your watch!'[16] The same was true in Poland, where for many years Polish children would 'play' Soviet soldiers by shouting: '*Davai chasyi*' – 'Give me your watch.'[17] A beloved Polish children's television series of the late 1960s included a scene of Russian and Polish soldiers during wartime, camping out in deserted German buildings having amassed a vast collection of stolen clocks.[18]

For many, these thefts heralded the bitter disillusion which would be experienced by those who had eagerly awaited the arrival of Soviet troops. Márai tells of an elderly man, a 'venerable and patriarchal figure', who received his first Soviet visitor with solemnity, and respectfully revealed to him that he was a Jew:

> the Russian soldier broke into a smile, removed the submachine gun from his neck, walked up to the old man, and, according to Russian custom, kissed him gently – from right to left – on the cheeks. He said he was a Jew, too. For a time he silently and heartily squeezed the old man's hand.
>
> Then he hung the submachine gun around his neck again and ordered the old gentleman to stand in the corner of the room with his entire family and to turn with raised hands toward the wall ... After this, the Russian robbed them slowly, at his leisure.[19]

Some Soviet soldiers also found this deeply disturbing. Years later, the writer Vasily Grossman told his daughter that the Red Army had 'changed for the worse' when it crossed the Soviet border. One night, Grossman remembered, he slept in a German house, along with several other Russian soldiers, including a 'majestic' colonel, with a 'good Russian face', who was so tired he seemed ready to collapse: 'All night, we hear noises coming from the room where the tired colonel is staying. He leaves in the morning without saying goodbye. We go to his room: chaos, the colonel has emptied the cupboards like a real looter.'[20]

What they didn't steal, they often destroyed. The street fighting in Berlin and Budapest caused plenty of what we would now call collateral damage, but the Red Army also engaged in wanton destruction, apparently for its own sake. In Gniezno, the cradle of Christianity in

Poland, Soviet tanks deliberately destroyed a thousand-year-old cathedral which had no military significance whatsoever. Photographs taken at the time (and then hidden for seventy years) show the tanks standing alone, in the town square, firing at the ancient building without provocation.[21] After taking the city of Breslau, Soviet soldiers deliberately set the buildings in the ancient town centre alight, burning to the ground the priceless book collection of the University Library as well as the city museum, and several churches.[22]

Both the robbery and the destruction would continue for many months, growing more sophisticated with time, eventually taking the official form of 'reparations'. But the unofficial robbery also went on for many months. As late as 1946, East German officials were complaining that Soviet officers in Saxony had set themselves up in private apartments and were ordering furniture, paintings and porcelain from the Saxon state collections to be sent to them from local castles: 'Once they leave the area they take them with them.' The owner of Castle Friesen near Reichenbach complained that he had lost a table worth 4000 Reichsmarks (the prewar currency), three carpets worth 11,500 Reichsmarks, a rococo chest of drawers worth 18,000 Reichsmarks and a mahogany desk worth 5000 Reichsmarks. There is no record that any of this was returned.[23]

More horrific, and ultimately of deeper political significance, were violent attacks on civilians which began long before the Red Army reached Berlin. They started as the Red Army crossed Poland, intensified in Hungary and reached an astonishing level as Soviet troops crossed into Germany. To those whom they encountered, the brutalized, angry soldiers of the Red Army seemed consumed by a desire for revenge. They were enraged by the deaths of friends, spouses and children, enraged by the burnt villages and mass graves which the Germans had left behind in Russia. Once, Grossman witnessed a procession of hundreds of Soviet children, walking eastwards on a road, leaving German captivity. Soviet soldiers and officers stood solemnly alongside the road, 'peering intently into their faces'. The men were fathers, looking for lost sons and daughters who had been deported to Germany: 'One colonel had been standing there for several hours, upright, stern, with a dark, gloomy face. He went back to his car in the dusk: he hadn't found his son.'[24] The Red Army may have been enraged by its own commanders, their heartless tactics and their constant use of threats and political spies, as well as its own losses. The historian Catherine Merridale, who interviewed hundreds of veterans, believes that they were often expressing political rage: 'consciously or not ... Red Army soldiers would soon be venting anger that had built up through decades of state oppression and endemic violence'.[25]

The women of the newly occupied territories would bear the brunt of this rage. Women of all ages were subjected to gang rapes, and sometimes murdered afterwards. Though more famous as the chronicler of the Gulag, the Russian writer Alexander Solzhenitsyn also entered East Prussia with the Red Army in 1945, where he encountered, and later put into verse – translated by Robert Conquest – scenes of horror:

> A moaning by the walls half muffled:
> The mother's wounded, still alive.
> The little daughter's on the mattress,
> Dead. How many have been on it
> A platoon, a company perhaps?
> A girl's been turned into a woman,
> A woman turned into a corpse.
> It's all come down to simple phrases:
> Do not forget! Do not forgive!
> Blood for blood! A tooth for a tooth![26]

These acts of vengeance were often apolitical, and they were not even necessarily directed at Germans or Nazi sympathizers. As Grossman noted, 'Soviet girls liberated from the camps are suffering a lot now. Tonight, some of them are hiding in our correspondents' room. During the night, we are woken up by screams: one of the correspondents couldn't resist the temptation.' In his memoirs, Lev Kopelev, at the time a political officer in the Red Army, recounts the fate of a Russian girl who had been a forced labourer in Germany, but who was mistaken for one of the enemy. She was 'beautiful, young, cheerful, hair like gold tumbling down her back – some soldiers, drunk I guess, were walking down the street, saw her – "Hey, Fritzie, hey, you bitch!" – and a spray from a submachine gun across her back. She didn't live an hour. Kept crying: "What for?" She had just written her mother that she'd be coming home.'[27]

Sometimes, the victims were Polish forced labourers, who had the bad luck to be in the Red Army's way: 'Just then there was a frenzied scream and a girl ran into the warehouse, her long, braided blonde hair disheveled, her dress torn across her breast, shouting piercingly, "I'm Polish! Jesus Mary, I'm Polish!" Two tank men were after her. Both were wearing their black helmets. One of them was viciously drunk.'[28] When Kopelev tried to intervene – theoretically rape was punishable by execution on the spot – his companions upbraided him, grumbling: '"Some commanders . . . They'll shoot their own men over a German bitch."' He was similarly reproached for objecting when fellow soldiers shot a feeble-minded old woman as a 'spy': 'Are you going to turn against your own people over a lousy German crone?'[29]

Both the rapes and the violence horrified local communists, who immediately understood what their political impact would be. In public, the rapes were attributed to 'diversionists dressed in Soviet uniforms'. In private, local communists petitioned authorities to help take control. One Polish security officer wrote to the propaganda boss of the Polish army in February 1945 to complain that Red Army troops 'behave towards Poles in a manner which is harming Polish–Soviet friendship and weakens the feelings of gratitude which the people of Poznań had for their liberators . . . rape of women is very common, sometimes in the presence of parents or husbands. Even more common are situations when soldiers, usually younger officers, compel women to their quarters (sometimes under the pretence that they will help with the wounded) and attack them there.'[30]

Others tried to deny what was happening. One young Hungarian, a communist at the time, explained that he hadn't known about any rapes: 'in our family circle one would have said that "this is Nazi nonsense" . . . at that time we were still convinced that they [the Soviets] were new men'. But over time, they found the 'new men' didn't quite conform to expectations. At one point, he was given responsibility for a group of young Russians: 'at night [they] were regularly jumping out of their windows and going to drink somewhere or pick up some whores or whatever else, which we were very embarrassed by. Very embarrassed by them. Didn't denounce them, but we knew about it . . .'[31]

Some were touched personally. Robert Bialek, one of the few active, underground communists in the then-German city of Breslau, arrived home after his first, celebratory encounter with the Soviet commandants who had occupied the city – as a communist, he wanted to offer them his help – to discover that his wife had been raped. This, for him, was the beginning of the end: 'The brutish instincts of two common Russian soldiers had brought the world crashing down about my head, as no Nazi tortures nor the subtlest persuasion had ever done.' He wished, he wrote, 'that I had been buried, like so many of my friends, under the ruins of the town'.[32]

It is frequently and correctly observed that this wave of sexual violence was not planned, in Germany or anywhere else, and there is no document 'ordering' such attacks.[33] Yet it is also true that officers such as Kopelev and Solzhenitsyn found that their immediate superiors weren't much interested in stopping them, and both rape and random killings were clearly tolerated, at least in the early weeks of occupation. Though decisions were left up to local commanders, this tolerance flowed from the highest possible level. When the Yugoslav communist Milovan Djilas complained about the behaviour of the Red Army to Stalin, the Soviet leader infamously demanded to know how he, a writer, could not 'understand it if a soldier who has crossed thousands of kilometers through blood and fire and death has fun with a woman or takes some trifle?'[34]

This sort of 'understanding' was enhanced by Soviet propaganda about the Germans and Germany, which became especially bloodthirsty during the final attack on Berlin, and by the desire to humiliate German men. 'Do not count days; do not count miles. Count only the number of Germans you have killed,' wrote one war correspondent, in an article reread and reprinted often after February 1945: 'Kill the German – this is your mother's prayer. Kill the German – this is the cry of your Russian earth.'[35]

Even if the looting, violence and rapes were not part of a political plan, in practice they had a deep and long-lasting political impact on all of the territories occupied by the Red Army. On the one hand, the violence made people doubtful about Soviet rule, and deeply suspicious of communist propaganda and Marxist ideology. At the same time, violence, especially sexual violence, made both men and women profoundly afraid. The Red Army was brutal, it was powerful and it could not be stopped. Men could not protect women; women could not protect themselves; neither could protect their children or their property. The horror that had been inspired could not be openly discussed, and official responses were usually oblique. In Hungary, the Budapest National Committee suspended the ban on abortions in February 1945, though without explaining exactly why. In January 1946, the Hungarian Social Welfare Minister issued an evasive decree: 'As an effect of the front and the chaos following it there were a lot of children born whose families did not want to take care of them ... I ask hereby the bureau of orphanages ... to qualify all babies as abandoned whose date of birth is from 9 to 18 months after the liberation.'[36]

Even individual responses were often wooden and perfunctory, and so they remained: what was there to say? Many years later, an otherwise eloquent East German pastor who had been a child at the time of the Soviet invasion still slipped and stuttered as he tried to describe what he remembered of that: 'The Russians came, then the rapes happened, it was incredible. One simply cannot forget that. I was 15 ... some women had gone into hiding, they'd got others, my mother, it was very difficult ... It was horrible and at the same time there was a feeling of relief, of having escaped alive. There was a strange tension inside me.'[37]

Only once in Soviet-occupied Europe was mass rape clearly and publicly discussed. In November 1948, the East German authorities organized a public debate on the subject in Berlin's 'House of Soviet Culture'. The meeting was inspired by the journalist Rudolf Herrnstadt – editor, at the time, of the *Berliner Zeitung*, the Berlin city newspaper, and later editor of the official party newspaper, *Neues Deutschland* – who had composed a provocative article entitled 'About the Russians and about Us'. The debate attracted an enormous crowd, so many that *Neues Deutschland* later complained the hall was 'too small to discuss this topic seriously'.

Herrnstadt himself opened the discussion by provocatively repeating the thesis of his article, which had been printed in *Neues Deutschland* a few days before. He declared that Germany 'could not overcome its present difficulties without unrestricted support of the USSR', and he dismissed the public's anger at and resentment of the Red Army. He belittled those in his audience who spoke of their 'brother-in-law who was standing on the side of the road and had his bicycle stolen, and he had been voting for the communists all of his life'. How was the Soviet army supposed to know that the man was a communist? Why wasn't this man fighting with the Red Army, against the Nazis? Why was the entire German working class standing by the side of the road, as it were, waiting to be saved?

The discussion lasted four hours, and would be continued the following night. But as the evening wore on, the focus gradually shifted away from stolen bicycles. At a key moment, a woman stood up and declared that 'many of us have experienced things which shape our reaction when we meet members of the Soviet army'. Still using euphemisms, she referred to 'that fear and this mistrust with which we approach everybody who wears a certain uniform'. Reading the transcript of the debate, it becomes strangely clear that everyone, immediately, understood that the real subject at hand was not theft but rape.

One by one, justifications for Soviet behaviour were presented. Germans must learn to use reason to overcome emotion. Germans must carry on with the class struggle. Germans had begun the war. German brutality had taught the Russians to be brutal. Still, there were a few counter-arguments – some women pushed back, others wanted to know how Russian women were treated at home – until finally, on the second night, a Russian officer stood up and effectively ended the argument. He declared that 'no one has suffered as much as we: 7 million people dead, 25 million lost their homes': 'What kind of soldier came to Berlin in 1945? Was he a tourist? Did he come on an invitation? No, that was a soldier who had thousands of kilometres of scorched Soviet territory behind him ... perhaps he found his kidnapped bride here, who had been taken as a slave labourer ...'

After this intervention, the public discussion was effectively over: no real response could be made to his argument. His words reminded everyone in the room not only of the German responsibility for the war and of the Red Army's deep desire for revenge but of the pointlessness of saying or doing anything about it.[38]

Official silence followed. But memories of the mass rape, of the looting and of the violence did not disappear in Germany, in Hungary, in Poland or anywhere else. They simply added to the 'fear and mistrust with which we approach everybody who wears a certain uniform', in the words of the woman at the Berlin discussion – a fear which persisted long after the violence stopped.[39] With time, it became clear that this peculiarly powerful combination of emotions – fear, shame, anger, silence – helped lay the psychological groundwork for the imposition of a new regime.

Violence was not the only cause of resentment. Within a few years of the war's end, the Soviet Union would encourage the rapid industrialization of Eastern Europe – but in the meantime Stalin wanted war reparations. In practice, this entailed the literal dismantling of industry across the region, sometimes with very long-term consequences. Like mass rape, the mass plunder of German factories often seems to have been a form of revenge as much as anything else. Equipment and goods which could not possibly have been any use in the USSR, bits of odd piping and broken machines, were hauled off alongside works of art, the contents of private houses, even masses of archival documents, ancient as well as modern (the archives of the Grand Duchy of Lichtenstein, of the Rothschild family, of the Dutch freemasons), which were of limited use to Soviet scholars. Random men, rounded up on the street for this purpose, were forced to pack up industrial equipment which required specialist treatment, and the goods were surely damaged as a result.

Unlike the thefts of watches and bicycles, these wholesale reparations were very carefully planned in advance, starting as early as 1943, although Soviet authorities did know what a backlash they might create. Just as the tide of the war was turning, the head of the Soviet Institute for World Economics and World Politics, Eugene Vargas (a Soviet economist of Hungarian origin, also known by his Hungarian name, Jëno Varga) wrote a paper anticipating mass reparations and arguing that they might 'alienate the working class' in Germany and elsewhere if done incorrectly. Vargas thought payments in kind were preferable to payments in cash, which might perhaps involve bankers and capitalism. He also thought that any former Axis state which adopted Soviet-style communism should be absolved from paying reparations altogether.[40] Vargas and the Soviet Foreign Minister, Vyacheslav Molotov, concluded by proposing a mixed form of reparations: the confiscation of German property outside Germany and radical agricultural reform within Germany, as well as the dismantling of German enterprises and their work forces (which could be brought to the USSR to do forced labour) and the reduction of German living standards to Soviet levels. These policies were later carried out, more or less as Vargas described, in the Soviet zone of Germany.[41]

The other Allies were aware of these plans. Stalin first spoke about them at the Tehran conference, and at the Yalta conference the Soviet delegation even proposed the dismemberment of Germany – the Rhineland and Bavaria would become separate states – along with the dismantling of three quarters of Germany's industrial equipment, of which 80 per cent would go to the Soviet Union. A figure was plucked from the air – $10bn – which Stalin said was 'owed' to the USSR. There was some mild argument, and Churchill pointed out that the harsh sanctions placed on Germany after the First World War had not exactly produced peace in Europe. But Roosevelt was inclined not to argue. His own Treasury Secretary, Henry Morgenthau Jr, was also pushing for the dismemberment and deindustrialization of Germany, which he imagined would become a purely agricultural society.[42] The matter wasn't resolved in Potsdam either, and although discussions of reparations continued through 1947, and although the USSR presented a bill for the total amount of destruction the Nazis had caused in the Soviet Union – $128bn, to be precise – no treaty to this effect was ever signed.

In the end, it didn't much matter, because no other Allied power was able to influence what the Red Army did in its German occupation zone, or anywhere else for that matter. By March 1945, a Soviet commission had already drawn up a list of German assets, and by the summer some 70,000 Soviet 'experts' had already begun to supervise their removal.[43] According to Soviet Foreign Ministry data collected by Norman Naimark, 1,280,000 tons of 'materials' and 3,600,000 tons of 'equipment' had been removed from eastern Germany between the invasion and the beginning of August.[44] These numbers may have been plucked from the air, just like Stalin's figure of $128bn, though it is reliably known that out of 17,024 medium and large factories identified by the USSR in their zone, more than 4500 were dismantled and removed. Another fifty or sixty large companies stayed intact but became Soviet companies. Between a third and a half of eastern Germany's industrial capacity disappeared between 1945 and 1947.[45] In a very real sense, this was the beginning of the division of Germany. Although the other Allies certainly 'recruited' German scientists and other experts, no comparable removal effort took place in the western zones of Germany. In the wake of Soviet reparations, the economies of the two halves of Germany began immediately to diverge.

Even these numbers don't tell the whole story. Factories can be counted, but there is no way to track the amount of currency, gold or even food products removed from the eastern zone. German bureaucrats of the Soviet zone tried to keep track. In the files of the Department of Reparations some sixty-five cards, with about twenty to thirty entries per card, form a partial record. They include everything from '68 barrels of paint' to geodetic instruments and lenses from the Zeiss Jena optical factory. According to these records, the Red Army even confiscated the feed for the animals from the Leipzig zoo in October 1945. A few weeks later, the Red Army confiscated the animals as well, and apparently took them to Russia.[46]

In addition to handing over their property, some companies were also forced to pay the transport costs. Others were forced to sell goods below price: the owner of a carpet factory in Babelsburg complained, indignantly, that he was required to lower prices for the Red Army. Farmers also complained that they were asked to sell goods to the Russians below the market price, or else not be paid for what they delivered.[47] The dismantling of a factory was even sometimes accompanied by the deportation of workers, who were simply put on trains and told to expect new job contracts upon arrival in the USSR.[48] Factory owners (as well as the Leipzig zookeeper) demanded compensation for the goods from Berlin, but to no avail. Listeners wrote letters to the Deutsche Rundfunk radio station – one of the few visible German authorities at the time – asking the same question: how would the German administration pay them back for goods taken by the Russians? When would people who worked for the Russians be paid?[49]

Private property also disappeared, sometimes on the grounds that it was Nazi-owned, whether or not this was actually the case. The Russians sequestered town houses, vacation houses, apartments and castles – and in their wake so did the German communists, who needed 'party headquarters', holiday homes and living quarters for their new cadres.[50] No private car was safe, and no furniture either. Marshal Zhukov himself was alleged to have furnished several Moscow apartments handsomely with his personal trophies.

German workers sometimes fought hard to save their factories, often appealing to the communist party, which they hoped could intervene with the Russians. The party leaders of Saxony wrote to party authorities in 1945 to protest against the dismantling of a company which was the only one able to supply industrial glass for local industry. 'If dismantled,' they declared, 'it will affect many other companies.' The company appealed to the local Soviet commanders, and to local and provincial party leaders, to no effect, and were now finally writing to the communist party in Berlin, hoping for an intervention. The economic department of the party's Central Committee received dozens of such letters in 1945 and 1946. In most cases, it couldn't help.[51]

But although the scale of payments was greatest there, the collection of reparations was not unique to Germany. As former Nazi allies, Hungary, Romania and Finland also had to pay huge reparations in the form of oil, ships, industrial equipment, food and fuel.[52] The Hungarian contribution had to be continually revisited because Hungary's galloping inflation made the prices of things difficult to calculate. Current estimates put the payments at $300m (in 1938 American dollars) to the USSR, $70m to Yugoslavia and $30m to Czechoslovakia. To put it differently, reparations shipments siphoned off about 17 per cent of Hungarian GDP in 1945–6, and a further 10 per cent in 1946–7. After that, the reparations payments accounted for about 7 per cent of GDP annually until the deliveries ended in 1952.[53]

There were other costs to Soviet occupation too. Feeding and housing the Red Army on its own proved an enormous burden for the Hungarians, who by the summer of 1945 were complaining that the cost already accounted for 10 per cent of the government's budget, and had led to the 'complete emptying of the food stores'. Hungarians also housed and fed some 1600 non-military Allied officials – Soviet, American, British, French – whose costs were not insignificant either. Among the expenses which the British and American officials scrupulously presented to their Hungarian hosts were bills for 'cars, horses, clubs, holidays, villas, golfing and tennis courts'. A clutch of florists' bills caused a great scandal in 1946, when details of these expenses appeared in the communist party's newspaper, *Szabad Nép* (*Free People*): members of the British and American delegations were sending great quantities of flowers to their new Hungarian girlfriends, and expected the Hungarian government to pay.[54]

No parallel scandal haunted the Soviet delegation, because Soviet officials did not present bills. Instead, they treated everything around them as booty, confiscating food, clothes, church treasures and museum exhibits. They routinely broke into office safes and locked storage boxes, removing bundles of the now worthless Hungarian currency, the pengő. In one celebrated case, an Anglo-American light bulb factory was dismantled by Soviet officers, despite Hungarian protests, and the contents shipped off to the USSR. About 100 other factories were also taken down in this period of 'wild' reparations too.

More complicated still was the matter of German property in Hungary which, according to the Potsdam treaty, had to be ceded to the USSR. Though an initial list was made up – first twenty large factories and mines, then a further fifty companies – it was not easy to say what was 'German' in Hungary and what was not. In practice, Austrian and Czech companies were confiscated, as well as companies which had some, but not necessarily a majority of, German shareholders. Jewish property which had previously been confiscated by the Germans was now confiscated by the Russians too. The Russians argued they had a moral right to this property, since 'these companies belonged to the German war machine, and served its goal of destroying the Soviet Union'.[55] Only in 1946, with inflation out of control and the economic stability of the country under threat, did the demands for reparations in Hungary slow down and eventually cease.

But Axis countries were not alone in paying a high price for occupation. Though few knew it at the time, Poland, in defiance of international agreements, was also made to pay reparations. Soviet military archives contain records of the dismantling and transportation, among other things, of the contents of a tractor factory near Poznań, a metal-working factory in Bydgoszcz, and a printing press in Toruń, all of which lay in regions of Poland which had not been

German before the war. The justification for such confiscations – that this was 'German' property – is highly dubious, given that much of the 'German' property in Poland had (as in Hungary) earlier been confiscated from Poles or Jews.[56]

Thanks to recent archival revelations, it is also now clear that the USSR also carefully planned the dismantling and removal of 'German' property from Upper Silesia, which had been a part of prewar Poland (Lower Silesia, which is confusingly to the north, had lain within the prewar German Reich). In February 1945, Stalin ordered a special committee to investigate and create an inventory of the property 'gained' in the war, with the aim of carrying it off to the Soviet Union. By March, the committee had already ordered the dismantling and shipping of the contents of a steel mill and a factory which made steel pipes, as well as furnaces and machine tools from other factories in and near Gliwice, part of prewar Poland. A single steel factory in Ukraine received thirty-two trainloads – 1591 wagons – of equipment.

In the months that followed, the Red Army proceeded to pack up factories as far from the German border as Rzeszów, in the south-eastern corner of Poland. Several electric power plants were dismantled, almost always without the foreknowledge of Polish authorities. Henryk Różański, then the Deputy Industry Minister, recalled later that the Russians took Polish train tracks, as well as Polish trains: 'There began a kind of game, involving painting and repainting the symbols on the trains – a game which became a serious conflict between Polish and Russian railway workers.' At one point, Różański travelled to Katowice, where locals told him that the Red Army was removing the contents of a factory producing zinc oxide. Unannounced, he paid a visit, and discovered machines and furnaces already lying about in the snow.

He protested to local Soviet authorities: after all, this was a Polish factory, in territory which had been Polish before the war. It had never had German owners. It had never been part of any reparations treaty. But they ignored him. Poland might have been an ally, but it was still, in Soviet eyes, an enemy.[57]

The Red Army's entry into Eastern Europe in 1944 and 1945 had not been carefully planned, and none of what followed – the violence, the theft, reparations, rape – was part of a long-term scheme. The Soviet Union's presence in the region certainly was the accidental result of Hitler's invasion of the Soviet Union, of the Red Army's victories at Stalingrad and Kursk, and of the Western Allies' decision not to push further and faster to the east when they had the chance. But it is incorrect to assume that the Soviet Union's leadership had never before contemplated a military invasion of the region, or that they were indifferent to the opportunity. On the contrary, they had already tried to overthrow the political order in Eastern Europe, more than once.

If the Red Army's soldiers were shocked by the relative wealth of Eastern Europe, the Soviet Union's founders would not have been surprised at all, for they knew the region extremely well. Lenin spent several months living in Kraków and the Polish countryside.[58] Trotsky spent many years in Vienna. All of them followed German politics closely, and all regarded the politics of Germany and of Eastern Europe as vitally important to their own.

To understand why, it helps to know some philosophy as well as some history, since the Bolsheviks read the works of Lenin and Marx not as they are read today, as texts in a university course, or as one of many theories of history, but as scientific fact. Contained within Lenin's oeuvre (and built up by Trotsky) was a very clear, and equally 'scientific', theory of international relations, which went something like this: the Russian Revolution was the first of what would be many communist revolutions; others would soon follow, in Eastern Europe, in Germany, in Western Europe and then around the world; once the entire world was run by communist regimes, then the communist utopia could be achieved.

Certain of this rosy future, Lenin himself referred to the coming upheavals with conviction and even a kind of reckless insouciance. 'Zinoviev, Bukharin and I, too, think that revolution in Italy should be spurred on immediately,' he wrote in a note to Stalin in July 1920. 'My personal opinion is that to this end, Hungary should be sovietized, and perhaps Czechia and Romania. We have to think it over carefully.'[59] A year earlier, he referred to the 'worldwide collapse of bourgeois democracy and bourgeois parliamentarism', as if it were imminent.[60]

The Bolsheviks did not intend to sit back and wait for these revolutions to unfold. As the revolutionary vanguard, they hoped to facilitate the coming turmoil through propaganda, subterfuge and even warfare.[61] In the spring of 1919 they had set up the Communist International, popularly known as the Comintern, a body officially dedicated to the overthrow of capitalist regimes according to a Leninist blueprint, as outlined in books such as *What is to be Done* (Lenin's furious denunciation of social democracy and left-wing pluralism, published in 1902).[62] In practice, as Richard Pipes has written, the Comintern constituted a 'declaration of war on all the existing governments'.[63]

In the chaos that followed the First World War in Europe, the possibility that all existing governments might collapse did not seem at all farfetched. In the first few shaky years, it even seemed as if Marx's prophecies would come true first in his own country. The Versailles Treaty and its punitive sanctions created immediate dissatisfaction in Germany. The German comrades, at the time the world's largest and most sophisticated communist party, immediately tried to use this to their advantage. In 1919, German communists staged a series of uprisings in Berlin. Weeks later, two veterans of the Russian Revolution helped lead a Munich rebellion which proclaimed, briefly and improbably, a Bavarian Socialist Republic. Lenin greeted these events with enthusiasm. Official Soviet envoys were dispatched to the Bavarian Workers' Soviet, arriving just before it collapsed.

These German rebellions were not flukes. A similarly chaotic end to the First World War brought a similarly short-lived communist regime to power in Hungary, another country that had been severely punished by a postwar settlement which eventually removed two thirds of its territory. Like the German uprisings, Hungary's short Marxist revolution also had deep Soviet connections. Its leader, Béla Kun, had taken an active part in the Russian Revolution, had founded the first foreign delegation within the Soviet communist party, and had even befriended Lenin and his family. Kun set out for Budapest in 1919 at Moscow's request. His brief but notably bloody rebellion imitated the Bolshevik Revolution in many ways. Among other things, the 133 days of the Hungarian Soviet Republic featured thugs in leather jackets calling themselves 'the Lenin boys', the transformation of the police into a 'Red Guard', and the nationalization of schools and factories. But Kun proved a sloppy political leader, just as he had been a sloppy conspirator (he once left a briefcase full of secret party documents in a Vienna taxi). The Hungarian Soviet Republic ended ignominiously, with a Romanian invasion and the founding of an authoritarian regime led by Admiral Miklós Horthy.[64]

Back in Moscow, the Bolsheviks perceived these setbacks as temporary. Of course, they argued, the reactionary forces would grow stronger in the face of growing working-class power. Of course the imperialists and the capitalists would fight tooth and nail to save themselves from destruction. According to marvellously flexible Marxist-Leninist theory, the growing power of the counter-revolution merely reflected the strength of the revolutionary tide. The greater the opposition, the more likely it was that capitalism would eventually fail. It had to: Marx had said so. Zinoviev, the Comintern's first leader, was so confident that this revolutionary wave was about to break that in 1919 he predicted 'in a year we shall already forget that Europe had had to fight a war for Communism, because in a year all Europe shall be Communist'.[65]

Lenin was confident too. In January 1920, just as the Russian Civil War was drawing to a close, he approved a plan to attack 'bourgeois' and 'capitalist' Poland. Though there were political, historical and imperial reasons for the conflict – the new border between Poland and Russia had turned former Tsarist lands over to the Polish state, and Polish troops were already fighting to take more of Ukraine – the true *casus belli* was ideological. Lenin believed that the war would lead to a communist revolution in Poland, and ultimately to communist revolutions in Germany, Italy and elsewhere, and so he ordered the creation of a Polish revolutionary committee ('PolRevKom'), which would start preparing itself to take power in Soviet Poland. Delegates to the Second Comintern Congress in Moscow that summer cheered the daily reports of Bolshevik victories, which were marked on a map that had been stuck up on a wall beside a discarded Romanov throne.[66] In London, the then junior cabinet minister Winston Churchill gloomily predicted that 'the Polish nation would emerge a Communist annexe of the Soviet power'.[67]

To everyone's immense surprise, the war ended with the decisive defeat of the Bolsheviks. The turning point came in August 1920 at the Battle of Warsaw, still remembered by the Poles as 'The Miracle on the Vistula'. Not only did the Poles turn back the Red Army, but they captured some 95,000 Red Army soldiers. The rest fled east in what turned rapidly into a total rout. The young Stalin played a minor role in this failed venture: as the political commissar of the south-western front, he botched communications during the Polish counter-offensive. By all accounts he continued to resent the 'Polish Lords' and the 'White aristocrats' who had dealt the Red Army such a blow for the rest of his life.[68]

Only in the wake of this embarrassing defeat did the Bolsheviks conclude that the time for revolution was not quite ripe. Poland's workers and peasants, Lenin bitterly observed, had failed to rise up against their exploiters, and had instead 'let our brave Red soldiers starve, ambushed them and beat them to death'.[69] It was left to Stalin, Lenin's successor, to explain this defeat with a new interpretation of Marxist theory. In 1924, he declared, with great fanfare, that it was now possible to achieve 'Socialism in One Country'. Banal though this sounds to us now, at the time this was a major shift in revolutionary thinking – and the beginning of Stalin's break with his internationalist arch-rival, Leon Trotsky.

It also marked a beginning of a shift in the Soviet Union's relationships with the outside world. In the wake of Stalin's announcement, Western countries began broadening their relations with Moscow. The UK granted diplomatic recognition to the USSR in 1924. Nine years later, the new American President, Franklin Roosevelt, established diplomatic relations with the Soviet Union too. He had been persuaded, in part, by Walter Duranty, the enthusiastically pro-Soviet Moscow correspondent who had notoriously (and knowingly) failed to report the existence of mass famine in Ukraine the previous year. Duranty assured Roosevelt that, as he had written in the *New York Times*, 'the word "Bolshevik" has lost much of its former mystery and terror over here'.[70] The USSR was becoming 'normal': more to the point, it seemed to have settled down within its borders.

As it turned out, the international revolution had not been abandoned. It had merely been postponed. And by 1944 the Soviet Union was preparing to relaunch it.

3

Communists

Whoever defames you, wants to slander us, The Party
  and the working class . . .
Those too stupid and blind to understand this will fall
  victim to the enemy . . .
You stand at the summit of our Party.

Poem written in honour of Walter Ulbricht[1]

Once, their names appeared on red banners, their portraits were carried in parades. No government office was complete without their photographs hanging on the wall. No national celebration could be held without them. They inspired awe and fear. Even their closest friends spoke guardedly when they entered a room. Yet in none of their respective countries are the men sometimes known as the 'little Stalins' – Walter Ulbricht of East Germany, Bolesław Bierut of Poland, Mátyás Rákosi of Hungary – now admired at all. Even at the height of their powers, none of them ever held total power. The cults created around them were mere shadow versions of the cult created around Stalin himself. His comrades frequently hailed Stalin as 'the great genius, the continuer of Lenin's immortal cause', something which was never quite said about Stalin's Eastern European imitators.[2] At the same time, no account of postwar Eastern Europe can be complete without a brief examination of the men whose names and faces were once ubiquitous in the streets of their respective countries.

Of the three, Walter Ulbricht was probably the most unpromising as a young man. The son of a poor tailor, Ulbricht left school early and became a cabinet-maker. He joined the Young Workers' Educational

45

Association, a socialist club of the sort that discouraged drinking and card-playing while encouraging earnest discussion and Sunday outings in the countryside. The club members would tie red handkerchiefs to their walking sticks and sing Marxist songs as they hiked along trails. That early experience seems to have left the future communist party General Secretary with an almost fanatically puritan sexual morality and a deep respect for long, heavy books.[3]

Like the rest of his generation, Ulbricht was drafted into the German army in 1915. But he deserted in 1918 – he loathed the military – and was profoundly impressed by the brief workers' revolution he witnessed in Leipzig that year. At about the same time he discovered Marxism. As one of his biographers writes, 'here was a seemingly simple, convincing formula that enabled him to categorize and explain everything he learned, heard and saw. Here was "truth" – the truth the ruling classes were bent on suppressing and keeping from people.'[4]

Ulbricht was to stick to that very simple, very clear faith for the rest of his life. When the Moscow show trials began in the late 1930s, he fervently supported Stalin's persecution of the 'Trotskyite spies of Nazi fascism'. He was never bothered by the fact that so many of his German comrades wound up in the Gulag, and perhaps this was not an accident. Ulbricht benefited directly from the arrest of dozens of leading communists – men better educated and more experienced – since their disappearance facilitated his own rise to power. In 1938, following a particularly vicious series of arrests, he became the German communist party's representative to the Comintern and moved to Moscow.

Even after the signing of the Hitler–Stalin pact in 1939 he stuck to his support for Stalin. This moment provoked a great crisis among German communists, most of whom were passionate and genuine anti-Nazis. Ulbricht was one of the few who did not waver. Even after Stalin sent several hundred German communists back to Hitler's concentration camps at Hitler's request, Ulbricht continued to agitate against 'primitive' anti-fascism, meaning anti-fascism which did not allow for nuances such as pacts with the fascists. Perhaps it was then that he won the Soviet dictator's trust.

Certainly it was not his charisma which brought him to power. A Nazi officer who encountered him in a Soviet camp recalled that although 'there are Communists who can handle themselves fairly well in the company of officers . . . the Party apparatchiks like Ulbricht, with their wooden "dialectical" monologues, are simply unbearable'.[5] Elfriede Brüning met Ulbricht before the war at the party meetings her parents organized in the back room of their shop. 'He was always in a hurry, never exchanged a personal word with us,' she wrote in her memoirs. ' "You really get cold just looking at him," said my mother.'[6] Ulbricht could not make small talk, and in later years was given to reciting monologues on topics such as 'the happiness of youth' (perhaps marginally more entertaining than his famously long speeches, which were devoted to subjects like 'the Tasks of the Political Departments of the Machine and Tractor Stations' and 'The Tasks of Trade Union Members in the Democratic Construction of the Economy', subsequently published in large volumes).[7] But because it was tacitly understood that Ulbricht was the USSR's man in Germany, his authority went unchallenged until Stalin's death.

Over the years, Ulbricht would repay the Soviet leadership's faith in him. During the early period of the Soviet occupation of Germany, Ulbricht would not tolerate any discussion of Red Army rape and looting. According to one of his colleagues, 'Ulbricht's workload amazed even his enemies. We kept asking ourselves, How can Ulbricht keep it up? – twelve or fourteen, sometimes sixteen hours a day . . .' Slowly, however, they began to realize that this 'was not so impressive', since 'apparently he received general directives from the Soviets; his skill lay in applying these instructions to specific areas'.[8] Towards the end of his life, his personal style even came to mimic Stalin's, and his birthday parties were celebrated with pomp, circumstance and poems dedicated to his glory. If imitation is the sincerest form of flattery, then Ulbricht was a great flatterer indeed.

By comparison to Ulbricht, Bolesław Bierut was a far shadier character – so shady that even his birthplace is disputed. He probably came from eastern Poland, a region which was part of the Russian empire until 1917, and it seems he went to a Russian-language school. Like Stalin's parents, Bierut's parents hoped he would be a priest. But after he participated in the strikes which broke out across the Russian empire in 1905 he was expelled from school and had to work. Some

sources think he might have joined the freemasons, but others dis-
agree. All do agree that he joined the party very early on, and that he
attended the Comintern's International Lenin School in Moscow in
the 1920s. He did not have a high position in the Polish communist
party before the war, and was hardly known in his own country at all.
Instead, like Ulbricht, he became a trusted agent of the Comintern,
and travelled on the Soviet communist party's behalf through Austria,
Czechoslovakia and Bulgaria. At one point he even became a leading
member of the Bulgarian communist party. His job in Sofia, as everywhere else, was presumably to make sure that local communist leaders
toed the Stalinist line. That he was a paid agent of Soviet influence is
beyond doubt.[9]

But the real mystery of Bierut surrounds his activities during the
Second World War. It is known that he was in Warsaw in 1939, that
he fled to the USSR after the German invasion, and that he lived in
Kiev until May 1941. This was an unusual place for a Polish communist to be in that period: most of them had made their way to the
newly Sovietized regions of western Ukraine and western Belarus,
where they were given important political or cultural offices, or else to
other parts of the USSR. After 1941, things become murkier still. A
confidential biography of Bierut put together by the international
department of the Soviet communist party in 1944 states that from
the moment Hitler invaded the USSR, 'information on Bierut is lacking'.[10] A Polish communist who met him in wartime Warsaw also
remembered that 'I knew nothing of his past. He simply appeared.'[11]

Bierut was probably in Białystok when Hitler's invasion of the
Soviet Union began in June 1941, and he probably travelled from
there to Minsk. But there the trail runs cold. He had a girlfriend and
child in Minsk, having left his first wife and children behind long ago,
as so many revolutionaries were wont to do. He also went to work for
the Nazi city administration, where he was probably, though not
necessarily, a Soviet agent. Rumours to the effect that Bierut had collaborated with the Gestapo, and even that he spent part of the war in
Berlin, have long been in circulation.[12] So have stories that Bierut was
simply a straightforward employee of the Soviet NKVD, the secret
police, from the beginning to the end of his career.[13]

Both might be true: Bierut may have simply switched sides a few times. Stalin is known to have favoured promoting people who had some deep character flaw or secret, supposedly because he liked to have an extra means of controlling his subordinates. Since Stalin had little faith in Polish communists in general, he might well have preferred a possible collaborator like Bierut to a true believer like Ulbricht. Anyone can lose their faith in communism, but blackmail is for ever.

Whatever the reason, Bierut did have unusually good contacts with the Soviet leadership, as well as lines of communication not necessarily open or apparent to others. He also remained, from the Soviet point of view, reliably subservient. The British statesman Anthony Eden witnessed an encounter between Bierut and Stalin and described the Polish communist as 'servile'. Władysław Gomułka – Bierut's most important party rival, and thus not an entirely dependable witness – claims to have seen Stalin shouting at Bierut, 'What kind of fucking communists are you', or words to that effect, in October 1944, when Bierut apparently ventured to suggest that an all-out attack on the Polish anti-Nazi underground might not be good policy. Some Polish communists even wanted to operate in tandem with the non-communist Polish partisans but Stalin did not like that idea at all – and thus neither did Bierut, who complied with Stalin's demands for the liquidation of the wartime underground, as well as his demands for an internal party purge in 1949, for the liquidation of the Polish officer corps, and for the imposition of socialist realism on Polish artists and architects. In the end, there is no record of Bierut ever defying Stalin on any issue at all.

Mátyás Rákosi, the third little Stalin, started out rather differently from his counterparts. Ulbricht was a worker, Bierut was (probably) a peasant, but Rákosi was the son of a small-time Jewish merchant. He was also relatively well-educated. Born in a Hungarian-speaking county of what is now Serbia, he was the fourth child in a family of twelve children, according to his autobiography. His father went bankrupt when he was six years old, and the family moved frequently after that. Mocked for his poverty by his schoolmates, the young Rákosi was attracted to the radical Left from childhood onwards. During his teenage years his school headmaster banned him from making political speeches. He also prided himself on his 'awful manners'.

He used deliberately rude forms of speech in order to offend people, especially if he thought they came from the upper classes.[14]

Following a brief period of military service and a couple of years as a political prisoner in Russia, in 1918 Rákosi helped found the Hungarian communist party. In 1919 he was one of the leaders of the short-lived Hungarian Soviet Republic. Somehow, within the three-month life of that regime, he managed to be commander-in-chief of the Red Guard, Commissar for Production and Deputy Commissar for Commerce. After the Hungarian Soviet Republic collapsed he made his way, via an Austrian prison, to Moscow, where in 1921 he had a brief meeting with Lenin. This event would, in time, be transformed into the myth of Rákosi as a 'friend and collaborator' of Lenin.[15]

Like Bierut and Ulbricht, Rákosi worked closely with the Comintern throughout the 1920s, and travelled through Europe on behalf of that organization and of the Soviet secret police. In 1924 – revealing a sense of humour he rarely exhibited elsewhere – he returned to Budapest disguised as a merchant from Venice. There he helped reorganize the communist party, banned since its disastrous period in power in 1919. Following his arrest in 1925, he became the focus of a celebrated and much-publicized trial. Despite an international campaign to release him, Rákosi then spent the next fifteen years in prison, where he learned Russian and taught Marxism to the other prisoners.

He was finally allowed to travel to the Soviet Union in 1940 when, following the Hitler–Stalin pact, the Hungarian authoritarian regime allowed a number of imprisoned communists to travel to the USSR. Upon arrival, he received a hero's welcome, and even stood beside Stalin during that year's celebration of the Great October Revolution. He quickly became one of the leaders of 'Kossuth Radio', which was already broadcasting Soviet propaganda into Hungary, and resumed his close relations with Comintern leaders.[16] Thoroughly at home in the USSR, he even managed to marry a Soviet prosecutor, a Yakut woman whose first husband had been a Red Army officer.[17]

Rákosi's career as Hungary's little Stalin followed that of his fellow dictators in another respect. Rákosi reckoned early on that the only way to get ahead and to stay on top was to slavishly follow the edicts of Stalin. Throughout the postwar period, the Hungarian communist party made no important decisions without Soviet approval, as Rákosi readily admitted. In his memoirs he wrote frankly, for example, that Stalin asked him to stay out of the negotiations which formed the first postwar government in 1945, on the grounds that Rákosi was too closely associated with the 1919 government – in other words he was 'too' communist – and also because he was Jewish, a fact which might be used against him by his political opponents. Rákosi did not object on either count.[18]

Without question, these three men were very different in character and personal style. Rákosi, garrulous and talkative, had been a well-known if not exactly beloved public figure inside his country for many years. Bierut was absolutely unknown to most Poles, including most Polish communists. Ulbricht was a familiar but not particularly popular face inside the German communist party, and wasn't much known outside it.

Yet as their biographies reveal, these three men did share certain things. All of them had worked closely with the Comintern. All of them had survived the war either by fleeing to Moscow or by obtaining Moscow's help. In the shorthand that later became popular, all of them were 'Moscow communists' – that is, Soviet-trained communists, as opposed to communists who had made their careers in their own countries, or communists who had spent the war in Western Europe or North America. From the Soviet point of view the latter two groups were less reliable: they might well have acquired suspicious views or dubious contacts in their years spent outside the USSR.

'Moscow communists' would play a key role in the formation of the first postwar governments all across Europe. Klement Gottwald, the Czechoslovak 'little Stalin', had been a Comintern leader, as had Josip Tito, the Yugoslav partisan leader who became the Yugoslav dictator. Georgi Dimitrov, Bulgaria's little Stalin, was actually the Comintern's boss for nearly a decade. Both Maurice Thorez, the leader of the French communist party during and after the war, and Palmiro Togliatti, who played that same role in Italy, were 'Moscow communists' too. Both men were intimately involved in Comintern affairs and, had the chance ever presented itself, they would have been Stalin's designated puppets in Western Europe. There were one or two exceptions – Romania's postwar communist party was run by Gheorghe Gheorghiu-Dej, a 'local' communist – but he still went out of his way to demonstrate his fealty to Stalin whenever possible.

Although their names and faces would appear most prominently on the placards and posters of the time, most of the little Stalins were also surrounded by other Moscow communists who reinforced their views, and who may also have watched over them on Moscow's behalf. Bierut's two most important sidekicks, Jakub Berman and Hilary Minc – the former in charge of ideology and propaganda, the latter in control of the economy – would eventually line up with him against 'Warsaw' or 'Home' communists such as Gomułka. In Hungary, Rákosi also headed a troika of Moscow communists. The other two members were József Révai and Ernő Gerő, again in charge of ideology and economics, respectively. Mihály Farkas, Minister of Defence between 1948 and 1953, was another important sidekick. All of them would eventually turn against the 'Budapest' communists too.

In Germany, Ulbricht's most important colleague, Wilhelm Pieck, had a long Comintern history, having been Secretary-General of the organization from 1938 to 1943. From the very earliest days of Soviet occupation, all of the German communists who returned to Berlin early, on planes flown directly from Moscow or in the company of Red Army troops, always had higher status than those German communists who found refuge in France (where many were harassed by French authorities), Morocco (they lurk in the background of the film *Casablanca*), Sweden (where Brecht lived for a time), Mexico (then very friendly to communists) and the United States. The Soviet leadership even considered them more trustworthy than the German communists who had stayed in Germany to the fight the Nazis. Even those Germans who had suffered as political prisoners in Hitler's concentration camps never enjoyed the confidence of the Soviet occupation authorities. It was as if their very presence in Nazi Germany had tarnished them in Soviet eyes.

Across Eastern Europe, the Moscow communists were united not only by a common ideology, but by a common commitment to the Comintern's long-term goal of worldwide revolution, followed by an international dictatorship of the proletariat. Though Stalin's declaration of 'Socialism in One Country' had brought to an end the open warfare between the Soviet Union and the nations of Western Europe, it did not prevent him and his secret services from plotting violent change, albeit using spies and subterfuge instead of the Red Army. In fact, the 1930s – W. H. Auden's 'low dishonest decade' – were a period of extraordinarily creative skulduggery for Soviet foreign policy. In the UK, Soviet agents recruited Guy Burgess, Kim Philby, Donald Maclean, Anthony Blunt and (probably) John Cairncross, the infamous 'Cambridge Five'. In the US they recruited Alger Hiss, Harry Dexter White and Whittaker Chambers.

In at least one respect, these Anglo-American agents had something in common with the Moscow communists of Eastern Europe: all of them were willing and eager to work closely with the NKVD. So too, at the time, were most European communists. In this, they were not exceptional. Though their links to the Soviet secret police are now felt, in retrospect, to have tarnished American and European communist parties, it did not bother the leaders of those parties at the time. Generally speaking, those in the West who believed in the desirability of world revolution also thought that this revolution would be led by the Soviet communist party and thus facilitated by the Soviet secret police. Even the American communist party took money from the USSR, sometimes channelled through the Comintern.[19] Many left-wing intellectuals at the time knowingly met NKVD agents on a regular basis, as a matter of course.[20] There was no stigma, as there would be in later years, in taking 'Moscow Gold', or in doing a few favours for the local undercover agents of the NKVD or, as it was later known, the KGB. To the truly dedicated, the goals of the USSR, of the Comintern, of the USSR's spies and of their own national communist parties would have seemed utterly interchangeable.

But the men and women who would become Eastern Europe's postwar leaders were linked not only by the ideology of the international communist movement, but also by its peculiar culture and rigid structures. Whatever their national origins, by the 1940s most European communist parties had copied the Bolsheviks' strictly hierarchical organization and nomenclature. They were all led by a General Secretary and a ruling group called the 'political bureau', or Politburo. The Politburo in turn controlled the Central Committee, a larger group of party apparatchiks, many of whom would eventually specialize in

particular issues. The Central Committee oversaw regional committees, which oversaw local party cells. Everyone at the bottom reported
to the top, and everyone at the top theoretically knew what was
happening at the bottom.

Those who lived in the USSR were particularly sensitive to the
rules of this hierarchy. For those in favour, the rewards were great.
Political émigrés – *polit-emigrants*, in Bolshevik slang – had, in the
1920s and 1930s, been a 'privileged caste':

> We lived in our own world, subjects of a state within a state. We
> received free hotel accommodations, generous monthly allowances,
> and free clothing. We spoke at meetings in factory clubs and schools,
> after which we were banqueted. There were free theater parties and
> amusements. Those *polit-emigrants* who were ill as a result of their suf-
> ferings in fascist and capitalist prisons were sent to exclusive hospitals
> and sanatoriums on the Black Sea. And here again, because of their
> special, privileged status, Russian girls flocked after the *polit-emigrant*
> for material considerations.[21]

The very highest ranking foreign communists – top Comintern
officials, national communist party leaders – were housed in the well-
appointed Hotel Lux, not far from the Kremlin. Their children went
to special schools. Both Markus Wolf, later East Germany's most
famous spymaster, and Wolfgang Leonhard, later its most senior
defector, attended the same Moscow high school for children of German communists. Those with a somewhat lesser status had jobs at
foreign-language newspapers, or at the International Red Aid society,
which agitated on behalf of communists in Western prisons. Some
worked in plants and factories scattered across the country.

Yet even at the highest level, and even when they were in favour,
these privileged foreigners had been utterly dependent on the goodwill of their Soviet hosts, and on the whims of Stalin in particular. The
diary of Dimitrov, the Bulgarian Comintern boss, illustrates this
deadly dependency with an almost comic repetitiveness. Over more
than a decade, he pedantically recorded his every meeting and every
conversation with Stalin, up to and including the time when he called
Stalin and the Generalissimo hung up as soon as he recognized
Dimitrov's voice.[22]

Like others, Dimitrov knew his privileged status might not last, and for some it didn't. In the late 1930s, when Stalin turned the focus of his purges on high-ranking members of the Soviet communist party, the 'international' communists in Moscow suffered too. At the height of the NKVD's paranoia, foreigners in the USSR became direct targets. The Polish communist party, which Stalin had never really trusted anyway (he had an NKVD agent specially appointed to manage their affairs in Moscow), was almost completely devastated. At least thirty of the Polish party's thirty-seven Central Committee members were arrested in Moscow, and most were shot or died in the Gulag. The party itself was dissolved on the grounds that it was 'saturated with spies and provocateurs'.[23]

Many prominent foreign communists were also arrested in Moscow, among them Leonhard's mother, and everyone was afraid of being next. In his carefully edited autobiography, even Markus Wolf wrote that his parents were 'anguished' by the arrests: 'When the doorbell rang unexpectedly one night, my usually calm father leapt to his feet and let out a violent curse. When it emerged that the visitor was only a neighbor intent on borrowing something he regained his savoir-faire, but his hands trembled for a good half an hour.'[24] In the hotels and dormitories where foreigners resided, the arrests came in waves – there was 'Polish night', 'German night', 'Italian night' and so on. In their wake, the hallways of the Hotel Lux acquired a 'stifling' atmosphere, in the words of the German communist Margarete Buber-Neumann. 'Former political friends no longer dared visit each other. No one could enter or leave the Lux without a special pass, and the name and particulars of everyone who did so were carefully noted down. All the telephones in the hotel were controlled by the [secret police] from the central switchboard and we could regularly hear the tell-tale click as the control switched in . . .'[25] Buber-Neumann was herself arrested and sent to the Gulag in 1938, a year after her husband had been arrested and executed.

If their lives were precarious within the USSR, dedicated communists were not, in the 1930s, necessarily any safer at home. Throughout the prewar period, European communists were often perceived by local authorities as straightforward agents of a foreign power (which, of course, some of them were). Following the Bolshevik invasion of

Poland in 1920, the Polish communist party was banned and many Polish communists spent long periods in Polish prisons – a piece of luck though they didn't know it at the time, as they were then safe from Stalin. The same was true in Hungary, where the interwar authoritarian regime led by Admiral Miklós Horthy persecuted the communist party because of its links with Soviet agents, because of the memory of the failed 1918 communist coup, and because of the disastrous policies of Béla Kun's brief dictatorship. In the illegal underground, Hungarian communists hid from the law and developed what one veteran called 'a severe, tough, hierarchical organization', one which tolerated very little internal democracy or dissent. Moreover, 'this way of organization was idealized and admired'.[26]

By contrast, the German communist party was a powerful and legal force in Germany after 1918, and at the height of its influence it could command some 10 per cent of the national vote. After Hitler came to power in 1933, the German communists were arrested, expropriated and persecuted as they were elsewhere. Many spent the war in concentration camps, and many did not survive. Ernst Thälmann, the party's charismatic leader, was arrested in 1933 and shot in the Buchenwald camp in August 1944. Had he survived he would no doubt have been treated with suspicion by the 'Moscow communists' too. In 1941 Stalin told Dimitrov that Thälmann 'is being worked on from all sides ... his letters show the influence of fascist ideology' – a judgement which did not prevent Thälmann from becoming one of the hero-martyrs of East Germany in the postwar years.[27]

Despite these obstacles, the international communist movement flourished in much of Europe in the 1930s, and it was in this period that Eastern European intellectuals began to join the party in larger numbers, largely because there were so few other options. To anyone residing in Eastern Europe, the Western half of the continent did not look attractive. They were horrified by the rise of Hitler and Mussolini and by the inability of their own leaders to confront either of them. They were repulsed by the weakness and small-mindedness of England and France, both of which were economically depressed, and both of which were then led by men who favoured the appeasement of fascism. After 1933, the Comintern had also been pushing legal communist parties to enter into 'popular fronts', movements which would unite communists, social democrats and other leftists against the right-wing movements which were then coming to power across Europe, and these seemed successful. A popular front coalition ruled France from 1936 to 1938, and another popular front contested the 1936 elections in Spain. Both of these coalitions, like their counterparts in Eastern Europe, were supported by the USSR.

At the same time many had become disillusioned with their own national politics, national traditions and national literature. The historian Marci Shore has traced the evolution of a number of Polish poets from the artistic avant-garde to the political left – or rather from the observations that 'God is Dead' and 'Realism is Finished' to the belief that Soviet communism would fill the resulting void. In 1929, the poet Julian Tuwim – formerly a member of the patriotic centre-left – became deeply disillusioned by the way patriotism was being exploited to the advantage of the ruling elite. He exhorted his compatriots:

> Throw your machine gun onto the pavement.
> The oil is theirs, the blood is yours.
> And from capital to capital
> Cry out . . .
> 'Gentlemen of the nobility, you do not fool us.'

This wasn't a Marxist *cri de coeur* – Tuwim had meant his poem as a statement of pacifism. But it was heading in that direction, and helps explain why Tuwim would cooperate, to some degree, with the communist regime after the war.[28] Wanda Wasilewska, one of the wartime Polish communist leaders, underwent a similar evolution at about that time. Her father had actually been a minister in one of the interwar Polish governments, and as a very young woman she was active in mainstream socialist groups. Only later, after Poland's shaky democracy collapsed into a small-time dictatorship, did she become truly radical. Disappointed with the failure of centrist, democratic politics, she enthusiastically joined a teachers' strike, lost her job and joined the movement.[29]

Shore's depiction of this milieu focuses on Poland, but the same evolution can be seen in many European countries, both East and West. Disappointment with the failures of capitalism and democracy pushed many Europeans to the far left in the 1930s. Many came to feel that their choices were limited to Hitler on the one hand or Marxism on the other – a polarization which was promoted and encouraged by people on both sides. Communism even acquired a certain avant-garde cachet among nihilist, existentialist or otherwise alienated intellectuals. The towering intellectual figure of the period, Jean-Paul Sartre, was an enthusiastic fellow traveller. Yet even he could never force himself to dwell too much on the Soviet regime's brutality. 'Like you I find these camps intolerable,' he told Albert Camus, speaking of the Soviet Gulag. 'But I find equally intolerable the use made of them every day in the bourgeois press.'[30]

Until 1939, it was possible for all kinds of vaguely leftist, committed anti-fascists to support the Soviet Union without thinking too hard about it. But in that year Soviet foreign policy changed again – dramatically – and made it much more difficult to be an unthinking fellow traveller. In August, Stalin signed his non-aggression pact with Hitler. As noted in the Introduction, the secret protocols of that pact divided Eastern Europe between the two dictators. Stalin got the Baltic states and eastern Poland, as well as northern Romania (Bessarabia and Bukovina). Hitler got western Poland, and was given leave to exert his influence over Hungary, Romania and Austria without Soviet objection. Following this pact, Hitler invaded Poland on 1 September 1939, and England and France declared war on Germany. Less than three weeks later, on 17 September 1939, Stalin invaded Poland too. The Wehrmacht and the Red Army met one another on their new border, shook hands and agreed to exist in peace. Overnight, communist parties around the world were instructed to tone down their criticism of fascism. Hitler was not an ally, exactly, but nor was he to be an enemy. Instead, the comrades were to describe the war as one 'between two groups of capitalist countries' who are 'waging war for their own imperialist interests'. The popular fronts, which had only 'served to ease the position of slaves under a capitalist regime', were to be abandoned altogether.

This tactical change was a great blow to communist solidarity. The German communist party was bitterly anti-fascist, and many of its members could not accept the idea of any accommodation with Hitler at all. The Polish communist party was torn in half between those who rejoiced at the Soviet invasion of eastern Poland – a change which created jobs and opportunities for many of them – and those horrified by the fact that their country had ceased to exist. Across the rest of Europe many communists were deeply confused by the new language they were supposed to adopt in response to these events. The Comintern itself dithered over its statement, drafting and redrafting its new 'theses' so often that one Politburo member acidly complained that 'By this time, Com[rade] Stalin would have written a whole book!'[31] In Moscow, great efforts were made to keep up morale. There is evidence that in February 1941 Ulbricht held a meeting of the German communist party in Moscow at the Hotel Lux, where he cheered them up by predicting, among other things, that the war would end with a wave of Leninist revolutions. The task of the German communists in Moscow, he told them, was to prepare for that possibility.[32]

Yet the Soviet Union and Nazi Germany were, for twenty-two months, real allies. The USSR sold oil and grain to Germany, and Germany sold weapons to the USSR. The Soviet Union offered the Germans the use of a submarine base in Murmansk. The Hitler–Stalin pact even resulted in a prisoner exchange. In 1940, several hundred German communists were removed from the Gulag camps where they had been imprisoned, and taken to the border. Margarete Buber-Neumann was among them. At the border, she wrote, these hardened German communists tried to ingratiate themselves with their old enemies: 'the SS and Gestapo men thrust their hands into the air in the Hitler salute and began to sing "*Deutschland, Deutschland über Alles*". Hesitantly, our men followed suit, and there were very few who did not raise their arms and join in the singing. Amongst these latter was the Jew from Hungary.'[33] Most of these loyal communists ended up in Nazi jails and camps. Buber-Neumann herself was sent directly from the border to a concentration camp, Ravensbrück, where she spent the rest of the war. She thus became a double victim, condemned both to the Soviet Gulag and a Nazi camp as well. These kinds of stories were quickly forgotten in Western Europe, where 'the war' was the war against Germany. But they were remembered all too well in Eastern Europe.

Paradoxically, Hitler's invasion of the Soviet Union in June 1941 gave the international communist movement a new lease on life. With

Stalin now a sworn enemy of Hitler, the Eastern European (and Western European) communist parties once again shared a common cause with the Soviet Union. In the USSR, enthusiasm for foreign communists also returned – now they were possible allies, fifth columns inside Nazi-occupied Europe – and Stalin's tactics changed to suit the new circumstances. Once again, the international communist movement was instructed to unite with social democrats, centrists and this time even bourgeois capitalists in order to create 'national fronts' to defeat Hitler.

Plans were made to send loyal communists back into their countries of origin, though not all of the earliest efforts met with much success. At the end of 1941, the Red Army helped the first group of 'Moscow communists' make their way into Nazi-occupied Poland, where, with radio equipment and contacts provided by the NKVD, they founded a new Polish Workers' Party (Polska Partia Robotnicza, or PPR) in January 1942.[34] Very quickly, they squabbled among themselves and with the rest of the resistance, and probably collaborated with the German secret police during at least one operation against the Home Army, the armed wing of the Polish resistance. One of them then murdered another in a notoriously convoluted incident. Eventually they lost radio contact with Moscow.[35] During the period of radio silence they elected a new leader of their own, Władysław Gomułka, who did not win Moscow's confidence, either then or later. Concerned, the Soviet Union sent in another leader. He was injured parachuting into the country, and wound up shooting himself. Gomułka thus remained the de facto wartime leader of the Polish Workers' Party, at least until Bierut could make it into the country at the end of 1943.

Now that the Soviet Union urgently needed to train new cadres, the Comintern suddenly became an important institution again. For reasons of security, its headquarters were moved to distant Ufa, the capital of the Central Asian province of Bashkortostan, where a new generation of Comintern agents could be trained without fear of bombing or attack. Far behind the front lines, the USSR began to prepare them for the postwar world. This was not the first time the Comintern had undertaken such a task: a special Politburo committee, which included Stalin, had supervised the organization of the first

Comintern training centre in 1925, in Moscow. High standards had been set for the first participants. They had to know English, German or French, were required to have read the most important works of Marx, Engels and Plekhanov, and had to pass a test administered by the Comintern as well as a very thorough background check. 'This is very important,' noted Comintern officials at the time, 'as the whole value of the university will be lost if the proper types are not selected.'[36]

From the very beginning, courses were heavy on Marxism – dialectical materialism, political economy, history of the Russian communist party – though they also tried to include 'practical' training, some-times with comic results. One attempt to teach students about life in Soviet factories ('so that they would learn about the dictatorship of the proletariat from the inside') ended badly when the designated factory, which specialized in metallurgy, could not find jobs for the untrained students, most of whom did not speak Russian. They became, as a result, 'figures of fun' and a distraction for the workers.[37] Worse, almost every national communist party had its splits and divi-sions, and there was always someone arguing that local circumstances in their country made it impossible to follow the Soviet line. The internal Comintern records from the 1930s are full of accusations and counter-accusations. Some students had 'hidden aspects to their pasts', or else bourgeois backgrounds which made them 'inappropriate people to be leading a workers' movement'. Disappointingly few appeared to be textbook revolutionaries.[38]

By 1941, the Comintern was a more experienced organization, and in the aftermath of the German invasion the recruitment of new stu-dents did follow some clear patterns. The foreign party leaders in Moscow immediately began the complex process of tracking down their comrades from the hiding places, refugee camps and prisons where they had found shelter from the war, as well as from Soviet camps and prisons. Those who had been arrested or had spent years in the Gulag were often rehabilitated immediately, no questions asked, if only they could be found alive.

The German leaders Ulbricht and Pieck were particularly assiduous about tracking down old comrades scattered across the Soviet Union, both in the Gulag and outside it. Among those they discovered was the young Wolfgang Leonhard, who had been deported to Karaganda, in Kazakhstan, at the start of the war, along with many other German residents of Moscow, where he languished in semi-starvation. Out of the blue a letter summoned him to Ufa in July 1942, without explanation. From then on, almost every aspect of his first encounter with the wartime Comintern was shrouded in an air of deep mystery. The entrance to the head office was flanked with large columns, but there was no sign on the door, 'nothing to indicate that this was the building which housed the headquarters of the Comintern'. Upon entering, he was immediately offered a meal – it seemed that many of the comrades who arrived there had not eaten in many days – which he wolfed down in silence. He then had a short meeting with the chief of cadres, who told him, still without explanation, that he would be travelling further: 'I will notify you of your destination.'

During the next few days he encountered many old friends, mostly children of German communists like himself, whom he had met in Moscow schools over the years and at meetings of the Komsomol, the communist party's youth wing. None of them would speak about their recent past or their future plans, or even use what he knew to be their real names. 'Gradually, I learned that different standards prevailed here: It was clear that what one did not talk about covered a much wider field.' After a few days he was again informed abruptly that it was time to leave. Still without any explanation, he was put on a boat, taken up the river, placed in a lorry and then finally told to get out and walk. At last he arrived at some old farm buildings, and learned that this, at last, was the Comintern school. In deepest secrecy, he began his training.[39]

Over the next few months, Leonhard and his fellow students heard the standard lectures – in Marxism, and dialectical and historical materialism – with an added emphasis on the history of the communist parties in their respective countries and the history of the Comintern. They had access to secret reports and papers unavailable to others in the Soviet Union. Because of the high status of their future missions, the students also received Nazi and fascist literature of a kind they had never seen or heard before. This was to enable them to better understand their enemies, as Leonhard remembered: 'Often one of us was required to expound in front of the group various doctrines of Nazi ideology, while others had the task of attacking and refuting the Nazi arguments. The student who had to expound the Nazi arguments was told to set them out as well and clearly and convincingly as he could, and his performance was actually assessed more favourably the better he represented the Nazi point of view.'[40]

But although they were allowed to read Nazi literature, they were kept well away from the writings of dissident or anti-Stalinist communists: 'whereas all the other seminars generally reached a respectable level of discussion, the seminar on Trotskyism was confined to furious partisan denunciations.'[41]

There were several such wartime schools, not only for communists but also for Polish officers who had been recruited into the 'Kościuszko Division', a Polish-speaking division of the Red Army, as well as for captured German officers who were being 're-educated'. A noteworthy number of the politicians who were later to play promiment roles in the postwar communist states studied at them – or sent their children to do so. Tito's son Zarko was one of Leonhard's colleagues, for example, as was Amaya Ibárruri, the daughter of the Spanish communist Dolores Ibárruri, better known as La Pasionaria, one of the celebrated orators of the Spanish Civil War.

Some of the teachers in the schools had equally illustrious careers in front of them. Jakub Berman, later the security, ideology and propaganda boss in Poland, taught Polish communists in Ufa from 1942 onward. Then, as later, Berman took great pains to toe the party line. Among other things, he kept in close touch at this time with Zofia Dzerzhinskaia, the Polish wife of the notorious founder of the secret police, Feliks Dzerzhinskii (who was also Polish). She functioned as a kind of godmother to the Polish communists in the Soviet Union, and Berman carefully preserved copies of his letters to her. Although these are stiffly written and not especially informative, they do shed some light on what life must have been like in wartime Ufa. Berman told Dzerzhinskaia that he often went to listen to other lecturers, including Pieck from Germany, Togliatti from Italy, and La Pasionaria from Spain. He carefully followed events in Warsaw ('with great eagerness we are following the news of the heroic battle in the country'). On the occasion of the twenty-fifth anniversary of the USSR, he solemnly informed Dzerzhinskaia that the Soviet Union is 'for us the best example of how to organize in the future the same kind of life in our country'.[42]

Berman also told Dzerzhinskaia that he was teaching courses on 'the History of Poland, the History of the Polish workers' movement' as well as instructing young Polish communists on contemporary politics. These were not easy subjects, given that Stalin had dissolved the Polish communist party in 1938 and killed many of its leaders. (Later, official party history would explain that the Polish communist party 'was created on a base of Marxism-Leninism, but didn't manage to finish off factionalist tendencies'.)[43] The party's replacement, Gomułka's Polish Workers' Party, was still very small, having been founded only in 1942. In another set of letters, to his comrade Leon Kasman, Berman was more open about the 'difficulties' these facts presented for anyone trying to teach the history of Polish communism. Obviously, it was necessary to tread very delicately when the 1930s were under discussion, since it was impossible to mention Stalin's role in the dissolution of the party, and even more impossible to mention his antagonism towards Poland.[44]

None of this prevented Berman from trying, as best he could, to indoctrinate young Poles and to teach them how to defend the Soviet Union. At one point, he even told Dzerzhinskaia that he had asked his pupils to listen to the broadcasts of the anti-Nazi and anti-communist Polish resistance movement, the Home Army, in order to be able to 'counter' their arguments. While German communists like Wolf and Leonhard were being taught to counter Nazi propaganda, Polish communists were thus preparing for the coming ideological struggle against the leaders of the mainstream Polish resistance. In one of his notes to Dzerzhinskaia, Berman wondered whether it might be possible to find 'healthy elements' – i.e. future collaborators – among the peasant leaders and even the far-right National Democrats. 'For this reason,' he explained to Dzerzhinskaia, 'it's absolutely necessary, I believe, to continue the tactics of the united front.' The Polish communist party must not show its true colours too early. First it would have to find allies and collaborators, and only later could it promote Soviet-style reforms.

He was not alone in making plans along these lines. At about the same time, Soviet leaders were also preparing once again to promote 'united fronts', coalition governments which could rule immediately after liberation, across Eastern Europe. In his long 1944 memo to

Molotov, Ivan Maiskii, the Soviet Foreign Minister, had speculated that the proletarian revolutions might take place in some thirty or forty years' time. But in the meantime he advocated keeping Poland and Hungary weak, perhaps dividing Germany – 'in the long term it will contribute to the weakening of Germany' – and, last but not least, ensuring that local communists worked in tandem with others. 'It is in the USSR's interests,' he concluded, for postwar governments to be 'based on the principle of broad democracy, in the spirit of the idea of the national fronts'.[45]

The word 'democracy' naturally must be taken here with a large grain of salt, for Maiskii also made it clear that these governments, created 'in the spirit of the national fronts', would not be able to tolerate the existence of political parties which were in any way hostile to socialism. In practice, this meant that in some countries (he mentions Germany, Hungary and Poland) 'various methods' of external influence would have to be deployed in order to prevent such parties from gaining power. He did not explain what those methods would be.

Persecuted in both East and West, European communists of all stripes came to inhabit a culture of conspiracy, secrecy and exclusivity. In their native countries they worked in cells, knew one another by pseudonyms, and communicated using passwords and dead letter drops. In the USSR, they kept their thoughts to themselves, refrained from criticizing the party, and searched their lodgings for secret microphones.[46] Wherever they were, they observed a 'rigid etiquette', which has been beautifully described by the writer Arthur Koestler, in both his novels and his memoirs. Koestler, much of whose fiction and nonfiction describes his relationship with communism, himself was drawn to the German party in the 1930s, not least because of his attraction to secrecy, conspiracy and intrigue: 'Even a superficial contact will make the innocent outsider feel that members of the Party lead a life apart from society, steeped in mystery, danger and constant sacrifice. The thrill of being in touch with this secret world is considerable even for people with an adult and otherwise unromantic mentality. Still stronger is the flattering effect of being found worthy of a certain amount of trust, of being permitted to perform minor services for the harassed men who live in such constant danger.'[47]

The lure of an elitist existence, complete with access to privileges and to privileged information, remained an important part of the attraction of communism for decades. At his special Comintern school Wolfgang Leonhard read for the first time the same high-level telegrams circulated among the party bosses and realized how much more they contained than the propaganda fed to the masses: 'I remember very well the feelings with which I held one of these secret information bulletins in my hands for the first time. There was a sense of gratitude for the confidence placed in me, and a sense of pride at being one of those officials who were sufficiently mature politically to be trusted with the knowledge of other points of view.'[48]

Their experiences of terror – mass arrest and purges, accompanied by rapid tactical changes – had a profound impact on European communists as well. At the Comintern school in Ufa, Leonhard was humiliated by being forced to make a ludicrous public statement of self-criticism. As he reflected on the experience, and on the smug behaviour of some of his comrades – notably a German woman named Emmi, later to become Mrs Markus Wolf – he suddenly wondered: 'Is our whole relationship at the school what it ought to be between Party members? There came back into my mind other critical thoughts, which I had had earlier in the period of the purges. Critical conversations came back to me, and I was frightened of myself. If I had already expressed critical thoughts like these, what was the end likely to be? I made up my mind in future to be much more cautious in what I said and to keep it to the minimum necessary.'[49]

These kinds of experiences eventually convinced Leonhard to flee East Germany, and eventually to leave the party altogether. But others, though humiliated in similar ways, did not flee or leave. Nor were they rendered any softer or more compassionate by their traumatic experiences. Far from being humbled by their wartime suffering, whether in Hitler's camps or in Western jails, the communists who remained in the party often became more devoted to the cause, not less so.

Many of those who physically survived the purges in the USSR – and intellectually survived the policy changes – emerged from the war not only with an increased sense of tribal loyalty, but an increased

2

feeling of dependence on the Soviet Union. And those who had remained faithful party members through the arrests, wild tactical shifts and confusion of the 1930s often emerged as true fanatics: totally loyal to Stalin, willing to follow the Soviet lead in any direction, they obeyed all orders they were given, if to do so served the cause.[50]

4

Policemen

More or less the following attitude developed among the
employees of the Ministry for State Security: We have been
particularly checked over. We are particularly good comrades.
We are, so to speak, first-class comrades.

Wilhelm Zaisser, Minister of State Security, GDR[1]

As the war drew to its bloody end, Stalin at last gave his East European
protégés the chance to prove themselves. One by one, as their countries were liberated, he sent the Moscow communists back into their
homelands along with the Red Army. All of them were fully conscious
of their tiny numbers, and all publicly declared an intention to found
or join a coalition government together with other, non-communist
parties. Bierut arrived in Warsaw in December 1943, just in time to be
named president of the new National Council (Krajowa Rada Narodowa, or KRN). This first attempt to create a popular front failed to
attract anybody except Władysław Gomułka's still-tiny Polish Workers' Party and a few fringe social democrats who had not joined the
mainstream resistance. But a few months later, the National Council
helped form a larger group, the Polish Committee of National Liberation (Polski Komitet Wyzwolenia Narodowego, or PKWN), whose
name, personally approved by Stalin, deliberately echoed De Gaulle's
French Committee of National Liberation.[2] Although based in Lublin, and although it now contained a few genuinely non-communist
politicians, there wasn't much doubt about who was backing the
Polish Committee of National Liberation. Its 22 July manifesto
sounded very liberal, promising that 'all democratic freedoms will be
reinstated for all citizens irrespective of race, religion and nationality;

those freedoms to be: freedom of free associations in political and professional fields, freedom of press and information, freedom of conscience'.[3] But the document was issued in Moscow, not Poland, and it was broadcast immediately on Soviet radio.

The creation of a Committee of National Liberation posed an immediate dilemma for the London government-in-exile, which had represented Poland abroad during the war, and still maintained close links to the Home Army and the mainstream Polish resistance. Though they struggled mightily to remain Poland's international voice, they lost that battle. In due course, the Committee transformed itself into the Provisional Government of National Unity (a group which became known as the 'Lublin Poles'), which all of the Allies would eventually recognize instead of the London government-in-exile (the 'London Poles') as Poland's legitimate rulers. The provisional government ran the country from the beginning of 1945, and was meant to organize the elections which would select the permanent government. Because Stalin was keen to boost its legitimacy, he agreed to allow Edward Osóbka-Morawski, technically a member of the Socialist Party and not the communist party, to become the provisional government's first postwar Prime Minister (Bierut would acquire a formal government title only in 1947). More importantly, he allowed the Prime Minister-in-exile, Stanisław Mikołajczyk, to return to the country and to join the provisional government as Minister of Agriculture and Deputy Prime Minister. For a short period, Mikołajczyk's Polish Peasants' Party (Polska Stronnictwo Ludowe, or PSL) would be allowed to function as a true anti-communist opposition. Officially there was no legal Soviet or Allied authority in Poland. In practice, an NKVD general, Ivan Serov, functioned as the senior Soviet adviser to the new government and to the new Polish security forces. It soon became clear that his influence was very broad indeed.[4]

Not long after Bierut's arrival in Poland, events began to move swiftly and a new authority was created in Hungary too. At the beginning of November 1944, Mihály Farkas, Ernő Gerő and Imre Nagy, three leading 'Moscow communists', were flown in Soviet planes to the liberated eastern city of Szeged. Immediately, they called a mass meeting to celebrate the anniversary of the Bolshevik Revolution, during which Gerő called for 'Hungarian rebirth'.[5] Rákosi arrived in

Debrecen after that city was liberated in January, also on a plane from Moscow. His orders were to set up a Hungarian provisional government there and to prepare for the Red Army's conquest of Budapest. He did so in conjunction with other Hungarian politicians who were now emerging from hiding or returning from abroad. Together, they negotiated the creation of a Provisional National Assembly, which selected a Provisional National Government. As in Poland, the latter was meant to rule Hungary until elections could be held.

Also as in Poland, this first Hungarian provisional government was a coalition. It contained four legal political parties: the communists (Magyar Kommunista Párt, or MKP), the social democrats (Szociál-demokrata Párt, or SZDP), the Peasants' Party and the Smallholders' Party. The last, a prewar party of small businessmen and farmers, rapidly developed into an anti-communist opposition party, and rapidly attracted wide support. Nevertheless, it did not dominate the new Provisional National Assembly or the new provisional government. Despite the fact that the Hungarian communist party had only a few hundred members at the time, the communists were awarded more than a third of the seats in the Provisional National Assembly as well as several key cabinet posts, in practice including the Interior Ministry. Even Gerő acknowledged the imbalance: 'the proportion of communist members was a little oversized. It was partly due to the hastiness, partly due to the overzealousness of local comrades'.[6] Under the terms of the Hungarian Armistice Agreement, signed in Moscow in January 1945, the Hungarian government in this interim period was also subject to the oversight of the Allied Control Council, a body which technically included American and British representatives but was in practice run by Marshal Kliment Voroshilov, a senior Red Army commander who regularly failed to consult the other Allies about anything.[7]

Finally, on 27 April 1945, the Red Army flew the 'Ulbricht Group' – several dozen communists, under Ulbricht's leadership – to join the First Belorussian Front on the outskirts of Berlin, whence they would enter the city. Wolfang Leonhard went with them. A few days later, the 'Ackermann Group', containing another several dozen communists, prepared to enter Berlin from the south with the First Ukrainian Front. Unlike Poland and Hungary, in eastern Germany there was no temporary or provisional government. Instead, a Soviet Military Administration ran its zone of Germany until the creation of the German Democratic Republic in 1949. But the Soviet administrators slowly created a German bureaucracy to help run the country beneath the Soviet umbrella.[8] In June 1947, this bureaucracy, by then a shadow government under control of the Soviet authorities, was blandly christened the German Economic Committee (Deutsche Wirtschaftskommission, or DWK). Many German communists, especially 'Moscow' communists, were immediately given senior roles to play in it. Eventually, the Economic Committee became the basis for the East German government when the German Democratic Republic achieved statehood in 1949.

The Soviet Union would also oversee municipal and local elections in Germany as elsewhere. Although the USSR actively encouraged the re-founding of the Social Democratic Party, the Christian Democratic Party and the Free Democratic Party in their zone of Germany, they still placed communist party members in key positions in the trade unions, cultural associations and other new institutions.[9] Wherever possible, non-communists were given public roles while communists took key jobs behind the scenes. Other kinds of political and semi-political groupings were reconstituted elsewhere, including Zionist and Bundist organizations in Poland and Hungary, some of which initially seemed to have a degree of real independence.

Separately, all of the communist parties in the region maintained their own internal structures, keeping to the Soviet model. They maintained Soviet-style hierarchies: Politburo on top, then the larger Central Committee below, then regional and local organizations. These structures would remain parallel to but separate from governmental structures until 1989. Sometimes Politburo members were also government ministers, but sometimes not. Sometimes Central Committee members also had roles in the state apparatus, but sometimes not. It was not always clear, even to people in positions of power, whether the party or the government had the final say in any given question.

If all of that sounds complicated, that is because it was meant to be: politics in Soviet-occupied Europe were designed to be opaque. As the war ended, the communist parties of Eastern Europe were clearly the most influential political grouping in the region, not because of their numbers but because of their Soviet 'advisers' in the NKVD and Red Army. At the same time, they were under strict instructions to disguise or deny their Soviet affiliations, to behave as normal democratic parties, to create coalitions and to find acceptable partners among the non-communist parties. With the exception of Germany, where the Soviet occupation regime immediately took control, Soviet influence was thus carefully camouflaged.

Throughout 1945 and 1946, the East European coalition provisional governments would therefore try, more or less, to create economic policy in tandem with other politicians. They would try, more or less, to tolerate the churches, some independent newspapers and some private business, all of which were for a time allowed to develop spontaneously and idiosyncratically. But there was one glaring exception to that tolerance. Everywhere the Red Army went, the Soviet Union always established one new institution whose form and character always followed a Soviet pattern. To put it bluntly, the structure of the new secret police force was never left up to chance, circumstance or local politicians to determine. And although there were some differences in timing and style, the creation of the new secret police forces followed remarkably similar patterns across Eastern Europe. In their organization, methods and mentality, all of the East European secret police forces were exact copies of their Soviet progenitor: Poland's Security Service (Urzad Bezpieczeństwa, or UB); Hungary's State Security Agency (Államvédelmi Osztály, or ÁVO); and East Germany's Ministry for State Security (Ministerium für Staatssicherheit, or later Stasi, the name by which it is now best known).[10] So was Czechoslovak State Security (Státní bezpečnost, or StB). The latter was organized, in the words of the Czech communist leader, Klement Gottwald, so as 'to best make use of the experience of the Soviet Union'. The same could be said of every secret police force in every country in Eastern Europe.[11]

Like the history of the East European communist parties, the history of Eastern Europe's 'little KGBs' begins well before the end of the war. The Polish secret police began to organize itself in 1939, following the Soviet invasion of eastern Poland. Upon entering the territories of what they now called western Ukraine and western Belarus, the Soviet officers tasked with carrying out the pacification of the region had trouble finding reliable local collaborators. Recognizing the need for more professional and more dependable partners, the NKVD created a special training centre near Smolensk in the autumn of 1940. Some 200 Poles, Ukrainians and Belarusians from the newly occupied territories were invited to attend. These first students completed their course of study in March 1941, after which some of the recruits were sent to do further schooling in the city of Gorky. Among this first generation of graduates were at least three men – Konrad Świetlik, Józef Czaplicki and Mieczysław Moczar – who remained influential leaders of the Polish security services through the 1950s and 1960s.[12]

With the outbreak of the Soviet–German war in June 1941, this training programme was abruptly halted. But a few months later, after the Soviet Union had recovered somewhat from the shock of the Nazi invasion, training resumed. After the battle of Stalingrad, when the war suddenly looked winnable, recruitment intensified. Candidates were at first chosen from the Polish-speaking 'Kościuszko Division' of the Red Army – mostly people who had previously lived in eastern Poland – through what seemed like a mysterious process to those selected. When, on a 'freezing afternoon in January of 1944' Józef Lobatiuk was approached by his commanding officer and told to come to his unit's headquarters to fill out some forms, no explanation was given. A month later, he was told to collect 'two weeks' dry rations' and to report for special training in Kuibyshev, a Russian city well behind the front lines. Again, no explanation was given.[13]

Only upon arriving in Kuibyshev did Lobatiuk discover that he had been sent to an NKVD officers' training school. He was delighted. Years later, describing his experiences for the Polish Security Service's in-house historians, he remembered being treated 'like a guest in someone's home'. After the rough conditions of the front, the school seemed luxurious. The 'students' were allowed out on weekends, and were not made to do watchman's duty. They had enough to eat. They were treated with civility. In the dining hall, waiters served food 'as if in a restaurant', even ladling out soup from real tureens.[14]

Actual lessons did not begin right away. Before any information was imparted, the new recruits were interrogated over several days by a commission of NKVD officers. They were questioned about their biographies, their family backgrounds and their political views. They were asked to repeat their life stories, more than once. Some did not pass the test and were sent back to their units, though they never learned why. In the end some 200 men remained. These were the *Kujbyszewiacy* – the Kuibyshev gang, as they eventually became known – the first graduating class of Soviet-taught Polish secret police officers. Immediately, they began preparing for 'operational work', under direct NKVD tutelage.

At this point in the war – the spring of 1944 – there was as yet no Polish government, other than the exile government in London and the underground 'state' which was connected to it, and no open Polish administration on the ground in what was still Nazi-occupied Poland. Nor had any international agreements been reached about the nature of postwar Poland: the Tehran conference had not come to any final conclusion about the Polish borders and the Yalta conference, during which Roosevelt and Churchill would cede de facto Soviet control over Poland, was still many months away. But the NKVD was already teaching the Polish officers in Kuibyshev to think in Soviet categories, so that when the time came they would act under Soviet orders.

This first course was very thorough. Some of the subject matter was theoretical – Marxism-Leninism, the history of the Bolshevik party, the history of the Polish 'workers' movement'. Some was practical: techniques of intelligence and counter-intelligence, detective work, interrogation. On fine days, they drove out to a shooting range on the Volga. Everything was taught in Russian – only one lecturer spoke Polish – which was a problem, particularly as few of the students had anything beyond a rudimentary education. There were no textbooks, so students met frequently outside class to compare notes. Whenever possible, the Russian-speaking students translated the material for those who had not understood it. Lectures and seminars took up ten hours a day, and six hours on Saturdays.

There wasn't much time to reflect on their new knowledge. This first course came to an abrupt end in July 1944, when the Red Army crossed the Bug River, Poland's new eastern border. The freshly minted security officers were deployed immediately. Most of the 200 men were sent first to the city of Lublin, where the Polish Committee of

National Liberation had just been set up, and where the provisional government was about to be formed. Conditions were rough – the men slept on floors and used their backpacks as pillows – but they were warmly welcomed. Stanisław Radkiewicz, Poland's first Security Minister, gave a dinner in their honour, together with a Soviet adviser. The two men handed out stars for the new officers to sew on to their uniforms.

As the Red Army advanced – first into Rzeszów and Białystok, later into Kraków and Warsaw – the Kuibyshev gang followed, always accompanied by Soviet advisers. In some areas, they first fought as partisans, alongside the Red Army. At this point in the war, there were dozens of different partisan groups in eastern Poland and the western USSR, some affiliated with the Polish Home Army resistance, some with the Ukrainian independence movement, some composed of Jews who had escaped the Holocaust, some containing criminal elements.[15] But the Kuibyshev gang, whatever their nationality, fought on behalf of the Soviet Union. And upon arrival in a newly liberated province, they always followed a predetermined plan. They set to work organizing regional and local police, identifying enemies, passing information to the NKVD and recruiting collaborators: 'We, the Kuibyshev gang, were supposed to be the backbone of the new force and the teachers of future cadres,' remembered one proudly.[16]

Not all of them were ultimately successful. Some would be kicked out of the service for theft and incompetence. A few were returned to the Soviet Union, presumably to take up similar work in the republics of Belarus or Ukraine, where many had come from. At least one rebelled, and joined the anti-communist opposition. But many of the others would rise high in the security services, and still others would train a new generation of cadres.

Lobatiuk took part, for a time, in the postwar 'fight against banditism', a euphemism which means that he joined the organized military action against the remnants of the Polish Home Army, some of whom were still holding out in the forests around Lublin, as well as Ukrainian partisans. In April 1945, he was sent to the city of Łódź, where he was told, again to his surprise, that he would become an instructor in a new Polish security police officers' school. He and the other Kuibyshev veterans who had been chosen for this task divided up the various subjects between them, according to who remembered which subject the best. Although they had been made to turn in their Kuibyshev notebooks when they left the USSR, they re-created them from memory. Eventually, they put together a textbook based on their recollections of what they had learned from the NKVD. This textbook would remain in use for the next several years, and thus would a whole generation of Polish secret policemen be trained according to Soviet methods.[17]

Over the next few months and years, the service expanded exponentially. In December 1944 there had been about 2500 security functionaries. By November 1945 there were already 23,700, and by 1953 there would be 33,200.[18] Hardly any of these new members fitted what later, in communist Poland, became the stereotype of the typical 'SB' functionary: a diabolically well-trained fanatic, highly educated, probably Jewish. In reality, the immediate postwar UB was overwhelmingly Polish by ethnic origin, and almost entirely Catholic. By 1947, 99.5 per cent of the SB was composed of Polish Catholics. Jews actually accounted for less than 1 per cent of the total, and were outnumbered even by ethnic Belarusians.[19] Of the eighteen founding members of the Lublin regional secret police force, only one was Jewish. The rest were Polish, Ukrainian and Belarusian.[20]

Far from being diabolically well-trained, these new recruits were also overwhelmingly uneducated. In 1945, fewer than 20 per cent had any education beyond primary school. Even in 1953, only half had made it past the equivalent of sixth grade. Throughout this period, the vast majority of the recruits were the children of Polish workers and peasants. Only a tiny number had families classified as 'bourgeois', and hardly any could be described as intellectuals.[21] Although the majority had joined the communist party by 1947, very few had any previous political involvement whatsoever.

It was probably not ideology but rather the possibility of rapid social advance which motivated them, as the story of Czesław Kiszczak, one of Poland's most notorious secret policemen, very well illustrates. Much later, Kiszczak would become the Polish Interior Minister – he organized the imposition of martial law in 1981 – but he was born in 1925 into an impoverished family in a poor part of southern Poland, the son of a factory worker who was unemployed throughout the

1930s. As a teenager in Nazi-occupied Poland, he was picked up and sent first to a labour camp, and then, after a series of adventures, to become a slave labourer in Austria. Between 1943 and 1945, by his own account, he lived in a workers' barracks in Vienna where he was the only Pole among Croats, Serbs and others, many of whom were communists. He worked on the Austrian train system until 7 April 1945, when the Russians liberated the eastern districts of Vienna. Soon after, again in his own words, 'the Red Army took me up, sat me on a tank, and I showed them around Vienna, I knew the streets'. He knew enough Russian and German to serve as a translator. At the age of twenty, with only a primary school education, he thus became a kind of Red Army mascot, cruising the defeated city of Vienna astride a Soviet tank.[22]

Eventually, Kiszczak returned to Poland clutching a document stating he had been part of the Austrian communist party. He immediately joined the Polish communist party, which in turn sent him to the secret police training school in Łódź. He was, he has said, then taken to Warsaw for further training, where he joined first the new Polish army and then Polish military intelligence, which was initially run entirely by Russians, though later a few Poles were brought in. Although he doesn't say so, many speculate that he developed a relationship of some kind with Soviet military intelligence as well.

Very soon afterwards, in 1946, Kiszczak was sent to London. This was, again, an extraordinary opportunity for a young man who was still only twenty-one. His version of this episode is benign. 'We wanted the remnants of the Polish army then in exile to return to Poland, with its arms and its soldiers. It would be a good gesture towards communist Poland … in the beginning there was a lot of joint spirit, the government supported the clergy, the clergy supported the government … Poland seemed friendly for everyone, it gave peasants land, promised higher education, new schools.' Other than that, he says his job in London involved 'normal intelligence work', collecting information on the British army, on Poles in London, and especially on the thousands of Polish soldiers who had fought with the Royal Air Force or other British armed forces during the war.

Much of this biographical information is impossible to corroborate, because Kiszczak apparently combed the archives for any documents relating to himself when he was Interior Minister, and removed or destroyed them. One or two have been found, however, including a summary of a report he sent home from London in July 1947, which had been tucked away in someone else's file. In ungrammatical Polish, it describes how the embassy was registering and monitoring Polish members of the British armed forces who expressed a desire to return home. The contempt which Kiszczak had clearly been taught to feel for these men, many of whom had been fighting since 1939, shines through:

> Registration takes place in a small room of about 4 metres by 3 metres in which there are five tables and five chairs and two cabinets containing the Consulate's books. Registration starts up at 10 or 11, and sometimes only at 2.30, as the British make special difficulties for us, and in this case deliberately send soldiers late for registration . . . The majority of these people would do anything they were told, they would agree to anything as long as someone would guarantee them a good standard of living in Poland. Those who aren't returning and are staying in England for material reasons would probably render certain services for money, as they are typical products of [prewar] Poland, people without deeper feelings, without ambition and honour . . . [23]

In the rest of the report, the now 22-year-old Kiszczak disparaged the older diplomats in the embassy, the military attaché who seemed insufficiently interested in collecting counter-intelligence, the colonel who was trying to demoralize him and others. In another report which survived, he was simply informing on his colleagues in a more straightforward manner. One consulate employee was constantly talking about information he had 'from unknown sources' about political violence in Poland, while others were conducting heated policy arguments and threatening one another.

It was a heady job for a young man, but he left soon afterwards. In an interview, he claimed that this was because he was lonely and homesick: 'I couldn't eat English sausages.' Or perhaps he had been told, accurately, that there were even better opportunities at home, and he decided to take them. In the chaos and poverty of postwar Poland the secret policemen, however modest their origins, had relative wealth and relative power. And no other state organs could arrest them if they abused it.

From the beginning, anyone with ambitions to become a secret policeman in Eastern Europe knew that the path to influence lay through Soviet connections. But it was not always easy to know which Soviet connections were the correct ones. In Hungary, the organization which eventually became the State Security department had not one predecessor but two, each one led by a Hungarian with his own set of Soviet friends and mentors.

One branch was created from above, in Debrecen, along with the Provisional National Government, in December 1944. In theory, the provisional government was a cross-party coalition. But although the newly appointed Interior Minister, Ferenc Erdei, was technically not a communist, he was secretly loyal to the party and his first documented comments on the new security services indicate that he knew which way the wind was blowing. In a report to his colleagues on his 'productive' meeting with General F. I. Kuznetsov, the head of Soviet military intelligence in Hungary, Erdei declared on 28 December that they needn't worry about security, because 'Russian guards will help us until we can find enough trustworthy policemen with proper uniforms'.[24] He worried, however, that General Kuznetsov was insufficiently interested in halting the crime and vandalism which had skyrocketed in the liberated half of the country: 'We discussed far more about the political police, about which he had much general advice and many proposals.'[25]

One of those proposals led to the appointment of András Tömpe to lead the new service. Tömpe was a Spanish Civil War veteran with longtime links to the international communist movement and a deep conviction that he alone had the authority to become the new Hungarian chief of secret police. He immediately began to organize his new force, requesting and receiving weapons directly from the Red Army. Thus prepared, he set out from Debrecen to Budapest, arriving in the eastern part of the city on 28 January, even while fighting continued in the western suburbs.

Unfortunately for Tömpe, he already had a rival. Just a few days earlier, the Budapest branch of the Hungarian communist party had also formed a political police department. Its leader was Gábor Péter, a member of the illegal Hungarian communist party since 1931 and a frequent traveller to Moscow in the years since. Throughout the 1930s, Péter had been in close contact with Kun and the other veterans of the 1919 revolution in Moscow, as well as with Rákosi. His wife, Jolán Simon, would eventually become Rákosi's private secretary.

Péter had long links to the NKVD as well. Before the war, he had specialized in underground logistics, among other things helping to make contacts between imprisoned communists and their families in both Vienna and Budapest. By his own somewhat self-aggrandizing account, Péter had long planned to lead the postwar political police, and clearly assumed that he had been promised the job. He may have had some justification for thinking this. For while Tömpe apparently had the support of Soviet military intelligence officers based in Debrecen, Péter, it seems, had the support of their political masters. Certainly it was true that in the middle of January – before Tömpe's arrival in Debrecen, and before the siege of Budapest had ended – Péter travelled to Soviet army headquarters in the eastern suburbs of Budapest to renew his acquaintances.[26] In February, at a presentation he made to high-ranking Hungarian party members, he sought to give the impression that he was already very much in control of things. He spoke of his ninety-eight employees ('87 workers and 11 intellectuals'), and already claimed to have arrested many 'fascists'. In the archives of the Hungarian communist party, a Russian-language version of that report is attached to the original, perhaps an indication that he expected the report to have Russian-speaking readers.[27]

Within weeks of the war's end, Tömpe and Péter clashed. Tömpe suspected Péter of lacking sufficient ideological sophistication. Péter blamed Tömpe for providing him with inadequate office furnishings. Tömpe was angry not to be invited to an event at which the press would be present.[28] Each later claimed to have been the first to set up headquarters in the gloomy building at 60 Andrássy Street, the headquarters of the Hungarian fascist police in the latter part of the war, despite the fact that this decision came back to haunt the Hungarian communist party. (The fact that both fascist and communist police used the cellars in the basement as a prison created an uncomfortable impression of continuity between the Nazi and Soviet regimes.)[29] Within two years, this comic opera dispute had been resolved in Péter's favour. After the election of November 1945, the Interior Ministry was officially placed under the control of the communist party and the fiction of a neutral secret police force was dropped. In 1946, Tömpe 'retired' to diplomatic service. He spent most of the rest of his career in Latin America.[30]

Petty though this struggle may seem in retrospect, Péter's successful struggle for power was an early and important defeat for Hungarian political pluralism. For one, this important debate about the nature of the new police force took place entirely within the confines of the communist party, and was heavily influenced by Soviet officials in Budapest. Neither then nor later did any non-communist politicians, even those operating legally at the time, ever have impact on the internal workings of the secret police. The nature of the victorious party – Péter and his 'Budapest police' – mattered too, since the Budapest police force was in effect an extra-legal structure, controlled not by the Interior Ministry or by the government but by the communist party alone. From 1945 onwards, in other words, the political police reported directly to the party leadership, flagrantly bypassing the provisional coalition government.

The special status of the secret police force was clear enough to those who worked for it. Though Péter had deputies from the Social Democratic and Smallholders' parties, he made no pretence of taking their advice, and no one in the department was ever fooled by their presence. A lower-ranking officer later remembered the non-communist deputies being 'isolated completely': 'it became common knowledge that their rooms were wiretapped so I had to be very careful during contacts with them what I said'.[31] When Vladimir Farkas, Mihály's son, went to work for ÁVO in 1946, he was explicitly instructed not to talk to Péter's two non-communist deputies: 'I was not allowed to give them any information about my work, even if I received a direct order from one of them.'[32]

Nor did the police force listen when non-communist politicians complained about police behaviour. In August 1945 a deputy minister from the Justice Department wrote a letter to the Interior Ministry complaining that the political police 'arrest prosecutors, judges without my prior approval ... The above mentioned practice seriously damages the authority of the justice system.' ÁVO did not respond. A year later, a member of parliament made similar complaints, but by the time his letter came up for parliamentary discussion, he had fled the country. By 1946, such critiques were no longer considered safe to make at all.[33] As in Poland, the Hungarian political police were accountable to no one except themselves. Also as in Poland, they grew quickly. In February 1946, Péter's organization in Budapest employed 848 people. By 1953, the once again renamed State Protection Authority (Államvédelmi Hatóság, or ÁVH) had 5751 employees in its headquarters, and far more informers.[34]

From the beginning, Soviet advisers stationed themselves throughout the organization. 'Counsellor Orlov', whom one Hungarian Interior Ministry official described as an NKVD officer 'dressed as a civilian', installed himself at 60 Andrássy Street in February 1945. Three other armed policemen – these in full NKVD uniform – were on hand to help him.[35] By March, a full chain of command had been established. At the top was General Fyodor Byelkin, officially a member of the Allied Control Council, but in practice the head of the NKVD's East European intelligence command, which was based in Baden outside Vienna. From 1947, the NKVD additionally maintained a permanent representative in Budapest – variously known as Lieutenant Kremnov or Kamenovic – whose fraternal assistance was later essential to the organization of Hungary's political show trials. Beneath them were a host of semi-permanent advisers. Even in November 1952 there were still thirty-three Soviet secret police officers plus thirteen of their family members on the official payroll of the Hungarian ÁVH. Along with relatively high salaries, they were provided with furnished apartments, travel expenses, free sports facilities including a swimming pool, chess, dominoes and ping-pong, as well as domestic staff. On the weekends they went hunting. According to one former Interior Minister these Soviet 'advisers' received daily intelligence reports, and were involved in frequent meetings with their Hungarian counterparts. (Their advice was accepted, but it seems they were never convinced of the loyalty of the nation they had chosen to serve. On the night of 29 October 1956 – when it seemed, briefly, as if the Hungarian Revolution might end in a Soviet withdrawal from the country – all of them, fearing the vengeance of the mob, boarded an aeroplane and flew back to Moscow.)[36]

The bosses of the Hungarian secret police kept in close touch with their Soviet mentors. Péter was in daily contact with Orlov, according to Farkas.[37] But the Russians also maintained other sources of influence in Budapest, via a small, mostly hidden but powerful community of Soviet or Sovietized Hungarians who had been born or had lived most of their lives in the USSR. One of them, János Kovács, an NVKD colonel of Hungarian origin, was Péter's deputy from January 1945 until his death in 1948. An even more significant role was eventually played by Rudolf Garasin, a man whose official biography seems hardly to do justice to his later influence – and whose life story illustrates that for Hungarians there were also hidden paths to secret police power.

Garasin had been born in Hungary, but wound up as a political prisoner in Russia as a teenager, following the First World War. Radicalized by these experiences, he joined the Bolsheviks, joined the Red Army and took active part in the Russian Revolution and then the Russian Civil War. Afterwards, he did not go back to Hungary – Béla Kun's short-lived revolution had already come and gone – but settled in the Soviet Union.[38] By his own account, Garasin's subsequent career in the USSR was unremarkable. According to a memo he wrote for Hungarian party historians, he was active in the Hungarian exile community in the USSR, studied engineering, and then worked for the Soviet Ministry of Light Industry. He rejoined the Red Army as an officer during the war, but, following an injury, wound up working behind the front line. In the spring of 1944, he wrote, he was abruptly called to Moscow, and taken to meet a political officer of the Red Army: 'While drinking tea, an Interior Ministry lieutenant appeared with a blue cap and, without saying a word, accompanied me to a car which drove to Marx-Engels Square. There another lieutenant waited for me, showed me a door which I entered, and left me there. There was nobody in the lobby.' Eventually, two figures emerged from the gloom and the mystery was solved: Rákosi and Mihály Farkas held their arms open to greet him.

As Garasin recounts the scene, Comrade Rákosi jovially scolded comrade Garasin for slipping out of sight for so long ('it had taken them half a year to find me') and then asked him for help: he wanted Garasin to select volunteers from one of the 'anti-fascist schools' in the USSR in order to form a partisan unit which would enter Hungary together with the Red Army, just as the Kuibyshev gang had entered Poland alongside the Red Army. 'Anti-fascist schools' was a euphemism: these were POW re-education camps, where captured Hungarian officers and soldiers were learning to become communists. Garasin did as he was told. He was introduced to the Hungarians at 'Institute 101', the renamed headquarters of what had been the Comintern. In due course he visited the 'anti-fascist school' at Krasnogorsk, where he was impressed by the enthusiasm of the candidates. So eager were most to return to Hungary and fight their former German allies, he recorded, that they volunteered without hesitation. Garasin also met the 'teachers' at the school, many of whom would later be leaders of the Hungarian communist government.

Garasin's attempt to form a partisan unit progressed rather slowly, Hungary and Hungarian partisans not being the Red Army's priority in the summer of 1944. The volunteers found it difficult to get to Ukraine, just behind the front line, where their training was supposed to begin. The unit's train was late getting started, there were mix-ups about clothing and equipment, and local commanders in Ukraine weren't prepared for their arrival. Eventually they began training, however, learning to use explosives and competing against one another in mock battles.

Occasionally, the team received notice that someone higher up was interested in their progress. One day they saw a Soviet plane circling overhead, trying to land, and they chased away some cows so that it would have a clear runway. As the plane's engine's roared, one of the better-known Hungarian communist ideologists, Zoltán Vas, stepped out of the cockpit, immediately losing his glasses in the melee. Vas gave a highly detailed and longish lecture anyway, describing the promising situation at the front and encouraging the men to fight hard. As he prepared to fly back to Moscow, Garasin joked that Vas should, in future, let the group know in advance when he planned to come, 'so we could practise shooting at the aeroplane!' This was presumably what passed for humour on the Ukrainian front.

The partisans shifted camp several times as the front moved, and various adventures ensued. In his unpublished memoir, Garasin confessed that he had an affair with a woman named Anna. He remembered constant difficulties with food supplies, resolved when the unit simply took over a local mill and confiscated its products, to the intense displeasure of the local peasants. Another low point came during a meeting with Rákosi, who attacked Garasin for having formed a 'purely Jewish company'. Garasin was 'so shocked I just stood there, I couldn't believe it'. He mulled over this strange outburst and made a point later on of telling Rákosi – who, as noted, was Jewish – that he had been much mistaken. When he counted them up, there were only six Jews in the unit.

Finally the moment of liberation arrived. At the beginning of February 1945, Garasin and his troops crossed the Carpathian mountains and he entered Hungary for the first time in thirty years. By 12 February they had reached Debrecen, the eastern city which had become the temporary capital. And that was the end of the adventure. Garasin, a Soviet citizen, was immediately assigned to work with the Allied Control Council. He lost touch with his partisans, drifted into propaganda and printing work and, according to the official version of events, returned to the Soviet Union.[39]

Unintentionally, Garasin's account of his life paints a witty and truthful picture of the Hungarian communist partisans. Later, they would be lauded by future communist leaders as war heroes, but at the time the Red Army clearly treated them as an afterthought. Garasin's story is also important for what it leaves out. In fact we don't really know what he was doing in the 1920s and 1930s or where he was in the years immediately following the war, and many have long suspected that he was working as a senior officer of the Soviet NKVD.[40] Later, Garasin would become known as the man who had 'imported' the techniques of the Soviet Gulag to Hungary.

Garasin's life story also illustrates the important role played in Eastern Europe in general, and Hungary in particular, by secret police officials who were not merely local collaborators or recruits, as the Kuibyshev gang mostly had been, but by people who were Soviet citizens, and probably Soviet secret policemen, from the very start. Garasin was a Hungarian by birth, but by his own account he was totally integrated into Soviet life. He had a Russian wife, a Russian education, and between 1915 and 1945 he lived in Russia. Garasin was not merely favourably inclined towards the Soviet Union, he was Soviet himself. It is hardly surprising that when he took charge of Hungary's labour camps in the early 1950s, he organized them very deliberately on Soviet lines.[41]

As we have seen, the NKVD had already organized reliable cadres among the German communists even before they entered Berlin. They had already selected their most experienced officer to lead them too. In April 1945, General Serov bade farewell to Warsaw and travelled to Germany, where he immediately divided Berlin and the other cities of the Soviet zone into 'operative sectors'. But he did not immediately give German policemen any real power. The Soviet officers considered Germans – even German communists – in need of far more tutelage than other East Europeans. Ordinary German policemen were not allowed to carry weapons until January 1946. Even after German authorities took control of the civilian police, all personnel decisions still had to be approved by the Soviet Military Administration.[42] Only in March 1948 did the Soviet Interior Ministry boss in the eastern zone even agree to inform the German communist party leadership about whom it intended to arrest.

Cautiously, and at first only on a small scale, the Soviet administrators did begin to set up a German political police force in 1947. Even then, not everybody approved of the idea. In Moscow, the Soviet Interior Minister, Viktor Abakumov, argued that a new police force would become a target of Western propaganda, and risked being seen as a 'new Gestapo'. More importantly, he still distrusted the Germans, complaining that there 'were not enough German cadres who have been thoroughly checked'. Recruitment began despite these objections, perhaps, as Norman Naimark suspects, because the NKVD had finally realized that its officers' poor understanding of German and Germany was creating massive resentment. Even so, it took some time for this new department – known as 'K5', or sometimes Department K – to gain real power. Originally set up to keep tabs on the police force itself, the employees of K5 took direct orders from Soviet Interior Ministry officials, bypassing the nascent regional and central government structures.[43] One of the few documents from that era to survive (most were removed by the KGB, or perhaps destroyed, in 1989 or before) mentions a departmental training meeting and includes a list of attendees. Topping the list is a group of Soviet advisers.[44]

In this sense, K5 did resemble the political police in the rest of Eastern Europe: as in Hungary, Poland and the USSR itself, this new political police force was initially extra-governmental, operating outside the ordinary rule of law. Only in 1950 did the new East German government pass a full-fledged 'Law on the Formation of a Ministry for State Security' which created the Ministry for State Security.[45] Even then the Stasi's Soviet masters were cautious. They dropped Erich Mielke, the organization's first boss – he had some suspicious holes in his biography, having spent part of the war in France – and put their own candidate, Wilhelm Zaisser, in charge of the new agency.[46]

Like the Polish UB or the Hungarian ÁVO, the Stasi was modelled closely on the NKVD (which also renamed itself after the war and eventually became known as the KGB), and the departmental structures of all three imitated those of the KGB. But the Stasi mimicked the KGB to an extraordinary degree. German secret policemen used Soviet methods of encoding and ciphering until 1954, and they even learned to sew police files together with thread, as Russian KGB clerks did in Moscow.[47] Soviet comrades were consulted on matters such as secret ink and microphotography.[48] More importantly, Stasi officers referred to themselves as 'Chekists', after the very first Bolshevik secret police organization, founded in 1918. They also used a symbol very similar to the KGB's symbol, the sword and shield, and made frequent obesiance to the Soviet 'friends' in their own literature.[49] An internal Stasi history manual explained that 'the Soviet Chekists under the leadership of Lenin and the Soviet communist party created the basic model of socialist state security organs'. All East Germans, the manual continued, knew that 'to learn from the Soviet Union means to learn how to win'. Members of the security services knew, in addition, that 'to learn from the Soviet Chekists means to learn to disarm even the most sophisticated enemy'.[50]

Initially, the Stasi recruited only from the existing staff of K5 and from communist party cadres. Even so, 88 per cent of the initial job candidates were rejected for having relatives in the West, for having spent time abroad or for having unacceptable political biographies of one kind or another. As elsewhere in the bloc, the recruiters, acting under Soviet advice, favoured the young, the uneducated and the inexperienced over older communists with prewar experience.[51] Some were 'graduates' of the training and indoctrination programmes set up in Soviet POW camps, but many of the first recruits had been teenagers at the end of the war, and had no experience at all. One early Stasi recruit describes his colleagues – 'our generation' – as 'people who had not been involved in the Third Reich, but who had been formed by the war'.[52] Many came from underprivileged or 'proletarian' backgrounds, and if they had any training at all it was heavily ideological. In 1953, 92 per cent were members of the East Germany communist party. In practice, they would need Soviet instructors and managers for many years.[53]

Wolfgang Schwanitz, a young law student who came to work for the Stasi in 1951, was, in this sense, a typical recruit. More than fifty years later, he remembered that 'I didn't know anything at all about the security organs, hadn't heard or read anything about them, and I was curious what was expected from me ... I was like a virgin before she committed a sin.' Convinced that it was 'necessary to protect the GDR', he agreed to take the job.[54] Over the next few months, Schwanitz underwent intensive training. Almost without exception his trainers were Soviet secret policemen: 'They really took us by the hand, the adviser would go through what I had to do during the day, and then in the evening would listen to what I'd done. He would tell me what had gone wrong or sometimes right.' They were taught practical skills – how to recruit an informer, how to set up a safe apartment, how to observe a suspect, how to conduct an investigation – as well as Marxist-Leninist theory and communist party history. Others had less training: another early recruit remembers having been 'thrown into the job'. Put in a room with two or three other people – with one motorcycle to share between fifteen men – he was told to go out and organize Stasi cells in various cities. Afterwards, the cells were meant to 'clone themselves'.[55]

Schwanitz was flattered by all of this intense attention, as were many others. Günter Tschirschwitz, a young policeman whose family had left Silesia at the end of the war, was only twenty-one when he was told simply to 'come to Berlin' for an interview in 1951. There he discovered that he was meeting with officers of the Stasi. His recruiters were older men, prewar communists: 'They told me stories from their anti-fascist past,' he told me. He was equally flattered to be recommended by his local party cell, whose letter of approval he kept for decades. The young man it describes certainly sounds promising: 'He has political knowledge above average. He tries hard to extend his knowledge by studying in his spare time. He industriously studies the German communist party, he is a class-conscious person. His attitude to the Soviet Union and the GDR is always positive. He is a member of the board of the fifth party cell, contributes actively to party work, and writes for the wall newsletter.'[56]

The recommendation went on to describe him as 'reliable' and 'comradely', and in the end he was accepted. According to his account, he was at one point considered for the job of interrogator, but wound up becoming a bodyguard, perhaps the most benign job in the secret police. This pleased him, he says, 'because I wouldn't have wanted to work indoors'.

Years later, Tschirschwitz's understanding of the role the Stasi had played in creating East Germany hadn't grown much deeper, and his positive feelings about his Soviet training had not changed. In a long conversation about his years in the security service, he mostly reminisced about the trips he had taken. In Prague there had been wonderful Bohemian food, in Vienna he was given 200 schillings to spend, and in Budapest the Hungarian security guards were hospitable. He told fond stories about the time he rode on the train to Moscow with Otto Grotewohl, East Germany's Prime Minister after 1949, and Wilhelm Pieck, and about the excellent cooperation he enjoyed with West German security guards during a trip to Bonn in the 1970s. His career in the Stasi had brought him social advance, a degree of material comfort, and education – all thanks to the fraternal comrades from the Soviet Union.[57]

The new recruits to the Eastern European secret police services learned espionage techniques, fighting skills and surveillance methods from the NKVD and later the KGB. From their Russian mentors, they also learned how to think like Soviet secret policemen. They learned to identify enemies even where none seemed to exist, because Soviet secret policemen knew the methods enemies used to conceal themselves. They learned to question the independence of any person or group which called itself politically neutral, because Soviet secret policemen did not believe in neutrality.

They were also trained to think in the long term, and to identify potential enemies as well as actual opponents of the regime. This was a profoundly Bolshevik obsession. In March 1922, Lenin himself had declared that the 'greater the number of representatives of the reactionary clergy and reactionary bourgeoisie we succeed in executing ... the better. We must teach these people a lesson right now, so that they will not dare even to think of any resistance for several decades.'[58] In an essay written for the benefit of future cadres, one of the Stasi's own historians explained that the organization 'from the beginning could not be restricted to defending the attacks of the enemy. It was and is an organ that has to use all means in the <u>offensive fight</u> against the opponents of socialism.'[59]

At the same time, Eastern European secret policemen were also taught to feel the Soviet Union's scorn and hatred for those whom it opposed. From the late 1930s, Stalin had begun to refer in public to the USSR's enemies in what one historian has called 'biological-hygienic terms'. He denounced them as vermin, as pollution, as filth which had to be 'subjected to ongoing purification', as 'poisonous weeds'.[60] Some of that venom is echoed in the young Czesław Kiszczak's reports from London, quoted earlier: 'Those who aren't returning and are staying in England for material reasons would probably render certain services for money, as they are typical products of [prewar] Poland, people without deeper feelings, without ambition and honour'.[61]

Finally, the Soviet comrades taught their protégés that anyone who was not a communist was, by definition, under suspicion as a foreign spy. This conviction would become very powerful everywhere in Eastern Europe once the Cold War was fully underway, supported by black-and-white propaganda depicting the peace-loving East in a constant battle with the war-mongering West. But in East Germany it quickly became an obsession. There, the proximity of West Germany and the relative openness of Berlin in the 1940s and 1950s meant that the new East German state really was surrounded, and infiltrated, by large numbers of Westerners. The Stasi's mentality was permanently shaped by the experiences of that era, to the point where its members later found it hard to distinguish between spies and ordinary dissidents. One internal Stasi historian described the postwar era as a period of struggle against the West German political parties as well as the 'so-called Committee of Free Lawyers', the Combat Group against Inhumanity (Kampfgruppe gegen Unmenschlichkeit, or KGU) and other human rights groups active in West Berlin at that time. These groups, in the Stasi's collective memory, had not been designed to promote free speech or democracy, but were rather intended to 'isolate the GDR internationally' and undermine the state. They had a 'strong social base in the GDR' only thanks to the persistence of capitalist forms of production and fascist ways of thinking, and thus it had been necessary to fight them and their 'libellous leaflets' with great energy.[62]

This fight against powerful, unidentified and carefully masked representatives of foreign states would take many forms. From the beginning, it certainly required close surveillance of anyone who had any contact with foreigners, any relatives abroad, or had made trips abroad in the past. The East Germans kept lists of anyone in contact with the Western press, especially Radio in the American Sector (Rundfunk im amerikanischen Sektor, or RIAS), which broadcasted under the auspices of the American occupation authorities. Special efforts were also made to place informers and spies at the station.[63]

The same was true in Hungary, where all Hungarians with foreign contacts were assumed to be spies. After Ilona and Endre Marton, two native Hungarians, were appointed correspondents in 1948 for the American wire services, the Associated Press and United Press, they were followed day and night by policemen and informers, as their daughter Kati Marton has since documented. A trip to a café, a flirtation with a colleague, an afternoon's skiing – all of this was recorded by the Hungarian ÁVO in a file which had reached 1600 pages by 1950. Although they were not spies – on the contrary, some American diplomats were very wary of them – when the Martons were finally arrested in 1955, the 'Plan for Mrs Marton's Interrogation' included discussions of 'the people she has met since 1945 and what sort of connection she formed with them', as well as 'her connections to the Americans and her spying' and 'her love of the Western way of life'.[64]

The fight against enemies also required the new security police-men, from the beginning, to master the delicate art of cultivating friends and informers. Because the enemy was hidden, the enemy could be uncovered only through subterfuge and careful collabor-ation with secret allies, both in one's own and in the enemy's camp. One early Stasi training document laid out very precisely how import-ant this kind of recruitment was:

> As it is the specific task of the [Ministry for State Security] to uncover and destroy the enemy in all areas using conspiratorial methods, unoffi-cial cooperation with both citizens of our republic and patriots in the enemy's camp is necessary. Those citizens who engage in this sort of cooperation are expressing an especially high degree of trust towards the MfS. Because this form of cooperation is of central importance to our work, all members of the MfS must be trained to love this import-ant task as well as to respect and appreciate the fighters and patriots at the invisible frontline.[65]

In practice, this meant that secret policemen had to be trained in the arts of persuasion, bribery, blackmail and threat. They had to convince wives to spy on husbands, children to inform on parents. They had to learn, for example, how to identify and monitor people like Bruno Kunkel, alias Max Kunz, who began to work secretly for the Stasi in 1950, and whose intact file reveals just how much secret policemen needed to know about their very closest collaborators, the people who worked for them in a conspiratorial capacity. Kunkel's file lists all of his political and professional affiliations (communist youth group, apprenticeship to a car mechanic) as well as all of his family members and their professional and political affiliations.[66] It also contains sev-eral psychological profiles of him, written by colleagues and superiors, not all of which are flattering ('K. does have a weak will. He has a light character and is superficial . . . His class-consciousness is only weakly developed. But he is friendly towards the Soviet Union and its anti-fascist democratic order'). By the time he was hired he had been thoroughly checked, but even so he was made to swear a dire oath:

> 'I, Bruno Kunkel, definitely declare to oblige myself to work for the organ of state security of the GDR. I oblige myself to find people whose

activities are directed against the GDR or the Soviet Union and to immediately report them. I vow to precisely carry out orders that my superior gives to me. It has been explained to me that my obligation for the organ for state security must remain secret and I oblige myself not to tell a second person, including my family members, about it. In order to keep all this secret I will sign the reports that I hand in in writing under the codename of Kunz. I will be severely punished if I spread this declaration, which has been signed by me.'[67]

He signed as both 'Bruno Kunkel' and 'Max Kunz', and was apparently a faithful secret employee, since he soon afterwards stopped his conspiratorial activity and went to work for the Stasi full time.

In the years which followed, tens of thousands of others across Eastern Europe had to be convinced to sign similar forms. Once they had signed, they then had to be carefully monitored to ensure that they really were keeping secrets, and that the information they were reporting was reliable. Informers kept an eye on the public, but the secret police had to learn to keep an eye on its informers. Eventually, Eastern Europe's secret policemen would strive to maintain an impossible level of vigilance against an unknown and often unidentifiable enemy, inside and outside the country, inside and outside the party, inside and outside their own organization. It was not a form of thinking conducive to democratic cooperation.

5
Violence

'It's quite clear – it's got to look democratic, but we must have everything in our control.'

Walter Ulbricht, 1945[1]

From the very beginning, the Soviet Union and the Eastern European communist parties pursued their goals using violence. They controlled the 'power ministries' of the Interior and Defence in every country, and they deployed both police troops and nascent armies to their advantage. After the war's end, this was not the mass, indiscriminate violence of the sort carried out by the Red Army during its march towards Berlin, but rather more selective, carefully targeted forms of political violence: arrests, beatings, executions and concentration camps. All of this they directed at a relatively small number of real, alleged and imagined and future enemies of the Soviet Union and the communist parties. They intended both to physically destroy them, and to create the sense that any armed resistance was useless.[2]

That was not what they said, of course. At least in the beginning, the NKVD and the new secret police forces loudly declared war on the remnants of fascism, while Soviet officials and local communist parties directed their fiercest propaganda at Nazi collaborators and quislings. In this they were no different from the restored national governments of France, the Netherlands and the rest of formerly occupied Europe.[3] But in every country occupied by the Red Army, the definition of 'fascist' eventually grew broader, expanding to include not only Nazi collaborators, but anybody whom the Soviet occupiers and their local allies disliked. In time, the word 'fascist', in true Orwellian fashion, was eventually used to describe anti-fascists who also happened to be anti-communists. And every time the definition was expanded, arrests followed.

Some of these 'fascists' had been identified in advance. The historian Amir Weiner points out that the NKVD had been collecting lists of potential 'enemies' in Eastern Europe – Poland and the Baltic states in particular – for many years (though Weiner makes a distinction between the NKVD's excellent 'knowledge' of Poland and its very poor cultural and historical 'understanding').[4] They collected names from newspapers, spies and diplomats. When they had no names, the NKVD prepared lists of the *types* of people who ought to be arrested. In May 1941, Stalin himself provided just such a list for the newly occupied territories of eastern Poland. He demanded the arrest and exile not only of 'members of Polish counter-revolutionary organizations' but also of their families, as well as the families of former officers of the Polish army, former policemen and former civil servants.[5]

Not all of the arrests took place right away. On a number of occasions, Stalin ordered East European communists to proceed cautiously while establishing the new social order. The then-tiny Polish communist party received a message from Moscow in the spring of 1944, ordering its leaders to work with *all* democratic forces ('all' was underlined) and to direct its propaganda at 'ordinary members' of other, more 'reactionary' parties.[6] Stalin's initial policy was to tread softly, not to upset the Allies and to win people over by persuasion or stealth. This is why free elections were held in Hungary, why some independent political parties were tolerated elsewhere and why, as late as 1948, Stalin told the East German communists to follow an 'opportunistic policy' which would entail 'moving toward socialism not directly but in zigzags and a roundabout way'. To their horror, he even suggested they might consider admitting former Nazis to their ranks.[7] The 'national front' model had been drilled into all of the local communists who had arrived by plane from Moscow or on foot with the Red Army: don't use communist slogans, don't talk about the dictatorship of the proletariat, do talk about coalitions, alliances and democracy.

Despite these moderate intentions, violence quickly accelerated, not always intentionally. Often, orders to move slowly could not be fulfilled because Soviet soldiers and officials were intellectually and psychologically unprepared for the consequences of such a policy. To a Soviet officer, educated in Bolshevik schools and trained in the Red Army or the NKVD, an active participant in *any* political group other than the communist party was a suspicious figure by definition, and probably a saboteur or spy. Politburo members in Moscow could speak in theory about the creation of 'socialist democracies', but Soviet administrators on the ground were often unable to tolerate anything other than a totalitarian state. They reacted with instinctive horror when newly liberated citizens began to exercise the freedom of speech, press and association which the new regimes' rhetoric appeared to promise.

The violence also accelerated because the expectations both of the new Soviet military administrators and of the local communists were so quickly dashed. In the wake of what the Red Army regarded as its triumphant march through Europe, local communists expected the working class to join the revolution. When that failed to happen, they would often explode in fury at their countrymen's 'incomprehensible spirit of resistance and complete ignorance', as one Warsaw party functionary put it.[8] Their frustration, coupled with the profound clash of Soviet and East European cultures, fed directly into the political violence too.

In some countries there was no initial 'liberal' moment of occupation. In Poland, the Soviet Union treated the Polish Home Army and especially its partisan divisions in the eastern half of the country with intense hostility long before the end of the war. The first Soviet invasion and occupation of eastern Poland in 1939 had been accompanied by mass arrests and deportations of Polish merchants, politicians, civil servants and priests. The violence culminated in the infamous mass murder of at least 21,000 Polish officers in the forests of western Russia, a tragedy known as the Katyń massacre, after the village where the first mass grave was discovered. Among the Katyń victims were many reserve officers who had worked in civilian life as doctors, lawyers and university lecturers – once again, the Polish patriotic and intellectual elite. The Polish Home Army, exile and underground leadership knew this story well: the discovery of one of the mass graves at Katyń by the Nazis in 1941 had led to a total break in diplomatic relations between the Polish exile government and the USSR.

At the time of the second Soviet invasion in 1944, the Home Army was nevertheless not primarily an anti-communist organization. By definition it was anti-Nazi and anti-fascist, having been formed in 1942 as the armed wing of the mainstream Polish resistance movement, the Polish Underground State. Anti-fascism was almost the only political sentiment which united its soldiers, in fact, among whom were members of socialist, social democratic, nationalist and peasant parties. At its height, the Home Army had some 300,000 armed partisans, which made it the second-largest resistance movement in Europe after the Yugoslav partisans, at least until the French resistance expanded in the wake of D-Day. The Home Army was legally subordinate to the Polish constitutional government-in-exile in London, which gave it both legitimacy and continuity with prewar Poland, something none of the smaller resistance movements in the country could claim.[9]

The Home Army itself operated on the premise that its leaders would play a large role in the formation of the postwar provisional government, just like Charles De Gaulle's followers in France. Its soldiers saw themselves, correctly, as Allies, along with Britain, France and the USSR. Faced with the imminent arrival of the Red Army, the Home Army was therefore determined to mobilize against the retreating Germans and engage in tactical cooperation with the Red Army. Home Army units had been under direct orders not to fight against Soviet troops since October 1943, when the Home Army commander had requested that the London government-in-exile make a 'historically transparent' decision on the matter.[10] Home Army partisan leaders were instructed to make themselves known to Red Army troops, and to assist Soviet soldiers as much as possible in fighting the Germans.[11] They were also to concentrate their efforts on liberating cities, the better to wield some political advantage later on.[12]

Some of the initial encounters went off smoothly. In March 1944, officers from a forward scouting unit of the Red Army met with their counterparts in the 27th Volhynia Home Army Infantry Division and agreed to cooperate in the liberation of Kovel, part of prewar Poland, today in western Ukraine. The Poles agreed to subordinate themselves to Soviet operational command during the battle, and the Soviets agreed to lend them ammunition and to acknowledge their political independence. Over three weeks, Polish and Soviet soldiers fought side by side, taking several villages and suffering many losses.[13]

If Soviet political goals had been different, that could have been a model for future cooperation. But it ended badly. In July, the Polish divisional commander reiterated his desire to continue to work with the Red Army, but declared that he would not cooperate with the new, communist-led, Polish national liberation committee in Lublin. Cooperation ended. The division was immediately surrounded by Soviet troops and disarmed. Some of its members were sent to labour camps, others were arrested.[14] Cooperation, betrayal, disarmament, arrest: most of the subsequent encounters between the Red Army and the Home Army followed exactly the same pattern.[15]

As the Red Army's second invasion of Poland got underway in the spring and summer of 1944, its interactions with the Home Army were of intense interest to the Soviet leadership. Lavrentii Beria, the brutal and duplicitous boss of the NKVD, filed detailed daily reports on the situation in Poland to Stalin, using language which could well have been designed to alarm the Soviet leader. On 29 June 1944, for example, Beria gave Stalin a list of 'Polish bands' (the word 'band' implying something vaguely criminal) which were then preparing for action in 'western Belarus' (formerly eastern Poland, the territory occupied by the USSR since 1939). These bands, he wrote, are 'organized according to the same principles as prewar Poland' (prewar Poland having been capitalist, 'aristocratic' and hostile to the USSR). He noted darkly that they maintain a 'direct connection to the military circles of the Polish government in England' and in a later note pointed out that they sometimes even met with envoys from London (which meant that they must be tools of Western influence). He reckoned there were between 10,000 and 20,000 armed men in the area, and he was deeply suspicious of all of them.[16]

Beria also noted that the 'bands' appeared to be preparing a major offensive against the Germans, which was true. At the end of June, Home Army soldiers in former Polish territories were indeed preparing for 'Operation Tempest', a series of uprisings aimed at liberating Polish cities from Nazi occupation in advance of the Red Army's arrival. The most famous of these was the Warsaw Uprising, but smaller uprisings were also planned for Vilnius and L'viv (or Wilno and Lwów, as the Poles still called them). Beria was also correct in surmising that the leaders of the Home Army kept in touch with London. Although their communication with the outside world was primitive and irregular, the partisan units in these eastern forests did consider themselves to be part of a regular army, operating under the command of the Polish government-in-exile in London. They also assumed that with the end of the war the Polish territories occupied by the USSR in 1939 would revert to Polish sovereignty, and that the country's prewar borders would be restored.

Eventually, Beria's communiqués went further. Not only did he imply darkly that the Home Army was a force of aristocratic capitalism, but he also implied that its leaders were collaborating with the Germans. Borrowing a term from espionage, he wrote to Stalin that the Warsaw and Vilnius Home Army 'centres' all 'work in service of the Germans, arm themselves at [German] cost, and conduct agitation against the Bolsheviks, the [communist] partisans and the kolkhozes, murdering communists who are left on the territory of western Belarus'.[17] Beria was profoundly suspicious of the motives of the local commander in eastern Poland, General Alexander Krzyzanowski – better known then and since by his pseudonym, Wilk ('wolf'). General Wilk, Beria wrote in July, was a shady figure who had arrived in the region 'illegally' from Warsaw during the period of German occupation. Worse, one of Wilk's underlings had already identified himself to the Red Army, and had asked the Soviet commanders for their cooperation in the liberation of Vilnius. Beria considered this request outrageous – 'the Poles think they have a right to take Vilnius!' – and complained that 'this Polish army disorients the population': the people of this region, he explained, ought to be under the impression that they owed their liberation to the Soviet Union, not to Poland.[18]

Some elements of Beria's rant against General Wilk ring true. Many Polish partisan groups in the regions around Vilnius, as well as in western Belarus and western Ukraine, were distinctly suspicious of communists, and with good reason. These were the territories that had already been occupied and terrorized by the USSR between 1939 and 1941, the territories from which half a million Poles had been deported into Soviet exile and concentration camps. The survivors were resentful, they knew about the Katyń massacre and they certainly did think they had the right to take back Vilnius, which had been a Polish city for many centuries and was at that time dominated by a Polish ethnic majority. They saw no shame in using the weapons stores which departing Germans had left behind either, if that would help them liberate their country in advance of the Red Army's arrival.

Yet to describe the Home Army battalions as working 'in the service of Germans' was ludicrous. There was nothing remotely fascist about General Wilk, who had been fighting the Germans since 1939. Neither he nor anyone else in a senior position gave orders to resist the Red Army, then or later. Beria's dislike of men like Wilk was ideological, and perhaps egotistical as well. He hated the idea that some upstart non-communist Poles might challenge Soviet officers.

This attitude was reflected all the way down the chain of command. In a report to headquarters in July, a Soviet commander of the First Belorussian Front reported meeting a Polish 'partisan' – like Beria, he put this description in quotations – who had, to the Soviet commander's astonishment, acted like his equal. He noted that the Pole had claimed to be a 'captain-commander of a division' and had requested arms and assistance. A few days later, another report from the field described an encounter with another group of Polish partisans who had come upon some downed American pilots. The Poles refused to turn these pilots over to the Red Army when commanded to do so. 'These aren't partisans,' complained the colonel in the field, 'they are Polish divisions loyal to the Polish government in London!'[19] Actually, they were both. But the colonel's mental horizon could not stretch to include a partisan who was not a Soviet partisan.

By the middle of the summer, all pretence of cooperation had been abandoned, and the USSR began to treat the Home Army overtly as a hostile force. Beria informed Stalin in mid-July 1944 that he had sent 12,000 NKVD troops to 'take the necessary Chekist measures' – that is, to use secret police methods – to root out the remaining Home Army partisans from the forest and to 'pacify' the population which had been feeding and housing them.[20] As noted, he also sent General Ivan Serov to command them. Serov had already supervised the deportation of 'dangerous elements' from eastern Poland and the Baltic states in 1939–41, and had organized the brutal deportation of the entire Tatar population from Crimea in 1944. The 'pacification' of small nations was his speciality.[21]

Serov acted quickly. On 17 July, Red Army commanders, acting on his orders, invited General Wilk to a meeting. Wilk arrived, and was promptly disarmed and arrested. Over the next two days, large numbers of his men were also summoned, disarmed and arrested. By 20 July, the Red Army had arrested and disarmed 6000 Home Army partisans, among them 650 officers.[22] Enticed by the promise of better weapons and support, almost all of them were caught by surprise. On 14 July, for example, Henryk Sawala, a young partisan fighter, was told that his unit would be joining a new Polish–Soviet division. His commander explained that they would receive six weeks of training. After that, they would continue to advance alongside the Red Army, with the support of Soviet artillery and tanks. Pleased by this prospect, Sawala presented himself on 18 July to the Soviet officers whom he believed would be leading this new division. He was immediately placed under arrest.

'We were met by a group of 50 [NKVD] soldiers and disarmed,' he recalled later. Some of his fellow partisans resisted arrest, preferring to 'die with honour'. But seeing that they were vastly outnumbered, most decided to avoid an unnecessary massacre and they put down their weapons immediately. All of them, including Sawala, were then marched, under armed guard and without food, to a temporary camp some forty kilometres from Vilnius. While the battle raged on in the west, these trained partisans – men who would have happily fought the retreating Germans – were forced to sit for days in cramped conditions, doing nothing: 'We slept beside one another like canned sardines,' he remembered, 'eating nothing but bread and herring.'[23]

Finally they were called to a meeting and offered a deal. A soldier in a Polish army uniform – Sawala remembered that he was 'hard to understand, because he used more Russian words than Polish' – exhorted them to join the Polish division of the Red Army and to reject the 'traitorous' London government. Jerzy Putrament, a Polish communist writer, then got up and repeated the same message. The response was not positive. The partisans threw mud in Putrament's face, and demanded the return of their commander. The agitator who spoke bad Polish then dropped his polite demeanour, and snarled that they'd all end up 'breaking rocks' somewhere if they didn't join the Red Army right away. Now furious, most of them refused. They were duly deported further east, to POW work camps. Some were sent further still into the Gulag system. Sawala himself landed in a camp in Kaluga, south-west of Moscow.[24] The attack on the Home Army was supplemented with violence directed at anyone who might be sympathetic to the Home Army's plight, including family members. In total, the NKVD arrested some 35,000–45,000 people in the former eastern territories of Poland between 1944 and 1947.[25]

As they moved into territory which even the USSR recognized as Polish, Soviet commanders did not become any less wary of the Home Army or any less suspicious of its leaders. On the contrary, as they moved deeper into Poland, the Russians became crueller, more decisive and more efficient. By the time they reached Poznań in western Poland, they needed only a week to arrest dozens of Home Army members, incarcerate them and subject them to brutal interrogation and torture. Following that, the NKVD conducted group executions of thousands of people in the forests outside the city.[26] At the same time, the Home Army stopped treating the advancing Red Army as a potential ally, and Home Army partisans stopped identifying themselves to the new invaders. Some dropped their arms and melted into the civilian population. Others stayed in the forest and hunkered down to see what would happen next.

Tales of what had happened in eastern Poland quickly reached Warsaw. Although the Home Army's leaders in the Polish capital had only sporadic contact with London, and although they knew little about the progress of the rest of the war, they did know that the Red Army was arresting and disarming their comrades. In an atmosphere of confusion and panic, on 1 August they launched the brave but disastrous Warsaw Uprising, in an attempt to overthrow the Nazis and liberate Warsaw before the Red Army entered the central part of the city. The Germans fought back, brutally. British and American planes, mainly flown by Polish and South African airmen, bravely dropped food and ammunition for the rebels, though not enough to make a difference. The Red Army, by then just across the river, stationed itself in the eastern suburbs and did nothing. Stalin refused permission for Allied planes carrying aid for the rebels to land on Soviet territory.[27]

Though Stalin would later affect to know nothing of the Uprising, the Red Army's spies watched the fighting in Warsaw very carefully, and they kept close track of the public mood. In early October, as the rebellion drew to a tragic and terrible end, a Red Army colonel described the situation in one of many detailed reports to Moscow. Though hundreds of thousands of people had died and the city had, in practice, ceased to exist – after the Uprising ended, the Germans systematically dynamited buildings that were still standing and forced all survivors into labour camps – his primary concern was the relationship between the remnants of the Home Army and the much smaller People's Guard, the Gwardia Ludowa, the armed wing of the communist party. The former, he complained, was not sharing weapons with the latter. Worse, Home Army leaders were spreading negative propaganda about the USSR:

> In bulletins, they emphasize the insignificant assistance that the rebels had received from Soviet air drops, and at the same time praise the Anglo-American effort. Thus is it clear that this organization is preparing action against the Red Army ... Rumours are also spreading to the effect that the Polish Army [the Polish troops under Soviet command] are Soviet spies who have nothing in common with Polish national interests.[28]

After the Uprising was over – after Warsaw was burned to the ground, the leaders of the Polish Underground State were dead or in German prison camps, and some 200,000 people had been killed – the tone of the field officers' reports to headquarters and of Beria's reports to Stalin grew harsher. On 1 November, Beria filed a report to Stalin describing the 'anti-Soviet activity of the White-Polish-Nationalist Bandit Revolutionary organizations', by which he meant the Home Army leadership.[29] Later that month, Soviet field commanders recommended an 'increase of repressive measures' against all armed Home Army members. Red Army troops were pulled from the front, more NKVD troops were procured and at last the forces of the new Polish secret police were sent to do battle, literally, with the Polish resistance.[30] Thanks in particular to the NKVD reinforcement, 3692 Home

Army members were under arrest by the third week of November 1944. By 1 December, the number was 5069.[31]

The bitter fighting in the capital radicalized the Polish public. Many of those who had hoped for a romantic, triumphant ending of the war now lapsed into nihilism. In later years, the Warsaw Uprising would often be remembered as a heroic last stand for Polish independence, and its leaders would become heroes, first of the anti-communist underground, later of the post-communist state. Contemporary Warsaw is filled with monuments to the Uprising, and Warsaw streets and squares are rightly named after its leaders and its fighters. But in the winter of 1944–5, as the reality of Warsaw's destruction sank in and as the Red Army's brutality increased, the Uprising was widely considered a terrible, disastrous mistake. Andrzej Panufnik, a deeply patriotic musician and composer, had been outside the city caring for his sick mother while the events unfolded. When his father finally returned from the city and began to describe the 'brave self-sacrifice of men, women and children', Panufnik 'became convinced that the Uprising had been an appalling mistake based on the false hope that the Russians would come to the rescue'.[32] Szymon Bojko, a Pole serving in the Kościuszko Division, the Polish division of the Red Army, arrived in the last days of the Uprising, and watched Warsaw burn from the other side of the river. 'I had a feeling of disaster inside me,' he remembered later: 'Nothing political. Just foreboding.'[33] In the words of the historian Andrzej Friszke, the failure created 'a deep gloom, a crisis of faith in the West, and a sharp realization of the country's dependence on Russia'.[34]

The gloom would deepen even further a few months later when news of the Yalta agreement filtered back to Poland. Poles pored over the treaty's vague language, especially its call for 'free and unfettered elections', which could not be monitored or enforced. Yalta was understood, then and later, as a Western betrayal. Finally, the reality sank in: the Western Allies were not going to help Poland. The Red Army would remain in power in the East.[35]

After Yalta, the leaders of the Home Army never again had the same authority. Following the Uprising, the organization had rebuilt its structures under the leadership of General Leopold Okulicki. But without Western allies, and without the tens of thousands of young combatants who had died in Warsaw, many Poles lost faith in their ability to fight the USSR. Aware of his lost legitimacy, Okulicki officially dissolved the Home Army in January. In his last, profoundly emotional message, he told his soldiers to keep the faith:

> Try to be the nation's guides and creators of an independent Polish state. In this activity each of us must be his own commander. In the conviction that you will obey this order, that you will remain loyal only to Poland, as well as to make your future work easier, on the authorization of the President of the Polish Republic, I release you from your oath and dissolve the ranks of the [Home Army].[36]

Having called upon his countrymen to renounce their membership of the resistance, Okulicki himself withdrew into deeper conspiracy. The remaining Home Army leaders kept themselves concealed too, waiting for a better future. But the future never came. At the end of February, the NKVD made contact with Okulicki and his commanders, and invited them to a meeting with General Serov in a Warsaw suburb. Aware that their identities had become known to the Soviet secret police, operating in the belief that the Yalta treaty still obliged the Soviet Union to include some non-communists in the new Polish government, hopeful of a better outcome, they went.

None returned. Like General Wilk before them, sixteen men were arrested, flown to Moscow, imprisoned in the Lubyanka, the Soviet Union's most notorious prison, and indicted under Soviet law for 'preparing an armed uprising against the USSR in league with the Germans'. They were accused, in other words, of 'fascist' sympathies. Most received long camp sentences. Three of them, including Okulicki, would eventually die in prison.

The arrests were intended both to serve as a lesson to the Polish underground, and to notify the outside world of Soviet intentions. They also sent a message to the Polish communists, at least some of whom had hoped to win over the Home Army's supporters legitimately. In notes he made later, Jakub Berman wrote that the arrests had 'shocked and worried' his comrades, who had planned to undermine the Home Army leaders through a policy of 'divide and rule', forcing them to squabble with one another so that, eventually, Okulicki and the rest would have become unpopular. Instead, the arrest of the sixteen men unified a large part of society against the communists.[37]

The abrupt abduction of the Polish underground leadership also caused the first major rupture in the alliance between the USSR and the Anglo-Saxon powers. In a letter to Roosevelt, Churchill described these arrests as a turning point: 'this is the test case between us and the Russians of the meaning which is to be attached to such terms as democracy, sovereignty, independence, representative government, and free and unfettered elections'.[38] As subsequent events would show, Churchill was right to question the Russians' interpretations of the words penned into the Yalta agreement, which very quickly came to appear not so much vague as meaningless.

After the arrest of the Home Army leadership, part of the Polish population decided there was nothing left to do except learn to live under a Soviet-style regime. But others drew the opposite conclusion, and decided that there was nothing left to do except fight. By the spring of 1945, one large group of anti-Nazi and anti-communist partisans, the National Armed Forces (Narodowe Siły Zbrojne, or NSZ), a nationalist grouping to the political right of the mainstream underground, had decided to take this path. Instead of following the Home Army's orders to end the struggle, their leaders decided to continue fighting. As the bulk of the Red Army moved west towards Germany, they regrouped in the forests of eastern Poland, especially around Lublin and Rzeszów, where they dedicated themselves to the new struggle.[39] Their goal, as a Polish secret police document not inaccurately put it, was 'the liquidation of the workers of the Department of Public Security' using either 'quiet disappearances (drowning, kidnapping, torture) or open shooting'.[40]

In the vacuum opened up by the dissolution of the Home Army, new groups began to form. The most famous was Wolność i Niezawisłość – Freedom and Independence – usually known as WiN. Jan Rzepecki, its leader, was a Home Army officer. Unlike the mainstream Home Army, he and his colleagues decided to remain underground after the failure of the Warsaw Uprising. They kept their identities secret, continued to observe the rules of conspiracy, and communicated using codes and passwords. Their intention was to remain a civilian organization, though they stayed in touch with armed partisans of all kinds. Until October 1946, they subsidized a newspaper, *Polska Niezawisła* (*Independent Poland*), whose editor argued that Poles should not be tempted to accept a status quo he characterized as 'Soviet terror'.[41] The NKVD identified and arrested Rzepecki not long afterwards, in November 1945. He was interrogated, and forced or convinced to reveal the names of his colleagues. He was freed on the condition that he call on the rest of the underground to reveal their identities, which some of them did.

Starting from scratch, WiN reconstituted itself once again. Its 'Second Executive' launched itself in December 1945, and lasted for almost a year, maintaining some communications with the outside world via long chains of couriers and messengers who passed inscrutable notes to one another over many weeks. Finally, after a woman working for WiN was captured on the border and found to be carrying an encrypted message, the chain unravelled, the ringleaders were again captured and tortured into naming names. Eventually, a Third Executive and a Fourth Executive were formed, both of which were penetrated by the Polish secret police from the start, probably according to a Soviet plan (the Bolsheviks had created a phony Russian 'opposition' at one point in the 1920s to attract foreign spies as well). After the Fourth Executive was disbanded the secret police created their own pseudo-WiN, which kept in contact with naive foreigners as well as those Poles too clueless to know that the 'clandestine organization' was a police operation. WiN existed in this sorry state until 1952, though a few of its former members did manage to live for long periods in hiding.

The story of WiN is often held up as an example of the pointlessness of anti-communist resistance in the immediate postwar period, and it was certainly perceived that way at the time. But it is also possible to view the sad history of WiN as a testimony to the Polish desire for resistance. Some 10,000 members of the organization were arrested, tortured and jailed. Hundreds were executed. Despite the amount of pressure on the group, and despite the obsession with which its members were pursued, at its zenith WiN had about 20,000–30,000 members.[42]

Among postwar Polish resistance groups, WiN was unusual in its size and in retaining some theoretical links to the old Home Army chain of command. Most other such groups were very small, often consisting entirely of young people who modelled themselves on an idea of the Home Army, which they themselves had not quite been old enough to join, or who called themselves 'NSZ' without really knowing what that organization was or what it stood for. A thirteen-member partisan group calling itself 'Home Army Youth' began to collect weapons in the forests south of Kraków after 1945, for example, and secretly practised using them until all were arrested in 1950.[43]

As Soviet troops moved west for the final assault on Berlin, the situation grew even more complicated. As the Red Army left a region, it often happened that partisan groups of all political stripes moved back in: NSZ groups, ex-Home Army soldiers, Ukrainian partisans who were fighting for Ukrainian independence. All of them were intent on fighting the Red Army and its Polish allies, but sometimes they fought with one another as well. Despite the chaos, some remained true to the ideals of the old underground. Others came to rely on theft to stay alive, and degenerated into semi-criminal gangs. Vicious battles often broke out between them, especially between Poles and Ukrainians.

Although the USSR had 'pacified' eastern Poland in the summer of 1944, by the following spring the east was thus convulsed by what should correctly be described as a civil war. For communists and their allies, the villages and forests around the city of Lublin became unsafe, and for a time even the city itself was a danger zone. According to one report filed in May 1945, the work of 'all party and government organs' had ground to a halt in the area. In four local districts, the police no longer existed, having been either disarmed by partisans or murdered outright.[44] Soon afterwards, Stalin, still celebrating the German surrender, was informed, in the most alarming terms, that 'in Poland the anti-state underground continues to be active, everywhere'.[45] Another five NKVD regiments, plus a motorized battalion, were duly called in to assist the hapless Polish secret police once again.[46]

In August 1945, the Minister of Public Security, Stanisław Radkiewicz, attended a regional meeting of the Security Department in Lublin and heard some hard truths. One local officer reckoned that no more than 20 per cent of the people in his county supported the new regime. Another explained that they had not managed to place any agents inside the armed anti-communist partisan movement because 'they don't want to cooperate'. Others thought the situation would improve because the peasants were tired of supporting the partisans, some of whom regularly stole food. But all present agreed that 'bands' were still a major problem. Some were hiding in the forests, others worked on their farms by day, but 'at an agreed signal they come together and carry out a criminal attack'.[47] They regularly assaulted security policemen, communist party officials and others who collaborated with them.

Yet even as it fought, the armed resistance already seemed aware of its tragic position. Its members were exhausted by the long struggle with the Germans. Many had already spent five or six years living in the forests. Often very young, they had missed months or years of schooling. They knew that surrender meant the end of their dream of national independence, but at the same time they were now fighting against a new and more amorphous enemy. In the course of their duties, they were required to murder not German occupiers but Polish communists and Polish policemen. Some of them considered these tasks fratricidal and wanted out. Others resented those who left. In 1946, one armed gang beat up a pair of schoolteachers, both former Home Army men, accusing them of 'collaboration' because they had returned to ordinary life.[48] Eventually, tens of thousands accepted one of a series of 'amnesties', turned in their weapons and joined civilian life.

Many were embittered by the experience. Lucjan Grabowski, the young man from the Białystok region, had stayed with his Home Army unit until he was asked to kill one of its members for treason. Suspecting the man was innocent, he refused to carry out the order. 'They were terrible times, brother was killing brother for any kind of reason.' Finally, 'I began to become conscious of a few facts which until then I hadn't paid attention to and hadn't thought much about. A lot of my friends, former partisans, had gone to the West. Others had started university courses, or were finishing high school diplomas and working. And I was still fighting, for the fifth year in a row.' Grabowski turned in his weapons together with forty other men, mostly from WiN. All had tears in their eyes: 'We left the secret police building without weapons and no longer the same people we had been a few hours earlier.'[49]

Others kept fighting. Tiny numbers of men – one or two dozen – remained in the forests for many years. One small group of NSZ partisans gave itself up in 1956, after Bierut's death. One lone operator, Michał Krupa, remained in hiding until he was finally tracked down and arrested in 1959.[50] But most of those who kept fighting did so knowing there was no hope.

Among them was an underground leader known by the pseudonym 'Mewa'. According to the Polish security police who tracked his movements, Mewa, who fought with the Home Army during the war, had returned to the armed struggle in 1945 out of desperation and disillusion: he was suicidal, a psychological profile of him explained, 'he wants to die'. Many of the 300 members of his gang – some former Home Army, some deserters from the Polish division of the Red Army – felt the same way. Most were from south-eastern Poland, and their morale was low. In May 1945, they held an outdoor mass and pledged allegiance to the Polish government-in-exile in London – a government which was no longer recognized as legitimate by its allies or by anyone else, as all of those present knew perfectly well.

From then on, Mewa's group slowly shrank. In the months which followed, many of Mewa's men drifted back to their family farms or decided to leave the area and head to the former German territories, now part of western Poland, in order to begin new lives. Some of those who stayed began to steal from the local Ukrainian population, at that time still a large percentage of the inhabitants of south-eastern Poland. More than once they burned Ukrainian villages to the ground. The archival record of their exploits says a lot about their desperation. In January 1945 they attacked a factory director, a Polish communist, and stole 100 zlotys of Polish currency. In April they stole two horses. In July they killed a Ukrainian peasant, and threw his body into the river. By the end of 1945, the local police were working hard, but not very competently, to break up Mewa's group. They infiltrated two agents into the gang, only to learn that one turned back against them and the other had been uncovered and murdered. His body was thrown into a river too. Over the year and a half of its existence, the group carried out 205 attacks and murdered many local communist officials – until finally, in July 1947, Mewa was captured. As he must have expected, he was sentenced to death.[51]

A decade later, the ambiguity of this moment was perfectly captured in *Ashes and Diamonds*, Andrzej Wajda's classic film about this period.

The movie tells the story of a partisan with a dilemma: he must choose between a girl he has just met and a political assassination he has been ordered to carry out. He chooses the assassination, but is shot himself while carrying it out. In the final scene he runs, stumbles and finally dies on a field full of garbage. The metaphor was clear enough to Polish audiences: the lives of the young men who joined the resistance had been thrown away on the trash heap of history.

Though precise figures are hard to calculate, the NKVD itself reckoned that between January and April of 1945 alone it had arrested some 215,540 people in Poland. Of this number, 138,000 were Germans or *Volksdeutsche* – local people who had claimed to be of German descent. Some 38,000 Poles were also arrested in this four-month period, and all were sent to camps in the USSR. Some 5000 died 'in the course of the operation and investigation'.[52] Among them must have been thousands of Mewa's men who fought until the end, knowing they would lose.

Once the war had ended there was no sustained or armed resistance to the Soviet occupation of eastern Germany. Hitler had hoped there would be: before his suicide he exhorted the Germans to fight to the death, to burn cities to the ground, to sacrifice everything in one last violent struggle. He also ordered the Wehrmacht to create youth battalions which would conduct a partisan struggle against the Red Army after his death.

These youth battalions were the 'Werewolves' who featured so largely in both Nazi and Allied propaganda, but who in reality were every bit as mythological as their name implied. With Hitler's death and Germany's defeat, they simply melted away: the spell was broken. Erich Loest, later a prominent East German novelist, was a 25-year-old Hitler Youth leader and a junior Wehrmacht officer when he was first recruited to the Werewolf movement. He was told of his new role in the final weeks of the war, and even given some partisan training in preparation for the Russian occupation. Yet when the Russians actually marched in to Mittweida, his home town in Saxony, the underground struggle was the farthest thing from his mind. Instead of fighting the Red Army, his family helped him escape to an aunt's farm further west, where he could safely surrender to the Americans.

Loest never spoke of his Werewolf training in the years immediately after the war – 'I am not stupid,' he told me – and he was never arrested. Others were less lucky. During the last days of the war, the SS ordered all of the teenagers in Mittweida to attend a lecture on the Werewolves. No training was given and no oaths were sworn, but an attendance list was passed around. Soviet authorities found the list after the war's end. 'Nothing had happened except for this lecture, but all of them were arrested. Arrested for one year,' explained Loest.[53]

The legal basis for such arrests was order 00315 of the Soviet Military Administration, issued on 18 April 1945. This edict called for the immediate internment, without prior investigation, of 'spies, saboteurs, terrorists, activists of the Nazi party' as well as people maintaining 'illegal' print and broadcasting devices, people with weapons, and former members of the German civil administration. The order resembled the regulations put in place in the other Allied occupation zones, where 'active' Nazis were also interrogated on a massive scale.[54] The difference between the Soviet zone and other zones was one of degree: in practice, the Soviet order made it possible to arrest almost anyone who had held any position of authority, whether or not he or she had been a Nazi. Policemen, town mayors, business people and prosperous farmers all qualified, on the grounds that they could not have been so successful unless they had collaborated.

By the time of the Potsdam Conference at the beginning of August, the definition of who could be interned had grown even broader. In an ugly Hohenzollern palace surrounded by green parkland, the Allies – Stalin and now Harry Truman and Clement Attlee (following Roosevelt's death and Churchill's electoral defeat) – issued a new declaration stating that 'Nazi leaders, influential Nazi supporters and high officials of Nazi organizations and institutions and *any other persons dangerous to the occupation or its objectives* shall be arrested and interned' (my italics).[55] For the USSR this was an ideal formulation: 'any other persons dangerous to the occupation or its objectives' is a very broad category indeed, and it could be stretched to include anyone whom the NKVD disliked for any reason.

The Red Army duly set up military tribunals, courts without lawyers or witnesses, which continued for several years. These were completely separate from the Nuremberg Trials, which were created jointly by all

VIOLENCE

of the Allies to try the most high-ranking Nazi leaders, and they had nothing to do with international law. Convictions were sometimes made on the basis of Article 58 of the Soviet criminal code, the statute which was used to arrest political prisoners in the Soviet Union and which had no relation of any kind to German law either. Sentences were sometimes translated into German but written out in Cyrillic, making them impossible for the accused to read. Prisoners were sometimes forced, after severe beatings and other kinds of torture, to sign documents they couldn't understand. Wolfgang Lehmann, aged fifteen, signed a document stating that he had blown up two trucks, though he didn't know it at the time. Other trials were held in Moscow, where prisoners were convicted in absentia by Soviet judges. Weeks later, they would learn what had happened.[56]

Some of those arrested really had been Nazis, though not necessarily important Nazis. Little attempt was made to separate real criminals from small-time bureaucrats or opportunists. But in addition to the Nazis, the arrests soon swept up thousands of people too young to have been Nazis – Manfred Papsdorf was arrested at thirteen – or many who, like the teenagers of Mittweida, were guilty of nothing more than being in the wrong place at the wrong time.[57] A few were arrested because their enthusiasm for liberation was too great. Gisela Gneist was fifteen years old in 1945 and transfixed by the idea of democracy, a word she heard frequently on American armed forces radio. Gneist lived in Wittenberg, and was resentful of the Soviet soldiers there, some of whom had created a brothel on the top floor of her apartment block. She wanted something better, and together with some other teenagers she created a 'political party', complete with its own amateurish secret codes. They had no idea of the potential danger, and they didn't have much of an ideology. 'My idea of freedom,' she remembered, 'was that people should be able to speak freely. I didn't know what communism was, had never really heard of it.'[58]

Gneist was arrested in December 1945, along with two dozen of her fellow 'party members', all teenagers. She was put in a 'cell without windows', together with twenty other women, some of whom were her schoolmates. The toilet was a milk bottle. There were bugs everywhere, and lice. A Soviet officer interrogated her in Russian for many days running, in the presence of a barely competent translator.

He also beat her on the back and on the legs until the blood ran. Gneist, not yet sixteen, eventually confessed: she admitted she had been part of a 'counter-revolutionary organization'. A military tribunal found her guilty in January 1946 and sentenced her, just like a real war criminal, to incarceration in Sachsenhausen.[59]

Surprising though it will seem to those unfamiliar with this odd twist of history, Sachsenhausen, a notorious Nazi concentration camp, underwent a metamorphosis after the war and lived a second life, as did the equally notorious concentration camp at Buchenwald. The American troops who liberated Buchenwald in April 1945 had forced the leading citizens of Weimar to walk around the camp's barracks and to witness the starving survivors, the mass graves and the corpses stacked like firewood beside them. Four months later, the Soviet troops who subsequently took control of the Weimar region had once again installed prisoners in those same barracks, and eventually buried them in similar mass graves. They followed the same practice in many places. Auschwitz was another one of many labour camps in Poland to be reused in some manner after the war too.[60]

The Russians renamed Buchenwald Special Camp Number Two, and Sachsenhausen became Special Camp Number Seven.[61] In total there would be ten such camps built or rebuilt in Soviet-occupied Germany, along with several prisons and other less formal places of incarceration. These were not German communist camps, but rather Soviet camps. The NKVD's central Gulag administration controlled all of them directly from Moscow, in some instances down to the last detail. The NKVD sent instructions from Moscow on how to celebrate the 1 May holiday in its German camps, for example, and carefully monitored the 'political-moral' condition of the guards.[62] All of the senior camp commanders were Soviet military personnel, although some had German staff too, and the camps were laid out according to Soviet designs. An inhabitant of Kolyma or Vorkuta would have felt immediately at home.

At the same time, the German Special Camps were not labour camps of the kind that the NKVD ran in the Soviet Union itself. They were not attached to factories or building projects, as Soviet camps usually were, and prisoners did not go out to work. On the contrary, survivors often describe the excruciating boredom of being forbidden to work, forbidden to leave their barracks, forbidden to walk or move. In the Ketschendorf camp, inmates begged to work in the kitchens so as to have some kind of activity (and of course to have access to more food).[63] In Sachsenhausen there were two zones, in only one of which people were allowed to work. Prisoners much preferred that one.[64]

The Special Camps were not death camps of the kind that the Nazis had constructed either. There were no gas chambers, and prisoners were not sent to Sachsenhausen to be immediately killed. But they were extraordinarily lethal nonetheless. Of some 150,000 people who were incarcerated in NKVD camps in eastern Germany between 1945 and 1953 – of which 120,000 were Germans and 30,000 were Soviet citizens – about a third died from starvation and illness.[65] Prisoners were fed wet, black bread and cabbage soup so bad that Lehmann, who was later sent to the Gulag, remembered that 'in Siberia the food was better and more regular'.[66] There were no medicines, and no doctors. Lice and vermin meant that disease spread quickly. In the winter of 1945–6, it was so cold that the prisoners in the women's zone in Sachsenhausen burned bed slats to keep warm.[67] As was the case in so many Soviet penal institutions, prisoners did not die because they were murdered, but because they were neglected, ignored and sometimes literally forgotten.

The explicit goal of the Soviet Special Camps in eastern Germany was not labour or murder but isolation: the Special Camps were meant to cut dubious people off from the rest of society, at least until the new Soviet occupiers had got their bearings. They were preventative rather than punitive, designed primarily to quarantine people who might oppose the system, not to incarcerate people who had already done so. In the Soviet Gulag some contact with the outside world was possible, and inmates could even sometimes receive visitors. By contrast, during the first three years of the existence of the postwar German camps, prisoners could not send or receive letters, and they had no news from the outside world whatsoever. In many cases, their families did not know what had happened to them or where they were. They had simply disappeared.

Over time, conditions did improve, in part thanks to pressure from outside. The sudden disappearance of so many young people made family members frantic, and they bombarded officials with requests for information. German authorities were usually of no help. In 1947, a local official advised family members in Thuringia that they 'might be able to learn more from the Russian prosecutor in Weimar'.[68] Soviet officials in turn passed such requests up the chain of command and, in the general chaos, people got lost. One German student disappeared in 1945 and was finally 'found' by his parents only in 1952.[69] That was four years after the Soviet Military Administration in Germany had agreed to allow prisoners to notify their family members of their locations.[70] In that same year, the NKVD had also increased the food allowances for the camps, in order to reduce the high death rate and to mollify the East German leaders who were petitioning the Soviet authorities for change.[71]

The arrests, along with the prolonged detention of Wehrmacht soldiers in the Soviet Union (some would remain there until the 1950s), became a major source of friction between the public and the new authorities. But they also helped create a new set of standards for public behaviour. Most of the newly liberated Germans were not communists, and did not know what to expect from the Soviet occupation forces. The arrest and incarceration of thousands of young people on the slightest suspicion of any form of 'anti-Soviet' politics immediately set the tone for others. It was a first lesson, for many, on the need to censor oneself in public. If a teenager like Gisela Gneist could be arrested for talking about democracy, then the penalty for more serious political involvement would obviously be much higher.

Former prisoners and their families were even more afraid. After their release, they rarely spoke about what had happened to them. Lehmann, who had been in the Ketschendorf camp in Germany as well as the Soviet Gulag, didn't tell his wife about either until after 1989.[72] The use of selective violence and the creation of camps for potential enemies of the regime were also part of a broader Soviet policy. The Red Army and the NKVD knew that in societies as uncertain and unstable as those of postwar Eastern Europe, mass arrests could backfire. But arrests carefully targeted at outspoken people could have a wider echo: if you arrest one such person, ten more will be frightened.

*

The Russians who arrived in Budapest in January 1945 knew little about the nation whose capital they had just conquered. Most assumed they had arrived in a country peopled entirely by Nazi collaborators – Hungary had been a German ally during the invasion of the USSR – and they were sometimes incredulous to find themselves treated as liberators. As in Germany, they were under orders to arrest all of the fascists they could identify. But whereas in Germany they had looked for 'Werewolves' and in Poland they tracked down the Home Army, in Hungary they seemed unsure of how, exactly, a fascist might be identified.

As a result, the first arrests in Hungary were often arbitrary. Men were stopped on the street, told they would be taken away to do 'a little work' – *malenkaya rabota* in Russian, a phrase which became Hungarianized as *málenkij robot* – and marched off in convoys. They would then disappear deep into the Soviet Union, and not return for many years. At the very beginning, it seemed almost anyone would suffice. An eyewitness from a town in eastern Hungary remembered that within days of entering his town, soldiers began collecting people: 'Not only men, but also children, sixteen- to seventeen-year-old kids and even a thirteen-year-old. No matter how we cried and begged, they did not react, just held their guns and told everyone to get out of the houses with sometimes nothing on, no clothes, no food, just the way they were there . . . We did not know where they were taken, they were just saying *málenkij robot, málenkij robot.*'[73]

Some were considered suspicious because they appeared to be wealthy, or because they owned books. George Bien, then aged sixteen, was arrested along with his father because he owned a shortwave radio. He was interrogated as a spy, forced to confess, and made to sign a thirty-page Russian document, of which he did not understand a single word. Bien eventually wound up in the camps of Kolyma, returning home only in 1955.[74]

Soviet troops also seemed to be under orders to look for Germans, who they had been informed would be quite numerous. In practice, this meant that people with German-sounding names (very common in the former Habsburg realms) were immediately treated as war criminals. József Révai, who was to become one of the most important Hungarian communists, complained to Rákosi in early January that Russian soldiers seemed to have 'fixed quotas' they had to fulfil, and that they took as Germans 'people who did not speak a word of German – people who were proven anti-fascists, had been interned'.[75] The result of these policies was that somewhere between 140,000 and 200,000 Hungarians were arrested and deported to the USSR after 1945. Most of them wound up in the camps of the Gulag.[76]

Many remained in Hungary as well. Internment – imprisonment without trial – had become common in Hungary in the late 1930s, but now it was expanded. 'People's Courts' were created to try, sentence and in some cases execute Nazi collaborators. A few of these trials were made into major public events, in the hope that they would educate Hungarians about the crimes of the past. Even at the time many observed that ordinary Hungarians mostly dismissed them as 'victors' justice'. A few years later, some of the verdicts would be overturned, on the grounds that it was time to drop the 'retaliatory character of the punishments'.[77]

Nor were they perceived as fair. Although decisions about internment and trials were nominally under Hungarian control, it was widely assumed that the NKVD influenced the courts. A. M. Belyanov, the Soviet official delegated to oversee security matters in Hungary, at one point berated a Hungarian politician about the slow pace of trials: 'He urged that the people's tribunals work faster, he criticized them for negotiating and talking too much. He wanted them to announce the verdict right after the prosecution speech. I told him that we had studied the Soviet justice system and there, in political cases, witnesses are heard publicly at the court. He smiled unwillingly and showed me his big yellow teeth, which were like those of a tiger . . .'[78] The Red Army also held its own trials near Vienna, in an elegant villa in the resort town of Baden. There was no pretence about Hungarian sovereignty there: Soviet military tribunals simply convicted Hungarians of political crimes under Article 58 of the Soviet criminal code, just as in Germany.[79]

The number of the accused was very high, and their nature very broad. A series of secret decrees had instructed the new Hungarian police forces to arrest, among others, former members of extreme right movements, including the fascist Arrow Cross movement, which had ruled Hungary during the final days fo the war, from October

1944 until March 1945; military officers who had served under Admiral Horthy, Hungary's interwar authoritarian leader, from 1920 until the Arrow Cross takeover; and also pub-owners, tobacconists, barbers and all of those who – in another hopelessly broad formulation – '*due to their regular contacts with the public were the primary disseminators of fascist propaganda*' (my italics). In practice, anyone who had ever worked for or praised any of the prewar governments, party leaders or politicians was at risk. The NKVD, together with the new security police, also acquired lists of young people who had been members of the *levente*, Admiral Horthy's paramilitary youth organization, and began tracking them down, just as they had tracked down Hitler Youth and alleged Werewolves in Germany. In total, Hungarian and Soviet security police interned some 40,000 Hungarians between 1945 and 1949. Around Budapest alone, the new regime built sixteen internment camps with a capacity to contain up to 23,000 prisoners.[80]

Not all of those arrested had collaborated with the Nazis. On the contrary, from the moment of the Red Army's entry into Hungary, the new Hungarian secret police – backed, of course, by the Hungarian communist party and its Soviet mentors – began to seek out and identify a different sort of 'fascist' as well. Although the Hungarian wartime underground was never as large or as well organized as its Polish equivalent, there had been cells of anti-German opposition even at the highest levels of society. Immediately after the war's end (much earlier than Hungarian chronology usually has it) the NKVD and the Hungarian secret police made these anti-fascists into a target. They were too independent, they believed in national sovereignty, and they knew how to create clandestine organizations. Many supported the Smallholders' Party, which played a large role in the provisional government and did actually win elections in 1945.

In a truly democratic postwar Eastern Europe, they would, like the Polish Home Army, have become the political elite. But even before the Hungarian government was fully under communist control, former members of the anti-German resistance knew they were under surveillance. István Szent-Miklósy, a member of one such secret grouping, later wrote that he and his friends 'felt somehow hunted but could not give any tangible reason' immediately after the war's end.

Unlike their Polish counterparts, these were not armed partisans: Szent-Miklósy's group was, he wrote, 'without formal structure, without lists of names, without pledges, emblems or identity cards, without clearly delineated rules, without even an encompassing philosophy'.[81] Many had been part of earlier groups such as the Hungarian Community, an anti-fascist (and also anti-semitic) secret society, or the wartime Hungarian Independence Movement, which was also more of an anti-German discussion circle than a full-fledged resistance organization. Some of the group were among the founding members of the postwar Smallholders' Party, and as such were trying to cooperate with a regime they thought might become a democracy eventually. They were hardly more than a group of friends who were vaguely anti-Soviet and who met in one another's apartments to exchange concerns.

In the end, they became objects of special interest not because of anything they'd done, but because the secret police got hold of a written summary of their wartime resistance activities. Then they were watched even more carefully, as Szent-Miklósy described:

> In the early fall [of 1946] my neighbor sublet the room adjacent to my living room to the Military Political section. From there they bored a hole through the wall and placed a microphone. As the hole lay behind my heavy Dutch colonial couch, the receiver did not pick up the voices in the room very clearly. Then my telephone was adapted to transmit the voices, and another microphone was placed in the front hall where, on a Biedermeier sofa, sat our neighbor's teenage daughter with her suitor, an MPS [military police] agent disguised as a university student.[82]

Szent-Miklósy was arrested in December 1946. He was taken to the secret police headquarters on Andrássy Street, where he was tortured. He was made to stand with his forehead angled against the wall and his arms outstretched for hours, and forced to shout, 'I am the murderer of my wife and my mother', both of whom, he had been told, were also under arrest. He was put on trial, along with a large group of co-conspirators. All were accused of agitating to overthrow 'the democratic state', and jailed for ten years. During the trial Szent-Miklósy 'confessed', at great length, to crimes he had never committed. His arrest was a kind of pre-emptive strike, typical of that time: he and his circle hadn't actually done anything of any significance – but the authorities feared they might.

★
ZERO HOUR

1. The Red Army in Western Poland, 142 kilometres from Berlin, March 1945

2. The Reichstag, April 1945

3. Soviet soldiers distributing food to German civilians, May 1945

4. Széchenyi Chain Bridge, Budapest, summer 1945

5. In the ruins of Warsaw, a Polish family's mid-day meal ...

6. ... and a woman selling bread on a street corner, summer 1945

★
ETHNIC CLEANSING

7. Germans expelled from the Sudetenland, awaiting deportation

8. German peasants ('Swabians') on their way out of Hungary

★ ARMED RESISTANCE

9. Polish partisans from the underground National Armed Forces (NSZ) who had fought the Germans and were preparing to fight the Red Army. All of these men were dead a few weeks after this photograph was taken in south-central Poland, spring 1944.

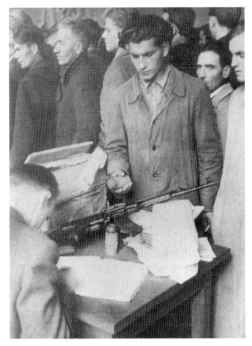

10. A Polish partisan accepts amnesty and turns in his weapons

★ ELECTIONS

11. Mátyás Rákosi addresses Budapest crowds, 1946

12. The Communist Party in Łodz, Poland, demonstrates against Western
imperialism and Winston Churchill, 1946

13. Election graffiti in Budapest, 1945: 'Black marketeers to prison! Victory for the Communist Party means more bread and more food!'

14. Voting in the Polish countryside, 1947

15. The Communist Party triumphant: the Hungarian elite gathers beneath portraits of Lenin, Stalin and Rákosi, 1949

A similarly pre-emptive strike against the independent-minded clergy followed soon after. The chief victim of that round was a charismatic and energetic Franciscan monk, Father Szaléz Kiss. Father Kiss ran a large and successful Christian youth group called Kedim, in and around the town of Gyöngyös, just fifty miles east of Budapest. Over the course of 1945, the new Hungarian secret police began to take a special interest in Gyöngyös because the communists had done particularly badly there in the elections of that year, and because the peasant-based Smallholders' Party had done particularly well.

Their Soviet mentors became even more interested when, beginning in September 1945, unknown gunmen murdered several Red Army soldiers stationed in the region. Under pressure to do something, the new Hungarian secret police launched one of their first big investigations. They arrested and detained some sixty people, including high-school-aged members of Kedim, and interrogated them all at great length. Their goal was to establish an elaborate spider's web of connections, between Kedim and the Smallholders' Party, between the Smallholders' Party and the 'Anglo-Saxon powers', between the US embassy and Father Kiss, and between Father Kiss and the young men who allegedly murdered the Russian soldiers. Put together, these links were said to expose a 'fascist terror conspiracy group' which was, at least in the imagination of the secret policemen, attempting to bring back the old regime.

The record of those interrogations, neatly preserved in a Budapest archive, does not make easy reading. One of the central suspects, a young law student named Jószef Antal, first denied everything. Later, he made a long and garbled confession, probably after having been tortured. Antal, who was described by a friend as having 'participated in the resistance against the German occupation', was a crucial link in the spider's web, since he worked in the local Smallholders' Party headquarters and was at the same time an acquaintance of Father Kiss. In his rambling statement, he recalled a conversation with a Smallholder politician about the 'coming war' between Russia and the Anglo-Saxon powers, and gave the impression that he had already started organizing for this 'armed conflict' together with Father Kiss. There are allusions to some guns and grenades being held at the Smallholders' Party offices, as well as to a weapons store 'in a castle' known to Father Kiss.[83]

Immediately afterwards, Antal retracted this confession. But an equally garbled statement was also obtained from Otto Kizmann, a seventeen-year-old Kedim member who confessed to having assassinated a Russian soldier. Kizmann, who was also probably tortured, went much further. He said that Father Kiss had 'showed us the business cards of influential persons who would bring us weapons', that the priest had 'told us to get weapons for ourselves until the foreign shipments arrive', and that he had declared that 'killing a Russian was not a sin'. Similarly wild tales were also extracted from a friend of Kizmann's, László Bodnár, also aged seventeen, who claimed Father Kiss had promised he would help them escape Hungary by aeroplane.[84]

Father Kiss himself did not confess to any of these unlikely crimes. On the contrary, he told his interrogators: 'I did everything I could to convince the young people to hide their weapons, and not to commit murder, because this was the most hideous crime.' He had, he said, once met a representative of the US embassy, a man who had given him some American newspapers. He had never received, and never sought to receive, any American weapons. He was condemned to death anyway, as were Kizmann, Bodnár and a sixteen-year-old boy. The sentences were carried out in December 1946. Other members of the 'conspiracy' went to jail or, in a few cases, to prison camps in the Soviet Union.

The 'Father Kiss conspiracy', like the arrest of Gisela Gneist in Germany or the sixteen Home Army leaders in Poland, was a harbinger of what was to come. The investigation into it was clearly inspired by the Soviet military authorities, as many later investigations would be. As was common in Soviet investigations, links were drawn between different organizations – Kedim, the Smallholders' Party, the church, the US embassy – based on chance encounters, distant acquaintanceship, or the imagination of investigators. The shadow of 'fascism' was cast over everyone caught in the net. The victims were mostly people in their teens and twenties, an age group which would remain of enormous interest to secret policemen across the bloc in years to come.

In the spring of 1946, at the time of the sentencing, the case also received massive publicity. On 4 May, the Hungarian communist party's newspaper, *Szabad Nép*, published a photograph of Father Kiss in handcuffs, under the headline 'Fascist conspirators confessed and pleaded guilty of murders.' An editorial alongside was entitled, simply, 'Hang Them.'[85] The case was also reported in the non-communist press, but with greater care. At first, *Kis Újság* (*Little Gazette*), the newspaper of the Smallholders' Party, at that time the largest party in the Hungarian parliament, simply published the official police press release. The following day, it reported the words of the Smallholder leader and Hungarian Prime Minister, Ferenc Nagy, who declared that 'if the information published in the official police communiqués proves even partly true then we demand the strictest investigation and the harshest punishment for the guilty'.[86] A few days later, he referred to the incident less ambivalently, as a 'fascist conspiracy'. Not for many years did anyone publicly suggest that the story might not have any truth to it at all.

Other cases followed, each accompanied by equally lurid propaganda, and each supported by equally ambiguous evidence. Internments came in consecutive waves, from 1945 onwards, without a break. First came the 'war criminals', fascists and anyone presumed to be a fascist; then military and civilian personnel from the Horthy regime; then members of legal political parties, especially the Smallholders; then social democrats; then communist party members themselves. Although the definition of an 'enemy of the state' changed over time, the mechanisms to deal with these enemies were put in place right at the very beginning.[87]

Theoretically, in 1946 Hungary was – like Czechoslovakia or eastern Germany at the same time – a democracy. The government was run by the majority Smallholders' Party, who were not communists. They ruled in coalition with communists, social democrats and others. But the Hungarian communist party controlled the security organs, not the Hungarian state, just as the Czechoslovak communist party controlled the Czech security organs, the German communist party would control the East German security organs, and the Polish communist party controlled the Polish security organs. Everywhere in Eastern Europe, their control over the secret police gave minority communist parties an outsized influence over political events. Through the selective use of terror, they could send clear messages to their opponents, and to the general public, about what kinds of behaviour and what kinds of people were no longer acceptable in the new regime.

6

Ethnic cleansing

The Bolshevik party is a model of the genuine international working-class party. From the day it was created it has fought nationalism in every form.

Educational pamphlet, published in Moscow, 1950

I came back to my native village for the first time in 1965. Once I had known every path there, every crooked tree. For the first few minutes, I didn't know what I was looking at. Tears filled my eyes, for a long time I couldn't say a word. They had ploughed up our beautiful Nietreba and planted a forest . . .

Ivan Bishko, a Ukrainian deported from his village in 1946[1]

One of the myths which the international communist movement propagated about itself was the myth of its own indifference to national and ethnic distinctions. Communists were internationalists by definition, 'soldiers in a single international army' with no national divisions between them. Raphael Samuel, son of a militant British communist and later a party member himself, once described the communism of his childhood as 'universalist':

> though allowing for the existence of national peculiarities (we only half believed in them), we thought of the transition from capitalism to socialism as being 'identical' in content everywhere. Communism, like medieval Christendom, was one and indivisible, an international fellowship of faith . . .[2]

In reality, there was no wartime leader so keen to manipulate and encourage national conflict as Stalin – with the exception, of course, of Hitler himself. Lenin appointed Stalin 'Commissar of Nationalities' in 1917, and the future Generalissimo acquired an expertise and interest in the issue which he never lost. From the 1930s onwards he directed waves of terror against minority ethnic groups living in the USSR, among them Poles, Chechens, Crimean Tatars, Volga Germans and, in the final years before his death, Jews. Following the Nazi invasion in 1941, he also drew heavily on Russian national and nationalist symbols – traditional army uniforms, the Orthodox church – to inspire 'internationalist' Soviet citizens to fight the Germans. He understood the political uses of nationalism very well: emotional calls for the defence of the Motherland inspired the soldiers of the Red Army far more than any Marxist, internationalist language could ever have done.

Ethnic conflict was also written into the agreement signed by the three Allied leaders at Potsdam in July 1945. A later generation of European leaders would react with horror at the notion of 'ethnic cleansing'. But Stalin, Truman and Attlee positively encouraged the mass transfer of populations. Their Potsdam agreement blandly called for the 'transfer to Germany of German populations . . . remaining in Poland, Czechoslovakia and Hungary', a sentence which affected millions of people.[3] By agreeing to move Poland's border with the USSR to the west, they also tacitly accepted that there would be transfers of millions of Poles to Poland from Ukraine, and millions of Ukrainians to Ukraine from Poland. Although transfers of Hungarians from Czechoslovakia and Slovaks from Hungary did not appear in the Potsdam agreements, nobody in the international community objected very much when they took place. For its part, the Soviet Union had already presided over the mass deportation of some 70,000 ethnic Germans from Romania to the USSR in January 1945, six months before the Potsdam treaty was signed.[4]

The only additional provision made at Potsdam was that 'any transfers that take place should be effected in an orderly and humane manner'. But by the time the treaty was signed, these 'orderly and humane' population transfers had already degenerated into chaotic and cruel mass movements of people. Ethnic conflict – deep, bitter, violent ethnic conflict, between many different kinds of groups in many countries – was Hitler's true legacy in Eastern Europe, so much so that any discussion of the expulsions of Germans from western Poland, the Sudetenland, Hungary and Romania after 1945 has to begin by recalling what had happened in the previous five years. To repeat: the object of the German occupation of Poland had been to destroy Polish civilization, to turn the Poles into an illiterate workforce, to eliminate the Polish educated class. Poles had been deported from historically Polish cities such as Poznań and Łódź, as well as from Gdynia, the new port city that the Polish state had constructed in the 1920s. They had been replaced by German colonists, had become second-class citizens, had in some places lost the right to speak Polish in the street or to send their children to Polish schools. Thousands wound up working either as slave labourers in Germany, or as prisoners in one of the dozens of slave labour camps the Germans constructed for that purpose on Polish territory.

The occupation of the Czech lands was milder, though also deeply degrading. Throughout the country, historical monuments and statues had been removed, local leaders murdered, the very notion of nationhood mocked. The German occupation of Hungary at the end of the war was shorter, though also very cruel. Even the earlier periods of uneasy Hungarian–German and Romanian–German collaboration were humiliating for those populations, since collaboration with the Germans had so quickly evolved into domination by the Germans. Everywhere, the Holocaust left a terrible legacy of guilt and hatred, among Jews and non-Jews alike.

Postwar tensions were worse in regions where local German ethnic populations had helped the Nazis maintain power. The Nazi party had secretly funded the fascist Sudeten German party, which won 85 per cent of the German ethnic vote in the Czech elections of 1938. The grateful Sudeten Germans had greeted their new Nazi rulers enthusiastically after the division of the country under the Munich agreement later that year, a fact much resented by the local Czechs.[5] Some of the German inhabitants of the Polish city of Bydgoszcz – about a fifth of the prewar population – actively assisted the Nazis in their 1939 slaughter of the town's leading citizens, including priests, teachers and even boy scouts. That didn't make them popular after the war either.[6]

As a result of this recent history, the Eastern European desire for revenge against the German populations in their midst was understandable, perhaps even justifiable. But it was not always just. Not all Germans had been Nazis, and not all of them had turned on their neighbours. Many of them had lived peacefully beside Czechs or Hungarians, and had been good citizens of Czechoslovakia and Hungary for centuries. Others, such as the inhabitants of Lower Silesia and East Prussia – territories which were an undisputed part of prewar Germany, and which now belonged to Poland – lived in towns and villages which had been part of German states for centuries.

For many individuals, the loss of their homes, furniture, livestock and family heirlooms was a tragedy from which they would never recover. Yet the ethnic Germans were not treated as individuals. They were treated as Germans. Gerhard Gruschka, a young Silesian who had refused to join the Hitler Youth because it interfered with his duties as an altar boy, was kept in a labour camp near Katowice where he was forced, by Polish commanders, to sing the Horst Wessel song while they jeered.[7] Ethnic Germans in Hungary who had been made to join the Wehrmacht against their will at the end of the war received the same arbitrary expulsion orders as those who had voluntarily joined the SS in 1943.[8] Herta Kuhrig, the daughter of a German communist in the Sudetenland, was expelled from her home along with the daughters of German fascists.[9] No distinctions were made between outright collaborators and committed anti-fascists, some of whom had suffered discrimination alongside the local population.

Knowing how much they were hated, the first Germans left Eastern Europe in a hurry, long before expulsions began. There was nothing organized about this mass movement of millions of people, many of whom ran from their homes in a panic, only to find themselves immediately engulfed by battle or overwhelmed by cold and hunger. Tens of thousands tried to escape across the Baltic Sea, only to drown when their ships were sunk by Allied planes. The 100,000 Germans living in the city of Łódź – most of them recent colonists – began to scramble out of the city on foot and on horseback on the morning of 16 January 1945, across roads and fields covered in snow. Many were caught in the Soviet bombardment of the city which began the same day.[10]

A few days later, Countess Marion Dönhoff began preparing to leave her family's ancient estate in East Prussia. Most of her neighbours had not yet left: they had been waiting for a Nazi order for evacuation, which never came. As the Red Army approached with unexpected speed, the East Prussians began throwing possessions on to carts and pouring into the streets of Preußisch Holland (now Pasłęk), as Dönhoff remembered: 'The town looked like a jammed turntable. The wagons had driven in from two sides and clogged up the whole thing and now there was no way to go either forward or backward.' She herself packed only 'a saddle bag with toiletries, bandage material and my old Spanish crucifix'. She ate a last meal, got up, left the food and dishes on the table, and went out of the house. She did not bother to lock the door behind her. She never went back.[11]

The actual expulsions of the Germans, when they began a few months later, weren't much better organized. The Czechs speak of the spring of 1945 as the time of 'wild' expulsions, a word which doesn't quite capture the depth of emotion surrounding these mass evictions. The prewar Czechoslovak president, Edvard Beneš, had advocated the deportation of ethnic Germans from his country ever since fleeing into exile in London, in 1938. For seven years he had travelled to Moscow, London and Washington trying to sell the idea. He had encouraged the deportation of Germans from Hungary too (in part so as to make way for the Hungarians he also hoped to expel from this own country). But despite these high-level discussions and advance preparations – and notwithstanding the 'orderly and humane' instruction about to be issued from the Potsdam palace – the first wave of expulsions from the Sudetenland took place in a maelstrom of fury, vengeance, nationalism and popular rage.

In a radio address in Brno on 12 May 1945, just after the Nazi surrender, Beneš declared that the Germans had ceased to behave like humans during the war, and as a nation 'must pay for all this with a great and severe punishment . . . We must liquidate the German problem definitively.' Following that statement, Czechs rioted in the centre of Brno, demanding German collaborators be turned over to the police. A few days later, the newly formed Brno National Committee forcibly evicted more than 20,000 men, women and children from their homes and forced them to start marching towards the Austrian border on foot, with whatever possessions they could carry.[12] Hundreds died before their arrival. According to Czech statistics, 5558 Germans committed suicide in the year 1946 alone.[13]

At about the same time, spontaneous expulsions also began in western Poland, near Poznań, sparked by a housing shortage as well as by a desire for revenge. There were many Germans still living in the region, Poles were returning home in increasing numbers, buildings were in ruins. In Wielkopolskia, the region around Poznań, the first local administrators to appear on the scene were communist secret police officers. They selected German deportees, put them on trucks and sent them to hastily organized transit camps, where they stayed until transport could be arranged to Germany. This wasn't the moment for finer feelings. Polish soldiers and security police were instructed to celebrate 'the expulsion of German filth from Polish lands ... Every officer, every soldier should be aware of the fact that today he fulfils a historic mission, for which generations have been waiting.'[14]

In this early period, when feelings were still raw, local populations often took their revenge by implementing the same kinds of laws and restrictions which Germans had imposed on them. In the summer of 1945, the Czechs forced Germans to wear white armbands marked with the letter 'N' – for *Nemec*, which means 'German' in Czech – painted swastikas on their backs and forbade them to sit on park benches, walk on pavements, or enter cinemas and restaurants.[15] In Budapest, it happened that crowds of Jewish survivors attacked and beat former fascist officials on their way to or from war crimes trials, in a couple of cases nearly lynching them.[16]

Poles made the Germans do forced labour – as they had themselves done forced labour during the Nazi occupation – sometimes in former Nazi concentration camps. In some cases, former prisoners now ruled over former guards, and they beat and tortured them just as they had been beaten and tortured themselves. As one Polish historian writes, the postwar use of these wartime camps, though shocking to us now, made sense at the time: they were intact in a period when little else was. Indeed, they often served multiple uses in quick succession.[17] More than 11,000 prisoners – mostly Poles, and some Soviet prisoners, including hundreds of children – were living in a small Nazi labour camp in the village of Potulice, near Bydgoszcz, for example,

until January 1945. Immediately after liberation, the camp was occupied by Russian soldiers, who made use of the barracks as well as
what was left of the leather in the tannery where prisoners had worked
during the war to repair boots. A few weeks after that, the camp's first
postwar Polish commander, Eugeniusz Wasilewski, found several
Soviet soldiers still in residence when he took possession of the property in February. He asked them to make way for the Germans and
the Nazi collaborators – among them the former German guards and
commanders of the Potulice camp – whom he had just arrested.

Wasilewski, a prewar member of the merchant marine – and, apparently, an unenthusiastic member of the communist party – then ran
the camp until July. Most of his employees were former prisoners, and
many of them were seeking revenge. By all accounts Wasilewski tried
to prevent the most egregious forms of mistreatment at Potulice, and
one former prisoner turned guard complained that he was too lenient:
'in my time things were worse'. But the camp grew from 181 prisoners to 3387 during the seven months he was in command and
conditions inevitably deteriorated.[18] A typhus epidemic broke out
after Wasilewski left in November, and in the following years the
camp employees were accused of fraud, neglect and alcoholism.[19]
Over the five years of the camp's existence, nearly 3000 Germans died
there of hunger and disease.

Though there are no archival records of such abuse at Potulice,
former guards and prisoners have also described, in interviews and
memoirs, scenes of torture and abuse there and in other camps for
German deportees. Germans were starved and beaten, they had excre-
ment poured on their heads, their gold teeth removed by force, their
hair set on fire. They were forced to repeat, 'I am a German swine',
and made to exhume the bodies of recently murdered Polish and
Soviet prisoners. The commandant of the prison at Gliwice, Lola
Potok – a Jewish woman who had survived Auschwitz but lost most
of her family, including her mother, her siblings and an infant son –
interrogated Germans about their Nazi affiliations, whipping them
both when they confessed and when they didn't, on the grounds that
if they didn't admit to collaboration they were lying. By her own
account, she 'recovered' after several months, regained her composure,
and began to treat the Germans like human beings. This was not

because she forgave them, but because, she said, she didn't want to become like them.[20]

Over time, the expulsions of Germans from Poland, Hungary and Czechoslovakia – and eventually Hungarians from Czechoslovakia as well – did become more orderly. The Czechoslovak president issued the Beneš Decrees, which gave a legal veneer to what had been spontaneous expulsions. These decrees authorized the seizure of German and Hungarian property in Czechoslovakia; the eviction of German and Hungarian residents; the resettlement of Czechs and Slovaks on German and Hungarian land; and the removal of Czechoslovak citizenship from Germans and Hungarians. As these decrees attained the status of law, transports became more regular, food was provided, expellees were allowed to take furniture and clothing. Commissions were created to deal with knotty questions of property or identity. The latter problem was especially acute in the ethnically mixed regions of Poland, where 'Polonized' Germans with Polish wives often wanted to stay in the country, as did a number of small ethnic groups such as the Kaszubians and Mazurians, whose members had been considered 'German' by the Nazis.

Most confusing were the cases of people who had declared themselves during the war to be *Volksdeutsche*, of German origin, a category specially invented for the Germanic but not necessarily German inhabitants of Nazi-occupied Europe. The *Volksdeutsche* were Romanians, Hungarians, Czechs, Poles or others with German-sounding surnames and perhaps German family roots. They weren't necessarily able to speak German and most had never been to Germany. When the Nazis asked them to sign *Volksdeutsche* lists they might have done so out of ethnic pride, but were just as likely to have done so out of fear, or simply a desire for better treatment. Some had been intimidated. In Poland one commission decided in November 1946 to 'rehabilitate' the *Volksdeutsche* and allow them to become 'Polish' again, but only if they could prove that they had signed the *Volksdeutsche* list under duress, and only if they had behaved 'in a manner befitting their Polish origin' during the war. Even so the security police sometimes authorized round-ups of *Volksdeutsche*, and forced them to work in labour camps alongside actual Germans.[21]

In Hungary, where many people had German-sounding surnames,

the only institution which actually knew who had signed the *Volksdeutsche* list was the Census Bureau, and at first its director refused to give it up. Even after a visit from the Hungarian secret police in April 1945, the Census Bureau's employees resisted: never before had the Bureau given data away, not for criminal investigations, not during the war, not even when the German occupation government in 1944 had tried to find out the identity of Jews. The Bureau finally relented after ten of its employees were arrested by the secret police – and when it was made to understand that the local Soviet authorities were involved in these arrests and would happily carry out more.[22]

By the time it was finished, the resettling of the German populations of Eastern Europe was an extraordinary mass movement, probably unequalled in European history. By the end of 1947, some 7.6 million 'Germans' – including ethnic Germans, *Volksdeutsche* and recent settlers – had left Poland, through transfer or escape. About 400,000 of them died on the way back to Germany, from hunger, or disease, or because they were caught in the crossfire of the advancing front.[23] Another 2.5 million had left Czechoslovakia, and a further 200,000 were expelled from Hungary.[24] German populations were also deported, or left voluntarily, from Ukraine, the Baltic states, Romania and Yugoslavia. In all, some 12 million Germans left Eastern Europe in the postwar period and resettled in both East and West Germany.

Once they'd made the trek across the border, German refugees received scant welcome. Almost everywhere they went in either the eastern or western occupation zones of Germany, they immediately formed an underclass. They spoke eastern dialects, had different manners and habits, and of course had no possessions or capital of any kind. In 1945, there had been no time to prepare any facilities for them, and many wound up wandering aimlessly in search of food. Epidemics of typhus and dysentery swept through the expellee population, and spread to others. So bad was this problem in the Soviet zone that the authorities appealed to local leaders directly to at least keep the expellees in one place, and to 'prevent people from wandering farther'. Representatives of the British and American zones also appealed for the expulsions to stop or at least slow down.[25]

In retrospect, blame for the initial chaos and the thousands of deaths has often been laid on the governments which expelled the Germans. But responsibility ought to be shared more widely. Of course, the expulsions would never have happened without the war, without the German invasion of the region and without Germany's brutal mistreatment of the East European population. The numbers were also high because so many German 'colonists' had moved to the region during the war, and, indeed, many Germans targeted for expulsion in 1945 did not have families and roots in the region at all. Among those expelled from Poland were ethnic Germans – sometimes from Germany, sometimes from other parts of Europe – who had been moved into Polish or Jewish homes and farms, following the murder or eviction of their owners. German officers or German businessmen and their families, many of whom had taken advantage of the privileges available to them in Nazi-occupied Europe, were also forced to leave. They had no moral claim to Polish land or property at all, though some later considered themselves 'expellees' and therefore 'victims' anyway. Erika Steinbach, a German politician who later became leader of the Bund der Vertriebenen, the powerful and vocal expellees' organization, was the daughter of a low-ranking German corporal, originally from Hesse, who happened to have been stationed in the Polish town of Rumia during the war. Her family had been 'expelled' – or rather they fled – because they were occupiers, and indeed they headed back home to Hesse, which is where Steinbach grew up.[26]

The expulsion policy also had the hearty approval of all of the Western Allies, who had thought about it a great deal even before the Potsdam Conference. In 1944, Churchill had told the House of Commons that the 'expulsion [of the Germans] is the method which, so far as we have been able to see, will be the most satisfactory and lasting' to achieve future peace. Roosevelt also approved of the ethnic cleansing policy, and cited the 1921–2 population exchanges between Turkey and Greece as a precedent.[27]

But the expulsions also had the full support of the Soviet Union. In a private, wartime conversation, Stalin had advised the Czechoslovak leadership to 'throw them [the Sudeten Germans] out. Now they will learn themselves what it means to rule over someone else.' He also advised the Poles to 'create such conditions for the Germans that they want to escape themselves'.[28] More importantly, Polish, Czechoslovak,

Romanian and Hungarian policemen who organized the deportation of Germans were all working with Soviet encouragement, in territories technically under the control of the Red Army. Stalin knew that both the Poles and the Czechoslovaks had talked of expelling Germans before the war's end, and had already assisted the Romanians. But the decision to redraw Poland's borders, replacing the eastern territories occupied by the Soviet Union with formerly German lands in the west, meant that the Poles had no choice but to go through with the expulsions, and on a much vaster scale than anyone could have imagined: in the end, the expulsion of the Germans was only possible with Soviet help.

The Red Army was also directly responsible for the expulsion and deportation of Germans from Romania and Hungary. The persecution of Germans in Hungary was launched by a Soviet order on 22 December 1944, which commanded all Germans in Hungary to report to the front line as forced labourers. Preparation for full-scale deportation began in February 1945, when the Soviet mission of the Allied Control Commission ordered the Hungarian Interior Ministry to 'prepare a list of all Germans living in Hungary' (the order which led to the dispute with the Census Bureau and the arrest of its administrators).[29] By that time, the NKVD had already presided over the deportations of Germans from Romania as well.[30]

At the same time, the expulsion of the Germans was undeniably popular in every country where it took place, so much so that local communist parties rapidly took control of it – and eventually took credit for it – wherever they could. The Polish communist party gained much-needed credibility from its leading role in the deportations, even winning some guarded approval from those on the political right, who had long advocated the creation of a 'homogeneous' Polish state – homogeneity being very much an acceptable political goal everywhere in Europe at that time.[31] The historian Stefan Bottoni also reckons that the Romanian communist party's dual policy towards Romanian minorities – harsh treatment of the Germans combined with efforts to integrate the Hungarian, Slavic and Jewish communities – helped it win legitimacy too.[32]

The Czechoslovak communist involvement in the expulsions was even more popular and possibly more important, since it made the party seem mainstream. After all, their policemen were simply upholding a popular government policy with exceptional vigour. Klement Gottwald, the Czechoslovak communist party General Secretary, even called on the nation to take revenge not just for the recent war, but for the Battle of the White Mountain in 1620, when Bohemia had been defeated by the Holy Roman Empire and its mostly German allies: 'You must prepare for the final retribution of White Mountain, for the return of the Czech lands to the Czech people. We will expel for good all descendants of the alien German nobility . . .'[33] The Slovak communist party's regional newspaper used similarly nationalist rhetoric against its Hungarian minority, sometimes endeavouring to give it a Marxist accent: 'The rich productive areas of Southern Slovakia whence the Hungarian feudal lords forced the Slovak farmers into the mountains, should be returned to the Slovak people.'[34]

All the ad hoc institutions set up to facilitate German deportation quickly proved to have other uses as well. In Poland, many of the deportation camps built or adapted to hold German expellees were eventually transformed into camps or prisons for opponents of the regime. In Czechoslovakia, the communist party created a paramilitary organization to assist with the expulsions – the same paramilitary organization which would help the communist party carry out its coup d'état in 1948.[35] In a very literal sense, the expulsions thus laid the institutional ground for the imposition of terror which would follow a year or two later.

Because their policemen had organized the expulsions, local communist parties often found themselves in charge, fortunately, of the redistribution of German property. Apartments, furniture and other goods suddenly fell into their hands, all of which could be usefully handed out to party supporters. The Germans also left behind farms and factories which could be nationalized immediately, to public applause, and put under the control of Polish or Czech officials. This mass property seizure helped prepare the psychological ground for popular acceptance of more widespread nationalization, which followed soon afterwards. Many had watched the Germans lose their houses and businesses with satisfaction, and felt that it was 'fair' to take property from the enemies of the nation. So why should it not be 'fair' to take property from the enemies of the working class?

Thanks to the efforts of vocal and powerful organizations of former German expellees, the expulsion of the Germans has become, in recent years, the best-known and most frequently discussed example of ethnic cleansing in postwar Europe. Yet it was only one of many mass ethnic-cleansing projects to be carried out after the war.

At almost exactly the same time as the Germans were being chased out of Silesia and Sudetenland, another population exchange was underway on the Polish–Ukrainian border. Curiously, the agreements governing this exchange – the second largest set of postwar deportations – were signed not between Poland and the Soviet Union, but between Poland and the Soviet Republic of Ukraine, an entity which at the time had no sovereignty, especially in matters of international relations. One Ukrainian historian reckons this was intentional. If the other Allies objected to the population transfer – or if the accompanying violence got out of hand – Stalin could always deny legal responsibility: 'it wasn't us, it was the Ukrainians.'[36]

As Stalin well knew, a full-blown ethnic war was raging in southeastern Poland and western Ukraine at that time. This is not the place for a full discussion of the rights and the wrongs of that particular conflict: suffice to say that it had its roots in longstanding economic, religious and political competition which had been inflamed and distorted by the Nazi occupation and two Soviet invasions, in 1939 and again in 1943–4. Nor was the cause of peace and ethnic harmony in eastern Poland and western Ukraine helped by the partisans of many nationalities – Polish, Jewish, Ukrainian, Soviet – and of many political persuasions who were vying for power at that time either. The violence reached a peak of horror and tragedy in the formerly Polish and now Ukrainian county of Volhynia in 1943, when Ukrainian partisans aligned to the Ukrainian Insurgent Army (Ukrayins'ka Povstans'ka Armiya, or UPA) became aware that the Germans were losing and that the Red Army was coming. They thought that the time to establish their own state might be approaching. The local leader, Mykola Lebed, called upon his followers to 'cleanse the entire revolutionary territory of the Polish population'. In the summer of 1943 his men – many of whom had been witnesses to or participants in the Soviet deportations of Poles in 1939 and the murders of Jews during the Holocaust – slaughtered some 50,000 Poles, almost all civilians, and chased tens of thousands of others out of Volhynia.[37]

Those who carried out the massacres that summer had absorbed both Nazi and Soviet lessons, as one Polish teenager's description of a mass execution in her village well illustrates. She, her sister, her two brothers and her neighbours had been herded into a forest outside their Volhynian village and told not to move. What followed was tragically similar to many other mass executions which had taken place in the same region, only a few months earlier:

> I lay down as if to sleep. I had a large scarf, and I covered my head with it, in order to see nothing. The firing came closer, I waited for death. But then I heard that the firing is growing more distant again, and I haven't been touched . . . [my sister and I] stood up, and looked at our brothers, aged 9 and 13, they had bullet wounds to the head. To this day I feel a weight on my conscience because I told them to take off their hats, maybe if they'd had their hats on they would have survived . . . [But then] where to go? We walked through the underbrush in the direction of Lubomal. We met an old Ukrainian lady with a girl. My sister started to ask if she would take us home with her, but she didn't want to . . . Luckily the nearest house was locked and empty, we drank water from the trough and kept going. My life as a wanderer had begun.[38]

The Poles took revenge. One Polish partisan, Waldemar Lotnik, recalled one of the return attacks which took place that same summer: 'They had killed seven men two nights previously; that night we killed sixteen of theirs, including an eight-year-old schoolboy . . . there were 300 of us in all and we met with no resistance and suffered no casualties. Most of us knew many of the people in Modryn, so we knew who was a Nazi supporter and who was a Ukrainian nationalist. We picked them out.' A week later, the Ukrainians retaliated, burned a village, raped all the women and killed anyone unable to escape. The Poles retaliated again, this time in the company of men 'so filled with hatred after losing whole generations of their family in the Ukrainian attacks that they swore that they would take an eye for an eye, a tooth for a tooth, and they were as good as their word'.[39]

Given this recent history, and given that it took time for the reality of the border changes to sink in, it isn't surprising that both Poles and Ukrainians resisted deportation. Initially, the Soviet and Polish sides both agreed that the population exchange would be strictly voluntary, and some on both sides willingly boarded trains to cross the border in the autumn of 1944. But winter came, the bulk of the Red Army moved west for the final battle for Berlin, and volunteers began to dry up. Polish Home Army partisans, believing that the USSR would soon be forced to hand back former Polish territories to Poland – surely another world war was about to break out – continued to conspire in western Ukraine through 1945. 'The territory of Western Ukraine will not be kept by the Soviet Union, it was and will be Polish territory,' one Polish inhabitant told an NKVD informer: 'America will never let the Soviet Union do that, because at the beginning of the war she declared that Poland would be the same as it was until 1939. And therefore it's not worth moving [to Poland].'[40]

Faced with this refusal and aware of the continuing ethnic conflict, Stalin made his policy towards ethnic Poles in the formerly Polish districts of what was now the Soviet Republic of Ukraine harsher. Nikita Khrushchev, then the Ukrainian communist party secretary, wrote to Stalin in September 1944, proposing to close down all Polish schools and universities in western Ukraine, to ban all Polish textbooks and to start rounding up Poles to work on industrial projects elsewhere in the USSR.[41] As a result of these policies (as well as of America's failure to come to the rescue, and the failure of the Third World War to break out) Poles finally did begin to board the transports heading west. Although the NKVD was still finding and arresting members of 'White Polish' organizations on Soviet territory as late as February 1946, those seem to have been the last cells of open resistance.[42] By October 1946, according to Soviet documents, 812,668 Poles had left Soviet Ukraine for Poland.[43] In total, 1,496,000 Poles would leave the USSR for Poland, moving from Lithuania and Belarus as well as Ukraine.[44]

This was a major cultural shift: the Poles leaving Lithuania, western Belarus and western Ukraine were abandoning towns and cities which had been Polish-speaking for centuries. Many were moving to towns and cities which had been German-speaking for centuries. The ancient

Jan Kazimierz University in Lwów, now called L'viv, left behind its buildings and moved what remained of its books and professors to Breslau, now Wrocław, where it took up residence in what remained of that city's equally ancient university. Peasants who had farmed the famously fertile 'black earth' of Ukraine found themselves relocated to the much sandier soil of Silesia, which required complex machinery and different farming methods. Sometimes resettled Poles walked into German houses where the tea kettles were still sitting on the stoves or where the previous owners, like Countess Dönhoff, had not bothered to do the dishes after eating a final meal.

In due course the Polish government would develop an elaborate mythology about this 'recovered land' (*ziemie odzyskane*, a phrase which sounds, in Polish, very much like 'promised land', *ziemia obiecana*) and about the Slavic kings who had ruled there in the Middle Ages. But in truth many of those who arrived in the 'recovered land' felt like trespassers. Their first harvests failed, as they were unused to the new conditions. They resisted making investments, as they feared the Germans would return. The fact that Poles from all over Poland journeyed to the former German cities in 1945 and 1946 to steal whatever the Germans had left is indicative: that isn't the way people treat a place which feels like home.

Ukrainians who found themselves on the western, Polish side of the new border were if anything even angrier and more resistant to moving. Having heard stories of the 1932–3 Ukrainian famine, engineered by Stalin in part to quell Ukrainian nationalism, most had no illusions about the Soviet regime. They didn't want to go to Soviet Ukraine and some who did go there soon tried to return. Throughout 1945 and 1946, partisans from the Ukrainian Insurgent Army, as well as the Organization of Ukrainian Nationalists (Orhanizatsiya Ukrayins'kykh Natsionalistiv, or OUN), attacked the repatriation offices, damaged the roads and train tracks meant to carry deportees, and even burned down villages where repatriated Poles had come from Poland to live.[45]

Polish communists fought back. In April 1945, the *Rzeszów* special operational group, including members from the militia, the police, the secret police and the Polish army, embarked upon a plan of forced deportation, intending to 'clean out' the Ukrainians from five Polish counties. Their efforts were embarrassingly unsuccessful. Local support for the Ukrainian Insurgent Army and the Organization of Ukrainian Nationalists was so strong that at one point *Rzeszów*'s leaders asked their secret police bosses for 'extra reconnaissance planes'. Since they couldn't catch Ukrainians on the ground, they thought they might do better spotting them from the air.[46]

By 1947, the Polish government was no longer interested in simple ethnic cleansing of the region. They faced a much more fundamental crisis: they had to preserve their own power in south-east Poland. Local administration was impossible, and in a few places the Ukrainian partisans had actually joined forces with the remnants of WiN, the Polish independence movement.[47] In March, Ukrainian partisans provoked a crisis by murdering the Polish Deputy Defence Minister, General Karol Świerczewski, following a battle with some 150 partisans who had been armed with artillery and machine guns. After that, the Polish communist newspapers practically boiled over with distinctly non-internationalist ethnic outrage, speaking of Ukrainian 'hangmen', 'bandits', 'butchers' and 'foreign mercenaries', accusing them of having murdered a gallant son of the Polish nation with 'fascist bullets'.[48] (Though Świerczewski was a longstanding Red Army officer, and one of the internal communiques about his death speaks of 'informing his family in Moscow'.)[49]

In the wake of that murder, the Polish regime finally mobilized itself to deport the Ukrainians, not to the Soviet Union – they might cause trouble there too – but to the formerly German lands in northern and western Poland. Trumpeting their intention to bring 'security' to the eastern part of the country – a goal the majority of Poles surely approved of – at the end of April they launched *Akcja Wisła*, Operation Vistula, a major military operation involving five infantry divisions, 17,000 soldiers, 500 militia, sappers, pilots and Interior Ministry troops. Militarized Soviet NKVD divisions and the Czechoslovak army provided support along the borders.[50] By the end of July, this enormous force had finally succeeded in evicting some 140,000 Ukrainians from their homes, placing them in filthy boxcars, and resettling them in the north and the west of Poland. It was a bloody, angry process, every bit as bloody and angry as the killings in Volhynia three years earlier. One Ukrainian, a child at the time, remembers Polish soldiers breaking up his cousin's wedding:

Suddenly the soldiers surrounded the house where the celebration was taking place, and set it alight with burning bombs. They killed the groom and several guests who couldn't escape; they threw the bloodied corpses onto a cart which already held those they'd got in Zagrod. When they were about to leave, the bride suddenly appeared, in a white dress, with a veil. She begged for them to leave the body of her husband, Ivan. The soldiers laughed, tied her hands together with rope, tied her to the wagon and set off. The girl first ran, then fell, and was dragged through the dirt. The soldiers shot at her, and finally cut the rope and left her dead in the road.[51]

Without their support network among the Ukrainian peasantry, the Ukrainian partisans could no longer maintain their resistance. Those who weren't killed were captured, interrogated and often tortured at Jaworzno, another former Nazi camp which had until then been used to hold Germans (like many Nazi camps, it had a long life, and served many functions). The Ukrainians were dispersed all over Poland. In the 1990s, I once encountered a group of their descendants living near Ełk, in the Mazurian lake district. They no longer spoke much Ukrainian. Because the Polish authorities ruled that no town in the country could consist of more than 10 per cent Ukrainians, they had slowly lost their language, their culture and their distinctiveness.

A few weeks after the end of Operation Vistula, the Soviet Union launched a similarly brutal action on the adjoining territories in Soviet Ukraine. Within the span of a few days in October 1947, the Soviet secret police arrested 76,192 Ukrainians in western Ukraine and deported them to the Gulag.[52] Several historians have speculated that the two operations were related. Both were intended to destroy, for ever, the fiercely proud and tightly knit west Ukrainian community which had generated so much resistance to Poles and Russians alike. Operation Vistula ensured that any Soviet Ukrainians who escaped arrest could no longer use Poland as a safe haven.[53] Both operations were popular. Polish peasants who had been tormented by Ukrainian partisans were delighted to see them gone – and grateful to the Soviet and Polish troops who had dispersed them.

Operation Vistula was a particularly brutal example of a population exchange within a single country but it wasn't the only one. When the Czechoslovak government failed to get approval from the

Allies, either at Potsdam or at the subsequent Paris Peace Conference, to deport Hungarians from Slovakia, they hit upon a similar solution. On paper, there would be no deportation of Hungarians from Slovakia, just a 'voluntary' population exchange. To encourage these 'voluntary' departures, Hungarians in Slovakia were deprived of citizenship, of the right to use their language in official places and of the right to attend church services in Hungarian. Between 1945 and 1948, some 89,000 Hungarians were thus 'persuaded' to leave Slovakia for the Sudetenland, where they replaced the missing Germans, or else to cross the border into Hungary itself. Some 70,000 Slovaks arrived from Hungary in their place.[54]

Not a word of protest was heard from outside the region. One Hungarian historian has declared that this was because 'the fate of the Hungarian minority did not interest anyone'.[55] But, in truth, the fate of none of the minorities interested anyone. The world hardly noticed the ethnic war between Poland and Ukraine, let alone Operation Vistula. Nor did it notice the 100,000 Hungarians who fled or were expelled from Romania, the 50,000 Ukrainians who left Czechoslovakia for Ukraine, or the 42,000 Czechs and Slovaks who returned from Ukraine to Czechoslovakia after the war.[56]

By 1950, not much remained of multi-ethnic Eastern Europe. Only nostalgia – Ukrainian nostalgia, Polish nostalgia, Hungarian nostalgia, German nostalgia – endured. In 1991, I went to visit a tiny hamlet near the town of Zablocko, in western Ukraine. It was occupied by a Ukrainian couple who in 1945 had been frightened by nightly visits from all kinds of partisans, frightened by the fighting and tired of war. Anxious for peace, they agreed to leave behind their beloved village on the river San, in eastern Poland. They piled all of their possessions on to a cart, and trudged east. They eventually moved into a wooden house on top of a hill, until recently the property of a Polish family, and there they stayed. Half a century later, their granddaughter, who had never seen Poland, still pined to go there. Was it, she wanted to know, 'as rich and beautiful as they say?'

In the end, most deported Germans went to Germany, Poles went to Poland and Ukrainians could go to Soviet Ukraine. But the Jews of Eastern Europe, already displaced into hiding places, concentration camps and exile, did not have an obvious homeland to which they could return in 1945. If they did return to their former homes, they found physical destruction, psychological devastation and worse. Indeed, their postwar fate is impossible to comprehend without understanding that they returned to towns and villages which had been – and often still were – enveloped in ethnic, political and criminal violence.

Accustomed to the idea that peace followed liberation, few Western Europeans find this easy to grasp. Nor is it easy to pick apart the myths and emotions which have wound themselves around the subject of the Jewish experience in postwar Eastern Europe in the years since. All of the postwar ethnic disputes are inflamed, from time to time, it is true, by contemporary politicians who want to use the past to influence the present. The associations of former expellees played a large and often awkward role in West German politics in the 1970s and 1980s, at times – including the critical moment of 1989 – agitating for a change in the Polish–German border and for the return of their homes. The Poles and the Ukrainians occasionally squabble over the memory of the Ukrainian Revolutionary Army, whom the former remember as murderers and the latter now revere as freedom fighters. In 2008, Slovak–Hungarian tensions rose to the point that Hungarians, angered by the arrest of Hungarian activists in Slovakia, actually blocked several border crossings in protest.

Still, there is almost no greater emotional minefield than the history of the Jews in postwar Eastern Europe, and especially of the Jews in postwar Poland. The tangled relationship of the Eastern European Jews to Eastern European communism is a large part of it: some Jews played prominent roles in several of the postwar East European communist parties, and were thus perceived as beneficiaries of the new regimes, even though other Jews suffered at the hands of those same regimes. At times, East Europeans and Jews have also engaged in a kind of competitive martyrology. The former resent the fact that the world knows about the Holocaust, but not about their own suffering at the hands of both the Nazis and the Soviet Union. At times, the latter have interpreted any discussion of anyone's wartime suffering other than their own as a denigration of their uniquely tragic experience. There have been arguments about money, property, guilt and responsibility.

An example of how these emotions play out arose in the 1990s, when a prosecutor at what became the Polish Institute for National Remembrance set out to investigate the unusual case of Salomon Morel, who – all agree – was a Polish Jew and a communist partisan. From February until September 1945, Morel was also the commandant of Zgoda, a labour camp for Germans, in the Upper Silesian town of Świętochłowice, on the site of what had once been an auxiliary camp to Auschwitz. After that, he remained an employee of the Polish secret police, eventually becoming a colonel and the commander of a prison in Katowice. Morel emigrated to Israel in the early 1990s.

Almost everything else about Morel remains in dispute. According to Polish investigators and prosecutors, Morel joined the Polish security police immediately after the war. He worked first in the prison of Lublin castle, where he assisted in the interrogation of Polish Home Army leaders. He was then transferred to Zgoda. During his tenure there, he became known for his cruelty to the mostly German prisoners, including women and children. He deprived them of food, allowed hygiene to deteriorate, tortured them for pleasure and sometimes beat them to death. As a result of the poor conditions, a typhus epidemic swept the camp in the summer and some 1800 prisoners died. According to archival documents, Morel was held responsible for the epidemic by the Interior Ministry, put under house arrest for three days and deprived of a part of his salary.

In 2005, a Polish prosecutor, having decided Morel was guilty of war crimes, sent an extradition request – one of several – to the state of Israel, where Morel then lived. He received, in response, a furious letter from the Israeli Ministry of Justice. Morel, the Israeli letter declared, was not a war criminal, but one of the war's victims. He had witnessed the murder of his parents, brother and sister-in-law at the hands of a Polish police officer during the war. His older brother was murdered by what the letter calls 'a Polish fascist'. According to the Israeli ministry official, the camp at Świętochłowice, when he ran it, contained no more than 600 prisoners, all of whom were former Nazis. Sanitary conditions were satisfactory. The Israeli official's judgement was not motivated by facts, but by emotions: Morel, he declared, had suffered from 'crimes of genocide committed by the Nazis and their Polish collaborators', the case against him was motivated by Polish anti-semitism and he would not be extradited.[57]

The exchange of letters caused a good deal of ill-will on both sides. The Poles felt that the Israelis were hiding a typical communist criminal. The Israelis felt that the Poles were attacking a typical Jewish victim. And yet Morel's story was not typical at all. Far from being a 'symbol' of unfairness to either Poles or Jews, his life story should have been treated as an exception.

To start with, Morel's story is unusual because, unlike most East European Jews, he survived the Holocaust. It's not easy to say exactly how rare this was, because precise numbers of survivors are not available. Not everybody who was Jewish registered as such in postwar Eastern Europe, and not everybody wanted to be in touch with Jewish organizations. Many had changed their names in order to pass as 'Aryan', and then simply kept those names after the war. But according to the best estimates, it seems that less than 10 per cent of the 3.5 million Jews who had lived within the prewar Polish borders were still alive after the war. Perhaps 80,000 survived in Nazi-occupied Poland. The rest had spent the war in the Soviet Union, and when the war ended most came home. By June 1946, there were about 220,000 Jews within the postwar Polish borders. This was, at the time, less than 1 per cent of the total population of Poland, which numbered about 24 million.[58]

Estimates are even more difficult to make in Hungary, where there was a long tradition of Jewish assimilation, intermarriage and conversion. As a result, the numbers given for Jews in Hungary in 1945 vary widely, from 143,000 up to 260,000. This was, again, a small percentage of the total Hungarian population of 9 million. But because the Nazi deportations in the latter part of the war, including the famous mass transport to Auschwitz, had affected mainly Jews in the provinces, almost all of the remaining Hungarian Jews lived in Budapest.[59] Within the city, which then had about 900,000 inhabitants, Jews were a very visible and vocal minority. With their families and professional networks intact, the Hungarian Jews quickly began to play an important role in public life. This was not the case in Poland, and certainly not the case in Germany. Only about 4500 Jewish survivors remained in the Soviet occupation zone of Germany after the war, a tiny fraction of the population of 18 million. They were, and remained, nearly invisible.[60]

Salomon Morel was also atypical in that he remained in Eastern Europe after the war. The vast majority of Jews who returned to their homes after the war stayed only just long enough to find out if their relatives were alive, and to see what property remained. Most were devastated by how little they found. In a 1946 memo, Polish Jewish authorities explained that many Jews were leaving the country mainly because it was impossible, simply, to live in towns or villages which had become 'the cemeteries of their families, relatives and friends'.[61] Some left because they had relatives abroad – sometimes their only living relatives. Others, especially those with wartime experiences in the USSR, left because they hated communism and feared, correctly, that Jewish businessmen and traders would have no future in a communist state.

But others left because they were afraid. Poland, Hungary, Czechoslovakia and Eastern Germany, like all of Eastern Europe, were violent places after the war. It was dangerous to be a communist official, dangerous to be an anti-communist, dangerous to be German, dangerous to be Polish in a Ukrainian village, dangerous to be Ukrainian in a Polish village. It could also be dangerous to be Jewish. Some Jews were welcomed home after the war, and treated with fairness and friendship. One Polish Jew who had joined the Red Army returned home to be welcomed by neighbours who fed him and protected him from local Home Army units who were hunting down communists. Other Polish Jews with communist party connections helped rescue Gentile Home Army partisans from the NKVD. Emil Sommerstein – a Zionist activist who was released from the Soviet Gulag in 1944 on condition that he join the Polish provisional government as Minister for Jewish Affairs – conspired secretly to send Home Army couriers to London, disguised as orthodox Jews.[62]

At the same time, there is both anecdotal and archival evidence of brutal and fatal attacks on Jews in the months and years immediately after the war in Hungary and Poland – as well as Czechoslovakia and Romania – though not much agreement on their scale. Numbers for 'Jewish deaths' in Poland in this period range from 400 to 2500.[63] This statistical disagreement is perhaps not surprising, given that there is no consensus on how many Jews had survived in the first place, but it also reflects a deeper set of uncertainties. With a few important exceptions, these attacks were isolated, and – unlike attacks on Germans in Poland or Hungarians in Slovakia – they were not part of an official government policy. Some were provoked by the return of Jews to homes occupied by others, some by political disputes, and it was not always clear which was which. Were Jews who returned to claim back their houses murdered for their property – or for being Jewish? Were Jews who joined the security services murdered for being communists – or for being Jewish? Were robberies of Jews acts of anti-semitism, or were they ordinary crimes?

Less ambiguous, at least in this narrow sense, were the anti-semitic riots, sometimes called pogroms, which also took place in this period. From 1945 onwards, outbursts of anti-Jewish violence unfolded in the Polish towns of Rzeszów, Kraków, Tarnów, Kalisz, Lublin, Kolbuszowa and Mielec; in the Slovak towns of Kolbasov, Svinna, Komarno and Teplicany; and in Ózd and Kunmadaras in Hungary.[64] By far the two most notorious riots took place in Kielce, Poland, on 4 July 1946, and in the Hungarian city of Miskolc a few weeks later, between 30 July and 1 August.

In Kielce, the ostensible cause of the riot – hard though it is to believe such a thing was still possible in the twentieth century – was a rumour of blood libel. A Polish child, probably to avoid punishment for not coming home on time, told his parents he had been kidnapped by the Jews, who intended to make him a ritual sacrifice. He had, he said, been kept in the basement of the Jewish Committee building in Kielce, a kind of dormitory and community centre where several dozen Jewish survivors were then living. His drunken father reported this to the local police; the police solemnly set out to investigate. But even as the occupants of the building were explaining to the police that they had no basement and thus could not have kept the child there, rumours began to spread throughout the town.

A crowd began to gather outside the committee building. An army unit arrived – forty soldiers from the Internal Security Corps. To the shock of the Jewish leaders inside, the soldiers began to fire not on the menacing crowd, but at the Jews. And instead of dispersing the crowd, they joined it, along with policemen and members of the citizens' militia. When their shift ended, workers from a local factory joined in as well. During the course of the day, Jews were murdered in different parts of town, on the outskirts of the city and on trains whose Jewish passengers had the tragic bad luck to arrive in Kielce. By nightfall, at least forty-two people were dead and dozens wounded. To this day, this ranks as the worst outbreak of anti-semitic violence in postwar Eastern Europe.[65]

Although there were blood libel rumours in Miskolc in the days leading up to the riots – and although stories about Jews and Christian children had sparked violence in Kunmadaras and Teplicany – the Miskolc breakdown was actually caused by the arrest of three black marketeers, of whom two were Jewish. The story of their arrest was quickly passed around the town, possibly by the police, and a crowd was waiting for the men on the morning of 31 July, when they were to be escorted from local custody to an internment camp. The crowd was already carrying signs: 'Death to the Jews and Death to the Black Marketeers'. When the prisoners appeared, the mob flung itself at them, murdered one of the men and beat the other so badly he wound up in hospital. The third – who was not Jewish – managed to escape.

That afternoon, the police, though notably absent during the earlier riot, arrested sixteen people for the public lynching. Outraged by these arrests, another angry crowd attacked and occupied the police station on the following day. This time, a Jewish police officer was murdered.

Genuine shock and outrage followed both of these events, which received a good deal of national – and in the case of Kielce, international – attention. The pogroms prompted fresh waves of emigration. As a Jew who lived in Łódź at the time explained, 'although we sensed that our existence was anchored in quicksand, we didn't allow this sensation to affect our consciousness. We wanted to resume living again as human beings. The Kielce pogrom woke us up from our illusion. One shouldn't stay here even for a moment.'[66]

Non-Jews were upset too. Polish and Hungarian intellectuals and politicians of all stripes wrote anguished condemnations deploring these remnants of anti-semitism, so repellent in countries where memories of the Holocaust were fresh. The Polish state conducted a judicial investigation and put some of the perpetrators on trial, eventually doling out nine death sentences. In Hungary, the communist party Central Committee openly discussed anti-semitism, probably for the first and last time, on the day following the Miskolc riot.[67] But the results of the subsequent police investigations and internal inquiries satisfied no one.

In both cases, elements of the regime were partly responsible. In Kielce, the police and security services not only failed to prevent the riot but actually joined the mob, along with the army: police participation had unleashed the crowd violence. In Miskolc, local police probably tipped off the crowds in advance that the speculators would be in the town centre, and certainly melted away when the violence started. More importantly, Rákosi, though himself Jewish, had been in Miskolc only a week earlier, on 23 July, when he gave a speech at a mass rally denouncing speculators: 'Those who speculate with the forint, who would undermine the economic foundations of our democracy, should be hung on the gallows.' At the same time, the Hungarian communist party put up posters and distributed brochures featuring caricatures of 'speculators' looking like caricatures of Jews.[68] Apparently, the party hoped to focus popular anger about hyperinflation and poor economic conditions on 'Jewish speculators' – and to deflect it from the communist party.[69]

In neither case is there any archival evidence of more careful advance planning, let alone international coordination, as some have alleged. Though Soviet agents and advisers were present in both cities – a Soviet NKVD officer in Kielce was even present at the riots – and despite the fact that these pogroms all took place in the same time period it isn't possible, so far, to trace any direct Soviet involvement in their organization.[70] Nor is it clear that either the Russians or the local communists felt that the riots had benefited them. Although both Hungarian and Polish authorities pinned the blame on the anticommunist movements and the church – a smear which, at the time, seemed to stick – in internal debates they recognized the riots as a sign of their own weakness. In Kielce, the different branches of the security services had argued with one another, failed to obey orders, and lost control of a mob on 4 July, after all, which was hardly evidence of their competence. In the wake of the riots, several local party leaders lost their jobs.[71] The Hungarian communists were also unnerved by Miskolc. Rákosi blamed the riots on 'fascist infiltration into our party' and vowed to prevent it from spreading.[72]

At the same time, both sets of riots undeniably had some popular support. As if from the depths of the Middle Ages, rumours that the Jews were killing Christian children, or that Jewish speculators were robbing Christian peasants, suddenly took hold in a few provincial East European towns, even as their countrymen looked on in horror. Some think the explanation for this moment of madness is economic: the Polish historian Jan Gross points out that the mass killings of Jews during the war created 'a social vacuum which was promptly filled by the native Polish petite bourgeoisie'.[73] Uncertain of their status, fearful of losing what they had so recently gained, threatened by the new communist regimes, this social strata, Gross speculates, focused its ire on the returning Jews. There was certainly something to that, and many witnessed the same phenomenon in other countries. Heda Kovály, a Jewish camp survivor, returned to her family's Czech country house in 1945: 'I rang the bell and, after a while, a fat unshaven man opened the door, stared at me for a moment and then yelled "So you've come back! Oh no! That's all we needed!" I turned around and walked into the woods. I spent the three hours until the next train back to Prague strolling on the mossy ground under the fir trees, listening to the birds.'[74] Fearing a negative popular reaction, in Hungary the communist party actually refused to advocate the return of Jewish property. In March 1945, *Szabad Nép* counselled Jews to have 'understanding' for the Gentiles who now occupied their apartments, even if those Gentiles had been collaborators with the fascist regime. Party officials in Budapest also suggested that returning Jews 'reach an agreement' with the inhabitants of their homes, something which, under the circumstances, was surely impossible.[75]

Others believe that something more profound than economic competition must have underlain the animosity. As the Polish historian Dariusz Stola points out, Poles – like Czechs, Hungarians, Romanians, Lithuanians – had seen, heard and even smelt the Holocaust to a degree unimaginable in Western Europe, including Germany:

> The psychological reaction to that kind of experience is complicated and completely irrational; the memory is a kind of convulsion, the feelings associated are intense and uncontrolled, and, most importantly, these aren't necessarily feelings of pity or sympathy . . . I'm not a psych-

ologist but I lean towards this theory because I don't see any other explanation for certain horrific forms of behaviour, for example when someone throws a grenade at an orphanage housing Jewish children.[76]

Stola is here referring to an infamous incident: on the night of 12 August 1945, an unknown assailant did indeed throw a grenade into a Jewish orphanage in the village of Rabka, and then kept firing at it for another two hours. Astonishingly, no one was killed. But the orphanage was soon shut down and the children moved away.[77]

Stola's explanation, although voiced in 2005, isn't so far from the views of many Polish intellectuals at the time. In 1947, Stanisław Ossowski, an esteemed philosopher and sociologist, came to the same conclusion. 'Compassion,' he wrote, 'is not the only imaginable response to misfortune suffered by other people ... those whom fate has destined for annihilation easily can appear disgusting to others and be removed beyond the pale of human relations.' He also observed, as others have done since, that those who had benefited in some material way from the destruction of the Jews were often uneasy or even guilt-ridden, and thus sought to make their actions seem legitimate: 'If one person's disaster benefits somebody else, an urge appears to persuade oneself, and others, that the disaster was morally justified.'[78]

Whatever the reason for the persistent hostility, it indeed helped persuade Jews to leave Eastern Europe and to emigrate to America, Western Europe and above all Palestine. Some 70,000 left Poland for Palestine in the three months following the Kielce riots. They were helped and encouraged by a handful of Zionist organizations, founded or supported by groups in Palestine or the US, which had been set up for this purpose. Under the terms of this arrangement, Polish Jews exited through agreed-upon border crossings in Silesia, then travelled on foot and in transport trucks through Czechoslovakia and eventually on to one of the Mediterranean ports, where they embarked for Palestine (though some broke off and headed for other countries along the way).[79]

Eventually, this mass movement began to embarrass the Polish regime – immigration to British mandate Palestine was still illegal, and the British press had begun to write about it – and it was halted for a short period. But after the establishment of the state of Israel, Jews were once again allowed to leave, not least because the Polish state, then in the course of imposing economic centralization, was more than happy to rid itself of the Jewish community's small businessmen. In order to encourage emigration, the new government of Israel also negotiated a trade deal advantageous to the Polish government, effectively guaranteeing Poland an inflow of hard currency. The Romanian government struck a similar deal with Israel, and it is likely that the Soviet Union actively approved both agreements.[80] In Hungary, Joint – the American-Jewish Joint Distribution Committee, a major Zionist charity – paid the Hungarian government $1m at about this time too. In exchange, 3000 Hungarian Jews were allowed immediately to leave for Israel.[81]

Behind the scenes, several Eastern European states were even more supportive, far more so than their leaders would later admit. All of them, with the exception of Yugoslavia, had voted for the partition of Palestine in 1947: at the time, the Soviet Union supported the creation of the state of Israel, not least because Stalin believed Israel would quickly join the communist camp. Enthusiasm for Israel was high in Eastern Europe too – so much so that in late 1947 the Polish, Czechoslovak and Hungarian governments all opened training camps for the Haganah, the Jewish paramilitary organization which formed the core of what would later become the Israeli Defence Force. The Hungarian army and secret police force trained some 1500 Hungarian Jews – and some 7000 Polish Jews meanwhile travelled to Bolków, a small town in Silesia, where they received training from both Red Army and Polish army soldiers, and eventually from Haganah fighters. At the time, this programme enjoyed both national and local support. In June 1948 the Central Committee of the Polish communist party allocated the group 'a certain amount of weapons and a military training ground for drilling'. In Bolków, drills took place in the open, the volunteers marched through the town singing and when the recruits left for Palestine, via Prague and Marseilles, 'there were flowers and banners – even Poles had a lot of sympathy for their freedom struggle', in the words of one ex-trainee. The programme lasted until early 1949, and was intended to have long-term benefits: the Polish secret police kept lists of who had been through the training courses. Those who were communist party members were asked to agree to cooperate as informers, 'even after they went on to Israel'.[82]

With Israel's attainment of statehood, all travel ceased to be clandestine. In 1948, the Polish state travel agency, Orbis, organized the first regular train transport, again via Czechoslovakia, Austria and Italy. After one or two successful trips (once Jews became convinced they were 'really going to Israel, and not to Siberia') the applications to emigrate began to increase again.[83] The numbers went down again in the early 1950s, almost certainly thanks to Soviet pressure: Stalin's initial support for Israel had by then hardened into suspicion and paranoia. Nevertheless, by 1955, no more than 80,000 Jews remained in Poland: more than two thirds of the survivors had left. The numbers were similar elsewhere in Eastern Europe. Between the years 1945 and 1957, 50 per cent of Romanian Jews left their country, along with 58 per cent of Czechoslovak Jews and 90 per cent of Bulgarian Jews. Between a quarter and a third of Hungarian Jews left Hungary too.[84]

Out of those remaining, a disproportionate member chose to stay because they were communists, because they had high expectations of a communist regime, or because they had jobs in the communist state apparatus. This is only logical: at a time when anti-communists of all kinds were being arrested and killed, anti-communist Jews left Eastern Europe. And this is the final unusual thing about Salomon Morel: he was exceptional because he was a Jew who not only stayed but also joined the security police. Popular Eastern European mythology to the contrary, the majority of Polish Jews did not join the secret police. How could they have done? Most of them had left or were planning to leave the country.

It is true that a small number of Jews did occupy very senior, very prominent positions in both the communist party and the communist security apparatus in Poland. Among them were Jakub Berman and Hilary Minc, Bierut's top advisers on ideology and economics, respectively; Julia Brystiger, who ran the secret police department dedicated to the penetration of the Catholic church; Józef Różański, the vicious chief secret police interrogator, and his deputy, Adam Humer; Różański's brother, Jerzy Borejsza, a writer who eventually came to control much of the postwar publishing industry; and Józef Światło, a senior secret policeman who later defected. This notorious group was never a majority. The best estimate, by the historian Andrzej Paczkowski, puts them at about 30 per cent of the secret police *leadership* in the immediate postwar period. After 1948 their numbers fell further. Without question, they attracted a disproportionate percentage of anti-communist resentment anyway.[85]

In Hungary, the situation was different because all of the leading Hungarian communists – Rákosi, Gerő, Révai – were of Jewish origin, as were many of the founders of the political police and the Interior Ministry, including Gábor Péter. Yet even in Hungary, it is not at all clear that the Jews in turn favoured the communists. Only a quarter of the Jewish population voted for the communist party in the 1945 elections. And although the number of visible Jewish party leaders remained high in the immediate postwar years, the percentage of Jews in the state apparatus began to fall after 1948, as the Hungarian communist party – like the East German communist party and the Romanian communist party – actively set out to recruit low-ranking members of the previous regime, especially policemen, in an open bid to become more popular in that milieu and to combat a stereotype of communists as 'elite' or 'alien' or indeed 'Jewish'. ('They aren't bad fellows, really,' Rákosi told an American journalist, speaking of former members of the fascist party. 'They were never active in it. All they have to do is sign a pledge and we let them in.')[86]

More importantly, the presence of Jews in leading positions in the East European communist parties did not produce anywhere a set of policies which could reasonably be described as 'pro-Jewish'. On the contrary, communists, including Jewish communists, were extraordinarily ambivalent about Jewish history and Jewish identity, even as the Holocaust was unfolding. While in Moscow in 1942, Jakub Berman began to hear horrible stories about what was happening to the Jews of Warsaw. In due course, one of his brothers would be gassed in Treblinka. But he steeled himself against pity: true communists could not let the Nazis define their politics. In one of the letters he wrote to Leon Kasman – who was also Jewish – he advised his friend not to be sidetracked or distracted by the unfolding tragedy. 'The situation of Jews in Poland is terrible,' he wrote: 'However, it seems to me that you can't put too much effort into this ... for although the question of mobilization of Jewish masses in Poland into an active struggle against the occupier is important and valid ... other things should be at the center of our attention.'[87]

After the war, this ambivalence increased. In 1945 and 1946, Rákosi worried that too many of the anti-fascist trials were focused on 'people who did something to the Jews', which might not be popular.[88] Notoriously, Rákosi threw anti-semitic comments into conversations, on one occasion offending the speaker of the parliament, Béla Varga, so much that Varga snapped at him, 'your mother was a Jew and do not deny your mother'. He would also issue blanket denials. When the Smallholder Prime Minister, Ferenc Nagy, commented at a cabinet meeting on the large number of Jews among the Hungarian postwar politicians, Rákosi calmly observed that the communist party didn't have this problem: 'Luckily all our leaders are Catholic.'[89] Even East Germany, with its almost non-existent Jewish community, made distinctions early on in the honours bestowed upon former 'Fighters Against Fascism', meaning mostly communists, and former 'Victims of Fascism', meaning mostly Gypsies and Jews. As Jeffrey Herf puts it, 'the old anti-semitic stereotype of the Jew as a capitalist and passive weakling would continue to lurk within the muscular Communist discourse of East German fascism'.[90]

Part of this queasy relationship between East European communists and East European Jews might be attributable to the anti-semitism of individuals, even the anti-semitism of Jewish individuals. Some of it reflected Stalin's own anti-semitism, which grew deeper with time, culminating in a purge of Soviet Jews in high positions just before his death. But at the deepest level, their uneasiness about Jews and Jewishness reflected the communist parties' insecurities about their own popularity. Knowing they were perceived as illegitimate by so many of their countrymen – knowing they were perceived as Soviet agents, to be more precise – they deployed traditional national, religious and ethnic symbols in an effort to win support. This was particularly true in 1945 and 1946, when they still thought they had a chance to take power through elections. While Rákosi spouted anti-black-market and anti-semitic rhetoric, the Hungarian communist party also championed the annual celebration of the 1848 'bourgeois revolution', and insisted, to the consternation of some old party members, that their followers carry national Hungarian flags as well as red party flags. As Rákosi explained, 'We still have a problem with our patriotic character. A lot of comrades are afraid that we are deviating from the

Marxist track. It has to be underlined demonstratively that we chose the red banner and the national flag . . . the national flag is the flag of Hungarian democracy.'[91]

The German communists did the same, resurrecting the German Imperial flag even as the war was still being fought, the better to attract ex-soldiers to their cause. They also bent over backwards to honour traditional German heroes, for example celebrating a Goethe Year in Weimar in 1949, and holding a quadrennial Bach competition in Leipzig. The Poles also organized a Chopin Year in 1949. In August 1944, Edward Osóbka-Morawski, leader of the Lublin provisional government, even publicly celebrated mass in honour of the 'miracle on the Vistula', the Polish defeat of the Bolsheviks outside Warsaw in 1920, a national holiday with distinctly anti-Russian overtones. That strange event was made even stranger by the presence of General Nikolai Bulganin, at the time the representative of the Soviet Council of People's Commissars, and later the Soviet Prime Minister.[92]

The communist indulgence of anti-semitism was part of this same way of thinking. Many hoped that by ignoring or even flirting with anti-semitism, their party would seem more 'national', more 'patriotic', less Soviet, less alien and more legitimate. In Poland, the thesis that the party's unpopularity was due to the presence of 'too many Jews' came originally from the party itself. In 1948, when he had fallen out of favour, Władysław Gomułka, the leader of the wartime Polish communists and Bierut's great rival, wrote a long memo to Stalin, declaring that the Jews in the communist party were making it difficult for the party to widen its base: 'Some of the Jewish comrades don't feel any link to the Polish nation or to the Polish working class . . . or they maintain a stance which might be described as "national nihilism".' As a result, he declared, 'I consider it absolutely necessary not only to stop any further growth in the percentage of Jews in the state as well as the party apparatus, but also to slowly lower that percentage, especially at the highest levels of that apparatus.'[93]

Like anti-German feeling in the Sudetenland, anti-Ukrainian emotions in Poland, and anti-Hungarian sentiment in Slovakia, anti-semitism finally became just another tool, another weapon in the party's arsenal. In this sense, the postwar history of the Jews belongs in the same chapter as the more vigorous forms of ethnic cleansing. In their quest for popularity, communist parties were willing to pump up hatred of Germans, hatred of Hungarians, hatred of Ukrainians, and, even in the region most devastated by the Holocaust, hatred of Jews. The Polish communist party would later return to this theme, expelling most of its own Jewish members in 1968.

And Salomon Morel? In the end, he was a 'typical' figure of this period in only one sense: like many people who lived through the horrors of the war and the confusion of the postwar years, he played different roles in different national narratives at different times. He was a Holocaust victim, a communist criminal, a man who lost his entire family to the Nazis and a man consumed by a sadistic fury against Germans and Poles – a fury which may or may not have originated from his victimhood, and may or may not have been connected to his communism. He was deeply vengeful, and profoundly violent. He was awarded medals by the communist Polish state, was prosecuted by the post-communist Polish state, and was defended by the Israeli state, though he had expressed no interest in moving to Israel until half a century after the war, and even then only after he started to fear prosecution. In the end his life story proves nothing about Jews or Poles at all. It only proves how difficult it is to pass judgement on the people who lived in the most shattered part of Europe in the worst decades of the twentieth century.

7
Youth

'Your anti-Fascist action group must be broken up at once . . . !
You're supposed to wait for instructions from the Central
Committee!'[1]

Walter Ulbricht, 1945

Those who own the youth, own the future
Slogan of the German Young Pioneers

In 1947, Stefan Jędrychowski, a communist veteran, member of the
Polish Politburo and minister in the government, wrote a memo to his
colleagues on a subject close to his heart. Somewhat pompously
entitled 'Notes on Anglo-Saxon Propaganda', the memo complained,
among other things, that British and American news services were
more influential in Poland than their Soviet and Polish equivalents;
that American films were too warmly reviewed; and that American
fashions were too readily available. He firmly suggested that Soviet
fashions be more prominently displayed and advertised, that strict
limits be placed on the British Council and other organizations which
taught English in Poland, and that the activities of Western embassies
be more closely monitored.

But above all, Jędrychowski was annoyed by the apparent clout of
Polska YMCA, the Polish section of the Young Men's Christian Association, an organization founded in Warsaw in 1923 and then banned
by Hitler. In April 1945 Polska YMCA had restarted itself with some
help from the international YMCA headquarters in Geneva and a
good deal of local enthusiasm. The YMCA was avowedly apolitical.

Its main tasks in Poland were the distribution of foreign aid – clothes, books, food – and the provision of activities and classes for young people. Jędrychowski suspected ulterior motives, however. The YMCA's propaganda, he wrote, was conducted 'carefully ... avoiding direct political accents', which of course made it more dangerous. He recommended that Comrade Radkiewicz, the Minister for State Security, conduct a financial audit of the organization and monitor carefully which publications were being made available and which kinds of courses were being taught.[2]

He was not the only one who was worried. At about the same time, the Education Ministry also received a report from leaders of the communist youth movement, then known as the Union of Fighting Youth (Związek Walki Młodych, or ZWM), which loathed the YMCA even more than Jędrychowski did. The young communists were irritated by the YMCA's English classes, clubs and billiards games. In Gdańsk, they complained, the organization sponsored dormitories and dining halls, and gave away used clothes. In Kraków it had rented a building with a seventy-five-year lease. Though they didn't say so, all of this was far more than they themselves were capable of doing.[3]

There may have been darker concerns: in the period just after the Bolshevik Revolution, a British agent named Paul Dukes had actually used the YMCA in Moscow as a cover for his espionage activities, though not with any particular success.[4] But the Polish communists wouldn't have needed to know that piece of history in order to find the Warsaw YMCA irritating. They hated the YMCA because it was fashionable, if there could be said to be such a thing as fashion in postwar Warsaw. The Warsaw YMCA was, for example, the abode of Leopold Tyrmand, a novelist, journalist and flâneur, as well as Poland's first and greatest jazz critic. Tyrmand rented a room in the half-destroyed building after the war as he later wrote, 'two and a half metres by three and a half metres – in other words a hole. But cozy.' All around was nothing but mud, dust and the ruins of Warsaw: this gave the building, a mere dormitory for single men, the air of 'a luxurious hotel'. It wasn't much, but it was clean and quiet.[5]

In the evenings, Tyrmand dressed in brightly coloured socks and narrow trousers, the latter specially made for him by a tailor who also lived at the YMCA, and went to the jazz concerts downstairs. There, 'between the cafeteria, the reading room and the swimming pool the best girls ambled about in the then-fashionable style of swing'. Both the Warsaw and Łódź YMCA branches were renowned for these concerts. One fan remembered that getting a ticket to a YMCA concert was 'a dream ... it was cultured, elegant, hugely fun, even without alcohol'. Above all it was entertainment: 'We didn't know anything about Katyń or about how one lives in a free country, we didn't have passports, we didn't have new books or movies, but we had a natural need to find entertainment, fun ... that was what jazz gave us.' Tyrmand himself wrote later that the YMCA represented 'genuine civilization in the middle of devastated, troglodyte Warsaw, a city where one lived in ratholes. Above all we valued the collegial atmosphere, the sportiness, the good humour.'[6]

But with enemies like Jędrychowski and the Union of Fighting Youth, the organization could not last. In 1949, the communist authorities declared the YMCA a 'tool of bourgeois-fascism' and dissolved it. With bizarre, Orwellian fury, communist youth activists descended on the club with hammers and smashed all the jazz records. The building was given over to something called the League of Soldiers' Friends. The inhabitants were harassed, first with early-morning noise, later with cuts in water and electricity, in order to get them to move out. Eventually, the young communists threw everyone's possessions out of the windows of the buildings and removed their beds.

Still, not everybody left, largely because they had no place to go. Tyrmand stayed. New people arrived, sometimes bringing wives and children. By 1954, the place was noisy and dirty, with washing hanging in the hall and the smell of cooking in the air. Whole families slept in the tiny rooms. The buildings had come to resemble a 'Parisian slum', wrote Tyrmand: 'The cheerful comfort of the old YMCA is now but a distant memory from an idyllic prehistory.'[7]

The reconstruction of Polska YMCA in the immediate postwar period was a classic example of what is nowadays called 'civil society', a phenomenon which has gone by other names in the past.[8] In the eighteenth century, Edmund Burke wrote admiringly of the 'little platoons', the small social organizations from which, he believed, public spirit arose (and which he thought were threatened by the French Revolution).

In the nineteenth century, Alexander de Tocqueville wrote equally enthusiastically of the 'associations' which 'Americans of all ages, all conditions, and all dispositions constantly form'. He concluded that they helped ward off dictatorship: 'If men are to remain civilized or to become so, the art of associating together must grow and improve.' More recently, the political scientist Robert Putnam has redefined the same phenomenon as 'social capital', and concluded that voluntary organizations lie at the heart of what we call 'community'.

By 1945, the Bolsheviks had also developed a theory of civil society, albeit one which was entirely negative. In contrast to Burke, Tocqueville and their own Russian intellectuals, they believed, in the words of the historian Stuart Finkel, that 'the public sphere in a socialist society should be unitary and univocal'. They dismissed the 'bourgeois' notion of open discussion, and hated independent associations, trade unions and guilds of all kinds, which they referred to as 'separatist' or 'caste' divisions within society. As for bourgeois political parties, these were meaningless. (As Lenin had written, 'the names of parties, both in Europe and in Russia, are often chosen purely for purposes of advertisement, the "programmes" of parties are more often than not written with the sole purpose of defrauding the public'.[9]) The only organizations allowed to have a legal existence were de facto extensions of the communist party. Even completely apolitical organizations had to be banned: until the revolution had triumphed, there could be no such thing as an apolitical organization. Everything was political. And if it was not openly political, then it was secretly political.

From that assumption, it also followed that no organized group was above suspicion. Associations that claimed to be interested in soccer or chess might well be 'fronts' for something more sinister. The St Petersburg academic Dmitri Likhachev – later Russia's most celebrated literary critic – was arrested in 1928 because he belonged to a philosophic discussion circle whose members saluted one another in ancient Greek. While in prison Likhachev encountered, among others, the head of the Petrograd boy scouts, an organization which would be later considered highly dubious in Eastern Europe as well.[10]

This profound suspicion of civil society was central to Bolshevik thinking, far more so than is usually acknowledged. Finkel points out that even while the Soviet leadership was experimenting with economic freedom in the 1920s (during Lenin's 'New Economic Plan') the systematic destruction of literary, philosophical and spiritual societies continued unabated.[11] Even for orthodox Marxists, free trade was preferable to free association, including the free association of apolitical sporting or cultural groups. This was true under Lenin's rule, under Stalin's rule, under Khrushchev's rule and under Brezhnev's rule. Although many other things changed, the persecution of civil society continued after Stalin's death, well into the 1970s and 1980s.

The Eastern European communists inherited this paranoia, either because they had observed it and acquired it for themselves during their many visits to the Soviet Union, because their colleagues in the secret police had acquired it during their training, or, in some cases, because the Soviet generals and ambassadors in their countries at the end of the war explicitly instructed them to be paranoid. In a few cases, Soviet authorities in Eastern Europe directly ordered local communists to ban particular organizations or types of organizations.

As in post-revolutionary Russia, the political persecution of civic activists in Eastern Europe not only preceded the persecution of actual politicians, but also took precedence over other Soviet and communist goals. Even in the years between 1945 and 1948, when elections were still theoretically free in Hungary and when Poland still had a legal opposition party, certain kinds of civic associations were already under threat. In Germany, Soviet commanders made no attempt to ban religious services or religious ceremonies in the first months of occupation, but they often objected strongly to church group meetings, religious evenings and even organized religious and charitable associations which met outside the church, in restaurants or other public spaces.[12] Despite Marx's belief that 'base determines superstructure' – meaning that economics determine politics and culture – the attacks on civil society preceded the most radical economic changes in the region too. Although the timing was not exactly the same in every nation of Soviet-occupied Europe, the patterns were very similar. In many places, private trade was still legal even when belonging to a Catholic youth group was not.

Nowhere is the significance of civil society to the new communist parties clearer than in the history of the region's youth movements, perhaps because there was no social group that the communists considered more important. In part, this is because their fascist opponents had considered young people important, and had enjoyed great 'success' in organizing them. As early as 1932, the German communist party boss, Ernst Thälmann, called upon his comrades to 'adopt sports, discipline and comradery, scouting games and marches' just like the Nazis: '"Why don't we pick up on the romantic-revolutionary sentiments of the masses of young workers? Why are we so dry and dull in our work? ... We have to create magnets to draw the proletarian youth ..."'[13]

The obsession with young people also reflected the deep belief in the mutability of human beings which was prevalent in communist circles in the 1940s (and in left-wing circles across Europe). Stalin's famous suspicion of genetics derived precisely from his conviction that propaganda and communist education could alter the human character, permanently. He championed quacks such as the anti-geneticist Lysenko, who held that acquired characteristics can be inherited, and who falsified his experiments to prove it. Any scientist whose work disproved Lysenko's theories risked persecution in the Soviet Union as long as Stalin was alive.[14] Stalin's reasoning was clear: if young people could be moulded and shaped by education and propaganda, and if they could then pass these acquired behaviours on to their children, then the creation of a 'new' breed of communist man – *Homo sovieticus*, about which more later – was possible.

Polska YMCA was only one of many youth groups to re-emerge from the rubble of the war. In an era before television and social media, and at a time when many lacked radio, newspapers, books, music and theatre, youth groups had an importance to teenagers and young adults which today is hard to imagine. They organized parties, concerts, camps, clubs, sports and discussion groups of a kind which could be found nowhere else.

In Germany in particular, the disappearance of the Hitler Youth and its female branch, the League of German Girls, left a real gap. Until the very end of the war, nearly half of the young people in Germany had attended Hitler Youth and League of German Girls' meetings in the evenings. Most had spent their summers and weekends at organized camps as well. Although those organizations were now utterly discredited, they had filled a real need, and as soon as the fighting stopped, former members and former opponents of the Nazi youth groups began spontaneously to form anti-fascist organizations in towns and cities across both East and West Germany.

These first groups were German, not Soviet, and they were organized by the young people themselves. All around them, adults were in despair. One in five German schoolchildren had lost his or her father. One in ten had a father who was a prisoner of war. Someone had to start reorganizing society, and in the absence of adult authorities a few very energetic young people took on this role. In Neukölln, a western Berlin district, an anti-fascist youth organization created on 8 May– the day before the armistice – had 600 members by 20 May, and had already set up five orphanages and cleared two sports stadiums of rubble. On 23 May, the group gave a performance in a Neukölln theatre which was attended by Soviet military officers as well as the general public.[15]

Wolfgang Leonhard, who had by then arrived in Berlin on Ulbricht's plane, met some of the members of this Neukölln group. These were the first non-Soviet political activists he had ever encountered: 'One could feel the genuineness of the enthusiasm combined with a healthy realism. Without waiting for directives, the [group's] members had immediately realized that the first thing was to organize a supply of food and water to alleviate the most urgent needs of the population.' He marvelled, among other things, at their efficient, businesslike discussions: 'More was accomplished in half an hour than in all the endless meetings I was used to in Russia.'[16] Similar groups began organizing food distribution and rubble clearance all across Berlin, which was entirely under Soviet control for the first couple of months after the armistice. The Western Allies arrived in July, and only then was the city divided into occupation zones. By that time, the Berlin magistrate reckoned 10,000 teenagers across the city had already joined spontaneous anti-fascist groups.[17]

But almost as soon as they had started, these groups attracted the attention and suspicion of the Soviet authorities in Germany. On 31 July, the Soviet Military Administration issued a declaration 'permitting' the formation of anti-fascist groups under the leadership of city mayors, but only 'in connection with formal requests'. Unless they received explicit permission, in other words, all other youth organizations, unions and sports clubs – even socialist groups – were banned. Separately, another declaration also commanded all youth groups to promote 'friendship' with the Soviet Union. After three months of spontaneous existence, these self-organized groups were already coming under state control.

Leonhard, who had just encountered spontaneous civil society for the first time in his life, was one of those tasked with destroying it. Not long after their arrival in Berlin, Ulbricht drew his attention to the 'Anti-Fascist Committees or Anti-Nazi Groups or Socialist Offices or National Committees or such-like' which had sprung up without authorization. Leonhard writes that he at first welcomed Ulbricht's interest in these groups, having been enormously impressed by his encounter with the Neukölln anti-fascists, and he 'took it for granted that the task Ulbricht was about to assign was to make contact with them and support their work'. He was wrong. All of these committees, Ulbricht told him, had been created by the Nazis. Most were cover organizations. He told Leonhard that they were designed to prevent the development of true democracy, and he issued an order: '"They are to be dissolved, and at once" ...' Leonhard, 'with a heavy heart', agreed to carry out the task. Only later did he understand why:

It was impossible for Stalinism to permit the creation by independent initiative from below of anti-Fascist, Socialist or Communist movements or organizations, because there was the constant danger that such organizations would escape its control and try to resist directives issued from above ... It was the first victory of the apparat over the independent stirrings of the anti-Fascist, left-inclined strata of Germany.[18]

But if Ulbricht and his Soviet partners did not want spontaneous committees, they did want young people to join sanctioned groups which had been properly registered with the Soviet authorities. Because Germany was deemed a 'bourgeois' democracy, and non-communist political parties were still allowed to exist, they did let some non-communist youth groups register themselves, provided they subjected themselves to full regulation. The centre-right Christian democrats were allowed to register an official 'youth wing' of the

Christian Democratic Party in July. In 1946, Soviet administrators would also issue instructions allowing the formation of certain artistic and cultural groups as well.[19]

The communist party also set up its own youth section, optimistically assuming that many young Germans would want to join. But they did not, or at least not in the numbers anticipated. In a report filed to the leadership in October 1945, the young (or youngish; he was then thirty-three) Erich Honecker, a trusted insider – he had arrived on the first plane from Moscow with Ulbricht too – informed his superiors that progress was slow. He worried that young Germans 'equate politics with the activity of the former Nazi party', and feared many were 'looking for individual solutions to their problems' or were 'giving in to an addiction to pleasure and black market dealing'.[20]

Others also found German young people to be insufficiently political. Robert Bialek – who had now left Breslau, and had temporarily recovered from his disillusionment with the Soviet soldiers who raped his wife – also complained that young Germans still thought and spoke using Nazi categories. Bialek had been named leader of the youth section of the communist party in Saxony, where he argued in favour of bringing former Hitler Youth into the new organization, the better to broaden its appeal. These were Germany's natural leaders, he declared: 'We might ostracize the former leaders of the Hitler Youth Movement but we could not eradicate, even by order of Marshal Zhukov, the authority these leaders had wielded.'[21]

Yet while the communist youth groups languished, the strength and appeal of other groups, particularly Christian groups, was clearly growing. In the moral wasteland of post-Nazi Germany, the church seemed a spiritual and ethical oasis. Ernst Benda, later a legal scholar, judge and eventually the president of West Germany's constitutional court, joined the youth wing of the Christian democrats in East Berlin at that time precisely because he believed that its doctrine derived from 'simple truths': 'be completely honest, do not lie, be truthful, be fair to your political opponent, be just – which means social justice'.[22]

Manfred Klein, a young man who had been heavily recruited by the communist party while still in a Soviet prison camp, also drifted back to the church in the autumn of 1945. Returning to Berlin at the war's end, he had initially helped Honecker organize the communist youth movement, but he soon grew uncomfortable. 'Being only twenty years old, we were pretty helpless when facing the closeness of this system and its seemingly complete and irrefutable logic,' he wrote in his memoirs: 'having been brought up on Catholic belief and having grown up with Catholic youth work I still held many reservations.' Eventually he joined the Christian Democratic Party's youth group. This infuriated his former communist colleagues, until they realized he could be of use to them. 'You are savvier than I thought you were,' Honecker told him, all smiles. The Soviet comrades approved of his decision too: now they expected him to be an agent within the Christian Democratic milieu, working on their behalf.[23]

By December 1945, the young communists realized they had to change their tactics. They were failing to attract young people in the same numbers as the other party youth groups, and so they decided to change the rules of the game. Honecker asked Bialek to begin surreptitiously organizing a 'spontaneous' popular movement for a 'unified' German youth movement. The push for the unification of all German youth groups under a single umbrella was to originate in Saxony, and would involve petitions, meetings and speeches. Youth leaders would also send letters to the Soviet authorities calling for a single, non-partisan youth group. Once the Soviet military leaders agreed to this plan, then the 'bourgeois' youth leaders would have no choice but to go along: all of the young people would then belong to the new group, and the relative weakness of the young communists would not be so noticeable.[24]

This was an idea born of failure: because the communist party could not compete for young people, its leaders decided to eliminate the competition. Though German in origin – it seems to have been Honecker's idea – the plan quickly found favour with the Soviet commanders. In January 1946, Wilhelm Pieck, at the time chairman of the party's Central Committee, made a note of a discussion held in Karlshorst, the Soviet headquarters in Berlin: 'the creation of a unified anti-fascist youth organization: Agree, but decide in Moscow.' Ulbricht duly took up the subject on his next trip to Moscow, and in early February he returned with Moscow's permission. Thus was born the Free German Youth (Freie Deutsche Jugend, or FDJ).

Bialek's 'spontaneous' call for unity took the other youth leaders by surprise. At a meeting called to discuss the matter, Honecker claimed that 'many' groups were demanding a unified, Free German youth movement. When Christian Democratic and Social Democratic youth leaders said they had not heard any such demands, they were shown several baskets containing hundreds of letters. 'The surprise was a success,' remembered Klein. 'We had not reckoned with such a suggestion at that time.' A founding congress was duly organized and a range of young people – Christian Democrat, Social Democrat, communist – agreed to attend. So did Catholic and Lutheran youth leaders, albeit cautiously. Klein discussed the meeting with Jakob Kaiser, then the leader of the Christian democrats in Berlin, who agreed that he should take part but advised him to be wary: 'None of us knows how long this will work.'[25]

This first meeting was held in Brandenburg in April 1946 and it started out optimistically. It began with a song ('The Ballad of Free Youth') and the unanimous selection of a praesidium which included Klein, Honecker and Bialek. There were several speeches of welcome. Colonel Sergei Tyulpanov, the cultural commissar of the Soviet occupation forces, told the young people that 'Hitler's ideology has left deep traces in the consciousness of German youth' and complimented those in the room, somewhat patronizingly, on having grown out of it: 'we know how hard you have worked in order to purge yourselves of all of that'.[26] Welcome speeches were followed by more speeches: on the achievements of youth, on the importance of the inclusion of girls, on the need for nationalized industry, on the perfidy of the West. Many of the speakers addressed the hall as 'comrades'. One or two Catholic representatives did get up to speak. Yes, we want to unite, said one, 'unite in the love of Germany'.[27]

But although the mood in the hall was reconciliatory, the atmosphere in the corridors was less so, and by day three the atmosphere had turned sour. That morning, some of the more radical communist delegates held a meeting in a side room, during which one of them had complained about the church group leaders. He thought they should be expelled. Bialek told him not to worry, the religious young people would be kept under control: 'we will give the churches ten blows a day until they lie on the ground. When we need them again, we will stroke them a little until their wounds are healed.'[28]

Unfortunately, one of the Catholic youth leaders overheard this little speech, took notes on the dialogue and reported back to his colleagues. Klein and several Catholic leaders announced they would refuse to join the new organization. Some shouting back and forth followed, and a Soviet officer intervened. Major Beylin promised the Catholics they could have some autonomy within the organization, whereupon they agreed to stay inside: the Soviet occupiers were, in 1946, still anxious for their occupation zone at least to appear democratic and multi-faceted.

That desire did not last. In the end, the congress elected sixty-two members to the new organization's central council, of which more than fifty were either communists or socialists. Separately, the communists allotted to themselves all the important jobs. Honecker, a communist of blind dedication, became and would remain the Free German Youth's leader until long after he had ceased to be a youth himself (he resigned from the Free German Youth in 1955, when he was forty-three years old). A Free German Youth training school was quickly opened in Bogensee. Here, Klein remembered, 'the real intentions of Honecker and his comrades became apparent very quickly . . . the boys and girls were trained in Marxist-Leninist-Stalinist ideology and got precise directives on what they had to do to help socialism win in the enterprises and the country'.[29]

The intentions of the Soviet comrades became clearer as well. In August 1946, authorities in Saxony sounded the alert because local churches had organized their own youth retreats and summer camps. The Soviet forces came to the rescue. Soldiers marched into the forest and, in the words of a report filed at the time, 'brought the children home'.[30] In October, there were ominous power cuts during a large Christian Democratic youth rally in West Berlin. Everyone present knew that electricity in Berlin at that time was all supplied by a power station in the Soviet-controlled half of the city. In a spirit of defiance, the rally continued by candlelight.[31]

Other groups were simply dispersed. In the spring of 1946, Soviet authorities discovered that an unregistered evangelical youth group,

Christian Endeavour (Entschieden für Christus) was active in Saxony, where it held Bible discussions and prayer meetings. 'This proved that control on the activity of German organizations is weak,' the Saxon authorities declared, and they immediately banned the organization.[32] Another group that set up an 'independent' cell of the Free German Youth in Leipzig met a similar fate. Although the leaders of the group argued that their members were more intellectually inclined than the 'workers' in the mainstream Free German Youth, and that they therefore needed their own organization, they were abruptly disbanded too.[33] One Soviet report complained that many of the groups which had religious affiliations 'act far outside the frame of religion' and were engaging in 'cultural-political work with youth', which is of course what church youth groups had always done.

In the winter of 1946, the Soviet authorities at Karlshorst also informed the brand-new German cultural administration – part of the German bureaucracy set up to enact Soviet policy – that artistic and cultural groups of all kinds, whether for children, young people or adults, were illegal unless they were affiliated to 'mass organizations' such as the Free German Youth, the official trade union organization or the official cultural union, the Kulturbund: 'otherwise they cannot be controlled'. A German inspector sent out to gauge the situation of 'associations' at this time discovered many such groups not aligned to mass organizations. She seemed particularly horrified by the large numbers of independent chess clubs. She called upon Soviet and German cultural authorities to eliminate these groups – chess clubs, sporting clubs, singing clubs – a task which was not finished until 1948–9. Other apolitical organizations were banned right away. Hiking clubs were strictly forbidden, for example, presumably because the Hitler Youth had a particular fondness for hiking (though the Wandervogel, the famous German hiking and nature clubs founded at the end of the nineteenth century, had once had left-wing as well as proto-Nazi sympathies).[34]

Klein kept working within the system. Though frustrated with his role as the 'token Christian' inside the Free German Youth, he spent a good bit of his time trying to organize the other token Christians into a voting bloc. He lobbied to keep the Free German Youth open to many different kinds of young people, but to no avail. Almost exactly a year after its founding, this brief Soviet–German experiment in non-partisan youth politics had come to an end. On 13 March 1947, the NKVD arrested Klein, along with fifteen other young Christian Democratic leaders. A Soviet military tribunal sentenced him to a Soviet labour camp. He remained there for nine years.

On 19 June 1946, *Szabad Nép*, the Hungarian communist party's newspaper, reported a shocking story: a Russian officer had been murdered at the Oktogon, a busy eight-sided intersection in central Budapest. During the shootout, another Russian soldier had also died, along with a woman described as a 'Hungarian working-class girl'. *Szabad Nép* explained that the murderer, a young man named István Pénzes, had been a member of a rural Catholic youth group, Kalot, and thus an 'enemy of our economic recovery and freedom'. Investigators found his charred body in an attic overlooking the square and concluded he had been part of a larger conspiracy: 'the traitors who lost their lands, the parasites of the hard-working Hungarian people, will try everything, in anticipation of the peace treaty and the currency reform, to make our nation's life impossible'.[35]

Little time was lost in drawing further conclusions about what quickly became known as the Oktogon murders. On the following morning, *Szabad Nép* filled its entire front page with an editorial entitled 'Youth and Democracy': 'It is high time for us to take the weapons and the grenades out of the hands of our misled youth ... After Monday's attack, we must tell the right wing of our democracy that fighting against the fascists is a national struggle, a national duty.'[36] The funeral of the two Red Army soldiers on the following day received equally lavish media coverage. 'Hundreds of thousands' participated in the ceremony for the dead soldiers, according to *Szabad Nép*. Led by Hungarian and Soviet officials, mourners had carried banners with slogans such as 'Death to the Traitors' and 'Liquidate Fascist Killers'. An editorialist repeated the call for stricter treatment of misled youth: 'Let us stop all reactionary criticism ... Let us prevent certain church circles from teaching our youth how to commit murder.'[37]

In his funeral oration, General Vladimir Sviridov, the recently arrived chairman of the Allied Control Commission in Hungary, also

spoke. Although 'the Red Army gave the Hungarian people the possibility to establish a new life according to democratic principles', he
declared, certain 'reactionary forces, like wild dogs, attack the greatest protector of the Hungarian people, the Red Army'. Sviridov
castigated Hungarian politicians: 'here in your country, which you
call a friend of the Soviet Union, fascist wrongdoers ambush Soviet
people. Here in your country you pay for all the blood spilled by the
Red Army with bullets.'[38]

Behind the scenes, all acknowledged that the true motives of the
Oktogon murderer were, and indeed remain, mysterious, if he was
even a murderer at all. In his memoirs, the Smallholders' Party politician Ferenc Nagy, Prime Minister at the time, claimed that Pénzes
had been a member of the Social Democratic youth group, not the
Catholic Kalot, and that he had acted out of jealousy. Allegedly, the
Soviet soldier was flirting with his girlfriend.[39] Another politician at
the time thought the matter had been a 'simple love triangle', which
explained why Pénzes, a poor student, had committed suicide afterwards: such was his distress at having murdered the woman he loved.
Some versions of the story had it that there was no murderer at all.
The two Russian soldiers had simply opened fire on one another, and
Pénzes had been murdered by secret policemen, who burned his body
to cover up their crime. Just about everyone agreed that the investigation had been delayed, inept and politicized.[40]

In the end, it didn't matter what had really happened. The Oktogon
murders, which followed close on the sentencing of Father Kiss – the
priest accused of organizing the murder of Russian soldiers – were
blamed on Kalot because Kalot was successful. Worse, Kalot was far
more successful than the communist party's Hungarian Democratic
Youth Alliance (Magyar Demokratikus Ifjúsági Szövetség, or Madisz),
with whom it had been in bitter conflict for the previous eighteen
months. 'Kalot' was an acronym meaning National Secretariat of
Catholic Agricultural Youth Clubs (Katolikus Agrárifjúsági Legényegyesületek Országos Testülete) and it predated Madisz by a decade.
Founded in 1935 by two energetic Jesuits, Father Töhötöm Nagy and
Father János Kerkai, Kalot had continued to function during the
war, maintaining its Catholic character and its credibility in the countryside by supporting land reform, peasant education and a mild form

of socialism. Kalot didn't have the urban cachet of Polska YMCA or the angry passion of the first anti-fascist groups in Germany. Some of its wartime leaders stand accused of anti-semitism.[41] But Kalot was authentic, it worked to improve peasants' lives, and it had maintained enough independence from the previous authoritarian and fascist regimes not to be compromised by their collapse. Above all, it was popular. At the end of 1944, Kalot had half a million members, spread among 4500 local organizations.

Madisz, by contrast, was brand-new, having been ordered into existence by Gerő, one of Rákosi's closest associates. Gerő's intentions were similar to those of Honecker in Germany: he wanted to create an organization which would 'unify workers, peasants and students' under a 'universal' and 'non-partisan' banner. He also wanted to prevent other political parties from forming youth groups of their own.[42] That plan failed almost immediately. At one of the organization's first meetings in Budapest in January 1945, a Madisz leader was already complaining that 'everybody thinks that Madisz is a cover organization' for the communist party. He told his comrades to fight this image: 'we must tell people that we have a communist character at the moment only because non-communists haven't yet joined us. We must recruit people from church organizations, scouts, and social democratic movements . . .' Young people would join if they could be made to understand the starkness of the choices before them: 'those who are not with us are against us . . . those who are against us are fascists'.[43]

Another young leader, András Hegedüs, wanted Madisz to use subtler means to attract young people too. 'The masses are in need of culture, we have to catch them through culture,' he argued: 'There is a golden opportunity in front of us, because for the moment there is no cinema, and no one who can offer other cultural possibilities to the masses. Later it will be more difficult.' Hegedüs – who was to become Prime Minister of Hungary, briefly, in 1956 – was not interested in culture for its own sake, 'but for the sake of drawing people into the movement . . . cleaning the ruins won't do it, it's not pleasurable enough'.[44]

Madisz did have some success in these very early days, particularly in Budapest, and particularly because its good connections with the Red Army gave its members access to food and to identity documents which could prevent them from being deported. But the group's attempts to organize mass meetings almost always failed. When only forty people came to a rally in January, the leadership blamed 'bad propaganda'.[45] Six months later, when it was still proving difficult to attract young people to meetings, the leadership wondered, echoing Rákosi, if there weren't 'too many Jews' in the organization, particularly in certain districts. It had been a mistake, some felt, to 'allow Zionists to march alongside us' in the recent May Day parades. It gave the wrong impression.[46]

Outside Budapest it was even more difficult to get anyone to acknowledge Madisz's natural leadership. Among rural young people, Kalot clearly had the lead – so much so that at one point Madisz tried to negotiate a deal: Madisz would manage Kalot's cultural activities and sports, and Kalot could remain in control of church and religious activities. Not surprisingly, the Kalot leaders refused.

Seeing that Kalot and other established youth organizations were not joining Madisz, Hungary's other legal political parties, most notably the social democrats and the Smallholders, began organizing their own youth groups. University and secondary school students also formed their own organization, the League of Hungarian University and College Associations (Magyar Egyetemisták és Főiskolai Egyesületek Szövetsége, or Mefesz). As these groups began mushrooming, and as it became clear that neither propaganda nor persuasion could convince them to unify beneath Madisz's umbrella, the group's tactics became more aggressive. Threats grew more frequent. In June 1945, Madisz authorities wrote a letter to the leaders of the Smallholders' Party's youth group, demanding that they apply for permission before forming new cultural organizations. 'Please respect these rules in the future,' the letter declared, 'because if not, we will apply the most radical methods.' (The letter was signed 'with democratic respect'.)[47]

Across the country, Madisz members, sometimes aided by local communist party leaders and police, attempted to confiscate Kalot property and to prevent Kalot from holding meetings. The Catholic church recorded twenty-seven occasions on which local authorities tried to ban a local Kalot group, and dozens of other incidents of harassment. Kalot responded to these threats by issuing its youth leaders with a set of guidelines, warning them not to recruit too heavily or put too much pressure on existing members: 'those members who want to quit should be allowed to do so, let them leave without comments, those who want to join should be welcome but do not comment on other organizations' difficulties in recruiting'.[48]

Antagonism grew anyway. In August 1945 the leaders of Madisz were already speaking among themselves of a plan to 'liquidate Kalot'. A series of articles in the Madisz newspaper attacked Kalot, questioning its wartime activities and especially its cooperation with the interwar paramilitary youth movement, the *levente*. The latter, though not especially ideological, had been drafted to fight the Red Army at the end of the war, and its leader had just been sentenced to death. Kalot responded with a booklet answering the accusations – the Catholic church had opposed the *levente*, as had Kalot – but the print run was confiscated by the secret police on the grounds that it was 'anti-Soviet propaganda'.[49]

Fearful for the safety of their members, some in Kalot tried to make accommodations. In January 1946, Father Kerkai, one of Kalot's co-founders, asked a Soviet official to arrange a visit for Kalot leaders to the USSR, so that they could 'get acquainted' with the Soviet system. Three months later, Kalot – over the objections of the church hierarchy – agreed to join yet another new group, the Hungarian National Youth Council. Also a creation of the young communists, this group was styling itself as an 'umbrella' organization which everyone could accept.

József Mindszenty, who had just become primate of Hungary and was slowly acquiring the anti-communist reputation which would make him famous, opposed Kalot's decision to join this new alliance. 'You have thrust a non-political movement into the swamp of daily politics,' he complained to Father Kerkai. In response, Kerkai pointed out that Hungary was going to have to learn to live 'in the neighbourhood of Soviet power' for a long time, and that a modus vivendi had to be found, one way or another.[50] Kalot's other leader, Father Nagy, even travelled to Rome to secure the Vatican's support against Mindszenty in this matter.[51]

In the aftermath of the Oktogon murders, it quickly became clear that no modus vivendi would be found. On 2 July, General Sviridov called openly for the dissolution of 'reactionary youth movements' at a meeting of the Allied Control Council, on the grounds that they 'educate their members in a fascist spirit'. In private, he complained to Moscow about the 'strengthening of reactionary circles' in Hungary, and told the Hungarian government, bluntly, that it must do something about the 'underground fascist organizations' which had found shelter behind these legal political parties and youth movements.

Without waiting for the government as a whole to agree, the communist Interior Minister, Lázsló Rajk, took up Sviridov's cause. Between 18 and 23 July, Rajk banned over 1500 organizations. The ban went far beyond youth groups. In the first wave he banned, among others, the Hungarian Athletic Club (described by *Szabad Nép* as 'the exclusive sports association of the highest, sharply antidemocratic circles'); the Prohaszka Work Community, a community service organization of Bishop Prohaszka; the Association of College Students; several Christian Democratic trade unions ('which made themselves known for their strike-breaking activities in the past'); and something called the Grand Order of Emericana, which was said to hold mystical ceremonies in the manner of the Ku Klux Klan. In the next wave Rajk banned the Hungarian Naval Association, a few local hunting clubs, the Count Széchenyi Association of War Veterans and the Association of Christian Democratic Tobacco Workers. Among the groups banned were professional associations and guilds, all of which were said to be working 'in the service of capitalist interests', as well as 'reactionary' social organizations, Catholic and Protestant organizations, and non-communist trade unions. Many were said to be working secretly on behalf of 'fascist' or foreign interests. Finally, Rajk banned all of the local branches of Kalot.[52]

After the ban, some Kalot members tried to reorganize their group under communist patronage, but nothing ever came of their efforts. In 1947, Father Nagy slipped out of Hungary, and made his way to Argentina. In 1949, the Hungarian security police arrested Father Kerkai and sentenced him to a labour camp. He would be released a decade later, in 1959, when he was half-blind and too ill to influence young people to become 'reactionaries' any longer.[53] In 1950, all of the Hungarian youth organizations were forced to unite and form a single organization, the League of Working Youth (Dolgozó Ifjúság

Szövetsége, or DISZ), putting an end to the alphabet soup of youth group acronyms, and to pluralism as well.

As time went on, the communist attack on civil society would change and become more sophisticated. In order to create competition for authentic civil society, the regimes would create ersatz 'official' civic groups, organizations which sometimes looked independent but were in fact controlled by the state.

They also set out to destroy some of the most powerful institutions of civil society not through outright bans but through trickery or subversion: the replacement of key leaders with regime loyalists, or the use of determined communist cells within looser organizations. Eventually, these kinds of methods would be used on churches and clergy throughout the region, and much later, in the 1970s and 1980s, they would be deployed against dissidents. But they were first tried out on the most recalcitrant youth groups, most notably the Polish scouting movement and the Hungarian People's Colleges.

Scouting had surprisingly deep roots in Eastern Europe, especially in states whose borders had been redrawn after the First World War. Leaders of these 'new' states – Poland, Czechoslovakia, Hungary – very much wanted young people to become engaged in the national rejuvenation and reconstruction projects of the time. With its emphasis on health, work and community service, Lord Baden-Powell's modern scouting movement seemed to show the way. Scouting, one Polish enthusiast wrote in a 1924 pamphlet, not only defined the vague notion of 'character' for young Poles, but offered them a concrete means to acquire it.[54]

In Poland, the scouts had acquired an extra layer of emotional and political significance during the war. Following the invasion of the country in September 1939, scouting leaders had taken the momentous decision to go underground and join the resistance. Under the name Szare Szeregi – the Grey Ranks – the scouts became messengers, liaison officers, radio operators, nurses and eventually partisan fighters in the Home Army. Scouts as young as ten or twelve fought and died in the Warsaw Uprising. Young men and women, sometimes still wearing their tattered grey uniforms, turned up in Soviet concentration camps after the rising failed and the Home Army was defeated.[55]

'This was a different scouting movement from today, we were brought up in the spirit of Poland,' wrote one.[56]

The underground Grey Ranks dissolved themselves at the war's end along with the rest of the Home Army. But scout troops began openly re-forming themselves on liberated territories even before the end of the war in Białystok and other eastern cities. Almost as soon as Kraków was liberated, several well-known prewar scout leaders started to organize new scout troops there too. They did not inform the provisional government in Lublin. Why would they? They hadn't had to inform anybody of their activities before the war. By the end of 1946, the movement had 237,749 members, both young men and young women. Enthusiasm was high, as one scout remembered: 'scouting, in the first months after independence, exploded like a powerful bomb. Scouts and scout leaders appeared as if from nowhere. Every night, campfires burned and scouting songs were sung in uncounted courtyards. Young people were extraordinarily enthusiastic, full of energy.'[57] Another recalled a summer scouting camp he had attended in July 1946:

> I remember the charm and the special atmosphere of the traditional campfire at that camp – in unplanned, lively discussions, using simple words, people spoke of what they had lived through in recent years, of their future plans, of the meaning of life, friendship . . . and when, by the smouldering coals of the disappearing fire, we folded our hands in the traditional scouts' prayer, our faces were thoughtful, serious, but glowing with happiness . . .[58]

To begin with, the Polish scouts set out to be apolitical. In this moment of national rebuilding, they wanted only to be useful. One former girl scout remembered working in orphanages during the week, while at the weekends her scout troop travelled to the formerly German territories around the Mazurian lakes to help create school libraries, catalogue historic monuments, even to 'take part in the committee for language changes', which was then translating German place names and street names into Polish.[59] But signs of official disapproval appeared almost immediately. In late 1944 and early 1945, the Polish authorities in Lublin created a temporary 'scouting council' to oversee the movement's activities. Although the council included some prewar troop leaders, it immediately made a few subtle changes to the scouting oath, which now referred to the scout serving 'Democratic Poland' and left out 'service to God'. It also created an umbrella organization, the Union of Polish Scouting (Związek Harcerstwa Polskiego, or ZHP), under which, theoretically, all scout troops were supposed to fit. The point was to make the spontaneously forming groups subservient to the communist administration, and it didn't work.[60]

By the end of 1945, there was clear tension between the government officials who were trying to control and direct the movement (they wrote yet another version of the scouts' oath, one in which scouts would pledge to create 'a better world') and the grassroots scouting groups, not all of whom kept the Warsaw-dominated Union informed of their activities. A number of well-known Grey Ranks leaders had entered the movement's leadership, and although they also remained officially apolitical, there were some political incidents. In Bydgoszcz, scouts marching past the local secret police headquarters during a parade in 1945 were stunned to hear two shots fired from the window. Two scouts died. No one was ever sentenced for the murders.[61] At a 'youth rally' in Szczecin in 1946, a shouting match between scouts and young communists turned into an open brawl. At least two girl scouts were badly beaten.[62] Scouts across the country were arrested after taking part in demonstrations on 3 May, Poland's traditional constitution day.

At several points in 1947, Polish authorities considered shutting the scouting movement down altogether. They worried, however, that a ban would send thousands of young people into the arms of the underground, or into the woods with the partisans.[63] So they waited. And eventually, they adopted the tactic which, as noted, would become a standard tool in the Eastern European communist arsenal: they resolved to destroy the movement from within. The Hungarian communists made a similar decision about their own, equally problematic scouting movement at about the same time.

Like their Hungarian and German counterparts, the political Polish youth groups had been unified into a single organization, the Union of Polish Youth (Związek Młodzieży Polskiej, or ZMP) in February 1948. After that, it was the turn of the scouts. The Education Ministry launched a 'reorganization' of the national movement, unifying the male and female scouts, removing many older leaders and replacing them with younger, less experienced and more ideologically pliable leaders. These changes were done gradually. First someone at the top was replaced; then he or she appointed a new deputy; then the deputy appointed a new regional leader, and so on. The new national scouting leaders began, subtly, to change the scouts' activities. In addition to the traditional scouting activities – hiking, camping, survival skills – troops should now 'take part in the daily life of the country'. They were sent to plant trees, help lay telephone cables, and work in pre-schools. They were directed to become, as one bureaucrat put it, a younger version of the 'Polish Service' (Służba Polska), the unskilled work brigades which at that time travelled from one construction site to the next. Some were even delegated to factories or workshops to learn a trade.[64]

The scouts ceased to be a cross-generational organization. Whereas, in the past, Polish scouting troops had included men and women in their late teens and twenties, scouts aged sixteen and older were now 'promoted' to the Union of Polish Youth, making scouting an activity for children. Organizationally and financially, the scouts eventually became a sub-division of the Union of Polish Youth rather than a separate organization. As such their main task was the political education of children. In practice, they began to look and act like Soviet Pioneers, the junior youth organization. They even wore similar white shirts and red ties.[65] In 1950, the scouting oath was changed for a third time. The new version now had the scouts swear an oath to People's Poland, and promise to promote 'peace and the freedom of nations'.

The scouts themselves understood what was happening. As one scout leader later remembered, 'Each month, new people began gradually infiltrating the scouting movement. There was one, Kosiński, said to be a scout leader. He was as much a scout leader as I am a ballet dancer. He was a [secret police] officer. An awful man.'[66] Those who cared gradually left the movement, drifting away to other activities. Those too young to remember how the organization had once looked weren't going to complain, and their parents, wanting their children to conform and not get into trouble, said nothing.

Those who wanted to form alternatives could pay a high price.[67]

A few scouting troops went underground and got hold of guns – still plentiful enough at that time – and began training themselves to fight. The secret police uncovered one such group in the town of Krotoszyn in 1947. The group had called itself Zawisza, a name with allusions to chivalry. Its leader, aged eighteen, committed suicide at the moment of arrest. The other members, some as young as fifteen, were arrested and sentenced. Another group of former scouts was 'liquidated' in Radzyminsk, also in 1947. The secret police sent their Polish Scouting Association membership cards to the Minister of Education as a kind of warning: this is what could happen if young people were not strictly, carefully and energetically controlled.[68] But unarmed objectors could face severe punishment too. In 1950, a seventeen-year-old Polish girl from Lublin decided to ask the members of her old scouting group to meet informally, just to discuss things not discussed in school. She and her seven friends were arrested in 1951, and all received sentences of two to five years: anything which looked like an authentic scouting troop had to be destroyed so that the ersatz scouts could take over.[69]

If anything, the Hungarian People's College movement presented an even more complex challenge to the Hungarian communists than the scouting movement did to their Polish colleagues. Whereas scouting was associated with prewar patriotism and the 'reactionary' (i.e. centrist) wing of the political spectrum, the People's Colleges were an explicitly populist, left-wing project. The original People's Colleges had been founded before the war by a group of romantic, reform-minded poets and writers. Designed to educate the children of peasants, the colleges were intended to function as schools, clubs, and living spaces in cities for students from the countryside. They were not ordinary schools, but rather had something of the spirit of the kibbutz about them, emphasizing communal living, democratic group decision-making, folk dancing and singing. But although they had strong socialist leanings, and although a number of their leading members joined the communist party during the war, they weren't Soviet or party institutions.

After the war, the founders of Györffy College, the first People's College to restart its programme in June 1945, were under the impression that they could carry on in the same spirit. In December 1944, some of the prewar students and teachers began meeting regularly at an old German language school in the liberated part of Budapest, and they began planning a new curriculum right away. The provisional government encouraged this enthusiasm and as soon as it could gave Györffy a new building, a garden with fruit trees and a vacation house on Lake Balaton. But Györffy's leaders intended to remain independent. At a conference held to mark the opening, the college's prewar leader, Lajos Horváth, called upon those assembled, many of whom were already communist party members, to 'fight for the autonomy of the college, and protect it from the party and the state as well'. In the months that followed, he and others helped to found Nékosz, the National Association of People's Colleges, which would eventually build dozens of similar institutions around the country.[70]

In fact, Nékosz's 'autonomy' was doomed from the start, for neither Györffy nor the other colleges had any independent means of financing themselves. Their buildings came from the government – castles, old garrison buildings, confiscated villas – and their students existed on government subsidies.[71] State influence came with state money, and the communist leadership had different goals from the leaders of the People's Colleges. At first, the conflict was hidden. Leading communists were publicly supportive of the college movement. Both Rajk, the Interior Minister, and Révai, the Culture Minister, gave regular lectures at the colleges, and Rajk helped found the Petőfi College in Budapest. The first generation of students were ecstatic simply to be there. Miklós Jancsó, a Nékosz graduate who became a film director (one of several People's College alumni to enter the movie business), portrayed the passion and zeal of the People's College movement in his 1968 film Bright Winds (Fényes Szelek), the title of which comes from the Nékosz anthem:

> Hey, our banner blows in the bright winds! Hey, on it is written, Let Freedom Live!
> Hey winds, blow! Bright winds, blow, for tomorrow we will change the entire world![72]

Afterwards, Jancsó was asked by a group of university students why he had written so much music into the script, the first half of which contains more singing than dialogue. He replied that this was pure realism: 'At that time, after the war, it was very common for young people to sing together on the streets.' Iván Vitányi, another People's College alumnus, also remembered that 'sons and daughters of the peasantry, we were singing all day long'.[73]

The enthusiasm came in part from the sense of opportunity experienced by these first students, for the colleges offered education to people who'd never had any before. Some were the first in their families who could properly read and write. By March 1948, the 158 People's Colleges contained 8298 people, of whom 35–40 per cent came from rural or peasant backgrounds and 18–25 per cent were working class. The majority were men, but some women graduates later became very prominent, including a handful of actresses. Some offered high-school education, some offered teaching certificates, some could provide higher education. The curriculum was often left wing but not necessarily Marxist. In its first year, Györffy College organized seminars on the revolutions of 1848 and the history of music; lessons in English, French and German as well as Russian; opportunities to study 'Hungarian realism' and the history of Hungarian industry. The students received free theatre tickets and were encouraged to use them, and they were given lists of books they were expected to read in their free time.[74] One of the other colleges, the Vasvari Academy, encouraged its students to study abroad for half a year.[75]

Left to themselves, the People's Colleges would have been content to produce a new generation of progressive intelligentsia. But the Hungarian communist party had a narrower goal. They saw that the colleges might help solve two of their most pressing problems: deep unpopularity in the countryside, and a lack of rural party members. In February 1945, Gerő wrote a note to Rákosi, pointing out that Hungary had a 'shortage of cadres, especially of leaders'. More to the point, 'the biggest problem is that many of them are of Jewish origin'. Although, as noted, Gerő and Rákosi were themselves Jewish, both feared that the Hungarian peasants would oppose the communist party if it was 'too Jewish'. The People's Colleges seemed to provide an answer: they could train peasants to become 'folk' communists – 'folk' being a kind of euphemism for 'non-Jewish' – and thus 'Hungarianize' the communist party.[76]

The transformation of the colleges began at first within the leadership, which from the beginning contained a handful of communists. They now set out to take control. András Hegedüs, a People's College student who had also been a founder of Madisz, the communist-backed youth movement, admitted in an interview years later that the communist cell at Györffy College was 'rather militant' and 'to a certain degree' it 'terrorized the rest of the group'. Another student, also a party member, agreed that it was a 'general law that an organized small group could impose its will on a larger heterogeneous group'.[77] Within the colleges, communists slowly took over the democratic self-government mechanisms. From this position of influence they brought in a more political element to student life. They organized students to work as advocates for land reform and cooperative production in the countryside, and to participate in mass communist party rallies which preceded the 1945 and 1947 elections. They also influenced the curriculum so that it more closely followed the communist party line. In 1946, the entry questionnaire for Györffy College required applicants to answer some distinctly biased questions: 'In your village, are churchgoers better people than those who don't go to church? Can you describe a reactionary priest? Are young people in your village religious?'[78] Sessions of criticism and self-criticism eventually dominated the evening meetings and colloquia within the colleges. During this same period, the leader of Györffy, László Kardos, who was given to using communist clichés – he spoke of 'having friendly relationships with democratic youth of the world' – began to play a much more dominant role in what had previously been a loose, almost anarchic, non-hierarchical institution.[79] But the change most bitterly remembered by nostalgic ex-students was the press attacks, which became increasingly bitter – students were accused of insufficient loyalty, unprofessionalism and, ironically, anti-semitism – as well as the internal students' 'courts', which began to expel those who failed to meet the ever more drastic standards of political correctness. All of the students were told to stay alert for ideological errors in themselves and others, and to search for evidence of 'peasant romanticism', which was now considered a bad thing, as well as petit-bourgois decadence'. Alajos Kovács, a teacher in one of the colleges at the time, remembered that 'we were shocked, we did not even know why they were attacking us, we could not understand what had happened. Because of this incomprehension, we began to try – in a masochist, self-defeating way – to understand what had gone wrong, what we had done wrong.'[80] One of these 'trials' forms the dramatic conclusion to the film *Bright Winds*.

The idealists might eventually have fought back, and there were numerous struggles for power throughout the larger Nékosz organization. But in 1949 the regime would run out of patience. The colleges were abruptly and decisively nationalized, on the grounds that they needed to become more 'professional'. They were absorbed into the rest of the state university system, the buildings were adopted by other institutions, the special reading lists and theatre trips were abandoned and the idealistic self-governing mechanisms, which had largely ceased to function in any case, were dissolved. The decision was justified by reference to Marxist theory. As Rákosi put it, 'I learned all about socialism from the famous old books. I learned about mass organizations, youth associations, women's organizations, trade unions . . . There is not a single word about People's Colleges in those books, and I don't think they are necessary.'[81]

In other words, the People's Colleges were an institution unknown to Marx, Lenin and Stalin, and nothing like them existed in the Soviet Union. And so they were destroyed, along with so many other groups which Marx, Lenin and Stalin had never mentioned. In the end, the fate of the Polish scouts, the Hungarian People's Colleges, the German Christian Democratic youth and a vast range of other institutions – mainstream and idiosyncratic, political and apolitical, from shooting clubs and fencing teams to folk dance troupes and Catholic charities – was the same. The nascent totalitarian states could not tolerate any competition whatsoever for their citizens' passions, talents and free time.

8

Radio

'One winter day, I stupidly wrote in the text of the script, 'There is a cold atmospheric front approaching us from Russia.' The broadcaster read it aloud ... in the morning they phoned me: 'Go and see the director.' I went to see the director, and was ushered in right away. 'Zalewski,' he told me, 'I thought you were more intelligent. From now on, remember that only warm, good things come from the East.' It didn't seem funny at the time ...'

Andrzej Zalewski, former Polish radio employee[1]

'*Hier Spricht Berlin.*'

'Here speaks Berlin.'

With those words, Berlin radios came back to life. It was 13 May 1945. They had been silent for nearly two weeks, since Admiral Doenitz had announced the death of Adolf Hitler on 1 May. Now the German capitulation was complete and the Soviet Military Administration had taken over the Reichsrundfunk radio building in Masurenallee, in the western half of the city. The building, which had been specially designed for radio broadcasting and had one of the most modern recording studios in Europe, had been saved from destruction by its location outside the centre and, more importantly, by the Red Army's deliberate protection. Even as the rest of Berlin lay in ruins, most of what had been Grossdeutsche Rundfunk's equipment was still intact, and many of the radio station's staff were still alive.[2] In that sense, the radio station was almost unique among Berlin institutions.

That first broadcast was only an hour long. It began with the Soviet, American, British and French national anthems, followed by an address from Marshal Stalin. Listeners then heard the terms of the unconditional surrender read aloud, along with statements from Churchill, Roosevelt, and Stalin again. News from around the world came next – including information on Himmler's arrest and plans for war crimes trials – interspersed with Soviet military music. The final part of the broadcast reported on the victory celebrations in Moscow:

> '... Millions of Muscovites held their breath and rushed out towards the loudspeakers. When the first melodious bars of the radio station began, more and more came to Red Square, to the Kremlin, and waited for the big news in front of Lenin's mausoleum. When they finally heard that Hitler's Germany had unconditionally surrendered, the celebration began ... A happy, melodious voice shouted, 'Three cheers for the Great Stalin!' This shouting extended across the whole square ...'[3]

Radio was important to Muscovites, listening in their dark apartments. The Red Army assumed, correctly, that it would be important to Germans listening in their dark apartments too. From the moment of their arrival, the Soviet occupiers invested heavily in programming and equipment for the new radio station, and in the days that followed the first broadcast, the new Berlin radio station expanded its repertoire with startling speed. On 18 May, the orchestra of the Deutsche Oper played Beethoven (representing German music) and Tchaikovskii (representing Russia) in one of its large recording studios. Two days later, Deutschland Rundfunk again broadcast Beethoven and Tchaikovskii, as well as Strauss and Borodin.[4] On 23 May, the radio broadcast its first children's programme.[5] Listeners could hear periodic news bulletins as well.

All of this activity was supervised by a group of Soviet officers who administered the new station and functioned as its first censors as well. They controlled in turn a group of Germans, including at least three members of the Ulbricht Group: Hans Mahle, a longtime communist who would later found East German television; Matthäus Klein, a Wehrmacht officer who had been 'converted' in the Soviet re-education camps for German soldiers; and, in a junior capacity, Wolfgang Leonhard, then aged twenty-four. They were soon joined by the 22-year-old Markus Wolf, Leonhard's Comintern school colleague and East Germany's future spy master.

Like the secret policemen of Eastern Europe, the 'new' German radio station already had a history in 1945. Though the Russians had not expected to have such an excellent facility immediately available, they had certainly thought to train some of the new radio broadcasters in advance. Both Klein and Mahle had been working for some years in tandem with political propaganda officers of the Red Army, from whose ranks many of the first Soviet cultural officers in Germany would later be drawn. As early as 1941 German-speaking Soviet officers and German communists jointly compiled leaflets which they dropped from aeroplanes over German lines. In November of that year, they also began to publish several newspapers aimed directly at German POWs.

After the battle of Stalingrad, in July 1943, the German communists in Moscow founded the National Committee for a Free Germany. They were joined by several POWs who had converted to the Soviet cause. Together, the two groups published a newspaper – edited by Rudolf Herrnstadt, later a prominent East German editor – which they delivered to German territories conquered by the Red Army, as well as POW camps. They also began active radio broadcasting. At different times different German-language stations transmitted news out of Moscow as well as constant invitations to German troops to lay down their arms and overthrow Hitler. Mahle worked on a number of these stations, including some which pretended to be Nazi stations in order to broadcast disinformation.[6] Wolf became an announcer and commentator, a job which brought him into close contact with Ulbricht. His wife Emmi – the woman who had once forced Leonhard into a humiliating public confession – walked up and down battlefields with a megaphone, shouting at German soldiers to lay down their arms.[7]

Though the National Committee was a Soviet front organization, its leaders were very careful not to appear 'too communist', particularly in 1943 and the first half of 1944 when they still hoped a *putsch* would overthrow Hitler. As noted, its members adopted the black, white and red flag of imperial Germany instead of the colours of the Weimar Republic or the USSR. A separate 'League of German Officers' was also created to work alongside the committee in order to encourage the participation of former Wehrmacht officers who might be squeamish about working directly with German communists.[8]

Something of this calculating spirit also infected the new Berlin radio station in the spring of 1945. Klein and Mahle had met many of the POWs, and they knew most Germans would be allergic to anything that seemed too radical or too Soviet. Superficially, they maintained much that was familiar about German radio, including its somewhat ponderous style and its heavy diet of serious culture and classical music. They retained the Nazi-era production staff and even many of the broadcasters, eliminating only those associated with the fiercest Nazi propaganda. As Wolf wrote to his parents in June, 'there are six of our men and one officer, and 600 of "them" ... sifting out the chaff is possible only to a small degree, since many, really most, are needed'.[9] Still, there was never any question about the station's fundamental political orientation. Nor did any of its leaders doubt that their political views would eventually triumph. Mahle understood that his job was to provide a 'mirror' for the masses in an interim period, while they were developing a 'democratic self-understanding'. During this process, there would be 'divergent voices' and open debates, and of course the media must express them: 'by publicly carrying out this dispute, the consciousness of the masses will be formed and their democratic self-consciousness will be strengthened'.[10]

Not all media, in this early period, followed such clear guidelines, and newspapers in particular provided many different viewpoints. In September 1945 Der Tagesspiegel, an economically liberal newspaper, began publishing in Berlin under American auspices, but it remained freely available throughout the city until 1948, as did the conservative Die Welt, which began publication in the British zone of West Germany in 1946. Even within the Soviet zone, all of the legal political parties – the social democrats, Christian democrats and liberal democrats – were at first allowed to publish their own newspapers on condition that they accept a certain amount of Soviet material.[11] These newspapers and others would provide real competition for the most important Soviet-sponsored newspapers, the Tägliche Rundschau, the voice of the Red Army in Berlin, and the Berliner Zeitung, jointly run by Herrnstadt and a Soviet colonel.[12] Later, the independent papers would run into trouble. Neue Zeit, the Christian Democratic paper, would be punished for political incorrectness by a reduction in its circulation (the authorities controlled all of the paper). Das Volk, the social democrats' paper, would be merged with the communist party's newspaper, *Deutsche Volkszeitung*, and transformed into *Neues Deutschland*, the official organ of the East German communist party from 1946 until its demise – and also edited, initially, by Herrnstadt.

But the radio was always different. Even if its biases were subtle and its attitude towards 'divergent views' more indulgent than would be the case later on, East German radio was a pro-communist and pro-Soviet monopoly from the very beginning. In later years, Mahle would recall that 'the Central Committee's understanding was that radio must play a direct, operative and organizational role in the transformation of life in Germany', and in 1945 and 1946 radio was certainly the most accessible form of media.[13] Workers, peasants and people of all kinds listened to it, particularly in a period of paper shortages and distribution glitches, and the communists intended to use it to their advantage.

Initially, they succeeded. In Berlin, the radio immediately had a special status as the only seemingly 'German' authority in the city – anyway the only public voice that clearly spoke in German – and indeed in the country as a whole. So high did the radio rank in the public's esteem that Germans wrote thousands of letters to the station in its first years of existence, asking about everything from Russian foreign policy to the price of potatoes. Some wanted more classical music, others asked for less. There were compliments – one writer liked a programme on Hölderlein, another a programme on fairy tales – but complaints as well. Indeed, these missives – which often began with the salutation 'Dear Radio' – could be brutally frank. Dozens demanded to know when their sons, husbands and brothers would be returning home from prison camps in the USSR. After a programme on that very subject, dozens more complained that the radio had presented an overly rosy portrait of those prisoners, most of whom 'come back from Russia miserable and sick'.[14]

Following Soviet practice, the station kept close track of all of these letters, counting how many were devoted to particular subjects (232 concerned food shortages in July 1947, for example) and carefully measuring whether the numbers of 'negative' letters was rising or falling.[15] At least in its first two years of existence, it tried hard to answer its listeners' most urgent concerns, and to convince them that the communist-led future would be better.

Perhaps the best-known attempt to soft-sell communism to the listening masses was Markus Wolf's signature programme, 'You Ask, We Answer'. For several months, starting in 1945, Wolf provided on-air answers to letters sent in by German listeners. Although the questions he received covered a huge range of subjects, and although they often required factual answers ('What is to become of the Berlin Zoo?'), he almost always supplied an ideological twist as well, just as he had learned to do in the Comintern school in Ufa. During the 7 June broadcast, for example, he responded enthusiastically to a listener who wrote in to say how impressed he was by the energy and spirit of the Red Army, particularly as 'we've always been taught that in Russia, those who achieve are not valued'. Wolf declared that 'all of those who believe the fairy tale about levelling down in the USSR have fallen victim to Goebbels' propaganda', and praised the Soviet system, which welcomed the 'creativity of the worker'.

Another listener wanted to know what, other than rationed food, would soon be available to eat in Germany. Wolf first reminded her that 'we are not going hungry' – the Germans should on that point feel themselves lucky – then noted that 'difficulties are being overcome with the help of the Red Army', and finally assured her that the 'nutrition department of the city council is doing its utmost to import vegetables, salad and so on, to Berlin'. He even used the question about the zoo to remind listeners of how much things had deteriorated during Hitler's final days, before promising them that better days were coming: the zoo still had 92 animals, including 'an elephant, 18 monkeys, 2 hyenas, 2 young lions, a rhino, 4 exotic bulls and 7 raccoons'.[16]

Wolf's answers rarely praised communism outright, and he didn't use Marxist language. But almost all of them praised the Red Army or the Soviet system, both of which were favourably compared to their German counterparts. And all of them explicitly contained the promise that life, which had become unbearable under the Nazis and during the final days of the war, would now quickly improve.

Other programmes took a similar tack. Late in 1945, one broadcaster visited Saxony to investigate the status of 'youth' in that region, and found many heartening developments. Several former Hitler Youth members told him they were 'delighted not to have to salute their leaders'. All professed to be thankful that the war had ended. Schools had not yet reopened and there were many hardships, but the reporter predicted 'a free and beautiful future for our youth'. The word 'communism' was not mentioned.[17] Yet another reporter visited Sachsenhausen, and produced a genuinely harrowing account of the final days at the camp. Though the Red Army was thanked profusely at the end, there was nothing especially ideological about that broadcast either.[18]

But as time went on, the station's tone changed. Following the Berlin municipal elections of 1946 – which provided the first great blow to the East German communist party – the propaganda became more strident, the announcers' communist affiliations more obvious. This change was immediately picked up by listeners, and reflected in the letters. 'Dear Radio,' wrote a listener in 1947, 'you have slowly started to become boring. Your evening programmes are starting to repeat themselves.' Another complained about the stridency of the language: 'One would think one had tuned into Radio Moscow.'

In part, the new tone was inspired by the Soviet officers who worked alongside the radio staff. Until 1949 they went on reading (and censoring) pre-prepared texts before they were broadcast, and they remained deeply involved in the finances of the radio, which in the early days they heavily subsidized. In 1945 and 1946 the radio consulted Soviet officials about hiring decisions, spending decisions, and the coordination of news policy with newspapers.[19] There was no secret about any of this involvement: on ceremonial occasions, Mahle paid official obeisance to his Soviet colleagues. It was, he said at a reception they hosted for the radio, 'an honour to thank them, especially Marshal Zhukov'. He also reminded his hosts that the radio was 'the largest cultural institution in the Soviet zone' and urged them to stay as closely involved as possible: the radio 'needs frequent meetings with its friends and powerful sponsors'.[20]

But the communist party's unpopularity among Germans in general, and Berliners in particular, would eventually give Mahle and his German colleagues reasons to worry. By 1946, the radio station would find itself in direct competition with Radio in the American Sector (Rundfunk im amerikanischen Sektor, or RIAS), which had livelier news programmes and, more importantly, better music. As the station sensed itself losing out in the competition with Western radio, and as East German communists began to recognize that living conditions were improving more rapidly in the Western zones of Germany, the radio's managers began an internal argument which would last for many years: how to win over the masses?

Some worried that the station was too elitist, that it was losing its connection to the party and that it had too little understanding of what 'the masses' really wanted to hear. 'We demand of the masses that they listen to us,' one radio party member declared during an internal discussion, 'but do we listen to them?' The radio should be a 'megaphone for the people', he declared. Many agreed that there should be more 'ordinary' voices on the radio, and far fewer party speeches. They also knew that the letter writers thought they were boring – and they feared it was true. In a 1948 discussion of how to promote the party's first 'Two Year Plan', some broadcasters argued that a simple broadcast of Ulbricht's speech on the matter wasn't enough: 'In order for listeners not to get bored, the radio must find ways to tell readers about the plan in a lively way.' The best reporters were to be commissioned, and they were to go out and interview people about how the plan would be put into practice. In a later discussion of theatrical performances, radio commissioners agreed that 'writers must be able to create lively and genuine scenes from material that is often very dry', and must learn to combine artistic technique with ideology: 'it's the special task of radio to train more and more such writers'.[21]

Others did not agree. As the communist party's unpopularity deepened, some at the radio, in the party and in particular in the Soviet headquarters at Karlshorst began to put forth another view. Russian cultural officers observed that the combination of ideology and culture didn't always work: during one organized 'culture week', they pointed out, people came to hear the music, but ignored the lectures.[22] They grew suspicious that attempts to lighten ideology would simply water it down. Others felt those long broadcasts of long speeches, however boring, had to stay in the radio's repertoire. Otherwise how could the people get to know their leaders? Their conclusion: there should be more ideology, not less – on the radio and everywhere else.

There was no Soviet occupation of the radio station in Poland, because in Poland there were no radio stations to occupy. By the end of the war there was almost no broadcasting equipment remaining in the entire country, since most of it had been confiscated by the Nazi occupiers. Polish radio went off the air in September 1939, to the sound of Chopin's *Nocturne in C Sharp Minor*, played by Władysław Szpilman, author of *The Pianist*. Transmissions began again, briefly, on 8 August 1944, following the outbreak of the Warsaw Uprising. For two months, the Home Army's Radio Błyskawice – 'Radio Lightning' – heroically issued four radio bulletins every day, covering military events as well as literature and culture. But it fell silent in the first week of October, when the Home Army capitulated.

Radio returned to Poland for good under Soviet auspices, and with the assistance of Soviet soldiers. Radio Pszczółka – 'Radio Honeybee' – began transmitting on Soviet equipment from a train wagon near Lublin on 11 August 1944, and advanced into the city with the Red Army. Once in Lublin, the radio station set itself up in a private apartment on Chopin Street. The 'studio' was placed in the sitting room, while another room doubled as a reception room and, in the evenings, the announcers' bedrooms. The first broadcasts – all live – consisted of military communiqués and situation updates, mostly intended for field commanders and partisans who might be expected to have radios. In liberated Lublin, Rzeszów and Białystok, the radio station employees also established *radiowęzły* – outdoor loudspeaker systems – so that people could gather in town squares and public places to listen to the broadcasts several times daily. At that point the radio began to add live music played by the many artistic refugees who found their way to the city after the failure of the Warsaw Uprising.[23]

As in Germany, some of these first Polish radio operators were communists. They weren't as prominent or as well-known to the Russians as those who would run the new radio in Berlin, but then prominent and trusted Polish communists were thin on the ground. The first director of Polish radio, Wilhelm Billig, was a prewar party member and a working engineer. Later, he became head of the Polish nuclear research agency (and much later he assisted the anti-communist Solidarity movement).[24] All of the first radio news broadcasts were written by propaganda officials of the Lublin provisional government, and then passed to the radio to be read out.

Some of these first employees found their way to the radio by accident. Stefania Grodzieńska, later a well-known actress and writer, saw a microphone for the first time in her life on 2 September 1944, and became an announcer for Polish radio on 3 September. In her memoirs, she describes the first, distinctly improvised, weeks of the Lublin radio station:

> On Chopin Street, aside from the announcers, there were a few technicians. The most popular of them was a Mr Nierobiec who lived in a village outside of Lublin and travelled in for work. He owed his fame to the large jug he brought with him, which was filled with moonshine. Around the neck of the jug hung a notebook with a pen, as well as a mug. Anyone who wanted a drink wrote his name and the quantity in the notebook – for example, 'Sikirycki – half a mug.' On payday Nierobiec stood with his notebook next to the cashier and took our contributions.[25]

As communist-era accounts had it, the months which followed were a heroic era for Polish radio. 'As the country was liberated,' one later report declared, 'Polish radio technicians followed right behind the front line, trying to save whatever radio equipment remained', bravely rebuilding transmitters and cooperating happily with the Red Army. At the end of 1945, Billig would publicly declare that the radio had succeeded thanks only to the 'noble and disinterested help of the Soviet Union'.

Billig was correct in his account of the speed of the reconstruction. Within three years, Polish radio technicians had built twelve stations and ten transmitters. He was also right to thank the Soviet Union, up to a point. During the course of 1945, Soviet money paid for a transmitter in Raszyn, a Warsaw suburb, which could transmit to the entire nation, and Soviet technicians came to help in its construction. According to Billig, Stalin personally approved the construction of the Raszyn transmitter, and there is no reason to doubt him, or to doubt that the Soviet Union wanted to rebuild Polish radio. But on the ground, the Red Army often seemed to have more ambivalent instructions as well. In theory the Soviet Union may have wanted to encourage 'communist' radio, but on the ground the NKVD also feared Poles might create rival Home Army radio stations, or perhaps that they might rig their radios to receive 'enemy' signals from London.

Though in principle committed to rebuilding Polish radio, Soviet officers were thus in practice suspicious of anyone who tried to build or reclaim transmission equipment. A letter to the central radio office from the Silesian city of Zabrze in June 1945, complained that the former employees of the radio station had been forbidden to transmit by the local Soviet commander. The writer was diplomatic about it: 'we believe this is the result of a misunderstanding and the matter will be resolved positively on the basis of Polish–Soviet friendship'. When local authorities tried to set up a radio station in Gliwice at about the same time, Soviet troops actually threatened them with guns. Authorities in Lower Silesia also had trouble persuading Soviet commanders to hand over radios and transmission devices. When they managed to obtain some equipment it was quickly confiscated by the Polish secret police.[26]

In the very early days, Soviet authorities treated even the redistribution of the radio sets confiscated by the Germans with caution. In August 1944 – just as Radio 'Honeybee' was starting its work – Red Army commanders issued an order commanding all Poles on liberated territory to surrender any radio transmitting or receiving equipment in their possession, 'regardless of its type and usage', and to hand it in to the Polish National Liberation Committee. Anyone who violated these commands would be treated as an 'enemy agent'.[27] A few months later, the Committee issued a more drastic version of that order: from 30 October, Bierut declared, anyone who owned a radio without a licence could be sentenced to death. At least one such sentence was carried out. On 1 May 1945, Stanisław Marinczenko of Poznań was executed for illegal possession of a 'Phillips' radio.[28]

Attitudes to newspapers, periodicals and publishing at this time were also uneven. In theory, the provisional government supported freedom of the press. All legal political parties were allowed to have their own newspapers – the communist party began to publish its paper, eventually to be called *Trybuna Ludu* (*People's Tribune*), in

1944 but there were several others. Throughout 1944 the Home Army and other resistance groups were also publishing dozens of small papers and periodicals, and one or two newspapers emerged thanks to the initiative of journalists, most notably *Życie Warszawy* (*Warsaw Life*). But paper was extremely scarce – 70 per cent of all paper mills had been destroyed, and they were producing one fifth of their prewar output – and by December of that year, thanks to nationalization of the remaining mills, most of the newsprint was under government control and most publishing was in the hands of a single company, Czytelnik.[29] A bill limiting private ownership in the printing industry had been passed by June 1945, and by 1946 newspapers unfavourable to the regime would have trouble getting hold of newsprint. Still, *Gazeta Ludowa*, the *People's Paper*, the most outspoken of the legal papers and the organ of the most outspoken political party, the Peasants' Party, continued bravely to publish open criticism of the government. Officials responsible for propaganda didn't necessarily control the party press either: some communist journalists reckoned they didn't have to listen to the propaganda bureaucrats because they were ranked higher in the party hierarchy, so even the party newspapers didn't always toe the line.[30]

Polish radio was not so bold, though it was initially not so professional either. Throughout 1945, the war dominated not only news programmes but everything else as well. Broadcasters reminisced about their experiences, got other people to do so, and read out long lists of lost family members on the air. Some told war stories for children. A broadcast on 2 February warned inhabitants of Warsaw to keep the wartime curfew, as the 'Hitlerite barbarians' had not yet surrendered, even though the frontline had moved west. Other common themes were the reconstruction of factories and schools, as well as the welcoming back of soldiers from abroad.[31]

The radio, like all other new state institutions in Poland at the time, also served other functions besides those it was meant to serve. The studios in Bydgoszcz in June 1945 had almost no equipment and produced very little programming, for example, but employed a cook who made lunch for 100 people every day.[32] Radio bosses from around the country constantly sent in pleas for more funding, especially on behalf of musicians, many of whom were starving. The list of the illnesses suffered by radio employees included tuberculosis, rheumatism, eye diseases and skin trouble, according to the letters they wrote to Warsaw.[33]

But just as the crowds cheered the first appearance of the Warsaw trams, the return of Polish radio was cheered as a sign of national revival, and it soon became a magnet for artistic talent. In his first live performance, Władysław Szpilman played, with great emotion, Chopin's *Nocturne in C Sharp Minor*, the same piece he had played just before the radio went off the air in 1939. Despite having lost his entire family in Treblinka and the Warsaw ghetto, Szpilman kept on composing music. He continued to work for the radio until 1963.[34]

Even as the radio portrayed itself as the voice of the whole nation, internal pressure to conform to Warsaw's ever harsher and ever narrower political views increased. After the Bydgoszcz radio station failed to transmit reports of Soviet victory celebrations on 9 May, the station chief felt obliged to defend himself. In a letter to Billig, he explained that his equipment was 'primitive, second-hand' and that it simply didn't function on that day. But the local Soviet military commander and the local secret police didn't buy that story. They claimed the transmission didn't happen because of 'disloyal technical personnel', and they sent a Soviet technician from Raszyn to investigate.[35] That kind of pressure, coupled with the general threat of violence, helps explain why the tone of the Polish broadcasts became distinctly more favourable to the new regime as the year wore on. There were material advantages available to those who cooperated as well – canteens and health care – whereas those who defied the Warsaw bosses lost their jobs and the ration cards which went with them.

If they hadn't been communists to start with, many broadcasters had at least learned to use communist language by the end of the year. The same Bydgoszcz radio boss who had defended himself against charges of disloyalty on 9 May wrote a letter a month later, explaining that he now met with the new 'propaganda' department of the local government at least three times a week. In September, he asked for (and was granted) a car and a megaphone. That would enable radio workers to travel to places their signal didn't reach: they could communicate by shouting slogans through the megaphone.[36] In the

autumn, the radio station in Katowice assured Warsaw it was producing more programmes oriented towards 'the world of work' and the
working class. At about the same time, broadcasters in Warsaw began
planning programmes celebrating the October Revolution and tout-
ing the advantages of central planning. In November, when the radio's
central authorities met to plan their future broadcasts, one executive
argued that they ought to produce more programmes praising the role
of the political police and militia: 'from the press we learn of more
and more acts of theft and murder from "bands" . . . the victims are
usually democratic activists, the people whom Poland needs most'.

At the same meeting, broadcasters discussed the forthcoming congress of the Peasants' Party, the one remaining independent force in
Polish politics at that time. Most thought information about the congress should be transmitted, but some felt that 'in our attitude to the
Peasants' Party we must be cautious' since it wasn't yet clear whether
the party had 'liberated itself from negative elements and joined the
democratic camp'. At that time, the Peasants' Party was still legal. But
that didn't, in the broadcasters' view, give it the automatic right to
transmit its message over the radio.

By the end of the year, the radio's tasks were clear, at least to its top
executives. In a speech he gave to his employees in December 1945 –
the same one in which he spoke of the 'noble and disinterested' help
of the USSR – Billig set out his vision for the radio's future. He spoke
of the need for more radio sets – 'we want the radio to be heard by
peasants, workers, the working intelligentsia' – and explained that
two new factories would produce some 15,000 in the coming year. He
pushed aside complaints that there was too much 'talk' on Polish
radio. Whereas prewar radio had focused on the mere entertainment
of the elite, he told his co-workers that the new radio could play 'a
colossal role as a propagandist. It's an amazing weapon.' And it was a
weapon which could reach everybody.

Radio, Billig explained, could help 'create the new type of person
which is coming to life in Poland . . . the main goal of radio is the
mobilization of society to carry out the basic task which history has
put in front of us: the reconstruction of the country, the strengthening
of democracy, the unification of the nation'.[37] During the years which

followed that speech, Polish radio would work hard to make sure that the nation defined those words – reconstruction, democracy, unification – in the same way as the communist party.

East German radio began with Moscow-trained communists. Polish radio began with Soviet equipment. Hungarian radio began with a decree, written in Russian and published by the provisional Budapest government on 20 January 1945, the second day of its existence. The decree re-established the Hungarian Press Agency as well as Magyar Radio, the national radio broadcaster. It named Gyula Ortutay director of both. Before he did anything else, Ortutay made his way to the radio's Budapest headquarters, which had been used as a stable during the final days of the war. The equipment was smashed, the rotting corpse of a dead horse lay on a side porch and a bomb crater scarred the courtyard. Ortutay taped a sign on the entrance of the wrecked building: 'Radio people: We will be waiting on the 21st for those who are still alive, in the shelter opposite the lift.'[38]

From the Soviet point of view, Ortutay was the ideal man for this task. A well-known ethnographer, literary critic and socialist intellectual who had worked for Magyar Radio before the war, Ortutay was also, as it happened, a secret member of the communist party, one of several who were then active in Hungarian politics. In public, Ortutay described himself as a member of the Smallholders' Party, one of the four parties which had been allowed to have a legal existence after the war, and throughout 1945 and 1946 he kept in close contact with leading Smallholder politicians. At the same time he privately took orders from the Hungarian communist leadership, which issued him with a party card under a false name at a secret ceremony in March 1945.

Ortutay's secret allegiances were known to Soviet commanders in Hungary, of course. Formally, the terms of the armistice gave the Allied Control Council responsibility for Hungarian media, and after the war's end this body allowed each of the legal political parties to set up a newspaper. The Hungarian communist party created its flagship, *Szabad Nép*, but the Social Democratic, Smallholders' and Peasants' parties were allowed to have their own newspapers too. Very quickly, *Kis Újság*, the Smallholders' Party paper, became the most popular in the country.[39] In Hungary, as everywhere else, the communists were more interested in radio, however, and Ortutay's presence guaranteed them extra influence over broadcasting. Very quickly, Hungarian radio would come to rely absolutely on Soviet equipment, transmitters and technicians, as well as on Soviet advisers. Soon it would reflect a distinctly Soviet worldview too.

None of this was immediately clear either to the general public or to the radio employees who read Ortutay's notice and returned to work. In the ruins of Budapest, they began planning the relaunch of Hungarian radio with tremendous energy. Conditions were difficult. Magyar Radio's day-to-day records note that, in May, 'Lajos Hernádi, pianist, asked for a seven-minute break due to the extreme cold in the studio.'[40] The initial 'wage' for radio workers was a daily cup of soup, but there were other advantages: they got an identity card, printed in both Russian and Hungarian, which could help the bearer avoid the street round-ups and waves of deportation.[41] Even so, it wasn't always easy to get to work in a city without public transport. Radio legend has it that on one morning, no one was in the building when the time came to start the day's broadcast. The cleaning lady put on a gramophone record and let it play until the others arrived.[42]

As in Poland and Germany, many of the technicians had worked at the station before the war – and others arrived by accident. Áron Tóbiás joined in the summer after high school in 1946, hoping to earn enough money to be able to go to college. His job consisted of selecting 'short stories of famous Hungarian writers to be read Sunday afternoon by actors', a task which seemed intensely glamorous to an eighteen-year-old. He never made it to university, and remained a radio journalist until 1955.[43] Still others were recruits. Among them was Gyula Schöpflin, a communist party member since the 1930s, who became the first programme director. In his memoirs – he defected from Hungary in 1949 – Schöpflin remembered that although Hungary was still in theory a multi-party democracy in 1945, Ortutay's personnel decisions were already influenced by his secret communist party membership: 'The hiring and firing of people had an entirely political character.' Ortutay also set political guidelines for programming: 'Avoid anything which could disturb the harmony and agreement between the great powers; beware of party politics; publicize, pro-mote anti-fascist international politics; promote the programme of the democratic government, reconstruction, land reform; always empha-size the Hungarian and international progressive traditions ...' Schöpflin himself visited the Hungarian party headquarters 'at least once a week', asking for 'guidelines, detailed party lines' for his broad-casts. He didn't get much help, mostly because the radio was already under the direct control of the Allied Control Council, and thus the Soviet Union. Hungarian communists didn't bother with it, as they assumed it was under Soviet control anyway.[44]

But if the Hungarian comrades didn't initially grasp the significance of the radio, the Soviet comrades did. Although they had banned the ownership of radios until the end of the war, they issued the new station with a licence, designated a Soviet officer as its permanent 'adviser' (and main censor) and allowed the station to get ready to broadcast.[45] By 1 May 1945, the radio was ready to go. At noon, loudspeakers placed strategically around Budapest played the new station signal – a few lines from a nineteenth-century anti-Habsburg revolutionary song – and the programme began. Each of the leaders of the four legal political parties spoke; news was read; music was played. A few major Hungarian musical works were performed – a Bartók piece, and then a Hungarian opera – followed by the Russian opera *Boris Godunov*. After that, the loudspeakers played a one-hour broadcast in Russian, for Soviet soldiers.[46]

Throughout most of 1945, radio broadcasts mostly kept within the boundaries set by Ortutay, judging from their topics – land reform, the Hungarian–Soviet friendship society, the founding of new trade unions, the war crimes trials and the history of the communist partisans – although the broadcasters were still reading aloud the works of 'bourgeois' – i.e. non-communist – writers, and playing familiar music.[47] Direct Soviet input presumably explains the preponderance of Russian-language programmes (e.g. 'We Learn to Sing in Russian'), and perhaps reflects the frustrations faced by the Red Army in occu-pying a country with such an impossible language. By the end of the year, the fledgling Hungarian secret police force had also established a presence at the station. Officers would periodically demand copies of transcripts with 'politically interesting' material. Secret police officers guarded the radio offices – another sign of radio's political significance – checking people who entered and left. Eventually, a separate secret police unit was sent to guard the technical department, allegedly because the engineers, many of whom had worked on the radio in the past, were politically untrustworthy.[48]

But most of the time, Magyar Radio's Soviet overseers relied on the intuition of the radio's communist employees to get the programming right. Even if they didn't have Comintern training, many had internalized the party line, and made judgements on that basis. At one point, for example, Rákosi ordered Schöpflin to broadcast live the trial of László Bárdossy, the wartime Hungarian Prime Minister who made the fatal decision to ally Hungary with Germany and to declare war on the Soviet Union. The trial took place a few days before the first Hungarian elections and was, as Schöpflin remembered it, a radio disaster: 'Bárdossy behaved as a gentleman, he answered bravely, with dignity and without emotions in response to the judge's erratic shouting . . . I was convinced that he was guilty but this attempt of ours to transform public opinion backfired.' Schöpflin – who was by no means the most doctrinaire of the Budapest comrades – stopped the live broadcast in the middle of the trial. Bárdossy was too appealing, and his words were too damaging to the communist cause. From then on, Schöpflin played only recorded excerpts from the trial.[49]

For a time, Ortutay managed to preserve at least the appearance of political diversity. Until 1945, Magyar Radio had been owned by a private holding company which produced news on the government's behalf. The same company also owned the press agency, an advertising agency, printing facilities and some small banks. After the war's end, its owners, who were linked in the public mind with the interwar Horthy regime, pushed hard to get their property back. They had some support from the Smallholders' Party, which wanted to compensate them, but which also argued that the majority of shares in the new station should belong to the government.

Ortutay fought against both ideas, and he won. By the end of the summer, the former owners were disenfranchised, their property was confiscated and the radio belonged entirely to a state-owned company called MKH Rt.[50] That company was run, in turn, not by the government – which at that time still contained a range of politicians –

but by a board composed of all major Hungarian political forces. There were two members each from each of the four legal parties – communist, socialist, Peasants' Party and Smallholders – as well as two members from the trade unions.

It looked even-handed, but in practice the two trade unionists were communists, so the communists had four board members. Many of the other delegates belonged to the far left wing of their respective parties, so they sided with the communists. Others were, like Ortutay, secretly affiliated with the communist party. By the beginning of 1946, only a year after the end of the war, the Hungarian communist party in practice controlled the personnel of the radio, the board of the radio and consequently the content of the radio, though neither the public nor the political class had been told that was the case. When the party decided a year later to tighten its ideological hold on the radio, nobody would be able to stop it.

9
Politics

The establishment of order in Europe and the rebuilding of national economic life must be achieved by processes which will enable the liberated peoples to destroy the last vestiges of Nazism and fascism, and to create democratic institutions of their own choice ... In these elections, all democratic and anti-Nazi parties shall have the right to take part and to put forward candidates.

Protocols of the Yalta treaty, 13 February 1945

'A shadow has fallen upon the scenes so lately lighted by the Allied victory ... The Communist parties, which were very small in all these Eastern States of Europe, have been raised to pre-eminence and power far beyond their numbers and are seeking everywhere to obtain totalitarian control.'

Winston Churchill, speaking in Fulton,
Missouri, 5 March 1946

Between the signing of the Yalta treaty, with its promise of free elections in Eastern Europe, and Winston Churchill's 'Iron Curtain' speech, which foretold the rise of totalitarianism, a year elapsed. During that year, a great many changes took place. The Red Army brought Moscow-trained secret policemen into every occupied country, put local communists in control of national radio stations and began dismantling youth groups and other civic organizations. They arrested, murdered and deported people whom they believed to be anti-Soviet and they brutally enforced a policy of ethnic cleansing.

These changes were no secret, and they had not been concealed from the outside world. The British Prime Minister himself used the phrase 'iron curtain' for the first time not in his famous Fulton speech but just as the war was ending in May 1945, only three months after Yalta. In a letter to Truman, Churchill wrote that 'an iron curtain is drawn down upon their front. We do not know what is going on behind.'[1] Churchill's love of grand language concealed the truth. He did know what was going on 'behind the iron curtain', because his Polish interlocutors had been telling him, much to his annoyance.

In fact, the warm relationship between the Anglo-Saxon powers and the Soviet Union had begun to break down much earlier. 'The alliance between ourselves and the democratic faction of the capitalists succeeds because the latter had an interest in preventing Hitler's domination,' Stalin told Dimitrov before the end of the war. '[I]n the future we shall be against this faction of the capitalists as well.' The tensions grew worse as the war drew to an end. Though the very first meeting of the American army and the Red Army on the river Elbe in April 1945 was an occasion of handshakes and celebrations, it was followed by petty arguments over where and to whom the Germans ought to surrender – in the end there were two ceremonies – and an abrupt American decision to end the Lend-Lease programme, which had been financing Soviet purchases of US goods during the war.[2] The first use of the atomic bomb in August set off another wave of Soviet paranoia. By the end of that month American and Russian soldiers were engaged in frequent night-time shoot-outs in Berlin.[3]

But events in Eastern Europe, and particularly in Poland, were the real trigger for the more profound mutual distrust which would soon become known as the Cold War. By the autumn of 1944, George Kennan had already concluded that those members of the Polish government-in-exile who continued to fight for democracy 'were, in my eyes, the doomed representatives of a doomed regime, but no one could be so brutal as to say this to them'.[4] Six months later, in May 1945, Harry Hopkins, one of Roosevelt's closest advisers, travelled to Moscow to meet Stalin and to transmit to him President Truman's concerns over 'our inability to carry into effect the Yalta Agreement on Poland'. In response, Stalin furiously denounced the Lend-Lease decision and declared that the USSR needed to have a 'friendly' – i.e. pro-Soviet – Poland on its borders.[5]

Still, Stalin had agreed to the Yalta protocols, and elections would be held, even in the odd circumstances. During the initial period of Soviet occupation and coalition rule of Eastern Europe – roughly 1945 to 1947 – some, though not all, non-communist political parties still had the legal right to exist. Some non-communist newspapers could be published. Political campaigns were conducted. The degree of political freedom varied from country to country, as did the degree to which elections were manipulated or falsified outright. But at least in the very beginning, the Soviet Union clearly intended to preserve at least the appearance, and to some extent the reality, of democratic choice.

And it expected to benefit. As I've noted, both the Soviet Union and its allies in Eastern Europe thought that democracy would work in their favour. This is an important point, often overlooked and worth repeating: though the sincerity of this expectation varied from country to country, most of the parties in the region held elections soon after the war's end because they thought they would win, and they had some good reasons for that belief. In the immediate aftermath of the war, almost all of the political parties operating in Europe advocated policies which, by modern standards, were very left wing. Even the centre-right Christian democrats in West Germany and the Conservatives in Britain were willing to accept a heavy role for the state in the economy in the late 1940s, up to and including the nationalization of some industries. Across the continent, just about everyone advocated the creation of extensive welfare states. Communist parties had done very well in European elections in the past, and seemed poised to do so again. The French communist party won the largest number of votes in the parliamentary elections of 1945. Why should the same not be true further east?

European communists also had ideological reasons to believe in victory. According to Marx, the working class would sooner or later become conscious of its own destiny, and would sooner or later put its faith in the communist party. Once this happened, communist parties would quite naturally be elected to power by working-class majorities. In a later interview, the Polish communist Leon Kasman explained:

We knew perfectly well that before the war the Party had the support of a minority of the population, but we believed that this was an enlightened minority, one which would lead the way to national progress. We also knew that if we took power and conducted politics correctly, we would win over people who didn't trust us, didn't believe us or were against us.[6]

Ulbricht, in a speech to his party in early 1946, expressed a similar optimism:

We have been asked: will you also hold elections in the Soviet zone? We are saying: yes, indeed, and you will see how we will organize those elections! We will organize them with the sense of responsibility that is required for the holding of such elections, and we will organize them in such a manner as to ensure that there is a working-class majority in all towns and villages.[7]

At least in public, Ulbricht never entertained the possibility that elections might *not* eventually lead to a working-class majority.

Stalin himself was more cynical, or perhaps he had never quite grasped what Europeans meant by 'democracy' and 'free elections'. During the war, he told a Polish delegation from London led by Stanisław Mikołajczyk, then the leader of the Polish government-in-exile, that 'there are certain people – both Left and Right – that we cannot allow in Polish politics'. Mikołajczyk pointed out that in a democracy, it was not possible to dictate who could be in politics and who could not. In response, 'Stalin looked at me as if I were . . . a lunatic and ended the conference.'[8]

Later, in August 1944, Stalin offhandedly told a group of Polish émigré leaders that the Soviet Union would look favourably upon the formation of a 'coalition' of 'democratic parties' in Poland – although these questions would, of course, 'be resolved by the Poles themselves'. By 'coalition' he meant a pre-electoral coalition, whose members would not compete with one another. By 'democratic' he meant pro-Soviet.[9] Clearly, he preferred the kind of 'election' which involved no competition whatsoever. In those sorts of circumstances, even the Polish communists had a chance of victory. As he told Gomułka in 1945, 'With good agitation and a proper attitude, you may win a considerable number of votes.'[10]

Several countries obligingly followed Stalin's formula and held elections without competition. Yugoslavia held exactly that sort of election – Tito needed no Soviet persuasion to persecute his opponents – in November 1945. The official results declared that 90 per cent of voters had voted for the Yugoslav People's Front, the only party on the ballot. The Soviet ambassador in Belgrade praised this exercise effusively, telling Molotov that these elections had 'strengthened' the country. He reckoned them a great success.[11] In Bulgaria, the communist party also organized several left-leaning parties into a coalition called the Fatherland Front in November 1945 elections.[12] In both countries the genuine opposition – parties of the centre and the centre-right which refused to join the coalition – called upon their countrymen to boycott the vote, and many did. The communist parties declared victory anyway.

Yet despite the best efforts of the NKVD and the local communists, not all of the region's politicians were willing to enter a unified electoral coalition, and not all of the working class became rapidly conscious of its destiny either. In 1945 and 1946 the region's economy was still in chaos. Political violence had created hatred and resentment of the Soviet Union. The result was that instead of confirming Marx's predictions, the first round of free and semi-free elections proved catastrophic for the communists in much of the region. In their wake, the communist parties' tactics grew much harsher.

In Poland, Stalin moved cautiously at first, at least in the matter of the elections. His envoys did not immediately bully the Polish political class into staging a one-party election, as in Yugoslavia or Bulgaria. Following the arrest and deportation of the sixteen Home Army leaders, the Western powers were watching Polish politics far more closely, and perhaps Stalin felt it was important to maintain the fiction of a coalition provisional government. Presumably with these considerations in mind, Stalin allowed one last, non-communist Polish leader, Stanisław Mikołajczyk – the politician who had tried to argue with him about democracy – to return to the country and operate legally in the spring of 1945.

Unlike the Polish communists, none of whom had taken part in prewar Polish electoral politics, Mikołajczyk was well-known to the general public. Before 1939, he had been president of the Polish Peasants' Party (Polska Stronnictwo Ludowe, or PSL) – a grouping with a rural base, a social democratic agenda and real legitimacy. Following the double German–Soviet invasion in September, Mikołajczyk had made his way to London, where he had joined the Polish government-in-exile. After the death of General Władysław Sikorski in a shocking plane crash in Gibraltar in 1943, Mikołajczyk himself became Prime Minister-in-exile. In that capacity, he negotiated with Stalin, Roosevelt and Churchill over the status of Poland at the end of the war, growing angrier and more ill-tempered as those negotiations went sour. During a particularly ugly meeting with Stalin and Churchill in Moscow in October 1944, he accidentally learned that despite reassurances from Roosevelt himself, the Allies had already ceded eastern Poland to the Soviet Union at the Tehran conference (the meeting at which Churchill suggested that Poland might 'move westwards, like soldiers taking two steps left close'). He shouted at Churchill and demanded a change of policy. The British Prime Minister shouted back at him: 'We'll become sick and tired of you if you continue arguing!'[13]

After the arrest of the sixteen Home Army leaders in March 1945, Mikołajczyk had little faith in the possibility of democracy in Poland. He decided to return to the country anyway. As Krystyna Kersten notes, Mikołajczyk was 'under the illusion that Stalin was serious when he declared that his goal was not a Communist Poland but only a democratic Poland friendly to the USSR'.[14] For this he was criticized by many Poles in both London and Poland who felt his return granted a spurious legitimacy to a government which was under de facto Soviet control already. One émigré newspaper made dark predictions: 'History teaches us that no one can stop dictatorial totalitarianism through even the farthest-reaching compromises ... The only road to deliverance is – the timely reversal of world opinion to our advantage.'[15] Mikołajczyk pointed out that the Yalta treaty had guaranteed 'free and unfettered elections as soon as possible on the basis of universal suffrage and secret ballot'. He was determined to take this promise at its face value.[16]

In June 1945, Mikołajczyk travelled to Moscow, where he took part in the discussions which led to the creation of the Polish provisional government. Present at this gathering were the 'Lublin Poles' – Bierut, Gomułka and other pro-Soviet politicians who had joined the Polish National Liberation Committee – as well as other PSL leaders. The resulting agreement created, as noted, a Provisional Government of National Unity, which was meant to rule Poland until elections could be held. PSL controlled one third of the delegates to this body. The party also received a few cabinet posts and an allotment of paper so that it could begin printing a newspaper. In his bitter memoir, written in exile, Mikołajczyk recalled that although this agreement 'brought additional disillusionment to a great majority of the Polish people . . . the day was to come when we gladly would have settled for the rights outlined in that agreement. For in the end, the [PSL] did not get even its one-third share. It got nothing.'[17]

For a very brief moment, his supporters might have had reason to hope for more. Mikołajczyk's first forays into the Polish countryside were triumphant. Thousands came out to the airfield to greet him when his plane landed in Warsaw in June 1945. A mob followed his motorcade through the city, and then clustered outside the new headquarters of the provisional government in the southern suburbs, cheering him on. When he visited Kraków a few days later, his jubilant supporters actually lifted his car and carried it through the streets. Later, they picked up Mikołajczyk himself and carried him on their shoulders. But even these euphoric meetings took place against a background of menace. As he stepped out of his first meeting with party leaders in Kraków on the evening following his arrival in the city, Mikołajczyk encountered a barrage of machine-gun fire. It was not meant to kill him. It was rather intended to scare him, which it did. Later, he discovered that everyone at that meeting was arrested after he had left.[18]

In the months which followed, Mikołajczyk and his dedicated followers conducted what was, in retrospect, an extraordinarily brave and amazingly blunt political campaign. He and his party fought first for the right to conduct open oppositional politics; then to make their mark on the first public referendum; and finally to obtain seats in the first postwar parliamentary elections. By 1947 they had lost all three battles, but not before scaring both the Polish communists and their Soviet advisers with the strength and scale of their support.

From the very beginning, the Polish communists did their best to isolate Mikołajczyk and the PSL. The electoral 'coalition' that Stalin had offhandedly proposed to Mikołajczyk quickly came into being. This pro-Soviet bloc contained the communists, the somewhat reluctant Social Democratic Party and, confusingly, two phony parties: an additional, ersatz 'Peasants' Party', controlled by the communists and intended to create confusion among the voters, and a 'Democratic Party' which was designed to do the same. The real PSL refused to join this deliberately muddled coalition, and thus became the only legal party to remain outside. As a result, Mikołajczyk attracted the support of every anti-communist in the country, from the mildest socialists to the most radical nationalists.

Within a few months, the communist leadership realized its mistake. At a meeting of the communist party's Central Committee in the winter of 1946, Gomułka gave a speech openly attacking the PSL for the first time. He described the party leadership as the new reactionary 'enemy', in league with Western imperialists. The PSL, he hinted, might well be more dangerous than the anti-communist partisans still hiding in the forests.[19] Włodzimierz Brus, at the time a young communist party economist, attended that meeting:

> Many people were surprised by the ferocity of this message, first of all because they had the sense that their [own] support in the country is not strong enough, so they would prefer some sort of truce, and not a fight. And secondly they were tired after this long war and these sacrifices, losses and victims ... I think that I myself was a bit surprised by the ferocity of this attack.

But, as Brus observed, others at the meeting greeted Gomułka's message 'with some satisfaction'. At last the party would 'destroy the reaction'.[20]

Mikołajczyk himself kept track of the verbal and physical attacks on his party. Serious harassment – including police violence, torture and murder – dogged his theoretically legal party from the beginning. As early as November 1945, he sent the first of what would be a long series of official complaints to the Polish secret police headquarters, complaining of 'mass arrests of PSL members in Tarnobrzeg, together with confiscation of valuables'. In that same month, police functionaries and communist party officials physically prevented people from attending a PSL meeting in Trzebenice; they warned people in villages around Oleśnica that anyone who attended such meetings risked arrest; they stole documents from a party office near Łowicz. On 9 January 1946, Mikołajczyk compiled a list of eighteen of his activists who had been arrested in the city of Wrocław. Later that month he listed eighty arrestees in Łódź.[21]

Often, PSL members were arrested for the actions of the armed underground. In March 1946, for example, local communists organized a political meeting in the town of Łapanów, south-east of Kraków, to which the PSL was not invited. On their way home, several communist politicians and secret policemen were ambushed by partisans armed with machine guns. Seven men were killed and three injured in the exchange of fire. The next day the police began to round up local PSL members at random, on the grounds that they hadn't been at the meeting so they must be responsible. They also set fire to the property of one local party leader, whose house and barn burned to the ground. Mikołajczyk complained that the functionaries 'act on the line of least resistance, neither investigating nor trying to find the guilty . . . It's unquestionably an abuse of power.'[22]

In the midst of this turmoil, the PSL began to publish *Gazeta Ludowa* – 'People's Paper' – an extraordinary achievement in its way. The publishers had a very limited access to paper, and didn't have the capacity to mail subscriptions. Periodically, they asked readers to limit themselves to one copy apiece – they weren't allowed to buy extras for friends – as there were always shortages. As Mikołajczyk remembered: 'we had enough requests for subscriptions for a daily print of 500,000 copies of *Gazeta Ludowa*, but we were never given newsprint for more than 70,000. Hundreds of copies of our paper were sabotaged by communists in the distributing plants and services . . . individual subscribers were warned that if they did not cancel their subscriptions, they would be fired from their jobs.'[23] Unlike the radio, *Gazeta Ludowa* clearly could not reach the vast majority of Poles. But its articles, appearing under frank headlines such as 'The mask is falling off' and 'The UB [secret police] tortures Poles', described reality in graphic terms for those who managed to get hold of a copy. *Gazeta Ludowa* printed names, dates and descriptions of arrests, and its journalists complained about Mikołajczyk's treatment during parliamentary meetings. Although his party allegedly controlled a third of the seats, whenever he spoke – or when any of his deputies spoke – the whole room would erupt in boos and catcalls, making it impossible to hear a word.[24]

The attacks on the PSL did not succeed in eliminating the party. On the contrary, funerals of murdered PSL members began to attract large and rebellious crowds. Priests – at that time still free to speak their minds – began to preach openly against the government. At one parish church, a priest purportedly declared that if 'someone were to ask who is the so-called reaction, we must declare clearly that we Christians are the reaction and we will win the battle with Marxism'. One Central Committee member carefully noted, in remarks to his colleagues, that 'the idea of a bloc [the left-wing coalition] has not been made popular enough among the masses'. Even the normally weak and cowed Social Democratic Party began to complain that the secret police were treating the PSL with too heavy a hand.[25]

Aware that they were losing support, the Polish communists tried a delaying tactic. Instead of holding elections in the autumn of 1945, as did the Hungarians, Bulgarians and Yugoslavs, Jakub Berman, the party's top ideologist, convinced Bierut to hold a referendum in the early summer of 1946. The point, he said years later, had been to 'survey' public opinion, to 'separate the grain from the chaff' and to force people to make a simple choice for or against Mikołajczyk.[26] The questions put to the public were designed to elicit a positive response. There were three: Do you support the abolition of the Senate [a prewar institution without much of a function]? Do you support land reform and nationalization of large industry while preserving private property? Do you wish to keep Poland's new territories and its new western border?

The correct answer to all of these questions was yes. Thus did the communist electoral campaign have a simple slogan: 'Three Times Yes!' Mikołajczyk took up the challenge, and instructed his followers to vote yes on the second two questions. As Berman recognized, it was hard for him to argue against the western territories, and both nationalization and land reform were then popular, especially since the question included the contradictory phrase 'while preserving private property'.[27] But Mikołajczyk did call upon his followers to vote 'Once No' on the meaningless question about the Senate.

In truth, no one cared in the slightest whether Poland did or did not have a second parliamentary chamber. Instead, the vote became a proxy contest between the communist party and Mikołajczyk's PSL, and the party did its utmost to win. Poland has probably never had an election campaign like it either before or since: the communist party printed over 84 million posters, leaflets and brochures, an extraordinary quantity of propaganda at a time when there were still paper shortages. An order went out to paint every wall and fence across the country with the slogan 'Three Times Yes!' Appeals were made on the radio and at public events, and they were aimed at all sectors of the population: women, peasants, workers, intellectuals. Sometimes they were crudely nationalistic – 'Three Times Yes does not appeal to the Germans' or 'Yes is the mark of your Polishness'. Others were populist and sentimental. Poles were told to vote 'Three Times Yes – if you don't want the landowners to return' or 'Three Times Yes – in the name of our children's prosperity and happiness'.[28]

As the campaign reached its height, threats began to follow the propaganda. The Kuibyshev-trained secret police boss in Łódź, Mieczysław Moczar, told the local PSL leader that he would arrest anyone who dared to campaign under the slogan 'Once No'. The regime also decided the referendum campaign might be an opportune moment to conduct open and heavily publicized trials of Home Army leaders, during which prosecutors hinted darkly at links between the partisan underground and the PSL. Of course all opponents of the regime, both armed and unarmed, were indeed supporting the PSL (though the PSL kept itself at a distance from the remaining partisans) and some of them were covertly going further, campaigning for a 'Twice No' or even 'Three Times No' vote. The regime grew alarmed by this. As voting day approached, both military and paramilitary organizations – the army, the border guards, the People's Militia and the secret police – were sent to organize meetings and demonstrations. Anyone suspected of supporting the 'wrong' vote risked arrest, interrogation, or worse.

But the propaganda backfired. On the night before the vote, some 20,000 fans gathered in Warsaw to watch a soccer match between Poland and Yugoslavia, one of the first international matches to be held since the war. During the half-time interval, a handful of communist politicians stepped forward, intending to encourage all present to vote. Realizing that yet another neutral occasion was about to become a political event and angered by the boring, stilted language of one of the speakers, the spectators began clapping and whistling – signs of disapproval in Poland. Someone started a rumour that Mikołajczyk was in the stadium, and the crowd began chanting his name. The Yugoslav team appeared disoriented – 'flabbergasted' in the words of a spectator – but the match proceeded (Poland lost). Towards the end, two truckloads of young activists, members of the Union of Fighting Youth, suddenly appeared outside the stadium and began to shout 'Long Live People's Poland and Long Live the National Army' as the crowd left for home, earning themselves nothing but jeers.[29]

The following morning – 30 June 1946 – more than 11 million people, 85.3 per cent of eligible voters, turned out at the polls, an extraordinary number. At first, the party rejoiced, believing that the high numbers meant the nation had swung behind them. Brus, the young economist, was on duty, receiving reports on the results from the provinces. He remembered that as his comrades heard the numbers, they turned from 'cautious to extremely enthusiastic'. There had been no boycott, as some had feared. If the working classes and the peasantry were turning out, that had to be good news. Immediately, the party leaders began to talk of holding a snap parliamentary election.[30]

The euphoria vanished quickly. Millions of people had indeed turned out, but the majority had followed Mikołajczyk's advice. The results were devastating. According to archival documents now available, only a quarter of the population had actually voted 'Three Times Yes'. A decisive majority had voted 'No' to at least one of the questions.[31] The communists pondered these distressing results for ten days. Finally, they released a wholly falsified set of figures which put the proportions the other way around. The PSL protested the obvious falsification. They didn't have access to the real numbers, but they knew from their informal exit polls that the majority had certainly not voted 'Three Times Yes'. The communists stood stonily by their fake result. The stage was set for an even nastier parliamentary election, which would not be held right away, but would rather be delayed for six more months.

What had happened? In its post-mortem discussion of the failed referendum campaign, the communist party bitterly concluded that the mass production of leaflets had backfired, and the mass painting of slogans had annoyed people. The propaganda had been over-whelming and too crude. As one inspector in the new Ministry of Propaganda wrote in an internal report:

> after the announcement of the People's Referendum, the most import-ant thing should have been to maintain moderation and caution while supporting the three positive answers, which were as obvious and clear as the sun in the sky. The out-of-control agitation for 'yes' created the suspicion that there must be something else going on.[32]

In future, they told one another, agitators had to be better trained to answer the two most frequently heard public complaints: Why had Poland's eastern territories been taken away? And why were Soviet soldiers still on Polish soil? Incompetent agitators were to be fired immediately. Conversations, not posters and leaflets, were to be used in the future.[33]

Even allowing for the 'mistakes' of propagandists, the communist party still found it hard to understand how workers and peasants could reject them in such numbers. Profoundly wedded to an ideology which was supposed to bring them victory – workers were supposed to support the workers' state, after all – they struggled to understand their countrymen. Even Poles living in the new western territories had voted "no" to their annexation.[34] One member of the Warsaw party committee concluded his countrymen were infected by 'con-fused thinking' on an inconceivable scale:

> This is connected with some kind of incomprehensible spirit of resist-ance and complete ignorance, even on the part of those individuals for whom democratic rule has been a blessing. Why, for example, did the districts with the most workers in Radom vote three times no in many cases? Why did the peasants of Iłża and Jędrzejów vote no for the most part? How can it be explained that even the army and the police, in many cases, gave negative responses?[35]

The referendum was an important turning point, even more so than the parliamentary elections which followed. For one, it represented the dawning of a realization which would still take many years to sink in: propaganda had its limits. Not only Polish communists, but communists of all kinds would eventually conclude that more did not mean better. More importantly, Poland's communists now knew they had no chance of a 'clean' electoral victory of any kind. Either they would have to threaten and intimidate Mikołajczyk's supporters, or they would have to falsify the election results altogether.

In the end, they did both. During the six months which elapsed between the failed referendum and the parliamentary election in January 1947, the secret police arrested all of PSL's Kraków leadership; they searched and sacked the party's headquarters in Warsaw; they interrogated and then arrested the entire PSL press department. The American ambassador in Warsaw wrote in a diplomatic cable that 'Even meetings arranged by PSL [which] are devoted to Polish–Soviet friendship have been broken up.'[36] All public electoral meetings were organized directly by the army because, as Brus put it, 'an army uniform is much more effective than a propagandist in civilian clothes'.[37] Under the guise of promoting security, detachments known as 'propaganda security groups' were sent out around the country to 'protect' the public from armed partisans.

As the vote grew closer, the regime's tactics grew more brazen. A week before the election, PSL candidates were struck from the ballot in ten out of fifty-two electoral districts – mostly in the rural southeast, a traditional Peasants' Party stronghold. On the final evening, the communist party sent thousands of fake telegrams to PSL officials, all identical: 'MIKOŁAJCZYK KILLED LAST NIGHT IN A PLANE ACCIDENT.' In his memoirs, Mikołajczyk described voting day, 17 January 1947, as 'a black day in Polish history':

> The millions who were ordered to vote openly gathered at their factories, offices and other appointed places, and with band music in the air were marched by armed guards to their polling places ... They were commanded to hold their voting slips – all number three [the number of the communist bloc] high over their heads as they stood in long queues in order that their guards might see.

And yet, he related, not everyone obeyed: 'Hundreds of thousands of these courageous people had concealed ballots with Polish Peasant Party numbers on them, and as they approached the ballot boxes, they managed to crumple the number three slips and insert slips of their own choice into the envelopes . . .'[38] Others ducked out of the line, and returned later when the soldiers were gone. Not that it mattered. According to the official results, 80 per cent of Polish voters cast their ballots for the 'democratic bloc'. Only 10 per cent voted for the PSL. Mikołajczyk resigned from the cabinet in protest. The parliament selected Bierut to serve as the Polish president, and Józef Cyrankiewicz, a social democrat who wanted his party to be unified with the communists, as Poland's Prime Minister. The British and American ambassadors lodged official protests and boycotted the opening day of parliament, but to no avail.[39]

Nine months later, in October 1947, Mikołajczyk slipped out of Poland, made his way to the British zone of Germany and flew to England. He said he had been covertly warned that he was at risk of immediate arrest. Though the British seemed to treat him as a mild hysteric, he was probably right. His Bulgarian counterpart, Nikola Petkov, the leader of the opposition Agrarian Party, had been arrested, tried and executed in the summer of 1947. His Hungarian counterpart, Ferenc Nagy, leader of the opposition Smallholders' Party, had been blackmailed into exile at about the same time. The PSL lived on in name, in the form of the phony 'shadow' party created for the 1947 elections, but played no further role in real politics, and after its demise there would be no authentic legal political opposition to the communist party in Poland for more than thirty years.[40]

In truth, the Polish communist party's electoral failure could not have been totally unexpected, at least in Moscow: Stalin had few illusions about the political allegiances of the Poles. But the Soviet Union had much greater faith in the electoral appeal of communist parties elsewhere. In eastern Austria, where the Red Army was still stationed, he thought the communist party might perform well in autumn elections, and there were high hopes for Romania too. But nowhere were expectations raised higher than in Budapest.

Indeed, the Hungarian communist party was absolutely confident of its success in the first postwar national elections, the first truly free and fair poll in Hungarian history. Full suffrage was extended to women, peasants and the uneducated for the first time.[41] Campaigning was open, conducted in the press and in public. Six parties put up candidates, each on a separate list: the Smallholders' Party, a party which was, as noted, quite similar in its sociology and its philosophy to the Polish PSL; the social democrats; the communist party; and three smaller parties.

Rákosi personally expected a major triumph. Unemployment and discontent were such that it was easy to get angry, aggressive-sounding crowds out into the streets, and the party did so as often as possible. Across the country communist leaders staged mass demonstrations, shouted slogans and put up posters. So overwhelming was their presence on the streets of Budapest that Rákosi confidently predicted victory for the left-wing coalition – the communist party plus the social democrats – even in the Budapest municipal elections which were held several weeks before the national poll. Together, the two left-wing parties would win 'Maybe 70 percent or maybe even more', he told the Central committee. General Voroshilov, then the highest-ranking Soviet officer in Hungary as well as the head of the Allied Control Council, suspected Rákosi was exaggerating, and complained to Molotov that the communist leader was over-fond of mass demonstrations.[42] True, Rákosi could get 300,000 people on the streets, but he had 'not even begun meticulous educational work among his members'. Voroshilov also felt Rákosi wasn't 'focused' enough on the economy – a euphemistic way of saying that his economic policies were already beginning to fail.[43]

Inside his party, few dared contradict Rákosi. Jenő Széll, who then worked in the communist party's propaganda office (and in 1956 rebelled against communist rule) was put in charge of managing election propaganda in the town of Pápa, in western Hungary. In advance of the vote, Széll was invited to a regional meeting to report on progress. As he listened to one glowing account of mass support after another, he began to worry: 'Everybody reported that the communist party is well ahead, the two workers' parties will get an absolute majority ... And I said to myself, "You unfortunate Széll, either you join the crowd and lie, or you tell the truth and get into trouble."'[44]

Széll screwed up his courage and answered honestly. He told the assembled activists that the left-wing coalition had little support in Pápa. The Smallholders' Party was very strong there, and might even win an outright majority (as it eventually did). Rákosi dismissed this information, declaring that Comrade Széll was misled, that he had met only with reactionaries, that propaganda would be increased in Pápa, that the public would be brought round. Eventually, Comrade Széll would see that everything would be all right.

But everything was not all right. The first shock came on Budapest's municipal election night, 7 October 1945. As the results were read out, the communists learned that the Smallholders had received more than 50 per cent of the vote. Rákosi, 'pale as a corpse, sank into the chair without saying a word'. The national elections on 4 November went no better. As the results came in to party headquarters, Széll saw one senior communist 'going white, going blue, going green, his lips becoming grey'. The counter-revolution was coming, the man declared, stumbling out of the room: 'the White Terror will follow'.[45] Rákosi, perhaps better prepared this time, reacted with more confidence. He entered the room, as Széll also remembered, 'with a great smile, saying "what news, comrades?"'

> We told him gloomily what news, and showed him the results. 'Come on comrades,' he said, 'these are just a few districts, a few rotten reactionary districts, don't be fooled by these results' ... I realized then what a politician he was ... he was completely aware of the fact that it was a total failure, but he played his role perfectly. He said he would go home, sleep, and 'you comrades prepare a full overall report of the results by 6 a.m. tomorrow'. Good work, he said, and left, seemingly in a happy mood ... I am convinced that the leadership started immediately meetings to find out how to correct the failure.[46]

The Smallholders had won hands down, with 57 per cent of the vote. The Socialist Party came second, with 17.4 per cent. The communist party finished a dismal third, with 16.9 per cent.

Though they had suspected Rákosi's optimism was exaggerated, the Soviet authorities in Budapest were alarmed by the scale of this defeat, and they looked for scapegoats. In his report back to Moscow, Major Tugarev of the Red Army's political department blamed 'the economic situation of the country' – inflation, coal shortages – as well as the 'right-wing leaders' who had somehow contrived to make the communists responsible for these failings. He accused the Smallholders of using anti-Soviet slogans and violence, and dwelled at some length on the perfidious behaviour of Cardinal József Mindszenty, primate of the Hungarian Catholic church. Clearly, Tugarev feared the Red Army would be blamed – thefts, rapes and deportations had taken their toll – and that there might be consequences for himself. Hungarians, he claimed, had 'provoked' Soviet soldiers into bad behaviour. They had given alcohol to soldiers, sent the soldiers to loot houses, and then taken the looted goods in exchange for food and more alcohol. The communist party, because of its close links to the Soviet Union, was then held responsible.[47]

Voroshilov pointed more forthrightly at his allies. He told Stalin that the Hungarian communist party had been infiltrated by 'criminal elements, careerists and adventurers, people who previously supported fascists, or were even members of fascist organizations'. More to the point, Voroshilov explained somewhat euphemistically, 'It is detrimental to the party that its leaders are not of Hungarian origin.' By this, he of course meant that there were too many Jews.[48] Within a few years, Rákosi would unleash waves of terror against precisely the same scapegoats identified in Voroshilov's report: the Smallholders' Party, Mindszenty, the church and the Jewish communists, or at least some of them.

Briefly, the Smallholders did try to benefit from their victory. Zoltán Tildy, the Smallholders' Party leader, and Ferenc Nagy, now the Speaker of the parliament, told Rákosi that the Smallholders wanted half the seats in the new cabinet – only reasonable since they had won more than half the votes – and that the other half should be divided among the other parties. They also tried to take the Interior Ministry away from the communists, and to put at least some of its functions under their own control.

They lost both arguments. Voroshilov – acting under the instructions of Molotov in Moscow – told Rákosi to inform Tildy and Nagy that although the communists had received only some 17 per cent of the vote, that 17 per cent represented the working class, the 'most active force in the country'. Moreover, 'the heavy burden of restoring the economy lies on the shoulders of the working class', and thus the working class deserved a much larger role in government. Aside from that, he explained, Tildy and Nagy needed to understand that

'Hungary is in a special situation. Although a defeated country, Hungary has, thanks to the great-hearted Soviet Union, received the opportunity to rapidly rejuvenate itself on a democratic basis.' A strong presence of the working class in the new parliament was a 'guarantee that Hungary would fulfil its obligations to the Soviet Union'.[49]

In normal circumstances, no democratically elected political party would have paid any attention to such menacing nonsense. But by November 1945, Father Kiss had been arrested. The memory of the Red Army's mass arrests was still fresh. The police had already begun to eliminate the youth groups and communist propaganda had infiltrated the radio. The Soviet advisers were angry – and Tildy gave in. The communists received the Interior Ministry – one of their stars, László Rajk, now became Interior Minister – and Rákosi became Deputy Prime Minister. Tildy became Prime Minister, but held the job only until February, when he was replaced by Nagy.

After that, the Smallholders' Party began to unravel with impressive speed. Under constant pressure, its leadership made one mistake after another. In the following months the communists formed temporary coalitions with the other parties, attacking first one Smallholder politician or faction and then the next, using mass demonstrations as well as harsh language in its newspapers and on the radio. In early March, the left-wing coalition organized a media campaign and then a huge demonstration calling for the expulsion of 'reactionary elements' from the Smallholders' Party. Two days later, Nagy caved in, and expelled these 'reactionaries' to appease the mob. Later, another Smallholder faction, led by Dezső Sulyok, decided to carve itself off and rename itself the Hungarian Independence Party. Sulyok hoped to distance his colleagues from Tildy and Nagy, who had now become hate figures in the left-wing media yet were regarded as weak by their own colleagues. The arrests of Smallholder sympathizers, including the members of the former anti-fascist resistance and the youth leaders, accelerated throughout 1946.

In the autumn, cryptic rumours of an impending police investigation began to circulate. At first covertly, then publicly, the newspapers, politicians and finally the Soviet authorities in Hungary accused Béla Kovács, the party's General Secretary and a close friend of Nagy, of plotting a coup. After the Soviet ambassador described Kovács openly as a 'conspirator', Rákosi advised Nagy to sack him. But Kovács departed for a 'vacation' in the country and the Hungarian police took their time about arresting him. And so the Red Army military authorities stepped in on 26 February 1947 and arrested Kovács themselves: 'In his own house, they read to him the Military Commander's order for his arrest; they searched the house, confiscated his files and took him away.'[50] Kovács would remain in the Soviet Union, in prison, for eight years.

Slice by slice, the Smallholders' Party was then whittled away with 'salami tactics', as they later became known. After Kovács disappeared, others began to go voluntarily. Leaders of the Smallholders' Party and of the other two legal non-communist parties slipped out of the country one by one. In May 1947, Nagy himself joined them, though it has never been clear whether or not he really meant to leave. Somewhat curiously, he chose that politically tense moment, when his party was unravelling and his colleagues were disappearing into exile, to take a vacation. Equally curiously, he took his wife, but left his young son behind. Having extracted a dubious promise from Rákosi not to enact any new nationalization legislation in his absence, Nagy drove to Switzerland, ostensibly to examine Swiss methods of agriculture ('It was not my plan to loaf in fashionable resorts,' he explained in his memoirs).

Almost as soon as he'd left the country, Nagy received a series of phone calls from Budapest, first ordering him to return and then warning him not to. His secretary was under arrest; he was being investigated for taking part in a conspiracy; he might not reach Budapest if he tried to get there, and 'it is also possible that some misfortune might happen en route', perhaps at the border. 'Don't take the situation so lightly,' Rákosi warned, when Nagy furiously called the conspiracy accusation 'a filthy concoction'. After several days of agony, Nagy finally chose exile. He wrote a letter of resignation, which he handed over in exchange for his son: 'At last, holding my child in my arms, I handed the Communist emissary my letter of resignation, the document they wanted so badly, to make their *coup d'état* "legal."'[51]

With Nagy out of the way – and with more politicians fleeing in his wake – the elections of 1947 were a foregone conclusion. Even so, the communists weren't taking any chances. In advance of the vote, they struck thousands of people off the electoral rolls, not only 'enemies' but friends and relatives of enemies, as well as people who had just returned from POW camps. During a campaign meeting in July, one leading activist laid out the party's intentions plainly. Overall, he hoped to exclude some 700,000 or 800,000 voters. 'Comrades,' he explained, 'you should not be too law-abiding ... We have to use whispering propaganda to disseminate that idea that the social democrats will merge with the communists after the elections. We must also spread the rumour that villages where the communist party wins a majority will have extra economic aid from the government.'[52]

Others suggested that activists should 'forget' to give registration documents to certain voters. In his district, Jenő Széll made sure that the communist party had the number one place on the ballot by asking a 'trustworthy lady' to choose the party's name out of a hat during a supposedly neutral selection process (the card was folded differently). Still others organized gangs of thugs to disrupt the meetings of other parties. Dezső Sulyok, now the leader of the Hungarian Independence Party, remembered what happened when he tried to speak at a public meeting:

> Loud shouting started: 'Throw him out of the window! Beat him to death! Hang him! Traitor!' ... When finally it was my turn, the attack of the crowd intensified. Since I could not say a word in that noise ... we stood up and started to sing the papal anthem, part of the crowd started to swear; others were singing the Internationale. This was the chance for our escape. While the crowd was standing and singing the Internationale, we quickly left the podium ... The crowd, however, noticed us and started to shout once again, 'Don't let them out, keep them back, throw them out of the windows ...'

Later he complained to the Interior Minister, Rajk, who was not sympathetic. 'As a communist,' Rajk told him, 'I can tell you that if it was up to me you would be all killed.'[53] Sulyok soon fled the country too.

By voting day, 31 August 1947, some 500,000 people had been eliminated from the voting rolls, about 8.5 per cent of all voters. Another 300,000 never showed up, possibly because they were too intimidated. Just to be certain, the communists carried out one final

225

fraud: they distributed tens of thousands of extra, blue-coloured ballots to special voting brigades – allegedly these were voters not in their home districts because of a 'vacation' – which raced from district to district casting multiple ballots. The brigades made little secret of what they were doing. They rode in Hungarian army trucks and even Soviet vehicles, laughing and singing, dashing from village to village, apparently happy to take part in this theatrical farce.[54]

Inside the country there were a few protesters. One of them was Sára Karig, a member of the Social Democratic Party since 1943, and a member of the anti-Nazi resistance since 1944. As a friend and colleague of the Swedish diplomat Raoul Wallenberg, Karig had helped hundreds of Hungarian Jews escape the ghetto, acquire false papers, hide their children in orphanages and leave the country. She had also helped Hungarian communists acquire false papers. (Her Budapest apartment, in one recollection, had been a 'birth certificate factory'.) After the war she remained politically active and in 1947, still a social democrat, she was named head of the election office of one of the central districts of Budapest. In that capacity, she set up an informal telephone line designed to keep in touch with voting stations throughout the district, the better to keep track of how many people were voting. By the end of the day, she knew there had been fraud. She reported several cases of double voting to the police. The fraudsters – all communist party members – were arrested, and almost immediately released.

On the following day Karig herself was arrested. She was picked up on the street without warning, dragged into a black Soviet limousine and driven immediately to the Red Army's headquarters in Baden, near Vienna. She was kept in custody for three months, interrogated and tortured, accused of spying and finally told that although there were no charges against her, she was being expelled from the country as an 'obstacle to Hungary's democratic process'. She eventually wound up in Vorkuta, one of the most distant Soviet Gulag camps. Back in Budapest, her friends, family and party colleagues were given no information about her. Rákosi and Rajk denied any knowledge of her whereabouts. Even the Soviet authorities in Budapest innocently said they knew nothing – perhaps she had emigrated to the West?

Karig returned home only in 1953, after Stalin's death.[55] In the meantime, the suppression of Karig's protest had been successful: within a year, the Hungarian government had dropped all real pretences of parliamentary democracy. The Hungarian communist party ruled alone.

Like their counterparts across the bloc, Ulbricht and his entourage believed the Left could and would win a popular vote in Germany. In September 1945, Wilhelm Pieck wrote confidently that Germany's workers not only 'understand that Hitler [has led] to disaster', but also understood that the Soviet Union would ensure 'strong growth and prospects for G[ermany]'. Therefore, they would favour politicians who were close to the Soviet Union. A few months later, Pieck also argued that elections would certainly produce victory for 'a proletarian regime'.[56]

The German communists remained cautious in one respect. Like the Hungarian communist party and the Polish communist party, they preferred to go to the polls in coalition with the German social democrats. If they could blur the line between the soft Left and the hard Left, they told themselves, they would easily win over Germany's workers. Eventually, all of the social democratic parties in Central Europe would be forced to dissolve themselves into the communist parties. But the first 'voluntary' unification of the Left – the abolition of social democracy as something separate and distinct from communism – took place in eastern Germany.

It was not an easy process. Social democracy had a long and venerable history in Germany and Eastern Europe, and many social democrats were profoundly anti-Soviet and anti-communist. For their part, German communists had long despised social democrats too.[57] In the early twentieth century, Lenin himself conducted a famous quarrel with Karl Kautsky, the founder of German social democracy, who had had the temerity to argue against revolution and in favour of attaining power through elections. In a famous 1918 pamphlet, 'The Proletarian Revolution and the Renegade Kautsky', Lenin dismissed his German colleague as a 'windbag' who spoke 'twaddle' and mouthed 'absurdities' about the nonsense of bourgeois democracy.[58] Elsewhere in Eastern Europe social democrats generally had a less radical programme than communists. They advocated what we would now call the welfare state, not the dictatorship of the proletariat, and they wanted evolution, not revolution. Above all, however, the communists hated social democrats because they were more popular, before the war and after.

But the experience of political failure and defeat at the hands of the Nazi party had demoralized Germany's venerable Social Democratic Party. In Weimar Germany, the Left had been divided and the Right had profited from that division. Now many believed that the Left's failure to unify had brought Hitler to power. Otto Buchwitz, a longtime social democrat, in March 1946 declared his support for the unification of the social democrats and the communists. 'Reformism' had failed, he wrote. Now it was time for his party to embrace 'revolutionary socialism' in partnership with the communists.

Soviet influence played a role as well. Otto Grotewohl, the leader of the social democrats in the Eastern zone of Germany, declared in August 1945 that his party had a right to independence and would not put forward a united list of candidates with the communists. He said the same to Kurt Schumacher, the Social Democratic leader in the Western zone, in October. Two months later, in December, he made a speech to a joint social democrat–communist meeting, listing ten reasons why he opposed unification. Above all, he declared, 'in our membership, a deep distrust of the communist brother party has materialized'.[59]

Very rapidly, he changed his tune. In February 1946, he told a British official that he was desperately worried. Personally he was under great pressure – he spoke of 'being tickled by Russian bayonets' – and the party was in trouble too: 'its organization in the provinces had been completely undermined,' he explained, and there was no longer any point in resisting the merger with the communists.[60] Grotewohl's view had changed because the communist party's tactics had changed, as had those of the Soviet Military Administration, in the autumn of 1945. The failure of communists to win elections in Hungary, the poor showing of the Austrian communist party (which had won only four parliamentary seats in national elections in November, despite high expectations) and the popularity of the Social Democratic Party in the Western occupation zones of Germany helped to convince first the East German communists, and then their Soviet minders, that the time for the unification of the Left had arrived. At the beginning of 1946, Red Army commanders were told to enforce the fusion of the two left-wing parties at the local level. Over the next few months, some 20,000 social democrats were 'harassed, imprisoned, or even killed' if they objected.[61] The Berlin city councillor Ruth Andreas-Friedrich, a dedicated social democrat, wrote a diary entry wondering 'who are we to stand up against the pressure of a world power? In the Eastern zone the merging process advances with steadfast relentlessness.'[62]

Grotewohl, like the social democrat Cyrankiewicz in Poland, might also have realized that if he played along, there was a good chance he would wind up with a top job (as indeed he eventually did: from 1949 until his death in 1964, he was Prime Minister of the GDR). Whether inspired by fear, opportunism or both, he agreed to the unification. At a special unification congress on 21 and 22 April 1946, the Socialist Unity Party (Sozialistische Einheitspartei Deutschlands, or SED) was born. 'Not a one-party system, but the consolidation of a united anti-fascist democratic front,' wrote *Neues Deutschland*, the communist party newspaper. 'Next to this party, which represents millions, there will be, in the long run, no room for any splinter groups.' In her diary, Andreas-Friedrich acidly summarized this statement: 'Not a one-party system, but, on the other hand, no room for any other parties.'[63]

But although Grotewohl caved in under pressure, not all of his party followed. During a tumultuous meeting of the Berlin social democrats, Grotewohl was shouted down with cries of 'Lackey!' or 'We don't want a forced unification! We won't let ourselves be raped' and more:

> The protests intensify. They turn more and more angry, more and more passionate. The speaker's words drown in them as if in a spring tide. 'Traitor . . . fraud . . . resign . . . stop . . .' . . . Someone begins to sing: 'Onward, brothers, to light and freedom . . .' His lips form the words automatically. And automatically the comrades join in. Everybody's face is glowing with pride and excitement. 'This time we didn't eat crow. For the first time in thirteen years we have defended our freedom.'[64]

More than 80 per cent of the Berlin social democrats voted against unification with the communist party, a vote which left both parties in an extremely odd position. Although it had ceased to exist in most of eastern Germany, the Social Democratic Party in the city of Berlin remained a major force. Not only that, the Berlin SPD (Sozialdemokratische Partei Deutschlands) had become radically anti-communist, maintaining close ties to the equally anti-communist western SPD. Kurt Schumacher opened an 'Eastern office' (Ostbüro) to aid eastern social democrats under Soviet pressure. Ulbricht railed against Schumacher in lengthy speeches, calling him a 'reactionary force' who promoted a 'policy of division'.[65]

Against this background, the first postwar German election campaign, launched in September 1946, proved a curious spectacle. From the beginning, the Soviet Military Administration and its propaganda division, led by Colonel Tyulpanov, planned the campaign with great precision. 'All of the SED's decisions,' Tyulpanov declared, 'must be agreed upon by the leadership of the Soviet Military Administration.' Tyulpanov persuaded higher officials to suspend temporarily the reparations programme, to increase the supply of raw materials to the zone, and even to increase food rations for children, babies and pregnant women.[66]

Though initially sceptical of the political talents of their German allies, the Soviet Military Administration began to feel more confident of victory by late summer. With unlimited access to paper, the German communists, like the Polish communists, printed hundreds of thousands of posters, and more than a million leaflets. Other parties had to fight to get any paper at all. The SED used deliberately anodyne slogans – 'Unity, Peace and Socialism!' or 'Unified Germany: Securing our Future!' – and avoided the word 'communism', as well as any references to the USSR. Across the five provinces of the Russian zone, Soviet officials also campaigned openly on the SED's behalf. In some regions, local commanders reserved the right to promote or veto specific candidates, and to approve or disapprove of electoral rallies.[67]

Even so, the result was far from reassuring. The SED failed to win majorities at the regional level, and would be forced to share power with the 'bourgeois' Christian democrats and liberal democrats. In Berlin, where the social democrats campaigned separately from the 'unified' SED – and where elections were held simultaneously in both the eastern and western halves of the city – the results were catastrophic. The social democrats won decisively, with 43 per cent of the vote in the Soviet sector and 49 per cent overall. The SED managed only 19.8 per cent overall, even falling behind the Christian democrats, who won 22.2 per cent.[68]

The party tried to put a positive slant on the results. The headline of *Neues Deutschland* declared the 'Great Election Victory of SED in the zone'. But behind the scenes the leadership was disappointed and the Russians were furious. In Moscow, the Soviet leadership debated a policy change, and considered removing Tyulpanov. In the Red Army's Karlshorst headquarters, some even expressed doubts that democracy could be 'created only through the bayonet', and advocated a more liberal policy.[69]

Instead of liberalizing, the Soviet Military Administration cracked down. One of the people who felt that pressure was Ernst Benda. In 1946, Benda was a law student at the Humboldt University in East Berlin, and the chairman of the Christian Democratic students' association. Christian democracy seemed to him an obvious choice at the time: 'After the experience we had with the Nazi regime it was necessary to become active in politics and to bring your religious personal convictions into politics, to try to form politics according to what you believe in.'[70]

The party gave Benda a small office at its headquarters on Jäger-straße, close to the university, where he was able to listen to the party leaders' internal debates. At the time, the CDU was divided between a strongly 'pro-Western' and anti-Soviet faction, led by Konrad Adenauer in the West, and another group, led by Jakob Kaiser in the East, whose members believed that it was still possible to find a compromise between East and West and thereby avoid the permanent division of Germany. There was nothing 'conservative' about the party in the contemporary sense: 'If you looked at the party platform [of the East Berlin CDU] today,' Benda explained in 2008, 'it would be to the left of the left.'

Yet even Benda's left-wing Christian democracy – at the time he advocated the creation of a welfare state and some centralization of the economy, along with private business and enterprise – led him into conflict with the communists at the university. He objected when, on the occasion of a communist party meeting in 1947, the university was draped in red flags, and, in conjunction with other activists, produced leaflets demanding to know where they were meant to be studying, 'Humboldt University, or Higher Party School?' The majority of the student council – which split along party lines roughly similar to those in greater Berlin – cooperated with Benda and his CDU friends. 'It is not important which party you vote for, it is more important which party you don't vote for,' Benda told a university election rally at that time: 'And everybody understood what I meant by this . . . You were either for or against the communists. If you were against them, it was not important whether you were a social democrat, a Christian democrat or anything else.'

As 1947 turned into 1948, these kinds of protests took place with ever greater frequency. They were also met with greater repression. Manfred Klein, the CDU leader who had tried to cooperate with the Free German Youth leaders, had already been arrested by the spring of 1947, and protests at the universities of Rostock, Jena and Leipzig led to more arrests. Another student leader, Arno Esch, was ultimately sentenced to death by a Soviet military tribunal.[71] The crackdown took a little bit longer to get underway in Berlin – the eastern half of the city was still being watched carefully by its western counterpart – but it finally came. Paul Wandel, the rector of Humboldt University and a longstanding communist, expelled three leading student activists. The student council, which was still led by a non-communist majority, voted to go on strike.

The end, for both Benda and the eastern Christian democrats, came soon afterwards:

> 'One day in March 1948 I heard that one of my friends, a CDU student, had been arrested at Friedrichstraße [the underground station which led to West Berlin] . . . Very clearly I recall that I immediately went over to the CDU headquarters, and called another friend, also a functionary at our student group, who was somewhere in Dahlem, in the American sector. I called him, told him what I had heard, and asked him, 'What can we do?' Then, just after I said this, somebody cut in our conversation from the outside. . . . In just four words he told me, "*Seien Sie nur vorsichtig: Just do be careful . . .*" I understood immediately: somebody whose job it was to follow telephone conversations had used this opportunity to give me a personal warning.'

Benda hung up the phone, left the office and went immediately to the subway station – not to Friedrichstraße, where his colleague had just been arrested, but to Kochstraße, another border crossing. After a few minutes he had entered into the American zone. He did not return to East Berlin for forty years.[72]

By the end of 1947, Mikołajczyk had escaped from Poland, and was living in Britain. Nagy was in exile, on his way to the United States. Jakob Kaiser had resigned as the leader of the Christian Democratic Party in the Soviet zone of Germany and would soon leave, along with Benda and many other colleagues, for West Berlin. Less than three years had elapsed since the end of the war, but almost all organized, legal opposition to the communist regimes had now been eliminated. Often 1948 – the year of the Berlin blockade – is said to mark the beginning of the Cold War as well as the onset of 'Stalinism' in Central Europe. But the Stalinization – or Sovietization, or totalitarianization – of Eastern Europe was already far advanced well before 1948 began.

By the autumn of 1947, Stalin had also stopped pretending to the outside world that he would adhere to the language of the Yalta treaty. During the war, he had shut down the Comintern, the Communist International, as a gesture of goodwill to the Western Allies. Now he created a new organization – the Communist Information Bureau, or Cominform – in part as a gesture of aggression towards those same Allies.

Although there had been some loose talk of re-creating an international body of 'revolutionary' communist parties, the immediate impetus for the creation of the Cominform was the news that Truman and his Secretary of State, General George C. Marshall, were launching a plan to help rebuild Europe's economies with large investments and big credits. In his 1947 Truman Doctrine speech, President Truman had declared that 'the seeds of totalitarian regimes are nurtured by misery and want'. The end result of that thought was the Marshall Plan, a generous fund for European recovery. Proposed in June 1947, the Marshall Plan was intended to rebuild European economies and – depending on your point of view – either help fend off the threat of communist revolution or help entrench Western capitalism. Writing at the time, one American advocate declared that 'The Plan will create an economic environment in Europe favorable for the growth and development of democratic processes and economic prosperity.' More to the point, the Plan can 'prevent a breakdown of the political and economic structure of Europe', and thus lower the chances of communist revolutions in Western Europe, which at the time were believed to be a real threat.[73]

At first, the Soviet Union was utterly flummoxed by the Marshall Plan. When the programme was announced, the Polish government, desperate to join, immediately requested guidance from Moscow. Molotov replied that as yet he had no information on the matter.[74] The Yugoslav government's instinct was to refuse, but it wrote to Moscow for advice as well.[75] Meanwhile, the Czechoslovak government – under the impression that it had a choice – voted to accept the offer and to attend a Marshall Aid conference in Paris. Stalin summoned Gottwald, the Czechoslovak communist party boss, and Masaryk, the non-communist Czech Foreign Minister, to Moscow. He told them that the Americans were 'trying to form a Western bloc and to isolate the Soviet Union' and they were to have no part of it. Bluntly, he ordered them to withdraw from the meeting: 'It is necessary for you to cancel your participation in the Paris conference *today* – that is, June 10, 1947.' They did.[76]

The Cominform was Stalin's response to Truman's challenge. Symbolically, the institution would solidify 'his' bloc, enabling its members to better respond to 'propaganda' from the West in future. With its creation, the notion of a uniquely 'Polish' – or German, or Czech, or Hungarian – path to communism was to be eliminated. All of the world's important communist parties were to adopt a single line, in Eastern Europe and in the West. Ten communist parties were invited to join, from Bulgaria, Czechoslovakia, Hungary, Poland, Romania, the USSR and Yugoslavia; Western parties from France, Italy and the 'Free Territory of Trieste' (at the time a disputed territory, eventually divided between Italy and Yugoslavia) joined as well.

Not all of those present at the organization's first meeting in September 1947, in the Polish mountain resort of Szklarska Poręba, seemed aware of its purpose. Gomułka, the forum's Polish host, emphasized the 'informal nature of the meeting' in his first speech and spoke naively of 'the need for exchange of experiences between the Communist Parties'. But there were no exchanges of experience. Instead, the Soviet delegation took over and imposed its agenda. Andrei Zhdanov, Stalin's culture boss, made a thundering speech in which he spoke of the 'new alignment of forces', the 'formation of two camps' and the 'American plan for the enslavement of Europe'. Finally, he provided the group with its draft resolution, which starkly described a Europe divided between 'the policy of the USSR' and its allies on the one hand, which was 'aimed at undermining imperialism and strengthening democracy', and 'the policy of the USA and Britain, aimed at strengthening imperialism and strangling democracy' on the other.[77]

The Cominform's creation is sometimes described as an ambush, a surprise assertion of Soviet power which sealed the fate of all present. Others have called it a turning point, the moment when the Soviet Union dropped its tolerance of Eastern bloc pluralism. In the revisionist interpretation of Cold War history, the Szklarska Poręba meeting is also sometimes portrayed as a panicked reaction to the aggression of the West, and in particular to the naked imperialism of the Marshall Plan.

Yet a close reading of the reports actually presented by the delegates at the meeting provides a different picture. By their own account, almost every one of the communist parties present at the meeting *already* had a stranglehold on power. Gomułka bragged that 'despite the coalition character of the government', Polish communist party members held all posts 'in the Ministry of Security and the Ministry of National Defence, from the highest to the lowest leading organs, and in the security organs the rank-and-file as well'. He also spoke at length about the communist party's elimination of the Polish socialists, bragged of the defeat of Mikołajczyk's PSL, and gleefully described the new, emasculated, pro-regime 'peasant party' which had replaced it.[78]

The Hungarian speaker, József Révai, sounded no less pleased: 'as a result of the last elections', he told the other delegates, 'we have become the leading party, whereas for 25 years we were essentially a small underground group'. He spoke of the 'liquidation of Ferenc Nagy', and of the break-up of the Smallholders' Party, in which 'American and British imperialism had set their hopes'. The Romanians also spoke of the success of their 'bloc of democratic parties', which had 'made possible an intensification of the process of democratic development' and the elimination of opponents. Even the Czech communist leader, Rudolf Slánský, bragged that his party, while not yet in full control (though it would be a few months later), already had created a 'regime of people's democracy' in Czechoslovakia.[79]

The Cominform did not turn out to be a permanent or even an especially influential institution. It never achieved much in the way of bloc coordination, and in 1956 would be dissolved. Comecon – the Council for Mutual Economic Assistance, founded in 1949 – would have more longevity and indeed did more lasting damage, since it distorted trade within the Eastern bloc for decades. But the Cominform's creation did mark the end of an era. In the wake of the Szklarska Poręba meeting, the East European communist parties eliminated even the fiction of opposition.

This meant, in practice, the elimination of all vestiges of social democracy. German social democracy had already been defeated. In 1948, the Polish social democrats were forced to merge with the Polish communist party too. The unified party was christened the Polish United Workers' Party (Polska Zjednoczona Partia Robotnicza, or PZPR), though it was widely referred to as the communist party, then and later. The Hungarian communists swallowed the Hungarian socialists in 1948 too. The name of their new party – the Hungarian Workers' Party (Magyar Dolgozók Pártja, or MDP) – was chosen in Moscow: the Hungarians had suggested 'Hungarian Worker-Peasant Party' but the Russians objected to the inclusion of the word 'Peasant'. Naturally, the MDP took over all of the property of the old socialist party, including its newspapers, and expelled any insufficiently enthusiastic members.[80] Its members were colloquially called 'communists' as well.

These changes had echoes in other institutions. Just before the unification of their two parties, Rákosi, the communist party leader, and Árpád Szakasits, the Social Democratic leader, arrived at the Hungarian Radio studios for what was supposed to be a live interview. Upon arrival, they closeted themselves in a room for an hour. They emerged, two minutes before the programme was due to start, and handed the radio reporter not only a list of the questions he was supposed to ask, but also the expected answers. 'Don't screw this up,' the reporter's boss whispered into his ear, 'and you'll get a 500 forint bonus.'[81] The pretence of democratic competition had been dropped. In its wake, the pretence of a free press dissolved as well.

Politics elsewhere in the bloc conformed to a similar pattern. Like the other fraternal parties, the Czechoslovak communist party now realized that its support was dropping. In 1946 the party had won 38 per cent of parliamentary votes. But in 1947 (partly thanks to the unpopular decision not to participate in the Marshall Plan) the party knew its candidates would be lucky to receive 20 per cent. Like his fellow little Stalins, Gottwald plotted an undemocratic path to power. He carried out a constitutional coup in February of 1948 and then proceeded to eliminate the remaining opposition.[82]

The same thing had happened in Bulgaria: following the victory of the left-wing Bulgarian Fatherland Front coalition, the Bulgarian communists had also dissolved the non-communist parties in the coalition (Stalin told Dimitrov that 'the elections are over and your opposition can go to hell') and murdered their only real opponent, Nikola Petkov, who had overcome terror and electoral fraud to win a third of the votes in the Bulgarian elections of 1946.[83]

In some countries, some of the 'bloc parties' or 'coalition parties' were allowed to go on functioning as a kind of democratic facade. Poland retained its castrated peasant party, also called the PSL. East Germany tolerated officially sanctioned 'Christian democrats' and 'free democrats' (FDP) who were nothing of the sort. But even these parties' leaders understood that their role was distinctly limited, if not entirely fictitious. They published regime-friendly newspapers and magazines, received sinecures and government privileges, and never threatened the hegemony of the communist parties at all. By the end of 1948, politics had not come to an end in the People's Democracies. But politics had become something which happened not between several parties, but within a single party. And so it would remain.

10

Economics

The new socialist human being should think like Lenin, act like Stalin, and work like Stakhanov.

Walter Ulbricht

The definition of socialism: an incessant struggle against difficulties which would not exist in any other system.

Hungarian joke of the 1950s

In classic Marxist thought, base determines superstructure. In other words, traditional Marxists believed that the shape of a society's economy – the division of labour, the means of production, the distribution of capital – determined its politics, culture, art and religion. No country, according to this way of thinking, can change its political system without changing its economic system first.

That was the theory. In practice, the new communist bosses of Eastern Europe had a chicken-and-egg problem. They believed that the economy would have to be transformed in order to create a communist society. At the same time, they knew they could not transform the economy in the face of popular resistance. In the first months following the war, the communist parties' priorities were therefore political: the police forces were put in place, civil society was subdued, the mass media were tamed. As a result, there was no economic revolution in Eastern Europe in 1945. Instead there was an institutional revolution, following which the state took control of the economy in small bites. The new regimes began with the reforms which they guessed would be most easily accepted.

238

The first and easiest change was land reform. Across the region, huge estates were empty and ownerless. Jewish properties which had been confiscated by the Nazis and German property abandoned after owners died or fled now lay fallow. In the eastern half of Germany, most of the largest landowners had escaped to the west in advance of the arrival of Soviet troops. Since much of this land seemed at the time to belong to no one, there were few objections when the state took it over.

In 1945 the notion of land reform did not strike everyone as a particularly 'communist' policy either, and it was not necessarily associated with the Soviet Union. In Hungary, the redistribution of land had been an important goal of many liberal reformers before the war, and was considered something very separate from the forced creation of collective farms. In Poland, both communists and non-communists expected the slogan 'land reform' to be popular, which is why the communists had included it in the referendum, though they hardly uttered the taboo word 'collectivization' at all. Far from heralding profound economic change, the first land reforms were a naked bid for support from the poorer peasantry, as they had been in the USSR, where the Bolshevik Revolution's first slogan had been 'Peace, Land and Bread!' From the moment they arrived, Red Army troops vigorously tried to enforce the same policy, confiscating land from richer owners and redistributing it to poorer peasants.[1] But in Eastern Europe, this simple formula did not have the impact that Soviet officers expected or that their communist colleagues hoped.

Although it would eventually affect everybody, land reform in Germany initially focused on the large estates owned by the Junkers, the former Prussian aristocrats. *Junkerland im Bauerhand* – 'the Junker's land in the farmer's hands' – was Wilhelm Pieck's conveniently rhyming slogan for the project. On 3 September 1945, the Soviet occupying powers issued a decree expropriating the property of anyone in the Prussian province of Saxony who owned more than 100 acres of land, along with anyone actively associated with the Nazi party. Some 7000 large estates were affected. The land was then redistributed in small parcels. Two thirds of it went to half a million landless farm labourers, unemployed town dwellers, and refugees from the East. The rest remained in state hands.[2]

Some of the recipients of this programme were of course pleased and grateful to the Soviet officers who had brought it about. Village halls were decorated with banners and flowers, songs were sung, the communists praised. But this kind of welcome was rare. More often the process was riddled with inequities and incongruities. Some of the commissions created to assist in the redistribution wound up being dominated by former Nazis. Other commissions used the procedures to settle scores, or even to manipulate the distribution of land to their members' advantage. In some areas, land reform led to the enlargement of estates rather than their reduction. Some 'new farmers' received property but no farm tools, draft animals or seed. They began to starve very quickly.

Not all of those who lost their land, even from the big Junker estates, fitted the stereotype of haughty aristocracy. So many heads of households were dead or in prison camps that the committees often wound up expropriating the land of women and children who were thereby utterly impoverished. Erich Loest, who worked as a farmhand in Saxony at this time, later described how a Saxon estate was seized from two kindly, elderly aristocratic sisters. Their expulsion won them a good deal of sympathy, especially when they were replaced by a group of Silesian refugees who had no interest whatsoever in the beautiful house they had just been given. 'No choir sang, no brass band played,' Loest wrote: 'it occurred to no one to hang garlands. It was completely different from what painters painted later in their commissioned works or scribes inscribed.' The Silesians were homesick, and wanted to go back to their own farms.[3] Because there were many similarly ambivalent situations, communist party membership in the countryside did not rise as rapidly as expected.[4]

Land reform was greeted with even greater suspicion in Poland, where 'collectivization' carried particularly negative connotations. In the eastern part of the country, many people had family and friends across the border in Soviet Ukraine, whose peasants had experienced first land reform, then collectivization, then famine. So strong was their fear of this scenario that many Polish peasants opposed partial land redistribution – even knowing they might personally benefit – on the grounds that the reform might be a prelude to the collectivization of all land (which in many places it proved to be). Even as a theoretical idea, 'land reform' had never been as popular in Poland as elsewhere. A few attempts at land reform in the 1920s and 1930s had foundered in part because the larger estates were generally well-managed, and many reformers thought that small farms were less productive.[5] Most of the country's very largest estates had in any case been in eastern Poland, which was now part of the Soviet Union.

Knowing this, the Polish communists proceeded cautiously, and small and medium-sized landowners were at first exempt. Instead, the 1944 decree on land reform called for the immediate confiscation of the land of 'citizens of the Reich who are not of Polish nationality' as well as 'Polish citizens claiming German nationality' (*Volksdeutsche*) and 'traitors' (a conveniently vague designation), as well as all farms larger than 100 hectares.[6] In total, some 10,000 estates were confiscated, and a further 13,000 estates were reduced in size.[7] About 20 per cent of all agricultural land was affected.

But even this policy – aimed squarely at the rich, at the Germans and at collaborators – was not as popular as some had hoped. In May 1945, Gomułka conceded as much at a meeting in Moscow. 'In this matter we have not conducted enough agitational work,' he explained delicately. Although land reform should have made peasants feel grateful to the regime, Gomułka noted that they were still wary, and still inclined to listen to 'reactionary forces'. To combat this problem, the Polish communist party had, he said, decided to come out loudly and clearly against collectivization. 'At this stage there isn't any sense in even thinking about Polish collective farms, we tell the farmers directly that our party is against collective farms, that our party will not oppose the will of the people,' he declared. The Comintern boss, Dimitrov, was annoyed by this. What if some farmers wanted to be collectivized, he snapped. Then what? 'We haven't got such a situation,' Gomułka replied.[8]

Land reform had a greater chance to be popular in Hungary, where the rural economy was still very nearly feudal. About 0.1 per cent of all landowners still controlled some 30 per cent of all Hungarian agricultural land in 1939, many of them living in ancient castles on vast latifundia. At the same time most peasant farms were tiny and most peasant farmers very poor. Populist land reformers had been thick on the ground in interwar Hungary, although they usually opposed

Soviet-style collectivization and called for the creation of private cooperatives to replace the vast aristocratic estates.[9]

After the war, most Hungarian politicians had reached an uneasy consensus about the necessity of land reform, but they had come to no agreement about scale or timing. Both issues were resolved for them by the Soviet occupiers, who forced the provisional government to carry out land reform immediately, in the spring of 1945, on the grounds that the redistribution of property would encourage any Hungarian peasants still fighting against the Red Army to drop their arms and come home. Soviet authorities also took a fast decision about the scale of the reform, which was very wide-ranging and very harsh. The decree on land reform in March 1945 expropriated all estates – land, livestock and machinery – larger than 570 hectares, along with all estates belonging to 'Germans, traitors and collaborationists'. Church property was not exempted.[10]

All of this property was redistributed to some 750,000 landless Hungarian peasants and farm workers. A ten-year moratorium was then placed on all land sales in order to prevent peasants, or anyone else, from re-creating large estates. In 1948, the reform was extended further: wealthier farmers lost the right even to lease land from other farmers. Instead, any unused agricultural land now had to be let out to farm workers and collective farms at very low rents.[11]

Many peasants thanked the communists for their new land. But many were made uneasy by the receipt of 'someone else's property', particularly as the clergy were often preaching against it. Rural Hungarians still had bad memories of Béla Kun's 1919 communist revolution, and like the Poles they knew something of what had happened in Ukraine. András Hegedüs, the dynamic young Madisz leader, was sent out to the countryside to agitate in favour of the reform, and encountered a wide range of reactions, from gratitude to hostility. In some villages, he was told that nobody wanted any land, in which case 'we were sure that there was a reactionary priest in that village'. At times, he had to use force. In one county, where he was constantly and mistakenly introduced as 'the comrade who came by aeroplane to Debrecen' (he had not, in fact, been on Rákosi's plane from Moscow), one of the local administrators, a member of the nobility, told Hegedüs he would not cooperate. 'I had to report to the Soviet commander,'

Hegedüs remembered, 'who came back with me and told the man he would stand him up against the wall and shoot him if he didn't fulfil the request in twenty-four hours.' Sometimes he too was threatened, once with hanging. Even at the time, he knew that the 'party leadership over-estimated the political impact of land distribution on peasants'.[12] In much of the country, land reform increased support not for the communist party but for the Smallholders' Party, whose rural ethos appealed far more to the new class of small landowners. Empowered by land reform, they gravitated to their 'own' party and to the church, not to the more 'urban' communists, even though the latter had pushed the reforms.[13]

Though collectivization was not mentioned in 1945 and 1946, both the Hungarian and the German communist parties did return to the idea in 1948 and 1956, respectively, as did other Eastern Europeans, though never the Poles. The Hungarians began with a programme of voluntary collectivization, which took advantage of a wave of rural bankruptcies. Between 1950 and 1953, they pursued 'kulaks' with a vengeance, demanding very high land taxes and insurance premiums while forcing them to accept low prices for their produce. The word 'kulak', borrowed from Russian, means 'wealthy peasant', and it sounds awkward and artificial in Hungarian. But like 'Trotskyite' or 'fascist', it rapidly became a political term which could also be used to mean 'anyone the communist party doesn't like'. The Germans also imposed 'voluntary' collectivization after 1956, thereby ensuring that thousands of East German peasants fled to the West. By then, many other economic refugees had done the same.[14]

Ulrich Fest was only ten years old when the war ended. His father was missing in action. Wittenberg, the town where his family had run a grocery store for several generations, now lay in the Soviet zone of occupation. As Fest remembered:

> 'Everything here was destroyed. The shop windows were smashed in and the people had looted all the groceries from the store. There was nothing left ... the doors had been locked but people had got into the shop by climbing through the shop windows. We nailed up the shop front with pieces of wood and then a panel – a glass panel – was taken out and made

IRON CURTAIN

into a shop front of sorts . . . a kind of peephole basically, measuring two
by one and a half metres or so. That became the shop window . . .'[15]

Faced by this catastrophe, his mother and grandfather had no doubt
about what to do: they reopened the shop, and went back into business. They were not alone.

Between the wars, Eastern Europe had not been as wealthy and as
industrialized as the western half of the continent.[16] Businesses were
small-scale, trade was limited and infrastructure was poor. Many
states in the region, most notably Nazi Germany, had practised forms
of corporatism which gave the state a large role in the affairs of business, especially big business. Nevertheless, at the most basic level,
Poland, Hungary, Czechoslovakia and the other nations of Eastern
Europe had been recognizably capitalist societies. Small workshops,
small factories and retail shops had all been in private hands. Some
wholesale distribution had been done through cooperatives, as in
Western Europe and the United States, but these were usually private
cooperatives, organized by merchants for their own benefit. All had
had established systems of commercial, corporate and contract law,
functioning stock markets and property rights.

After the war, small businessmen like the Fests were initially allowed
to continue operating. This was not because the new authorities liked
or admired small businesses. Lenin himself, correctly spotting the
importance of small-scale enterprises to a healthy free market economy, once wrote that 'unfortunately, small-scale production is still
widespread in the world, and small-scale production engenders capitalism and the bourgeoisie'.[17] Although they didn't necessarily say so
in public, most communist leaders shared Lenin's loathing for small
business. At a Central Committee meeting in October 1946, for
example, German communist leaders discussed not *whether* private
shops should be brought under state control, but *when*. One of those
present argued against acting fast: an overly rapid dismantling of the
sector would lead to chaos, which would drive people into the arms
of the reactionaries. Another argued for greater speed, on the grounds
that dangerous liberal economic ideas were taking hold among small
businessmen: 'we must prove to retail that a planned economy is a
higher form of people's economy'.[18]

All present were clearly hostile to private business, though anxious that they should not appear to be. The public might react badly to an overnight nationalization of all trade. More to the point, all present knew that private trade was still necessary, because there wasn't anything else. In the ruins of the Eastern European cities, there was no way to stop starving people from trading, and indeed there was no alternative means of distributing food. In the most devastated parts of the region, it would have been difficult even to organize rationing. The Italian writer Primo Levi, upon being liberated from Auschwitz, immediately trudged to the nearest city:

> The market of [Kraków] had blossomed out spontaneously, as soon as the front had passed by, and in a few days it had invaded an entire suburb. Everything was bought and sold there, and the whole city centred on it; townsfolk were selling furniture, books, paintings, clothes and silver; peasant women, padded out like mattresses, offered meat, poultry, eggs, cheese; boys and girls, with noses reddened by the icy wind, searched for tobacco-addicts to buy their ration . . .[19]

But as the occupying authorities across the region began to impose rationing, tax laws and regulation, that sort of market acquired a sordid reputation and became known as a black market. The people working in it were no longer traders, but rather black marketeers. In order to rid squares and plazas of (in their eyes) messy and uncontrolled capitalism, communist authorities set out to nationalize the retail and wholesale industries right away, in just about every country in the region. In eastern Germany, for example, the Soviet authorities resurrected a prewar cooperative, Konsum, setting it up to behave exactly like a state company. Instead of serving its members as it had before the Nazis shut it down, Konsum received privileged access to wholesale goods and could choose to whom to sell them.[20]

Though their businesses were technically legal in 1945 and 1946, Eastern Europe's small capitalists understood right from the start that they were operating in a hostile environment. In Fest's retelling of his family's story, his grandfather's decision to reopen his shop during that period acquires the attributes of a heroic struggle. Immediately after the war, the Fests had to fight just to get allotments of flour and sugar from the state offices (Handel und Versorgung), which had quickly taken over the distribution of basic goods, all of which were eventually allotted through ration cards. 'We didn't get nearly enough merchandise to match the amount people wanted to buy,' Fest remembered. So he and his family would collect customers' ration cards and take them over to Konsum, where they used them to purchase the goods which they hadn't been able to procure themselves. They made no profit from this activity, which they saw as a favour to customers. They hoped it would build loyalty, and help keep the shop open.[21]

Down the street from the Fest establishment, Ulrich Schneider's family business, a textile and clothing shop, underwent a similar transformation. Schneider's shop had also been in the family for several generations, and was also the focus of enormous hopes and fears. In the final days of the war, his father had hidden their inventory – coats, dresses, rolls of fabrics – in friends' houses and barns. What remained in the store was plundered by the Russians in May 1945. The Red Army then adopted the family house as a provisional headquarters, using the shop windows to lay out their dead in coffins. Schneider and his parents moved into an apartment above the shop. In August his father – who had not been in the Nazi party and somehow avoided Soviet arrest and deportation – received a permit from the occupation regime, to resume trade.

Like the Fests, the Schneiders boarded up their shop windows with wood, leaving only a few small openings so that some of their wares – whatever had been rescued from the local attics and basements – could be displayed and sold off. They dragged a few sewing machines out of hiding, and began doing alterations and making rag dolls. 'There wasn't anything else to do,' remembered Schneider.

After a few weeks, Schneider's father began making regular trips to the Erzgebirge, the mountains on the German–Czech border, the traditional home of the textile industry. Though the region was hundreds of kilometres away, he went by horse-drawn cart: 'it was very trying, because there were checkpoints everywhere and he was held up wherever there were Russians'. He had no other options because there was no other source of goods. But what he brought back he could certainly sell.[22]

Hope that things would improve kept the Fests, the Schneiders and other small entrepreneurs open throughout the years of 1945 and 1946. By 1947, however, it became clear that things were not going to get better. The Leipzig Fair, reopened that year for the first time since the war, proved a major disappointment and was for textile merchants like the Schneiders a turning point. Although the fair, a central feature of German commercial life since the Middle Ages, was hailed with much fuss and propaganda, no textiles or fabrics were actually for sale. In the past, 'you met other companies there or caught up on things – what there was, what was new,' Ulrich Schneider explained. But now the fair had become a propaganda event, not a place to exchange real business information.

The year 1947 was a turning point in Poland too. Following the parliamentary elections in January, the 'victorious' communists launched a series of reforms designed to increase the number of industrial workers, who presumably might support them in future, and to cut down on private industry and retail, which did not support them at all. This was the infamous 'battle for trade', launched by the Economics Minister, Hilary Minc. Personally appointed by Stalin, Minc was a prewar communist who had acquired a real gift for Marxist economic jargon. 'The struggle for the conquest of the market does not mean the elimination of market-capitalist elements,' he told the Central Committee plenum in April: 'it means only a struggle for control over these elements by the People's Democratic State.'[23] There would be a 'free market', in other words, but it would be kept under firm government control – which meant it would not be free, of course.

In practice, Minc tried to kill off private enterprise without ever quite saying so. The 'battle for trade' took the form of rigid price regulation and high taxation, accompanied by criminal penalties for the failure to fill out proper forms, as well as a massive licensing and permit system. All entrepreneurs had to have business licences which required them to prove they were 'professionally qualified', whatever that meant in the postwar chaos. Limits were placed on the numbers of people whom one entrepreneur could employ and on what quantities of goods could be taken in and out of the country and even in and out of Warsaw. As in Germany, the Poles also effectively nationalized the wholesale industry. Private businesses were prevented from buying and selling specific commodities, including food, at whole-sale prices.

Officially, the communist press trumpeted the 'battle for trade' as a resounding success, and official Polish historiography continued to do so until the 1980s. But the economist Anders Åslund notes that this success was short-lived: 'it is difficult to join in the exultation, since the "battle for trade" dealt a savage blow to trade as a whole'. Between 1947 and 1949, the number of private trading and distribution firms fell by half, and the state sector was not able to replace them. Thanks to the death of wholesaling, the remaining private shops and busi-nesses, especially in small towns, had no legal access to goods of any kind.[24] The imposition of these new rules was unpredictable: 'from one day to another, specified economic activities lost their legal basis of existence,' recalled one economist.[25] But the result was perfectly predictable: the rapid development of more black markets (now clan-destine), the chaotic distribution of goods – and chronic shortages of everything. A former auditor of a rural cooperative – a fancy name for what was, in practice, a state-managed wholesaler – remembers that it was difficult to know whether the shortages in her sector were the result of theft or incompetence. As a part of her job, she was required to inspect the account books of her company's regional branches, and they were full of mistakes: 'I didn't always know the reason for the missing money ... all the shop girls were uneducated, they couldn't add or measure.' By 1950, the cooperative had expelled whatever remained of the prewar 'blue-blooded' management, and replaced them with reliable members of the working class, in one case a hair-dresser. Not surprisingly, the situation failed to improve.[26]

Overnight, the rule of law disappeared, as the only way for many to stay in business was to break the law. Small businessmen ceased to be respectable, and instead became *prywaciarze*, 'privateers', semi-outlaw figures. The daughter of a talented engineer who ran a very small manufacturing business in that period remembers being embar-rassed to tell her friends what her father did for a living.[27] Some bent rules that limited the number of employees by employing family mem-bers, or bent rules limiting the size of a business by appointing family members as 'owners'. Private businessmen also learned to avoid big investments – they attracted too much attention from the tax authorities – and to focus on business plans which could be started and halted very quickly, as the legal situation changed. Long-term planning was impossible.

Over time, businessmen also learned how to work together. Many renamed themselves 'craftsmen', a designation which allowed them to maintain tiny businesses and workshops without the stigma of being 'capitalists'. They also created guilds, state institutions which did sometimes act in the interests of their members. The guilds tried to organize access to raw materials for private shops at official, state-controlled prices. They also altered registration rules so that car mechanics, plumbers and others could become 'craftsmen'. A former guild boss – technically a state employee – recalls 'bending the rules' on more than one occasion, in the expectation that sooner or later the whole system would be improved: 'I thought people would change, as they studied more, learned more, that the system would become more intelligent.' Alas it did not.[28]

In Hungary, the nationalization of retail proceeded more slowly, not least because in 1945 and 1946, the communist party didn't initially have a large enough parliamentary majority to control every aspect of economic policy and wasn't able to impose harsh regulations and taxes. The party conducted a 'war on trade' anyway, not through regulation but through its propaganda organs and police. From the summer of 1945, the communist party's invective against small businessmen, small traders and informal street markets grew ever fiercer, until it was nearly as harsh as its attacks on fascists. In July, the Budapest police chief declared he intended to 'liberate the workers of Budapest from the hyenas of the black market'. By September, some 600 policemen, accompanied by 600 Soviet soldiers and 300 detectives, had detained 1500 'black marketeers', mostly in the course of two raids on large Budapest street markets.

The anti-business propaganda campaign quickly spread beyond the street markets. Later in July, *Szabad Nép* printed a series of photographs showing workers laying tram rails while people sat in cafés nearby, sipping coffee – and enjoying themselves, in other words, while the working class worked. Police raids on cafés, bars and restaurants in Budapest followed soon afterwards. The police even shut down the Café New York, a beloved prewar institution, confiscated the food found in its storerooms and ostentatiously distributed it to returning prisoners of war.[29]

Through bribery and connections some restaurants stayed open. But that led to another campaign and another series of raids a year later. In June 1946, *Szabad Nép* reported that ten 'luxury' restaurants had been shut because 'by serving the most expensive banned meat products to satisfy the needs of the few, they endangered social peace and public calm'. That might well have been true: the communist campaign was intended to be popular, and among some people it probably was. In a period of shortages, inflation and real hunger, resentment of those who could eat well must have been running very high.[30]

Other articles tried to make private restaurants seem not just immoral, but laughable. Some mocked the 'bourgeois' practice of tipping, and one made fun of the tailcoat, the traditional garb of the Budapest waiter:

> This out-of-date outfit is still widespread, waiters are still dressed in them, as if displaying the spirit of the lackeys of old times. ... In the near future the trade unions will abolish the wearing of tails by waiters ... this unhealthy, uncomfortable piece of clothing will hopefully vanish, to make room for a better, more appropriate, more comfortable and more tasteful outfit.

The secret police followed up, investigating private business for all manner of fraud and impropriety. A baker in an elegant district was detained by the police after they discovered that 'not a single gram of salt is added' to his bread, although he had received 400 kilos of salt as a part of that month's ration.[31] He was suspected of selling the salt on the black market. Another target was the owner of the Baghdad Café, whose aesthetics were deemed immoral. 'The entrance of the restaurant leads the visitor into a wardrobe with mirrors on the wall, beside a painting depicting ladies dressed in evening dress in erotic positions with their thighs uncovered,' the police report complained. Worse, 'two negroes are members of staff'. This last observation reflected not merely racism, but also a deep suspicion of an establishment able to retain such exotic foreign employees.[32]

Hoping to stay in business, restaurateurs tried various strategies to stay afloat. One café owner transformed herself into a street vendor; others joined the communist party, with the hope that this would absolve them of political suspicion. Eventually, many café owners volunteered to be 'nationalized', the better to ensure their own future as 'managers' of their former businesses. One such petition, filed by Mrs Lászlóné Göttler in 1949, reads like a for-sale advertisement:

> I hereby request the Management of the National Company to take over my restaurant in operation from 1923 at Benierky street 19, Sasha-lom, and to keep my person as a manager. . . . It is a corner house consisting of a winter-pub and a separate room, an open veranda, a terrace, a buffet and a kiosk in the garden. Up until today it has been a unit of good revenues close to the canning factory without unpaid taxes . . .[33]

Some of them succeeded. Klára Rothschild, proprietress since 1934 of the Clara Salon in Váci Utca, Budapest's most exclusive shopping street, managed to stay in charge of her shop following its nationalization, not least because she was so popular among party leaders' wives. Rothschild followed Paris fashions, and adapted them to Budapest tastes. Because of her high status, she was even allowed to travel to Paris in order to keep *au courant* with French styles.[34]

Over time, nearly all private restaurants in Budapest became 'people's' cafeterias or state-owned 'proletarian' pubs. The names changed too: instead of the 'New York Café' they adopted short, Hungarian-sounding names – 'Adam's buffet' or 'Quick Café' – or else simply a number. Waiters and tips disappeared. Queues replaced good service. In a city which had fuelled itself on espresso and cream cakes for decades, these were truly revolutionary changes.

Land reform came first, because land reform was thought to be popular. Retail came later because the communists knew its elimination would be unpopular. But industry – especially heavy industry – was the main prize. Industry had always interested communists far more than 'backward' sectors like farming and 'irrelevant' sectors like retail. In the Marxist view of the world, manufacturing was the future. Steel plants, mills and machine-tool factories would modernize the country, eliminating old-fashioned ways of thinking. The goal of industrialization was ultimately political: once everybody was an industrial worker, then everybody would support the communist party, or so the theory went. In the meantime, the destruction of the property-owning class would deprive the opposition of powerful allies.

The most profound changes had to wait until the period of Soviet reparations and generalized theft came to an end. Thanks to the poor election results, the USSR agreed to slow down its collection of reparations in Hungary in 1946, and in 1948 reparations demands were decreased by 50 per cent.[35] German reparations on a large scale also came to an end in 1948, largely thanks to the pleas of Ulbricht and others who knew what damage they had done to the communist party's reputation.[36] In Poland and Czechoslovakia there had never been any official acknowledgement of reparations, and so there was no official acknowledgement of their end. Still, by 1947–8 the most visible forms of Soviet and Red Army theft had stopped.

But the damage had been done. In the postwar period, everything had been up for grabs and nobody's property had been sacrosanct. In that atmosphere, the first wave of large-scale nationalizations won some public acceptance. Many people were no longer shocked by the sight of mass confiscations. Others thought that only state ownership could bring order to the economic chaos. In October 1945, for example, the Polish provisional government abruptly nationalized all the land within the boundaries of the city of Warsaw, homes and factories included.[37] Such a decree would have been considered outrageous before 1939, and is unthinkable now. But in 1945, the nationalization of urban land, mostly covered in rubble, seemed only logical to many Poles.[38] The provisional government's January 1946 decree, nationalizing all factories across the country with fifty or more workers, didn't encounter much resistance either. Many of these factories had no owners anyway, and the previous managers had died or fled. When these businesses became the property of the state, the situation was actually more stable: at least the ownership was clear.[39]

In Germany, the newly unified communist party initially portrayed the nationalization of major industry not as an economic policy, but as a piece of anti-fascist politics. Just like the Junkers, the German industrialists were accused of complicity with Nazism: if they'd owned anything of consequence before the war then they deserved to lose it.

As a precaution, the communist party decreed that nationalization of industry should be the policy of the 'anti-fascist bloc', and none of the legal political parties were permitted to oppose it. Initially, the Eastern German Christian Democratic leader, Jakob Kaiser, baulked. Though he approved in principle (later he became a proponent of nationalization in West Germany), he feared that if the Soviet zone implemented nationalization on its own, then the policy would split Germany into two different economies – as it eventually did. Under pressure from the Soviet Military Administration, Kaiser did finally agree, however. As a final piece of propaganda, the communists decided to hold a referendum on nationalization in 1946. Anxious not to botch their referendum like the Poles, they limited the vote to the state of Saxony, and they restricted the ballot to one question: did voters want to place 'the factories of war criminals and Nazi criminals into the hands of the people'? It passed.[40]

At the same time, Hungarian nationalization took place in stages. First the coal mines, then the largest industrial conglomerates, and eventually the banks. In March 1948, the government nationalized all remaining factories with over 100 workers, putting 90 per cent of heavy industry and 75 per cent of light industry in state hands. By 1948 there was very little major private industry anywhere in the country.[41]

This 'success' had a political price, in Hungary as everywhere else. In practice, nationalization had very little effect on the daily lives of ordinary workers: they were paid the same wages, did the same work, had the same grievances. What difference did it make if their foremen worked for a capitalist or for the Ministry of Industry? Buoyed by consciousness of the rightness of his cause – he was an employee of 'the people' after all – a state manager might even be more arrogant than a private owner. Instead of making the communist party more popular, nationalization often made workers more wary, and even led in some places to strikes. The historian Padraic Kenney described what happened next in the textile city of Łódź:

> at the Jarisch mill, strikers successfully argued that [the mill director's] actions harmed the workers as well as the state. By carelessly setting norms too high, without regard to the ability of the worker or of the machine, he

made it impossible for many workers to earn bonuses (which often made up most of one's pay). He also offended workers' dignity by using them instead of horses to haul wagons.[42]

The conflicts in Łódź reached a peak in September 1947, when some 40 per cent of the city's workers went on strike. Not every factory in Poland followed the same pattern. Kenney also notes that in the formerly German city of Wrocław, populated almost entirely by refugees, strikes were far fewer because social ties were much looser. Still, Łódź was not an exception. Miners and factory workers went on strike in Silesia in 1946. A strike in the ports of Gdańsk and Gdynia in that same year ended with two men dead.[43]

This was not unusual: nationalization politicized ordinary workplace conflicts almost everywhere. When factory workers were angry about pay or conditions in their state-owned factories, they aimed their protests directly at the state. In 1947, when strikes broke out in Csepel, a working-class district of Budapest, workers hijacked twenty trucks and drove into the centre of town to demand that the government raise their wages. That afternoon, Interior Minister Rajk went to Csepel, accompanied by the boss of the official government trade union. Both were heckled by workers. Retribution was swift: the political police immediately entered the striking factory and arrested 350 people. Taking no chances, the police stepped up their reliance on informers after that, and began 'cleansing' other factories too. They recorded evidence of discontent – 'we had better treatment during the old reactionary period than now in this so-called democracy,' one worker grumbled, according to the police files – and they began to identify and dismiss 'troublemaking' workers. The Diósgyőr Steel Mill instigated 113 'political' disciplinary procedures in May and June of 1948. From 1949 onwards, any discussion of strike action was considered an 'anti-democratic' crime against the state, and workers could be expelled from the party even for suggesting it.[44]

In the longer term, nationalization of the economy prolonged the shortages and economic distortions created by the war. Central planning and fixed prices distorted markets, making trade between individuals as well as between enterprises difficult. These problems were compounded by weak, non-existent or competing national currencies. In 1944 and 1945, the 'occupation' Polish zloty, the Soviet ruble and the Nazi Reichsmark were all circulating in Poland. Yeast and alcohol served as currency in some places too.[45] In their zone of Germany, Soviet officials had closed all banks and expropriated all bank accounts by August 1945. Only those accounts containing fewer than 3000 Reichsmarks remained accessible to their owners. With those moves, they simultaneously wiped out the wealthiest Germans in their zone, deprived the private economy of capital and hastened bankruptcies across all sectors.

Like the British, French and Americans, the Soviet military authorities in Berlin also issued a new currency for their zone of Germany. They called it the 'M-Mark', decreed it could be exchanged for Reichsmarks on a one-to-one basis and used it to pay troops and purchase goods. Though they never admitted to doing so in public, they immediately began printing M-Marks as fast as possible – 17.5 billion between February and April. The other allies would eventually be forced to carry out a currency reform in 1946 just in order to stave off hyperinflation.[46]

In Hungary, the combination of a newly floating currency, the threat of impending nationalization, the high cost of reparations and general economic insecurity did create, for about a year and a half, what may have been the most extreme bout of hyperinflation ever to take place anywhere, at any time. At its zenith, in the summer of 1946, the Hungarian pengö was counted in thousand millions. Its value halved every day, and prices changed every hour. A Budapest artist, Tamás Lossonczy, kept a diary at the time:

> Yesterday at 10 in the morning I went to the Cultural Ministry to collect the money for a painting of mine they had bought for the museum. The deal was 10 grams of gold. I asked about the price of gold from a jeweler on the way. In the morning, one gram of gold was worth 190–200 thousand million pengö. A dollar was 170 thousand million pengö.

Lossonczy was paid 2000 thousand million pengö. But by the time he finished the transaction, it was afternoon:

> ... by 2 p.m. the price of gold had risen to 280 thousand million and the dollar to 260 thousand million. I wanted to use the money for setting glass in the windows of the studio, which cost 11 dollars, which, according to the exchange rates of noon yesterday was 2860 thousand million, so I'd have a loss of 860 thousand million.[47]

Barter inevitably replaced cash. A few days later, Lossonczy recorded the sale of one of his paintings for 'twenty kilos of wheaten flour'. In August, the government finally carried out a currency reform. One unit of the new currency, the forint, was worth 400,000 quadrillion pengő.[48]

Not all of the distortions were reflected in inflation. Despite angry propaganda, police actions and political pressure, the semi-legal black market kept expanding, taking the form of everything from primitive street hawkers of the kind Primo Levi saw in Kraków to sophisticated smuggling operations. In the months immediately following the war, most East Germans spent a few hours a day 'working' (or 'shopping') in the black market. Berliners then spent their weekends in the countryside, looking for food, for purchase or for barter.[49] Staple goods were rationed almost everywhere. But while this ensured basic subsistence and kept people alive, it also meant that black market or free market prices skyrocketed, creating even more discontent. As a Polish propaganda official reported, 'The lack of goods and inefficient distribution make for a lot of malcontents. The Łódź worker cannot accept the fact that his children can only gaze at cake from afar, and he is not satisfied that one like himself who works hard earns so little, while some parasite makes big money on the free market and the state gets nothing from him.'[50]

As nationalization progressed, the shortages worsened, causing difficulties for factories as well as shoppers. In desperation, the Leuna Chemical Works in East Germany began bartering fertilizer for food:

> Fourteen train wagons of potatoes and vegetables that were to be transported illegally out of the Haldensleben district were sent back. No official found it strange that the Leuna works sent out an entire train with fertilizer in order to set up an exchange with the farmers in the villages of Nordge[r]mersleben and Gro[ß S]antersleben, although the farmers of these villages have not yet fulfilled their mandatory orders of potatoes and vegetables.[51]

Though that story dates from 1947, it could also have taken place in 1967, or even 1987. Shortages and imbalances plagued the People's Democracies from the very beginning and lasted until the very end. The economies of Eastern Europe grew after the war, because they were starting from nothing – they began literally from ground zero –

but they quickly fell behind their counterparts in Western Europe. They never did catch up.

Strange though it may sound to say so, party economists often understood perfectly well what was wrong. The archived files of the Polish Ministry of Trade and Industry, Minc's fiefdom, contain many letters from clear-eyed bureaucrats around the country: one after the next, they patiently explain the negative effects of increased state control. Private businesses, many argued, were more productive than their state-owned counterparts. Rapid nationalization of both large and small enterprises was making the economic situation worse. A letter to the minister from an institution called the Central Bureau of Technical Inputs in the spring of 1947 argued that private enterprises 'are smaller entities than state enterprises ... and are therefore able to carry out orders faster and more effectively, and usually at lower prices, than state enterprises. This is the result of the fact that private and cooperative companies are directly interested in profits and a quick turnover of capital.'[52]

The letter, in effect a plea for clemency for private business, also contained a list of things that private companies were producing, including pumps, thermometers, machine parts, scales and building materials. 'To sum up,' the Bureau of Technical Inputs concluded, 'we confirm that private and cooperative companies supply us with a wide range of articles, so that we may better and more quickly orient ourselves in the means of carrying out the most cost-effective production.'

Individual enterprises also tried to argue against nationalization, sometimes marshalling support for their cases within the government. In June 1946, the managers of the Anczyc printing house in Kraków, a business specializing in high-quality illustrated books – and owned by the same family for seventy years – wrote to the Education Ministry. The 'democratic character' of their company, its excellent treatment of its workers and its unique graphic expertise should make it exempt from the nationalization laws, they argued: 'now, when we are rebuilding Polish culture and art ... we will put our illustrated scientific and artistic publications at risk if we remove the individual influence of the owner'.[53] The Anczyc owners attached supporting letters from various other institutions – the Kraków Society of Book Lovers, the Jagellonian University – as well from their own print shop workers, who testified that although they favoured nationalization 'in principle', they were convinced that 'private ownership will not harm our material situation'. This deluge of support won over the Education Ministry, which passed the printer's request on to various other institutions. Despite all of this support, the effort failed. A bureaucrat at the Ministry of Information and Propaganda decreed that 'the firm, under the pretext of acting for the good of the printing industry and the high quality of its work . . . wants to remain a profit-making enterprise and exploit the excess labour of the technical workers and employees'. The printing house was nationalized in 1949, and the owners' property confiscated.[54]

Evidence that private enterprises could be both profitable and popular among their workers proved equally annoying to German communists, who conducted a survey of the private sector in 1950 and passed the results to the economic department of the Central Committee. The committee members must have found them depressing reading. Party inspectors had discovered that productivity was higher in private companies, workers appeared more satisfied in private companies and private owners were still very popular. At one firm, the owner 'gave 12,500 marks to his employees for Christmas'; another granted his employees two weeks' extra wages and a food package for the holidays, including butter and sugar.

Though some of these factories contained communist party cells, the report noted that within private factories 'the question of class struggle was hardly discussed', and the workers were unenlightened. One had shockingly declared that the factory owner 'is not an exploiter, but an entrepreneur'. Another said that if his company were nationalized 'we would earn less and there would be no Christmas celebration'. The bureaucrats' response to this was frankly ideological: the Central Committee members decided that the 'educational and propaganda work in private enterprises must be systematically improved'. Trade union work must be stepped up as well.[55]

Their response to the relative success of private retail was no different. There is no 'trade' in the Soviet zone of Germany, one economist complained in 1948, only 'distribution'. But instead of creating better conditions for trade – that would have meant freeing prices and allowing the growth of private retail and wholesalers – the government resolved to create a substitute: a chain of state-managed 'free' shops, the Handelsorganisation. At these 'HO' shops, people could buy consumer goods and food unavailable elsewhere, without ration tickets, at what purported to be market prices.

The public received them with mixed feelings, as the party surveys recorded. One woman welcomed them because 'now we will be able to buy important goods for daily life'. Others complained that 'free shops are very nice but not at these prices', that 'a worker cannot buy anything there with the money he earns', or that they were 'only for people with a lot of money'.[56]

It quickly became clear that even these 'free' shops couldn't compete with the private sector, a problem which continued to puzzle party economists. At another meeting of the economic department of the Central Committee a few years later, the group analysed the figures. The number of people employed in the private sector had plummeted, which was not surprising given the financial and political pressures on private owners. Yet the private sector's turnover was increasing. Private retail had maintained its 'business connections' to private industry, the bureaucrats speculated, which might be helping shops get 'uncontrolled goods' from the state sector. The private sector also seemed more flexible, and it had a more stable customer base.

The conclusion: a commission should be formed. Fewer permits for the creation of private wholesalers should be granted. Taxes on profits should be raised, and commercial space was not to be rented out to private businessmen. Private retail, the committee concluded, must 'lower its turnover by 10%'. If reality was not conforming to ideology, then it would be forced to do so.[57] In 1949, the East German Politburo even decreed that every state enterprise would have, in addition to its economic leadership, a deputy director responsible for politics. He would have to set an 'example of discipline and constant vigilance', to keep workers apprised of all national events and to keep them informed about the Soviet Union: 'employees have to be convinced that the victory of progressive democratic forces in Germany can only be attained with the support of the USSR'.[58]

The response was no different in other spheres, or in other Eastern

European countries. Strikers' demands, public discontent and poor economic performance did not persuade the communists to loosen up the system. Instead of backing away from ideology, they grimly stepped up their propaganda, increased the pace of 'reform', and sought new ways to persuade their compatriots to conform to the rules of the new system. As in the sphere of politics, failure spawned greater radicalism.

More control, not less, was what the communist parties of the region believed would stop the strikes, fix the shortages and raise living standards to the level of the West. And so, one by one, East European governments began drawing up complex, multi-year, Soviet-style central plans, setting targets for everything from road construction to shoe production. Hungary launched its Three Year Plan in August 1947, and would announce a Five Year Plan in 1950. Poland also launched a Three Year Plan in 1947, and a Six Year Plan in 1950. Germany launched a Two Year Plan in January 1949 and then a Five Year Plan for the years 1951–5.

The targets set in these first plans were often pulled from the air, and the understanding of pricing mechanisms was unsophisticated, to say the least. One of Poland's first economic bureaucrats tried to keep track of the fluctuating prices of coal and bread in the months before the first plan went into effect, imagining that would eventually help him set the 'correct' prices for all goods – prices which, of course, would never need to be changed again, he thought, since there would be no inflation in a communist economy. Poles also debated, at one point, whether they should simply set the same prices for basic goods in Poland as in the USSR, which had presumably already discovered the secret of correct pricing.[59]

The numbers were no less arbitrary at the micro level. Jo Langer, the wife of a prominent Slovak communist, worked in a Bratislava export company in 1948, and witnessed the imposition of planning from the ground up:

> My first shock came when in December the head of the planning department asked me to make out a table showing exactly how many tooth-brushes (what sort of bristles, what colours, etc) I was planning to deliver to Switzerland, England, Malta, Madagascar and so on during the first

half of the coming year. I said that I couldn't possibly know, as our agents in various places were ordinary mortals and as such were subject to illness and death . . . My objections were waved aside and I was told to draw up my forecast without delay.

Langer writes that 'with a bad conscience', she presented her invented statistics. Her boss was satisfied:

His staff was then kept busy drawing up a neat chart summarizing similar data received from our other departments. In Prague, the chart was incorporated into an even more artistically drawn-up table which was at last launched on its way to even higher places. On its way up it was mated with similar creations from other economic branches, to give birth in the end to the Plan with a capital P: the ultimate basis of our national economy.[60]

Despite their fantastical origins, the communists had great faith in the Plans, which became the focus of massive national propaganda campaigns. Enormous banners hung from buildings and factories, calling on people to 'fulfil the Plan' or 'work for the Plan' or 'achieve socialist victory with the Plan'. The word *Aufbau* – 'construction' or 'building up' – was used frequently and positively as well, on posters, on banners and on pamphlets. Radio stations discussed the Plan to the point of obsessiveness. In 1948, East German radio scriptwriters were told to comment 'repeatedly' on four numbers which had been written into the Plan: the 35 per cent increase in production, the 30 per cent rise in productivity, the 15 per cent increase in wages and the 7 per cent reduction in budgets.

In order not to bore listeners (or, as the radio authorities more delicately put it, in order not to 'evoke apathy') the writers were also instructed to liven up their repetition of these four figures with interviews and reports from the ground. It was suggested that they present profiles of enterprises which had overfulfilled their production plans, and that they offer 'positive criticism' of delays. Success was thus to be contrasted with failure (reversible failure, of course), which would presumably make the programmes more interesting.[61] In the offices of Polish radio, 'discussion of the Six Year Plan' appeared on every list of every programme's political priorities, from sport to culture to politics, from 1950 until 1956.

At the same time, the Plans were touted as the solution to myriad problems. East German radio told its listeners in 1948 not to worry about the West German currency reforms, which were then shaking up eastern Germany: 'The fulfilment and over-fulfilment' of the Plan will 'take us across this hard but necessary currency trouble'.[62] Nor were they meant exclusively for industry. 'What we need from our artists,' wrote an East German newspaper, are 'works of art that help us in our daily struggle in fulfilling the Five Year Plan'.[63] German cultural bureaucrats drew up annual and quarterly plans, and also issued annual and quarterly reports on their fulfilment. They included general goals – 'propagating the economic and cultural development in the Soviet Union', for example – as well as more specific targets. One 1948 plan required every museum in the country to construct, rapidly, an exhibit describing and explaining the Two Year Plan.[64]

In Poland, the reconstruction of Warsaw became one of the central focuses of the Six Year Plan, which was launched in January 1950. To mark the occasion, a lush, 350-page photo album was published under the authorship of Bierut himself. The album contained pictures of Warsaw as it was – piles of rubble, children squatting in the ruins, women hanging laundry on broken balconies – and drawings of Warsaw as it would be: austere socialist realist skyscrapers, imposing government buildings, wide boulevards. There would be space for 'mass meetings and demonstrations', sports palaces and parks.[65]

But Poland's Six Year Plan ran out of steam even before six years were up. It stuttered to a halt after Stalin's death in 1953, and much of what had been planned was never finished. Though reconstruction of the city continued, many of the buildings in the Warsaw album were never built, while others were modified drastically. For that, a later generation of Warsovians was grateful.

PART TWO

High Stalinism

II

Reactionary enemies

We teach that it is proper to render unto Caesar the things that are Caesar's and to God the things that are God's. But when Caesar sits himself on the altar, we respond curtly: he may not.

Cardinal Stefan Wyszyński, 1953

By the end of 1948, the Eastern European communist parties and their Soviet allies had already enacted enormous changes in the new People's Democracies. They had eliminated the most capable of their potential opponents. They had taken control of the institutions they considered most valuable. They had created, from scratch, the political police. In Poland, the armed opposition had been destroyed and the legal opposition had been dismantled. In Hungary and East Germany, spontaneous 'anti-fascist' movements no longer existed, and genuine opposition parties had been eliminated. In the Czech Republic, a successful coup d'état had left the communists with absolute power. Loyal, pro-Soviet communist parties now ruled Bulgaria, Romania and Albania. Social democracy, despite its deep roots in the region, had vanished from the political arena, along with large private companies and many independent organizations.

Yet the socialist paradise was still far away. The regimes had acquired some collaborators and some true believers, and they were attempting to educate more. Many tens of thousands of people had joined the party and its affiliated mass organizations, including the youth movements, the women's organizations and the official trade unions. But the communist parties were unpopular, and their support was still shaky, even in their most trusted institutions. Millions of

Eastern Europeans still considered communist ideology to be alien, and still thought the party represented a foreign power. The Eastern European communist parties had not won legitimacy through elections, and they had not won legitimacy through their economic policies either. Already, their economies were slipping behind those of the West. The East Germans, especially East Berliners, saw this most clearly after the West German currency reform in 1948. But anyone with Western relatives or access to Western radio knew it too.

Even Stalin didn't really trust his East European followers, and so he concluded that they now needed harsher methods in order to stay in power. For the next five or so years the Eastern European states would directly mimic Soviet domestic and international policies in the hopes of eliminating their opponents for good, achieving higher economic growth and influencing a new generation of firm supporters through propaganda and public education. Until Stalin's death in 1953, all of the region's communist parties would pursue an identical set of goals using an identical set of tactics. This was the era of High Stalinism.

Although the rhetoric of High Stalinism always sounded supremely confident, the period began in crisis. In March 1949, Bierut, now the unchallenged leader of the Polish communist party, outlined his problem in a letter he wrote to Molotov, which was then passed on to Stalin. Bierut first praised the Polish secret policemen who had 'repulsed the attacks of the enemy' in 1945 and 1946. Not only had Poland's Soviet-trained security officers vanquished the underground and 'destroyed Mikołajczyk's PSL', but they had become a 'sharp instrument of the people's power in the battle against the class enemy and the penetration of foreign espionage'. Yet he was not satisfied. For all of their many achievements, the secret police had still not managed to 'decisively reorganize its work in order to conduct a more successful battle against the activities of the enemy'. Among these enemies Bierut listed not only the underground movements, but also the 'clerics', the Polish social democrats, the former members of the Home Army and even former communists who had been 'excluded from the party'.[1]

Bierut then went on to list the many 'insufficiencies' of the Polish secret police, and to recommend solutions. These included the complete closure of the western land and northern sea borders; the infiltration of the potential 'enemy' groups; increased security for factories and party offices; and careful 'tactical' work among the clergy, using everything from 'coercive methods' in some cases to 'neutralization' in others. The tone of Bierut's letter is deeply paranoid, with multiple references to spies, Anglo-American agents and enemies of various kinds:

> In the course of recent months it was possible to observe signs of self-satisfaction, underestimation of the enemy's ability to reconstruct its organized networks, insufficient watchfulness in relation to the enemy's activities, a tendency to adopt mechanically old methods of struggle which are clearly not sufficient for the current situation . . .[2]

Bierut's paranoia was in a certain sense justified. There was indeed great dissatisfaction among many Polish clerics, as well as in ex-Home Army, ex-communist and ex-social democratic circles. Large portions of Polish society were certainly more pro-American than pro-Soviet, and many felt more deeply attached to the ideals of the disbanded Home Army than they did to those of the new Polish army, which was visibly dominated by Soviet officers.

But Bierut's paranoia was surely amplified by Stalin's own paranoia, which notoriously increased in 1948 and 1949 as well, and for some of the same reasons. Millions of Soviet citizens had experienced the wealth and freedom of Western Europe for the first time during the Second World War, and had now returned home to a world devoid of material goods. 'Bikes were old, of pre-war make,' wrote Joseph Brodsky of his postwar Soviet childhood: 'and the owner of a soccer ball was considered a bourgeois.'[3] The dissatisfaction, even among believing communists, was real. Stalin knew it, and the Soviet secret police knew it. During a private telephone conversation, taped and recorded by the KGB, a Soviet general who had returned home from the front told a colleague that 'Absolutely everyone says openly how everyone is discontented with life. On the trains, in fact everywhere, it's what everyone's saying.'[4]

As a result of its wartime conquests and the bloody suppression of resistance movements, the Soviet Union had also acquired whole new categories of highly suspect residents. Because its borders had moved several hundred kilometres to the west, millions of inhabitants of prewar Poland, Romania, Czechoslovakia and the Baltic states were now Soviet citizens. Many were naturally unsympathetic to what they perceived as a new form of Russian imperialism, and the secret police knew that too. From 1945, the KGB viewed all of the citizens of the new western territories as potential agents of foreign influence, saboteurs and spies. Even after the majority of political prisoners were released from the Gulag following Stalin's death, Baltic and Ukrainian nationalists remained in Soviet prisons well into the 1960s.[5] To stifle the general discontent, and perhaps to scare new Soviet citizens into compliance, Stalin ordered a major wave of arrests in the years 1948–9, comparable in size to the 'Great Terror' of 1937–8. After a postwar lull, the camps of the Gulag began to fill up again. They would reach their peak, in terms of both numbers and economic significance, between 1950 and 1952.[6]

Stalin's heightened paranoia also helped provoke the Cold War – which in turn fuelled his anxiety further. Western doubts about Soviet intentions in Europe had solidified by the time of Churchill's 1946 'Iron Curtain' speech, and had become policy by 1947, when President Truman declared America's intention to 'support free peoples who are resisting attempted subjugation by armed minorities or by outside pressures', a statement which became known as the Truman Doctrine.[7] Eventually, 'support for free peoples' would take many forms, ranging from the fanciful – balloons carrying propaganda leaflets were floated over the East–West borders – to the pragmatic.[8] By far the most effective Cold War 'weapon' was Radio Free Europe, a broadcasting service based in Munich, funded by the US government but staffed by émigrés and exiles, broadcasting in their own languages. Radio Free Europe ultimately proved effective not because it offered counter-propaganda, but because it reliably reported the news of the day.[9]

Western fear of Soviet intentions combined with Stalin's paranoia eventually led to deeper military and diplomatic changes, all very well described in the many excellent histories of the Cold War.[10] In April 1949, the Western Europeans ratified the North Atlantic Treaty, and created NATO. In October 1949, Stalin abandoned the pretence that there would be an imminent reunification of Germany, and the

German Democratic Republic – also known as East Germany, the GDR or the DDR, from Deutsche Demokratische Republik – became an independent state. The rearmament of Germany, unthinkable a few years earlier, slowly picked up pace on both sides of the German–German border with the creation of the Western Bundeswehr, the Federal Defence Force, and the National People's Army in the East. Extra measures were taken to ensure the loyalty of other Eastern European armies. In November 1949, a senior Soviet general, Konstantin Rokossovskii, was named Polish Defence Minister. Though of Polish origin (and though his family still insist heartily that he was born in Warsaw), Rokossovskii had made his career in the Red Army, and he never gave up his Soviet passport. His presence in the Polish government thus established, symbolically and practically, Soviet control over Poland's armed forces and foreign policy.[11] Other Soviet officers, some of whom spoke no language other than Russian, received senior jobs in the Polish and Hungarian armed forces at this time as well. In both armies, younger officers from working-class and peasant backgrounds were promoted rapidly while older officers were eased out.[12]

But in 1948 the Soviet Union also received three additional, specific blows to its prestige in Eastern Europe. The first was the arrival of the first tranche of Marshall Aid money, some $4bn of which would be distributed over the subsequent two years. The Marshall Fund was not the sole reason for the Western European economic recovery which now picked up pace, but it did provide a critical moral and financial boost. 'Marshall Money' became one of the common explanations for the real prosperity gap which was now developing between the eastern and western halves of the continent.[13]

The second blow was the result of a Soviet provocation which backfired. Following the Western Allies' announcement of a currency reform and their introduction of the West Mark (eventually the Deutsche Mark) into their occupation zones in June 1948, the Soviet Union responded with what would become known as the Berlin blockade. Soviet occupation authorities cut off electricity as well as road, rail and barge access to West Berlin, and halted deliveries of food and fuel. The currency reform did accelerate the economic divergence of East and West Germany but the purpose of the blockade was not just to

IRON CURTAIN

protest against the new West Mark. It was clearly intended to push the Americans out of Berlin, and perhaps out of Germany as well. The Red Army was confident it would succeed. One Soviet administrator later recalled that when the blockade was announced, the employees at the Soviet military headquarters in Karlshorst loudly cheered, believing that this was the beginning of the end: at last the Western Allies would depart Berlin![14]

Famously, that did not happen. Instead, between 24 June 1948 and 12 May 1949, the Western Allies organized a massive airlift, bringing thousands of tons of food and fuel into the Western sector of Berlin every day, enough to sustain 2 million people. Allied commitment to the Berlin airlift, and to the maintenance of a Western presence in Germany, took the Soviet leadership in Moscow very much by surprise. Soviet intelligence had massively underrated the airlift's chances of success, and had confidently predicted a quick Western withdrawal. Within a few weeks, the analysts were forced to change their minds. The superb logistics stunned the Russians in Berlin. To one Soviet officer, it seemed as if 'the aircraft deliberately flew low over Karlshorst to impress them. One would appear overhead, another would disappear over the horizon, and a third emerge, one after another without interruption, like a conveyor belt!'[15] The success of the airlift eventually forced the Soviet leadership to lift the blockade, and in the months that followed, West Berlin began agitating to become a formal part of West Germany. Soviet intelligence in the region began reporting back to Stalin threats of impending war. He was inclined to believe them.[16]

The third major blow to Stalin's prestige came from within the bloc. Josip Broz Tito, the 'little Stalin' of Yugoslavia, was the only Eastern European communist leader who did not suffer from the knowledge that he was deeply unpopular. Although he had plenty of enemies, and although he disposed of them quite brutally, the Yugoslav communist party also had its own sources of legitimacy. Having led the anti-Nazi resistance, and having created his own loyal army and secret police, Tito – uniquely in the region – had no need of Soviet military support in order to stay in power. Nor did he want much Soviet interference. Although tensions had been brewing for some time, the break became official in June 1948, when the rest of the bloc agreed to expel Yugoslavia from the Cominform.

If the success of the Berlin airlift had compounded Soviet paranoia about lurking Western conspiracies and Anglo-American spy rings, Tito's departure from the bloc fuelled Soviet fears of internal dissent. For if Tito could escape Stalin's influence, then why not others? If the Yugoslavs could design their own economic policies, then why shouldn't the Poles or the Czechs? Eventually 'Titoism', or 'right deviationism', became a very serious political crime: in the Eastern European context, a 'Titoist' was someone who wanted his national communist party to maintain some independence from the Soviet communist party. Like 'Trotskyism' the term could eventually be applied to anyone who objected (or appeared to object, or was accused of objecting) to the mainstream political line. 'Titoists' also became the new scapegoats. If Eastern Europe was not as prosperous as the West, then surely 'Titoists' were to blame. If shops were empty, 'Titoists' were at fault. If Central European factories were not producing at the expected level, 'Titoists' had sabotaged them.

Within the boundaries of the Eastern bloc, the year 1948 was an important turning point in domestic politics too: it was the year in which the Soviet Union's Eastern European allies abandoned all attempts to win legitimacy through an electoral process, and stopped tolerating any forms of genuine opposition. The full power of the police state was now turned against the regime's perceived enemies in the church, in the already-defeated political opposition and even within the communist party itself.

Violence, arrests and interrogation were deployed against regime opponents, but they were not the only tactic. From 1948, the communist parties also began a very long-term effort to corrupt the institutions of civil society from within, especially religious institutions. The intention was not to destroy churches, but to transform them into 'mass organizations', vehicles for the distribution of state propaganda just like the communist youth movements, the communist women's movements, or the communist trade unions.[17] In this new era, the communist parties felt it was no longer sufficient to scare opponents. They had to be exposed in public as traitors or thieves, put through humiliating show trials, subjected to extensive attacks in the media and placed in new, harsher prisons and specially designed camps.

The renewed attack on the enemies of communism was the most visible and dramatic element of High Stalinism. But the creation of a vast system of education and propaganda, designed to prevent more enemies from emerging in the future, was just as important to the Eastern European communists. In theory, they hoped to create not only a new kind of society but a new kind of person, a citizen who was not capable even of imagining alternatives to communism orthodoxy. During a turbulent discussion about falling listenership at East German radio, a high-ranking communist argued that 'it is necessary in every detail, in every programme, in every department to discuss the line of the party and to use it in daily work'.[18] This was precisely what was done across society: from 1948 onwards, the theories of Marxism-Leninism would be explained, expounded and discussed in kindergartens, schools and universities, on the radio and in the newspapers, through elaborate mass campaigns, parades and public events. Every public holiday became an occasion for teaching, and every organization, from the Konsum food cooperative in Germany to the Chopin Society in Poland, became a vehicle for the distribution of communist propaganda. The public in communist countries took part in campaigns for 'peace', they collected money in aid of communist North Korea, they marched in parades to celebrate communist holidays.[19] From the outside – and to some on the inside as well – High Stalinism looked like a political system whose attempt to achieve total control might well succeed.

From the earliest days of Soviet occupation, the church had been subject to harassment, and worse. Religious leaders, as prominent and influential members of civil society, had been among the first victims of the Red Army's initial wave of violence. Polish Catholic priests were sent to Soviet camps in large numbers. The German postwar camps contained both Catholic and Protestant clergy, with a particularly large number of Catholic youth leaders. Soviet occupation authorities had gone out of their way to ban religious youth camps and retreats. In Hungary, the wave of violence against youth groups had begun with the arrest of Father Kiss, the priest accused of organizing the murder of Red Army soldiers in 1946, and had continued with the banning of the Catholic youth group Kalot, with slander campaigns against Calvinist and Lutheran clergy, and many other forms of legal and personal harassment. As early as May 1945, a Lutheran bishop, Zoltán Túróczy, was put on trial before one of the People's Courts and sentenced to prison, presumably to scare others.[20]

Communist leaders instinctively hated and feared church leaders, and not merely because of their own doctrinal atheism. Religious leaders were a source of alternative moral and spiritual authority. They had independent financial resources and powerful contacts in Western Europe. Catholic priests in particular were feared, both because of their close links to the Vatican and because of the perceived power of international Catholic charities and societies. In many countries, notably Poland and Germany, church leaders had also been associated with the anti-fascist or anti-Hitler opposition during the war, which gave them additional status and legitimacy after the war's end. The church's organizing power, even aside from its ideological power, was formidable. It owned buildings where dissatisfied people could meet, as well as institutions where they could be employed. Every Sunday, priests and preachers had a guaranteed audience. Church publications had a guaranteed readership. That made the church an essential component and supporter of civic, charitable and educational organizations of all kinds.

Yet in the early years, both the new regimes and their Soviet allies had demonstrated a substantial measure of caution in dealing with the churches. In 1945 the Red Army did not, as a rule, shut down, sack or destroy churches as the Bolsheviks had during the Russian Revolution and Civil War, nor did it carry out mass shootings of priests.[21] Much of the time, Red Army soldiers in Germany went out of their way to facilitate the reopening of religious institutions – churches, schools, even theological colleges. They allowed the new radio stations to transmit sermons, and sanctioned the printing of bibles and other religious literature. This was deliberate. They wanted to distinguish the new occupiers from their Nazi predecessors, as one Soviet official in Germany wrote in a later analysis: 'By giving churches full freedom in their activities, the Soviet occupation authorities demonstrated their tolerance of religion' and eliminated 'an important part of the arsenal of anti-Soviet propaganda'.[22] Their sheer ignorance of religion did lend an arbitrary quality to some of their behaviour.

In 1949, for example, the local Soviet commander became suspicious of the young people preparing for a Lutheran confirmation service in the town of Nordhausen, and demanded to know why 'such additional propaganda is necessary'. What, he blustered, was the purpose of a special confirmation service: 'Is it to agitate against Marxism and Russia?'[23]

Deference to the church was even greater in Poland, where communist leaders, anxious to be perceived as 'Polish', and not 'Soviet' (or indeed Jewish), initially made obeisance to Polish national symbols of all kinds, the church hierarchy included. Senior communists marched alongside senior clergy in the annual Corpus Christi processions, and communist leaders attended mass on multiple occasions. Behind the scenes, the Polish party leadership described this policy as one of 'bypassing' the church: they would reform other institutions first, tempt young people away from the church, and hope that older churchgoers would eventually die out.

As in Germany, the new government very much wanted some formal Catholic institutions to reopen in Poland as proof that 'normalcy' had returned, and that the Red Army's presence did not constitute a new occupation. The most prominent Catholic institution in the country, the Catholic University of Lublin, opened its doors in August 1944, a decision which infuriated the London government-in-exile, as it implied a tacit recognition of the status quo. Soon afterwards, the archdiocese of Kraków received official permission to publish *Tygodnik Powszechny* (*Universal weekly*), the intellectual Catholic weekly which quickly became one of the most important in the country. The writer and communist intellectual Jerzy Borejsza also organized meetings of communist and Catholic intellectuals in Kraków in the hope of orchestrating a ceasefire between the church and the party.[24]

In Hungary, the party also tried to appear accommodating, though the word 'appear' must be stressed. In November 1945, Rákosi told a Central Committee meeting dedicated to church matters that 'We have to work carefully, we have to see how and in which form we attack.'[25] 'Working carefully', at least in the early days, meant that Hungarian communists never assaulted the church openly and that communist brigades helped restore bomb-damaged churches, for which they were publicly praised.[26] Yet at the same time, church leaders were portrayed in the official media as corrupt 'reactionaries' seeking to restore the Horthy regime.

Attacks on the churches were also carried out under the guise of other programmes. During the land reform, the Hungarian state deliberately deprived the Roman Catholic church of more than three quarters of its land, and the Protestant churches of nearly half.[27] In public, the authorities described this confiscation of church property as a legitimate by-product of economic reform rather than an open attack on religion. No compensation was paid. Priests and other church functionaries assumed the dubious status of state employees as religious organizations became completely dependent on state subsidies for the first time.

But by the end of 1947, most of the region's communist parties, knowing they remained unpopular, prepared to abandon any remaining nuances. Young people were taking too long to become enthusiastic communists, and religious people were not dying out fast enough. In September, József Révai, at the time responsible for ideology, had already begun to speak of 'terminating the clerical reaction'.[28] In October, the regional Polish secret police bosses gathered in Warsaw to hear Julia Brystiger, head of Department V, the secret police department responsible for the clergy, declare that 'the battle against the enemy activity of the clerics is without a doubt one of the most difficult tasks in front of us'. Brystiger, one of a handful of deeply loathed secret policewomen, laid out several new methods of attack, ranging from a 'systematic' investigation and penetration of the church in the provinces to the recruitment of clergy as informers and the use of 'youth activists' to monitor the religiosity of teachers and educators.[29] In due course, these tactics became standard practice across the bloc.

In East Germany, both the secret police and the ordinary police force, the Volkspolizei (People's Police) wasted little time in refocusing attention on 'enemies' in the religious youth groups. By December 1949, the Volkspolizei's general inspector had already identified what remained of the Junge Gemeinde, the Protestant youth movement, as a hostile organization whose central goal was the destruction of the Free German Youth. In an exchange with the Free German Youth leadership, the inspector declared that 'If criminals meet under the cover of a religious cult, we will of course decisively lash out against them with all legal means.'[30] Rapidly, the language grew even harsher. Ulbricht called the Junge Gemeinde an 'agents' centre' which is 'in touch with the so-called youth groups' in West Berlin. In East Berlin, administrators received a special directive to 'thwart and destroy the work being carried out by reactionary groups within the church and the Junge Gemeinde, on behalf of foreign imperialists, to damage socialist construction, to sabotage the struggle for peace and to prevent Germany unity'.[31]

Before 1949, harassment had been focused on a handful of influential Christian youth leaders. But now anti-church propaganda became more blatant. The regime banned the *Kreuz auf der Weltkugel* – a cross atop a circle, symbolizing the globe – the Junge Gemeinde's symbol. Free German Youth gangs appeared at church meetings and heckled those inside. (One Free German Youth report describes with satisfaction a 'steeplechase of motorcycles' which had been organized around one Christian group meeting.)[32] The Free German Youth also organized meetings in high schools designed to 'protest against fascist terror in West Germany' and to 'uncover and dismiss hostile elements' from the premises, which meant Catholic and Protestant students. School 'tribunals' interrogated children suspected of having religious leanings. These were huge, public occasions and often very dramatic. One such spectacle took place in a school theatre in Wittenberg: students who refused to join the Free German Youth or insisted upon going to church were named, condemned and expelled one by one, before the whole school. Many left the stage weeping.[33]

In 1954, the state would even introduce the *Jugendweihe*, a secular alternative to Protestant confirmation services, a ceremony which was supposed to impart to young people 'useful knowledge in basic questions of the scientific world-view and socialist morality . . . raising them in the spirit of socialist patriotism and proletarian internationalism, and helping them to prepare themselves for active participation in the construction of developed socialist society and the creation of the basic preconditions for the gradual transition to communism'. Pastors protested, but although only about a sixth of young people participated at first, by the 1960s more than 90 per cent would take part in this ceremony.[34]

Many children were expelled from school for refusing to publicly renounce religion – estimates vary from 300 to 3000 – and far more were expelled from universities. Some made their way to West Germany or West Berlin, where the West German Interior Ministry arranged tuition and accommodation for those forced to flee school, a policy which naturally increased the paranoia in the eastern half of the country.[35] Others from religious famlies simply never tried to attend university at all. Having refused to join the Free German Youth in school, Ulrich Fest, the Wittenberg shopkeeper, knew he and his friends weren't ever going to qualify for higher education: 'We were a very small group that somehow mutually thought, "No, we're not doing that."'[36]

Events followed a similar pattern in Hungary: first dark talk of espionage, then harassment, bans and arrests. Rákosi kicked off 1948 by agreeing with Révai: 'by the end of this year we have to terminate the clerical reaction'.[37] Hundreds of church schools were nationalized within months, sometimes in the face of bitter objections. In an infamous incident in the village of Pócspetri, locals gathered to protest at the loss of their school and policemen attacked them with clubs. A gun went off, killing one of the police. Afterwards, a local notary and a priest were arrested, and the notary was subsequently sentenced to death and executed. Suspicions (for which there is now some documentary support) that the entire incident had been provoked and organized by the political police have hung over the case ever since. At the time, the incident was used in the propaganda war against church schools. In June, more than 6500 of them were forced to relinquish their religious identity and become state schools.[38]

The closure of monasteries followed soon afterwards. Nuns in the city of Győr were given six hours to pack up and leave. In southern Hungary, 800 monks and some 700 nuns were removed from monasteries in the middle of the night, told they could take 25 kilos of books and clothing, placed into transport trucks and removed by force. Across the country, some 800 nuns were told they could no longer work in hospitals – a decree which forced many of these hospitals to cut services. Some nuns were subsequently sent back to their families or to work in factories, others were eventually deported to the Soviet Union.[39] Sándor Keresztes, a former Catholic politician who was himself under constant police surveillance – he had eight children, which was itself considered suspicious – quietly hired a group of nuns and set them to work repairing nylon stockings, in order to enable them to stay together and not starve.[40]

In Poland, the party's change of tactics in 1948 coincided with the death of the Catholic primate, August Hlond. With his passing, the widespread conviction among clergy that the regime would soon fail, and that the Western powers would have to force the USSR out of Eastern Europe, began to fade.[41] The church was further demoralized by the arrests of priests, by edicts forbidding the teaching of catechism in any schools, and by the shuttering of seminaries. Catholic hospitals and nursing homes were also closed, along with any remaining charitable organizations. At the beginning of 1950, a new taboo was breached when the regime launched an attack on Caritas, the most important Catholic charity. Caritas operated 4500 orphanages, looked after 166,700 orphans, maintained 241 soup kitchens and distributed aid from abroad, mostly from the United States, which had helped reconstruct churches, schools and convents. In the months after the war's end, Caritas had been one of the few sources of medicine in Poland. But its power, prestige and independence meant that the party's attack was especially harsh. In January 1950, the Polish press agency announced that Caritas had fallen under the control of 'aristocrats' and Nazi sympathizers, and that most of its leaders were under investigation for misappropriation of funds. Caritas was immediately placed under state administration and its leadership was removed. In effect, the charity was nationalized. Stunned, the Polish episcopate jointly denied all of the charges against Caritas and denounced the attack:

> concern for the public welfare . . . is [not] intended here, but the destruction of *Caritas* as a Church institution, and at the same time, the heaping of insinuation and calumny on Catholicism, in order to disrupt the Church in Poland. This impression is made by the large scale campaign staged in the press and on the radio, and by organized conferences and meetings . . . In some instances, the hunting down of priests has been organized. They have been pulled out of bed in the early morning by militia armed with rifles, who sometimes did not permit the celebration of Holy Mass or forced the interruption of religious services . . . priests were sometimes brought in still wearing liturgical vestments.[42]

Priests who protested against the nationalization of Caritas were punished severely. One priest who read a protest aloud to his congregation was fined 75,000 zlotys, a fortune at the time.[43] After a group of parents in Katowice wrote a letter opposing the closure of the local Catholic school, priests in the area were repeatedly hauled into the local offices of the secret police. One internal church report noted, 'It would be hard to find in the Katowice diocese a priest who had not been called in, and not once but two, three, four and more times to the State Security, where, after long, sometimes five- or six-hour interrogations, they were forced to sign various protocols and statements.'[44]

After that, the church leadership discouraged others from staging similar protests. By 1954 there were only eight Catholic elementary schools left in the country, of which six were closing down their operations. The remaining two stayed open only because there were no local alternatives. Catholic hospitals and nursing schools had also been eliminated, along with the last independent religious groups, among them Bratni Pomoc (Brotherly Aid) the oldest student charitable organization in the country. Some monasteries and convents remained open, but they too were under pressure. Nuns were no longer allowed to study in nursing schools which had formerly belonged to their orders, and the remaining monks were carefully watched. Uniquely in Eastern Europe, the Catholic University of Lublin did remain open. But its rector was under arrest for blocking the Union of Polish Youth's organizations on campus, and the faculty was under heavy pressure to conform.[45]

Across the bloc, priests were arrested in almost arbitrary waves – by 1953 about a thousand were behind bars in Poland – and they were watched with acute suspicion. A parish priest in Krotoszyn was investigated as a 'definite enemy of the current reality, which he reveals in sermons with double meanings, individual conversations and confessions'.[46] An informer in Budapest heard 'careful, well-measured' but nevertheless clear evidence of counter-revolutionary sentiment in a sermon on the heroic behaviour of St Paul. He also found it suspicious that a church choir performed a 'little-known song full of complaints and desperate prayers'.[47] Among those incarcerated in Germany were several priests, including Johannes Hamel in Halle and Deacon Herbert Dost in Leipzig, both of whom had large youth followings, as well as lay leaders such as Erich Schumann, who was charged with violating the German constitution.[48] Campaigns to discredit the church were discussed at the highest levels. In Hungary, the Politburo agreed that factory managers should 'organize seminars on the role of the church as the main support of capitalism', and that secret police should launch 'whispering campaigns' in workplaces and residential areas which would place the blame for unmet production targets on clerical sabotage.[49]

But the most terrifying assaults were not those carried out in secret. By the end of the 1940s, the most senior church leaders in the region were also under open attack. In the winter of 1952–3, senior figures in the archdiocese of Kraków underwent a macabre trial, featuring fabricated evidence, invisible ink and forged documents.[50] The investigation into Archbishop József Grösz, the second-highest ranking Catholic clergyman in Hungary, also led to arrests of priests and laymen for 'armed conspiracy' and terrorist plots.[51] Earlier attacks had smeared a Hungarian Calvinist bishop, László Ravasz, and a Lutheran bishop, Lajos Ordass. The latter was arrested in August 1947 and sentenced to two years in prison on charges of illegally trafficking in foreign currencies.[52] Of all of these 'criminal' cases, however, two stood out for the obsessiveness and single-mindedness with which they were pursued. These were the attacks on Eastern Europe's two most important Catholic leaders, Cardinal József Mindszenty, appointed Hungarian primate by the Vatican in 1945, and Cardinal Stefan Wyszyński, his Polish counterpart, appointed in October 1948.

One way or another, the clergy had to function within a political system which described them as its most important enemies. Some thought a degree of cooperation and even collaboration with the communist parties was the only way to survive, and the only way to protect the faithful. Others disagreed vehemently. Nobody had the benefit of hindsight, and it was not always clear at the time what the 'right' or 'moral' choice ought to be. This ambiguity becomes very clear when examining closely the stories of Cardinals Mindszenty and Wyszyński, two extraordinary men who made very different choices at this time.

Sociologically, the two men had much in common. Both were the

MOSCOW COMMUNISTS: HUNGARY, EAST GERMANY, POLAND

16. left to right: István Dobi, Mátyas Rákosi, Ernő Gerő, Mihály Farkas, József Révai

17. left to right: Wilhelm Pieck, Walter Ulbricht, Otto Grotewohl

18. Bierut (centre) receiving congratulations on his 60th birthday

★ THE CHURCH

19. The Party makes early concessions to the church: Deputy Defence Minister Jaroszewicz marches alongside the Primate, Cardinal August Hlond, in a Corpus Christi procession, 1947

20. The crackdown begins in Hungary: Cardinal Jószef Mindszenty with an army escort in Budapest, 1947

★ THE MEDIA

21. Soviet soldiers distributing newspapers in the eastern zone of Germany, 1945

22. Hungarian peasants gathered around their village radio, 1951

★ YOUTH

23. The Free German Youth helps to form young minds

24. The Free German Youth makes good use of its summer vacation

25. The Union of Polish Youth rebuilds Warsaw

26. The Union of Polish Youth puts on a gymnastic display

★ WORK

27. Polish shockworkers in Gdańsk register their daily output

28. 'The carefully-posed picture was intended to educate.' Zsófia Teván and Júlia Kollár, posing for the camera on a building site in Sztálinváros

29. Adolf Hennecke, the German coal miner who dug 287 per cent of his production quota, sitting beneath a portrait of himself holding a drill

30. Ignác Pióker, the Hungarian factory worker who achieved 1470 per cent of his production quota (and completed his personal five-year plan four years ahead of schedule)

31. The Palace of Culture, Stalin's gift to Warsaw

sons of devout, provincial farmers of modest means, and both owed their education and their careers to the church. In his memoir, Mindszenty writes with gratitude of his parents' decision to send him to secondary school, which wasn't common among his peers.[53] Wyszyński's earliest childhood memory was of gazing up at two holy pictures in his bedroom: the Black Madonna of Częstochowa, a figure his father adored, and the Blessed Virgin of Ostra Brama, the icon most revered by his mother.[54]

Both men were patriots, and both had established records of resistance to tyranny. The short-lived Hungarian communist government of 1919 had arrested Mindszenty briefly, and the Hungarian fascist Arrow Cross government had arrested him again in 1944, when he refused to take an oath to their leader, Ferenc Szálasi.[55] Wyszyński too had worked as an 'underground' teacher in Warsaw during the Nazi occupation, after the university was closed. He remained closely linked to the Home Army throughout the war. During the Warsaw Uprising he served as chaplain to the Żoliborz district and the hospital in Laski, to the north of the city.

Both men were politically savvy and alert to the dangers of their own positions. Following his appointment in 1948, Wyszyński noted wryly that he was frequently offered books on the subject of martyrdom, as well as holy pictures of martyrs. Everyone around him expected the police to come at any moment: 'my impending arrest seemed so certain that even the chauffeur was on the lookout for a new job'.[56] In the same year, also fearing arrest, Mindszenty issued a statement forgiving in advance any Catholics who might be forced to sign letters or petitions against him: 'I do not wish that any Catholic should lose his livelihood because of me. If Catholic faithful sign letters of protest against me, they can do it in the knowledge that it is not done of their own free will. Let us pray for our beloved Church and our precious Hungary.'[57]

During their initial years in office, both men thought deeply about the role of the church under a communist regime, discussing the possible options with their colleagues, praying for guidance. Both also acted in good faith, according to what they thought best for religious institutions and for believers. Yet as their respective memoirs illustrate, they eventually came to very different conclusions about the best path to follow. For deeply religious people, the choices were neither easy nor obvious.

Of the two, Mindszenty was the more political, the more outspoken and the more openly antagonistic to communism. His conflict with the Hungarian government began very early. During a 1945 visit to the Vatican, his first as primate, Mindszenty obtained a promise of charitable aid for Hungary from American Catholics. This infuriated the communists, who tried to prevent the aid from reaching Hungary. Mindszenty denounced this manoeuvre in public: 'these American donations were a sign of the all-embracing solidarity of the world Church. World Bolshevism did not like them at all.' He was equally blunt about the communist party's disregard for the rule of law. Before the elections in October 1945, he issued a letter which did not mention any party by name, but which denounced police violence and arbitrary arrests, declaring that 'it seems that a totalitarian dictatorship is starting to replace the previous one'. Rákosi called an emergency meeting after Mindszenty's letter was released, and in some places police tried to prevent priests from reading it aloud in church.[58]

As pressure on Catholic and Protestant youth groups grew, Mindszenty took on the responsibility of loudly and publicly defending them. In May 1946, he marched alongside the Catholic Parents' Association in demonstrations against the proposed closure of church schools. In March 1947 he publicly condemned the abolition of religion in all schools, warning that, 'promising freedom of religion while creating institutions of irreligiousness is the height of hypocrisy'. After Hungary's bishops declared 1947 a holy year – a Marian year – Mindszenty threw himself into the celebrations. Hundreds of thousands of pilgrims turned out to meet him at mass gatherings around the country, despite artificially constructed obstacles such as 'broken' trains and 'closed' roads. He rallied them with powerful and provocative speeches: 'The Catholic parishes must be on the alert in such times of struggle ... We harm no one, and will not do so in the future. But if there be an attempt made to destroy justice and love, the foundations that sustain us, we then have the right of legitimate self-defense.'[59]

Mindszenty did not mince his words, and he did not compromise or negotiate. He responded to every attack on the church with a counterattack. He would not sign any agreement with the state until the regime agreed to restore the church's confiscated buildings and funds, revive the disbanded associations and establish diplomatic relations with the Vatican. Clearly, these were not conditions that the communist party was going to meet, and in the autumn of 1948 the party press launched a campaign under a new slogan: 'We will annhilate Mindszentyism!'

After Christmas, he was arrested. He was immediately stripped of his robes and his possessions, repeatedly interrogated and tortured for many weeks. He writes of being beaten on the soles of his feet and of being kicked on the floor of his cell. Eventually he was forced to undergo a humiliating show trial, during which he publicly 'confessed' to a series of ludicrous crimes, including plotting the theft of Hungary's crown jewels and conspiring to return Archduke Otto von Habsburg to the Hungarian throne. Afterwards he remained in prison until October 1956.[60]

Wyszyński's fate was different, both because Poland was different, but also because the Polish primate chose different tactics. By nature, he was inclined to seek compromise. Although he too was openly harassed from the very beginning of his term in office – he became primate after Hlond's death in 1948, just as the propaganda campaign against the church gathered pace – he nevertheless sought to avoid open conflict. He eschewed fiery sermons and public criticism of the regime, preferring to protest behind the scenes. In his memoirs, he regretted that people were not always aware of these hidden tactics: 'the public knew nothing about the many letters, memoranda, protests submitted ... in defense of the Church's rights'. He even sought to identify some points of potential agreement with communist ideology, pointing to the church's traditional advocacy of 'social justice' and declaring himself in favour of economic restructuring and land reform, which he considered to be long overdue. He admitted that their 'narrow atheism' made cooperation with communists difficult, but he sought to find common ground anyway.[61]

From the moment he took office, Wyszyński also began to negotiate what would later be known as the 'agreement of mutual understanding' between the state authorities and the church. Three senior bishops were sent to meet regularly with communist officials. They continued the meetings even as heavier restrictions were placed on church activity, and even as the communists created obstacles and delays.

Famously – or infamously, depending on one's point of view – Wyszyński finally signed the document in April 1950. Among other things, it compelled Polish church leaders to 'tell the clergy that their pastoral work, in accordance with church teachings, should foster respect for the laws and prerogatives of the state among the faithful'.[62] In effect, the church undertook not to support the underground resistance, or indeed any anti-communist resistance of any kind. The agreement was controversial and remained so for many years. To many, it seemed a step too far, a shameful compromise which contributed to the regime's legitimacy and weakened the church. One priest who was under police interrogation in 1950 was told about the agreement while still in prison. He wrote later that he had assumed it must be a lie, designed to rob him of the will to resist. It was impossible, unthinkable that a Polish Catholic primate had signed something so profoundly collaborationist.

Wyszyński himself agonized over the decision to sign this agreement, and at times he appeared to regret it. In 1953, he told a conference of the episcopate that all of their attempts to cooperate with and accommodate the regime had been perceived simply as 'weakness': 'the government has never stopped looking at the church through a political lens. The church is the Vatican, the bishops are agents and spies.' He seemed almost relieved when he was finally arrested in September 1953 because that gave his position some clarity, as he told a fellow priest: 'workers, peasants, intellectuals, all kinds of people from all over the nation are in prison, it's good that the primate and priests are in prison too, since our task is to be with the nation'.[63]

Wyszyński understood why so many disliked the church–state agreement, and he also knew that Mindszenty had refused to sign a similar document. His decision to negotiate did not mean he had any illusions about the nature of the regime: he knew he gained nothing by signing an agreement except some extra time. But time was precisely what he wanted. The Polish church had suffered terribly during the war, he later wrote: thousands of Polish priests had been arrested, thousands had died in both German and Soviet concentration camps, and the clergy needed time to recover. The church must avoid at all costs the destruction which had been inflicted on the Russian Orthodox church after the Russian Revolution: 'we had to gain time and strength to defend

God's positions'.[64] He saw the agreement as a necessary compromise, one which would give the church some breathing space and would at least make it difficult for the regime to claim that the church was obstinate or recalcitrant.

These two different positions produced different results. Mindszenty's open confrontation had the merit of clarity. At the time, he was widely admired for his insistence upon the truth, and he is still admired for that today. Church schools and institutions had been destroyed, innocent people had been arrested and killed, and he had the courage to say so. His openness later made him an important symbol for anti-communists in Hungary and around the world. When he was finally freed by Hungarian rebels in 1956, ecstatic crowds awaited him outside the prison.[65] Yet his courage did not prevent the Hungarian church from suffering severe repression. After his arrest, torture and humiliating public show trial, the Hungarian bishops were forced to sign an 'agreement of mutual understanding' of the sort Wyszyński had reluctantly signed, but under far worse terms.[66] The Hungarian version not only acknowledged the constitution of the Hungarian People's Republic, but also called upon believers to help fulfil the Five Year Plan. It explicitly warned priests not to oppose the collectivization of agriculture. A week after it was signed, the state issued the order dissolving Hungary's monastic orders.[67]

Wyszyński's more pliable tactics had the merit of flexibility. He sought to avoid confrontation, to keep priests out of prison and to keep as many church institutions open as possible. His approach didn't have the same moral clarity as that of Mindszenty, nor the same inspirational quality, and his soft-spoken sermons left ordinary people feeling confused about the church's real attitude to communism. But his non-confrontational style may help explain why Wyszyński was arrested relatively late, in 1953 instead of 1949; why he was never put on trial; and why the Polish church emerged from the Stalinist period relatively intact, at least as compared to its Hungarian, Czechoslovak and German equivalents. Wyszyński himself believed that his conciliatory tone had made it more difficult for the communists to attack the Polish Catholic church. They could hardly accuse him of reactionary intransigence when he agreed to so many of their demands. At least until the 1980s, Wyszyński's attitude set the tone for other Polish clerics, most of whom publicly accepted the party's legal authority. Throughout the communist period, the vast majority of Polish priests sought to avoid open political conflict while continuing to carry out their traditional duties. By contrast, the Hungarian churches, both Catholic and Protestant, were more thoroughly demoralized in the Stalinist period, and more deeply penetrated by the secret police in the 1970s and 1980s. Unlike the Catholic church in Poland and the Protestant churches in Germany, the Hungarian churches did not play a large institutional role in the political opposition to communism which developed in the 1980s.

Both of their approaches had advantages and drawbacks, and indeed the different choices made by the region's two outstanding Catholic leaders had their echo among ordinary clergy as well as lay believers. Some chose defiance and prison. Others chose the less satisfying path of negotiation, compromise and protest behind the scenes, believing that it was better for their parishoners. Hans-Jochen Tschiche, a Lutheran clergyman in East Germany, told himself that 'We are not only the church for the strong ones, but for the majority. The church is for the weak and the fearful and if I enter into a large conflict with the state that might be too threatening to them.'[68]

But those were not the only choices open to the faithful under the new regime. Very quickly, other kinds of opportunities opened up as well.

From the first days of Soviet occupation, the new secret police services sought to recruit priests and religious people secretly into their ranks, just as they sought to recruit members of many other professions. But in the case of the clergy, secret collaboration was not enough: they also wanted the clergy to function openly in the service of the regime, as an arm of the communist party. This was an explicitly Soviet idea.[69] According to Józef Światło, a senior Polish secret police officer who defected in 1953, General Serov himself had proposed 'not the liquidation of the church, but slowly making it into a tool of Soviet politics'. The idea was to 'penetrate it on the inside, divide it into squabbling factions as much as possible – as happened in Russia before 1929 – and weaken its authority on the outside'.[70] This had been the fate of the Orthodox church in Russia, which by the 1930s was in effect a state institution.

Stalin himself laid out this policy very clearly in October 1949, before a Cominform meeting in Karlsbad, when he ordered the bloc's communist parties to adopt harsher tactics, starting in Czechoslovakia:

> It is necessary that we isolate the Catholic hierarchy and drive a wedge between the Vatican and the believers. Depending on our success in Czechoslovakia, we will build up Catholic activities in Poland, Hungary and in the other countries. We must also make full use of the question of the finances of the lower-level priests. Our measures will divide lower-level priests from the hierarchy. Governments should order priests to take the citizen's oath, communist parties should force priests to spread the ideas of Marx, Engels and Lenin through religious classes and sermons, and whenever they have direct contacts with their believers. We have to fight a systematic war against the hierarchy; churches should be under our full control by December 1949.[71]

In Hungary, the authorities followed precisely these tactics, and they did so in concert with the mass 'peace campaign' launched nationwide in 1948. This peace movement, as noted, did not resemble its spontaneous, grassroots counterparts which eventually developed in some Western European countries: it was organized from above by the government, and carried out with the aid of communist party activists who organized peace parades, peace races and peace conferences, and who collected money for peace bonds. Journalists were commissioned to write about the peace campaign, and designers were set the task of creating posters and brochures promoting peace.

In Hungary, as elsewhere, activists also launched a major peace petition drive. Petitions were passed around schools, offices and factories, where party members vied with one another to see who could get the most signatures. In the spring of 1950, this campaign reached an almost hysterical intensity. By the beginning of May, 24,583 'peace activists' had collected 6,806,130 signatures on a petition calling for world peace, an enormous percentage in a country which at the time had some 9 million inhabitants.[72]

Priests were asked to sign the petitions too, and some did. Others evaded or dodged the campaign altogether, arguing that they didn't know whether their vows permitted them to sign a political petition. Finally, Archbishop Grösz, who had replaced Mindszenty as the

Hungarian primate after his arrest, resolved the issue. In public, he declared that the Catholic church had always promoted peace. However, only the Vatican was entitled to decide whether any Catholic clergyman could join an international organization or sign any treaties. As a result, he would not sign this peace petition, or any other petition, and no other Hungarian priest should do so either.[73]

That statement gave the communist party and its sympathizers the ammunition they needed. Party journalists immediately attacked the church for war-mongering. György Lukács, the Hungarian philosopher who sometimes collaborated with the communist party and sometimes did not, attacked the archbishop's 'hypocritical' decision. The communist party leadership was delighted: the secretariat decided that the peace movement should now be 'used to make lower-level priests oppose their superiors'.[74] Pressure on low-ranking clergy would intensify – and rewards would be offered to those who defied Archbishop Grösz and agreed to join the 'peace movement'.

Quickly, the potential collaborators were identified and József Révai orchestrated the 'peace rally' which would become the founding meeting of the organization of 'peace priests'. Everything about the meeting was planned in advance, including its concluding declarations, which would eventually be signed by 279 priests and monks, about 2 per cent of the clergy in the country. Even the mood of the participants was determined in advance. At one Central Committee meeting, János Kádár – later to become Hungary's post-1956 dictator – declared that 'the atmosphere of the meeting should neither be too convivial, nor too reserved':

> An atmosphere of war should be created. They have to emphasize Mindszenty's policy mistakes, criticize the episcopacy's policies towards authorities . . . priests should report on threats they received because of their democratic convictions and because of their planned participation in this meeting . . . Speeches should contain remarks against bishops, speakers should demand the episcopacy change its opinion towards democracy and peace, speakers should not be too radical, so as not to endanger the feeling of unity at the meeting.[75]

A similar level of planning went into the organization of the Polish 'progressive' priests, as the Polish communist party called them.

(Colloquially – and ironically – this group of clerics was widely known as the 'patriotic priests'.) These Polish clergymen were not attached to the peace movement, as in Hungary, but rather to the 'official' organization of war veterans, the Union of Fighters for Freedom and Democracy (Związek Bojowników o Wolność i Demokrację, or ZBoWiD), which had been created by the communist party because the authentic veterans' groups, linked by informal relationships and close emotional bonds to the Home Army, were too dangerous for the regime to tolerate.

Priests who joined immediately received privileges such as access to doctors and sanatoriums, as well as building materials for church construction. Following the dissolution of Caritas in January 1950, the possible rewards for collaboration grew even larger. Priests who cooperated with the state could take control of Caritas assets, offices and projects. By that point the Polish secret police had begun to encourage the creation of 'official' Catholic publications and organizations as well. An 'official' Catholic newspaper, *Today and Tomorrow* (*Dziś i Jutro*) was already in existence, as was Pax, an 'official' Catholic pseudo-political party, of which more later. In the wake of these changes, the progressive priests orchestrated a membership drive and planned a national conference, which was indeed attended by some 350 priests in 1952.[76]

But the church fought back. In Hungary, the bishops' council dismissed peace priests from their posts. In Kraków, Cardinal Sapieha demanded a personal meeting with the local progressive priests and ordered them to resign from the movement. In both countries, pro-regime priests were also, at times, harassed by members of the public. In one Hungarian village, the faithful 'stopped confessing and taking holy communion with the peace priest' and interrupted his sermons with shouts.[77]

As a result of such hostility, the movements never did become mass organizations for the distribution of pro-communist literature and the support of the regime. They did grow, but not as much as the regime had hoped: at the movement's zenith, there were some 1000 progressive Polish priests, plus another 1000 sympathizers. The Hungarian group never published an official count of its members: at one point the leadership claimed more than 3000, though Radio Free Europe, the American-backed broadcasters based in Munich, later put the number of true activists at 150. Both groups published newspapers – *The Chaplain's Voice* in Poland and *Cross* in Hungary – and held periodic meetings.

The motives of those who stayed out of these movements are easy to understand: both their hierarchy and their system of values argued against it. Much harder to understand are the motives of those who joined. The historian József Gyula Orbán reckons that a small proportion, about a tenth, collaborated out of an honest desire to cooperate with the new ruling powers. Some were themselves Marxists or left-wing socialists who had some faith in the party's economic programme. Others hoped that by working together with the communists they could improve the lives of their parishioners. The Polish church historian Father Tadeusz Isakowicz-Zaleski also speculates that some of the progressive priests, especially survivors of German concentration camps, were psychologically weakened by their wartime experiences and therefore easily manipulated by the communists.[78]

Others were clearly blackmailed or beaten into submission. The eventual leader of the Hungarian group, Bishop Miklós Beresztóczy, had been arrested in 1948 and tortured brutally. Another priest joined after he had been accused of arson (a haystack in his parish had burned) and he hoped to avoid prison. Światło, the secret police defector, claimed the Polish security services were disappointed by the movement: 'the patriotic priests are creatures of the [security services], in many cases broken physically and morally by Soviet or Nazi camps'.[79] A few of those who attended the official gatherings were no more than secret police agents dressed in cassocks. Observers in Hungary at the first meeting of peace priests noted mysterious 'Franciscans' whom no one had ever seen before and no one met later.

Still others joined in expectation of promotions and privileges, and indeed the secret police actively sought out priests who were disgruntled, thwarted in their ambitions, or in conflict with their superiors. Father Henryk Weryński, a Polish priest who had once been a firm supporter of the prewar regime, fell very much into that category. Before the war, Weryński had worked for the Catholic press agency and had strong political and literary ambitions. He had even tried to run for parliament, but with no success. After the war he switched sides – and from then on his career progressed at a rapid pace.

Very early on, Weryński agreed to become a working agent of the secret police. They paid him a monthly stipend of 5000 zlotys and ensured that his pro-government articles would be printed in all of the Catholic newspapers which had hitherto rejected them. In return, he helped them to identify other potentially 'progressive' priests. He informed on all of his Kraków colleagues, both clerical and lay people, reported regularly to the authorities, and expressed his gratitude in public. At a meeting of the local progressive priests' committee in Krynica in 1951, he declared that the prewar government, 'though beloved by many priests, never took such good care of them' as the communists.[80] According to Światło, Weryński had even supplied police agents with information he obtained from hearing confessions. Światło claimed that he personally gave Weryński a coupon to purchase a cassock.[81]

Fear, the stifling politics of Stalinism and doubts about the future must have affected many priests as well. Cardinal Mindszenty's arrest and disjointed 'confession' terrified Catholic priests all across the Soviet bloc. The nationalization of Caritas and other religious charities in Poland, the liquidation of the monasteries in Hungary and the destruction of church schools everywhere may have seemed, to many, like the beginning of the end of the traditional church. So gloomy was the Polish Cardinal Sapieha in this period that he issued a statement declaring that if he were arrested, no one should believe in the authenticity of any statements or 'confessions' he made afterwards.[82] In this atmosphere, the decision to collaborate might not have seemed so morally dubious as it did later on.

Similarly mixed motives also explain not only public clerical collaboration but secret clerical collaboration. Sándor Ladanyi, a historian of the Hungarian Lutheran church and the son of a Lutheran pastor, notes that although many priests who became informers had been tortured, and although many others were careerists like Weryński – priests, theology students, teachers who felt thwarted in their careers or wanted to study abroad – there were many more ambiguous reasons for collaboration as well. Priests and pastors were under constant pressure to speak to the secret police – more pressure than others – and some cooperated voluntarily, hoping to deflect the authorities' interest while at the same time striving to assist them as little as possible. Some agreed to be informers, but said nothing. A number of Hungarian informer files end with the statement that a given priest's name should be removed because 'the information he provides is no good'. Still others were blackmailed, openly or more subtly. Protestant clergymen in particular were thought to be susceptible to blackmail because they had families. Their children's education could be at stake, or their wife's medication (Catholic priests, who did not have wives and children, were thought to be harder to 'turn' and were often therefore treated more harshly).[83]

Certainly the peace priests and the patriotic priests were not in the end of much real value to the regime. Behind the scenes, Hungarian authorities criticized the peace priests for making 'insufficient progress in the fight against clerical reaction'. In Poland, the movement was never truly embraced by either the party or the public: eventually, the very phrase 'patriotic priest' evolved into a term of abuse. As they became alienated from the mainstream of the church, and easier to ignore, they also became less useful to the regime as mouthpieces for propaganda. Nevertheless, their presence seems to have had a dispiriting, even debilitating effect on the rest of the clergy, and they occupied a good deal of church leaders' time and energy. Cardinal Wyszyński met with the progressive priests frequently, including several times in the months preceding his arrest in 1953. For a short period, the prospect of a wholesale 'conversion' of Catholic priests to the communist cause must have seemed perfectly plausible.

Above all, the existence of a vocal and pro-communist clergy contributed to the moral confusion of the period. Was the church supporting or opposing communism? Was the new Caritas charity in Poland authentic or ersatz? Were the peace priests really in favour of peace, and if so – shouldn't everyone support them? Collaborationist priests also encouraged the collaboration of others: if 'holy' men could accept gifts and favours from the regime in exchange for cooperation, why shouldn't anyone else?

12

Internal enemies

The Party promises only one thing: after the victory, one day
when it can do no more harm, the material of the secret
archives will be published. Then the world will learn what was
in the background of this Punch and Judy show . . .
            Arthur Koestler, Darkness at Noon, *1941*[1]

A person that's beaten will give the kind of confession that the
interrogating agents want, will admit that he is an English or
an American spy or whatever we want. But it will never be
possible to know the truth this way.
        Lavrentii Beria, speaking at a secret Politburo meeting
            after Stalin's death in 1953, from archival documents
                            published after 1991[2]

'Reactionary clerics' were obvious targets in the paranoid atmosphere
of High Stalinism. But there were many other potential enemies.
Following a series of strikes and economic disasters, the Polish secret
police decided that it needed 'a thorough study of the workforce on
the shop floor and at all levels of the administration . . . intelligence
concerning the precise political influences to be found among the
workforce, in the past and at present'. They rummaged through their
files and identified twenty-five categories of 'enemies'. These included
anyone who had been in the Home Army, anyone who had been at all
active in the prewar social democratic movement or any other political party, and anyone who had served in the Polish armed forces
abroad. Many who had been released from prison in 1947 or had

accepted amnesty after the war immediately fell under new suspicion too. Eventually, this list grew to forty-three categories. By 1954, according to Andrzej Paczkowski, the 'register of criminal and suspicious elements' contained 6 million names, or one in three adults. In 1948 there were 26,400 political prisoners, by mid-1950 there were 35,200, and by 1954 there were 84,200 political prisoners in the country, incarcerated all over Poland.[3]

Similar processes unfolded across the bloc. In Hungary, the secret police kept its focus on 'potential' enemies. In East Germany the Stasi sought to identify real and imagined Western spies. In Czechoslovakia police sought out anyone who had opposed the communist coup d'état of 1948, or anyone who might be presumed to oppose it. The Romanians launched a special operation in May 1950, targeting any remaining government ministers from the period 1919–45, including some very elderly men, as well as Greek Catholic and Roman Catholic priests.[4]

In this second wave of investigations and arrests, peasants and rural landowners were frequently victims too. In the autumn of 1952, the secret police arrested tens of thousands of Polish peasants who had failed to comply with requirements for compulsory delivery of grain.[5] Between 1948 and 1953, some 400,000 Hungarian peasants were arrested for failing to deliver their production quotas, and an extraordinary 850,000 were fined.[6] In 1949, nearly 3000 rural Romanian landowners were evicted from their properties within the space of a few minutes to make way for collectivization.[7]

But mass, Soviet-style arrests created a Soviet-style problem: where should all of these unreliable enemies be kept? In Poland, authorities simply allowed prisons to become overcrowded and let conditions deteriorate. Wacław Beynar, a former Home Army partisan, was arrested in 1948, and found himself in an airless cell in the Rakowiecka prison in Warsaw. So humid was the cell that prisoners, among them many veterans of the Warsaw Uprising, removed their shirts and waved them in the air in order to create the illusion of a breeze. There was no toilet in the cell, and prisoners were taken out to use one only twice a day, a system which quickly became a form of torture for those who got diarrhoea from the prison food. During interrogations, Beynar was beaten 'primitively', hit in the face, kicked in the side and given a death sentence which he heard 'with neutrality: I just couldn't believe it, that I'm a criminal'.

Eventually Beynar was reprieved, given a long prison sentence and sent to Wronki, a much larger prison near Poznań which held some 4000 mostly political 'criminals'. Upon arrival, 'we all cried like children,' he remembered, though the prisoner who suffered most was one who had been in the camp at Dachau. To him it felt simply like déjà vu.[8] Another fellow prisoner was Stanisław Szostak, arrested along with General Wilk outside Vilnius in 1944, rearrested in Szczecin in 1948 and immediately thrown into a cell with Nazi collaborators. Wronki, he recalled, was 'full of lice, lacked air, was hot in the summer and cold in the winter'. Both he and Beynar would be freed only in 1956.[9] Lublin castle, a forbidding medieval structure which had been used as an emergency prison and execution site for Home Army soldiers in 1944 and 1945, also remained open until 1954. Its gloom, dirt and silence were thought to increase prisoners' terror.[10]

Not everyone went to a domestic prison. Tens of thousands of Poles were sent straight into the Soviet Gulag, as were many Germans. Many of the latter had been picked up directly by the NKVD – sometimes off the streets of West Berlin – and put directly on trial in the USSR. Several hundred cases of Germans arrested in Germany after the war, tried in Moscow and put to death there have since been documented.[11] The Hungarians also adopted another Soviet penal practice and began sending ex-aristocrats, prewar military officers, former landowners and 'politically untrustworthy people' living near Hungary's Austrian or Yugoslav borders not to prison but into exile, in small villages in eastern Hungary. This policy of relocation had two additional advantages: it freed up large apartments in major cities for the new legions of party bureaucrats who needed suitable accommodation, and it provided rural communities with a new pool of unskilled labour, though not necessarily a productive one.[12] A similar policy in Romania led to the removal of some 44,000 people living near the Romanian–Yugoslav border. Entire families were loaded on to trains, taken to a sparsely populated region, the Bărăgan steppe, and left in fields to fend for themselves.[13]

Still others were sent to concentration camps. By 1949 the NKVD's

Gulag camps in Germany, described in Chapter 5, had been disbanded, on the grounds that they were attracting too much Western
attention and creating bad publicity for the Soviet occupation regime.
But at about the same time, other Eastern European governments
founded brand-new camp systems. Although not part of the Soviet
Gulag, they were modelled on it. As in the USSR, prisoners were
meant to work in exchange for food and were meant to be 'useful' to
the economy.

Between 1949 and 1953 the Czechoslovak regime maintained a
group of eighteen such camps near Jáchymov, in north-west Bohemia,
where prisoners worked in uranium mines, extracting raw materials
for the new Soviet nuclear weapons programme. The prisoners were
given no special clothing or protection against radiation, and death
rates were high.[14] The Romanian regime also created a network of
camps, the best-known of which were built along the Danube–Black
Sea canal, a Soviet-backed construction project with dubious economic returns. At its height, the canal 'employed' some 40,000
prisoners, about a quarter of the 180,000 Romanian camp inmates.[15]
The Bulgarian regime also built several notably sadistic labour camps
(and maintained them well into the 1960s and 1970s, long after the
majority of Soviet camps had been disbanded).[16] Despite its 'anti-
Stalinist' political orientation, Tito's Yugoslavia built labour camps
too, including one on an Adriatic island, where water was scarce and
the main torment was thirst.[17]

Even on this list of grim institutions, Recsk, Hungary's most notorious labour camp, deserves a special place. Internment – imprisonment
without trial – had been a feature of the Hungarian system from the
very beginning, and internment camps had been constructed all
around Budapest and other major cities.[18] But by 1950–51, the regime
considered these temporary arrangements neither harsh enough nor
secure enough to deal with especially dangerous political criminals. In
search of a better solution, the Hungarian leadership turned for advice
to Rudolf Garasin.

After his wartime exploits as a marginally successful partisan –
described in Chapter 4 – Garasin had returned to the Soviet Union.
There, according to his official biography, he served as the deputy
director of a state printing company until 1951, when he suddenly

returned to Hungary and took a series of high-ranking government jobs, first in the Justice Ministry, and then in the Interior Ministry.[19] In an internal party questionnaire, he later described himself with a little bit more detail, as having been 'commander of a unit of Siberian military construction in the forests around Novosibirsk' during the early 1940s – an era when 'construction in the forests around Novosibirsk' was almost exclusively carried out by the Soviet Gulag.[20] In Hungarian government archives, his name also appears in correspondence with Rákosi, with whom he discussed 'the situation in labour camps' on several occasions. In June 1953, for example, he sent Rákosi a report containing statistics and information on people who had been interned as well as the numbers of people employed by the camp directorate.[21]

Though it was never publicly stated, leading party members, government officials and prisoners all in fact regarded Garasin as the man who had 'imported' the techniques of the Soviet Gulag to Hungary.[22] His reappearance in Budapest in 1951 coincided with the creation of a new 'directorate for public works' – the Hungarian acronym is KÖMI – in December. This new department was supposed to support 'on the one hand the interests of the people's economy, and on the other hand the interests of law enforcement'.[23] Just like the Soviet Gulag, in other words, KÖMI aimed to create profitable companies which would make use of prisoner labour in factories, quarries and construction projects. The department was first part of the Justice Ministry, as was Garasin. In 1952, both Garasin and the department were shifted to the Interior Ministry. By January 1953, KÖMI 'employed' some 27,000 prisoners.

Recsk was only one of the camps in Garasin's empire, a vast department which also included notoriously disorganized transit and internment camps at Kistarcsa, Kazinbarcika and Tiszalök. But Recsk held the most prominent and distinguished prisoners, and Recsk's existence was shrouded in the deepest secrecy. It was not given an official number, as were other camps, and prisoners there were forbidden any contact with the outside world. Few documents are available on the camp's early days – possibly because the decision to build it was taken by János Kádár, Hungary's later leader.[24]

Recsk also became, in Hungarian national memory, a symbol not only of secrecy but of the absurd twists which fate could hand out to people in the era of High Stalinism. Recsk only existed for a short time – it opened in 1950 and was dissolved in October 1953 – but in that period people became prisoners there for political reasons, economic reasons, or for nothing in particular. Many of the prisoners were Smallholders or social democrats, especially social democrats who had opposed the merger of their party with the communist party. Others were former aristocrats, or people with foreign contacts – even very slight foreign contacts. One prisoner, Aladár Györgyey, was a student of art history who briefly befriended a French student visitor.[25] Another man was sent there after his car crashed into Rákosi's car. He had been late to a wedding and was in a hurry.[26] György Faludy, the Hungarian poet, was sent to Recsk after he returned to the country from exile in the United States. He became active in the Social Democratic Party, went to work for its newspaper, there made the acquaintance of several people swept up in the show trials of the time – and was sentenced as an American spy.[27]

As in previous waves of arrests, a large number of Recsk inmates were also former members of the wartime anti-fascist resistance. One of them – the member of a group which in 1944 broke away from the Hungarian regime in order to fight the Germans – was beaten up during interrogation by a guard who shouted 'someone who was able to organize a plot in 1944 can easily be an enemy of the people after 1945'.[28] The regime wanted them out of the way even before they had begun to think about starting to fight again.

By comparison to the vast Soviet camps in whose shadow it was built, Recsk was very small. At its height, Recsk held only 1700 prisoners, and many of the buildings used on or near the site – those where the staff lived, for example – were just large farmhouses, left over from before the war. The camp itself was in a cleared piece of forest; the quarry was a short walk away; the guards lived in a small manor house nearby. On the day I visited, in 2009, not much remained of the barracks. One or two have been rebuilt, to house a museum on the site, but the rest are gone, their locations indicated by a sign or a mark on the map. Local archaeologists have marked out the other important sites – the location of the punishment cell, the foundations of the other barracks, the entrance to the camp – but the overwhelming impression is one of mud, the same mud Faludy described as so thick the men lost their boots in it.

Like the Soviet camps after which it was modelled, Recsk was built from scratch by prisoners, who then cut timber and worked in a quarry to 'earn' their food, which they ate standing up outside, in sunshine, snow or rain, as Faludy also remembered:

> We consumed the half pint of barley coffee we received for breakfast, the soup and vegetable we got for lunch and the vegetable served us as dinner standing on the hillside in front of the camp kitchen, where the cauldrons and cooks were protected against the rain by corrugated sheet-iron mounted on four posts. We poured the hot soup down our throats, spooned out the vegetable (automatically counting the little pieces of horse meat put in it three times a week) . . . [29]

As in the Gulag, there was a hierarchy in Recsk – former social democrats were treated better than former members of centre-right parties, for example, and some prisoners were allowed to collaborate and become foremen. The prisoners called them *nachalniks*, the Russian word for 'boss'. Also as in the Gulag there were elaborate systems of control and punishment. The prisoners were regularly made to stand and be counted, no matter the weather. This took a long time because the guards' knowledge of numbers was so weak. Those who disobeyed any of the rules could be put in a punishment barrack and deprived of food or could be sent to spend the night lying on a plank in a 'wet' cell, where water seeped in from the sides, sometimes knee-deep. To observe all of these Soviet innovations, and presumably to offer suggestions for improvement, Soviet advisers paid periodic visits to the camp, as did Rákosi. As in the USSR a Potemkin village was created in anticipation of their arrival: prisoners were cleaned, workplaces were tidied up, flowers were even planted around the camp perimeter.

Just as the Gulag began to close down after Stalin died, so too did Recsk cease to operate after the Soviet leader's demise. Garasin's reward – or perhaps his punishment – for importing a Soviet-style concentration camp to Hungary was to become, in subsequent years, the Hungarian ambassador to Mongolia. His party files also contain pleas for help from his Hungarian comrades – he needed money for throat operations which could only be done in Moscow, and his pension was very low. On his seventieth birthday, someone wrote a letter recommending that the Hungarian Politburo give him a medal. Soon after that, he died.[30]

On the list of 'enemies' which Bierut sent to Molotov in the spring of 1949, there was one very special category: 'party members excluded from the party'. As 1949 turned into 1950, this category of enemy assumed far greater importance. Across the bloc, communist party and sometimes military leaders became the focus of suspicion, arrests and then of show trials. Hitherto loyal party members and decorated generals were 'revealed' to be traitors or spies. Among the communists with long records of loyalty who now fell into this category were László Rajk, the Hungarian Interior Minister, and Gábor Péter, the founder and leader of the secret police; Rudolf Slánský, General Secretary of the Czech communist party; Władysław Gomułka, General Secretary of the Polish communist party; Paul Merker, leading member of the East German Politburo; and Ana Pauker, the Romanian Foreign Minister. There would be Albanian and Bulgarian victims too.

The spectacle of the revolution devouring its children was nothing new. Precisely the same set of obsessions had consumed the Soviet leadership in the late 1930s, the period of the 'Great Purge' and the 'Great Terror'. For the diplomats, observers and journalists who witnessed them, the show trials of that era – featuring the humiliating confessions of internationally admired revolutionaries such as Lev Kamenev, Grigorii Zinoviev and Nikolai Bukharin – had seemed a grotesque spectacle, proof that Stalin's mad drive for power knew no limits. Fitzroy Maclean, a British diplomat who witnessed Bukharin's trial, described these staged events as 'fantastic public confessions, orgies of self-abasement' accompanied by the 'bloodthirsty ravings of the Public Prosecutor'. One by one, he recalled, senior figures stood before the court, eyes glazed, and confessed to 'a long catalogue of improbable misdeeds'.[31]

Book after book has been written in an attempt to explain the rationale behind the Soviet show trials of 1936, 1937 and 1938. Obviously, they were intended to create political terror, but the timing, the methods and the politics remain controversial. Theories

abound. Long after he had fled East Germany, Wolfgang Leonhard –
by then Professor Leonhard – addressed the question in a famous
annual lecture at Yale University, as a part of his undergraduate course
on Soviet history. Among the possible explanations for the 'Great
Purge', Leonhard listed Stalin's insanity, Russia's historic fear of
foreign invasion – and an outbreak, in the 1930s, of highly active
sunspots.[32] But in their way, the Eastern European show trials of 1949
and 1950 shed some light on those earlier show trials in Moscow. If
nothing else, the very fact that they were carefully choreographed in
conjunction with Soviet advisers and in close imitation of the
Moscow trials proves that Stalin judged those earlier trials to have
been a political success, a tactic worth repeating in his new client
states.

Certainly both sets of trials marked similar turning points in the
respective histories of the Soviet Union and Eastern Europe. In both
late-1930s Russia and late-1940s Eastern Europe, the party's economic policy was failing, and the party members themselves were
becoming disillusioned. The trials diverted the blame for manifold
economic failures away from Stalin (in the 1930s) and the little Stalins (in the 1940s). Simultaneously they rid the party leaders of their
most dangerous internal enemies by terrorizing potential party opponents into silence. The show trials also served a public function, aside
from whatever they achieved within the inner circles: like practically
every other Stalinist institution, they had an educational purpose. If
communist Europe had not surpassed capitalist Europe, if infrastructure projects were flawed or delayed, if food supplies were poor and
living standards low, then the show trials provided the explanation:
foreign spies, nefarious saboteurs and traitors, posing as faithful communists, had hijacked progress.

Soviet secret policemen were involved in the Eastern European
show trials from the beginning. A plethora of documentary and anecdotal evidence proves beyond doubt that officials in Moscow ordered
the arrests, helped choose the victims and managed the interrogations. At the congress of the Czechoslovak communist party in May
1949, Byelkin, the senior NKVD general in Hungary, took aside the
Hungarian Defence Minister, Mihály Farkas, and told him Moscow
had 'come to the conclusion that Rajk was the *rezident* [the spy chief]

in Hungary of a European Trotskyist organization, which was in contact with the Americans'. This party jargon was a message that the 'documents of the constructed trial were already being prepared'.[33]

In Poland, the fate of Gomułka was foretold in a memorandum of April 1948 prepared for Mikhail Suslov, the secretary of the Soviet Central Committee, entitled 'On the Anti-Marxist Ideological Orientation in the Leadership of the Polish Workers' Party'. The authors, three Soviet party bureaucrats specializing in ideology, complained of the 'nationalist tendencies' of some Polish communists who 'kept silent about the experiences and successes of the Soviet Union' and 'ignored Leninist-Stalinist teachings'. They identified Gomułka as the leader of this tendency, contemptuously dismissed his notion of 'Polish Marxism', and complained about his categorical refusal to collectivize Polish agriculture. In fact, they suspected Gomułka of 'right-deviationism', another way of saying 'Titoism', which was itself another way of saying he might not be sufficiently loyal to the USSR. They feared the Polish United Workers' Party might be moving closer to 'social democracy', and also expressed great concern about the ideological direction of the Polish army, whose leaders were also never quite pro-Soviet enough for Moscow's taste, even though General Rokossovskii was now firmly in charge.[34]

Having caught wind of these conclusions, Gomułka paid a visit to Moscow in December to argue his case. Afterwards, he wrote his infamous memo, cited in Chapter 6, complaining that the Polish communist party had been taken over by Jews, and declaring that he had always seen the Soviet Union as 'the best friend of Poland' and Stalin as a great 'teacher'.[35] Despite these efforts, Gomułka's closest colleagues were soon arrested – including General Marian Spychalski, a fellow Politburo member – as were a large group of Polish army officers. Bierut kept Stalin regularly updated on the progress of their cases. Gomułka himself was finally arrested in 1951.[36]

Soviet ideologists prepared a similar document on the Czechoslovak communist party, which they also sent to Suslov in 1948. Entitled 'On Several Mistakes of the Communist Party of Czechoslovakia', this document is broader, more theoretical and more rambling than the Polish equivalent, identifying deep problems in many spheres. But it does get in a few digs at Slánský, accusing him of having made mistakes in recruitment to the communist party.[37] That document prepared the ground for Stalin's message to Klement Gottwald, sent via an emissary in July 1951, effectively ordering the Czechoslovak communist party boss to arrest Slánský.[38] This was extremely awkward for Gottwald: the Czechoslovak communist party had just launched a national campaign to celebrate Slánský's fiftieth birthday. A coal mine had just proudly renamed itself the Partisan Slánský mine, and other factories were clamouring for the same privilege.[39]

Not trusting their Eastern European colleagues to get it right, Moscow sent Soviet secret police officers – Byelkin to Budapest and Alexander Beschasnov to Prague, where the local policemen had been resisting Soviet 'advice' on this and other matters – to direct the investigations.[40] They brought with them teams of advisers prepared to plan and orchestrate the trials. In Prague, Beschasnov and his group all lived together in a suburban villa, where they employed four full-time translators and sent regular reports to Stalin.[41] In Budapest, the Hungarian investigators were accompanied at all times by Soviet mentors. When a Polish officer arrived from Warsaw to be briefed by the Hungarians on their 'progress', he was struck by the presence of a red-haired NKVD general, recently arrived from Moscow, who appeared to know a lot more than the Hungarians about 'the real motivations of the whole affair', even though he said nothing directly to the Poles during their stay.[42]

The identities of the arrestees and the nature of their alleged conspiracies also fell in line with Stalin's own obsessions of the time. Though the rules were not ironclad, certain types of people were more likely to be arrested than others. Potential 'right-deviationists' and 'Titoists' like Gomułka were suspect. So were 'left-deviationists', also known as 'cosmopolitans' or 'Zionists' – in other words, Jews. As noted, this latter category of enemy had come to the forefront of Stalinist paranoia following the establishment of the state of Israel in 1948, after which he launched a broad campaign against Soviet Jews. Jewish doctors – who were allegedly trying to kill or poison party leaders – would become one of the obsessions of his final years. In Eastern Europe, he may have had some more pragmatic motivations as well. He and his henchmen clearly believed, not without justification, that the persecution of Jewish communists would be welcomed by everyone else.

Communists who had spent the war away from Moscow, either at home or in Western Europe, were another target. Anyone with connections to foreign communist parties, anyone who had fought in the international brigades of the Spanish Civil War, and anyone with family connections outside their own country, was also at risk of being named a left-deviationist or right-deviationist. Rajk had fought in Spain and spent the war in Budapest. Merker, a Jew who waited out the war in Mexico, was another obvious target. Gomułka had spent the war in Warsaw (which was when Bierut had been scheming against him: as early as June 1944 he had told the Comintern leadership that Gomułka was not qualified to be secretary of the communist party and had asked for Moscow's help in replacing him).[43]

The Soviet scenario was not always followed with precision. Across the bloc, leaders also played for time, altered the orders, and arranged both arrests and trials in accordance with their own political needs. Gottwald delayed Slánský's arrest until he himself was threatened. Gomułka's trial was never held at all: although happy enough to arrest the popular party boss, Bierut never tortured him and never subjected him to a show trial, despite being under some pressure to do so. He may have feared that Gomułka would eventually emerge more popular, not less, from a show trial and he may have doubted whether his rival, in many ways the more confident figure, could be made to confess to imaginary crimes. Bierut may also have feared the long-term consquences of Gomułka's destruction, just as Gottwald seems to have feared the long-term consequences of Slánský's demise. Although neither man had any qualms about arresting and torturing priests or senior military officers, the murder of the General Secretary of the communist party – the job held by both Gomułka and Slánský at the time – could be extremely dangerous for everyone else. Any one of them might come next, as one Hungarian historian notes: 'When the ax was directed at the head of the party, the move triggered within the other party leaders ... a defense mechanism, aimed at self-preservation.'[44]

In East Germany the leadership had other reasons for hesitation, and in fact senior German communists were at first largely spared when arrests began elsewhere in the bloc. At the time, the Allied Control Council still had a large presence in Germany, and events in Berlin were very much the focus of international news. Later on, after the official establishment of East Germany – the German Democratic Republic – a belated party purge began. A dozen-odd German communists were arrested, and several were eventually executed. But because both the Soviet and the East German leadership worried about how they would be received in West Germany, no public show trials were ever held. Aside from the possible bad publicity, the 'success' of such trials depended on the creation and portrayal of a conspiracy, and there were too many German communists now residing in the West who would be able to pick apart a contrived 'conspiracy' story and expose it as fiction.

Yet even countries which never held show trials did prepare for them, conducting arrests and interrogations under Soviet direction. As the investigations progressed, ever more international coordination was required. To be successful, Soviet secret policemen thought that show trials needed a complex story line, a conspiracy involving many actors, and so Soviet advisers pushed their Eastern European colleagues to link the traitors of Prague, Budapest, Berlin and Warsaw into one story. In order to do so, they needed a central figure, someone who had known some of the protagonists and who could plausibly, or semi-plausibly, be accused of recruiting all of them. Eventually, they hit on a man who fitted these requirements: a mildly eccentric Harvard graduate and American State Department official named Noel Field.

In his lifetime, Field was notorious. Since then, he has been described as an American spy, as an agent, as a double agent and as a provocateur sent by the CIA to cause havoc among the Eastern European communists.[45] In his 1954 'rehabilitation' testimony – recently discovered by the Hungarian historian Mária Schmidt – Field declared himself, simply, to be a communist, working alongside the NKVD. A number of other documents now testify to that as well. Field wrote that he had been secretly working for the USSR since 1927, living an 'illegal life completely separate from my official life', and had been well acquainted with fellow members of the American communist party, among them Alger Hiss and Whittaker Chambers.[46]

But although he also knew Allen Dulles – a US intelligence officer in Switzerland during the war and later Director of the CIA – and might even have had some dealings with him, there isn't any evidence that Field ever became an American agent as Hungarian, Czech and Polish prosecutors would allege. Nevertheless, from the Soviet point of view, Field was the perfect victim. He had left the State Department in 1936. He had spent the war in Geneva, working for the Unitarian Service Committee, an organization which offered assistance to refugees fleeing Hitler. Naturally, many of these refugees were communists and thus he had friends and acquaintances all across Eastern Europe.

Ironically, Field fell into Soviet hands because he wanted to capitalize on those friends and acquaintances. In the spring of 1949, Field was unemployed and afraid to return to the United States, where his name had already been mentioned during the public hearings on Alger Hiss. He travelled from East Berlin to Prague to Warsaw, apparently looking for a job, as the Unitarians were closing their Swiss office.[47] He returned to Prague in May – and promptly disappeared. His wife Herta went to look for him, and in August she disappeared too. Field's brother, Hermann, and his stepdaughter, Erica Wallach, also vanished, the former in Warsaw, the latter in East Berlin.

Field's communist sympathies didn't prevent Soviet and Eastern European prosecutors from weaving an elaborate web of theories around him and his family, or from inventing stories about him which bordered on the fantastical. Indeed, to do true justice to this bizarre piece of the Eastern European Stalinist story would require another book the size of this one. Suffice to say that, after 1949, knowing Field or even having met him briefly was enough to incriminate anyone living in communist Europe, however high their rank and however excellent their connections. Even those who weren't arrested fell under Field's shadow. Jakub Berman, Poland's ideology boss – second only to Bierut in the communist party hierarchy – lived under a cloud of suspicion for years because his secretary, Anna Duracz, had once met Field briefly.

Field's arrest in Budapest set off a rapid chain of events. His incarceration was quickly followed by the arrest and interrogation of Tibor Szőnyi, an anti-Nazi activist who had lived in Switzerland during the war and had known Field as well as Rajk. The Hungarian investigators were pleased because this implicated Rajk, along with dozens of others, by association. Eleven East Germans alleged to have known Noel Field were arrested in Berlin in 1950, Merker among them. Two years later, when Slánský and thirteen associates confessed to Titoism, Zionism, treason and conspiracy, they were also alleged to have been organized by the 'well-known agent' Noel Field.

Although he lay at the centre of the case, Field himself never went on trial. But others confessed, in public and in great detail, that they had been guided by his evil hand. At his show trial, Szőnyi declared that Field and Dulles had persuaded him to impose a 'chauvinistic and pro-American spirit' on the Hungarian diaspora in Switzerland.[48] Rajk confessed that he, Field and Tito had plotted the assassination of the Hungarian leadership. Béla Szász confessed to an absurd conspiracy involving a Danish nanny he had known slightly and an Englishman he had met once while in exile in Argentina. His guilt was proven by the fact that he had briefly passed through Switzerland during the war, even though he didn't meet Field there and had never heard of him.[49] Gejza Pavlik, a Czech arrested by the Hungarians in 1949, confessed that he had joined a vast Trotskyite movement organized by Field and the CIA which was planning to insinuate itself into the leadership of the Czechoslovak communist party.[50] In Prague, Slánský confessed that under the influence of Field he had 'allowed hostile elements to penetrate the highest levels of the Central Committee', and had organized an 'anti-state centre' with the support of freemasons, Zionists and Titoists, among others. Otto Šling, a Czech regional party boss, confessed to working on behalf of the British secret service since the war. Bedřich Geminder, the head of the party's international department, confessed that he was in touch with 'Israeli diplomats'. That they really were diplomats, and not spies, hardly mattered. In a world in which Noel Field was a criminal mastermind, any foreign consul, however junior, was a dangerous secret agent.[51]

Soviet advisers both wrote the scripts of these show trials and helped 'persuade' victims to make the necessary confessions, using techniques they had tried before. The art of forcing confessions had already been honed to perfection in the Soviet system, where the 'usual methods', as one Czech report later put it, began with an 'endless interrogation of the victim, with the officers working in shifts so that he or she received only a minimum of rest'. In addition to this there were 'beatings, torture by hunger and thirst, confinement in the dark chamber, the inculcation of fear about the fate of the prisoner's family, subtly staged confrontations, the use of stool pigeons, the bugging of cells, and many other refinements'.[52] Most of the time, this kind of torture was referred to with euphemisms. Bierut and his sidekick Berman frequently ordered the police to create 'such conditions that they tell the truth'.[53] Czech interrogators were told that 'these kinds of people are very obstinate and we cannot give them time to get ready for the trials'.[54]

The precise methods did vary from person to person and case to case. Szász was left standing for 'seven times twenty-four hours', and over the course of his imprisonment suffered five broken ribs: 'Whether on instruction or simply for fun, they used me to relieve their boredom. They ordered me to stand motionless, then yelled at me or kicked the door, and on the pretext that I had moved, fell upon me and struck and kicked me all over . . .'[55] Polish interrogation protocols contain records of guards who burnt prisoners' feet or hands, pulled their hair out, made them kneel with their arms in the air for hours, or forced them to stand on one leg for hours.[56] General Spychalski was kept naked in a damp, dark, mouldy cell.[57] The Czech police beat a pregnant woman so badly that she miscarried. Another Czech woman, also pregnant, was made to sleep without clothes, mattress or blankets for ten days. When she asked for a doctor, she was told that 'it would be better if another beast like me would never be brought into the world'.[58]

Interrogations were also intended to 'break' the victim psychologically. Prisoners were shown photographs of their spouses in prison, or were told that their children would suffer if they didn't confess, or were persuaded to put their trust in a 'kind' interrogator or an apparently sympathetic cellmate. In the case of the Eastern European communists, interrogators found it particularly effective to return again and again to the past. Incidents which had taken place decades earlier were rehashed over and over again. The suspect's years in the underground were discussed at length, as were his wartime experiences. This obsession with the past was deliberate, as István Rév has brilliantly observed. After all, no one who had ever been in the communist underground could ever be absolutely certain about what had happened during those years of conspiracy. He could never be sure with whom he had really been speaking, and what secret games had been played without his knowledge:

It was not only out of chronological accuracy to start the investigation of the political trials with questions related to the recruitment of the accused into the ranks of the 'fascist' political police, but in order to render the accused uncertain and defenseless. The accused himself has never been in the possession of all the relevant facts; the logic of illegality provided only partial, fragmentary information always open to doubt . . . He could never be absolutely sure, he could not clearly answer all the questions, all his previous acts could be presented under a new description.[59]

Almost anybody who had ever worked underground could be tripped up, confused or misled. Anyone could be made to feel guilt about something he might have accidentally said, or unknowingly done. Some openly said so, either at the time or afterwards. During his long interrogation, Gomułka was plied with endless, repetitive questions. Day after day, month after month, he was asked to tell the same stories over and over again, from different angles, by different people, almost all of them concerning 'controversial' incidents in the now distant past. He was asked how he had met particular people, when he first heard the names of others. He was asked to recall events which had taken place a decade before. Sometimes, an entire day was spent on a single person or incident.[60]

Several times Gomułka was asked about Spychalski, who had been the leader of the wartime communist militia and in that capacity had led an operation against the Home Army, allegedly in concert with the Gestapo. He was questioned about some more recent comments Spychalski had supposedly made about the need to rid the Polish army of Soviet advisers. He was also asked in enormous detail about the murder of the communist Marceli Nowotko, which took place during the Nazi occupation and which was probably carried out by one of Nowotko's communist comrades. Gomułka was also accused of knowingly hiring 'unreliable' people. In response, he told his interrogators that he had done so because he thought the 'unreliables' in question were Soviet agents, and that he was obliged to make use of their talents.

The questioning took its toll. Gomułka's interrogators at first described him as 'calm'. Later, however, he became 'nervy' and 'weepy'. From time to time he wrote plaintive letters to the Central Committee: 'as of today I still do not know either the reason for my arrest or the state of my case, although 11 months have passed since I was placed in isolation'. He began to complain of leg pains, a lack of exercise and poor medical care. He wrote plaintive letters to his son, wondering if he had been forgotten: 'Sooner or later I'll have a breakdown.' All of this was reported to Moscow. Later, after Stalin had died and Gomułka was released – in due course he would replace Bierut as the communist party boss – Nikita Khrushchev would inquire sweetly after Gomułka's health, even offering to send Soviet doctors to help him recover.

Behind the 'nerves' and the 'weepiness' surely lay far greater fears. Gomułka knew enough about communism to understand that torture and death might come next. But from his account, and from accounts of the interrogations of Slánský, Spychalski and others, it's also clear that the recollection of the past – the murky, confusing, conspiratorial past – created emotional and psychological trauma even when no violence was used at all. The Soviet comrades appear to have understood very well that the people they were dealing with could be made to feel uncertain, uneasy and even guilty about their lives. This was true of those who had been arrested as well as those who had not been – or not yet. Before he himself was imprisoned, the Czech communist Oskar Langer told his wife that 'These men are perhaps not guilty in the everyday sense of the word. But just now the fate and interests of individuals are of secondary importance. Our whole future, maybe the future of mankind, is at stake.'[61] Perhaps in the grander scheme of things, which ordinary mortals could not understand, the arrests were somehow necessary. 'In the dark,' writes Rév, 'it is always difficult to explain appearances in a clear way, for nobody follows normal rules.'

Others felt uneasy as well. Indeed, an ominous sense of déjà vu enveloped communists, communist sympathizers and former communist sympathizers in both Eastern and Western Europe. Arthur Koestler, the German-Hungarian writer, sat weeping beside his radio in London, '"convulsed" for two days' by the public confessions of his old comrade Otto Katz, on trial in Prague.[62] He and others had witnessed all of this before, though many had repressed these bad memories for the sake of the battle against fascism. Now the duplicitousness of the Soviet regime was staring them in the face once again. And once again all of the party slogans looked empty and ominous. 'My life is at an end,' said the Czechoslovak victim, Geminder, 'and the only thing I can do is to embark on a road of truth and thus save the party ... I am walking to the gallows with a heavy heart but relatively calm ... the air is becoming purer and one obstacle along the victorious road to socialism is being removed. The party is always right ...'[63]

The political impact of the arrests and convictions of leading communists between 1949 and 1953 is not easy to measure. By that time, show trials were a familiar spectacle in Eastern Europe. Home Army soldiers in Poland had been subjected to them; priests and pastors had been subjected to them; Cardinal Mindszenty himself had publicly confessed to plotting the launch of the Third World War. But the sight of the nation's heroic leaders confessing in public to absurd crimes left ordinary citizens feeling both afraid and confused.[64] If the accusations weren't true, then that meant the party had reached new levels of paranoia. But if they were true, then the country really had been penetrated by enemies and spies. Even among members of the secret police the confessions simultaneously produced a strange mixture of fear and disbelief. Szász's interrogator laughingly called the truncheon he used to beat prisoners the 'people's educator', and yet at the same time his cynicism was 'interwoven with some sort of bigoted and sentimental blind faith'.[65]

In the long run, the trials planted doubts about the reliability and even the sanity of the communist leadership, though these were not necessarily expressed at the time. One historian tells the story of two Hungarian sisters, both loyal communists, who separately grew disenchanted with the regime during the trials. Despite living in the same apartment, each remained convinced that the other was still a believer, and both continued to repeat Stalinist slogans, even to one another, just as they did outside the house.[66] Like the accused, the public were also expected to act as if they believed the truth of what was being said, even if they had private doubts.

In the short run, the arrests of leading communists did contribute to the public paranoia which reached new levels in 1949, which remained high until Stalin's death in March 1953, and which had a real impact on the public, the leadership and the secret police. Because the accused were alleged to be foreign spies, their arrests were accompanied by a wave of especially vicious anti-American and anti-Western propaganda. In 1952, the propaganda department of the Polish communist party's Central Committee handed out a pamphlet to party agitators containing sample speeches. One of them, using language typical for the time, proclaimed that the 'American imperialists are rebuilding the neo-Nazi Wehrmacht and preparing it to invade Poland' while the Soviet Union was 'helping to develop Polish technology, culture and art'.[67] At about the same time, East German activists were also presented with pamphlets instructing them on the proper way to explain West German politics to their East German listeners:

> Just who are these 'German' politicians? They are monopoly capitalists whose property was seized in the German Democratic Republic, along with their cronies in West Germany. They are the Junkers who lost their land and moved to West Germany. They believe that they can regain their estates through a new war. They are the war criminals and militarists who dream of new deeds of 'heroism' and the lackeys of the Anglo-Americans, like Adenauer, Blücher, Kaiser, Schumacher, etc.[68]

Both the Polish and the German propagandists also received instructions on the conduct of the 'battle against the beetle', national campaigns to rid the Polish and German potato crops of a deluge of Colorado potato beetles which invaded Central Europe that summer – a scourge which both *Trybuna Ludu* and *Neues Deutschland* blamed squarely on the Americans: US pilots, they declared, had thrown thousands of the parasites down from aeroplanes over East Germany, whence they had made their way east. Polish schoolchildren were urged to form brigades to find, catch and kill them, and factory workers spent their weekends in the fields, searching for them.[69] The East Germans, who christened the bugs *Amikäfer*, meaning Ami (American) beetles, invited sympathetic foreign journalists from China, Poland, Czechoslovakia, France and Italy to witness the damage done by *Amikäfer*. Afterwards, the journalists and their German colleagues signed a joint protest note: 'Colorado beetles are smaller than atomic bombs, but they are also a weapon of US imperialism against the peace-loving working population. We journalists who serve peace hereby condemn this new criminal method of the American warmongers.'[70]

Though that kind of language sounds ludicrous in retrospect it had real and tragic consequences at the time. In Hungary, food shortages were widely and angrily blamed not on beetles but on kulaks, wealthy peasants who were allegedly hiding their produce in order to undermine the regime. 'Enemies of the state try to prevent us from making bread for the whole nation' declared a 1950 newsreel. In that same year, an elaborate case was launched against a peasant who made a small campfire in a field to cook his lunch, knocked over the pot and lost control of the flames. Although nobody was injured and the harvest was not harmed, the man's field burned. A local prosecutor investigated, and was at first inclined to dismiss the case as an accident.

The prosecutor changed his mind after he was visited in the middle of the night by secret policemen who told him that this case involved a kulak, criminal arson and a crime against the state. On the following morning, officials from the Justice Ministry also called to tell him that he had three days to finish the trial, which was being observed very closely by the highest officials. Amidst a burst of national publicity the man was quickly convicted. He received a death sentence which was enacted immediately. As his daughter remembered, 'when we were entering the courtroom, we could see the gallows under preparation for the afternoon'.[71] The authorities had clearly been looking for just such a case, as Rákosi's personal correspondence from that period reveals. From 1948 onwards he had been complaining about over-lenient sentences for peasants convicted of crimes such as food hoarding or illegal animal slaughter. 'We must take class origins into consideration in these verdicts,' he declared in a note to Gerő.[72]

In this period, the early training of the East European secret police forces also finally began to bear fruit: they had been taught that all independent organizations were suspect by definition, that all foreign contacts most likely involved espionage – and now the evidence at the highest levels proved that those warnings had been correct. Following each arrest of a leading communist, the victim's relatives, colleagues, employers and employees fell under suspicion too, and many were arrested. After the arrest of Pál Justus, a social democrat who was implicated in the Rajk trial, the secret police then came, one by one, for Justus's wife, his secretary, his friends and then the acquaintances of his friends, of whom György Faludy was one. 'They'll get you too comrade Faludy,' his driver told him without emotion, and a few days later they did.[73] Almost everybody felt they could be accused, and almost everybody took measures to prove their innocence. At the offices of the newspaper where Faludy worked, the entire staff had gathered to hear Rajk's sentence read aloud over the radio:

> These burnings of heretics were regarded as festive and joyful occasions, as in a certain sense they really were: they came as climaxes to long weeks of uncertainty, and put an end to campaigns of arrest so that everyone could feel safe for at least a few weeks until a new wave of arrests began. But if the heretic on the stake was widely known as a faithful believer, the audience – namely the whole country – felt [implicated] in the same suspicion and thus it was advisable to be present at such collective radio-listenings and at the party meeting after them unless one wanted to be accused of complicity.[74]

Even those who were not arrested became pariahs. Jo Langer was away from Prague on holiday when she learned of her husband's arrest. Her companions immediately showed 'shock, curiosity, sympathy, helpfulness, tearful embraces, yes. Not many words. Above all, no comments. We were six of us in the hotel room when the call came, all good friends. But at such a moment and in those times, who dared to trust five other people? Or, for that matter, the walls.' In subsequent months and years, Langer lost her job, her apartment and most of her friends. She and her young daughter barely survived. Only a few courageous people would speak to the wife of an enemy of the state.[75]

By the early 1950s, in other words, the stage was set for the region's secret policemen to finish the task they had begun in 1945: the elimination of any social or civic institutions still remaining, along with anyone who might still sympathize with them. Among those finally destroyed were the Hungarian freemasons.

The freemasons had deep roots in Eastern Europe, where they had long been linked to projects of modernization and, originally, the Enlightenment. The first Hungarian lodge was opened in 1749 – freemasonry was imported into the country simultaneously from both Poland and France – and freemasons were an important force in the

Hungarian revolution of 1848. Treated sceptically in the interwar period and banned by the Nazis, the freemasons had lain low until 1945, when a group of them founded the first postwar lodge. The seventy-six new members were, in the words of a current member, 'ordinary bourgeoisie' – doctors, lawyers, university professors, civil servants. With the blessing of the provisional city mayor, himself a freemason, they got back their old building, a splendid structure in central Budapest.[76] By definition they were an international organization and they received some aid from abroad. They began organizing concerts, lectures and charitable events.

By the end of 1950, the organization no longer existed. The organization had been banned, the secret police had ransacked their building and confiscated their books and paintings.[77] Major investigations into the activities of all the leading freemasons were already underway. Of these, the most important and most comprehensive was the investigation of Géza Supka, Grandmaster of the main Budapest lodge. Supka, aged sixty-seven in 1950, had by that time enjoyed a long and admirable career. A trained archaeologist, he had been director of the National Museum, a member of parliament, and a founder of a leading literary periodical as well as, after the war, a short-lived centrist newspaper. He had not collaborated with the fascists, he had not compromised himself during the war. He devoted much of his life to charitable and patriotic causes.

Nevertheless, in the view of the security services, Supka represented a dangerous threat to Hungarian national security. In his thick and detailed police file, a summary of his life, written in 1950, describes him as a 'representative of Anglo-Saxon interests in Hungary' and as a traitor plotting to overthrow the regime: 'According to our agents' reports, Supka had received a note in August 1949 from Count Géza Teleki in the United States, advising him to keep regular contact with political personalities on whom they can both count after the regime change. Supka establishes widespread contacts for this purpose . . .'[78]

During the previous year, the Hungarian secret police had detained and interrogated many of Supka's friends and acquaintances. Many had cooperated, as his police file demonstrates. A journalist who had worked for his newspaper was threatened – or tortured – into declaring that Supka was a 'man of the Americans', that he had been recruiting 'sympathizers for his movement' since 1944, that he frequently read foreign newspapers and that after the war he had often visited the American embassy 'to speak to his boss'. The journalist claimed to have visited the US embassy in Supka's company, where he had observed that Supka had suspiciously good relations with everyone there. Worse, 'I have knowledge of his participation in cocktail parties with the Anglo-Saxons.' At about the same time, the secret police began opening Supka's mail, copying letters and placing them back in envelopes. Among the copied 'evidence' against him were notices from Paris about the renewal of his magazine subscriptions.

Nevertheless, the most harrowing element of the file is a series of frequent, almost daily reports filed by someone very close to Supka. Although not named in the police file, this informer must have been a close friend or personal secretary, for his knowledge of Supka's movements, conversation and intimate thoughts is very precise. Supka confided many times in the informer, who then gave full reports to the authorities. The resulting report unintentionally provides a glimpse into the life of a man who knows he is in danger, who knows he is being watched, but who still has a naive faith in the goodwill of people who are close to him, including the informer.

As the atmosphere in Budapest grew more stultifying, Supka at first thought of emigration. 'Political changes will not come soon,' he told the informer on 20 December 1949, and he wondered if he should leave the country, as some of his friends were doing, including the vice-president of the national bank. He wasn't certain, however, and he was afraid to apply for a passport, as that would draw the authorities' attention. The informer sent this information back to Supka's case officer, who in turn ordered him to go back 'to find out the exact content of the conversation between him and this bank vice-president, and at the same time to observe Supka and report as soon as he sees any preparation for immigration'.

The informer complied. He also continued to report Supka's views on a wide range of topics. In January, Supka told him he was disappointed with American diplomacy in China, which was too indecisive: he had expected the Americans to be more firmly anti-communist. However, he was cheered by the appointment of General Bradley to replace Eisenhower, as Bradley was a freemason – as, he said, were Truman and MacArthur. (Supka's case officer here made a note: 'all these reports support our assumption that Supka kept in close contact with agents of imperialist powers'.)

Supka also told the informer that Hungary had two strong links to the West: the church and the freemasons. The latter, he felt confident, could evade secret police observation. A few days later, however, the file notes that 'when our agent left at a quarter to midnight, an unknown young person showed up at Supka's apartment from the British embassy, bringing a bulletin and newspapers . . .' The case officer leapt upon this detail as proof of his thesis: 'Supka is the most prominent representative of the imperialist powers in Hungary. On the basis of his statement, we conclude that the focus of their activity is the freemason movement . . . the person coming from the UK embassy proves that Supka has direct and regular links with Western powers.'

Beginning in the spring of 1950, the informer began reporting on Supka's thoughts and movements almost every day. Supka told the informer that he was prepared to be detained at any time, and that he'd already made contact with well-connected friends who he hoped would help him if and when this happened. He told him that he knew his name had been dropped from invitation lists, as people were becoming wary of him, and that he knew he was under observation. But now he had decided not to emigrate, due to his old age and ill-health, and he asked the informer for help in evading what he thought was inevitable arrest. He was trying to get an academic posting in the distant countryside, and perhaps the informer could help him find a suitable place.

In July, Supka and the informer discussed the Korean situation, and the fact that several freemasons had been arrested. In September, they discussed the church–state agreement, and the possibility of an American war in Europe. In June 1951, Supka told the informer that police had visited his house, and confessed he was once again frightened of being deported. Among other things they also discussed the defection of Gyula Schöpflin, the former radio director, to Great Britain; the Rajk trial, about which Supka had many doubts; and Supka's health, which was not good. Still, Supka had many visitors. His cleaning lady gave all of their names to the informer, who passed them on to the case officer.

After that, Supka plunged into depression, fearing his arrest. He obtained some medical documents from a doctor, which he hoped would help him avoid detention or deportation. He tried to make contact with some people he knew in the communist party leadership. He reached out to a couple of freemasons who seemed to have made their peace with the regime – one of them wore a brand-new suit and had a new car – and he discussed rumours that people like himself were being sent to work on collective farms in the Soviet Union. In August 1952, he told the informer that he now left his apartment only rarely. Supka didn't want to see the world of the present, the informer declared in his report to the secret police, it had become so completely different from what he had imagined:

> He added that he often asked himself whether it had been worth it to fight against so many things, now that he knew it would end this way. He is almost 70 years old and is unable to adapt to present-day condi-tions. This makes everything he believed in irrelevant. He still believes in freedom, and although he doesn't know well the condition of the United States, he knows that in England civic freedom is still alive. He thinks he won't see the day when the third world war which he thought would be inevitable would come, but he is convinced that a world built on freedom, not the fake freedom of the fake October revolution, would come someday. His greatest sorrow is that the freemason lodge was banned and he considers this a major attack on civic freedom ... All his life he had been anti-religious and anti-clerical, but even so he could not agree with the persecution of church and of priests ... his sympathy was for the persecuted.

Though a collective celebration was impossible, friends did come to visit the former Grandmaster in small groups on Supka's seventieth birthday. After that he was often ill, according to the informer's reports, though he still liked to discuss politics. Géza Supka finally died in May 1956, five months before the Hungarian Revolution. Some 400 people came to his funeral. As the informer reported, 'there were several wreaths and several people put acacia leaves on them, symbol of the freemasons . . .'

13

Homo sovieticus

> We watched the procession, the masses carrying red flags, the
> girls in white dresses. Grigorev was with us, the Soviet adviser
> to the Allied Control Commission ... When the whole square
> was full of people, he turned to me and asked: 'Say, these
> 200,000 proletarians gathered here – six months ago they
> were just as enthusiastic for the Arrow Cross fascists, weren't
> they?
>
> *Gyula Schöpflin in his memoirs*[1]

The show trials, the arrests and the assaults on clergy attracted
national and international attention during the era of High Stalinism.
But pressure from above was only one of the tools the regimes
deployed to convince their fellow citizens of their right to rule. They
also attempted to create enthusiasm and cooperation from below. If
the immediate postwar period had been characterized by violent
attacks on the existing institutions of civil society, after 1948 the
regimes began instead to create a new system of state-controlled
schools and mass organizations which would envelop their citizens
from the moment of birth. Once inside this totalitarian system, it was
assumed, the citizens of the communist states would never want or be
able to leave it. They were meant to become, in the sarcastic phrasing
of an old Soviet dissident, members of the species *Homo sovieticus*,
Soviet Man. Not only would *Homo sovieticus* never oppose communism, he could never even conceive of opposing communism.[2]

In the era of High Stalinism, no one was exempt from this ideological instruction – not even the very youngest citizens. Though teenagers
had long been a communist priority, now the focus was expanded to

include kindergarteners. As Otto Grotewohl, the new East German Prime Minister, declared in 1949, the youngest German children were 'our cleanest and best human material'. They were 'the gold reserve for our future'. They must not 'fall prey to reactionary forces', and they should not 'grow wildly, without care and attention'.[3]

The notion of small children as blank slates or lumps of clay which the regime could mould at will was not a new one in Germany: the Nazis had used very similar metaphors (as had the Jesuits, among others). But the content which German communists poured into the allegedly empty brains of infants would not be Nazi. As early as June 1945, a Berlin newspaper wrote of the damage already done to children by years of Nazi education:

> Let's consider the following facts. The beginning of the strongest sensitivity and memory of the child lies between the fifth and the seventh year. Add to this the length of Nazi rule, and we get the horrifying result that all young people . . . have been growing up exclusively under the influence of lies which have been hammered into them in school and the Hitler Youth.[4]

Right away, the Soviet occupation force banned private kindergartens and forbade former Nazis and Nazi fellow travellers – a loosely defined category – from teaching in any kindergartens. When that edict led to a teacher shortage, the Soviet occupation regime, which surely had more urgent matters on its plate, organized six-month courses to train new preschool teachers.[5]

More was to come. Indeed, the extent and nature of the Soviet Union's desired influence over education came as a shock to many Eastern European and especially to German educators, many of whom had enthusiastically anticipated that a left-wing regime would support the progressive, avant-garde pedagogy advocated in the 1920s, with its emphasis on spontaneity, creativity and what would nowadays be called 'child-centred' education. There had been Montessori kindergartens in Budapest and Berlin since before the First World War; Janusz Korczak, a progressive educator and children's author, had experimented with the idea of 'self-government' in his Warsaw orphanages, encouraging children to write their own rules and form their own parliaments.[6]

Instead, Eastern Europe's educators learned that the 'correct' methods of instruction would not be found in Montessori textbooks but rather in the works of Soviet educational theorists, and most notably in the writings of Anton Makarenko, a particular favourite of Stalin. In the 1930s, Makarenko had been the director of the Gorky colony, a reform school for juvenile delinquents. His methods were heavy on peer pressure, repetition and indoctrination, and he emphasized collective living and working. The most eloquent passages of *The Road to Life*, his book about the Gorky colony, are dedicated to the glories of collective labour: 'It was a joy, perhaps the deepest joy the world has to give – this feeling of interdependence, of the strength and flexibility of human relations, of the calm, vast power of the collective, vibrating in an atmosphere permeated with its own force.'[7]

Like Lysenko, the fraudulent Stalinist biologist who believed in the inheritability of acquired traits, Makarenko believed in the mutability of human nature. Any child, however unpromising his background and however reactionary his parents, could be transformed into a good Soviet citizen. Put him in a team, tell him that everybody works for the good of the group, patiently repeat slogans in his presence and he will learn. While the real Makarenko was surely more sophisticated than his followers, crude 'Makarenkoism' (like crude 'Lysenkoism') looked a lot like ordinary ideological brainwashing.

Progressive educators were forced to make a rapid retreat. 'I overemphasized children's independent activities, underestimated the necessity of political leadership, and [mistakenly] believed that people become educated through the acquisition of experience,' one German educational theorist declared in her apologetic memoirs. She also regretted not following the advice of Erich Honecker, who, though of course not an expert in early childhood education, 'approached all questions with a clear political-ideological class viewpoint' and thus reached the 'right conclusions'.[8] At about the same time, Korczak – who had died tragically in Treblinka, together with his orphans – was denounced in Poland for promulgating 'education in the spirit of mindless subservience to the existing order'.[9]

With only six months of training, the army of brand-new kindergarten teachers in Germany would have had difficulty understanding these theoretical debates, let alone deploying them in the classroom. But the basics, as they and their colleagues across the bloc soon learned, were not difficult. Politics was to lie at the centre of the curriculum for every child, from kindergarten onwards. Acceptable topics included the history of the working class, the Russian Revolution and the achievements of the Soviet Union. Children were to participate in the party's various campaigns for 'peace', for North Korea, for the Plan. Teachers who did not teach these topics or pursue these campaigns risked losing their jobs.

Naturally, some of the material had to be changed for the benefit of small children. In Poland, the cult of Stalin was transmitted through the study of an utterly fictional version of the Soviet dictator's childhood, which had in reality been rather grim. Polish children were taught to call him by his childhood nickname, Soso (they also learned to call Feliks Dzerzhinskii, the terrifying founder of the Soviet secret police, by the nickname 'Franek'), and they read of his various exploits and youthful successes. Popular children's magazines contained tales designed to stoke admiration of Stalin, such as the story of a child who asks his mother the meaning of the word 'Generalissimo'. She explains that because 'the whole Soviet nation deeply loved their leader' the USSR had granted him this special title as a gesture of thanks. Impressed by this deep faith, the child determines to learn how to spell the difficult word 'generalissimo' and remember it for ever.

The glories of central planning were meanwhile conveyed through books such as *Six Year Old Bronek and the Six Year Plan*.[10] The evils of capitalism were transmitted though tales like the story of Mister Twister, an American who visits Leningrad and is shocked to find a black man staying in his hotel – or through poems about American plans for war:

> In crazy America
> They dream of war
> And the front lines are painted
> On maps with human blood[11]

Novelists also worked hard to supply the children of the new era with reading material. In the late 1940s and 1950s, Alex Wedding – a communist whose books had been burned by Hitler in 1933 – published a series of children's books in eastern Germany. The first was *Die Fahne des Pfeiferhansleins*, the tale of a fifteenth-century peasants' rebellion which features a flute-playing rebel leader, a *Pfeifer*, who dreams of 'a free homeland' without rulers and ruled. The rebellion ends badly, but the rebels don't give up hope: 'Someday the sun of freedom will break through the clouds. Someday even our exile will end, and we will see our motherland again, a beautiful motherland, free of the arbitrary rule of the dukes and lords ... and then the flag of the *Pfeifer* will wave from all towers ...'[12]

Existing children's stories were sometimes rewritten to conform to the new ideological spirit. A beloved Polish children's comic strip – 'The Adventures of Matolek the Goat' – reappeared with a few subtle changes. Before the war, Matolek had looked down upon Warsaw and seen the Royal Castle and the spire of a church. After the war, he only saw the Palace of Culture, a towering monument to Stalin. Before the war, policemen in trench coats had swung their batons at Matolek for breaking traffic regulations. After the war, as one reader remembered, 'nice socialist militiamen politely point him in the right direction'. The original Matolek discovered a treasure which he gave to 'poor children in Poland'. Because there were no poor children under communism, postwar Matolek gave the treasure to the 'dear' children in Poland instead.[13]

Textbooks also had to be rewritten to reflect the new reality. In November 1945, at a time when its bureaucrats were still collecting shoes and sweaters from the UN relief agency and handing them out to desperate teachers, the Polish Education Ministry ordered the writing of a new history of education, designed to emphasize 'the fight for democratic education' and set up a committee to write new history textbooks as well.[14] When that rewriting process didn't take place fast enough, more drastic measures were used: for a brief period, in 1950–51, only Soviet history texts were allowed in Polish schools.[15] In eastern Germany, the rewriting efforts were more successful. The history curriculum for thirteen-year-olds described the postwar period as follows:

> With the help of the Soviet occupation authorities, the democratic forces ... managed to disempower the monopoly capitalists and land owners in the eastern part of Germany and to establish an anti-fascist democratic order. This anti-fascist democratic order ... enjoys the support and help of the great socialist Soviet Union, which respects

the national rights of the German people and represents its national interests.[16]

Most urgently of all, teachers had to be retrained – or replaced – and not only kindergarten teachers. The Soviet military regime first proclaimed the 'democratic renewal of the German school', in August 1945, in an order which also called for a 'new type of democratic, responsible and capable teacher'. Soon afterwards, educational policy in the Soviet zone of Germany was handed over to the most senior and most trusted 'Moscow' communists: Anton Ackermann, a leader of the wartime National Committee for a Free Germany; Paul Wandel, a member of the Soviet, not the German, communist party; and Otto Winzer, a member of the Ulbricht Group.[17] Soviet authorities would in due course use educational reform as a type of de-Nazification, as well as a means of offering ambitious, pro-regime young people a path to rapid advancement.[18] A whole generation of *Neulehrer* – 'new teachers', often with minimal training – were rapidly deployed in place of old ones, and they were expected to show their gratitude to the new regime by following every one of its precepts.

By contrast, most Polish teachers were left alone in the immediate postwar chaos, despite the close links between the wartime underground and the teaching profession. In much of Poland, children had been prevented from attending school at all during the Nazi occupation – the Germans had intended to make the Poles into a nation of illiterate serfs – and many children could not read or write. The resumption of normal schooling was considered a national priority. In September 1945, the Minister of State Security, Radkiewicz, even signed an internal decree declaring that in light of the 'destruction wreaked on schools', secret policemen should 'arrest teachers only when absolutely necessary'. If they had to be incarcerated, then their cases should be investigated and reviewed as fast as possible.[19]

Over time, however, those who did not conform to the ideology would be intimidated, threatened and eventually fired. Their actions and behaviour would be observed by local secret policemen, by school directors sent from outside, by each other – or even by students themselves. In 1946, the Education Ministry learned that in the small town of Człuchów, the teenage son of a secret policeman had been threatening both his teachers and his classmates. Bragging that he had 'access to the UB building at any minute, without a pass', he told one child he would be 'locked up', and threatened another for playing a 'religious' Christmas carol ('Silent Night') on the piano. After a teacher described 'Russia's historical push towards Constantinople' in a geography class, he told another student gleefully that 'the old man's just done himself in'. Though the boy was failing ('he can't do simple maths . . . and in French he is hopeless') he bragged that, thanks to his father's influence, he would pass without doing any work. When the school director finally summoned his parents to complain, she herself received a summons to the offices of the local secret police two hours later.[20]

That particular case was resolved in the school's favour, not least because even secret policemen didn't like children of their employees threatening schoolmates with arrest. But other stories ended less happily, for example when teachers were made responsible for their pupils' politics. They could lose their jobs for having presumably exerted 'bad influence' over children who displayed 'reactionary' or anti-communist views.[21] In January 1947, a group of about thirty armed secret policemen entered a Polish secondary school near Sobieszyn, burst into a classroom and told everyone present to put up their hands and march outside. Some students were separated, questioned and beaten; the school director's protests were ignored. An officer brusquely explained that the students came from 'bandit' families, and that several teachers from the school had already been arrested. The raid was designed to punish the entire institution, in other words, for failing to maintain an ideologically correct atmosphere.[22]

By 1948, however, the mood had changed more decisively, and the Polish Education Ministry set out to 'verify' the 'values, ideological and professional', of all school directors, teachers and educators; to 'deepen the ideological offensive among teachers and students'; and to 'raise the consciousness' of future teachers.[23] At about the same time, one German educational bureaucrat declared that Soviet education, after thirty years of experimentation, had finally reached its zenith: the Soviet Union's experience proved that education 'on the basis of socialist humanism' could be successful. All German teachers who aimed to become 'qualified progressive pedagogues' must therefore 'get acquainted with, study and increasingly learn to apply

Marxist educational science as founded by Marx and Engels, spread by Joseph Dietzgen, August Bebel and Karl Liebknecht, and further developed by Lenin and Stalin'.[24] Similar programmes were arranged for teachers all across the bloc.

From 1948, Marx, Lenin and Makarenko were added to the curriculum in teacher-training colleges across the bloc. Careful attention was now paid to the class background of new teaching cadres, and enormous efforts were made to secure teachers with the 'right' class origins. According to the Polish Education Ministry, 52 per cent of new teachers-in-training in 1948 were of working-class origin, 32 per cent were peasants and 7 per cent were children of 'craftsmen'. If these statistics are correct, only 9 per cent of teachers that year came from 'intellectual' families.[25]

The proletarianization of the professoriate proved a trickier task. In East Germany, a number of university rectors tried to regroup in May 1945 in order to reconnect to the 'German university tradition', but they were almost immediately dismissed by Soviet officials who were horrified by their 'reactionary philosophical worldview' as well as their previous Nazi connections. A wave of de-Nazification followed, both mandatory and voluntary, as dozens of German professors fled to the West. By the time of the opening of the winter semester in January 1946, three quarters of the professors at universities in Berlin, Leipzig, Halle, Greifswald and Rostock were gone, and Soviet officers began to play an active role in recruiting new ones.[26] As they didn't have the resources to run the university system themselves they created a German body, the Central Education Administration, to which they sent often unrealistic demands. In March 1947, the Soviet Military Administration issued an order 'on training the next generation of academics' which called upon the Central Education Administration to find '200 active antifascists' within ten days. As one German member of the administration noted, 'we cannot in all of Germany get hold of 200 active antifascists who are also academically qualified'. The Germans did eventually come up with seventy-five names of 'politically open-minded' professors, but the Soviet administrators rejected thirty-two. Of the rest, most were over fifty and thus not exactly good candidates for a training programme.[27]

From 1948, the authorities in East Germany as well as Hungary and Czechoslovakia launched a more systematic attack on the faculties of philosophy, history, sociology and law, all of which were transformed into vehicles for the transmission of ideology, just as they were in the Soviet Union. History became Marxist history, philosophy became Marxist philosophy, law became Marxist law and sociology often disappeared altogether. Most remaining humanities scholars left at this time, though Soviet authorities did make some effort to keep scientists. As one German cultural bureaucrat put it, 'when a reactionary philosopher or historian leaves [for West Germany] we smile. But the situation is different with physicians, mathematicians or technicians, whom we need and cannot replace.'[28] Scientists were part of the educational establishment, however, and the changes affected them too. When one chemist decided to leave for the West, he told two communist functionaries his reasons. Among other things, they reported back, 'He can no longer accept responsibility for educating his children at our high schools.'[29] The end result was the near total transformation of East German universities. In a relatively short period of time, a new generation of much younger professors – either more ideological, more cynical or more easily cowed – filled all of the teaching posts and controlled all future academic appointments as well.

The situation in Poland was different, in part because the war, the Warsaw Uprising and the Katyń massacre had more thoroughly devastated the Polish intellectual class. In 1939 the Nazis had sent the entire faculty of the Jagellonian University in Kraków, the oldest in the country, to Sachsenhausen (where they were incarcerated alongside more than a thousand students from universities in Prague and Brno).[30] It wasn't easy to fire a Polish professor, because there might not be anyone remotely qualified to replace him and as a result there were far fewer ardent young ideologues in university faculties than there were in East Germany. As late as 1953, law students in Kraków could still study most of their subjects, including the history of Polish law, legal theory and logic, with prewar professors. Only one or two obligatory courses in Marxism-Leninism were taught by new appointees. As John Connelly points out in his definitive study of High Stalinist East European universities, the culture of Polish academic life was also different. Many academics who survived had worked in the 'flying universities' during the war, teaching students in secret, and the habits of patriotism were strong. It was quite common for academic administrators to pay lip service to the regime, but to teach, lecture, hire and fire without any regard to politics. Even in the late 1940s and early 1950s, older professors habitually protected younger students and colleagues from police investigation.[31] Ties of family, loyalty and academic influence often proved stronger, at least behind the scenes, than fear of the party or the secret police.

But the proletarianization of the student body was, for the communist parties, far more important. Bourgeois professors would die out, eventually, and then they could be replaced by eager members of the working classes. In Polish, the term for this wave of academic affirmative action was *awans społeczyny*, a rather ugly bureaucratic phrase which translates, more or less, as 'social advance'. The term took on enormous significance over time, referring both to a policy – the rapid promotion of peasants' and workers' children into higher education – as well as to the 'socially advanced' class which emerged as a result. A similar form of social advance was a central goal of every country in Eastern Europe. In a speech to the 1949 German party congress, Grotewohl proposed to single out and promote 'workers and peasants' from among the Young Pioneers. They had, he said, 'experienced a different kind of learning from early childhood' and could therefore be transformed into a 'genuinely new, democratic, socialist intelligentsia ... which we will need to command our economy and to carry out socialist measures'.[32]

The attempts to create a 'new, democratic, socialist intelligentsia' to replace the old, suspect, bourgeois intelligentsia ranged from the admirable to the absurd. In Poland, where schools of all kinds had been forcibly closed throughout the duration of the Nazi occupation, the postwar illiteracy rate was an extraordinary 18 per cent. The party launched a mass 'battle to liquidate illiteracy' campaign in 1951, preceded by a school reform that emphasized technical education.[33] The success of this programme persuaded many intellectuals of the party's good intentions. One former Polish schoolteacher, though not a communist himself, spent the first part of his career teaching adult literacy classes to refugees from Ukraine and marvelled at the impact: 'they became different people'. Participating in the campaign helped convince him that the party, though it made mistakes, ultimately meant well.[34]

But the mere teaching of reading and writing would not by itself create a new elite. Across the bloc, other forms of more aggressive affirmative action were also put in place. The children of workers and peasants had privileged access to university places, training programmes, jobs and promotions. In East Germany, education bureaucrats actively recruited workers and peasants to join special courses designed to move them quickly up the ladder. Students could qualify for these pre-university entrance courses if their parents came from the correct social background and if they could submit 'political character references of democratic organizations', either trade unions or youth groups.[35] In Poland, Union of Polish Youth activists actually took control of the university admissions process through the institution of 'technical secretaries', functionaries who were placed in deans' offices where they 'through self-sacrificing work contributed to the improvement of the action'. Thanks to these efforts, between 1945 and 1952 the number of students of worker and peasant origin at East German universities rose from 10 to 45 per cent of the total. In 1949, the numbers of worker-peasant students at Polish universities rose to 54.5 per cent.[36]

Polish communists also created their own alternative institutions of higher education to increase the speed of this social advancement further. Students with no high school education were offered the chance to obtain a Polish baccalaureate – the *matura*, similar to a high school graduation certificate – in six months at the Central Party School. With this so called 'small' *matura*, they could enter university. Although other institutions offered faster degrees at this time as well – many young people completed the two-year preparatory course to enable them to enter university without finishing high school – the Party School had different criteria: 'political consciousness' was considered far more important than the ability to read and write well.

The result was predictable. In 1948, the Central Committee Secretariat complained that some 20 per cent of the students at the Party School course – overwhelmingly young, working-class men with no secondary education – couldn't finish the course, because they weren't competent enough to take lecture notes.[37] More than fifty students at the Humboldt University in East Berlin reportedly had nervous break-downs in the 1950s.[38] Professors, particularly in Poland, sometimes quietly advised young workers at the beginning of their courses that they weren't going to make it and should return to their factories. There were also reports of Polish students faking their social origins: 'sons and daughters of merchants, kulaks, and prewar colonels came to the examinations in dirty overalls' and pretended to be workers, as one indignant report had it.[39] In Hungary, some students from bour-geois families were instructed outright to spend a bit of time working as labourers, and then to reapply for university places. Minor displays of loyalty, such as becoming a youth group leader, helped secure uni-versity places too.[40] Material gaps between the worker-peasant university students and the children of prewar intellectuals remained, however – the former often lived in shabby university dorms and the latter lived at home – and the two groups often kept their distance from one another.[41]

In Germany, some of the attempts to retrain workers to fill cultural jobs also ended in fiasco. At one point, the writer Erich Loest was assigned to teach a group of factory workers to become *Volkskorres-pondenten*, people's correspondents. The logic was straightforward: if the proletariat could be trained in journalism, then newspapers would by definition become ideologically correct, and there would be no need for bourgeois journalists. Or so the theory went. In practice, Loest's particular task – the training of workers to become theatre critics – was less than successful:

> There were fifteen people – twelve women, three men – they were workers. They had been asked at their enterprise, 'We need people for this group, who of you likes going to the theatre?' And they had put their hands up and been selected: 'Well, Hildegard, you are a member of this group now.' We went to the theatre together and afterwards or the next day we met. And I told them, tried to tell them, what a theatre review is about. And then we wrote a review together. I was twenty-five by then and I had liked going to the theatre . . . It was horrible. We were all unhappy. I was unhappy, they were even more unhappy . . . They were supposed to write a theatre review, they could not do that and they did not learn it with me. After half a year the whole thing col-lapsed. We carried on for one winter.[42]

But, in a narrower sense, these policies succeeded: eventually they changed the composition of the urban intelligentsia. One Pole remembers that at his elite Warsaw school in the 1950s, almost everybody came from a rural background. When the teacher asked the children where they were going on summer vacation, they answered almost in unison: 'I'm going to stay with my grandparents in the countryside.' It took him many years to realize that in most European capitals, the vast majority of people did not have grandparents who lived on tiny farms and grew potatoes.[43] The social advance policy did also produce a generation of loyal if not necessarily talented communist party leaders. As one historian explains, some people saw right from the beginning that the system could provide them with a clear path to upward mobility, regardless of their background and regardless of their abilities, if they played by the rules:

> They were active in the party, they always had something to say at meetings and consultations – and it was always something 'in line' and 'correct' as we said back then. They defended the position of the directors and the party organization, they took part in after-work 'cultural' activities and made other social contributions. Whatever the quality of their work and their professional training, they advanced quickly, though not necessarily in the workplace. More often they were promoted into the administration, or sent away on courses ... sometimes they wound up in the party apparatus.[44]

A glance at the sociological backgrounds of the Eastern European communist leadership in the 1980s reveals that many activists from modest backgrounds did eventually climb to the very top. Mieczysław Rakowski was born into a peasant family, operated a lathe as a teenager, received a doctorate from the Warsaw Institute for Social Sciences in 1956 and became Prime Minister of Poland in 1988. Miloš Jakeš was born into a peasant family, worked in a shoe factory, obtained a degree from the Moscow Higher Party School in 1958 and was named General Secretary of the Czechoslovak communist party in 1987. Egon Krenz was the child of East Prussian refugees, became the leader of the Pioneers in the 1970s, and was named Prime Minister of East Germany in October 1989, a job he held until December 1989. All of these men were among the most outstanding beneficiaries of the 'social advance'. And all of them reached the summit of power too late to enjoy it.

During the school and work day, the communist educational establishment could keep children, students, young people and young workers safe from the forces of reaction. But after school – at weekends, in the summers – they could still be exposed to any number of harmful ideas. Makarenko had believed that Soviet children and teenagers should be occupied at all times, with collective work, sport or study. By the late 1940s, bureaucrats in Eastern Europe were striving towards the same ideal. At a 1951 Polish teachers' conference, much time was devoted to 'Extracurricular Education'. Those present agreed that it should be used 'to deepen and broaden education obtained in school ... to create conditions for collective life, and to support valuable, socially useful character traits in the spirit of socialist morality.'

More to the point, one speaker declared, afterschool programmes would keep children safe from bad influences: 'The failure to organize the time children spend outside school creates conditions which encourage hostile activity on the part of reactionary priests as well as other reactionary elements and imperialist agents.' Examples of such negative activity, as presented at the conference, included the 'organization of children's daycare in the basement of the Warsaw basilica' as well as the 'participation of priests in various sporting and other organizations for children' (though not that many priests, at that point, were in a position to do so).[45]

In order to keep children and young workers away from these reactionary contacts, the educational establishments across the bloc created a vast programme of afterschool and evening clubs, teams and organizations, all of them under state control though not necessarily political. Some of these official afterschool programmes were even deliberately apolitical, including everything from music and folk dancing to painting and needlework. Chess clubs were especially popular. The idea was to draw children into a place where they could be subtly influenced. If nothing else, organizers had the satisfaction of knowing that children were singing, sewing or checkmating one another in rooms where Stalin's portrait hung on the wall, under the supervision of ideologically reliable educators. All of these activities were free, and hence very attractive to working parents.[46]

More overtly political activities were also available. In Poland, the 'Society of the Friends of Children' organized not only afterschool clubs but 'mass actions' such as the decoration of communal New Years' trees (as opposed to Christmas trees). In Hungary, the Young Pioneers organized 'Michurinist' clubs, which experimented with cotton and other plants in the manner of Ivan Michurin, a botanist colleague of Lysenko and an opponent of genetics.[47] The German Young Pioneers also participated in 'young technician' and 'young natural scientist' clubs, all intended to lead children in professional directions useful to the party.[48]

But the real prize, for dedicated communist educators, was the summer vacation, two long months of idleness which presented enticing possibilities for those who wanted to influence the young. At summer camp, young people were not only away from their families and any other reactionary influences but inside an environment which, in theory, the party and the youth movements could control down to the last detail. Of course, summer camps were nothing new in this part of the world. But in Eastern Europe only the state was allowed to organize youth summer camps – and the state took them very seriously indeed. In Germany, summer camps were of sufficient importance to merit Politburo and Central Committee debate. In Poland, the Education Ministry set up a special 'Commission on the Matter of Summer Vacations for Children and Youth' in 1948.[49]

At first, such experiences were available only to the most ideologically correct. In the first few years after the war, only about 10 per cent of German children attended summer camps. But the German Politburo soon saw that it was the ideologically *incorrect* children who most needed camps which could teach them 'firm friendship with all peace-loving human beings, especially with the people of the great Soviet Union and the best friend and teacher of all children, the great Stalin'. In 1949, the German communists therefore launched a new campaign – *Frohe Ferientage für alle Kinder* ('Happy Holidays for all the Children') – and obliged state companies to sponsor it. By the summer of 1951, some 75 per cent of children in the Soviet zone of Germany attended some kind of overnight summer programme.

Once these camps were up and running, no detail was left to chance. In Germany, guidelines for the directors of the camps were composed by the central council of the Free German Youth and the communist party Central Committee. These dictated everything from the number of hours to be spent swimming during the three-week camp session (eighteen) to the number of hours to be spent singing (two and a half). Campers were to be instructed in the merits of the Five Year Plan, and taught the history of the Komsomol, the Soviet youth association, 'the vanguard of the democratic youth of the world'. There would be group readings of *How the Steel was Tempered*, a novel by the Soviet writer Nikolai Ostrovskii. Every day would start with gymnastics and a morning roll call, and on certain days special ceremonies would be observed: 18 July, the 'Day of the International Brigades'; 6 August, the anniversary of the bombing of Hiroshima; 18 August, the day Ernst Thälmann had been murdered in Buchenwald.[50]

Traditional games – tag, hide-and-seek, 'capture the flag' – were also adapted for the new era. In 1950, for example, one observer described a German summer camp game as follows:

> Boys and girls were hidden on the slopes, under bushes and trees, crawling forward under camouflage ... We happened to come across a Pioneer leader with a red armband and asked her what the children were playing. She explained to us that the children were divided into two armies, the People's Army and the capitalist army. She pointed to the Free German Youth banner placed on a mountain, which was to be conquered by the capitalist army ... On a different hill the 'People's Army' were calling to the capitalist army: 'Do not fight for the capitalists, defect to the People's Army' and similar slogans. During the fight they had to rip off the armbands of the opponents. A Pioneer without an armband was considered dead.

Afterwards, a camp leader explained that these war games were preparing the children to 'struggle for peace': 'The children must know what to defend!'[51]

Nor was teaching only confined to games. At about this time, the central council of the Hungarian youth movement also issued instructions to directors of summer camps in Hungary. Among other things, they advised them on the correct methods of dealing with rebellious campers. Cliques should be broken up, but 'not with violence'. To command the respect of the campers, the group leaders should set an example: every morning, they should get up and get dressed before anyone else.

If all else failed, punishments should be meted out – but only punishments which, in the manner of Makarenko, would have a positive impact on the group as a whole. Punishment through 'excommunication' was highly recommended, for example: if a camper refused to go along with group activities, other campers should refuse to call him 'comrade', and refuse to speak with him. Not only would this peer pressure make the recalcitrant camper change his mind and rejoin the group, but others would see that it is a great honour to be called 'comrade', and would strive hard to be worthy of the title.[52]

As the camps expanded, standards slipped. It was one thing to declare that every child must attend summer camp; it was quite another to build and supply the camps and to train the instructors at short notice. An inspection of some day camps in the Hungarian countryside in 1950 revealed that although children were in theory busy from eight in the morning until six in the evening, in practice they went home much earlier. Some even left before lunch. By the time the camp leaders were preparing the all-important, end-of-day flag-lowering ceremony, 'everybody was gone'. The inspectors complained that the camp leaders lacked organization and initiative: 'in none of these camps did we see organized group activities, hours devoted to education'. Worse, some of the camp leaders 'didn't understand the importance of fighting against clerical reactionaries ... one group leader was playing the organ in the church'. The proposed solution: 'more ideological education'.[53]

As a result of these kinds of problems, the employment opportunities for enthusiastic youth activists were virtually limitless, although these jobs were not easy. Krzysztof Pomian was the leader of the young Polish communists in the Warsaw district of Mokotów in the early 1950s:

'To be a youth leader meant endless meetings, lasting until very late hours in the night, even for schoolchildren. Meetings, group singing sessions, marches, demonstrations, checking whether everyone was at the May 1st celebration, at the 22 July celebration . . . Those who went to these meetings with a feeling of responsibility were deadly serious, others took it all with a grain of salt . . . Green shirts, red ties, singing the "Hymn of Youth" before lessons – it was all easier for me because I came from a communist family, and the forced communist "liturgy" didn't bother me as much as it did others.'[54]

Still, those who stuck with it could remain 'youth leaders' for many years. Honecker finally resigned as the Free German Youth leader in 1955, at the age of forty-three, whereupon he slid seamlessly into the leadership of the East German communist party. Józef Tejchma, a Union of Polish Youth activist from 1948 until 1956, when he was twenty-nine, went on to become Minister of Culture in 1974. András Hegedüs, who attended the founding meetings of the young Hungarian communists in 1945, found himself unexpectedly named Prime Minister of Hungary a decade later, just before being forced to flee the country following the Hungarian Revolution. For those who played the game, the rewards could be high – but so could the price.[55]

Children and young people offered the most enticing prospects to party propagandists – they were, literally, the party's future. But party activists also felt that they had a special mission to win over blue-collar industrial workers, the men and women (but mainly men) in whose name the revolution had been carried out. In order to raise the consciousness of the working class, they therefore turned factories and workplaces into centres for ideological education too, using some of the same techniques – lectures, banners, posters, rallies – as they deployed in schools. By the late 1940s, work itself had been redefined as a political activity. To do a factory job, especially in heavy industry, became a form of service not just to the state or to the economy but to the party itself.

In fact, ideology filled a very important gap in the economy of the period. In state-owned factories better performance did not bring a salary increase, wages were set by central government bureaucrats and there was no incentive to produce more or better. The temptation not to work – or to work slowly and poorly – was very strong. The new factory managers knew they had to find a way to motivate people, and they now did so by tying the performance of individuals directly to the national Five Year or Six Year Plans: industries had a daily 'norm' or quota, factories had a daily quota, workers had a daily quota, and workers would be paid according to how well they met their quota. They would also battle one another in 'socialist competitions', racing not only to fulfil their quotas, but to overfulfil them, and thus to overfulfil the national plan.

Once again, this idea was not a new one. Socialist competitions had been used in the Soviet Union before the war in response to similarly unmotivated workers, low productivity and an urgent need for faster economic growth. Like their Eastern European counterparts of the late 1940s, the Soviet leaders of the early 1930s were also anxious to prove the superiority of their economic model, which they still expected would soon outpace the capitalist West. In order to inspire their sluggish working class, Soviet propagandists had focused on a select group of high-performing (or allegedly high-performing) examples. These were the 'shockworkers', the Heroes of Labour. They dug more coal, produced more iron bars and constructed more kilometres of road than anyone else. Their model was Alexi Stakhanov, a Donbass miner who on 31 August 1935 supposedly dug 102 tonnes of coal in five hours and forty-five minutes, fourteen times his assigned production quota. Stakhanov's achievement was brought to Stalin's attention, and subsequently turned into a miniature cult of personality. There were articles, books and posters about Stakhanov as well as Stakhanov streets and Stakhanov squares. A Ukrainian town was renamed 'Stakhanov' in his honour. Heroes of Labour were renamed Stakhanovites after him too, and Stakhanovite competitions were held all over the Soviet Union.

The Eastern European communists would have known the Stakhanov cult very well, and some of them imitated this model with great precision. Eastern Germany's Stakhanov was Adolf Hennecke, a coal miner who astonished his comrades in 1948 and dug 287 per cent of his production quota. This was far lower than Stakhanov's record – a German could not be expected to surpass a Russian – but Hennecke's name soon appeared on posters and pamphlets anyway. October the 13th, the anniversary of his great feat, was for several years celebrated as a national holiday.

Poland had a coal-mining shockworker too, Wincenty Pstrowski.

He achieved 273 per cent of the norm in 1947, and then endeared himself to the authorities by issuing a challenge: 'Who can extract more than I?' Pstrowski was a rather less successful figure than Hennecke. Although he had a clean ideological background – he had emigrated from Poland during the war, and joined the communist party in Belgium – he wasn't an entirely reliable propagandist. In public meetings he would often reminisce weepily about his years in exile instead of lecturing the enthusiastic crowd about the joys of hard work. Worse, he died unexpectedly in 1948, possibly because of a dental operation which went wrong. (He had wanted to look better in his photographs, but apparently contracted blood poisoning after a surgeon pulled too many teeth at once.)[56] After his death, Poles invented a little poem about him:

> Chcesz się udać na sąd boski
> Pracuj tak jak górnik Pstrowski.

In rough translation it means, 'If you want a shortcut to heaven, work as hard as miner Pstrowski', but in Polish it rhymes. Hungarians made similar rhymes about their most famous shockworker: 'I don't care about girls any more, I'd rather watch Ignác Pióker.' Pióker was a factory worker who achieved 1470 per cent of the norm by 1949, and had finished his personal five-year plan in 1951, four years ahead of schedule.[57] But not everyone was laughing. For a time, some East European workers really did compete with one another to match the feats of Hennecke, Pstrowski and Pióker, and not just in factories. In Germany, one historian records:

> a 17-year-old girl sorted 20,000 cigarettes in a single day, surpassing the previous record of 14,000. A 16-year-old boy installed 20 radio tubes per hour. A Leipzig train conductor spearheaded the '500 Movement', whereby every locomotive had to be driven 500 kilometers per day. A truck supervisor outdid that: he launched the '100,000 Movement', whereby his truck drivers would travel 100,000 kilometers without repair. Not to be left out, a '4,000 Liter Movement' enlisted Hero of Labor cows to contribute 4,000 liters of milk annually.[58]

Since plans and quotas were in existence everywhere, shockworkers were eventually found, or created, in a wide variety of fields and professions. East Germany held Hennecke academic competitions for schoolchildren, and Hennecke contests for university students, who vied with one another to complete their studies in record time.[59] There were also 'hero brigades' such as the Hungarian 'youth brigade' at the Sztálinváros steel factory which worked so fast it ran out of bricks. Realizing that they needed 14,000 more bricks, youth activists attached to the brigade came to the rescue: 'they saw the problem and mobilized young people from other parts of the construction site . . . from 10.30 in the morning until 2.30 a.m. the brigade transported bricks to where they were needed, in knee-deep mud and heavy rainfall. This helped the brigade fufil their pledge and finish one month early.'[60]

For a brief period, successful Heroes of Labour really were a privileged group with an important role in the communist narrative. Successful workers were praised locally and sometimes nationally, not for merely setting records but for achieving great things for the benefit of the whole of society – or, increasingly, for the benefit of the party – and the rewards were more than material. Their names appeared on signs and billboards. They were celebrated in the newspapers and on the radio, and they featured in public events, newsreels and parades. Sometimes they received unexpected perks, as one female Polish textile worker remembered:

> 'In 1950 or 1952 . . . I don't remember exactly . . . I was chosen as the best Stakhanovite in my factory. I did 250 per cent of the quota . . . One day I went to work, of course in my daily clothes, because you do not go to work in your Sunday clothes. And they gave me a ticket saying that I am going to the Stakhanovite ball. I said I was not going because I was not dressed up, but they ordered me to go. So I went with the others. It was an amazing experience: me, an ordinary worker of a sewing department visited President Bierut himself. Bierut welcomed us, and thanked us for our good work. I received a letter of commendation. We returned home in the morning. My mother started to shout at me – where had I been? I showed her the letter but she didn't believe me. I wept and tried to convince her that I was in Warsaw with Bierut! After some time she started to believe me. And when she started to believe she was proud, so proud.'[61]

Yet in purely economic terms, the shockworker movement was a failure. For one, it created perverse incentives: workers competed to finish quickly, and ignored quality. As a result, 'socialist competitions' never made the economy more productive, in the Soviet Union or any-where else. The economic historian Paul Gregory reckons that in the USSR the Stakhanovite movement had no impact on labour product-ivity whatsoever: the cost of the expensive prizes and higher wages for the Stakhanovites cancelled out whatever value industry might have gained from the superhuman effort of individual workers.[62]

In political terms, the movement's impact was more mixed. In some places, the daily quotas became a bone of contention, particularly as they began to rise faster than wages and living standards, and the party had to invent new techniques to stop the complaining. In 1952, one large Budapest factory called in party activists to lecture its employees on 'how workers lived during the Horthy regime', 'what is the true situation of young workers today', 'what the future will bring' and 'the consequences of the international situation and the struggle for peace'. The workers were told how much worse things had been in the past, how much better life had become, and how much wealth-ier they would be in the future, once capitalism had been defeated.[63]

In Germany, the party countered some of the complaints about high quotas using *Betriebsfunk*, workplace radio stations. Party activists helped workers write and organize radio programmes which were then broadcast throughout the larger factory complexes using loud-speaker systems. At a meeting to discuss the national *Betriebsfunk* effort in 1949, German radio bureaucrats agreed that such broadcast-ing was of the highest significance. 'We must find the language to reach people who are working hard,' said one of them: perhaps those who had 'lost trust in the radio' would feel differently when they heard reports from their own enterprises. Plans were made to organize lunch-time broadcasts and after-work broadcasts for workers waiting for transportation to go home. The idea was that 'the achievements of employees should be recognized and repeated every day' (although some thought it was 'a mistake to be too political', even on the *Betriebs-funk*, and so music and light entertainment were also thrown in).[64]

But the movement did have some political successes. In the USSR, Stalin had used the shockworkers as a tool to replace the Soviet Union's technical and managerial class. At a speech to the Stakhanovite Con-gress in 1935, he had called on the gathered shockworkers to 'smash the conservatism of some of our engineers and technicians' and to 'give free range to the new forces of the working class'.[65] Many of these 'engineers and technicians' were subsequently blamed for the system's failure to produce rapid economic growth and wound up in the Gulag. In Eastern Europe, the movements filled a similarly revolutionary, though slightly different, function. In practice they often pitted younger, inexperienced but more 'ideological' workers against older and more skilled foremen. The older workers remembered prewar factory conditions, which though not necessarily better had not been necessarily worse. Some had once been part of authentic trade union movements too, and they knew that the state-run trade unions, beholden to the government and thus to the factory bosses, were not the same thing at all.

In many factories, older workers quickly became hostile to the work competitions, suspecting, correctly, that they were designed to get everyone to work harder for the same wage. That hostility is reflected in the official biography of Jószef Kiszlinger, a Hungarian Stakhanovite who came into direct conflict with older workers: 'Sometimes he worked with a different knife and managed to overfulfill his quota. The older ones attacked him: "Are you insane? You're undermining us!" Even one of the union officials came to warn him: "Watch yourself, son. This isn't a good idea. Don't go for too high a percentage." '[66]

A young woman who threw herself into the work competitions at the Eisenhüttenstadt combine in Germany – 'we always did our best, so that we would win,' she told an interviewer – also encountered hostility from her older male colleagues. One of her colleagues told her that if the factory management were ever to plant trees, 'you will be the first to be hanged from them'.[67] It isn't hard to see how enthusiastic young people who voluntarily carried bricks in the mud until 2.30 a.m. quickly became annoying. Their efforts set a precedent others would have to follow.

This generational conflict had been created deliberately, and it was deliberately sustained through propaganda as well. Industrialization was proceeding rapidly, and the party had to integrate thousands of inexperienced and mostly rural labourers into the work force. In Budapest, *Szabad Nép* declared that 'in the Stakhanovite movement a new kind of worker has appeared: the first signs of the new communist working class have emerged . . . From the practice of their everyday life the toiling masses learn the truth of what theory tells us, that the construction of socialism . . . is tied to an increase in the welfare of the workers.'[68]

By 1950, many who had refused to join the competitions were disappearing. In Hungary, an investigation into 'sabotage' in the construction industry in September concluded that hundreds of senior people were responsible for the collapse of a dam: the whole industry would have to be cleaned of 'enemy elements'.[69] By 1951, some 250 'prewar foremen' had been deliberately removed from their jobs in Warsaw too. They were replaced by younger, more ideological colleagues. In due course, the party expected them to be more reliable too.

If propaganda for the young didn't cease at the end of the school day, propaganda for adults didn't end with the work day either. After-work clubs, 'houses of culture' and theatrical expeditions for young workers were organized at the larger factories. Many workplaces also organized discussions and lectures on political themes as well. But in addition to these more mundane events and meetings, the party also planned countless commemorations, festivals, anniversaries and holidays. These were designed both to educate the general public, and to ensure that the general public was kept fully occupied during its scant free time.

By the late 1940s, every communist country had established an official calendar, a list of holidays designed to replace traditional saints' days and religious feasts. May Day (1 May), the Anniversary of the October Revolution (7 November) and Stalin's birthday (21 December) were common to all. Each country also had holidays of its own, including 22 July in Poland, the date the Polish Committee of National Liberation had published its manifesto; 16 April in Germany, Ernst Thälmann's birthday; 19 March and 4 April in Hungary, which respectively marked the launch of the Hungarian Revolution in 1919 and the completion of the Soviet conquest of Hungary in 1945. Each country celebrated its own leader's birthday as well. All of these holidays were marked by parades, often including floats, music and gymnastic displays, as well as flags, banners and speeches, special editions of the newspaper and special programmes on the radio, all of which required quite a bit of time and energy to set up.

Some of these occasions were deliberately designed to push older holidays out of the way. In Poland, 1 May came into direct conflict with 3 May, the anniversary of the signing of the country's first democratic constitution in 1791. In Hungary, 19 March, the anniversary of the 1919 communist revolution, clashed with 15 March, the anniversary of the revolution of 1848. Illegal celebrations of the 'wrong' holidays became a feature of public life and a form of low-level opposition in both countries for many years.

There were rewards for participation in the 'right' holidays: May Day celebrations often included free sausages for those who marched in the parade. But the behaviour of the celebrants at all of these events was also carefully observed. According to an inspector who attended several commemorations of Rákosi's birthday in 1950, the results were sometimes mixed. At one meeting of the Pioneers, a Hungarian child, overwhelmed by the intensity of the propaganda, broke into tears and cried that 'he had no father, but even if he had a father he would love comrade Rákosi more'. But at another meeting, a child was overheard telling another that 'I wish Rákosi had never got out of prison.' The remark was reported to his school director, who spoke to the child's parents as well as the parents' employers. Both children were expelled from the Pioneers, and presumably had to find other ways to occupy themselves after school.[70]

Special plans were made for round-number anniversaries. Rákosi's sixtieth birthday in 1952 was marked by a specially commissioned biography, which was rapidly translated into several languages, as well as multiple ceremonies and a special exhibition containing photographs of the leader as a young man, paintings of events in his life and gifts presented to the leader from his grateful people, including elaborate peasant embroidery, ceramics, carvings and dolls.[71] Bierut's sixtieth birthday in 1952 also required the publication of a biography, as well as a special poetry anthology. Pledges were made to honour him with extra output at factories, and congratulatory letters were sent from around the country. Elaborate ceremonies were held, including at two factories which had decided to name themselves after the leader. A mountain village ('Bierutowice') did the same. At the main ceremony in Warsaw, Bierut's photograph was placed between busts of Lenin and Stalin.[72]

Equally elaborate plans were laid to celebrate Ulbricht's sixtieth birthday in 1953. Three volumes of his speeches were due to be published, two busts were to be carved, prints of his portrait were to go on sale in shops, a special issue of *Neues Deutschland* was to contain congratulatory articles and messages, he was to be named an honorary citizen of Leipzig and a grand dinner was to be held for him in the evening.[73] Alas for Ulbricht, Stalin died before this festival was to take place and most of the events were cancelled after East Germany's Soviet advisers complained of the extravagance. (One of them snorted that Lenin had celebrated his fiftieth birthday by 'inviting a few friends to drop in for dinner'.)[74]

But the regimes planned celebrations with more universal themes as well. Parades, floats, spectacles and speeches were also dedicated to older or more universal cultural figures, with an aim to winning over a wider public and appealing to national pride. When the German communist party realized that 28 August 1949 was not only the 200th anniversary of the birth of Johann Wolfgang von Goethe, one of Germany's most revered writers, but that Goethe had fortuitously been born in Weimar, an East German city, the party, the Culture Ministry and even the Stasi launched an almost frantic effort to claim this aristocratic Enlightenment figure as a kind of proto-communist. Meticulously, they planned an elaborate festival which was designed to show the West that communists cared more about high culture than did capitalists, to show their own people that communists were true German patriots, and to involve as many different kinds of people in as many events as possible.

Their ultimate intention was not just to organize high-brow literati, but to inspire mass enthusiasm. In a speech to the Central Committee in February 1949, one cultural bureaucrat explained that the Goethe celebrations would 'contribute to the democratic education of our people' and also have a 'propagating effect' across the borders: 'in this eastern zone we don't want to be just an economic and political example but also a cultural model for a [future] unified Germany'. The party, he conceded, would not be able to 'keep silent about the contradictions in the life and work of . . . this greatest of all Germans' – unfortunately, Goethe had been sceptical about the French Revolution, and indeed revolutions in general. Still, 'if you look at

Goethe's work you can see that he always worked towards [Marxist] dialectical materialism, without realizing it.'[75] The Soviet Military Administration approved, and indeed they had some background for this kind of work.[76] The USSR had adopted a similarly hagiographic cult of Pushkin, the nineteenth-century Russian poet who would surely have found the Bolsheviks horrifying.

Cultural festivals were nothing new in Germany. But everything about this one seemed exceptionally lavish, especially given the poverty of most East Germans at the time. Celebrations kicked off with a Politburo decree on 8 March. This was followed by lectures in the National Theatre; recitations of Goethe's poetry; performances of Goethe's plays; conferences on Goethe's legacy; commemorative speeches on Goethe's greatness; and a festive week in Weimar.[77] A special event was held for young people, organized by and for the Free German Youth, including a long speech from Honecker and an even longer speech from Grotewohl – the published version was eighty pages – which called on German youth to 'complete the great work of Goethe'. A Goethe Prize was presented to the writer Thomas Mann, whose controversial appearance in Weimar was considered a major propaganda coup for East Germany, even though he made a point of giving exactly the same speech at West Germany's Goethe festival in Frankfurt. East German radio took the opportunity to trumpet his presence, broadcasting best wishes to Mann from 'young pioneers and workers', as well as thanks from various dignitaries, including the mayor of Weimar (though Mann later wrote to the mayor and pointedly declared himself happy to be both an honorary citizen of the city and a genuine citizen of the United States, as he by then was).[78]

The aesthetic highlight of the festival was the Free German Youth's torchlight parade, a truly dramatic spectacle: hundreds of young people carrying blazing torches marched through the darkened, crowded streets of Weimar, finally gathering at the Goethe–Schiller monument where they laid their torches on the stones. This event raised some eyebrows in both East and West Germany, if only because the Hitler Youth had been fond of torchlight parades too.[79] Nevertheless, the entire event was rated a major propaganda and educational success, and similar festivals were planned in its wake. A Bach Year followed in 1950 (the great composer had lived for many years in the

East German city of Leipzig) and a Beethoven Year in 1952 (trickier, as he was born in the West German city of Bonn) as well as a Karl Marx Year in 1953 and a Schiller Year in 1955.

In Poland, musical enthusiasts began planning their own festival, a Chopin Year, right after the war's end. At first, the prewar Chopin Institute was in charge of the events. But by the time it actually took place, also in 1949 – the 100th anniversary of Chopin's death – the festival was firmly under the control of an 'honorary committee' of which Bierut was the ceremonial president. Almost as lavish at the Goethe Year, the Chopin Year celebrations included publications of new editions of Chopin's music; a new scholarly biography; a new popular biography; collections of essays on Chopin; photo albums; and repairs to the composer's birthplace in Żelazowa Wola. For the masses there were 'workers and peasants' concerts, recordings specially designed for factory cultural centres and radio concerts.[80] Every county formed a 'Chopin committee'. Most important of all were the national Chopin competitions as well as the traditional international one, the first to take place in Poland since the war. Talented pianists from around the world duly arrived in Warsaw, and throngs turned out to see them.

The emotions experienced by Chopin's admirers were complicated, as they must have been for Germans who loved Goethe. On the one hand, Chopin was a true national Polish hero, whose music had been restricted by the Nazis and had been played at hundreds of secret wartime concerts. Millions of people were genuinely overjoyed to hear it celebrated again. On the other hand, the regime milked the events for as much popular support as possible, and many had doubts about the competition's conclusion. The judges declared two winners: a Russian and a Pole.[81] Even more mixed emotions accompanied celebrations of the 150th anniversary of the birth of Adam Mickiewicz, Poland's national poet, who had written a number of notably anti-Russian works. Some of his poems were read aloud and some of his plays were performed. Others were banned, however, and the regime found it hard to get the same enthusiastic crowds as for Chopin.[82]

National culture was not the only focus for mass events, however. Sporting events were very high on the communist agenda too, and had also been thoroughly monopolized by the state. The German communists had systematically eliminated non-communist sporting groups by 1948, declaring them 'a form of illegal children's activity'.[83] The only legal sporting clubs in East Germany were state-run sporting clubs, and these acquired an almost paramilitary seriousness. Sports, one Free German Youth directive declared in 1951, could help turn children into 'healthy, strong and strong-minded human beings, who love their fatherland and are prepared to work and to defend peace' – in other words, soldiers.[84] In 1952, the German Young Pioneers were likewise told to 'strengthen your bodies for the building of socialism and the protection of our fatherland'.[85] The Hungarian youth movement meanwhile launched a campaign to 'be prepared for work and battle', promising to procure sports equipment in schools, and to reconstruct a new stadium for the use of young people and children on Margit Island, in central Budapest.[86]

The communist parties also understood very early on the propaganda value of international sports competitions. In subsequent decades, the East Germans in particular would become famous for their brutal sports training academies, their use of performance-enhancing drugs and their militaristic assault on the Olympics. But the use of sports in communist propaganda predates the infamously masculine East German female swimmers. As early as 1946, two party sports journalists, a Czech and a Pole, conceived the idea of the Peace Race, an international, Prague-to-Warsaw bicycle competition. The first competition took place in 1948, and enthusiasm was mandatory: well in advance of the event, Czech and Polish communist leaders instructed local party leaders along the race's route to mobilize spectators. The Peace Race, they explained, was meant to 'attract the attention and interest' of people who were unmoved by 'other means of propaganda'; to demonstrate 'the rise in living standards of the broad masses and the growth of the national economy'; and to be a 'symbol of brotherly cooperation between peace-loving nations, and Polish–Czech friendship in particular'.

In the early years of what became an annual race, the cyclists launched the event by marching in a May Day parade on 1 May. The race itself began on 2 May. Sporting commentary emphasized the 'collective' nature of a bicycle race, during which individual performers were sometimes sacrificed for the glory of the team. To lend the event more credibility as an 'international' competition, cyclists from the Soviet Union and the other People's Democracies were invited to join, and, in 1952, the route was lengthened to include eastern Germany. The organizers intended the Peace Race to compete for prestige with the Tour de France – a competition which Czech, Polish and German communists denounced as vulgar and commercialized – but they never quite succeeded, not least because the Peace Race never could offer similarly attractive prizes.[87]

The history of the race also illustrates how the politicization of a sporting event could backfire. One competitor in the Peace Race complained that once the riders entered Czech territory, the Czech media ignored the 'internationalism' of the contest, coverage 'acquired elements of Czech chauvinism' and cyclists from other communist countries were booed. This was not an isolated incident. In the early 1950s, Rákosi once had to explain to Andropov, the Soviet ambassador in Budapest, why Soviet sportsmen were booed during an international athletics competition in the city, even when they won. Delicately, Rákosi explained that this was just 'fans' fever': naturally Hungarian spectators thought of the USSR as their most important opponent, and they cared most about contests which involved Soviet sportsmen. This didn't please Andropov, who worried that the booing could 'serve as a pretext for journalists of capitalist countries to create a false picture of the feelings of the Hungarian people for the USSR'. All Rákosi could offer in response, again, was more ideological education: the Central Committee, he promised lamely, would 'take all necessary steps to strengthen the education of Hungarian sportsmen'.[88]

Culture and sport, singing and dancing, mass rallies and meetings all had their place in the High Stalinist calendar. There was one event, however, which combined them all. This was the World Festival of Youth and Students, a biannual meeting held first in Prague in 1947, and then in Budapest in 1949. But although these first two festivals were extravagant productions by the standards of the time, the third festival – now renamed the World Festival of Youth and Students for Peace – held in East Berlin in 1951, far surpassed them both. The East Berlin youth festival might even be said to mark the zenith of High Stalinism: at one of the tensest moments in the Cold War, it provided

a focus for Soviet and East European propaganda, and it put East
Germany on display on an international stage for the first time.

From the beginning, the Berlin festival was conceived on a grand
scale. As one concerned Western analyst noted, the festival was
intended to fill sixteen Berlin theatres, with a total capacity for 20,000;
103 cinemas, serving 40,000; the brand-new Walter Ulbricht Stadium,
which would seat 60,000; and the brand-new swimming stadium,
which had room for 8,000. Open-air events would be held in forty
squares and parks.[89] To accommodate the expected crowds at the
mass demonstrations, the Berlin authorities cleared a huge pile of rubble in the centre of the city. They also renovated some of the monuments
on Unter den Linden and prepared the Berlin Museum to receive a
major exhibition from the People's Republic of China. Hotels, youth
hostels and private homes were equipped with 120,000 mattresses to
accommodate the visitors from abroad. East Germans – at least
80,000 of them – were housed in tents.[90]

The Stasi prepared well in advance too. In May, the policemen
began careful monitoring of the 'atmosphere' around the festival
planning. They collected informers' reports and scanned the letters of
800 students and 100 teachers at Leipzig University, 500 students and
40 teachers at Rostock University and 800 students and 100 teachers
at Jena University, to get a sense of what was being said about the
event.[91] In June, the Stasi unveiled 'Operation Sunrise', the police
action designed to monitor and control all of the West German participants. The 'Sunrise' team – headed by the Minister of State Security
himself, Erich Mielke – was to take all West German delegates directly
from the border to reception camps where they would be registered,
and from there to collection camps where they would stay. At the collection camps, Stasi functionaries – posing as drivers, catering staff
and organizers – were immediately to begin recruiting potential secret
agents and to be on guard against spies.[92] Other informers were also
assigned to find out 'which members of the bourgeois political parties
are meeting who' and to observe 'whether priests try to prevent people
from participating or whether they oppose the World Festival in their
sermons'.[93] Statistics were to be kept in the run-up to the events and
weekly reports were to be written, partly encrypted. Each of the West
German states was to be given a codename (Schleswig-Holstein was

Mercury, Lower Saxony was Jupiter, North Rhine-Westphalia was Mars, and so on).[94] In addition, the ministry would send extra contingents of armed policemen who were instructed, curiously, to bring their own toothbrushes, razors and musical instruments.[95]

All of this meticulous advance preparation in some sense paid off. The Third World Youth Festival was indeed a marvel of mass choreography and crowd planning. There were opening and closing ceremonies, a Day of Solidarity with Young Girls ('because they are active defenders of peace') and a 'demonstration of German Youth against the remilitarization of Germany'.[96] Pablo Neruda came, as did his friend Bertolt Brecht. A newsreel created to promote the festival shows participants releasing doves. Special homage was paid to the North Korean delegation, as the newsreel announcer explained: 'the youth of the world wants to show you courageous people that we are standing on your side'. During another ceremony, flowers were also laid on the graves of Soviet soldiers in Berlin ('Youth from around the world gave thanks to the Soviet Union'). At the opening ceremony there were flags, marchers and choreographed displays on a scale not seen in Germany since the war.[97]

For those already enthusiastic about the communist regimes, the Berlin youth festival was a glorious, even an ecstatic experience. One Free German Youth functionary recalled the opening parade with enthusiasm decades later: 'that was an amazing experience, the people who walked down Unter den Linden, Friedrichstraße, who came from all parts of the city, from everywhere, it was an amazing experience . . .'[98] Jacek Trznadel, a young Polish writer, received ration cards for a new suit so that he could attend the festival along with other members of the 'young literary generation'. He encountered a Berlin which was 'poor and grey, still filled with rubble, but bedecked for the celebration with red banners'. Afterwards he remembered very little except a 'portrait of Stalin in the sky – and a young German girl with whom I exchanged addresses . . . there were such euphoric sentiments'.[99] Hans Modrow recalled being moved to tears by the closing ceremony, which involved hundreds of people from all over the world. Modrow was also part of an enthusiastic group of Free German Youth who decided to internationalize the festival even more: they locked arms, marched to the border and picked a fight with the West Berlin police. Much later,

Modrow reckoned that this seminal experience had reinforced his sense of righteousness, as well as his faith in the new regime.[100]

But for anyone who felt at all sceptical, either about East Germany or about communism, the festival also had an ominous side. So soon after the end of the war, some found it was strange to see young Germans marching in uniform, performing perfectly coordinated gymnastics and shouting in unison. One Polish youth activist, Józef Tejchma, remembered the opening ceremony had left him both with admiration and something like fear: 'it made an enormous impression on me, of a vast machine, an explosion of energy . . . all of that order, that Germanness . . . I had the feeling that these young people had enormous power, that they were functioning according to a particular scenario.' Although he was 'impressed that you could organize something like that' he also felt uneasy.[101] Werner Stötzer, later a well-known East German sculptor, had even more mixed feelings. Along with Modrow, Stötzer was part of the Free German Youth group which marched to the border, an event he recalled rather differently from how Modrow did. It all began in a good-humoured manner, Stötzer wrote in his memoirs – but then the mood changed:

> suddenly one of the older ones started ordering us about. It happened very quickly, people were confused, but before entering a wide street we formed into a kind of company. The banner bearers shouldered their banners in the way as if they had been practising secretly in the past five years and the mass of people started to change from ambling about into walking firmly. I noticed too late that people were marching and did the 'Eyes left!' Straight legs from behind me kicked my back, I was insecure, stumbled and suddenly familiar people from the right and the left hissed 'Twerp', 'Stupid one', 'Bastard'. And just before we reached the stands I was kicked out from the rally and I felt very miserable and ran to the S-Bahn station in Friedrichstraße . . . and went to West Berlin without a ticket.[102]

As the Polish communists had learned during their first referendum, more propaganda was not necessarily more convincing. And more chanting young people, more banners, more parades and more coordinated gymnastic displays were not necessarily more reassuring, to the Germans or to anyone else.

14

Socialist realism

Literature must become party literature ... Down with non-partisan literature!

Vladimir Lenin, 1905[1]

A typical Warsaw joke described the result of a competition for a memorial sculpture to Pushkin ... The prize-winning monument was a gigantic, seated figure of Stalin holding a tiny book, on the cover of which were printed in minuscule letters just two words: Pushkin – Poems.

Andrzej Panufnik, 1949[2]

In one corner, a bureaucrat in a suit, briefcase under his arm, strides forward with confidence; from the opposite corner, a young family – father, mother and baby – smile and wave a flag, on their way to a parade. In between, engineers huddle over their designs. Workers lay down railroad ties. From their tractor, peasant farmers hail a blonde peasant girl with a sheaf of wheat in her arms. Young people dressed in the blue uniform of the Free German Youth and the blue ties of the German Pioneers march and clap their hands in the air, to the accompaniment of accordions and a guitar.

Factories, apartment blocks and a stadium rise up in the background behind the figures. And at the very centre, a young worker grasps the hand of a white-haired party boss. A man in a flat cap and high leather boots – the familiar uniform of the policeman – smiles enthusiastically at them both, as if giving his blessing. The colours are bright, the surface is shiny. All of the figures have symmetrical, idealized faces and a somewhat weightless quality, as if they belonged in a children's cartoon.

But they are not in a cartoon. All of these figures feature in an eighteen-metre mural, grandiosely entitled *Aufbau der Republik* – 'Construction of the Republic'. The mural was designed by Max Lingner, a German communist painter, executed on Meissen porcelain tiles – hence the shiny surface – and then mounted on the side of what had been Göring's Air Ministry in Berlin, one of the few monuments of Nazi architecture to survive the war. Soviet forces had used the building briefly, but from 1949 until 1991 it was known as the House of Ministries of the German Democratic Republic, and it contained the GDR's most important government offices.[3]

Aufbau is of course a work composed in the spirit of *Socrealismus*, socialist realism, at its most zealous moment. If parades, festivals, work competitions and summer camps were meant to occupy the daily life and the leisure time of *Homo sovieticus*, the images of socialist realism were meant to occupy his imagination and his dreams. Painting, sculpture, music, literature, design, architecture, theatre and film in Eastern Europe would all eventually be shaped by the theories of socialist realism, one way or another. So would the lives of painters, sculptors, writers, actors, directors, musicians, architects and designers – as well as the experiences of ordinary people who came to live in socialist realist buildings, read socialist realist fiction and watch socialist realist films.

Aufbau is a typical work of High Stalinist socialist realism. But it was not a typical work for its painter. Lingner had been born in Germany but emigrated to France after Hitler came to power in 1933. While in Paris, he was influenced by the bright colours and abstract designs of his French Postimpressionist colleagues, and he began painting in that vein. He also achieved a certain renown for his sharp, dark, satirical illustrations in the French communist press. Although this graphic work was highly politicized it was not mawkish or bland, and it never looked like a children's cartoon. *Aufbau* was, for him, a new departure. For that reason the story of Lingner's mural – how it came to be painted, why it looks the way it does – is also the story of how socialist realism came to dominate, for a brief period, the fine arts everywhere in Eastern Europe.

Lingner was not the only East German painter whose prewar work had been dissonant, eclectic, satirical or abstract. Before 1933, German painters such as Emil Nolde, Max Beckmann, Franz Marc and George Grosz had been among the most energetic and innovative in Europe. German art schools and movements – expressionism, the Bauhaus – had influenced artists and architects around the world, from Edvard Munch and Vassilii Kandinskii to Marcel Breuer and Philip Johnson. Many of these artists and movements had links to the political left, and after the war several of the most famous names in German culture – Otto Dix, for example, and in 1948 Bertolt Brecht – returned deliberately to East Berlin, hoping to build a socialist Germany.

An unusually talented group of Soviet cultural bureaucrats awaited them. To the immense surprise of those Germans who had been horrified by their first, often brutal contacts with Soviet troops, a handful of their new occupiers spoke fluent German, read German literature and admired German culture. One or two even knew more about German art than most natives. Two of the most important – Alexander Dymschitz, head of the cultural division of the Soviet Military Administration, and Grigorii Weispapier, the first editor of *Tägliche Rundschau*, the Red Army's newspaper in Berlin – had once been classmates at the Art History Institute in Leningrad. Others had training in philosophy. Several were Jewish. They arrived with a mandate to make the eastern half of the city more culturally dynamic than the West, to oversee the 'bourgeois revolution' in culture, and to prepare the way for the communist cultural revolution which would follow. In contrast to most of their countrymen, who treated the natives with disdain and brutality, they cultivated contacts with German artists and literati, attended performances and visited exhibitions.

In the very early days the East German cultural scene was just as chaotic as everything else. In the immediate wake of war, a series of random people 'reoccupied' the Reichskulturkammer, the Chamber of Culture, where files on all of the artists, performers and writers in Germany were still extant. The first to arrive was one Elizabeth Dilthey, a former Nazi. She produced bogus Russian credentials, declared herself in charge of the new Kulturkammer, moved into the building and immediately gathered around her cultural luminaries such as Martin Gericke, a hairdresser and theatrical makeup artist. When the American army arrived in July, Gericke, now describing himself as a 'philosopher', became their informant. Next, Klemens Herzberg – who had only marginally better credentials – ousted Dilthey and had himself proclaimed 'Plenipotentiary of the City Commandant of Berlin for Cultural Affairs', a title he kept for ten days, during which time he threw some excellent parties. Finally the Soviet administration replaced him with an elderly and politically neutral actor, Paul Wegener.[4]

For a short time, the Kulturkammer was a critical institution for artists and intellectuals in Berlin, who used the building as a club, dining room and meeting place. More importantly, it was also the centre for the distribution of ration cards, a central concern for every Berliner. Even in the first weeks following the war's end the Red Army granted those with artistic credentials the coveted 'first' ration, a larger piece of bread and more meat and vegetables. Asked why, Dymschitz declared that 'it is possible that there is a Gorki among you. Should his immortal books remain unwritten, only because he goes hungry?'[5] So powerful did this tool of cultural influence become, however, that the Soviet authorities decided to wield it with more force. The Kulturkammer had been a spontaneous creation, after all, and within a few months they had taken away its more important function – the distribution of privileges – and given it to an institution of their own creation, the Cultural Union, or Kulturbund.

In its way, the Kulturbund was an archetypical postwar Eastern European institution. Its central figure was not an accidental grifter but a 'Moscow' communist, Johannes Becher, who had spent twelve years living in exile in the Soviet Union. Its founding and formation were not spontaneous, but planned in advance. As early as September 1944, Becher had attended Soviet meetings on Germany's future, where he spoke of the need to win over educators and pastors as well as actors, directors, writers and painters. Like the Free German Youth, the Kulturbund was intended to be a mass organization, and it immediately set up branches around the country.

Like many other institutions at the time, the Kulturbund also maintained two very separate sets of policies. Internally, its leadership was loyal to the Soviet occupation force and to the German communist party. Becher kept in constant touch with Dymschitz and other Soviet cultural officers about everything from the showing of Soviet films to the design of stamps.[6] At internal meetings, the leadership also used recognizably communist language. In January 1946, the organization's inner circle agreed that it was time to launch 'the struggle against reactionary influences and tendencies', and reprimanded regional leaders who had become too 'autonomous'. Everyone present understood that 'too autonomous' meant 'not pro-Soviet enough'.[7]

Externally, the Kulturbund presented itself as non-partisan, apolitical and certainly not communist. Hoping to attract the 'bourgeois intelligentsia', Becher placed the Kulturbund's headquarters squarely in Dahlem, the elegant western Berlin suburb where many of them lived. At the opening meeting, he called for the creation of 'a national front of all German intellectuals', and in an early declaration he said the organization was 'oriented neither to the East nor to the West'.[8]

For a time, the Kulturbund succeeded in maintaining this dual role. Thanks to its Soviet patrons, the Kulturbund could procure not just ration cards and coal deliveries – Becher and his colleagues got a regular supply in the winter of 1945 – but commissions, theatres and exhibition space. Very quickly, the Kulturbund also began allocating apartments, villas, seaside vacations and government salaries. Those connected to the Kulturbund could have new editions of their previously banned books published in large numbers, or see their plays produced before big audiences.[9] The Kulturbund also helped organize the first major postwar exhibition of German art, the first time that the paintings Hitler had scorned as 'degenerate' had appeared in a German gallery since 1933.

The Kulturbund did sponsor a lively cultural life, at least for a time, and in December 1945 a group closely linked to the Kulturbund began to publish a satirical magazine, *Ulenspiegel*, which was sharp, pointed and actually funny. The era's best artists, cartoonists and writers all contributed. The editor, Herbert Sandberg, was a Buchenwald survivor as well as a talented and amusing satirist and cartoonist. The magazine's covers daringly mocked Germany's strange, divided existence, and its writers seemed prepared to take on anything. We 'bubbled with activity and believed that the golden age had begun', said Sandberg later on.[10]

Seeing what appeared to be the beginnings of a true cultural flowering, émigrés began to write in. Hanns Eisler, one of Brecht's musical collaborators, politely appealed to the Soviet administration in 1946: 'I would be very pleased if I could be of use: even a destroyed Berlin is still Berlin for me. Above all, I am thinking of the chairmanship of a music department ...'[11] Brecht himself announced that he was returning to the country, and would like to be met by car at the German border – as long as it was a *large* car. If a suitable vehicle could not be found, he told the Kulturbund, he would prefer to make the journey to Berlin by train.[12] The large car was procured, and in October 1949 he and Helene Weigel were transported in high style, first to Dresden – where photographers, radio reporters and local dignitaries greeted him – and then to Berlin, where he was installed in what remained of the Hotel Adlon. Becher, Dymschitz and dozens of others spoke at a reception for him the following day.[13]

Even artists and writers with a Nazi past were forgiven and offered new jobs if they were famous enough, much to the annoyance of some German communists. At one meeting of the Kulturbund praesidium, a member complained that the organization was constantly being asked to procure 'a farm, or a villa by the sea' for cultural figures who had belonged to the Nazi party. Politically dubious artists were receiving privileges at the expense of the workers: 'my hair sometimes stands on end when I see how we at the Kulturbund draw up lists of intellectuals who are to receive Christmas parcels from the Soviet Military Administration ... I have a bad conscience towards the working-class comrades when I see how little is being done for them.'[14]

Weimar artists who had been on the political left – and there were many – were courted most fiercely of all. György Faludy, the Hungarian poet, has described how these kinds of approaches could be deeply embarrassing: a communist functionary once tried to win him over with a 'nauseating, clumsy and to me almost physically painful glorification of my greatness as a writer. Then he said that the party would rebuild for me a damaged villa ... After the inflation – which would last only a few more weeks – they would give me, naturally in secret, a considerable monthly salary.'[15]

Max Lingner found this kind of approach appealing. The new department for 'people's education' (*Volksbildung*), set up under

Soviet auspices but run by German bureaucrats, issued an invitation to him in 1946: 'we urgently need you to return right away to Berlin'. He struck up a correspondence with Ulbricht, among other things sending him a manuscript about art education. He was unwell – he had survived the occupation of France and at the age of sixty had both heart and liver complaints – but nevertheless thought it was his duty, as a Marxist, to return and help build communism.

Lingner finally came back to Germany in March 1949. Like Brecht he was greeted as a hero, which pleased him enormously. *Neues Deutschland* called him a 'great painter, known by all the world, but not by the Germans'.[16] He received several large exhibitions, and a commission to decorate Unter den Linden, Berlin's central boulevard, for the May Day parade. He was placed on the jury for the second national fine arts exhibition. In 1950, he helped found the new German Academy of the Arts.[17]

But 1949 was not 1945, and the East Berlin which seemed to welcome Lingner so warmly was undergoing a dramatic transformation. The creeping influence of the Cold War was part of the change. In 1947, the Western Allies kicked the Kulturbund out of West Berlin, on the grounds that it was a communist front operation – which, of course, it was – and forced it to move its offices to the Soviet sector of the city. In May 1948, *Ulenspiegel* followed the Kulturbund from West to East. Though Sandberg stayed on, his co-editor quit, as did a number of others.

Growing Soviet paranoia about the unreliability of the Eastern European allies was behind the change too. In March 1949, when the European department of the Soviet Foreign Ministry drew up a list of suggestions for 'the strengthening of Soviet influence on the cultural life of Poland, Czechoslovakia and other countries of Eastern Europe', they knew they faced a problem: 'A part of the Polish and Czechoslovak intelligentsia is still under the thumb of the most reactionary leaders of the bourgeoisie, who are linked by a thousand threads to reactionary imperialist circles in the West.'[18] They made a similar analysis of Hungary, Bulgaria, Romania and Albania, and concluded, once again, that more ideological education was needed: the translation and distribution of Soviet films and books, the construction of Soviet cultural centres and Soviet-style schools, more cultural exchanges.[19]

The Soviet cultural officers on the ground wanted not just to bring in Soviet art, however, but to transform Eastern European culture into something fundamentally different. Dymschitz proclaimed this policy in an article, 'On the Formalist Direction in German Art', published in the *Tägliche Rundschau* in November 1948. 'Form without content means nothing,' he declared, before launching a sustained attack on abstract and modern art of all kinds. He mocked the 'formalist artists' who 'like to pretend they are revolutionaries ... they act as if they were agents of renewal' and specifically attacked Picasso, a communist and a heroic figure for many German painters. He did not quite use the word 'degenerate' – *entartet* – as Hitler had done, but he did call formalist art 'decadent' – *dekadent* – which is very close. German intellectuals and artists responded in subsequent days. Some approved, and some were angry. Sandberg launched a vigorous defence of Picasso. Most, however, were simply surprised: left-wing artists had simply not expected the 'progressive' Soviet Union to favour 'conservative' art.

A few of them knew that similar debate had already taken place in the Soviet Union of the 1920s and 1930s, when experimental poets and constructivist architects had been banned in favour of artists more to the regime's liking. All of them knew that a version of this 'formalism debate' had also been conducted in Weimar Germany in the 1920s and 1930s, when the theatrical world had been divided between traditionalists, who favoured classical productions in the manner of Lessing and Goethe, and radicals such as Brecht, who argued for the avant-garde.[20] Painters had also at that time split roughly into those who thought that there was still a social or political role for the fine arts and those who believed in 'art for art's sake'.

But the new formalism debate – which soon took the form of numerous turgid essays, interminable committee discussions, and unreadable books – had an aspect which the earlier debate had lacked: because the definition of 'formalism' was political as well as aesthetic, it was extremely slippery. In truth, no one could ever be certain what politically correct, socialist realist art was supposed to look like. It was easy enough to condemn artists who valued beauty over politics, or who worked in pure abstraction, atonal music and experimental verse. It was also possible to dictate topics and subjects. One artistic competition in Poland in 1950 suggested painters produce works illustrating subjects such as 'the technology and organization of cattle slaughter', 'the rationalization and mechanization of the industrialized pig farms' or 'bull and swine breeds in Limanowa, Nowy Targ and Miechów'.[21]

Other judgements were more difficult, even for the most committed socialist realist critic. Did a portrait of a worker have to be precisely realistic, or could the artist's brushwork show? If the lyrics of a song were 'progressive', did it matter whether the tune was difficult to sing? Could a non-rhyming poem still express positive socialist attitudes, or did communist poetry need to follow a certain form? In practice, these questions were decided not by critics or artists but by cultural bureaucrats whose judgements were often made for political or personal reasons. One Polish art historian has argued that what mattered was the attiude of the artist: if he agreed to abandon all pretence of individualism, if he strove to create the right mood on his canvas – however the right mood was defined at that particular moment – then he was a successful socialist realist.[22] A pliant, regime-friendly artist might therefore be allowed to get away with the odd splash of unnatural colour, a green face or a purple sky, and a cooperative poet would be allowed some difficult figures of speech. But those who were under suspicion for whatever reason might well have their work banned for precisely the same things.[23]

In practice, cultural bureaucrats used their constantly evolving definition of what was 'good' socialist realism in order to keep artists and intellectuals under control. After it was premiered for a select group in 1951, for example, the opera *Lucullus* – music by Paul Dessau, libretto by Brecht – was sent back for an overhaul. Some of the critics had found that the music contained 'all the elements of formalism, distinguishing itself by the predominance of destructive, caustic dissonances and mechanical percussive noise'. The party was probably more bothered by the opera's anti-war message – the Korean conflict had just begun – as much as by the aggressively non-traditional music (nine kinds of percussion instruments, no violins). Brecht wrote to Pieck, promised to add three arias which were 'positive in content' and eventually *Lucullus* opened again in October, though only for one night. The changes had been very minor: the main point of the delay, presumably, was to make sure Brecht and Dessau understood that the party, not its artists, had the final say.[24]

Other artists fell victim to changes in socialist fashion. In 1948, Horst Strempel painted a mural entitled 'Clear the Rubble! Rebuild!' in the new Friedrichstraße underground station. Abstract and metaphorical, the mural was highly praised – at first – as a 'colourful symphony of reconstruction'. But after Dymschitz's article, Strempel publicly registered his objections to the Soviet attack on 'formalism'. The party's critics retaliated and denounced the mural for its 'slave-like lack of clarity'. Eventually the *Tägliche Rundschau* called it a 'senseless product'. In February 1951, just as Lingner was working on his own design for the *Aufbau* mural, Strempel's mural was painted over and lost for ever.[25]

The artistic establishment also exercised control because it could. In Germany, just as everywhere else in Eastern Europe, the artists' union – the Association of Fine Arts – had ceased to be a self-organizing organization in the 1940s. By 1950 it had become a centralized bureaucracy, with a single registry of membership. In order to buy paints and brushes, artists had to have a tax number issued by the association, and a membership card confirming the tax number. Anyone who wanted to paint, in other words, had to conform at least enough to remain a member of the association.[26] Choosing not to join could mean choosing not to work as an artist at all.

A similar situation pertained in Poland, where the prewar Union of Polish Fine Artists had been reconstituted in Lublin in 1944, and had remained close to the communist party ever since. The union saw its tasks as including 'the control and assessment of artistic production' as well as the organization of exhibitions and courses and even, in the early days, making living arrangements for artists. Control over artists was also exerted through art schools and academies. Over the course of 1950 and 1951, for example, the directors of the department of painting at the Academy of Fine Arts regularly discussed the poor material conditions of their students and the lack of artistic materials. They also regularly announced that they were searching for student 'volunteers' to complete political tasks – exhibits dedicated to Stalin, decoration of conference halls for party celebrations – for which they would receive lucrative payments. Clearly, some of this 'voluntary' work may have been nothing more than a lifeline for penniless art students.[27]

Like its German counterpart, the Polish artists' union was also, along with the party, the government and occasionally factories, one of the primary buyers of art. Private galleries had disappeared almost entirely, along with the rest of the private sector. A Polish Ministry of Culture document from 1945 stated explicitly that 'because of the changes to structure of the economy, the state as well as local governments must take on the role of the client who purchases art'. If artists wanted to sell their works, they had to stay in the union's good books. By 1947 the union had nearly 2000 members all over the country, as well as branches such as one in Częstochowa which proudly reported that its members executed 'posters and portraits' for the local government as well as decorations for events, lectures and May Day demonstrations.[28] Not all of its branches were so cooperative: traditionalists, 'colourists', realists and a young avant-garde competed for influence in Kraków throughout this period.[29]

There were carrots as well as sticks. Artists such as Otto Nagel, long an outsider in Germany – he had even spent time in Sachsenhausen – now found themselves warmly embraced by the state for the first time in their lives, and discovered that the state could meet all kinds of needs. In 1950, the president of the German Academy of Art issued Nagel ration cards for a pair of shoes as well as fabric for a good suit and an overcoat lining. Nagel also received a personal letter from Pieck upon joining the Academy – 'as a child of Berlin workers, you have been long associated with workers' – and when he helped with some designs for the Berlin youth festival, he received warm personal thanks from Honecker.[30]

Lingner would have known every detail of Strempel's fall from grace and of the rewards available to Nagel and others. He also would have known that despite being a member of the artists' union, he still had much to prove. He had spent more than twenty years outside the country, his links were to the French communist party, not to the Soviet Union, and at one point he was directly accused of 'formalism'. In a 1950 letter to the leadership of the German trade unions, he apologized for the 'difficulties' which had arisen with his May Day parade decorations (the colours had faded due to bad weather). He felt obliged to reassure them on political grounds as well. For two decades, he said, he had 'put pencil and brush to the service of the progressive working class in France', but of course he would now do the same for Germany: 'You can be sure that you and the Berlin working class, and not only the Berlin one, can always count on me.'[31] His apologies were accepted and he was awarded the commission to paint *Aufbau* – but only on the condition that he design it in close collaboration with Otto Grotewohl, at that time the Prime Minister of East Germany.

The official art world was enthusiastic about this arrangement. In a pamphlet published at the time, an art critic explained that with the Grotewohl–Lingner partnership, the relation between the party and the Artist had been 'taken to a new level, one which now corresponds to the new relationship between Art and the People'.[32] From now on, the critic declared, artists would cease to paint for themselves, for their friends or for rich patrons. Instead, they would paint for the party, under the party's tutelage.

What this meant, in practice, was that Grotewohl criticized each draft of Lingner's mural, compelling him to add and subtract figures, change colours and emphasize different details. Following the first draft, he declared that 'the painter had not understood the importance of industry to the development of socialism', since 'heavy industry was not presented as the first precondition to future success'. He also objected to the fact that the main figure at the centre of the painting was an intellectual, not a worker: 'It is the working class who is the real initiator and agent of this alliance.'[33] Following the second draft, Grotewohl's commentary was more directly aesthetic: he felt the colours were unbalanced, and he found some of the figures too static. They failed to reflect society's great march forward, he declared: those looking at the painting would thus be drawn to particular details, instead of concentrating on the meaning of the painting as a whole.[34]

Lingner took all of these comments on board, and worked on several more drafts, some of which were shown to 'scientists, women and Young Pioneers' as well as parliamentarians and other politicians, all of whom were allowed to have their say. In the course of this process, Lingner went through a kind of psychological transformation as well. He had to learn to abase himself before his political critics, and soon he began to do so in other ways as well. During the course of the project, he even composed an essay of self-criticism. He had, he said, been reproached on the grounds that 'I have lost touch with life in the GDR and therefore only depict schematic schemes and masks.' But he would now change his tactics:

I studied those works that I had created since returning to Germany and came to realize that these reproaches are rightfully made. I have suffered from intellectual laziness, my inability to adapt to an environment from which I had become estranged after twenty-four years of absence, and a certain tendency to rest on old laurels ... I have resolutely addressed these deficiencies and hope to very soon be able to present a draft for a mural that has come into being during several months of collaboration with the head of the government.[35]

This 'confession' was not the result of direct violence or fear of arrest: Lingner *wanted* to conform. He was now receiving commissions and acclaim in his own country for the first time in decades. He was no longer an exile, but had instead found acceptance at home. He also appeared to believe, at some level, that the party really did know best: if he himself was unable to understand the purpose of some of Grotewohl's commentary, if he thought the painting ugly, then that must be because he himself was insufficiently enlightened.[36]

Aufbau was finally unveiled in 3 January 1953 – Wilhelm Pieck's birthday – to general acclaim which rapidly faded. Too obvious a work of propaganda, and too clearly the product of a political discussion, it eventually became something of an embarrassment. In a catalogue of Lingner's work published in the final years of the German Democratic Republic, the East German art establishment held itself at arm's length from the mural: 'Was it the very short delivery time, or was it because the enlargement of the draft and the transfer of the drawing on to tiles could only be done by a third hand? Or was it that this "painting" is more than 25 metres wide, and that this is not the right place for it?' Whatever the reason, the critic concluded: 'The result satisfied neither one side nor the other.'[37] Lingner died in 1959, though his mural remains. In the final years of his life, he supposedly avoided even walking past the House of Ministries, so as to avoid looking at it.

'The masses were cut off from the beautiful things of everyday life, as well as from the greatest joy of all: the joy of developing their artistic gifts.' In the introduction to her 1954 book, *Folk Creativity in Contemporary Design*, the director of the Polish Industrial Design Institute, Wanda Telakowska, painted a dark picture of prewar Poland. The 1920s and the 1930s had, she wrote, been 'characteristic of the capitalist epoch'. The wealthy had 'sought confirmation of their own worth through possession of the most ostentatious objects'. Those lacking means had been forced to seek cheap and tacky imitations. Factories, mostly belonging to foreign capitalists, 'followed foreign design – third-rate of course, since the better designs were reserved for their own means of production – as a result of which output for the masses was ugly, and above all incompatible with our culture'.[38]

Telakowska did not begin her career using the language of orthodox Marxism. At different times an art teacher, designer, critic and curator, Telakowska had previously been best known for her association with a Polish artistic group called Ład. Connoisseurs of design history would recognize Ład as a cousin of the British Arts and Crafts movement. Its members sought to study the folk and peasant craftsmen who still thrived in parts of southern and eastern Poland, and to use their work as the basis for a new and authentically 'Polish' vernacular design. The artists associated with Ład believed that 'contemporary' did not have to mean 'modernist' or futuristic. Not everything had to be sleek or simplified in the machine age: folk designs for furniture, textiles, glass and ceramics could, they believed, be brought up to date and even used as inspiration by industry.

By instinct and by training, Telakowska was no communist either. Although many left-wing artists of the time, including the Bauhaus designers in Germany, spoke of sweeping away the past in the name of revolution and starting from scratch, Telakowska retained a distinctly un-communist determination to find inspiration from history. But she also wanted to continue Ład's work after the war, and towards that end she joined the new communist government. She quickly found that her project – which favoured peasant and folk art over the slicker modernism of urban intellectuals – overlapped with some of the aims of the communist party.[39] As one cultural bureaucrat pointed out, folk art was more likely to appeal to the Polish labourer: 'Our working class is closely linked to the countryside and feels more connected to the culture of folk art than to the culture of intellectual salons.' By the end of the 1940s, Telakowska's promotion of peasant art also fitted in with the assault on formalism which had been launched in Poland at the same time as in Germany. In the constipated words of one approving Marxist critic, 'Unlike the art produced by the nobility and the Court, which became increasingly divorced from the national foundations, the uncontaminated culture of the country-side was able to resist cosmopolitan tendencies and to protect itself successfully against ossified formalism.'[40]

In Polish terminology, Telakowska was a 'positivist', or what an English speaker would call a pragmatist. She accepted the communist regime as inevitable and was determined to work with it – even within it – in order to achieve goals which she believed to be in the national interest. In the spring of 1945 she joined the new Ministry of Culture, even though that made her a member of the communist-dominated provisional government, and in 1946 she created the wonderfully named Bureau for Supervision of Production Aesthetics (Biuro Nadzoru Estetyki Produkcji, or BNEP). Under its auspices, she conducted surveys of folk artists and folk art groups around the country and persuaded Polish artists from Ład and from the Warsaw School of Fine Arts to work on her most ambitious project: the provision of Polish factories with new designs which could be mass produced. Though this had long been her goal, she made an economic argument to her superiors. Better design could increase the appeal of Polish products: 'beauty and elegance raise the value of objects such as furniture, fabric, printed materials, curtains, clothes ... French, Viennese and German objects control the world market only because of their artistic form, not because of the quality of the materials.'[41]

At first, the artistic community was suspicious. Fearing that this new project might herald a crackdown on painting and sculpture, the artists' union issued a defence of 'pure' art, as opposed to 'useful' art. More importantly, many didn't want to collaborate with the Polish communists, who in 1946 were escalating their campaign against the Home Army. But Telakowska won at least some of them over, partly through her personal contacts, partly because she offered material help, and partly because she was genuinely passionate about her cause. One Polish painter, Bohdan Urbanowicz, remembered meeting her on his return to Poland from a German prisoner-of-war camp in August 1945:

I travelled back to Poland full of fears and uncertainty, without any papers. After crossing the border at Cieszyn, I headed for Warsaw. Soviet trucks passed me, decorated with seals and slogans. Herds of cattle are being driven to the east ... At last, Warsaw. I'm lost in tunnels of former streets.

There is a provisional bridge across the Vistula. In an enormous building in Praga, the former Headquarters of the State Railways, there sits the Ministry [of Culture]. A dark stairway leads up to the department of fine arts. A big room, full of people, chatter and smoke . . . And suddenly, I am embraced. I've found myself in the arms of Wanda Telakowska.[42]

Telakowska reached into a drawer, pulled out 2000 zlotys and gave it to Urbanowicz, 'without any accounting'. She also found him a place to stay and arranged for him to join the artists' union. For several years, he and many others remained under her influence and protection. Because he also felt that he had a responsibility for the 'reconstruction of our destroyed culture', he too went to work at the ministry.[43] Telakowska didn't have the resources available to Becher in East Berlin – postwar Poland in general had less to offer returning émigrés – but neither was she competing, as Becher was, with an alternative, non-communist Germany: the alternative to communist Poland was exile. Telakowska brought people on board by appealing to their patriotism and by convincing them it was important to reconstruct Poland, no matter what Poland's political leadership might be.

Many did cooperate. Under the slogan 'Beauty is for everyday and for everybody' Telakowska's Bureau commissioned and purchased dozens of strikingly original designs for fabrics, furniture, cutlery, dishes, crockery, ceramics, jewellery and clothes.[44] She sent one group of artists to a glass factory in Szklarska Poręba and another group to a glass factory in Silesia. Both were meant to cooperate with the workers and the management in order to create attractive, popular designs which could be mass produced. One group created a series of glasses, etched with calligraphy in a prewar style. The other used older antique glass for inspiration. Telakowska also persuaded a prominent Polish sculptor, Antoni Kenar, to return to Poland from exile in Paris in order to organize a woodcarving workshop, and she sent designers to the Carpathian mountains, where they worked with women weavers, helping them to update their designs. At one point, her Bureau held a competition to encourage peasant carvers to design new wooden 'folk' toys, prompting one art critic to exult that 'a new type of toy-making is being born, one which breaks decisively away from the objects which, in the 1920s, persuaded children to play at "war"'.[45]

*

In her enthusiasm, and in her positivism, Telakowska was not alone. The powerful desire to rebuild their ruined country was the one sentiment that unified Poles of all political persuasions in the immediate postwar years, and nowhere more acutely than in Warsaw, a city so profoundly destroyed that many believed it should be left in ruins as a monument to war. The writer Kazimierz Brandys remembered feeling that 'this must not be touched. Let it stand, just as it is ... we, who had loved that city, we wanted at that time to love its scattered bricks.'[46] Others thought reconstruction impractical or impossible. Alexander Jackowski, a young officer at the time (and later an eminent historian of Polish folk art), said simply that 'I didn't believe it could be rebuilt in my lifetime.'[47]

Within days of the war's end, the city's former inhabitants had nevertheless begun to clear the streets and volunteer their services as builders and engineers. Such was the magnetic pull of Warsaw that as soon as it was possible, people began squatting in the rubble, making do with whatever was left of their ruined homes. The communist leadership leapt to attach itself to this outpouring of energy and sentiment: in the reconstruction of Warsaw, they saw a way to become, if not popular, then at least grudgingly admired. If nothing else, they could make common cause with people like Telakowska and Urbanowicz, who were enthusiastic about the restoration of the country's artistic and architectural heritage, even if they didn't sign on to the entire communist project. In February 1945, the provisional government created the Bureau for the Reconstruction of the Capital (Biuro Odbudowy Stolicy, or BOS) and appointed Józef Sigalin, an architect who had spent the war years in the USSR, to take charge.

Immediately, Sigalin was deluged with advice. Some wanted to wipe away the ruins and construct a shiny, modern city of steel and glass, in the then-popular International Style. At the Polish School of Architecture, founded by exiles at the University of Liverpool during the war, a group of young Polish architects created a series of architectural drawings which looked no different from those created at the time by their British colleagues. Jerzy Piatkiewicz reimagined the medieval section of Warsaw, the Old Town, keeping the street plan but substituting glass-fronted modern buildings for the baroque facades. Others proposed concrete apartment blocks and massive buildings in the style which came to be known in Britain as 'brutalism'.[47]

From the very beginning, popular sentiment went in precisely the opposite direction. Most of the public wanted the old Warsaw back, and many architects did too. 'Our sense of responsibility to future generations obliges us to rebuild that which was destroyed' is how one put it.[49] In particular, the reconstructionists argued that the oldest parts of the city – its medieval, baroque, renaissance and eighteenth-century buildings – should be put back exactly as they had been, brick for brick, so that the country's architectural heritage would not disappear for ever.

By 1949, a third strand of thinking had developed too. Neither functional glass boxes nor strict reconstruction fitted very well into the Soviet Union's new push for 'socialist realism', after all. Nor did either option entirely satisfy the Polish communists' mania for re-education, or reflect their belief in environmental determinism: if people could be subtly influenced by their surroundings, then Warsaw's architects had a responsibility to help create the new reality, the spaces within which *Homo sovieticus* would eventually live and work. In a major speech on the reconstruction of Warsaw in 1949, Bierut declared that 'The new Warsaw cannot be a copy of the old, it cannot simply repeat, slightly altered, the hodge-podge of the capitalist class's private interests which constituted the city before the war . . . the New Warsaw must become the capital of a socialist state.'[50] But at the time, there was only one city that qualified as a true 'capital of a socialist state'. And thus did much of the official 1949 plan for the reconstruction of Warsaw come to derive directly and almost slavishly from the architecture of Moscow.

In the period of High Stalinism, Soviet architecture was deliberately designed to impress and intimidate. Offices, public monuments and apartment blocks in Moscow were massive, heavy and ornate. Streets were impressively wide but difficult to cross. Public squares were broad, flat and covered in concrete, perfectly suited to mass demonstrations though monotonous to behold. Distances between buildings were great, and pedestrians had to rely on trams or buses. Because their design was supposed to be 'comprehensible' to the workers who would inhabit these palatial structures, architects relied heavily on familiar, even clichéd classical elements such as columns, balconies and archways.[51]

Soviet city design was, in other words, totally unsuited to Warsaw, a city which had been designed for horses and pedestrians in an era before the automobile, and whose plan had revolved around churches and shopping streets. Squares and parks had been created for leisure, not for mass demonstrations, and they had been filled with grass, not concrete. Nevertheless, the 1949 designs for Warsaw are classic examples of High Stalinist socialist realism: the Ministry of Agriculture with its two layers of columns, the wide boulevards designed for May Day parades, the decorative concrete lampposts and balconies.[52] Though these designs did not derive from any existing Polish tradition, one art historian writes that 'The compulsion to adapt themselves to "the example of the Soviet Union" did not come to the architects as an order. It came upon them as a heavy pressure that was just as hard to resist as its consequences were hard to accept.'[53] By the time construction was really underway, the city's land was all state-owned, the city's architects were all employed by the city Bureau, the national architectural periodicals – as in Czechoslovakia, Hungary and East Germany – were state-owned, producing regular articles and special supplements on Soviet architecture. In 1946–7, state printing presses even produced an anthology, Soviet Architecture, which lauded Soviet architectural achievements and attacked Russian 'dissident' cultural figures, including the poet Anna Akhmatova. By 1949, no one had to be told that the party had the last word on all major building projects in Warsaw – though, at the same time, no one had to be forced to work on them.

In this sense Polish architects resembled German painters, none of whom had been forced at gunpoint to paint cartoonish works of propaganda either. On the contrary, just like Max Lingner in Germany, some of them did their best to convince themselves of Soviet architecture's merits. In 1948, Sigalin travelled to Moscow to meet Edmund Goldzamt, a Polish architect who had sought shelter in the Soviet Union during the Nazi occupation, had completed his architectural studies in Moscow and seems to have been inclined to stay (he returned there in the 1970s). Goldzamt described the theory of Stalinist architectural socialist realism to Sigalin in a memorable, all-night conversation. 'We have to have it,' Sigalin allegedly responded, and he persuaded Goldzamt to return to Warsaw as an adviser.[54]

Goldzamt would not have described himself, at that time or later, as a Soviet lackey. Like Telakowska, he was an admirer of the British

Arts and Crafts movement, with its emphasis on traditional patterns and designs. Later in his life, he wrote a book about William Morris (with chapter titles such as 'The Place of Morris in the Class Struggle').[55] But in his work, and in the work of his disciples, these theories played themselves out very differently than they had in the designs produced for Telakowska's Bureau for Supervision of Production Aesthetics, let alone in Morris's own workshops. In theory, Goldzamt believed that buildings were to be 'socialist in content, but national in form'. In practice, he thought architects should impose 'national' motifs, i.e. kitschy decorations, derived from historical buildings and folk art, on to massive, Soviet-style structures.

Warsaw's Palace of Culture and Science, the most famous piece of High Stalinist architecture in Poland, was also the building which most clearly reflected Goldzamt's theories. To this day, the Palace of Culture and Science looms over Warsaw, occupying an incongruous amount of space at the very heart of the city and depriving central Warsaw of any aesthetic continuity. The building was a gift from Stalin to the Polish people – a gift which it seems to have been impossible to refuse. Poland's Economics Minister, Hilary Minc, apparently tried to suggest the erection of a housing estate instead, but Stalin wanted 'a palace that would be visible from any point in the city', according to Jakub Berman, whose responsibilities included culture as well as the secret police.[56] Many communists disliked the design (Berman conceded years later that 'they didn't do a very good job of it') but Bierut admired it, or said he did. The Palace of Culture was not a cheap present: though the Soviet Union paid for the construction materials, the Poles had to pay for the Soviet workforce, on whose behalf a brand-new suburb was constructed, complete with a cinema and a swimming pool. The Polish government was also responsible for clearing the space in the centre of the city, during the course of which many inhabitable houses were destroyed, along with the traditional street plan.

The Palace of Culture was designed by Russian architects and executed in part by imported Russian workmen, using imported Russian tools and materials. But the Palace of Culture was supposed to be 'socialist in content, national in form', and so the Russian architects, led by Lev Rudinev, solemnly toured the country. They visited the ancient cities of Kraków, Zamość and Kazimierz, sketching baroque and renaissance motifs as they went along. They consulted with Sigalin and other Polish architects too.[57]

The result was, and remains, peculiar. From a distance, the Palace of Culture looks like an exact copy of the 'wedding cake' skyscrapers which are scattered around Moscow, with a spire on top and four additional buildings grouped around the bottom, variously containing theatres, gyms, exhibition space and a swimming pool. Up close, the 'Polish' elements stand out. The tops of walls are lined with decorative elements copied from the Renaissance facades which the Russians had seen in their Polish tour. Massive, oversized statues are grouped around the base, mostly showing 'workers' in various grand poses, though their metaphorical significance is unclear. For decades, the Palace was Warsaw's only skyscraper – from 1955 to 1957 it was the tallest building in Europe – and it still seems out of place, though taller and more modern skyscrapers have now been constructed nearby. The building's only merit is that it looks exactly like what it is: a Soviet imposition on the Polish capital, the wrong size and the wrong proportions, constructed without regard to the city's history or culture.

A few other examples of Soviet architecture were also completed. Not far from the Palace of Culture, the architects of Warsaw managed to construct a socialist realist housing estate – the Marszałkowska Dzielnica Mieszkaniowa, or MDM – with monumental entryways, columns, grand stairways and the same ambiguous sculptures of 'workers' staring out into space. Soviet elements can also be seen in Muranów, a housing district built on the site of the old Warsaw ghetto, and in a few other places too.

But the 1949 plan was unpopular, or at least not universally popular, as the communists themselves well knew. And so even as the Palace of Culture was under construction, the city Bureau also began to rebuild Warsaw's medieval Old Town and its historic main thoroughfare, Nowy Świat, in excruciating, painstaking detail. The party was somewhat embarrassed by this: Bierut explained that healthy, sanitary contemporary apartments would be constructed behind the old-fashioned facades, and would be handed immediately to worthy members of the working class.[58] But despite the addition of indoor plumbing, the Old Town eventually looked so familiar that some found it eerie. One former resident of the medieval city centre described the effect years later: 'The house I was born in was destroyed violently . . . but I can go into the bedroom I had as a boy, look out of the exact same window at the exact same house across the courtyard. There's even a lamp bracket with a curious twist in it hanging in the same place.'[59]

This, at last, was popular, and for a while the Old Town was a powerful advertisement for the regime. Each new section was opened with great fanfare – the cutting of ribbons, the drinking of toasts – often on 22 July, the anniversary of the creation of the Polish United Workers' Party, or another communist holiday. Photographs of the reconstructed Old Town taken in the 1950s show people strolling and gazing 'at the miracle of reconstruction'. What had been a dark, picturesque, decaying part of the city became well-lit, open and full of tourists.

As far as urban planning went, the combination of the recon-structed Old Town and the Palace of Culture was never successful, particularly when cheap, prefab apartment blocks were constructed around and in between them in subsequent decades. But, in the end, the plan for the reconstruction of Warsaw was defeated not by its aesthetic mistakes, but by Stalinist economics. Remarkably, the ori-ginal plans had been drawn up without any consideration of costs. Because the heavy, elaborate buildings were expensive to construct, the money ran out before the facades were complete and the foun-tains and public sculptures were built. The grand rooms of the Palace of Culture also wasted heat, electricity and space. No one had planned for energy efficiency, and the high cost of upkeep meant that the interiors quickly began to look tawdry. The reconstruction of the Old Town was not economically efficient either, for it did not take into consideration Warsaw's urgent housing shortage. In the early 1950s, many young people still lived in primitive wooden dormitories, and they did not want to wait for the elaborate buildings to be finished. Within a very few years, all enthusiasm for both Stalinist projects and historical reconstruction had vanished. The city architects acknow-ledged, among themselves, that the Bureau had failed to create any kind of coherence. In 1953, Sigalin told a group of them that 'form was still lagging behind content'. He had not achieved an intellectual breakthrough after all.

At about the same time, Wanda Telakowska's Bureau for Super-vision of Production Aesthetics was defeated by socialist economics too. Despite the care which had been lavished upon them – and des-pite, in some cases, their high quality and originality – the hundreds of samples and avant-garde designs produced by Telakowska and her colleagues were never turned into elegant consumer products. As it turned out, Polish factories had no incentive to produce elegant con-sumer products: because there were shortages of everything, anything that any factory produced would always find a buyer. Since prices were controlled, companies couldn't charge more for a nicer vase designed by a team of famous artists than they could for a cheap and ugly vase and they couldn't pay more to the people who produced one either. Since factory managers were government employees on government salaries, they saw no need to exert any special effort.[60]

'Design for the workers' was ultimately of no interest to provincial bureaucrats and state factory managers. One art critic tactfully explained that 'the leadership of the Industry Ministry completely understood the need to make art widely available – but at the level of the individual workplace, it was still not popular'. There was a Marx-ist explanation as well: 'In the People's Democracy, anarchy in the area of production has been replaced by socialist planning. However, in the realm of the aesthetic production of the articles of everyday life, anarchy, inherited from the era of capitalist economy, still remains . . .'[61]

By comparison to Western Europe, Polish consumer production – like East German, Hungarian, Czech and Romanian consumer production – remained very poor in quality. Polish exports of glass and ceramics, historically a major source of income (as they are now once again), remained low. The bureaucrats responsible for choosing which products to export did not necessarily have the taste or instinct for good design.[62] Output for the masses became, if anything, uglier than it ever had been, mostly because the vast majority of consumer products were rushed down assembly lines as cheaply and as quickly as possible.

Nor did the Bureau for Supervision of Production Aesthetics succeed in preserving traditional folk culture. The marketing of folk art was quickly taken over by another state company, Cepelia, which eventually became known for the production of repetitive wooden souvenirs. Cepelia has its defenders, including Jackowski, Poland's pre-eminent scholar of folk art, who believes that Cepelia helped peasants make a living in a particularly difficult economic period. The 'violent urbanization of the countryside' was going to destroy folk culture anyway, he argues – and besides, the demand for kitsch came from the cities, from the workers who eagerly purchased it.[63]

Telakowska herself went on to found the Institute for Industrial Design, which she ran for several years before resigning in 1968. Her influence did not last. A later generation of Polish artists dismissed her as a Stalinist, and then forgot about her. She had proved that it was possible to work in conjunction with the communist state, even if one was not a communist – but she had not proved that such cooperation could succeed.

By the time Vsevolod Pudovkin paid his two visits to Budapest in 1950 and 1951, his days as a revolutionary Soviet film-maker were long over. Along with Sergei Eisenstein, Pudovkin had been one of the founders of Soviet experimental cinema. Famously, he once declared that film was a new art form and should be treated as such: movies should neither mirror everyday life nor duplicate the linear storytelling of a traditional novel. He had been so opposed to strict realism that he initially objected to the use of sound, on the grounds that it would force movies to become too much like plays. His most famous film, *Mother* – based on the novel by Maxim Gorky – was a 1926 silent movie which made liberal use of the then-new technique of montage. Pudovkin was one of the first directors to juxtapose different scenes and different points of view in order to heighten the emotional reactions of his audience.[64]

Unfortunately for Pudovkin – and for Eisenstein and the rest of the Soviet avant-garde – Stalin himself was an avid film buff, and he very much admired linear storytelling. As Stalin's power increased, Pudovkin's popularity declined. His films first failed to please the leader. Then they failed to please Soviet critics. Then they failed to please the cultural bureaucrats, who prevented Pudovkin from making any more of them. Eventually he dropped his old theories, abandoned experimental montage and began making 'realist' films in which communism triumphed, one way or another, over its enemies.[65] It was at this late point in his no longer illustrious career that Pudovkin was sent to Budapest.

In principle, Pudovkin should have found it extremely difficult to teach Hungarian directors anything at all. Before the war, the Hungarian film industry had been the third largest in Europe and one of the world's most sophisticated. In its technology and in its directors' experience, it was far ahead of the Soviet Union. Hungarian film distribution was sophisticated too. A network of 500 cinemas had operated around the country before the war, at least half of which had not been destroyed and were still fully functional in 1945, far more than in Poland or Germany. Although anti-semitic legislation had divided the industry in the 1930s (and resulted in an exodus of an extraordinarily talented group of Hungarian Jews to Hollywood), much of the equipment remained. In Poland, by contrast, the postwar film industry was relaunched with cameras 'captured' in Germany and removed as war booty.

The postwar Hungarian film industry had not started out with the goal of propagating communism either. In the summer following the liberation of Budapest, Hunnia, the most important Hungarian studio, applied successfully to the Soviet occupation forces for permission to begin operation as a state company. Hunnia's carefully balanced new board of directors included three communist party members, two social democrats, officials from three government ministries and some non-communists as well. Private film production companies optimistically opened their doors for business at the same time. All of the four major parties founded film production companies, and theoretically divided the movie theatres between them. In this, as in so many other things, the communist party was more equal than others: together with the social democrats the communists controlled the majority of the cinemas, as well as most of the funding.

Despite this relatively optimistic beginning, inflation prevented much progress – only three films were made in 1945, and none in 1946 – and by the beginning of 1947 politics began to intervene too. In the summer of that year, István Szőts, a talented young director – he had won the main prize at the Venice film festival in 1942 – began work on a film in conjunction with a private production company. The film, *Song of the Cornfields* (*Ének a búzamezőkről*), was based on an older novel about the tragic impact of the First World War on a Hungarian peasant family, and it included a love affair between a Hungarian girl and a Russian POW. By all accounts Szőts adapted it with great success. But despite the Hungarian–Russian love theme, which he thought would protect him, Szőts had trouble with the censors. They disliked the religious scenes, which were a touch too powerful for their liking. They disliked the pacifist message, which was no longer politically correct. They also disliked the fact that the Hungarian peasants in the movie were so deeply attached to their land: that was an ill omen for a regime which was planning further land reforms and eventually collectivization. Szőts was surprised but he made some changes, declared the film finished and, at least initially, received rapturous praise from those who saw the early screenings.

The praise did not last, as Szőts later remembered:

> The premiere date and place were fixed when critics began attacking the film, saying it was reactionary, religious and even that it supports Mindszenty ... Ten days before opening night, the film was banned without any justification ... Finally the film was shown at party head-quarters, though not to the end because Rákosi, when he saw the first scenes of the procession [people] praying and singing for the beloved sons in the faraway country, stood up and went out in a demonstrative way ... The case was closed, the film was banned.[66]

Song of the Cornfields never appeared in theatres. Nor, after that, did any other privately produced films. In 1948 the industry was com-pletely nationalized, Hunnia's carefully balanced board of directors was dropped and all pretence of artistic freedom was abandoned as well. Following Stalin's example, József Révai, now Minister of Cul-ture, began monitoring every aspect of film production, from planning to shooting. Wanting to leave nothing to chance, he immediately turned to the Soviet comrades for aesthetic advice. He invited the Soviet Deputy Minister for Film to visit Budapest, who declared that 'the first thing I can advise Hungarian film artists is that they must thoroughly study Soviet film ... great art can only be made if you add your special Hungarian Bolshevik aesthetic to what you learn from us'.[67] An invitation to Budapest was immediately extended to Pudovkin. Like schools, workplaces and public space, cinemas were to become another venue for ideological education, and the Soviet director could show the Hungarians how to do it.

In later accounts, the Pudovkin who arrived in Budapest in 1950 is often described as a 'broken man'. In his case the cliché seems accurate. His instincts for experimentalism had been quashed long ago. He had just been awarded the Stalin Prize for *Zhukovskii*, a dull, hagiographic film about the founder of the Soviet aeronautics industry. He could certainly teach Hungarians the psychology of subservience, but not much else. Pudovkin's own descriptions of his experiences in Hungary are disappointingly stiff and not very revealing. If he was impressed by the architecture or the material culture of Budapest, which even after the war was still far wealthier than Moscow, he never said so. If he admired anything about prewar Hungarian film, he never said that either.

Unusually, for a film director, there is no folk memory of Pudovkin flirting with Hungarian girls or drinking in the bar after work either. Instead, in a short book he published in Hungarian in 1952, he expounded on the importance of theory: 'to understand life it is necessary to know Marxism-Leninism ... without political education it is impossible to make a movie.' He also wrote of the need for what Hollywood would call happy endings: 'the drama has to show the struggle and the victory ... of peoples walking on the path of socialism'. He highlighted the significance of positive role models: 'creating a positive character is one of the most difficult but beautiful tasks a socialist artist can ever have'. He criticized Western movies as 'pessimistic', and praised the 'organic optimism' of Soviet films.[68] The director also gave extensive interviews to the press, one of which Szőts, now an ideological pariah, read with horror. In essence, Pudovkin argued that a historical film had to be ideologically accurate, not factually accurate:

> 'The important thing, he said, is that a film should follow events as determined by the ideological argument. Everything that did not fit into that was considered false 'naturalism', something different from the ideological, historical reality necessary for this kind of film ... No matter how much I had previously respected Pudovkin ... after these comments I read in the press, I was glad not to have been introduced to him.'[69]

378

But Pudovkin's impact extended far beyond bland statements. In the Hungarian film industry, as in the Polish film industry, film projects had in the past been spearheaded by directors who conceived, designed and organized the production of a new movie. In the Soviet Union, the leading role was played by scriptwriters who discussed with censors every aspect of a film, the themes as well as the dialogue, even before they began to write. Ironically, or perhaps tragically, Pudovkin – a director who had been an early master of visual, soundless imagery – imported this system to Hungary, and thus created a Hungarian studio system dominated by obedient scriptwriters and cultural bureaucrats. There was no avoiding his advice or influence: from 1948, anyone wishing to work as a director had to be a graduate of the Hungarian Academy for Theatre and Film Art. Until 1959, they could offer their services to only one studio, Hunnia, later renamed Mafilm. During that period, every film script had to pass through several stages of ministerial approval, as did every finished film.

While he was in Budapest, Pudovkin sat in on many script discussions at the Ministry of Culture. Most of his contributions focused on a given movie's political and social themes, rather than visual or technical issues. He chided the scriptwriters of a film about peasants joining a cooperative movement for their focus on the moral rather than the practical and material advantages of the cooperative: 'this is a serious deficiency'. He proposed the creation of new characters and plot twists which would dramatize the advantages of the cooperative. There might be a child, he suggested, for example, who was devastated by his father's refusal to join the cooperative and who feared his future might be compromised as a result.[70] On another occasion, Pudovkin criticized a film because a worker died in the final scene, a conclusion he found insufficiently optimistic. In both cases his critique was accepted without argument. The written account of one of his meetings ended with a single sentence: 'We accept the proposals of Comrade Pudovkin and we will correct the movie as suggested.'[71]

Pudovkin also worked directly on several Hungarian films. One of these was *Katalin's Marriage* (*Kis Katalin Házassága*), a film about two factory workers, Katalin and Jóska, whose relationship begins to falter when Katalin loses interest in her work and her studies and

begins to mope around the house. Instead of helping her, Jóska con-
centrates on his own work. Katalin moves back home with her mother,
but is eventually 'saved' by Barna, the party secretary at the factory,
who teaches her how she can become a shockworker, a good student
and even a party member. Eventually Jóska realizes it is he who must
learn from her. As the film's scriptwriter explained at the time, 'The
film shows how both of them are put back on track by the party, and
it also shows how it is possible that one member of the couple works
in the factory shop and the other in an office.'[72] Following the principle that the 'best' socialist realist films contained multiple lessons, the
movie also contained an episode involving a saboteur. From *Katalin's
Marriage* viewers were thus meant to learn about the leading role of
the party; the significance of work competitions; the need to battle
against reaction; the value of different sorts of work; and the importance of marriage. They also got to see some scenes shot outdoors,
outside the studio. As Pudovkin put it, 'the movie has to show the
truth of life'.[73]

Any Hungarian film-maker who wanted to direct or write a film
had to work within these kinds of parameters. The only other option
was to leave the profession – or starve. After the disastrous cancella-
tion of *Song of the Cornfields*, István Szőts was invited to become a
state director:

> 'I did not take this opportunity because I knew that I would never
> shoot a film, a script which was full of lies, loud propaganda and pol-
> itics . . . So I tried to survive . . . which was not an easy task since I had
> no revenues. I sold my flat . . . I also started to sell whatever I had, the
> camera, the lenses, and realized that you could live out of such trade
> but it was not very well seen by the authorities, they considered it black
> marketeering, since I had no documents whatsoever for these activities.
> After a while I started to be afraid to be sitting in a café, I was afraid
> that if I was asked for my documents I would have to say I had no job
> and I would end up in an internment camp.'

And thus the year 1951 saw the release of *A Strange Marriage*
(*Különös házasság*), the story of a man forced to marry a girl who had
been made pregnant by a priest – a Hungarian classic, which happened to fit nicely into the party's campaign against the 'reactionary

clergy'. In the same year, Mafilm released *Underground Colony* (*Gyarmat a föld alatt*), a movie about American sabotage of Hungarian oil refineries. The hero is the secret policeman who uncovers the sabotage, and the film ends happily, with the nationalization of the Hungarian oil industry. At about the same time, the East Germans were exploring anti-capitalist and anti-American themes too, notably in *The Council of the Gods* (*Der Rat der Götter*), whose plot revolved around the collusion between American chemical companies and I. G. Farben, the Nazi chemical company which produced the Zyklon-B gas used for mass murders, and thus between American officials and the Nazis.

Yet the harsh systems of control over film-making put in place by Pudovkin in Budapest, by the Soviet authorities in Berlin and briefly by communists in Warsaw did not last. Directors and scriptwriters initially agreed to make socialist realist movies because there was no choice. But as soon as it was possible, they began searching for ways around the rules. In later years, directors of Eastern European films and plays would raise the non-verbal 'joke' – the unspoken visual political commentary, comprehensible to viewers but invisible to script-reading censors – into something close to an art form of its own. Andrzej Wajda, one of the founders of postwar Polish cinema, notes that in Poland:

> 'We knew from the very beginning that there is nothing we can do about dialogue ... the censors had their eye on our words, which is understandable because ideology is expressed in words ... But although we knew there was no chance to express ourselves in words, pictures were completely different. A picture can be ambiguous. The viewers might understand the message in a picture, but the censors do not have any basis for taking action.'[74]

Wajda's film *Ashes and Diamonds* (*Popiół i diament*) contains, for example, a scene in which two characters sit at a bar and set glasses of vodka on fire, each time repeating a name. Nobody says that these are memorial candles for friends who died in the Warsaw Uprising, an event which was by then taboo, but audiences understood immediately what was happening. Hungarian cinema would eventually develop similarly elaborate metaphors, perhaps most famously in

Mephisto, István Szabó's modern-day *Faust*. Set in Nazi Germany, *Mephisto* tells the story of an actor who agrees to collaborate with National Socialism in order to advance his career. The audience watching the movie knew that this story was also a commentary on the recent communist past: actors in Stalinist Hungary had collaborated in order to advance their careers too.

Hints and allusions could also be found in plays, both contemporary and classic, and directors made full use of them. In communist Poland, even Shakespeare became a form of contemporary political commentary. The line 'Denmark is a prison' could be understood as an allusion to the Soviet occupation of Poland. 'Something is rotten in the state of Denmark' had the same force. Even the division of King Lear's kingdom could be seen as a metaphor for the division of postwar Poland and the loss of the eastern territories.[75]

Odd though it sounds, genuine realism – spontaneity, authentic-sounding dialogue and scenes which viewers would recognize from their own lives – was also a tool which could be carefully deployed against the 'socialist realism' imported from the USSR. This technique paid off in a Hungarian film with the unpromising title *State Department Store* (*Állami Áruház*). Though there was nothing radical about the plot or the setting – a state department store, in fact – the film included a few charming scenes by the Danube, during which people jump in and out of the water, splash one another, and generally move about in a messy and disorganized fashion, just as in real life, and not as in a carefully constructed May Day parade. In another scene, customers mob the department store when they hear a shipment of goods has arrived – a familiar sight to filmgoers at the time – though fortunately truckloads of goods arrive in time to sate them. Everyone watching would have known that this was ridiculous: in reality there would have been no truckloads of goods, and thus it became a kind of insiders' joke.

Wajda's first film, *Generation* (*Pokolenia*), released in 1955, deployed this kind of 'realism' too. Though it contained several scenes which might well have been designed to please communist bureaucrats, it also included several which seemed spontaneous, as indeed they were. Several of the young actors, including a teenaged Roman Polanski, had been part of the resistance as children and remembered the occupation well. When they scampered up and down stairways and hid in alleys from the Gestapo, they were simply playing themselves and behaving as they remembered behaving during the occupation. Audiences understood that too.[76]

In due course, the most obviously Stalinist films became embarrassments to their directors, some of whom denounced or disavowed them after his death in 1953. The crudest High Stalinist paintings, sculpture, poetry, fiction and architecture met the same fate. Wisława Szymborska, a distinguished, Nobel Prize-winning Polish poet, rarely spoke about her Stalinist poetry, and didn't include it in later collected editions of her work. The very titles became embarrassing: 'Lenin'; 'Welcoming the Construction of a Socialist City'; 'The Youth Building Nowa Huta'; 'Our Worker Speaks about the Imperialists'. Her elegy for Stalin – 'That Day' ('Ten Dzień') – includes the immortal lines, 'This is the party, the vision of humanity / This is the party, the power of people and conscience / Nothing from His life will be forgotten / His party will push aside the gloom'. She went on to write beautiful and enigmatic poems about many other subjects, and in later years avoided discussion of this difficult era altogether.[77]

But even after it had passed, the moment of High Stalinism left its mark on the culture of the region. East German painters went on arguing about definitions of 'realism' for decades. Ágnes Heller, one of Hungary's most distinguished philosophers, remained focused on the problem of totalitarianism most of her life. Milan Kundera, the exiled Czech writer, wrote stories about censorship, secrets and collaboration. The best-known novel by the East German writer Christa Wolf, *The Quest for Christa T.* (*Nachdenken über Christa T.*), is a story about a woman's struggle against the pressure to conform.[78] Wajda kept returning to themes of totalitarianism and resistance throughout his life, whether during the French Revolution or the Second World War. For myriad reasons – historical, political, psychological – some Eastern European artists did agree to become 'socialist realists' between 1949 and 1953. But they, their contemporaries and their successors often spent the rest of their lives trying to understand why, and how, this had been possible.

15
Ideal cities

O my steel mill! Mother of the countless masses
Who work together for your glory
You strengthen my heart
I grew up on your soil . . .

From 'To My Steel Mill',
Urszula Ciszek-Frankiewicz[1]

I looked for the city. I came through the village and ended up
in a big puddle . . . With some compassion the workers looked
across to a man carrying a briefcase – back then many of these
came to give directives – whose small car had got stuck in the
mud. The circumstances were chaotic. People arrived in droves
and didn't know each other.

Jószef Bondor, a party functionary,
remembering his arrival in Sztálinváros[2]

Like so many photographs of its era, the carefully posed picture was
intended to educate. On the left, a young woman with her hair tied
back in a peasant scarf stands with her hands behind her back, listening attentively. She wears a gingham shirt and overalls. On the right,
another woman, her foot placed firmly on a step, points into the middle distance. She wears a more formal skirt and blouse, carries a
pencil and paper, and is giving instructions. Both women are members
of an all-female construction brigade, and they are hard at work on
the new steel mill in the new city of Sztálinváros – Stalintown. The
woman on the right with the pencil is Zsófia Tevan, an engineer and

architect. The woman on the left in the gingham blouse is Júlia Kollár, a bricklayer.

Kollár had arrived in Sztálinváros in 1951. The daughter of peasant farmers, she finished school at the age of thirteen just after the war and then went immediately to work – 'at that time we accepted any job that was offered to us' – eventually making her way to a construction site in the town of Mohács, near the Yugoslav border in southern Hungary, where work had begun on a major steel mill. In the summer of 1949, special courses were organized in Mohács for unskilled workers like Júlia. She learned how to mix mortar and how to lay bricks. She also joined the communist youth movement, by then known as the League of Working Youth (Dolgozó Ifjúság Szövetsége, or DISZ). But after only a few months, work at Mohács came to an abrupt halt. The authorities announced that the building site would be moved to the village of Dunapentele, situated along the Danube in central Hungary. All of the Mohács workers and supervisors were invited to move as well.

Kollár accepted, received five further months of training at the Construction Ministry in Budapest, and arrived at the new construction site in the spring of 1951. At first, she was shocked by the conditions. In Mohács, she had lived in a house with her mother and her siblings, but in Dunapentele the young workers slept in tents and makeshift dormitories: 'there were five or six people in a single room, people were sleeping in bunk beds'. She almost gave up and went home, but was convinced to stay by Tevan, her work supervisor.

Unusually, Tevan had her own apartment: 'there was a hostel for engineers but since everybody was a man, I got a separate room in a half-ready building. The walls were not plastered, the room was so damp that I had to sleep with my clothes on and by the morning all my clothes had become wet.' But the apartment did have indoor plumbing and a small kitchen, and Tevan lived alone. Though she didn't tell Kollár at the time, her fiancé was then in prison, having been swept up with dozens of others in the wake of the Rajk trial. She invited Kollár to stay with her, and the two women lived together until Kollár married a year later.

For Kollár, the period which followed seemed, in retrospect, a very happy one. When I met her in 2009 she remembered her first years on the steel mill construction site with immense nostalgia. Early on, she had joined the first all-women's construction brigade at Sztálinváros, along with Tevan, at the time an enormous honour. Launched on 8 March – International Women's Day, according to the Soviet calendar – with great pomp and circumstance, the brigade had mixed success. Although placing tiles on walls and floors was a perfectly acceptable job for women, Tevan remembered that 'pouring concrete was not, especially as we did not have the right equipment . . . it was physically very difficult, even though the women were enthusiastic'. Because the brigade's progress was carefully watched by the media it couldn't be allowed to fail: when they had trouble meeting deadlines, one of the men's brigades would surreptitiously help the women bricklayers finish their tasks quickly.

Though her brigade worked from early in the morning until late in the evening, Kollár was also very active in her League of Working Youth section. In her own words, she 'did voluntary work, carried out social campaigns, bought peace bonds'. Kollár served as a mentor to new girls on the site, went to dances and helped to put on plays and concerts: 'it was a community, and people need community. We are social creatures, we need others.' When she heard that the League of Working Youth would be sending a delegation to the international youth festival in Berlin, she went to see Elek Horváth, head of the youth cadres at the factory, who was running the selection committee. They ran into one another on a staircase – she found him strikingly handsome – and she asked to be chosen.

But he did not select her. Later, Horváth told her he didn't want her to go to Berlin because 'she might have met someone there'. He had fallen instantly in love, and they were married a few months later. The civil ceremony, held at the brand-new registry office, was simple – 'no special dresses' – and Tevan was a witness. The bride almost arrived late, having spent the morning cleaning the one-room apartment they had received from the city the day before. No photographs were taken, since there weren't any photographers. Afterwards, they went out to a restaurant. On the following Monday they all returned to work.[3]

At the time of its construction, the vast steel mill that shaped the early lives and careers of Kollár, Tevan and Horváth was the largest and most ambitious industrial investment in Hungary. Everything about the project was highly politicized, and everything about it was shaped by Soviet advice and Soviet concerns from the very start. The design was selected at a meeting between Hungarian officials and their Soviet counterparts in Moscow, in 1949. The original site was also selected jointly – Mohács had been chosen for its proximity to transport and the quality of its soil – but after the Soviet spat with Yugoslavia it was deemed too close to the border. As Rákosi told the Hungarian Polit-buro in December 1949, the new site in Dunapentele, along the Danube, was less advantageous in some ways, and the sandy soil would eventually complicate construction. But it was nearer to Buda-pest and further from Tito, and that was what mattered most.

Once the site had been chosen, the project moved forward with Soviet-style haste. Construction began even before planning had fin-ished. In the early months there was no time to build housing, so workers like Kollár lived in tents and primitive barracks, and there was no time to plaster the walls of new apartments. Workers from nearby farms pitched in as 'Sunday help' so that construction could continue through the weekends. When it got dark, night shifts worked under powerful lights. In the summer, youth groups came from all over the country to help too.[4]

Sztálinváros was unique in Hungary, but not in the Soviet bloc. It was one of several 'socialist cities', all founded around vast new steel mills, which collectively represent the Eastern European communists' most comprehensive attempt to jump-start the creation of a truly totalitarian civilization. The steel mills were intended to accelerate industrialization, and thus the production of armaments. The huge construction sites were meant to draw the peasantry into factories and thus enlarge the working class. The new factory complexes, built from scratch, were intended to prove, definitively, that when unhin-dered by pre-existing economic relationships, central planning could produce more rapid economic growth than capitalism.

The architecture and design of the new cities were also meant to facilitate the development of a new kind of society, one which would facilitate the spread of *Homo sovieticus*. In these brand-new commu-nities, traditional organizations and institutions would have no sway, old habits would not hinder progress and communist organizations would exert enormous influence over young people because there weren't any others. The socialist city, as one German historian writes, was to be a place 'free of historical burdens, where a new human being was to come into existence, the city and the factory were to be a laboratory of a future society, culture and way of life'.[5]

The new factories and the new cities beside them were shaped by communist imperatives from the beginning. Sztálinváros was moved away from the Yugoslav border for security reasons, but the new Polish steel town of Nowa Huta was deliberately placed beside the city of Kraków, with its longstanding aristocratic, historical and intellectual traditions, for ideological reasons. 'They wanted to change the character of Kraków,' explained Stanisław Juchnowicz, one of Nowa Huta's original architects: 'they wanted to create a working class who would change the city.'[6]

Even at the time, this was controversial: dozens of Kraków institutions protested against the decision to place an enormous steel mill directly beside an ancient city with a medieval university, but to no avail. According to an account written at the time, the Soviet engineers who helped select the site 'stated their surprise at discovering that the proposed construction of a steel mill next to Kraków created suspicion and opposition among representatives of the society, not enthusiasm'. They suspected city authorities might simply be shirkers who 'feared the hard work' that the project would entail. The protests were ignored and the decision went ahead.[7] By the 1970s, heavy air pollution had indeed turned all of the medieval buildings of Kraków black. Juchnowicz, later a founder of the city's ecological society, explained that 'at the time, our consciousness of this problem was pretty low'.[8]

The placement of East Germany's first major steel town, Eisenhüttenstadt – rechristened Stalinstadt in 1953 – was similarly political. A new steel combine was a particular imperative in East Germany because the prewar German coal and steel industries were located almost entirely in the western half of the country. A number of sites were considered, including one on the Baltic, the better to import iron ore from Sweden. This plan was quashed by Ulbricht, probably following a conversation with Stalin, who didn't want 'his' Germany to become too dependent on the West. Finally, at a meeting with the industrial experts charged with planning the new site, Ulbricht settled the question of the new mill's location with a flourish. He took out a compass and put it on a map of Germany which was spread out on a table. 'Look here,' he declared, and drew a half-circle from the US bases in Bavaria. Then he spread the compass and pointed to one suggested site: 'That's about seven minutes' air raid warning.' Then he extended the compass to the town of Fürstenberg, on the eastern border of the GDR, and said: 'That's about fifteen minutes' air raid warning.' One of those present pointed out that this kind of reasoning could not be made public. 'Of course not,' Ulbricht replied. The new steelworks were being placed in the east in order to take advantage of iron ore coming from central Ukraine and coal from Poland. 'And so it will be a work of friendship, and that's how we are going to argue about it.'[9]

Fürstenberg had other advantages, including high numbers of refugees who could be put to work on the site. There was no large town in the vicinity, and that was a good thing too.[10] Ulbricht, like his Polish and Hungarian colleagues, was personally committed to the idea of a city 'uncontaminated by old workplace values'.[11] Fürstenberg had no industry, and thus no workplace values of any kind.

Like the combine at Sztálinváros, the mills in Nowa Huta and Stalinstadt were of Soviet design, and Russian engineers were involved in their construction from the very beginning. In both Hungary and Poland, all of the planning and instructional materials – provided by Giprometz, a Soviet state company – had to be translated from Russian, which caused multiple misunderstandings. (Even the laudatory official accounts of Nowa Huta's construction allude to the 'language difficulties' which resulted.)[12] The Russians also sent equipment, much of which had to be 'modified' for Polish conditions or even remodelled entirely.[13] In Germany, meanwhile, the decision to use Soviet technology was laden with multiple ironies. The plans brought to Stalinstadt were the same as those developed by American advisers for the steel combine at Magnitogorsk in the Urals in the 1930s. Not only were they therefore 'capitalist' in origin, but they were also less sophisticated than those subsequently developed in Germany and already in use in the western half of the country.[14]

The urban architecture of the new cities was no less political.

Socialist realist architects treated the designs as an important experiment. Honoured foreign visitors were brought to witness their progress. The workers and engineers of Stalinstadt paid ceremonial visits to Nowa Huta and Sztálinváros, and vice versa. In due course, artists and writers would be invited to record the new lives being lived in the new cities. Many elements of High Stalinist culture thus came together in the planning of these three cities: the cult of heavy industry, the cult of the 'shockworker', the youth movements and socialist realist aesthetics.

The stakes were high: by the early 1950s, the Eastern European communists were desperate to prove that their failing economic and political theories could work. Many believed that one final, superhuman effort to raise workers' living standards and create 'new men' might finally win the communists the legitimacy they needed.

But what did a 'socialist' city look like? Once again, nobody knew. In 1950, a small group of Eastern German architects went to Moscow, Kiev, Leningrad and Stalingrad to find out. They rode the Moscow metro, attended the 1 May celebrations in Red Square, and even caught a glimpse of Stalin, as they reported later on: 'we were standing on the side of the [Lenin] mausoleum where the stairs go up to the stand, and he walked past us on the stairs . . . the storm of enthusiasm grew immensely. We were very sorry not to be inside the demonstration, just being observers . . . Such a colourful picture is indescribable. The flags, the posters and pictures, the variety of colours . . .'[15]

Duly impressed by the spectacle, they listened attentively in the meetings which followed. They learned that the Soviet Union had built over 400 new cities and that in each one 'the planning bureau solves all questions on where to place things and how to organize them'. They showed their Soviet colleagues their plans for the reconstruction of central Berlin, which the Soviet colleagues – ironically, given their scorn for German history – found unacceptably ahistorical: 'The only time they criticized us directly was with the reproach that the great traditions of German city planning were not cherished in Germany.' New cities, they were told, had to take up regional traditions, from Berlin classicism to North German gothic. That would make them more 'democratic'.

In addition, they learned that their Soviet colleagues favoured urban over rural ('the city demonstrates the political will and the national consciousness of the nation'), heavy industry over agriculture and services ('cities are built largely by industry and for industry'), and multi-storey apartment blocks over leafy suburbs ('it is impossible to change a city into a garden'). In fact, they had no interest in suburbs of any kind. The character of a city, the Soviet architects declared, 'is that people live an urban life. And on the edges of the city or outside the city, they live a rural life.'

The group returned to Berlin filled with evangelical zeal. They organized meetings and conferences, held seminars and training sessions designed to pass on what they had learned. Walter Pistonek, one of the German architects, gave seventeen public lectures between May and November 1950, and published more than a dozen articles. Eventually, the group published 'Sixteen Principles' of socialist planning which became part of East German law, and remained so until 1989. Ulbricht became so enthusiastic about the new plans that he approved the construction of a Stalinist 'wedding cake' skyscraper in Dresden, much like the Warsaw Palace of Culture. Fortunately, it was never built.

Yet despite the general enthusiasm for socialist realist architecture, the concept was no clearer in practice to German town planners than it had been to Polish town planners. In Stalinstadt, many of the architects at first built what they knew how to build: simple, streamlined structures in the Bauhaus tradition (which had itself been a left-wing movement dedicated to the construction of 'homes for the workers'). But when Ulbricht visited the first completed apartments in January 1952, he declared that they were too small and too plain, like 'undecorated boxes'. New plans were made and discarded more than once.[16]

Finally, the East German leadership appointed a new chief architect. Karl Leucht increased the size of the city planning office from forty to 650 employees, accelerated the speed of the project and declared that in future the city's buildings were to be 'an expression of the growing wealth of socialist society' and a reflection of the high status of the working class. A new and more 'monumental' phase of construction began. Apartment blocks were linked by high archways. Doorways were flanked by columns. Elements intended to evoke the classical tradition in German art (this was deemed the most 'progressive' period of German culture) were mounted on facades, though sometimes in an almost haphazard manner. The new city was designed around the factory: though separated from the city by a green belt, the factory gates could be seen in the distance from the main streets, much as Berliners can see the Brandenburg Gate from the far end of Unter den Linden. Until 1981, no churches were built in the city at all. Instead, Leucht designed a town hall with a spire.

The construction of Nowa Huta followed a similar trajectory. In the early period, the city architects wanted to continue building in the styles they had pursued before the war. In Poland, this was not strict Bauhaus design but rather garden suburbs of the kind built in Britain in the 1920s and 1930s: low, one- or two-storey buildings, surrounded by green plots and trees. Although these were diametrically opposed to the socialist realist ideal, several such developments were completed. But the tone quickly changed in Nowa Huta too: party authorities declared these new buildings to be insufficiently ideological and insufficiently reflective of Poland's national character.

New plans for the city were drawn up in Warsaw at great speed and in an atmosphere of high tension. Nobody was allowed to see them before they were made public, and they were transported to Kraków under armed guard.[17] Like the Russian architects who had placed Renaissance decorative elements on the Palace of Culture, the Nowa Huta architects also decided that the moment when Poland had been most Polish was the sixteenth century. While the real sixteenth-century buildings of Kraków were thus put at risk by air pollution, Nowa Huta duly acquired a neo-Renaissance factory headquarters with an elaborate, crenellated facade. A town hall was designed in the style of Zamość, a Renaissance city in south-east Poland, though it was never built. Like Stalinstadt, Nowa Huta was also the first Polish city in many centuries to have been constructed without a church.

Equally grandiose designs were drawn up for Sztálinváros. According to the plans, the city would contain canteens where people would eat collective meals, instead of cooking at home; nurseries and pre-schools would be in walking distance; theatres and sports halls would be in close reach. People would also need spaces where they could gather to express their support and love for the regime. Accordingly, the city's architects drew up plans for a wide boulevard – Stalin Street – which would stretch from the factory to the central square and was ideal for May Day marches. The square itself was meant to have one side open to the Danube and a larger-than-life statue of Stalin in its centre.[18]

Outward appearances were not the architects' only concern. The socialist cities were to be, in the words of Leucht, 'a visible expression for the economic and cultural upswing of the German Democratic Republic'. Implicitly or explicitly, the new cities promised their workers a higher living standard. They might be living for the moment in primitive barracks of the sort which horrified Julia Kollár, but they all believed that this was temporary. 'You knew, from the beginning you believed, that it would work out with an apartment at some point. Even if you didn't say so, in the beginning,' one German woman remembered.[19] Another told the city newspaper that her definition of a 'socialist' city was one in which there was 'light, greenery, air and space everywhere'.[20] In Sztálinváros the authorities duly set themselves the ambitious goal of completing 1000 new apartments every month while leaving plenty of space for parks.[21]

Expectations were high, and the authorities raised them even higher. Workers' apartments were not only to be plentiful; they were to be large, comfortable and equipped with the most up-to-date designs. After Ulbricht's visit to Stalinstadt in 1952, construction authorities drew up a protocol stating that the height of rooms in the flats was to be raised from 2.42 to 2.7 metres; that window frames and ledges were to be of higher quality than normal; that buildings were all to be of the same height.[22] Leucht declared that apartment buildings must have central heating and the new occupants must 'have a say' in their construction. Architects alone should not decide how much space people got.[23]

The Prime Minister, Grotewohl, also paid a visit in 1952. He inspected some newly constructed apartments, and 'came to the conclusion that the workers had not been given sufficient advice on how to furnish and equip their new homes'.[24] An exhibition of 'show apartments' was duly created in order to teach people how to decorate an apartment, if and when they received one. The furniture on display was 'factory made', and thus 'more advanced' than the primitive furniture which the new workers had previously used, back when they were still peasants. Of course only those worthy of living in one of these socialist homes would receive one: because some 80 per cent of these new living spaces belonged to the steel combine, they quickly became part of the 'workers competition' awards system, and were used to encourage shockworkers to fulfil their norms even faster.[25]

Shops were to be of high quality too. In Nowa Huta, great effort went into the design of those which lined the central square. One of them, now part of the Cepelia chain, still retains its 1950s decor, including an enormous ceiling light which looks like a Renaissance chandelier as conceived by someone who has never seen a Renaissance chandelier. Shops were also meant to be full, and in some cases they were. In Sztálinváros, many who came from peasant families, Julia Kollár included, sent food home to their families.[26] Nowa Huta also had a reputation for having a better range of goods than nearby Kraków.

Stalinstadt initially had more trouble meeting its inhabitants' material demands, so much so that the shortages there became a matter of national concern. In August 1952, the East German Minister for Trade wrote an angry letter to one of the city authorities:

> when I visited EKO [the steel combine] on Saturday, 16 August, many workers as well as members of the party organization within EKO told me that for workers' families the supply of vegetables, fruits and other goods is very bad. I was told to get in touch with the housewives to get more information ... I was told to 'dress warmly' in anticipation of the reproaches that I would hear. The shopping street in the new district, which was to be finished on 1 May of this year, is still incomplete, allegedly because of disagreements over interior decoration.[27]

After receiving this letter, city authorities agreed to organize special 'shopping fairs' in the city, supplying, among other things, 740 bicycles, 5000 buckets, 2400 pairs of shoes and 10,000 metres of bed linen.

Last but not least, a 'socialist' city was supposed to be one in which the workers would not only eat and sleep, but would enjoy leisure activities of the sort only the bourgeoisie had enjoyed in the past.

Visiting Sztálinváros in 1952, Zoltán Vas – the Hungarian communist who lost his eyeglasses while visiting Hungarian partisans in 1944 – arranged a meeting with young engineers and asked them what they did after work. Upon hearing that 'there was nothing to do, so usually after work we went to sleep', he ordered city planners to build a restaurant. They did.[28] (On the same trip, Vas asked the head of the central planning bureau where he could get a taxi. 'We don't even have roads,' he was told.[29]) Juchnowicz also once received, out of the blue, a phone call: 'Build a theatre,' he was told.[30] He did. The Nowa Huta's People's Theatre was completed in 1955. Stalinstadt finished its theatre – named in honour of Friedrich Wolf, Markus Wolf's father – in the same year. Designed to resemble a Greek temple, the Stalinstadt theatre was not connected to the city's heating system, and for a long time had to be kept warm with the help of an old locomotive engine. But the projects kept coming. Sztálinváros, also under pressure to raise the cultural level of the city's inhabitants, opened a new hotel, the Arany Csillag ('Golden Star'), in 1954. The building was described by one newspaper as 'the most beautiful in the city' and its restaurant was meant to be the 'best in town'. Waiters and cooks were imported from Budapest, and the mayor grandly declared that in this restaurant, ordinary people would be served before dignitaries.[31]

In addition to entertainment for the workers, the socialist cities were also meant to provide cultural inspiration for everyone else. In the early 1950s, artists, writers and film-makers all came to visit in order to 'learn from the workers'. The Russian composer Dmitri Shostakovich came to Stalinstadt in 1952. The East German director Karl Gass made a laudatory newsreel there in 1953. Though his equipment was too primitive to do interviews, Gass filmed the construction of the steel furnace in monumental detail.[32] An East German novelist, Karl Mundstock, also published a book based on his experiences in the city. *Helle Nächte* (*White Nights*) contained a lyrical description of the construction site:

> Piles of wood, scaffolding, finished barracks, furnaces, tables, chairs, beds, piles of gravel, all of this lay about wherever there was any space . . . But soon the rows of barracks, the shops, the storage for material, could be seen, proving that a rational system underlay the

apparent chaos. Soon the bulldozers cleared the canal, which had turned into a river of mud in the ten years since the war. And soon the saws began to sing, and the road to the centre of the steelworks, the road of friendship, had been built.[33]

Tadeusz Konwicki also spent parts of 1949 and 1950 working at Nowa Huta, using the material gathered there to write *Przy Budowie* (*At the Building Site*), possibly his worst novel. The plot concerns a work crew who have to meet their construction deadline but are frustrated by class enemies and insufficiently enlightened colleagues. Naturally, they overcome all difficulties and fulfil the Plan.[34]

But it was not just the experience of work that writers and artists sought at the new city building sites. In some cases, they were also looking for an opportunity to remake themselves, much as the workers were remaking society. In 1952 the painter Oskar Nerlinger came to Stalinstadt, hoping to cure himself of any remaining traces of bourgeois formalism. Nerlinger had been an active member of the prewar avant-garde, and after the war was appointed director of the Hochschule der Bildenden Künste, the School of Fine Arts in West Berlin. His close association with his communist counterparts in the East, his loud opposition to 'capitalism' and his support for the East German 'peace' campaigns soon won him many enemies, however. After taking part in some exhibitions on the eastern side of the border, he was dubbed one of the West's 'rotten professors', and – like several others – lost his job.[35] In the early 1950s, it was not only communists who were intolerant.

With a great flourish, Nerlinger emigrated across the border in 1951 – one of the few to make the move from West to East – and joined the East German artistic establishment. Yet he remained, in his own words, 'insecure in his artistic attitude'. His wife, Alice Lex-Nerlinger, had trouble having her paintings exhibited in the East, even though, as she complained in a letter to the authorities, 'my whole life as an artist I've done nothing but work for Peace'.[36] Nerlinger himself felt it was a 'relief' to be in the East, but the aesthetics were hard to understand for someone best known as a highly abstract painter. Hoping to educate himself out of his 'pessimism' and to acquire 'optimism' like the workers, he determined to live for a time in the new socialist city.[37]

Nerlinger received a commission from the factory management to paint a mural, and thus became an employee of the steel mill, with the 'rights and duties of a factory worker'. Determined to experience every aspect of his new colleagues' lives, he visited their apartments, their restaurants and their sports stadium. By day, he sat 'wrapped in blankets in the winter mud, stood by the furnaces, experienced the construction of the great ovens, listened to the many noises of the machines', hoping to learn from 'the wonderful human beings who have caused this courageous project to rise from former forests'. In the evenings, he studied technical engineering literature. He tried to paint workers as they worked, which wasn't easy: 'The factory was noisy and dangerous, and the camera didn't help because the glow of the metal was too hot and bright.'[38]

His first results didn't please his subjects. They thought the scenes were too gloomy and unpleasant – 'like in a bad West German company' – and they began to advise Nerlinger on how he should change them. Nerlinger complied. He began to paint the factory as a brighter, more cheerful place. He painted the workers looking happier, more optimistic. He thought it important to show the engineers looking 'proud' of what they were doing. His worker-critics approved, so much so that he made prints for them which they hung in their apartments.[39]

His style had indeed changed, as he himself boasted at an exhibition of his sketches, studies and works in progress which took place in November 1952 – the very first art exhibit in Stalinstadt. To demonstrate how far he had come, Nerlinger brought four of his prewar paintings, and introduced them as evidence that 'it could not go on like this'. In the words of an art critic who reviewed the show, these older works included 'an icy depiction of a very solemn factory' (1930) and 'a melancholic, dark landscape' (1945), behind which lay 'the tragic situation of an artist whose political openness had led him astray'. Fortunately 'his progressive spirit turned against the paralysing pessimism. In the pulsating rhythm of the Eisenhüttenstadt combine, the depressing fears of growing lonely in a studio became the utopian dream of a new reality . . .'[40]

The factory workers were pleased with this first exhibition. 'Dear colleague Nerlinger,' wrote one in the visitors' book that evening,

'I was very happy when going through the exhibition, I could see how you, with a warm heart and unbroken creativity, have addressed new problems . . . I hope the finished work will be a great success.' Another declared that 'our conviction that the human being lies at the centre of all of our efforts cannot remain a mere saying, it must be expressed in art'. Representatives from friendly socialist countries wrote admiring notes in Polish, Hungarian and Czech.

A few weeks later, there was a discussion in the factory itself. Nerlinger began by asking for 'the helpful criticism of the workers'. Some of the responses were surprisingly precise. One comment was signed by three trade union members: 'we like the black and white drawings very much, but the watercolours must be lighter and more natural'. Another complained that in one of the pictures he couldn't recognize the faces of individuals, the figures were too generic. A representative from the Free German Youth was more enthusiastic: 'This is probably the first time in the history of our people that an artist presents his work for critical discussion to the workers who gave him motivation and strength.'[41]

Nerlinger's critical triumph was complete, and his psychological transformation had progressed as well. Like Max Lingner, he had truly wanted to conform to the spirit of his era, and he knowingly underwent a process of 're-education' so that he would better fit in to his new surroundings. In that sense, Nerlinger had a good deal in common with the workers who appeared in his paintings, as well as the workers of Sztálinváros and Nowa Huta. They too were allegedly being re-formed and reshaped by their surroundings – and they too were supposedly going to conform to the spirit of their cities.

The dreams of the socialist city planners went far beyond bricks and mortar. From the beginning, their ambitions included not just the transformation of art and urban planning, but the transformation of human behaviour. Sztálinváros, in an early description, was supposed to be a 'city without beggars, and with no periphery' – i.e. with no slums on the outskirts.[42] Inside the socialist city, workers were meant to follow a more 'cultured' way of life than they had known in the past – a way of life which bore an overwhelming resemblance to the life of the prewar bourgeoisie. In Sztálinváros, a glimpse of this appealing future finally became available in the summer of 1952, by which time the apartment blocks along 1 May Street were relatively orderly, the street itself was covered in asphalt, and the building debris and rubble had been carried away. The area had become a place where well-dressed people could go for a leisurely Sunday walk, and it soon became known as the 'Switzerland of Sztálinváros'. This, in the words of the historian Sándor Horváth, was exactly what was supposed to happen. The new urban spaces would breed a new kind of worker, the 'urban human':

> The 'urban human' leads a sober life, visits the cinema and theatre or listens to the radio instead of going to the pub, wears modern and comfortable ready-made clothing. He likes going for walks and loves to spend his spare time 'sensibly' on the beach. In contrast to the villager he furnishes his flat with urban furniture, preferring furniture from a factory to that designed by carpenters, and he lies on a practical sofa. In the urban human's flat there is a bathroom where he regularly takes a bath. He does not use the bathtub for his animals or to store food. During the day he eats at the factory, and only uses his kitchen to cook light meals. The rest of the time he spends with his family in the living room. The urban human sunbathes on the balcony of his modern, light and airy flat, or lets his children get fresh air there. He does not dry clothes on the balcony, but uses the communal laundry in the building.[43]

But the Switzerland of Sztálinváros was tiny. In 1952, it consisted of only a single street. Daily life on the rest of the building site, and on the building sites of Stalinstadt and Nowa Huta, looked rather different.

During their first decade, the socialist cities met one of their goals with stunning success: all of them achieved extraordinarily rapid growth. Nowa Huta, founded in 1949, had 18,800 inhabitants by the end of 1950, and would have 101,900 inhabitants by 1960.[44] Sztálinváros had 5860 inhabitants at the end of 1950, but the number had more than doubled to 14,708 a year later.[45] Stalinstadt had 2400 inhabitants in 1952, and 15,150 in 1955. In any developing country such rapid growth was guaranteed to bring chaos, disorganization, mistakes and worse. And so it did. As Józef Tejchma remembered, 'it was all . . . incredibly primitive'.

Tejchma arrived in Nowa Huta in 1951 at the age of twenty-four, the same year he attended the Berlin youth festival. Born into a peasant family in an isolated village in south-eastern Poland, Tejchma had finished high school thanks to the free education which his parents would never have been able to afford before the war. He had joined the Peasants' Party's youth movement as a student and when it merged into the Union of Polish Youth (ZMP) in 1948, he automatically became a member. Talented and enthusiastic, he was quickly invited to work in the Union's headquarters in Warsaw. Though he had hopes of attending university, there were other, more urgent tasks. Unexpectedly, the head of cadres in Warsaw called him into his office and told him there was an urgent need to open a ZMP office in Nowa Huta. Would Tejchma become its first leader? He agreed. And thus, as he remembered, he became 'the leader of several tens of thousands of young people. I was responsible for their education, for culture, for sport – for everything.'[46]

Tejchma stayed for three years, during which time he encountered 'the vast complications which accompanied the transfer of young people straight from the countryside into big factories'. Many of those who arrived in Nowa Huta were illiterate or semi-literate. They had never left their small villages, had never been away from their families and knew nothing of the outside world. Tejchma did not immediately see this as an insurmountable problem. He himself was the product of an impoverished village, and the modest 'corner' he inhabited in a workers' hotel in Nowa Huta was more luxurious than anything he'd known growing up: 'there was water, electricity'. He also had a secretary and a salary, paid by the ZMP, which made him independent of the factory.

At first, Tejchma's days were packed with interest. Though he had instructions from Warsaw, telling him how to organize lectures and parades, he also had a good deal of independence. He walked around the building site, 'interesting myself in how the young people were working, maybe intervening, making suggestions, looking at the dining hall, the educational system'. He brought his conclusions to the construction bosses and argued for changes. In order to prevent workers from 'lying around on benches' after work, he organized a fleet of construction site trucks to take a group of workers, many of whom had never been inside a theatre before, to attend a performance at a Kraków theatre. Tejchma also organized meetings with the important writers, artists and poets who came to Nowa Huta in search of creative inspiration. At the same time, Tejchma kept track of who was meeting construction norms, and who had beaten them. True to the spirit of the age, he encouraged 'socialist competitions' and rewarded the victors. Some people listened: 'they engaged, they tried to do well, they raced against one another. But of course it didn't look, in real life, the way it did in the newsreels.'

Very quickly, Tejchma's job became a disappointment. Some of his new charges appreciated his work, wanted to broaden their horizons, learn the history of the workers' movement, become acquainted with theatre and literature. But others were not only bored by his efforts, they were actively hostile. Many of them 'had no cultural standards at all. No education, no need for higher things. They were constantly drunk, they entertained themselves by fighting. They had no sense of unity. They wanted nothing that we had to give them.'

He was not the only one to come to that conclusion. In 1955 – after Stalin's death, by which time the press was much freer – the young journalist Ryszard Kapuściński visited Nowa Huta on behalf of *Sztandar Młodych* (*Banner of Youth*), the newspaper of the Youth Union. In the recently completed apartment blocks, Kapuściński met many people who were satisfied with what they had achieved. 'I've been here two years and won't leave for anything,' one man told him. But in the barrack cities on the outskirts of town, he found dramatic, even Dantesque living conditions, and an emerging underclass of impoverished and degenerate factory workers:

Not long ago, a fourteen-year-old girl infected an army of boys [with venereal disease]. When we met her, she described her achievement with such vulgarity that we wanted to vomit. She isn't alone. Not all of them are so young, but there are many. Go to the Mogilski forest, to 'Tajwan', to 'Kozedo' [names of pubs] ... In Nowa Huta there are apartments where in one room the mother takes money from men, and in the other the daughter makes it up to them. There is more than one such apartment ...

And now look at the life of a young man here in the factory. He gets up early, he goes to work. He comes back at three. That's it. At three, his day ends. I've walked around the dorms where such men lived. I've looked inside: they are sitting. Actually that's the only activity they do. They don't talk, what is there to talk about? They could read, but they aren't used to it, they could sing, but that would bother others, they could fight but they don't want to. They just – sit. The more active wander around the streets. Hell, maybe there is somewhere to go, something to fill half the day? There are a lot of bars. But some don't want to go there, others don't have money. Besides that there isn't anything . . . [47]

Tejchma made the same observation. He tried to hold group discussions with the most apathetic workers, but while they would happily complain about working conditions, it was impossible to get them to talk about much else. When famous writers came to visit, they mostly sat silent, as if waiting to be instructed by these visitors from a different world. Tejchma began to warn these literary figures in advance, even advising them against overselling Nowa Huta. He told Kazimierz Brandys, at the time a leading Stalinist writer, to tone down his description of the building site: real life was not so optimistic, so joyful as it appeared to be in Brandys's work. There was a vast gap between daily life as it was actually lived, and daily life as it was described in the newspapers, the newsreels and the novels.

Vast gaps were also emerging between the different districts of the socialist cities. Not far from 1 May Street, the Switzerland of Sztálinváros, there were barrack cities with names like 'Radar' and 'South'. These were in fact slums, with no running water, no indoor toilets and no asphalt streets. Rubbish collection was irregular. People kept pigs and chickens in sheds alongside the barracks – and sometimes in the half-finished apartment blocks nearby. When it rained the mud was so deep that parents had to carry children to kindergarten on their backs. Sometimes two, three or more families lived in spaces meant for one.[48] For entertainment, the inhabitants of the barrack cities visited not theatres and hotel restaurants but pubs. The most notorious – Késdobáló, which literally means 'The Knife-Thrower' as well as 'pub' or 'joint' in Hungarian slang – was, according to press reports, a place of drunkenness, wild singing, fights and stabbings. Of another pub – Lepra, or 'The Leopard' – it was jokingly said that one had to fire into the air upon crossing the threshold, and if no one shot back then it was possible to enter. Periodically the police tried to close these establishments, but the pubs had become gathering places for former peasants, who defended them vigorously against the 'urban' police and media.[49]

Stalinstadt was equally divided. In one part of the city, the lucky few were able to move into new flats, and were genuinely enthusiastic about their new circumstances. Elsewhere, things were harder. Most of the workers who came to the site in the early days were young people, who came from all over Germany – one in three was a refugee from Poland, Sudetenland or elsewhere in the former Reich – without their families. They lived in barracks, ten to a room, and their main entertainment was drinking. One remembered going 'over the rail tracks to Fürstenberg', where, as in Sztálinváros, there were bars with non-utopian names like 'The Wild Boar' and 'The Cellar'.[50] Another remembered a pub which was so crowded it was difficult to enter – unless you were lucky enough to get there after a fight, when the clients had all been tossed out.[51]

The speed of the construction, the use of night shifts, the long working days and the inexperience of both workers and management also meant that there were frequent technological failures in these supposedly ideal construction sites. The loose, sandy soil of Sztálinváros caused enormous problems and slowed down progress. Tevan remembered waking up early on Sunday mornings and sneaking out to the construction site to make sure that 'the walls and the buildings were still there'.[52] Her piece of the factory survived, but a wing of one of the local schools did collapse and had to be reconstructed. In 1958 the entire sewage system had to be refurbished. Ideology itself was the source of technical problems: at one point Tevan requested that a much-applauded brigade of shockworkers be removed from one of her projects because they were so anxious to finish quickly and collect their rewards that they cut corners and did the work badly. That kind of problem arose at many other building sites and in many other factories in this era, but heightened propaganda made the problem worse in the socialist cities.

Technical problems arose within the steel mills too. At Stalinstadt, a furnace designed to produce 360 tons of raw iron was initially only able to produce about one and a half tons. After about two months of repairs and adjustments, it could produce around 205 tons – which meant, at least, that the Plan could be 'fulfilled by 58 per cent'. The output eventually improved, but poor planning and engineering failures meant that parts of the steel production process at the Stalinstadt mill would be carried out in the Soviet Union for many years. Decades after the mill was 'complete', unfinished materials still had to be shipped back and forth across the border for processing. The entire plant, encompassing all of the stages of the steel production cycle, would not be completed until the 1990s, after East Germany no longer existed.[53]

Rapid development often leads to these kinds of mistakes and failures in poor countries. But in the new socialist cities the gap between the utopian propaganda and the sometimes catastrophic reality of daily life was so wide that the communist parties scrambled constantly to explain it away. Certainly mass propaganda campaigns were organized in the socialist cities on a broader and more frantic scale than elsewhere in the country. The campaign to change Dunapentele's name to Sztálinváros was carried out precisely in order to mobilize the city's work force, for example, and perhaps to encourage the Soviet Union to pitch in as well. As Gerő wrote in a letter to Rákosi in 1951:

> with the new name we could have a big boost in the organization of work contests on the construction sites. We could organize the name change in such a way ... that the overwhelming majority of the workers identify with the plan, and ask the government to fulfil their demands for the name change ... Also I think that naming the Duna Steel Mill after comrade Stalin would morally oblige Soviet economic organizations to offer us the necessary help in planning and supply ...[54]

A 'spontaneous' campaign was duly set in motion. From all over the city, workers wrote letters to Rákosi, pledging to achieve higher work norms and faster deadlines if only the Hungarian leader would agree to change the city's name. 'I promise that with all my efforts and knowledge I will help this little tree planted in this small village Dunapentele to reach the skies in the wondercity of Sztálinváros,' wrote one. 'I beg comrade Rákosi to bring this letter to our father Stalin,' declared another. Some wrote poems:

> By the Volga, there is Stalingrad, by the Danube we have Sztálinváros,
> Comrade Stalin is the greatest guardian of peace, his name will protect
> our city . . .

Finally, a workers' delegation went to see Rákosi and presented him with all of the letters, bound into a large leather book which is preserved today in the city museum. He shook hands with them and told them he had agreed: the city could be renamed. A three-day 'naming' celebration was scheduled for the anniversary of the October Revolution, complete with folk dance performances, theatre and opera, sporting contests and a book fair with all of Stalin's books. A huge portrait of Stalin was hung on the party headquarters, carefully lit up, in the words of a local journalist, 'as if the light of gratitude of the Hungarian people would shine upon his face'.[55]

In East Germany, the party leadership took a grimmer approach to their socialist city's failures. Particularly concerned by the engineering mistakes, the East German party leadership organized a meeting of the Stalinstadt party bosses in 1952. Behind closed doors, all of the problems were aired: the lack of supplies, the lack of protective clothing for workers, the poor transportation, the filthy barracks, the dysfunctional furnaces. The result was a blistering report, laying most of the blame on the Minister of Metallurgy, Fritz Selbmann, who was charged with 'arrogance' and fined. He was told he could keep his job, but only on the condition that he led a commission of experts to oversee work at the factory for the next three months, and only if the commission made swift changes.

Separately, the East German secret police carried out their own investigation into the poor performance of the brand-new furnaces. The Stasi boss, Wilhelm Zaisser, personally commissioned a report entitled 'On Suspicion of Sabotage in Project Planning and Construction of Eisenhüttenstadt'. At the suggestion of his Soviet advisers, Zaisser once again laid much of the blame for technical failures on 'the completely irresponsible behaviour of Minister Selbmann', and there was some dark talk of a show trial (perhaps along the lines of the Soviet 'Shakhty Trial' of the 1930s, during which several hapless engineers had been blamed for a whole range of industrial failures). Selbmann and his colleagues were only saved from arrest and public humiliation by the arrival of a group of Soviet engineers. After examining the project, they applauded the construction of the furnaces but criticized the 'inexperience' of their German colleagues: the low production rate was not caused by sabotage, but by an incorrect mixture of coke and iron ore.[56] The pressure on Stalinstadt engineers remained so strong that the technical director of the mill, Hans König, openly complained of constant attacks and accusations. In 1955 he slipped over the border to the West.[57]

Ordinary workers shouldered some of the blame too. The Sztálinváros press openly blamed glitches and delays on the 'criminals, prostitutes and déclassé elements' who had found their way to the city by nefarious means and were now allegedly pushing up crime rates and sabotaging the effort of others. There was some truth behind these accusations. Sztálinváros was the biggest construction site in the country, and all kinds of people drifted there to seek their fortunes. The appalling living conditions – the overcrowding, lack of entertainment, the housing shortage – might have made workers behave worse than they might have done too, though not always. Tevan had several ex-prostitutes in her women's construction brigade: 'some of them of course continued their jobs in Sztálinváros, but some of them really wanted to start a new life. I had one such employee who I helped a good deal, and who later became a local shop manager. Every time I went to shop there she gave me the best produce, she was so grateful.'[58]

But the majority of the workers who came to the socialist cities were not criminals or prostitutes, just as the majority of those who went to the makeshift pubs were not gun-toting thugs. In the end, the mythology of Sztálinváros as a lawless 'gold-rush' town, where anything could happen and all rules were broken, was more useful than true. Like the accusations of industrial sabotage, it helped explain why living standards weren't rising, why apartments weren't complete and why even Soviet-designed steel mills built from scratch weren't able to fulfil the communist party's ambitious plans.

The campaigns against shirkers, 'criminals' and other spoilers may have had their successes. But the gap between propaganda and reality eventually became too wide to disguise, and in time even many enthusiastic socialist city-dwellers became disillusioned. After a few years as a youth activist, Elek Horváth was drafted into the army and given an officer's commission. Júlia Kollár – now Júlia Horváth – was invited to attend a party training school in Budapest, where she got in trouble for voicing her opposition to the 'peace bonds' campaign. As a League of Working Youth leader, she had been obliged to sell these 'bonds' – a tax, in effect, since the money went back to the state – to her fellow workers: the more bonds you sold, the higher your standing inside the youth movement. She came to feel it was wrong to persuade people to go into debt in order to purchase peace bonds, and she didn't want to do so herself, even if it meant that the Horváths would no longer be considered 'exemplary cadres'. She said so aloud. Soon afterwards, someone asked her if she was proud to have a husband who was an officer at such a young age, and she said no, she didn't like his job because it meant that he was away most of the time. Both that conversation and her comments about the peace bonds were reported to the school director. Summoned to explain herself, she told him that this was not 'enemy behaviour', just an expression of her opinion. The incident ended there and she returned to Sztálinváros as a party activist. But she never returned to construction work, and she has no nostalgia for the later years she spent in the city.

If the enthusiasm did not last, neither did the utopian dream of a 'socialist' city. After Stalin's death in 1953, not everything changed right away – the names Stalinstadt and Sztálinváros remained in use until 1961, when the two cities were quietly rechristened Eisenhüttenstadt and Dunaújváros, respectively. But new architectural principles were put into practice right away. In December 1954, less than a year after Stalin's death, Nikita Khrushchev launched a campaign to promote the 'industrialization of architecture'. In a speech which heralded some of the political battle still to come, he spoke enthusiastically of pre-fabricated buildings, reinforced concrete and standardized apartments. He dismissed architects who were too concerned with appearances: 'he needs a beautiful silhouette, but what people need are apartments'. And he stamped roundly on the extravagances of Stalinist socialist realism:

> Certain architects have a passion for adding spires to the tops of buildings, which gives this architecture an ecclesiastical appearance. Do you like the silhouette of churches? I don't want to argue about tastes, but for residential buildings such an appearance is unnecessary ... This produces no extra convenience for residents and merely makes exploitation of the building more expensive and puts up its cost.[59]

In line with this new set of policies, the Soviet Central Committee passed a decree on 'the elimination of unnecessary extravagance in architecture'. Eastern Europe followed suit. In January, Khrushchev's speech appeared in a German translation. In February 1955, the party Central Committee in Berlin declared that all new construction was to go forward under a new slogan: 'Better, cheaper, faster.'[60] Pre-fab tower blocks – the infamous *Plattenbau* – began going up in Stalinstadt and other East German cities not long afterwards.

In the end, the town hall with the soaring spire planned for Stalinstadt was never built. Nor was the cultural centre on Nowa Huta's central square, a space which has been renamed Ronald Reagan Plaza and today marks the intersection of streets named after General Władysław Anders, Pope John Paul II and the Solidarity trade union. Only half of the main square in Dunaújváros was completed, leaving the 'square' somewhat lopsided and causing architectural controversy in the city even today. Investment in the Stalinstadt steel mill was reduced in 1954 from 110 million to 34 million marks, and construction of some pieces of the production cycle were put off indefinitely.[61] Investment in the Sztálinváros mill was frozen in 1954. Although the Nowa Huta mill continued to grow, its location became more controversial with time.

Because of the immense amount of publicity and propaganda which had initially been focused upon them, all three socialist towns continued to play symbolic roles in the subsequent history of their respective countries. In the summer of 1955, Nowa Huta and its workers became the subject of one of the first openly anti-communist poems to appear in print in Poland after Stalin's death. Adam Ważyk's 'Poem for Adults' bitterly mocked the peasants-turned-workers, the pretensions of the Nowa Huta management and the glowing communist propaganda:

From villages and little towns, they come in wooden carts
To build a factory and dream out a city,
To dig out of the earth a new Eldorado.
An army of pioneers, a massed crowd,
They cram into barns, barracks, and hostels,
Walk heavily and whistle loudly in the muddy streets:
A great migration, carrying confused ambitions,
The crucifix of Częstochowa on a string around their necks,
A stack of curses, a feather pillow, a gallon of vodka, the lust for girls . . .

The huge mob, pushed suddenly
Out of medieval darkness: an inhuman Poland,
Howling with boredom on December nights . . .[62]

Later, this same 'army of pioneers', with their crucifixes and their vodka, featured in Andrzej Wajda's film *Man of Marble* (*Człowiek z marmuru*). The story of a Stalinist shockworker who fades into insignificance and disappointment, *Man of Marble* was approved for distribution in 1977 thanks to the intervention of Józef Tejchma, the former Nowa Huta youth leader, who was by then the Polish Minister of Culture.

In subsequent decades, the first Polish city to be built without a church also became the focus of an enormous political and religious struggle. In 1957, the archdiocese of Kraków applied to build a church in Nowa Huta. In 1959, the Archbishop of Kraków, Karol Wojtyła, celebrated outdoor mass in the open field where the church was supposed to be constructed. Throughout the 1960s and 1970s, clergy and the authorities tussled over funding and permits until finally, in 1977, the church was built. Cardinal Wojtyła consecrated it, an act which elevated both his national and his international stature. Six years later, Wojtyła – now Pope John Paul II – celebrated mass there before a triumphant crowd. Nowa Huta had become, and remains, a symbol of totalitarianism's failure in Poland: failed planning, failed architecture, a failed utopian dream.

16

Reluctant collaborators

She gave us everything
Sun and Wind, always generous
Wherever she was, there was life,
We are what we are because of her
She never abandoned us
Even in a frozen world we were warmed . . .
The party, the party, she is always right!
And Comrades, so it will always remain
Since he who fights for the right, is always right . . .
He who defends mankind is always right . . .
As raised to life by Lenin's spirit, as welded by Stalin
The party, the party, the party

'The Song of the Party', 1949

'This is the difficult thing to explain to people: that song – 'the
party, the party is always right' – we thought it was really
the truth, and we behaved that way.'

Herta Kuhrig, Berlin, 2006[1]

To the modern ear, or perhaps more accurately to the post-modern
ear, the lyrics of 'The Song of the Party' ('Das Lied der Partei'), cited
above, are not exactly emotive. On the contrary, they seem absurd,
and in the years since East Germany ceased to exist they have been
mocked, parodied and even sung by Mickey Mouse in a YouTube
production.[2] Without an intact ideology to support them, the words
of the chorus – 'The party, the party, she is always right' – sound not

merely outdated, but laughable. It is difficult to imagine how anyone could have sung them with a straight face.

But those who sang this song in Stalinist East Germany were not laughing, and the words had certainly been composed in earnest. Their author was a Czech-German communist named Louis Fürnberg, who had fled to Palestine during the war and returned to Prague in 1946. As both a Jew and a former émigré, he had become a figure of suspicion in Czechoslovakia by 1949, and was thus excluded from the party congress of that year. In sorrow – or perhaps with the hope of reversing his status – he composed 'The Party is Always Right'. But then he got lucky. Instead of going to jail with Slánský, he was sent to East Germany as a diplomat. His song was performed at the Berlin party congress in 1950, where it was much admired. Eventually, it was adopted as the German party's anthem. After that, the 'Song of the Party' was performed regularly, at official and party occasions, right up through the 1980s, often with apparent gusto.[3]

Why? Some sang because they were afraid not to sing. But quite a few of them simply didn't listen to the words, or weren't interested in them. Indeed, many of those who clapped at the leaders' speeches, or who mouthed slogans at meetings, or who marched in May Day parades did so with a certain odd ambivalence. Millions of people did not necessarily believe all of the slogans they read in the newspaper, but neither did they feel compelled to denounce those who were writing them. They did not necessarily believe that Stalin was an infallible leader, but nor did they tear down his portraits. They did not necessarily believe that 'the party, the party, the party is always right', but nor did they stop singing those lyrics.

There isn't a straightforward explanation for why they did not resist more openly, though some may now think so. For the extraordinary achievement of Soviet communism – as conceived in the 1920s, perfected in the 1930s and then spread across Eastern Europe after 1945 – was the system's ability to get so many apolitical people in so many countries to play along without much protest. The devastation of the war, the exhaustion of its victims, the carefully targeted terror and ethnic cleansing – all of the elements of Sovietization described earlier in this book – are part of the explanation. Both the memory of recent violence and the threat of future violence hovered constantly in the background. If one person in a group of twenty acquaintances was arrested, that might suffice to keep the other nineteen afraid. The secret police's informer network was ever-present, and even when it wasn't people thought it might be. The unavoidable, repetitive propaganda in schools, in the media, on the streets, and at all kinds of 'apolitical' meetings and events also made the slogans seem inevitable and the system unavoidable. What was the point of objecting?

At the same time, some of the language the authorities used was very appealing. Reconstruction, though it would have happened faster and more efficiently under a different political system, was clearly moving forward. Though they often overreached, communist authorities did call for a war on ignorance and illiteracy, they did align themselves with the forces of science and technical progress, and they did appeal to those who hoped that society could be remade after a terrible war. Jerzy Morawski, a Politburo member in the 1950s, remembered wistfully that 'at the beginning, I was enormously impressed with the enthusiasm. I thought we were going to create a new Poland, different from prewar Poland ... that we would take care of all of those who had been maltreated in the past.'[4] Another Pole, a junior officer at the time, remembered that 'work waited for people and not the other way around, Warsaw was being rebuilt, industry was being rebuilt, everyone could study. New schools were built, high schools, and everything was free.'[5]

Meanwhile, the systematic destruction of alternative sources of authority and of civil society, also described in previous chapters, meant that those who questioned the system and its values felt isolated and alone. The satirist and writer Jacek Fedorowicz grew up in a family with grave doubts about the regime, but had no idea what his classmates thought about communism and never asked them: 'The terror was such that one didn't speak of it.'[6]

The communists also had a claque of influential supporters in the West, among them intellectual luminaries such as Jean-Paul Sartre and Pablo Picasso, who gave a sheen of legitimacy to communist ideology and made many Eastern Europeans feel they weren't merely Soviet subjects but rather part of a continental avant-garde. Much of Western Europe was turning to the Left, after all, so why shouldn't Eastern Europe do so too? Picasso himself visited Poland in 1948 to attend the World Congress of Intellectuals for Peace. Although he tore off his headset and refused to listen to the translation when the Soviet guests began insulting existentialism and T. S. Eliot, he did seem to approve of much else.[7] He stayed two weeks, donated some hand-painted ceramics to the National Museum and sketched a mermaid, the symbol of Warsaw, on the wall of one of the new socialist realist 'apartments for the workers' in central Warsaw. Alas the workers became annoyed by the numbers of people who wanted to visit the sketch, and they eventually painted it over.[8]

There were also outright bribes. These came in many forms, from the well-paid jobs and exclusive villas offered to famous writers and artists to the pay rises offered to the German technicians and scientists who agreed to stay in the East. Further down the scale, state employees often had very cheap or free meals, better housing and ration tickets. At the highest levels, the privileges could be very elaborate indeed, especially by the standards of the time. In 1946, the party secretary in the Hungarian town of Csákberény held a grand dinner in the villa he had confiscated from the local gentry. One guest remembered the evening well:

> The villa was illuminated, decorated with torches. On the right side of the entrance, the hunting club stood guard in their uniforms, on the left side stood party youth leaders in blue shirts and red tie ... [outside] some American limousines were parked beside two Soviet military jeeps, several motor-bikes and some horse-carriages. One police car was also there. ... Inside on the long table there was a roasted pig, caviar and turkey, and also wild boar, pheasant, and studded goose. Strong Meran wine from the confiscated vineyards was poured in crystal glasses from crystal bottles ...[9]

In Budapest and Berlin, party leaders had the pick of the villas left behind by the displaced bourgeoisie. In Warsaw, the party elite generally spent their time outside the city, in the suburb of Konstancin, where they had their own dining facilities and cinema, and where they were protected by armed guards under Soviet command. According to Józef Światło, the secret policeman who defected in 1953, the garden surrounding Bierut's villa was 'swarming with men in dark suits and briefcases, or with their hands in their pockets', when Bierut and his mistress were in residence: 'they are there just in case "the masses"

want to greet him, God forbid'. This description might be over-col-
ourful, but it does have an echo in Joel Agee's memoir of his childhood
spent in the home of his stepfather, an East German writer who also
lived in a heavily guarded enclave outside Berlin. Wilhelm Pieck's villa
was just nearby, as Agee remembered: 'Many black limousines stood
in front of it, and armored cars and jeeps. A ring of barbed wire surrounded the place, patrolled by guards. You could sense it was best
not to go too near it.'[10]

Secret police employees could offer other services too. All of Bierut's
cooks, waiters and cleaning ladies were Security Ministry employees,
according to Światło, and their salaries were paid from its budget.
Other dignitaries enjoyed similarly large staff and similarly large resi-
dences. Radkiewicz, the security police boss, had an apartment in
Warsaw, a villa in Konstancin and four cars with four drivers to get
him back and forth. But even further down the scale, deputy ministers
and high-ranking security policemen like Światło 'had free apartments
with servants, and cars at our disposal' as well as free clothes, shoes,
blankets, linen and even socks, gloves and briefcases.[11]

There were also outright financial rewards for people willing to
work secretly on behalf of the regime, especially if they agreed to
switch sides. One of the Stasi's most successful early espionage operations, *Aktion Pfeil*, was made possible because a low-level courier for
the West German Federal Intelligence Service (the Bundesnachrichten-
dienst, or BND) was so easily purchased. The courier, Hans-Joachim
Geyer, was a former Nazi party member and had been a BND
employee for only a few weeks when he was caught. Under interrogation he immediately pleaded guilty, but declared that 'he thought he
could be of help . . .'

The Stasi put Geyer on the payroll immediately: his first payment
went through on 12 December 1952. Geyer continued to travel to
West Berlin to meet his contacts. Every time he reported to the Stasi
he presented them with receipts, some of which have been lovingly
preserved in the Stasi archive and remain there today. These include,
among other things, an optician's bill; six tickets to the circus; and
sales receipts for books, for sporting equipment and for leather goods.
Geyer's Christmas shopping list (presumably presents for family)

included chocolate biscuits, coconut, a pair of children's stockings, marzipan, apricots, a new suit and handkerchiefs.

Apparently he was worth it. Thanks to Geyer, one officer wrote, the Stasi had been able to 'arrest 108 BND spies in East Germany', and obtain hundreds of original documents. Although he was eventually brought home in the autumn of 1953 after his cover had been blown, he received multiple medals from the East German state, and even after his death the GDR continued to pay a hefty pension to his widow.[12] The Stasi even paid all of his sons' educational fees, including medical school tuition. Both eventually became doctors.

Consciously or unconsciously, the Stasi background file on Geyer reveals a good deal about the personality type of someone who could be bribed into cooperation. Geyer, his case managers wrote, 'wants to please everybody'. In addition, 'he is devoted to his wife and children and to the property where he lives. He doesn't drink too much. Nothing immoral can be found out about him.' He was 'politically indifferent' but 'easy to influence', and it was suggested that instructors train him in 'logical thinking and the dialectical method'. Presumably he went along with that too.

For a select few, the communist system also offered dramatic promotions – the 'social advance' described in Chapter 13 – and excellent opportunities for those who conformed. The new educational system and the new workplace ideology certainly created losers – teachers and intellectuals with a prewar sensibility, older skilled workers, young people who would not or could not conform – but it created many winners as well. Among them were new teachers and workers who replaced the older ones, new writers who replaced older writers and new politicians who replaced their elders too. Jacek Kuroń, a Union of Polish Youth activist at the time (and later a renowned dissident) observed the results of the 'social advance' policy in his Warsaw neighbourhood during the 1950s:

> In the ruling committee of the local Union of Polish Youth group one could see it with the naked eye. Who came there? Many young people from the poorest houses in Marymont, from the pre-war slums, from shacks built after the war with bricks taken out of the rubble, as well as the former officers' villas in Żoliborz, which had become dormito-

ries for the unemployed and were now slums as well. In fact, the people who came had been, until recently, the absolute lowest rung of society. And everyone knew someone in power. An uncle, a brother-in-law, a friend who had once hung around the neighbourhood and was now in the Security Department, the army, the militia, the local or regional party committee . . . Of deep significance was the fact that these young people felt themselves to be in charge. And for a certain period, particularly on the neighbourhood level, they were.[13]

The communist regime required very little in exchange for this brandnew sensation of control and power: it just asked the beneficiaries to close their eyes occasionally to contradictions between propaganda and reality. To some, this seemed a very small price indeed to pay for rapid social mobility.

Yet most people in the communist regimes did not succumb to dramatic bribes, furious threats or elaborate rewards. Most people wanted neither to be party bosses nor angry dissidents. They wanted to get on with their lives, rebuild their countries, educate their children, feed their families and stay far away from those in power. But the culture of High Stalinist Eastern Europe made it impossible to do so in silent neutrality. No one could be apolitical: the system demanded that all citizens constantly sing its praises, however reluctantly. And so the vast majority of East Europeans did not make a pact with the devil or sell their souls to become informers, but rather succumbed to constant, all-encompassing, everyday psychological and economic pressure. The Stalinist system excelled at creating large groups of people who disliked the regime and knew the propaganda was false, but who felt nevertheless compelled by circumstances to go along with it. For lack of a better expression, I'll call them 'resistant' or 'reluctant' collaborators.

Upon returning from a labour camp in Siberia, for example, Wolfgang Lehmann wanted to get a job in construction in East Germany. Because of his record, he wasn't accepted anywhere. The chief engineer advised him to join the German–Soviet friendship society. He did. For good measure, he got a Russian friend to write a letter certifying that he'd been a good friend to the USSR while in the Gulag. He got the job.[14] Michał Bauer, a Home Army soldier who also spent time in the Gulag, found himself working at a state company a few years later. Every day the entire staff had to gather to listen to readings from the morning's newspapers. Sometimes he had to preside over these sessions, even though he never had any sympathy for communism at all: 'they would say Bauer, tomorrow you've got press duty, find a theme . . . if you didn't do it, you could be thrown out of work'.[15]

The musician Andrzej Panufnik also had no love for a system which he found 'artistically and morally dishonest . . . My musical imagination turned somersaults at the thought of reflecting the "struggle of the people victoriously marching towards socialism" . . .' After the war, Panufnik wanted nothing except to rebuild his country and compose music. But in order to be allowed to do so, he had to join the Union of Polish Composers. And when all Union members were ordered to compete to compose a new 'Song of the United Party', he was forced to do that too: if he refused, he was told, not only would he lose his post, the whole Union would lose the financial support of the state. He wrote a song 'literally in a few minutes, setting the ridiculous text to the first jumble of notes which came into my head. It was rubbish, and I smiled to myself as I sent it off to the adjudicators.' To his eternal embarrassment, he won first prize.[16]

These examples are by no means unusual. By the 1950s, most people in Eastern Europe worked in state jobs, lived in state-owned properties and sent their children to state schools. They depended on the state for health care, and they bought food from state-owned shops. They were understandably cautious about defying the state except in dramatic circumstances. And, much of the time, their circumstances were not dramatic, because in peacetime, most people's circumstances are not dramatic.

In 1947, for example, the Soviet military administrators in East Germany passed order number 90, a regulation governing the activity of publishing houses and printers. In essence, the rule said that every printing press must be licensed and that licensed printing presses could only print books and pamphlets which had been approved and stamped by the official censors. Failure to comply with these simple guidelines did not lead to murder or arrest, but could cause the printer to be fined, or the printing press to be shut down.[17] The order presented the owner of a printing press in Dresden or Leipzig with a very straightforward choice. He could comply with the law, and print only what was permitted. Or he could break the law and lose his printer's licence, and therefore his livelihood. For most people, it just wasn't worth it. For those who had a sick wife, a son in a Soviet camp or an ageing parent to support, the incentive to stay within the law was even higher.

But once the Dresden printer had made that compromise, others would follow. He might dislike communist ideology, but when presented with the collected works of Stalin, he would agree to print them. He might dislike communist economics, but when presented with a Marxist textbook, he'd probably go ahead and print that too. Why not? There were no consequences: no one would be hurt or go to jail. But if he said no, then he and his family could have real problems, and someone else would soon print it in any case.

Meanwhile, all across East Germany, other owners of other printing presses were making the same decisions. After a while – with no one being shot and no one going to prison and no one even suffering any particular pangs of conscience – the only books left to read were the ones approved by the authorities. After a little more time had passed, there were no private printing presses any more either. None of the printers involved would necessarily have considered himself a collaborator, let alone a communist. And yet every one of them had somehow contributed to the creation of totalitarianism. So did everyone who endured a university course in Marxism-Leninism in order to become a doctor or an engineer; everyone who joined an artists' union in order to become a painter; everyone who put a portrait of Bierut in his office, in order to keep his job; and, of course, everyone who joined the crowd in singing 'the party, the party, the party is always right'.

The experience of living in a society which forced everyone to sound enthusiastic all of the time, and which forced many people to say and do things they didn't believe in, eventually had profound psychological consequences. Despite all of the state's efforts, despite the education and the propaganda, many people retained an inner sense of disjunction or discomfort. 'I was shouting from a tribune at some university meeting in Wrocław, and simultaneously felt panicked at the thought of myself shouting . . . I told myself I was trying to convince [the crowd] by shouting, but in reality I was trying to convince myself,' remembered the writer Jacek Trznadel.[18] Panufnik, the composer, agonized over how and what to write – he couldn't bear the 'nineteenth-century musical language' which the regime preferred, but did not want to be accused of 'professing the art of the rotten West' either, especially after his daughter was born. He sought refuge in the restoration of old Polish music from the sixteenth and seventeenth centuries: 'Thus I could help to reconstruct a small part of our missing inheritance, working more as a scholar than as a composer.'[19] If the genius of Soviet totalitarianism was its ability to get people to conform, this was its fatal flaw: the need to conform to a mendacious political reality left many people haunted by the sense that they were leading double lives.

Lily Hajdú-Gimes, a trained Freudian psychoanalyst, was perhaps the first to diagnose this as a problem in patients, as well as in herself. 'I play the game which is offered by the regime,' she told friends, 'though as soon as you accept that rule you are in a trap.' Hajdú was a member of Hungary's Association of Psychoanalysts, a once influential and largely Jewish community which had been decimated by the war. Determined to regroup and reintegrate, the Association had begun to hold bi-weekly meetings in March 1945, and a number of its members, including Hajdú, had joined the communist party. A few made intellectual efforts to reconcile Freud with Marxism, by examining, for example, the role of economic insecurity in the development of neurosis. The new Ministry of Health permitted the group to open two consulting rooms, and several joined university medical schools, hoping eventually to have their speciality recognized with its own department. Hajdú eventually went to work in the main state psychiatric hospital.

This brief rebirth ended quickly. Freudian psychoanalysis had long been taboo in the Soviet Union – it was too focused on the individual, too accepting of irrational and subconscious behaviour, and too uninterested in politics – and so it would have to be banned in Hungary as well. Attacks against the group began in 1948, following the publication of a vicious scholarly article entitled 'Freudianism as the Domestic Psychology of Imperialism'. Once that had appeared, others began to use words like 'bourgeois-feudalist', 'anti-social' and 'irrationalist' to describe the profession too.[20] The philosopher György

Lukács called analysts 'reactionaries' who longed for Anglo-American class dictatorship.[21]

Some psychoanalysts quit the profession altogether. Others sought a middle ground. In an attempt to reconcile themselves to the new order, Hajdú and a colleague, Imre Hermann, went beyond their previous attempts at reconciliation and wrote a letter to Lukács agreeing with some of his criticism – 'imperialists in their own countries try to make use of psychoanalysis for their own purposes' – but objecting to the latent anti-semitism in some of the attacks.[22] They received a stinging rebuke: 'I would urgently request you, comrades, not to divert important ideological debates to the roadside of common demagoguery.' Frightened, the Association voluntarily dissolved itself in 1949. Hajdú and Hermann signed a declaration that 'psychoanalysis is the product of decaying capitalism and anti-state ideology'. Books by Freud, Adler and Jung were banned, Hermann was expelled from his university post and several analysts were arrested.[23]

After that, Hungarian psychiatrists followed Soviet practice, which mostly relied on the cruder methods of electroshock and insulin therapy – also popular in much of the West, of course – and whose primary goal was to persuade people to conform. One analyst who was in training at this time remembered that 'exhaustion' was one of the main postwar diagnoses, and medically induced sleep one of the main forms of therapy: 'Even people who were traumatized because of the concentration camps or the Holocaust were not diagnosed as such ... there was no talk of trauma, there was a denial because psychoanalysts themselves were in denial.' He thought Hajdú, one of his teachers, had also been in denial about her own tragic past. Though she had lost her husband in the Holocaust, she never mentioned it.[24]

She may have been in denial in other ways too. For Hajdú, Hermann and a few other dedicated Freudians continued to practise their true profession in secret. Hajdú saw patients at home, and even conducted Freudian training sessions in private apartments. In public she accepted the official view of the human psyche as innately conformist. In private, she listened as patients, including Holocaust survivors and children of imprisoned or executed communists, described their very individual and very unique personal demons. One such patient later remembered the experience of psychoanalysis in 1948 Budapest as very strange, since honesty in that period could be dangerous: 'I told the whole truth . . . I was also under threat as I was analysed. I asked myself: Did he know that? Could I rely on him? Would he give me away?' The position of the analyst was no less precarious. After one of Imre Hermann's patients was sentenced to death during the Rajk trial, he himself was suddenly endangered: if his client mentioned his name, he could be arrested.[25] For Hajdú, the strain of living such a life eventually proved too much, especially after the regime executed her son following the 1956 revolution. In 1960 she killed herself.[26]

Hajdú's double life was particularly traumatic, but it was not unique. Antoni Rajkiewicz fought with the 'peasants' battalion' of the Home Army during the war, joined the party afterwards, quit in disgust in 1946 and was briefly arrested in 1948. But he was also intelligent and ambitious, he wanted to get a doctorate at one of the most prestigious universities, the School of Central Planning and Statistics, and he wanted to make some positive contribution to his country's development. He reckoned he could accept some of the party's ideas – the emphasis on education and scientific progress, for example – even though he rejected others. Besides, there were no other options. He applied and was accepted. He studied with several Russian professors who had been imported to explain central planning to the Poles, using textbooks translated from Russian. He rejoined the party and also began, in his own words, to live a double life: 'You had to behave differently, speak differently, at official meetings and party meetings, and differently among your friends.'[27]

Rajkiewicz, like many young party members, stayed in touch with his friends from the Home Army and freely discussed politics with them. At the same time, he was careful about what he said when at the university. No one gave him instructions, but 'it was possible to intuit, from newspapers like *Trybuna Ludu*, what would be allowed and what would not'. Rajkiewicz was never ignorant of the flaws in the system, and he was not blind to its injustices. But he saw no other way to study, work and live in communist Poland. Like Wanda Telakowska, he was a positivist who believed in pragmatic solutions and in getting on with things. His 'double life' persisted until Stalin's death, when the circle of people with whom one could speak honestly grew wider.

For Rajkiewicz, the split was between his friends and his professional life. For Jacek Fedorowicz, later an actor and cabaret artist, the split was between home and school. Fedorowicz intuitively understood, even as a child, that there were things he was allowed to say in his house which could not be repeated at school. As a contemporary of his notes, 'it seems curious how quickly we learned this code, even in primary school, with almost zero knowledge of politics ... we knew exactly what could be said in different settings, at school, among close friends and not so close, at home and on holiday'.[28] Like Rajkiewicz, Fedorowicz came from a Home Army family and his father was refused permission to work in Gdańsk, forcing the family to move. His parents reinforced his childish impression of the different rules – even the different definitions of words – which applied at home and at school. Once, when told to take the scouting oath, he went home and asked his mother whether it was right to swear allegiance to 'democracy', if 'democracy' had been brought to Poland by the Russians. She explained to him that there were two kinds of democracy: 'real' democracy and 'Soviet' democracy. He should admire the former and keep his distance from the latter.

Fedorowicz also picked up clues from children's books and magazines – clues which had been placed there, unwittingly, by their authors. He was particularly addicted to a children's magazine called *Świat Przygód* (*The World of Adventure*), which he liked to read because it contained comic strips. But at a certain point, the magazine changed its name to *Świat Młodych* (*The World of Youth*), ceased to be interesting and stopped printing comic strips. (Presumably comic strips, as a capitalist invention, were deemed ideologically incorrect.) But as the official world became more boring, he felt an ever greater internal distance from school and an ever greater disinclination to speak honestly when he was there.

Fedorowicz did have some teachers who also kept their distance from the regime – he remembered one who would carefully explain that 'Marxists think like this' while 'we think like that'. Years later, he reckoned that almost everyone had overrated the effectiveness of communist propaganda and as a result overestimated the number of people who supported the system. But like Lily Hajdú he also thought it impossible to live in a communist country and not somehow be touched or deformed by the system: tiny compromises, whether the mumbling of a song or the signing of a peace petition, were impossible to avoid.[29]

If anything, the childhood experiences of Karol Modzelewski were even more contradictory and confusing. Modzelewski was born in Russia, the son of a Russian officer and his Polish communist wife. Three weeks after his birth in 1937, his father was arrested, and he was sent to a Russian orphanage, where he lived for several years. But he was removed from the orphanage after his mother remarried. Karol's new stepfather was Zygmunt Modzelewski, a communist who was the Polish ambassador to the USSR in 1945–7, and later Polish Minister of Foreign Affairs. Modzelewski learned of his biological father's arrest only in 1954 – by accident, from a schoolmate – when he was seventeen years old, and only then did he discuss the true story of his father's life with his mother.

Years later, he reckoned even that conversation was only possible because Stalin was already dead: 'Before, no one told such things to children – there was always a threat that the child would let out the secret. It was dangerous for the child but also for the parents.' Modzelewski's wife had been expelled from kindergarten at the age of three after Stalin's death because she told her teacher, 'My grandfather says Stalin is already burning in hell.' The teacher sent her home, not as punishment but because the danger to the grandfather and to the school was so great.

So carefully did his parents shield Modzelewski from their own growing doubts about the Polish political system that as a child he was terrified by their occasionally critical comments. After the arrest of General Wacław Komar in 1952, in connection with the show trials of the time, he explained to his father, echoing his schoolteachers, that Komar was a spy: 'My father shouted at me . . . he never cursed me so much as then. I said that he had been arrested. My father replied, "Arrested does not equal guilty." It was a banal truth but at that time I felt it like an earthquake. If he was right, it meant that the authorities are arresting innocent citizens. Who could say this? Only an enemy . . .'

He drew similar conclusions after he once asked about a change to the food rationing system. His father snapped, 'It is so that people eat less and work more.' Modzelewski was shocked: 'only the enemy could say something like that ... I remember that because it was a tremendous stress at the time, I had to deny it somehow in order to decrease the dissonance ... I did not recognize him as the enemy but he was speaking like one. I remember that feeling even today after all those years that have passed.'[30]

The Modzelewskis were not alone in dealing with difficult information by keeping silent. Krzysztof Pomian, another scion of a communist family, remembered that 'it was simply not done to speak about arrests, they were accepted without comment. And since this wasn't a topic for discussion, it wasn't a topic for reflection either.' In 1952, he and a Jewish friend sat together and read accounts of the show trials in Prague. The friend asked him what he thought of the Slánský trial and Pomian replied that he didn't think anything of it: 'It's just another trial.' The friend exploded: 'You don't see that this is an anti-semitic story?' That was his first conversation with anyone about any of the trials, and it did make him think for the first time too.[31]

Feelings of divided loyalty haunted some who were even closer to the centres of power. Jerzy Morawski, a Union of Polish Youth leader at the time, didn't doubt in retrospect his own youthful enthusiasm for the communist cause, even in the Stalinist 1950s. But even then he knew that party meetings were, to put it bluntly, boring: 'It was all stiff, all of that. And there was an enormous amount of intolerance. Everyone was supposed to agree. Everybody was supposed to think identically, act identically ... that stiffness destroyed the enthusiasm.'

Later, Morawski became a leading propaganda bureaucrat; more precisely, he was the man who decided which Stalinist slogans would be used in public spaces. But even in this position of high authority, he had mixed feelings about this work: 'Something inside me always said that this is not right, it's aesthetically unappealing ... but on the other hand, that's how we win people over.'[32] This may not be an entirely honest recollection – of course, it's easy in retrospect to say that one was uncomfortable – but the problem of divided feelings was acknowledged by others, even at the time. 'People have become cunning after twelve years of the Nazi regime,' one Leipzig professor told a party acquaintance: 'if they suspect that a certain person has anything to do with state power – and this applies to members of the Party as well – they shut their mouths.'[33]

Splitting one's personality into home and school, friends and work, private and public, was one way to cope with the requirement to collaborate. Others tried what Iván Vitányi called 'a brainwashing made by myself'. This wasn't quite the same as Oskar Nerlinger's determined effort to transform himself from an abstract painter into a socialist realist, but something more like self-silencing. After the war, Vitányi had been an enthusiastic activist at one of the People's Colleges in Budapest, and an avid student of peasant music and folk dancing. But after objecting to the removal of the Nékosz leadership in 1948, he was expelled from his college and given an internal party trial. He was not, in the end, expelled from the party. But the Rajk affair had begun and a sense of menace had crept into the media. Although he was himself a member of the regime, having taken a job at the Ministry of Culture, he decided, in his own words, 'I shall not think and I shall not deal with the country. I don't know anything, I don't want to know. I want to do my work.'

From having been a talkative and even argumentative young man, he became silent. And although he agreed years later that one could debate about whether this 'self-brainwashing' was a good tactic or not, 'I survived.' He behaved as he knew he should in public. He kept his thoughts to himself. He was not arrested. This, at the time, counted as a major professional success.[34]

Instead of remaining silent, others deliberately chose to forget parts of their biography or to ignore, quite consciously, uncomfortable facts. Those were the tactics deployed by Elfriede Brüning, the East German journalist and novelist who had belonged to the communist party before the war – she had even met Ulbricht as a child – and had been jailed by the Nazis. By the end of the war she was living quietly in the country home of her husband's parents, where she joyfully anticipated the arrival of the Russians and celebrated when they finally came.[35]

After the war's end, Brüning threw herself enthusiastically into the work of the cultural life of communist East Berlin. She joined the Kulturbund and went to work for its weekly publication, *Sonntag*, hoping to become a journalist. In one of her first articles, she described her arrival in Berlin, riding on a truck full of onions and carrots. Arriving in the city, the truck was besieged by beggars and women holding up children: 'One carrot for my child, one carrot!' She handed the article in to her editor, who dismissed it: 'Give that to *Tagesspiegel*,' the West Berlin newspaper, he told her. She looked at him blankly: did he really want her to give it to *Tagesspiegel*? In the East, he explained scornfully, 'We are to radiate optimism.' Her article was too negative, it must show the present as it ought to be, not as it was.

Brüning never considered giving her article to *Tagesspiegel* and never considered working for a Western newspaper either. All of Brüning's friends were staying in the East, and she herself belonged, culturally and intellectually, to the communist movement. And so she convinced herself that 'optimism' was important, and that in any case what mattered were communism's ultimate goals, not the mistakes made along the way. She disliked many things about the new system: 'the personality cult of Stalin . . . the ridiculous banners everywhere . . . slogans like "Every artificially inseminated pig is a blow to the face of imperialist warmongers"'.[36] She objected to the ration cards which divided the population into classes, and the system of double canteens at workplaces, 'one with stew for the workers and one [with better food] for the engineers and heads of departments'. But she persevered: 'We were steeped in the wish to help the construction, and to convince people who had believed in Hitler not long ago that we wanted the right thing now.'

In her autobiography, Brüning makes clear that at some level she continued to believe that she had done the right thing. She frequently contrasts the achievements of the East with those of the West: 'Didn't we send workers' children to university? Hadn't we liberated women from their immaturity, given them access to all professions and guaranteed them the same rights as men, including the same wage for the same work – a demand that has not been fulfilled in the Western state until today? We were, that was our belief, the better state . . . we were proud of our alleged independence and thought ourselves to be on the right track.'[37]

Brüning learned to rationalize her choices, to put things into a larger context and to take the long view. But she never convinced herself that black was white, or that there was nothing wrong with the system she had chosen. In 1968, following the Soviet invasion of Czechoslovakia, she briefly considered emigrating, but did not. In time, she grew friendly with Susanne Leonhard, Wolfgang's mother, who had spent many years in the Soviet Gulag but eventually returned to East Berlin. Inspired by Leonhard's life story, she began to interview others who had spent time in the Gulag. After 1989 she published the collected interviews in a book, *Lästige Zeugen* (*Annoying Witnesses*). The words of her preface could be about herself: 'For too long they were forced to remain silent, to conceal ... Therefore, it is high time we let these men and women have their say, they who fell victim to the Stalin era and must finally be granted full justice ...'[38]

In a 2006 interview, I spoke with Brüning for several hours about her life. We talked about her career, the early days of the Kulturbund and her life in East Berlin after the war. Among other things, she told me she had known nothing at the time about mass rapes and theft carried out by the Red Army in 1945, and nothing about the mass arrests that followed. I didn't press. But a few days later, she called back. Yes, she had known about some of these things, she said, and she would like to talk about them. We met for a second time.

It was true, Brüning explained, that she had celebrated the liberation. But her pleasure had quickly faded. In the spring of 1945, Soviet soldiers occupied her parents-in-law's home and began stealing books and other things to sell on the black market. Her husband approached their commander and asked them to stop. In revenge, one of the soldiers planted a pistol in his suitcase. It was 'discovered', and Brüning's husband was arrested as a saboteur. Pleading her long membership in the communist party, she managed to obtain his release. But as a result of this incident, her husband turned on communism (and on her) and emigrated to the West. She never remarried.

It was also true, as Brüning had said in our first conversation, that out in the countryside there were no mass rapes. But after the war, she had visited Berlin to find her parents. Not only had she heard a good deal about rape in the city and met many victims, she spent several days hiding from Soviet soldiers who were looking for women in her parents' neighbourhood.

A few months after that, Brüning spent some time in the seaside town of Ahrenshoop, where the Kulturbund wanted to set up a writers' colony. But in order to have a writers' colony, the Kulturbund had to get hold of somewhere for the writers to stay. To solve that problem, charges were trumped up against the owners of some of the more attractive seaside villas. Those who were not arrested fled to the West. The cultural bureaucrats moved in.

We did hear about these things, Brüning told me, 'but you must understand, I had welcomed the arrival of the Red Army and we wanted to build socialism – well, even today I sometimes reproach myself – we did not inquire closely enough . . .' Her voice trailed off – and that was all. She had just wanted me to know that she knew.

The splitting of one's personality into public and private, home and school, friends and work, was not the only solution for those who wanted to live successful lives in a communist regime. Instead of hiding their mixed feelings, a small and unusual group of people displayed them openly. Instead of feeling conflicted, they tried to play dual roles, staying within the system and maintaining some independence at the same time. This kind of ambiguous role could be played, for example, within the official 'opposition' parties, the phony political parties which had been created to replace the real ones after their leaders had fled or been arrested, parties which were loyal to the regime in every way that mattered. East Germans who remained active within the rump Christian Democratic Party were allowed to be publicly religious, although they were expected to adhere to the principles of Marxism-Leninism at the same time. Poles who remained within the rump Polish Peasants' Party were allowed to be advocates on behalf of farmers, as long as their advocacy didn't come into conflict with official policy.

No one in Eastern Europe ever played this particular game with greater skill than Bolesław Piasecki, a politician whose extraordinary career took him from the radical Right to the radical Left within a decade. Assessments of his life range widely. As early as 1956, Leopold Tyrmand denounced him as a man for whom 'all morality in politics is a harmful myth'.[39] More recently, one of his biographers called him a 'tragic figure'.[40] Judgements of Piasecki fall almost everywhere else in between. To some, his is a classic collaborationist story. To others, his life is a tale of survival.

Piasecki's career began in the turbulent 1930s, when as a very young man he made his name as an activist of a faction of the far-right Polish National Radical Party. Known by the name of their publication, *Falanga* – a clear allusion to Spanish fascism – the Falangists believed that they were living through a time of moral and economic crisis. Like the communist parties of that same era, they also believed that Polish society was deeply corrupt, and that the weaknesses of democracy and the 'nonsense' of democratic liberalism were to blame. But although they were anti-semites, and though they admired authoritarian regimes in general and Italian fascism in particular, the Falangists were Polish nationalists, and thus, with one or two exceptions, they did not collaborate with Hitler.[41]

Piasecki himself was imprisoned by the Gestapo in 1939. Upon his release, he joined the resistance and eventually the Home Army. In the summer of 1944, just as the Warsaw Uprising broke out, he and his partisan unit were captured by the Red Army in the forests to the east of the city. By November, he was imprisoned in the Soviet occupation force's headquarters, probably in the notorious cellars of Lublin castle. What happened next is a matter of no little controversy.

Most of the sources agree that Piasecki held nothing back. He gave the Soviet officers leading his interrogation an accurate account of his career in the resistance. He also gave away the names, and possibly locations, of many of his Home Army colleagues, though by that time much of that information was already known. He hinted heavily at his own importance. He told his Soviet interrogators that he had been in charge of the 'clandestine operations' of the Home Army, and had already been named leader of a new, secret section of the underground. This was an exaggeration. But the tactic paid off.

Piasecki's guards halted his interrogation. They removed him from ordinary military supervision, and took him directly to Ivan Serov, the Soviet general who had organized the 'cleansing' and pacification of eastern Poland in 1939, and who had been brought back to carry out the same task in the rest of Poland in 1944. Serov had already organized the arrests of General Wilk and General Okulicki, and was trying to find out as much as he could about the Home Army. To Piasecki's immense surprise, Serov was not much interested in Piasecki's Falangist past: like most Soviet officials, he considered anyone who was not a communist to be 'far right' by definition, and distinctions between social democrats and radical right-wingers did not concern him. He was far more interested in Piasecki's wartime underground activity, in his alleged 'clandestine' connections, in his political views and in his declared contempt for the London government-in-exile.[42]

By his own account, Piasecki was pleased to discover that he had much in common with the Soviet general. He admired men of power, he was delighted to talk philosophy, and he had some positive things to say about the new regime. He told Serov that he approved of the communist-dominated provisional government and admired the land reform. He enthusiastically endorsed the expulsion of the Germans and the acquisition of the Western territories. He lauded the 'idea of a bloodless social revolution and the transfer of power to workers and peasants'. But he also told Serov that the new communist government was going to have difficulties attracting the loyalty of Poles, with their deep anti-Russian prejudices and their paranoia about occupation. Which, of course, was true.

He offered to help. 'I am deeply convinced,' he told Serov in a memo, 'that through my influence I can mobilize the reluctant strata of society for active cooperation.' He promised, in other words, to persuade the patriotic, nationalist elements of the underground to support the new regime. Piasecki's memo was eventually forwarded to Colonel Roman Romkowski, the secret policeman in charge of counter-intelligence, as well as to Gomułka, then the communist party boss.[43]

In the decades afterwards, this enigmatic conversation – an exchange between a famously cruel NKVD general and a famously charismatic Polish nationalist – attained an almost legendary status in Warsaw. No one knew at the time exactly what had transpired, but everyone had a theory. In 1952, Czesław Miłosz wrote a fictional version of the encounter in *Zdobycie Władzy* (*The Seizure of Power*), a novel he published after emigrating to the West. Of course, Miłosz's account is imaginary. But as one of Piasecki's biographers points out, Miłosz was in Warsaw in 1945, he would have heard accounts of this famous meeting and he had himself been tempted into cooperation with the new regime. His account thus has a ring of authenticity, particularly when Kamienski, the Piasecki figure, warns the Soviet general that 'you are hated here', and tells him to expect resistance:

'Ah,' said the general, leaning his chin on his hands – 'you are counting on internal opposition . . . But conspiracy, in our system, is impossible. You know that. Encouraging more murders will just increase the numbers of victims. We are starting to build trains and factories. We have got back the Western territories, which of course were always Slavic, almost to Berlin – and if I'm not mistaken, that was your pre-war programme. Those territories can only be held with our help. And so?'

Eventually, the general in the novel comes to the point: Kamienski/Piasecki would be set free, even allowed to publish a newspaper, on the condition that he 'recognize the status quo, and help us reduce the number of victims'. Kamienski/Piasecki deliberates, and then agrees. The general, satisfied, leans back and states that he is not surprised:

> 'You have already understood that anyone who wants to change the world can't continue to pay lip service to phony parliamentarianism, and you know that the liberal games of merchants were a short-lived bit of excess in human history.'[44]

Whether or not he used those exact words, archival evidence makes clear that Serov really was impressed by Piasecki, and apparently hoped to jump-start his political career by naming him mayor of Warsaw. (When reminded of Piasecki years later, Serov is said to have asked, 'And so – did he become mayor of Warsaw?')[45] But Serov left soon afterwards for Berlin, along with most of the rest of the Red Army leadership. He never returned to Poland.

That left Piasecki in an odd position. He had clearly obtained a blessing of some kind from the Soviet Union. But Polish communists, who understood the significance of his Falangist past quite well, were more suspicious of him and his motives and did not at first promote his political career; nor did they make him mayor of Warsaw. Still, in November 1945 they allowed him to publish the first edition of communist Poland's first 'official' Catholic newspaper, *Dziś i Jutro* (*Today and Tomorrow*).

From the start, the paper offered harsh criticisms of the then-legal PSL and of its leader, Stanisław Mikołajczyk, and it urged Poles to support the communists in their 'Three Times Yes' referendum. After that referendum had failed to provide a ringing endorsement for the new regime, Piasecki wrote to Gomułka. The current system, he argued, 'should be enriched by the political representation of Catholics'.[46] He also published an interview with Bierut, in which the communist leader declared grandly that 'Polish Catholics have no more and no fewer rights than other citizens' – a comment which implied they might even have a right to their own party. Eventually, this came to pass and in 1952 Piasecki founded Pax, a loyal, legal, pro-communist Catholic 'opposition' party, the only one which would ever be allowed to exist in communist Poland or indeed anywhere else in communist Europe.

Both Pax and Piasecki existed in a strange, undefined and ambiguous political space. On the one hand, Piasecki expressed his loyalty to the regime enthusiastically and often. 'Our main goal,' he wrote at one point, 'is the reconstruction of a Catholic doctrine with respect to the ongoing conflict between Marxism and capitalism.' At the same time, Piasecki was one of the few people in public life who never quite cut himself off from the traditions of the wartime underground, and was never forced to denounce his Home Army comrades. Those in his circle, many of whom had had extensive Home Army careers, never had to renounce their pasts either, and they were never arrested.

All of this was extremely unusual in public life at the time, and it created, in the words of Janusz Zabłocki, one of his former colleagues, 'an enclave of freedom' around Piasecki, as well as an aura of mystery. Nobody quite knew why the leader of Pax was exempt from the rules – at one point he even managed to expel a police informer from his inner circle – but everyone saw that he was. Most assumed that 'there must have been an agreement at the highest political levels' which allowed Piasecki such leeway – presumably an agreement with Soviet officials – and many hoped that his position would grow even stronger. Zabłocki joined the staff of *Dziś i Jutro* under the influence of this belief. So did Tadeusz Mazowiecki, the Catholic intellectual who would become Poland's first non-communist Prime Minister in 1989. Both men reckoned that Pax would sooner or later play an important role in governing the country.[47] Piasecki himself hoped the same.

Throughout his career, Piasecki's ambiguous status made everyone uneasy. Perhaps because he did have a separate relationship with Soviet officials, the Polish communists never trusted him. Although he continued to play their game (at one point he offered to send Pax observers to North Korea, to promote 'peace') the government left him out of the creation of the union of 'patriotic' priests and did not ask him to help negotiate the church–state accord. At the same time, his public Catholicism did not endear him to the church as much as he might have hoped. Cardinal Wyszyński loathed Piasecki, and at one point forbade clergy to subscribe to his publications, which eventually came to include *Słowo Powszechny* (*Universal World*), a daily newspaper, as well as *Dziś i Jutro*. Wyszyński was particularly infuriated by Piasecki's management of Caritas, the Catholic charity – Pax took it over after the real organizers were removed – especially when unscrupulous Pax priests were caught selling donated penicillin on the black market.[48] The rivalry between the two men may well have been encouraged by the communist party, of course, which had no interest in seeing Pax and the church create a united front. In later years the party allowed rival 'official' church groups to proliferate precisely in order to create competition among them.[49]

In the end, Piasecki failed in what he apparently set out to do. He never did persuade 'reactionary forces' to join the new system. Nor did he persuade the communist party to make Pax an equal partner. He guessed, correctly, that someday the party would hand over power to an opposition grouping of its choice, which is indeed what happened in 1989. But he appeared on the scene too early to take advantage of such a situation himself, and he paid a very high price for trying. In 1957, his teenage son, Bohdan, was kidnapped and murdered, probably by a faction within the Polish secret police, in circumstances that remain murky to this day.

Piasecki did open what seemed, at the time, to be a window of freedom for a few people, and he did ensure that an avowedly Catholic discourse remained part of public life. The books and newspapers published by Pax provided some Catholic education for a generation of readers. More importantly, from Piasecki's point of view, he survived. At a time when other ex-Home Army officers were dead or in prison, he and his colleagues had their own party, their own newspapers, a stable position within the system. And they had influence in all kinds of places. In 1955, Mazowiecki, Zabłocki and several others rebelled against his leadership. But after they quit their jobs at *Dziś i*

Jutro or Pax, all of them found it difficult to get new jobs elsewhere: every potential employer was warned off by the secret police, and no one wanted them around. All learned a lesson: a fight with Piasecki was dangerously close to a fight with the regime.[50]

Odd though it may sound, newspapers and magazines also provided a way out for reluctant collaborators. Of course, those who wrote about politics had few options in this era. They had to accept the telephone calls from the party brass, listen to instructions and write as they were told. But others had more leeway. Leopold Unger, a correspondent for *Życie Warszawy* (*Warsaw Life*) in the early 1950s, remembered that even then it was possible to write freely and critically about all kinds of things. The potholes in the streets, for example, or the lack of public buses: 'it just wasn't possible to criticize the system itself'.[51]

Newspapers were not all about politics, even then, and there were other kinds of publications as well. Alexander Jackowski, after trying and failing to find his way in Poland's Foreign Affairs Ministry in the late 1940s, began editing a folk art journal in 1952 'by accident', as he recalled. He kept that job for forty-six years. During that period, he became a renowned expert in the subject of folk art, which he genuinely came to know and love. He didn't challenge the system in that job, but nor did he spend any time defending it.[52]

At some level, the regimes themselves understood the need for apolitical outlets, both for the reading public and for journalists. That's the best explanation for the East German regime's decision to begin publishing the *Wochenpost* (*The Weekly Post*) in the autumn of 1953. Although the first issue appeared after Stalin's death, plans for the newspaper had been laid a year earlier. Originally, the idea was Soviet: a senior Red Army general stationed in Berlin felt the East German press was not succeeding in reaching the entire population, especially women. The general approached Rudi Wetzel, a journalist then out of favour with the regime, and asked him for some ideas. Wetzel made a proposal which seemed to come to nothing.

But behind the scenes a discussion had been sparked. Official reports bewailed the 'colourlessness and uniformity of material about life in the republic', as well as the absence of articles on 'gardening, medicine, housework'.[53] The East German leadership, ever conscious of how boring its propaganda could be, finally approached Wetzel and proposed that he start a magazine. Their suggestions were identical to those Wetzel himself had made to the Soviet general. And thus the *Wochenpost* was born.

From the start, the newspaper tried to be different. Wetzel went out of his way to find journalists who were ambivalent about the regime, at one point even describing the first editorial board as a 'journalistic penal colony, full of ex-convicts'. Their articles, at least by comparison to the political tracts found in *Neues Deutschland*, seemed remarkably fresh and entertaining. The first issue, published in time for Christmas, contained gardening hints, light features and a 'womens' page'. The cover showed a child blowing out a candle, and the words 'To all who are of goodwill'. Later issues would feature travel writing, long pieces of reportage, even articles for children. But the *Wochenpost* never tried to become an opposition newspaper, in any sense of the term, and this may have been part of its appeal. As the journalist Klaus Polkehn has argued, the *Wochenpost* was 'no more opportunistic than its readers'.[54] The newspaper didn't push the limits, and neither did they.

Polkehn would have known both his colleagues and his audience very well, since he worked at the *Wochenpost* from the very beginning until almost the very end. Many years later he was still nostalgic about his career there, and it isn't hard to see why. Polkehn was aged fourteen at the end of the war, and aged seventeen when he left school to become a typesetter at a newspaper. He was encouraged in these choices by his father, Hugo Polkehn, a communist and journalist who thought his son should 'get experience in real life'. After the war, Polkehn senior became editor of *Tribune*, the East German trade union newspaper. But in March 1953 he was suddenly arrested: *Tribune* had made a typesetting mistake in Stalin's obituary. Instead of writing 'Stalin was a great friend of peace' a typesetter accidentally set 'Stalin was a great friend of war.' Both Hugo Polkehn and the typesetter were sentenced to five years in prison, of which they would serve three. At the time of the trial Klaus Polkehn lost his job, and was told he would 'never work again as a journalist'. The *Wochenpost* hired him right away.

For the subsequent four decades, Polkehn remained loyal to the newspaper which had given him this second chance. He maintained, until the end, that it had also allowed him an extraordinary amount of freedom within an extraordinarily constrained system. Because of his father, and because he was in any case dubious about many aspects of the regime, he stayed well away from domestic politics. Instead, he became the magazine's travel writer, eventually filing stories from all over the world. Polkehn was allowed to go everywhere, so long as he stayed within certain boundaries. Before he went to Egypt, for example, he was told not to write critically about Anwar Sadat, who was then exporting a lot of cotton to East Germany. But in Cairo, 'I got a whole day at the pyramids . . . that was my privilege.' At a time when few East Germans could travel at all, that was a great privilege indeed.

There was a price to pay for that kind of freedom. Polkehn, like the other *Wochenpost* journalists, had to learn to read between the lines, to follow the political signals, and above all not to cause 'trouble'. When I asked him what 'trouble' meant, he explained that it would begin with a phone call from someone on the communist party Central Committee, berating you for crossing the invisible lines. Trouble could continue with a reprimand, a meeting, maybe being fired from an excellent job at a relatively open-minded newspaper. Polkehn sought to avoid this at all costs. Only once, when he had violated an unwritten code and written something which crossed one of the invisible lines, did he get the telephone call, and a request: 'Please give a written statement, explaining why this article was published.' That was enough for him to make sure it never happened again.

He was aware, even then, that he was lucky and that others resented him. He sometimes had letters from readers: 'As long as we can't travel, we don't want to read your articles either.' Many of his compatriots were wary of journalists in general – they were seen as a part of the communist establishment – and would refuse to be interviewed. But he brushed away the idea that he might have taken part in more open dissent: 'It seemed pointless to me.' He disliked the dissidents who later became part of East Germany's political scene, finding them 'conceited, indecent people'. He suspected that some of them adopted their pose of opposition in order to secure an exit visa to West Germany.

Polkehn did contract ulcers, which mysteriously disappeared in the 1990s, after both the *Wochenpost* and East Germany had ceased to exist. Perhaps this was not surprising: his life required him to walk a kind of political tightrope, keeping away from all sensitive subjects while producing articles which he believed had integrity. But he felt pride in his work, even years later. He loved writing, he loved travelling, and there were modest material advantages as well as intellectual pleasures. His job at the *Wochenpost* was relatively well-paid, by East German standards. There were two holiday homes, one near Berlin and one by the Baltic Sea, which the journalists were allowed to use every third or fourth year. The newsroom also had access to a tailor's shop and a cobbler as well as a dentist: 'it saved time. He was very good.' As at almost every workplace in East Germany, there was a very cheap canteen for meals.

Polkehn didn't change anything about the system he lived in, but nor did he feel responsible for its more brutal aspects. He kept well away from the secret police, well away from those in power and well away from controversy. Like Piasecki, he prospered, flourished and remained nostalgic for his years as a travel writer. 'It was my dream job,' he told me.[55]

17

Passive opponents

The time had now come when we must listen with devoted
expressions to Soviet orders, smiling only with the wrinkles in
our bottoms, under our trousers, as did the lackeys of the Byz-
antine emperors. Heroic gestures would be of no avail; we
would have to speak the language of flowers, be patient and
cunning, as we had been under Hitler. The essential thing was
to survive.

György Faludy, paraphrasing Jan Masaryk, 1946[1]

A thing is funny when it upsets the established order. Every
joke is a tiny revolution.

George Orwell

By the year 1950 or 1951, it was no longer possible to identify anything so coherent as a political opposition anywhere in Eastern
Europe. There were a few Poles who kept their pistols hidden in the
barn, waiting for a better day, and one or two still hiding in the forests. There were some officially tolerated regime opponents like
Bolesław Piasecki, whose real views were opaque. There were a few
people who were able to criticize the regime's less important decisions
in public, and were even encouraged to do so, as long as they kept the
right tone. As Bierut had declared, 'there are different kinds of criticism. There is creative criticism and hostile criticism. The first is
helpful to our development, the second is an obstacle ... criticism
shouldn't undermine the authority of the leader ...'[2]

But the remaining Polish Home Army leaders were in prison or in the Soviet Gulag. The Hungarian regime's most powerful opponents were imprisoned in Recsk. East Germany's critics had left or fallen silent. The public sphere had been cleansed so thoroughly that a tourist visiting Warsaw, Budapest or East Berlin – or Prague, Sofia or Bucharest – in the early 1950s would have observed no political opposition whatsoever. The press contained regime propaganda. Holidays were celebrated with regime parades. Conversations did not deviate from the official line if an outsider was present.

The tourist might even have assumed that all were united in support of the regime, and various distinguished visitors did indeed form that impression. Upon returning from Warsaw in 1950, one British socialist, the wife of a Labour MP, told a crowd at Trafalagar Square she had seen 'no signs of dictatorship' in Poland. On the contrary, she declared, the only 'iron curtain' in existence was the one around Great Britain (the British government had just refused visas to Eastern European delegates who had wanted to attend a world peace conference in Sheffield).[3] One of her compatriots, equally impressed with her visit to the East, said that to be in Warsaw was 'like changing worlds, like stepping into the sun after being in the rain'.[4] Though these were extreme views, they reflected a broader prejudice. The Western notion that the Eastern bloc contained an undifferentiated group of countries with identical regimes and indistinguishable people – 'Siberia starts at Checkpoint Charlie' – dates precisely from this era.

And yet there was opposition. But it was not an active opposition, and certainly not an armed opposition. It was rather a passive opposition, an opposition which sought outlets in jokes, graffiti and unsigned letters, an opposition which was often anonymous and frequently ambivalent. It existed in all classes and among all ages. Sometimes the regime's passive opponents and reluctant collaborators were actually one and the same. Many people felt embarrassed or ashamed by the things they had to do in order to keep their jobs, protect their families and stay out of jail. Others were appalled by the hypocrisy of public life, bored by the peace demonstrations and parades which impressed outsiders. They were stultified by the dull meetings and the empty slogans, uninterested in the leader's speeches and the endless lectures. Unable to do anything about it openly, they got their revenge behind the party's back.

*

Not by accident were young people the most enthusiastic of the passive resisters to High Stalinism, if 'enthusiasm' is a word which can be used in this context. They were the focus of the heaviest, most concentrated and most strictly enforced propaganda, which they heard at school and in their youth groups. They bore the brunt of the regime's various campaigns and obsessions, they were sent round to collect the subscription money, gather signatures and organize rallies. At the same time, they were less cowed by the horrors of a war which they didn't necessarily remember, and less intimidated by the prospect of prison, which they had yet to experience.

As a result, examples of low-level opposition among young people abound. Organized protest was relatively uncommon but it was not unknown, and young people sometimes paid a high price to join it. In 1950, Edeltraude Eckert was arrested aged twenty for distributing pro-democracy leaflets. She received a twenty-five-year prison sentence, which became a death sentence after an accident in an East German prison factory led to an infection which killed her. From her cell, and then from her hospital bed, she sent hopeful, optimistic notes home. 'The world is so beautiful you just have to believe in it,' she wrote to her mother, a few months before her death.[5]

Jokes, insults and tricks, often aimed at the sombre and humourless youth leaders, were much more common, and there are dozens of examples from the late 1940s and early 1950s. At an election in one of the youth group cells in a Polish mining town, for example, someone wrote in 'Adenauer' – then the Chancellor of West Germany – as a joke candidate. The ballot was treated as evidence of 'enemy tendencies', and an investigation was conducted into the identity of the author. In a youth workers' brigade, another young man was reprimanded for composing rhyming couplets. One of the few obscenity-free verses read like this:

> Cleanliness prevails in the camp
> When you want to wash yourself there is not a drop of water
> But someone can weep tears over you.[6]

At times these things were taken extremely seriously. Between 1948 and 1951 alone, some 300 East German high school and university students were arrested and sentenced to hard labour, many for similar pranks. A group of young boys in Jena received ten years apiece for throwing stink bombs at school officials during a formal celebration of President Wilhelm Pieck's birthday. By 1950, East German camps and jails held 800 boys and girls under the age of seventeen. Some were being held for having made faces during a lecture about Stalin, or for having scribbled an 'F' (for *Freiheit*, or freedom) on city walls at night.[7]

But young people also had some less verbal forms of protest available to them. Just as Western teenagers were beginning to discover that long hair and blue jeans could be an enormously effective means of registering discontent, East European teenagers living under Stalinist regimes discovered that narrow trousers, shoulder pads, red socks and jazz could be a form of protest too. In different countries, these early 'youth rebel' subcultures had different names. In Poland, they were called *bikiniarze*, possibly after the Pacific atoll where the United States tested the first atomic bomb – or, more likely, the Hawaiian/Pacific/Bikini-themed ties which some of the truly hip *bikiniarze* managed to obtain from the care packages sent by the United Nations and other relief organizations. (The truly lucky also got hold of *makarturki*, sunglasses of the kind General MacArthur wore.) In Hungary, they were called the *jampecek*, a word which roughly translates as 'spivs'. In Germany – both East and West – they were the *Halbstarke*, or 'half-strong'. There was a Czech version – the *potapka*, or duck – probably named after the ducktail hairstyle, and even a Romanian version, the *malagambisti*, named after a famously cool Romanian drummer, Sergiu Malagamba.[8]

The fashions adopted by these youth rebels varied slightly from country to country as well, depending on what was actually available in flea markets or from those Western care packages, and what could be made from scratch. Generally speaking, the boys favoured narrow, drainpipe trousers (in Warsaw there was a tailor who specialized in making them out of ordinary ones). The girls at first wore tight pencil skirts, though later they switched to the 'New Look' then being sold by Christian Dior and copied everywhere else: dresses with small waists and wide skirts, preferably in loud colours and patterns. Both favoured shoes with thick rubber soles – a distant echo of the American sneaker – which in Hungary came to be called *jampi* shoes. Brightly coloured shirts were popular too, since they contrasted so starkly with the conformist uniforms of the communist youth movements, as were wide ties, often hand-painted. The idea was that shirts and ties should clash. Particularly popular was the combination of a green tie and a yellow shirt, known in Polish as 'chives on scrambled egg'. In Warsaw, Leopold Tyrmand popularized the wearing of striped socks as well. He did so, he once said, to demonstrate 'the right to one's own taste'.[9] He maintained some ironic distance from the *bikiniarze*, who mostly belonged to a younger generation, though in general he approved:

> Certainly this was a poor, unwashed, provincial Polish version of the 'jitterbug' style . . . it provoked a certain amount of disdain even among those who didn't fight it, but it also inspired respect for its tenacity, for its battle against the arch-powerful officialdom, for the challenge it threw down to the greyness and total poverty all around.[10]

As in the West, the clothes were associated with music. Like their West European counterparts, the *bikiniarze*, the *jampecek* and the others started out as jazz fans, despite – or thanks to – the young communists who went around smashing up jazz records. Once it had been forbidden, jazz music became politicized. Even to listen to jazz on the radio became a political activity: to twiddle the dials of one's father's radio in an attempt to catch different stations through the static became a form of surrogate dissent. Radio Luxemburg was weirdly popular, as were the jazz programmes on Voice of America later on. This would remain a dissident activity until the communist regimes collapsed forty years later.

In their clothes and in their music, the youth rebels of Poland or East Germany had a lot in common with American rockers and zoot suiters, as well as British Teddy boys. But because of the nature of their regimes, their fashion choices had a much deeper political significance than they would have done in the West. From the authorities' point of view, these young hipsters were by definition implicated in black market trading. How else could they have obtained such unusual clothes? They were also by definition admirers of American-style consumerism. Like Western teenagers, they wanted possessions. In particular, they wanted possessions which the communist system could not provide, and they went out of their way to get them. One former Hungarian *jampecek* remembered the lengths to which he went to get hold of the thick-soled shoes:

'There were dealers in the southern district, three of them. I don't know their names, Frici somebody-or-other, they brought the stuff in. I think from Yugoslavia or the South . . . It was a big thing that you could buy it on the side, in instalments. You had to have connections to get hold of it . . . People envied each other for where they'd bought stuff . . .'[11]

The regime also suspected that admiration for Western fashions implied an admiration for Western politics. Very quickly, the press began to accuse the youth rebels not just of non-conformism, but of propagating degenerate American culture, of plotting to undermine communist values, even of taking orders from the West. At times the youth rebels were called saboteurs, or even spies. Perversely, this kind of propaganda had the effect of making these inchoate groups seem, and eventually become, more powerful and more important than they might have been otherwise. One Polish newspaper described American pop culture as 'a cult of fame and luxury, the acceptance and glorification of the most primitive desires, the filling of a hunger for sensation'.[12] Other official media equated the *bikiniarze* with 'speculators, kulaks, hooligans and reactionaries'.[13] Jacek Kuroń reckoned that this sort of language actually drew young people to jazz, to 'Western' dancing, and to more exotic forms of dress. He argued that the *bikiniarze* became a genuine counter-cultural movement only after the press began to rail against them: 'They were told, "You are *bikiniarze*", and they responded, "We are *bikiniarze*." And that gave them the political programme that they'd been missing.'[14]

Sándor Horváth, a Hungarian historian who has studied the *jampecek* movement in depth, argues along similar lines that the Hungarian youth subculture was created by newspaper propaganda and not vice versa. In addition, he speculates that the crusade against the *jampecek* was probably inspired by the Soviet drive against 'hooliganism' which took place at the same time. He even questions whether the *jampecek* really existed, in the beginning – or whether the communist authorities, needing something against which to define themselves, had in fact invented them, deriving their description from the 'Westerns, gangster films, dime novels and comic books' which made their way across the Hungarian border. In order to promote the character of a 'good' communist they needed 'bad' capitalists, and the *jampecek* fitted the bill.[15]

Once they had been defined as outlaws, these fashionable groups began to attract people who really were looking for a fight. In Poland, there were frequent, serious squabbles between *bikiniarze* and *zetempowcy* (a nickname derived from the Polish acronym of the Union of Polish Youth, ZMP), as well as between the *bikiniarze* and the police. In 1951, a group of young people from a Warsaw suburb went on trial for alleged armed robbery. *Sztandar Młodych*, the official youth newspaper, described them as 'young bandits serving American imperialism', and claimed they had been dressed in the characteristic narrow trousers and thick-soled shoes. One young communist activist wrote in to *Sztandar Młodych* to complain that he too had been convinced that 'admirers of the American lifestyle are hostile to People's Poland' after having been beaten up by a group of young 'hooligans', dressed as *bikiniarze*. He had been wearing his red Union of Polish Youth tie. Krzysztof Pomian, at the time a Union of Polish Youth leader in Warsaw, was also once attacked in a park and beaten up by people he never saw. A schoolmate was arrested for the crime, but later freed.[16]

The reverse was also true. Young communists, sometimes in tandem with the police, hunted *bikiniarze* in the streets: they would catch them, beat them up, cut their hair and slash their ties. More than one 'official' youth dance party was ruined when *bikiniarze* began to dance 'in the style' – meaning the jitterbug – after which they were beaten up by their 'offended' peers.[17] Kuroń himself remembers being told by a local party secretary that since the '*bikiniarze* and the hooligans' hadn't been persuaded by the press, the radio, and the comic caricatures of themselves in posters and books it was time to get a group of young, healthy workers and go after them: 'From that moment, whenever *bikiniarze* jumped onto the dance floor, the young communists hauled them off and beat them up.'[18] Similar situations occurred in Hungary too.

In East Germany, the problem of youthful rebellion was made more acute by the undeniable influence of American radio, which was available not just on crackly, distant Radio Luxemburg but right next door on RIAS, 'Radio in the American Sector', which was broadcast directly from West Berlin. West German sheet music was also available for dance bands, and to the great consternation of the regime it was very popular. At a German composers' conference in 1951, an East German musicologist denounced this 'American entertainment kitsch' as a 'channel through which the poison of Americanism penetrates and threatens to anaesthetize the minds of workers'. The threat from jazz, swing and big band music was 'just as dangerous as a military attack with poison gases', since it reflected:

> the degenerate ideology of American monopoly capital with its lack of culture . . . its empty sensationalism and above all its fury for war and destruction . . . We should speak plainly here of a fifth column of Americanism. It would be wrong to misjudge the dangerous role of American hit music in the preparation for war.[19]

In the wake of this conference, the East German state took active measures to fight against this new scourge. Around the country, regional governments began to force dance bands and musicians to obtain licences. Some banned jazz outright. Though the enforcement was irregular, there were arrests. The writer Erich Loest remembered one jazz musician who, when told to change his music selection, pointed out that he was playing the music of the oppressed Negro minority. He was arrested anyway, and went to prison for two years.[20]

The regime also sought alternatives, though tentatively. Nobody was quite sure what progressive dance music was supposed to sound like, after all, or where it was supposed to be played. At the German Academy of Art, a learned commission of musicologists came together to discuss the 'role of dance music in our society'. They agreed that 'dance music must be purposeful music', which meant it should be only for dancing. But those present could not agree on whether dance music should be played on the radio – 'merely listening to dance music is impossible, the listener will forget what its purpose was supposed to be' – and they feared young people would ask for 'boogie-woogie' instead of 'real' dance music anyway.[21]

In May 1952, the Culture Ministry tried to solve this problem with a competition and prizes to be given to composers of 'new German dance music'. The competition failed, as none of the entries were deemed sufficiently attractive by a committee which was probably looking for a modern version of Strauss's Vienna waltzes. As the new 'Dance Commission' of the Central Committee complained, much of the work submitted was based on unprogressive, uneducational themes such as sentimental love, nostalgia or pure escapism. One song about Hawaii, the committee declared, could just as well be set in Lübeck.

Much of the time, young East Germans responded to this sort of thing with howls of laughter. Some bands openly mocked letters they had received from party officials and read them aloud to audiences. Others simply flouted the rules. One shocked official wrote a report describing the 'wild cascades of sound at high volume' and the 'wild bodily dislocations' he'd heard and seen at one concert. Inevitably, there were escapes as well. One band, a particularly notable 'propagandist for American unculture', caused a sensation by fleeing to the West and then immediately beaming its music back into East Berlin on RIAS.

In truth, the problem of Western music and Western youth fashion never went away. If anything, both became even more alluring after the first, sensational recording of *Rock Around the Clock* reached the East in 1956, heralding the arrival of rock and roll. But by that time, the communist regimes had stopped fighting pop music. Jazz would become legal after the death of Stalin, at least in some places. Rules on leisure clothing would relax, and eventually Eastern Europe would have its own rock bands too. As one historian notes, the battle against Western pop music was 'fought and lost' in East Germany even before the Berlin Wall was built – and it had been 'fought and lost' everywhere else, too.[22]

For adults who had to hold down jobs and maintain families in the era of High Stalinism, flamboyant clothing was never a practical form of protest, though a few professions did allow it. Marta Stebnicka, an actress who spent much of her career in Kraków, put a great deal of effort into designing interesting hats for herself in the 1950s.[23] Leopold Tyrmand, the Polish jazz critic with the narrow ties and the coloured socks, was an adult style icon too.

But adults who couldn't or wouldn't dress up could still play pranks. They could also tell jokes. So ubiquitous and so varied were the jokes told in communist regimes that numerous academic tomes have since been written about them, though the use of jokes as a form of passive resistance in a repressive political system was nothing new. Plato wrote of the 'malice of amusement' and Hobbes observed that jokes often serve to make the joker feel superior to the objects of his humour. George Orwell observed (as quoted above) that 'A thing is funny when it upsets the established order. Every joke is a tiny revolution.' In the communist regimes of Eastern Europe, where there were so few opportunities either to express malice towards authority or to feel superior, and where the desire to upset the established order was both strong and forbidden, jokes flourished.[24]

Jokes also served a wide variety of purposes. The Soviet dissident Vladimir Bukovskii probably expressed their main function most precisely when he pointed out that 'The simplification of the joke exposes the absurdity of all propaganda tricks . . . In the jokes you can find the thing that has left no trace in the printed sources: the people's opinion of events.'[25] Certainly jokes allowed the joker to refer aloud to otherwise unmentionable truths, such as the fact that the Soviet Union bought Polish coal and other Polish products far below the international market price:

Negotiations are going on between Mao and Stalin. The Chinese leader asks the Soviet leader for help: 'We need a billion dollars, 50 million tons of coal, and a lot of rice.' Stalin turns to his advisers: 'Dollars, ok. Coal, ok. But where will Bierut get the rice?'[26]

Also the fact that the Polish army, in the 1950s, was led by a Soviet general with a Polish surname:

Why did Rokossovskii become a Marshal of the Polish army?

Because it's cheaper to dress one Russian in a Polish uniform than to dress the whole Polish army in Russian uniforms.

Or the fact that even artists had to be forced to conform under communism:

What is the difference between painters of the naturalist, impressionist and the socialist realist schools?

The naturalists paint as they see, the impressionists as they feel, the socialist realists as they are told.

Or the fact that supporters of the deeply unpopular regime were too embarrassed to admit it:

Two friends are walking down the street. One asks the other, 'What do you think of Rákosi?' 'I can't tell you here,' he replies. 'Follow me.' They disappear down a side street. 'Now tell me what you think of Rákosi,' says the friend. 'No, not here,' says the other, leading him into the hallway of an apartment block. 'OK, here then.' 'No, not here. It's not safe.' They walk down the stairs into the deserted basement of the building. 'OK, now you can tell me what you think of our leader.'

'Well,' says the other, looking around nervously, 'actually I quite like him.'

As was the case in so many spheres of life, the communist monopoly on power meant that jokes about anything – the economy, the national soccer team, the weather – all qualified, at some level, as political jokes. This was what made them subversive, as the authorities understood perfectly well, and this is way they went out of their way to quash them. A letter from Budapest youth movement authorities to Hungarian summer camp counsellors solemnly warned them to be prepared: campers might well indulge in 'vulgar' joke-telling sessions. In case such a thing should happen, the counsellors should cheerfully participate in these occasions in order to divert the crowd towards more tasteful and politically acceptable forms of humour.[27]

Not all youth leaders were so understanding. In reports sent to the Education Ministry about the general mood of students in Poland, 'chants, jokes, rhymes and graffiti' were judged a sign of 'oppositional feelings', perhaps even evidence of 'contact with the underground'.[28] For the wrong joke, told in the wrong place at the wrong time, one could even be arrested, not only in the 1950s but later on as well. This was the premise of Milan Kundera's 1967 novel *The Joke*, the book which first gained the Czech writer an international audience: its protagonist writes a joke on a postcard to a girl, and is thrown out of the party and sent to work in the mines as a result.[29] In 1961, members of an East German cabaret troupe really were arrested after a performance entitled 'Where the Dog's Buried' which included the following skit:

> Two of the actors start dismantling a wall, brick by brick. 'What are you doing?' asks a third. 'We're tearing down the walls of the brick factory!' they reply. 'Why are you doing that? There's a shortage of bricks!' the other responds. 'Exactly,' say the two labourers, continuing with their work. 'That's why we're dismantling the walls!'

The cabaret also featured a bureaucrat who answered every question with a quotation from Ulbricht, 'just to be absolutely on the safe side'. It was all rather clumsy, but the authorities were not amused. In the report filed afterwards, a local party boss fumed, 'the show consisted of provocative defamations of the press, workers, Party officials, and youth leaders'. The actors remained in jail for nine months, during which time several of them were isolated in solitary confinement. Much later, one of them discovered that hundreds of his jokes had been reported to the secret police.[30]

The incident does illustrate the distinct absence of a communist sense of humour. It also underlines the delicate balance which had to be struck by satirists, cabaret artists and others who wanted to perform legally. On the one hand, they had to be funny, or at least pointed and sharp, if they were to attract an audience. On the other hand, they had to avoid telling the jokes that people around them were actually telling, or even alluding to the topics that others found so amusing. Official media faced the same dilemma. Hungarian state radio made an attempt at tackling this problem in 1950 with the launch of a political cabaret. Their aim was clear: 'Every good laugh is a blow to the enemy. The new programme will radiate the optimistic joy and strength of our society.' The programme lasted two months, and was then abandoned.[31]

Almost no one in the Eastern bloc wrestled with this problem in the Stalinist period so diligently as Herbert Sandberg, the Buchenwald survivor who became the editor of *Ulenspiegel*, briefly East Germany's funny satirical magazine. Although the magazine's offices were originally located in West Berlin and the magazine was first registered under an American licence, Sandberg's superb team of artists and writers all came from the intellectual left, and from the beginning they were close to the Kulturbund and the communist party. Sandberg himself was not at all ideological, however. He regarded laughter as 'healing', and believed he could play a role in reconstructing society if he and his colleagues focused their sharp pens on caricatures of Germany's Nazi past and its present division.

At least to begin with, *Ulenspiegel* very much reflected Sandberg's sensibility. The 1 January 1947 issue contained, among other things, a satirical article about Adenauer, a review of an underrated exhibit of children's books (no one was talking about the exhibit in over-serious Berlin because 'it's about fun and love and magic') and a critical piece about Wilhelm Furtwängler, the conductor who had stayed in Germany during the war and kept silent about Nazi atrocities. There were cartoons criticizing the moribund de-Nazification process ('Are there really no Nazi party members left?') and much open discussion of the Third Reich. A few months later, Sandberg's ambivalence about the deepening division of Germany and of Berlin was reflected in the 2 May cover, which showed a blind man standing between the four flags of Berlin's four occupying powers. The headline – 'An Uncertain Future' – did not clearly blame either the Americans or the USSR for the division.

This neutrality could not be maintained for long, and eventually Sandberg had to take sides. As East–West tensions grew, so did communist influence over the magazine's content. Its satire shifted to focus more sharply on capitalism, on the United States and on Germany's helplessness in the face of Western 'warmongering'. By December 1947, its Christmas issue cover featured a German child asking, blandly, 'Mother, what is peace?' By the spring of 1948, the magazine had lost its American publishing licence. In May, the first issue produced under Soviet licence showed several bridges. The ones marked 'currency unity' and 'economic unity' are still intact; the one marked 'political unity' has been blown apart.[32]

Covers mocking Truman, De Gaulle and Western promises of demilitarization followed, although Sandberg resisted becoming yet another propaganda tool. He took the 'wrong' side in the formalism debate, insisting on expressing his admiration for 'formalist' artists such as Picasso. This compromise did not last long. By 1950, the party Central Committee's cultural department could no longer tolerate anything other than total conformity. As one of its members argued, 'we need support by our satirical press in the republic'. The magazine, another declared, was attempting to conform – 'We believe that Ulenspiegel has constantly and intensively worked on improving itself' – but doubts remained.[33] None of this mattered, because its readership had collapsed. No one wanted to buy a satirical magazine which wasn't funny, and the authorities shut it down in August. Although it was later reincarnated under the similar name of Eulenspiegel it was never quite the same.

Yet in private, behind closed doors and when they were on their own, even the authorities told political jokes. Günter Schabowski, an East German journalist and later a member of the last East German government, once told a British journalist that 'At . . . *Neues Deutschland* we told each other jokes in the canteen. We weren't blind to the failings of the system, but we convinced ourselves that this was only because it was early days and the class enemy was perpetrating sabotage wherever he could. One day, we thought, all problems would be solved and there wouldn't be any more jokes because there wouldn't be anything left to joke about.'[34] There were even jokes about that. For example this one, quite possibly imported from the USSR, and alluding to two of the Soviet Union's most famous Gulag construction projects:

'*Who built the White Sea Canal?*'
'*Those who told political jokes.*'
'*And who built the Volga–Don Canal?*'
'*Those who listened.*'

Humour could not always be controlled. Clothing could not always be controlled. As it turned out, religious emotions could not always be controlled either. Some of those in communist Europe organized themselves under the church's umbrella in a careful manner, planning and measuring their involvement, calculating the personal price they might have to pay. Józef Puciłowski was part of a Union of Polish Youth section whose leaders took a decision to go, as a group, to a priest for private catechism instruction on a regular basis. The risk paid off: no one in the group ever told the authorities.[35] As a young man, Hans-Jochen Tschiche decided to become a Lutheran clergyman. Although at the time, in the late 1940s, he was able to study in West Berlin, he deliberately went back to work in the East, in order to pursue his vocation there. Part of the appeal of the clergy for him was its openness: one was allowed to read a wider range of literature, to discuss material not available to most people in the East, to make contact with Western priests and churches while at the same time avoiding conflict with the regime and being of some help to its victims.[36]

But others did not calculate, did not measure and did not plan. Occasionally, suppressed religious feelings simply burst into the open.

Perhaps the largest spontaneous outburst took place in 1949, in the Polish city of Lublin. It began in the summer, on 3 July, when a local nun noticed a change on the face of a Virgin Mary icon in the city's cathedral. The Madonna – a copy of the Black Madonna of Częstochowa, Poland's most revered icon – appeared to be weeping. The nun called for a priest. He witnessed the miracle too, and both began to pray. Others followed suit. With astonishing speed – this was before telephones were common – the news of the miraculous weeping virgin spread across the city. By evening, the doors of the cathedral could not be closed because of the size of the crowds.

In the days which followed, the news spread further and pilgrims from all over Poland began to make their way to the cathedral. Of course, there was no public announcement of the miracle, and the regime did what it could to discourage the faithful. The authorities blocked public transportation into the city and placed policemen along the roads to prevent people from getting there, but to no avail, as one eyewitness remembered:

> It was in July 1949. Five of us went on foot since they had already stopped selling tickets for the train to Lublin. When we got to the cathedral we stayed there all night and in the morning there were already thousands of people, and at about seven o'clock they began standing in a queue waiting for the cathedral doors to open. After some time a policeman came and took away the priest but people still waited longer. And then they came again and took the keys to the cathedral and still people waited.
>
> And then a bishop came and told people to go home because the cathedral was not opening so then people were really shocked and sang and prayed and that went on until afternoon when I went to the side entrance of the cathedral and at first I didn't understand what was happening and then . . . I saw that they were breaking down the doors and I am helping and people are singing and praying and shouting 'Don't close our church' . . .

Eventually, he entered. He saw the face of the Virgin Mary light up. Tears of blood flowed down one of her cheeks. 'I believe it was a true miracle,' he wrote.[37]

Communist officials were stymied. At first, they kept the story out of the newspapers, in the hope that it would go away. But as more and more people came, and as the cathedral square filled up with pilgrims they changed tactics. On 10 July they launched an 'anti-miracle action': an extra 500 policemen arrived from Warsaw and Łódź, and the newspapers were given the go-ahead to begin a negative propaganda campaign. The pilgrims were described not as 'peasants' (a positive word in the communist lexicon) but rather as a 'crowd' or 'mob' of 'country people', naive illiterates, even 'speculators' or 'traders' who could be spotted carrying vodka bottles in the evening. Government authorities solemnly examined the miraculous painting, declared it had been damaged during the war, and said that any apparent markings on the face must be due to humidity. Church leaders, including Cardinal Wyszyński himself, were pressed to declare the miracle false. Fearing that the pilgrims could face terrible repercussions, clergymen told the faithful to go home.

But the faithful kept coming, pitching their tents in front of the cathedral doors. The following Sunday, 17 July, the inevitable confrontation took place. Local party leaders organized a demonstration in Litewski Square, in the city centre. They denounced 'reactionary clerics' through megaphones so powerful they could be heard inside all of the city's churches. Inside one of them, the Church of the Capuchins, the congregation began to sing a hymn: 'We Want God!' As mass came to an end and people poured out on to the streets, arrests began. The churchgoers tried to escape from the town centre, but policemen blocked the side streets and herded them into armoured trucks – a scene, one historian remarks, not so different from the street arrests which the Nazis had carried out in Lublin a few years earlier. Some remained under arrest for a few hours, some for up to three weeks.[38]

By August, the authorities had found a way to fit the event into their overarching narrative. How had it happened that news of the 'miracle' had travelled so quickly, even to places hundreds of miles away from Lublin? Who spread this fantastic rumour through the whole country? Polish radio had the answer: the organizers of the 'miracle' in Lublin turned out to be reactionary cliques of clerics, acting in concert with enemies of the Polish nation and the People's Republic, together with 'Voice of America'. This, the reporter ominously concluded, was hardly surprising: 'Voice of America was very pleased that in Poland people abandoned positive work in the fields, and ordered them to gather in front of the cathedral in indescribable conditions ... This was not a manifestation of faith. It was an organized demonstration of medieval fanaticism ... for purposes which had nothing to do with religion.'[39]

Eventually, the fuss over the Lublin miracle died down. But it was not the only such event in Stalinist Europe. In the Hungarian village of Fallóskút, two years earlier, a young woman named Klára ran away from a violent husband, spent the night in the fields, and had a dream in which the Virgin Mary told her to look for a spring. She found the spring, and then had a second dream, in which the Virgin Mary told her to build a chapel. Despite her poverty, 'belief would be enough' to pay for the chapel, according to the Virgin, and so it proved. Klára convinced others to help, and the chapel was erected beside the spring at the end of 1948. A priest came to inaugurate the building.

Even though the fearful episcopate refused to recognize the miracle, the Virgin nevertheless appeared to Klára several times again in 1949, after which she was sent to a psychiatric hospital and given electric shock treatment. She was released, but then sent back to the hospital once more in 1952 and diagnosed as schizophrenic. In the meantime, many others began to support the chapel, including Klára's repentant husband. Later, in the 1970s, she made two trips to the Vatican in an attempt to secure papal recognition for the miracle. Eventually recognition was granted, though only after her death in 1985.[40]

Fallóskút never attracted the crowds which briefly deluged Lublin cathedral. But the chapel eventually came to play a special role in Hungarian gypsy culture. These most passive of all regime opponents demonstrated their belief by quietly making their way to Klára's source, and by quietly observing the miracles the holy water wrought. Several patients with eye trouble were cured by the water. A mute boy was said to have begun to speak. No one who came to pray at the chapel had to say a word about politics, communism, democracy or opposition. But everyone who came to Fallóskút understood why they were there and why others were not.

*

Miracles, pilgrimages and prayer were not the only form of passive opposition which the church could offer. However curtailed, persecuted and oppressed, religious institutions did continue to exist during High Stalinism. However pressured or threatened, not every priest was 'patriotic' either, and not every Catholic intellectual was in search of a public career. Those church authorities who were willing to operate discreetly were even able to create unusual living and working arrangements for people who wanted nothing to do with communism at all. Precisely that sort of odd arrangement helped Halina Bortnowska survive High Stalinism with her conscience intact.

Bortnowska, the daughter of a teacher who taught her to 'take life seriously', was thirteen when the war ended. She and her mother had escaped from Warsaw during the uprising, and made their way to Toruń. In the spring of 1945 Bortnowska returned to school. Classes had resumed spontaneously. There was no order from above: teachers simply began teaching again, and the children simply wanted to learn. The teachers were the same as they had been before the war, and they taught in the same way, using the same textbooks. Not everything was absolutely normal. In May, Bortnowska remembered, or perhaps June, a rumour spread that Russian soldiers were coming to deport Polish children. The teachers sent everyone home from school. But it was a false rumour, and things continued, at least for a time.

Bortnowska's scouting troop resumed spontaneously too. Led by several young women who had been part of the Szare Szeregi, the Home Army scouts, the troop set out to make itself useful. They organized aid for refugees then arriving from the east, assisted orphans and children who had been displaced. They behaved as they wanted, and answered to no higher authorities, despite some of the threatening signs around them.

In 1948, things changed. The school director was replaced, and many of the teachers left as well. The scouting movement in Warsaw was taken over by Union of Polish Youth leaders, pressure came from above to conform, and the young women instructors decided to disband their troop. 'Scouts can't exist in a dishonest organization,' they told Bortnowska and her friends. In their case, no one thought of forming a secret or conspiratorial troop: 'We understood that there was no point.' Bortnowska looked for other outlets. She managed to join Sodalicja Mariańska, a Catholic student group, on the day before it was disbanded. She was too late to work with Caritas as well.

Frustrated, but still determined to stick to her family's principles and her own Catholic ideals, Bortnowska sought other small outlets for rebellion. A turning point came when she and a friend were asked to sign the Stockholm Appeal, one of the many peace petitions which had gone round the school. They signed – and then thought better of it. They went to the school director, and asked for their names to be removed. Those who had managed not to sign in the first place went unnoticed. But Bortnowska and her friend, then in their final year of secondary school, 'caused a fuss, and attracted attention to ourselves ... the whole town was talking about it'. With that kind of black mark on their records, the possibility of higher education suddenly evaporated for both of them.

She could have gone to work at a factory, and she thought about doing so. But because Bortnowska had friends within religious institutions, there was one more option. She entered the Catholic Institute in Wrocław, and began to study to become a *katechetka*, a teacher of religion in elementary schools. The Catholic Institute, despite its imposing name, was in fact a temporary, unofficial institution, recognized by nobody except the church. Soon after its founding in the city of Wrocław, the Institute's buildings were confiscated and it moved to shabby rural premises near the town of Olsztyn.

At the Institute, the students studied and taught at the same time. They survived off money from local parishes, free meals from grateful parents and food donations from churchgoers. They cooked for themselves and cleaned for themselves. They stayed out of the way. 'We didn't exist, from the point of view of the authorities,' Bortnowska recalled. There was still enough administrative chaos, especially in the former German territories, for them to remain under the radar.

Bortnowska remained at the Catholic Institute until 1956, when things began to loosen up and she was able to apply to a real university and get a real degree. But for six years, she survived in communist Poland and did not collaborate. During that time she taught the rudiments of religion to schoolchildren, and had enough to eat, and somewhere to sleep. She did not pose a threat to the regime, and the regime probably took no interest in her. She played no public role and

★ HIGH STALINISM

32. A 1952 Warsaw May Day parade, featuring Stalin and Bierut behind a banner: 'Long Live the Avant-garde of the Working Class, the Leading Force of the Nation, the Polish United Workers' Party'

33. A 1949 Budapest May Day parade featuring a papier-mâché Lenin

★
SOCIALIST REALISM

34. A detail from Max Lingner's mural *Aufbau der Republik*, 1952

35. András Kocsis at work on his sculpture, 'Agricultural Brigade', 1954

★
SOCIALIST CITIES

36. The Women's Construction Brigade, Sztálinváros

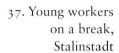

37. Young workers on a break, Stalinstadt

BERLIN YOUTH FESTIVAL, 1951

38. Delegates march in to the Walter Ulbricht Stadium

39. A Free German Youth fanfare corps performs

★ WARSAW YOUTH FESTIVAL, 1955

40. Spontaneous dancers ...

41. ... carefully planned displays

★ REVOLUTIONS

42. Demonstrators throwing stones at Soviet tanks, Berlin, June 17, 1953

43. Carrying away the wounded, Berlin, June 17, 1953

44. Hungarian rebels on a tank, Budapest, October 1956

45. Shots fired at
Bierut's portrait,
Poznań, October 1956

46. Soviet tanks return, Budapest, November 4, 1956

took no political positions. She had no children and no family, and thus did not have to worry about ensuring their future. Her mother was able to look after herself.

Asked, more than half a century later, whether she'd been afraid during that time, she shrugged. Yes and no, she said: 'It's impossible to be afraid all the time. A person gets used to it, you stop paying attention.' And so, hidden in the countryside, she did.[41]

For those who could not or would not collaborate, for those unable to find shelter within the church or take comfort in humour, there was one, final, dramatic option: escape.

In this, the East Germans had it easiest. Poles who left Poland or Hungarians who left Hungary left not just their homes and families but their language and culture. For them, to leave the country was to become for ever a refugee. After 1949, passport regimes across Eastern Europe were strengthened and borders reinforced, which made even this heartbreaking choice more risky and difficult, since anyone caught crossing the border risked arrest and imprisonment. According to Interior Ministry statistics, only 9360 Poles crossed the Polish border for any reason in 1951, of whom only 1980 were travelling to capitalist countries.[42]

For Germans the same choice could be very difficult, especially for those who owned property or had family in the East. But it was not quite so dramatic. West Germany was still Germany, after all, and the national language was still German. The logistics were easier too. Unlike the Poles, who had to find a way across East Germany, Czechoslovakia or the Baltic Sea to the West, Germans who wanted to leave East Germany in the 1950s had only, in theory, to cross the border into the West.

This apparently simple task did become more complicated as time went on. In the early days, the obstacles were often on the western side of the border. Because the flow of refugees was almost entirely from East to West from the very beginning, the US Army in Bavaria and the British Army in northern Germany initially tried to slow it down. Fearing it would be overwhelmed by large numbers of refugees entering their occupation zones, the US Army actually began defending the borders of its zone in March 1945, controlling who could and could not enter. Though these efforts weren't particularly successful – refugees still crossed through forests, or found their way around border posts with the help of smugglers and bribable Soviet soldiers – they did help set a precedent. In due course all of the Allied armies in Germany set up border posts and road blocks, monitored routes leading in and out of their respective zones, and required those crossing 'internal' German borders to carry passes and visas.[43]

Inevitably, there began to be border 'incidents' – Soviet soldiers shooting into the American zone and vice versa – as well as arguments over where, exactly, the new German–German border was supposed to be. Nineteenth-century stone markers which could be stealthily moved at night became a focus of contention, and a number of towns in the Soviet zone applied to be transferred to the American zone.[44] The Red Army began to establish what would later become 'No Man's Land', an area along the border where no one was allowed to live. Later, whole villages in these border areas would be evacuated. A series of Allied negotiations were held to discuss travel problems, and various commissions were set up to find the answers. Rules were created to govern the issuance of passes and permits.

All the while, Germans kept moving from East to West. Between October 1945 and June 1946 some 1.6 million people crossed into the American and British zones from the Soviet zone. By June 1946, the Red Army, not the American army, was demanding a ban on inter-zonal travel, and American soldiers, not Red Army soldiers, were helping Germans sneak across (by dressing up German women in American uniforms, among other things, a trick which was apparently not hard to see through).[45]

From 1949, the West German authorities also stopped treating people arriving from the East as illegal immigrants. Instead, they came to be regarded as political refugees and victims of communist oppression. They received places in refugee camps and help in finding housing and work. In accordance with these changes, the Soviet authorities also began to enforce stricter controls, sending Red Army troops to patrol their border and build ditches, fences and barriers.

Berlin remained the exception. Although the city lay inside the Soviet zone, it was not easy to set up an enforceable 'border' within it (though the construction of the Berlin Wall in 1961 would eventually

prove that it was possible). More importantly, the USSR did not at
first want the city's division to become official. The Soviet authorities
preferred Berlin to remain unified, albeit anchored securely in the
East. This anomaly quickly created another odd dynamic, as East
Germans began flocking to East Berlin in order to cross the border
into West Berlin, and to make their way from there to West Germany
by closed train or air. The mystery and intrigue of Berlin, so attractive
to spy novelists and film-makers, date from this era, when Berlin was
the gateway to freedom.

The Berlin blockade of 1948–9, described in Chapter 11, was designed
to end this flow of people, as well as to persuade the Western Allies to
abandon the western part of the city. Though the blockade failed in
that latter task, the reinforcement of the border within the city did
make it more difficult for Berliners to cross. Border police, ostensibly
looking for black marketeers, monitored all forms of transportation,
checking passports and visas, sometimes arresting would-be refugees.

The real clampdown came in 1952, after the East German
government created a special commission to deal with the problem of
those 'fleeing the Republic'. Naturally, their solutions included
propaganda – denunciations of the Western spies who enticed East-
erners across the border with false promises of riches – as well as
promises of better employment and housing for anyone who came
back. The secret police began to collect information about people
who had left, the better to understand their motives. Eventually, all
remaining crossings along the German–German border were closed
to ordinary traffic, including as many in Berlin as feasible. It was at this
point that the East German police and the Red Army began to monitor and block the roads into East Berlin from East Germany as well.

Yet still people fled. Despite all of the border controls, the guns and
the tanks, despite the risk of arrest or capture, nearly 200,000 people –
197,788 to be precise – left East Germany for the West in 1950. In
1952, after the border had been newly fortified, the number dropped
only slightly, to 182,393. Even then it began to pick up again, and
would hover around 200,000 annually until the construction of the
Berlin Wall halted the traffic. In total, 3.5 million people, out of a
population of 18 million, are thought to have left East Germany
between 1945 and 1961.[46]

Of these 3.5 million, some might have become the regime's opponents if they had stayed. Ernst Benda, the young Christian Democratic activist who slipped over the border after receiving an odd phone message, went on to become a legal scholar, an early supporter of the Free University of West Berlin, and eventually president of the West German Supreme Court. Gisela Gneist, imprisoned in Sachsenhausen for founding a democratic youth group at the age of fifteen, crossed the border after her release. Decades later she helped create the memorial to Soviet prisoners at that camp. Gerhard Finn, also arrested as a teenage 'Werewolf', crossed the border and threw himself into the anti-communist movement in West Berlin. Among the émigrés were artists, writers and musicians of all kinds who, if they had stayed, might well have developed into cultural dissidents.

Not all of the refugees were political. One factory in Köpenick, required to explain its employees' departures, told the authorities that people left because their relatives were in West Germany, because the factory had not granted them a leave of absence to study, because they had debts and because they thought they could make more money in the West. This was probably an accurate reflection of many émigrés' motives, which were undoubtedly mixed. The last point in particular was surely influential. By the early 1950s, West Germany's economy had left East Germany's economy far behind, as everyone could see.

But not all of those who remained were unhappy, and it is a mistake to imagine that only a sullen, apolitical rump population remained behind after this exodus – or that, as the German scholar Arnulf Baring once wrote, 'anyone who showed initiative or was energetic and determined, had either left in time or was thrown out later on'. At least until the Wall was built in 1961, those who stayed behind had extra leverage: if not given housing, better wages or a top job, they could always threaten to leave. Those in certain critical professions – doctors, for example – were showered with privileges designed to persuade them to stay, and some of them reckoned they were better off for it. When, after Stalin's death, her husband told her that changes in regime policy might mean that many who had fled west might be coming back to East Germany, Herta Kuhrig, then aged twenty-three, thought: 'Oh my god, if they return, we might have to leave our flat.'[47]

Knowing its citizens had a choice, the East German government refrained from cutting wages, and probably kept the police regime lighter than it would have been. Fear of a mass exodus might even help explain why there were no show trials in East Germany.[48] Not all of those who stayed were admirers of the communist system, but they had assessed the situation, worked out how much compromise would be required and how much passive opposition would be possible. They made what they thought was the best choice for themselves and their families, and then waited to see what would happen next.

18
Revolutions

After the uprising of the 17th June
The Secretary of the Writers' Union
Had leaflets distributed in the Stalinallee
Stating that the people
Had forfeited the confidence of the government
And could win it back only
By redoubled efforts. Would it not be easier
In that case for the government
To dissolve the people
And elect another?

Bertolt Brecht[1]

On 6 March 1953, Eastern Europeans, like the rest of the world, awoke to hear stunning news: Stalin was dead.[2]

Across the region, radios played funereal music. Shops closed their doors. Citizens were urged to hang flags from their homes, and millions voluntarily wore black clothes and black ribbons. Newspapers appeared with black borders around the edges, black sashes were placed on Stalin's photograph in offices, and schoolchildren took turns standing as honour guards before his portrait. Delegations from factories and ministries trooped through the offices of Soviet commandants in East Germany, where they signed condolence books in mournful silence. In the town of Heiligenstadt, Catholic churches rang their bells and priests said an 'Our Father' in Stalin's name.[3] Enormous crowds of mourners filled Wenceslas Square in Prague, and tens of thousands gathered around the Stalin statue in Budapest. A moment of silence was observed on Alexanderplatz in East Berlin.[4]

In Moscow, Stalin's acolytes and imitators gathered for his funeral. Bierut and Rokossovskii, Rákosi and Gottwald, Ulbricht and Grotewohl, all of them were there. So were Gheorghe Gheorghiu-Dej from Romania, Enver Hoxha from Albania and Vulko Chervenkov from Bulgaria. Mao Tse-tung and Chou En-lai came from China, Palmiro Togliatti came from Italy and Maurice Thorez from France.[5] Malenkov, Beria and Molotov gave funeral orations, although they did not, one observer noted, 'exhibit a trace of sorrow'.[6] Emotions must have run high, however. Gottwald suffered a heart attack after the funeral, and died soon after.

Change followed swiftly. By the time of his death, Stalin's colleagues had grimly concluded that things were not going well in the Soviet empire. For many months they had been receiving regular, accurate and extremely worrying reports from Eastern Europe. The Soviet ambassador to Prague had written of 'near-total chaos' in Czech industry in December 1952, for example, along with steep price rises and a dramatic drop in living standards. Following the deaths of Stalin and Gottwald, strikes across Czechoslovakia again picked up pace. In May, thousands of Czechoslovak workers marched three kilometres from the Škoda factory to the city hall in Plzeň, where they occupied the building, burned Soviet flags and threw busts of Lenin, Stalin and Gottwald out of the window – a symbolic protest against the defenestration of Jan Masaryk, the former Foreign Minister, an anti-communist who had been thrown out of a window of the Foreign Ministry in 1948.[7] Strikes also began to spread among tobacco workers in Bulgaria, until then one of the most obedient countries in the bloc. The Soviet Politburo found this particularly disturbing: if hitherto loyal Bulgarian workers were restless, then the rest of the region must be even more unstable.[8]

The news from East Germany was not good either. Despite ever-increasing border security, despite police controls and barbed wire, traffic over the internal German border was accelerating. More than 160,000 people had moved from East to West Germany in 1952, and a further 120,000 had left in the first four months of 1953.[9] One report warned of 'growing unrest among the [East German] population stemming from the hardline policies of the GDR leadership'.[10] Beria himself penned a very accurate, perfectly clear-eyed analysis:

The increasing number of flights to the West can be explained ... by the unwillingness of individual groups of peasants to join the agricultural production cooperatives that are being organized, by the fear among small and medium entrepreneurs about the abolition of private property and the confiscation of their possessions, by the desire of some young people to evade service in the GDR armed forces, and by the severe difficulties that the GDR is experiencing with the supply of food products and consumer goods.[11]

Even with the evidence in front of them, the Soviet leaders did not publicly question their own ideology. The ideas of Marxism were still correct – but, they concluded, the people in charge had failed: they had been too harsh, too arbitrary, too hasty, too incompetent. In particular, the East Germany party bosses had failed. On 2 June, the Soviet Politburo summoned Ulbricht, Grotewohl and Fred Oelssner, the ideology chief, to Moscow to tell them so. For three days, the Politburo lectured their German comrades. They told them to abandon celebrations of Ulbricht's birthday, to liberalize their economic programme and to postpone, indefinitely, the planned announcement of East Germany's imminent transition to 'full socialism'. This 'incorrect political line' was to be replaced by a 'New Course'. The Germans naturally obeyed. On 11 June, *Neues Deutschland* published a statement from the party leadership on its front page, apologizing for the 'grave mistakes' of previous years, calling for an end to collectivization and even for the rehabilitation of victims of political trials.

Soviet–Hungarian talks followed a week later. This time, the Politburo attacked Rákosi, along with Gerő, Révai and Farkas. Beria – who had himself personally conducted brutal interrogations in the Soviet Union – led the charge: Rákosi, he said, had initiated an insupportable 'wave of repression' against the population, even giving personal directions as to who should be arrested and beaten. Beria's colleagues also accused the Hungarian leader of 'economic adventurism'. Well aware of 'discontent among the Hungarian population', shortages and economic hardship they ordered Rákosi to step down as Prime Minister, although they allowed him to remain General Secretary of the Hungarian communist party.[12]

They replaced him with Imre Nagy, the little-known Agricultural

Minister. Nagy was also a 'Moscow communist' who had lived in the Soviet Union before the war – where, as the historian Charles Gati argues, he had probably worked as a secret police informer and maintained informal links to some of the Soviet leadership. But he had long favoured a more gradual transition to communism and, more importantly, was not Jewish, which the Soviet Politburo seemed to think was an enormous advantage.[13] He set to work designing a New Course for Hungary, and within a few weeks he was ready to announce it. In July he made his first speech to parliament, stunning his party and his country. Nagy called for an end to rapid industrialization, an end to collectivization and a more relaxed approach to culture and the media. 'In the future,' the Central Committee would soon declare, 'the primary goal of our economic policy will be to raise constantly and considerably the standard of living of the people.' Nagy remained a Marxist, and described all of his policies using Marxist language – his long, dull and almost unreadable written defence of the New Course quotes Stalin and Lenin with alarming frequency – but in the context of the time he seemed fresh and very different.[14]

The Soviet Politburo had never intended East Germany and Hungary to make these changes on their own: the liberalization was meant to be instituted across the bloc, in order to stem the tide of protest and discontent. Some of them may even have imagined, eventually, that similar changes would take place in the USSR, where, for a few short years – a period known in the USSR as 'the Thaw' – it would also seem as if truly radical change were possible. Certainly in all of their conversations with their Eastern European partners in 1953, the Soviet leaders made it clear that their criticism was intended 'not just for a single country but for all the people's democracies'.[15] Talks with the Albanian leader Enver Hoxha followed those with Ulbricht and Rákosi. More conversations, plotting more New Courses, were planned for late July. The Politburo also intended to invite the Poles, the Czechs and the Bulgarians to Moscow, where they would also be told to change direction and make themselves popular – or risk catastrophe.

But catastrophe came anyway, though in a form nobody had expected.

*

The weather broke bright and clear in Berlin on 17 June 1953. Nevertheless, many Berliners stepped into the sunshine with trepidation, not sure what the morning would bring. The previous day, East Berlin had witnessed its first major mass strikes since the war. Emboldened by the announcement of the New Course, cheered on by Stalin's death, frustrated by the fact that the new policies didn't seem to include lower work quotas, Berlin's workers had taken to the streets to protest. Lutz Rackow, an East German journalist, had walked down Stalinallee on 16 June alongside several thousand construction workers. They carried banners – 'Berliners, join us! We don't want to be slaves to our work!' Few had dared. But as soon as he got to Stalinallee on 17 June, Rackow immediately saw that things were going to be different: 'This time people were joining. Not only that, workers were coming into the city from as far as Henningsdorf to join, even though public transportation had been halted and the walk took three hours.'[16]

Erich Loest, the novelist who had tried to teach workers to write theatre reviews, was on his way into the city that morning from Leipzig and he saw strikers too. But he also saw Soviet tanks and lorries moving northwards from bases near Schonefeld and Ahlsdorf. They were heading for the centre of Berlin at about the same speed as his train. On another train from Leipzig – or perhaps even the same one – the writer Elfriede Brüning saw the same tanks. She was sitting with a colleague, who read aloud a newspaper headline: 'Tumult in Bonn,' it declared. Her friend laughed, and made a daring joke: 'How is it that the government has heard only about the tumult in Bonn, and not the uprising in Berlin!'[17]

On the Western side of the city, Egon Bahr, then the chief political editor in West Berlin for RIAS, Radio in the American Sector, was anxiously waiting to hear what was happening. A couple of days earlier, a delegation from East Berlin had come to his office to ask him to publicize their planned strike. He had agreed to broadcast the strikers' demands – they wanted lower work quotas, lower food prices and free elections, among other things – and he had continued to do so until the radio's American controller, Gordon Ewing, burst into his office and told him to stop: 'Do you want to start World War Three?' Ewing told Bahr that American responsibility and American security guarantees ended at the border, and he'd better be clear about that in his broadcasts. As Bahr remembers, 'This was the only order I ever got from the US government at RIAS.'[18]

On the Eastern side of the city, most of the Politburo had left their homes early and made their way to Karlshorst, where they could hide from the expected crowds. In fact, they wound up spending the entire day there, standing around the office of the Soviet ambassador, Vladimir Semyonov. This was not a voluntary activity. At one point, Ulbricht asked to return home, and Semyonov snarled at him: 'And if anything happens to you back in your apartment? It's all very well for you, but think what my superiors will do to me.'[19] It was perfectly clear who was in charge: at lunchtime, the Politburo learned that the Russian authorities had unilaterally imposed martial law on East Germany. The Soviet 'state of emergency' would last until the end of the month.

The Politburo were not the only ones who didn't know what to do with themselves on 17 June. After watching the march on Stalinallee, Rackow went to his office. But hardly any work was done that day. Journalists wandered about aimlessly, and the chief editor was locked into an office with the party cell leader, unsure what to do or what their line should be. Meanwhile, both Brüning and Loest made their separate ways to a long-planned meeting of the Writers' Association, where no one could talk about anything except the strike. The General Secretary of the association put a call in to the Central Committee. Then he made an announcement: the writers should go out and discuss the situation with the workers. 'And don't let yourselves be provoked!'[20]

Loest went out, together with a colleague. As a precaution, they put their party badges in their pocket. Elfriede Brüning waded into the crowd as well. So did the journalist Klaus Polkehn, who had taken the U-bahn into the centre of town and wanted to find out what was going on. By then, tens of thousands of people were walking down Unter den Linden and towards the House of Ministries, the headquarters of the East German government, the outside of which was adorned with *Aufbau der Republik*, Max Lingner's mural.

Walking beside them, Loest saw right away that things were getting out of hand. Dozens of young men, 'the fighting type', dominated the scene. 'I was standing on the side,' he remembered thinking with surprise: 'they were on strike, the workers were on strike against the Workers' and Peasants' Party, against myself.' A newspaper kiosk was in flames. No Volkspolizei – German policemen – were to be seen. This was deliberate: Ulbricht didn't trust them, and they only arrived later on. But there were plenty of Russian soldiers. They had 'immobile faces', Loest remembered, 'their caps fastened to their chins, their guns between their legs. Officers were standing beside them, not moving.'[21]

These soldiers were merely the advance guard. The real demonstration of Soviet force came later in the morning. Loest was standing at the corner of Unter den Linden and Friedrichstraße when he saw the tanks roll in. A few hundred yards away, Karl-Heinz Arnold, also a journalist, watched the same tanks through the window of a building on the corner of Leipziger Straße and Wilhelmstraße. From above, he could see the crowd gathering outside the House of Ministries: 'The people there were definitely "eight penny" boys from West Berlin. You give them eight pennies and tell them to go and pick up trouble. They were completely different from the demonstrators on Stalinallee, those were our construction workers.'[22]

Hans-Walter Bendzko, a border control officer, was watching the same crowd, but from the other side of a barricade. That morning, he had been told to report for special duty, and had been sent to the House of Ministries as a security guard. He didn't know who was in the crowd, East German construction workers or West Berlin provocateurs. He only knew that it was not a 'normal' demonstration, with banners and slogans, but rather 'a dark mass that moved back and forth'. 'I thought they wanted to storm the ministry, I was afraid that there would be a fight, but I did not know what was going on.' When Bendzko heard the tanks, he panicked, thinking, 'this is the moment when the Americans will interfere'. But as they approached, he saw – with enormous relief – that they were Soviet T-34 tanks, with red stars. Arnold, looking down from his window above, was also relieved: 'It was a kind of liberation. It stopped the pressure.' Two of the tanks slowly drove into the crowd around the building. People moved aside to let them through. One of them halted in front of the House of Ministries, and, as Bendzko looked on, the commander of Soviet troops in Berlin emerged.

He got out and walked through our cordon to the House of Ministries. And then he came back, got up on the tank, said something which, of course, nobody understood. Maybe he was announcing martial law. Then the tanks turned away again and moved towards Potsdamer Platz. And everybody ran away. Some were caught and arrested ... The troublemakers started to attack the tanks. One of them got a large beam from among the rubble and put it under the wheel of the tank so the chains wouldn't move ...[23]

Some of the tanks began firing when they reached Potsdamer Platz; others had already started shooting on Unter den Linden. Some of the Volkspolizei belatedly began using their pistols. Most people ran away, and hardly any fought back. What was there to fight back with? A few people threw stones, but there wasn't anything else. Some fifty people are thought to have died that day, though the numbers have never been confirmed.[24] Hundreds were arrested, of whom thirteen were eventually sentenced and executed as traitors. Not all of the victims were demonstrators: in Rathenow, a Stasi functionary died after an angry mob dragged him into the canal and prevented him from getting out again.[25]

In the melee, Polkehn was arrested. He was dragged into a truck, waving his press card to no avail, and taken to Soviet headquarters at Karlshorst. He spent two days there, emerging filthy and hungry but relieved. Most of his fellow prisoners seemed to be there by accident: they had joined the demonstrations out of curiosity, or perhaps naive conviction. Not all of them were from Berlin. Indeed, demonstrations took place in all of the major cities and industrial centres that day, especially those with a strong communist or social democratic tradition: Rostock, Cottbus, Magdeburg, Dresden, Leipzig, Erfurt and Halle. In total, about 500,000 people in 373 towns and cities went on strike in about 600 enterprises. Between a million and 1.5 million people took part in demonstrations of some kind.[26]

Nobody was more surprised by the geographic spread of the strikers than Bahr, who had assumed the protests would be confined to Berlin. But he felt a peculiar thrill of responsibility when he heard that some of the demonstrators outside the capital had voiced demands which were the same, word for word, as those he had played on the radio the day before.[27] As it turned out, the Russians had been right in 1945: radio really was the most important mass medium of its time, and the only one which could reach a broad audience. But RIAS's audience turned out to be much broader than the audience of state radio. 'June the 17th proves how many people listen to RIAS,' an angry East German communist argued at a meeting a few weeks later. 'We've done so much education and training, but none of it was absorbed.'[28]

In Berlin, the appearance of Soviet tanks had ended the demonstrations. But by the time Semyonov sent his first cable to Moscow at 2 p.m., a good deal of damage had been done in the city and across the country. The windows of government offices had been smashed and a bookstore selling Russian books in central Berlin had been ransacked. In the town of Görlitz on the Polish border, a mob of 30,000 had destroyed the headquarters of the communist party, the offices of the secret police and the prison. In Magdeburg, the party headquarters and the prison had actually been set on fire, and in factories near Halle workers had overwhelmed the police.[29] There were some more subtle rebellions as well. In one factory, workers struck up a 'whistling concert' in order to drown out the propaganda coming out of the sound system.[30]

East Germans reacted to these events in many different ways. Communist sympathizers, as Loest was at the time, were shocked by the idea that the workers could be protesting against the Workers' Party. Günter Schabowski – whose out-of-context comments at a press conference led to the opening of the Berlin Wall in 1989 – recalls that 17 June 'showed us how endangered was the communists' seemingly immovable and firm creation'.[31] Functionaries like Arnold, seeking to explain the situation, sought to blame the violence on troublemakers from West Berlin. Those inclined to make excuses for the regime agreed with them. Though he later became more ambivalent (wondering, in the poem cited in the epigraph to this chapter, whether the government shouldn't 'dissolve the people' and elect another), Brecht's first reaction was to blame 'organized fascist elements' from the West. In a *Neues Deutschland* article published a few days after the riots, Brecht, who was living at the time in Berlin, praised the Soviet intervention: 'It is only thanks to the swift and accurate intervention of Soviet troops that these attempts were frustrated.'[32]

More careful observers, Polkehn included, knew that many of the people involved in the strikes were dissatisfied workers and innocent bystanders – though even Polkehn, decades later, also thought that

Western provocateurs must have been involved, somehow. It was too difficult and demoralizing to believe otherwise.[33] Rackow insisted differently: 'It's nonsense that it was a Western plot, nobody believed that. Even those saying it didn't believe it.'[34]

The Soviet authorities, with their excellent informer networks and multiple spies, were less surprised by the strikes than some of their East German comrades. They had expected demonstrations on 17 June and had known in advance that they would have to support the East German police. They were not shy about bringing their tanks on to the streets. But they had not expected demonstrations on such a large scale, with such evidently broad support and with such clearly anti-Soviet intentions. One memorandum sent to Khrushchev mentioned the 'abuse', 'vulgar insults' and 'violent threats' directed at Soviet soldiers and officials, not to mention the stones thrown at them. 'The mass of the population have retained a hatred towards Soviet officials, which has now been inflamed again,' the memo concluded: 'This hatred was openly on display during the demonstrations.'[35]

Initially, the Soviet authorities did not blame the West at all. In his first reports, Ambassador Semyonov spoke about strikers, workers and demonstrators. Later his language changed, and he began speaking of provocateurs, ringleaders and rowdies. Eventually, Soviet reports spoke of a 'great international provocation, prepared earlier by the three Western powers and their accomplices from the circles of West German monopolistic capital' – though even then they conceded that there was still a 'lack of factual material' to justify this thesis.[36]

For the Soviet diplomats and officers in Germany, the 'provocation' explanation may have been a face-saving measure, a way to conceal their own failure to predict or prevent the riots. But it also might have been the only explanation which made sense to them. According to their ideology, their education and their prejudices, this sort of thing wasn't supposed to happen. Not only was it impossible for workers to rise up against the workers' state, but Germans were not supposed to oppose any authority at all. Stalin himself had once laughed at the thought of political protests in East Germany: 'Revolt? Why they won't even cross the street unless the light is green.'[37] But Stalin was dead.

*

The riots in East Berlin had one immediate and unexpected casualty. Nine days later, on 26 June, Khrushchev engineered a dramatic coup against Beria. The Soviet secret police boss was taken by surprise, arrested by his colleagues, jailed and eventually executed. Khrushchev's motivations were largely personal. He feared Beria's influence over the secret police and probably suspected, no doubt correctly, that Beria held compromising material on all of the Soviet leaders. But instead of saying so openly, he found it convenient to justify his arrest by blaming Beria for the 17 June riots. Although none of the Soviet Politburo members had objected to the New Course, and although all of them had pressed Ulbricht to implement it, they self-righteously deemed the riots evidence of Beria's dangerous 'deviationism', his traitorous instincts, his high-handedness and his arrogance.

Like all Politburo politics, Beria's arrest had an echo in Eastern Europe. The 'hardliners' in Germany now attacked the 'reformers' – principally Rudolf Herrnstadt, then the editor-in-chief of *Neues Deutschland*, and Wilhelm Zaisser, the Stasi boss – for their alleged affiliations with Beria. In Budapest, Rákosi also began to drop knowing hints about Nagy's lack of support in Moscow and his own imminent return to power.[38]

Yet although German communists threw Beria's name around during the angry internal debates which followed the 17 June riots, his supposed influence was not really what was at stake. On the contrary, the argument which began in Germany in the summer of 1953 was part of a much wider debate about the nature of Eastern European communism. Should the regimes liberalize, allow more pluralism, open up debate and bring back economic freedom? Or should they keep harsh, punitive and controlling policies in place? Would liberalism lead to chaos? Would a crackdown cause a revolution?

In July 1953, both views were voiced in Berlin. At a stormy, angry Central Committee plenum in July, Anton Ackermann, previously an opponent of Ulbricht, declared that the party's enemies were growing stronger and the media should be more strictly controlled: 'only letters to the editor which have been checked for factual correctness should be published'.[39] Another functionary present agreed, calling on the party to 'intensify the fight against formalism, in favour of social realism', and to 'persuade the masses to develop a love for Soviet art'.[40]

But the liberalizers were not defeated altogether. At the same meeting, Zaisser reminded his comrades that the 'change of course' had been designed, among other things, to prevent people from fleeing the country, and '17 June was an even more alarming signal' of mass discontent. Johannes Becher, the former head of the Kulturbund, also spoke out in favour of looser controls on media and culture. Even in the USSR, he said, it would be 'unthinkable for a Goethe museum to contain [Free German Youth] posters', as one did in East Germany.[41]

In the wake of the 1953 German riots, the argument between neo-Stalinists and liberalizers intensified in the other Eastern European capitals as well. In Warsaw, Bierut and Gomułka's battle for personal power had long ago turned into a struggle between neo-Stalinism on the one hand and a more 'Polish', less Soviet form of communism on the other. Gomułka's cause received a sudden boost in December 1953 when Józef Światło, a senior secret policeman – the boss of Department X, responsible for watching party members – unexpectedly defected to the West. A few months later, Światło began broadcasting an extraordinary series of reports on the Polish service of Radio Free Europe, describing the privileged lifestyle of the party elite, the role of Soviet advisers and the arrest and incarceration of Gomułka in lurid detail. Millions openly tuned in to listen, even in government offices. In its own report on the broadcasts, the Security Ministry noted with alarm that previously reliable informers were now refusing to cooperate, and were demanding to know whether Światło would reveal their names.[42] By December, Gomułka had been freed from house arrest.[43]

In Budapest, the party took a radically different turn. Rákosi – still the communist party's General Secretary – used the Berlin riots as an excuse to call for renewed 'vigiliance' and to begin preparing for a comeback. Taking advantage of Moscow's general disorientation, he contrived to reverse the Hungarian New Course. By 1955 he had convinced the Soviet Union to dismiss Nagy from the Prime Minister's job and to replace him with a more pliant sidekick, András Hegedüs, the former youth leader. Nagy retaliated with an even more vociferous attack on Rákosi's harsh policies.[44] But while these arguments were

473

going on at the very top of society, other things were happening far below.

If the first hint of discontent in Berlin came in the form of construction strikes, the beginning of the end of Stalinism in Poland came in the form of a large party. More precisely, it came in the form of the Fifth Youth and Students' Festival of 'World Peace and Friendship' in the summer of 1955.

Like its predecessor in Berlin, the Warsaw Youth Festival was designed to be a vast propaganda exercise, a meeting place for Eastern European communists and their comrades from Western Europe, Asia, Africa and South America. Also like its predecessor in Berlin, it was meant to be carefully planned and orchestrated. Advance propaganda and enthusiastic coverage brought hundreds of thousands of Polish spectators to Warsaw for the five days of the festival. They travelled from all over the country to watch the dancing, the theatre and the other attractions – a Hungarian circus, a puppet show and an opera were all performed on the first day – as well as sporting contests and economic debates.[45]

Yet from the very first day of the events, the crowds in Warsaw were not primarily interested in politics, culture or even sports. The real attraction was the foreigners. Strolling the streets of the Polish capital for the first time since the war were Arabs in long robes, Africans in native dress, Chinese in Mao jackets, even Italians in striped shirts and French girls in flowered skirts. Maciej Rosalak, a child at the time, remembered the shock:

> Grey, sad, poorly dressed people living among ruins and the rubble of streets were suddenly replaced by what seemed to be a different species. The newcomers smiled instead of listening to the static on Radio Free Europe like our parents, and they sang instead of whispering. Warsaw children ran among them and collected autographs in special notebooks. An Italian drew us a picture of his country, shaped like a boot, with Sicily and Sardinia alongside; a Chinese man left mysterious symbols; and a beautiful African wrote her exotic name and tousled our hair . . .[46]

The contrast between Poles and foreigners – especially those from Western Europe, who were culturally similar but so much richer and more open – struck everybody. *Trybuna Ludu*, the party newspaper, quoted a factory worker declaring that the dresses of the French girls were 'amusing, happy and tasteful ... can't Polish clothes be more beautiful?'[47] The same newspaper also observed the contrast between the unsmiling Polish youth leaders – 'we were sad, gloomy, incredibly stiff, uptight' – and their more cheerful foreign counterparts. 'It turned out that it was possible to be "progressive", and at the same time enjoy life, wear colourful clothes, listen to jazz, have fun and fall in love,' wrote Kuroń, who had been one of those unsmiling youth leaders at the time.[48] Particularly shocking, many noted, was the sight of young people kissing in public.

The political implications of this non-political experience were clear even at the time. Jacek Fedorowicz, whose cabaret group Bim-Bom played in one of the theatres during the festival, remembered that 'suddenly everything had became colourful, in a manner which was unbelievably unsocialist'.[49] It was, he reckoned, 'a propaganda mistake: without warning, they had let a crowd of multi-coloured outsiders into grey Warsaw'. A decade's worth of anti-Western rhetoric was shown to be false: 'Young people from the capitalist world were healthy and well-dressed, even though we'd been told that everything there is bad ...'[50]

Spontaneity, the human quality most vigorously repressed by the communist regimes, suddenly flowered. To the horror of the festival organizers, Poles, Germans, Hungarians, Czechs and others from the communist bloc actively socialized with one another and with the more exotic visitors, not only in the streets but in private apartments all over the city. Romances, friendships and drunken evenings unfolded in an uncontrolled and unmonitored manner. A student meeting at the library of the University of Warsaw developed into an argument when it turned out that not all of the French delegation were actually communists. For young communists such as Pomian, this was the first experience of open public debate.[51]

Many officially planned events seemed somehow to go wrong too. At the old city Arsenal, young Polish artists put on a show dedicated, of course, to 'peace'. But what attracted visitors and garnered attention was not the theme but the extraordinary variation in what was on display. There were many paintings executed in heavy paint and harsh colours. Brushwork was visible. Allegories were obscure. The

images were different, unexpected – and abstract and avant-garde.
It was the end of an era. After the Arsenal show socialist realism
vanished from the visual arts in Poland for ever.

Spontaneity in art led to spontaneity in behaviour. At times, crowds
grew ugly. When the sound system broke down at one event, the riot-
ing and anger were so great that the sound technicians had to escape
to their van and drive quickly away.[52] People complained loudly about
the shortage of food, the poor quality of some of the duller events and
the propaganda emitted by the ubiquitous loudspeakers. 'In Warsaw,
one dances in the name of something, or against something,' one party
writer had solemnly declared in his summary of the festival, a sentiment which almost everybody else found annoying.[53] There were
many tedious performances, from stiff folk dancing to unsmiling
waltzes, from which the crowds turned away in droves.

And yet – sometimes the crowds grew spontaneously joyous as
well. At one point, the Bim-Bom cabaret group was supposed to have
an official meeting with a Swiss delegation. But instead of a stiff
exchange of greetings, moderated by a translator and presided over
by a Union of Polish Youth official, someone began to play jazz. The
young people started to dance. And this time, the cabaret artists and
their new Swiss friends were dancing, neither for something nor
against something. They were dancing just for fun.[54] At that moment –
as they did the jitterbug to the jazz music, as they ignored the distressed
officials, as they sang along to the songs and paid no attention to their
surroundings – the totalitarian dream suddenly seemed far away.

In the summer of 1955, Union of Polish Youth members were slipping
away from their dull rallies to dance with Mexican communists and
French fellow travellers. By autumn, their Hungarian counterparts
had begun to breathe life into their turgid League of Working Youth
meetings too. These efforts had begun on a very small scale, when a
group of young staff members at the Hungarian National Museum
decided to organize a literary and political discussion group. They
asked one of their friends, a poet named István Lakatos, to lead them.
Lakatos opened the debates with a lecture on the Hungarian Enlightenment. He read from the works of Hungary's most prominent
Enlightenment poet, György Bessenyei. In conclusion, he called upon

the group to endorse Enlightenment values, albeit 200 years late, and they decided there and then to form a society, the 'Bessenyei Circle'.

It was a tiny, elite and somewhat esoteric effort. But it was nevertheless a matter of concern for the League of Working Youth, for whom any spontaneously organized group was a threat. A few years earlier, they would have banned a group dedicated to Enlightenment values. But Stalin was dead, and angry debate about Nagy's 'New Course' was still raging. They decided to replace the group's leaders and to channel their efforts towards more politically correct, contemporary topics. Fatally, they also decided to name the group after Sándor Petőfi, the young poet of the 1848 revolution, whom they thought more appropriate to a progressive society than the 'bourgeois' Bessenyei. Thus was born the Petőfi Circle, a debating club whose ostensibly academic discussions quickly became open debates about censorship, socialist realism and central planning. Initial discussion topics included the peasants' revolt of 1514 (a pretext for a debate on agricultural policy) and an analysis of Hungarian historiography (a pretext for a debate about the falsification of history in communist textbooks).[55] The choice of name quickly proved 'double-edged', as one Hungarian writer put it: Petőfi had been a revolutionary fighting for Hungarian independence and the group bearing his name soon felt empowered to become revolutionary too.[56]

Changes had been taking place in other regime institutions at the same time. At *Szabad Nép*, the communist party's hitherto reliable newspaper, reporters had become restless. In October 1954, a group of them, sent to cover life in the country's factories, returned wanting to write about faked production statistics, falling living standards and workers who had been blackmailed into buying 'peace bonds'. In a published article, they declared that 'though the life of the workers has changed and improved a great deal in the last ten years, many of them still have serious problems. Many are still living in overcrowded and shabby apartments. Many have to think twice about buying their children a new pair of shoes or going to an occasional movie!' The following day, the reporters got the dreaded phone call from the Politburo member responsible for *Szabad Nép*: 'What do you mean by this article? Do you think we will tolerate this agitation?' Instead of backing down, the editors held a three-day staff conference, at which one reporter after another stood up and called for honest reporting, supported Nagy's reforms, and attacked senior party officials as well as their own editors. Several of these overly honest reporters lost their jobs, including Miklós Gimes, the son of Lily Hajdú, the Freudian psychiatrist who had practised in secret. But a precedent had been set.[57]

Meanwhile, the Hungarian Writers' Association – the group responsible for imposing political correctness on Hungarian prose and poetry – also began to re-examine its previous views, to discuss taboos and to welcome back its banned members. By the autumn of 1955 this formerly hard-line group even felt brave enough to issue a statement protesting against the dismissal of pro-Nagy editors from their posts, demanding 'autonomy' for their association and objecting to the 'anti-democratic methods which cripple our cultural life'.[58]

Most of these new or newly re-formed groups, clubs and debating societies quickly came to be dominated by disillusioned young communists and former communists, mostly in their twenties and thirties. This was a generation which wasn't supposed to be revolutionary – or rather counter-revolutionary – at all. Old enough to have been traumatized by war, young enough to have studied in communist institutions, many were products of the 'social advance' promised by the communist system and many had already enjoyed rapid promotion and early success. Tamás Aczél, active in the Writers' Association debates, had been named chief editor of the party's publishing house at the age of twenty-nine, and by the age of thirty-one had received both the Stalin Prize and the prestigious Kossuth Prize for his work. Tibor Meráy, another Writers' Association activist, had also received a Kossuth Prize at the age of twenty-nine.[59] István Eörsi, also an active member of the Petőfi Circle, had been a published poet from a very young age too.

At the same time, many in this generation had been personally affected by the destruction of civil society, the terror and the purges which had ended just a few years before. All of them knew what it meant to be forced to play the 'reluctant collaborator'. Tibor Déry, one of the leaders of the new Writers' Association, had watched as his once celebrated works of fiction had been attacked and barred from publication as insufficiently ideologically correct.[60] Gábor Tánczos, the leader of the Petőfi Circle, had been an idealistic graduate of Györffy College, one of the Hungarian People's Colleges, until its abrupt and brutal closing in 1949. Another People's College graduate, Iván Vitányi – the music critic who had 'brainwashed' himself after being expelled from the party in 1948 – spoke about folk art and music at some of the early public meetings of the Petőfi Circle.[61] One account describes the early meetings of the Circle as 'reunions' of activists from Nékosz, the People's College movement, and Mefesz, the short-lived university students' union which had been forcibly submerged into the League of Working Youth in 1950. At some of their early meetings they even sang songs together, just as in the old days.[62]

In particular, these young (or youngish) intellectuals were all deeply disturbed by what they now knew had been the unjust arrest, imprisonment and torture of their colleagues. In 1954, Nagy had begun to rehabilitate political prisoners, and they were slowly trickling back to Budapest from prison, from Recsk and from exile. Béla Kovács, the Smallholders' Party leader, came back from the Soviet Union along with several colleagues in 1955.[63] Mindszenty was released from prison and placed under house arrest in a castle outside Budapest. Even Noel Field was rehabilitated that year. Aczél and Meráy have described the deep emotions many Hungarian writers felt when they encountered old friends who had been in prison, suffering while they were penning socialist realist fiction and winning prizes: 'They were ashamed of what they had written and of what they had not written. Now they looked with disgust upon the volumes that they had once upon a time caressed with their eyes – the volumes that had won them the recognition of Kossuth Prizes; and they had no other desire than to unwrite them.'[64]

At the same time, many were also seeking to justify themselves, to make up for the damage they had caused and to put their left-wing projects back on track. This was 1956, not 1989, and not everybody was yet convinced communism was doomed to fail. As Eörsi put it, 'they wanted to rehabilitate, together with their own guilty person, the credibility and the good scientific reputation of Marxism too'.[65] Many turned back to the original texts of Marxism for inspiration and instruction, in Poland as well as Hungary. Karol Modzelewski, a student radical at the time – he was part of a group of activists who took over the Union of Polish Youth at the University of Warsaw in 1956 – explains this dynamic very well: 'We had learned that if a political system is bad, what should one do? Start a revolution. And we were taught, through all of those years, how to make a revolution . . . The workers should do it, with the help of the intellectuals who bring the revolutionary consciousness to the working classes.'[66]

Modzelewski and his colleagues soon began agitating in Polish factories, hoping to create a more equitable economic system, just as Marx had advised: 'It was like a myth turning into real life.'[67] Hungarian intellectuals had the same idea, and for the same reason. As Eörsi wrote later, 'That is the common trap of all quasi-revolutionary systems: the people begin to take seriously the real message of the officially declared ideology and the nationalized heroes of the system.'[68]

Paradoxically, ties between workers and intellectuals were reinforced by their experience of mistreatment under communism. These two social groups had been the most heavily targeted and manipulated by communist propaganda in the previous decade, and had the most profound sense of disjunction and disaffection as a result. If anything, Hungarian workers were even angrier than Hungarian students and Hungarian intellectuals. While writers and journalists felt guilty, the workers felt betrayed. They had been promised the highest possible status in the 'workers' state', and instead they had poor working conditions and low pay. In the immediate postwar period, they had directed their anger at state factory bosses. But now they were inclined to blame the state itself. Miners in the 1950s 'denounced the system and grumbled that despite the difficulty of their work the pay was low', while industry workers in general believed they were exploited by 'a bloodsucking government'.[69] Though *Szabad Nép* had been scared away from reporting too closely on factory life a year earlier, the previously moribund Writers' Association magazine, *Irodalmi Újság* (*Literary Gazette*), now picked up this theme quite frequently, printing interviews and letters from workers, such as this one from a blacksmith:

> How many times have I been obliged to accept the opinion of others, one which I perhaps don't share. As that opinion changes, it's demanded that mine change equally. And that makes me feel sick, sicker than if I'd

been beaten. I'm a man, I too. I also have a head which I use to think. And I'm not a child. I'm an adult, who gives his soul, his heart, his youth and his energy for the construction of socialism ... I do it willingly but I want to be considered like an adult who lives and knows how to think. I want to be able to speak my thoughts without having anything to fear – and I want to be heard as well ...[70]

The Petőfi Circle meetings proved an excellent forum for interactions between the rejuvenated young intellectuals and their radicalized working-class counterparts. In the winter of 1955 the major Budapest factories began sending regular delegations to the meetings, and the demand for tickets soon exceeded supply, forcing the Circle to meet at larger premises. The meetings were open and informal, even raucous at times, and they touched on issues of industrial and economic reform which were of interest to many. Still, they might well have become nothing but a forum for criticism and complaints, had greater events not intervened.

Unexpectedly, Nikita Khrushchev, now the General Secretary of the Soviet communist party, was the man who pushed the students, the workers and the Petőfi Circle participants much further and faster than they had ever expected to go. On 24 February 1956, with no forewarning, Khrushchev stood up in front of the Twentieth Party Congress and denounced 'the cult of personality' which had surrounded the late Stalin:

> it is impermissible and foreign to the spirit of Marxism-Leninism to elevate one person, to transform him into a superman possessing supernatural characteristics, akin to those of a god. Such a man supposedly knows everything, sees everything, thinks for everyone, can do anything, is infallible in his behavior. Such a belief about a man, and specifically about Stalin, was cultivated among us for many years.[71]

This was Khrushchev's famous 'secret' speech – though thanks largely to the Soviet Union's Eastern European friends, it did not remain secret for long. Polish officials leaked it to Israeli intelligence, who leaked it to the CIA, who handed it to the *New York Times*, who published it in June.[72] But even before that, Eastern European communists were poring over it for clues to Khrushchev's thinking. The Soviet leader had lauded Lenin, attacked Stalin, and deplored the

arrests and murder of Soviet party members and military commanders during the purge years of the 1930s, but his *mea culpa* was not
complete. He had not mentioned other arrests and other crimes such
as the Ukrainian famine, for which he himself was partly responsible.
He had not called for economic reforms or institutional reforms. He
had certainly not apologized for anything the Soviet Union had done
in Eastern Europe, and he offered no clear proposals for change.

Nevertheless, it was in Eastern Europe where the most dramatic
reactions ensued. The speech literally killed Bolesław Bierut. The Polish leader went to Moscow for the Twentieth Party Congress and – like
Gottwald at Stalin's funeral – died there of a stroke or a heart attack,
presumably brought on by the shock. Lower down the hierarchy,
many previously loyal party members were stunned: 'People had
trouble believing it,' remembered a Pole who was a junior army officer
at the time: 'The revelations about Generalissimo Stalin, leader of half
the world . . . it was incredible.'[73]

Others were energized, even radicalized by the speech. At the end of
May, a few months after the Twentieth Party Congress, the Petőfi Cir-
cle organized an open, public discussion entitled 'The Twentieth Soviet
Party Congress and the Problems of Hungarian Political Economy'.
Very quickly, that discussion turned into an 'all-out denunciation of
Rákosi's megalomania; his policies of senseless industrial construc-
tion, forced industrialization, the proposed new Five Year Plan and
the lack of realism of his agricultural policy'.[74] In early June, György
Lukás, Hungary's most famous Marxist philosopher, praised 'inde-
pendent thinking' and called for a 'dialogue' between theologians and
Marxists.

Two weeks later, a half-forgotten figure from the recent past stood
up and gave the most devastating denunciation of all. On the evening
of 27 June, Júlia Rajk, aged forty-four and only six months out of
prison, took the podium in a large, neo-classical meeting room in the
very heart of Budapest. 'I stand before you,' she told hundreds of
members of the Petőfi Circle, 'deeply moved after five years of prison
and humiliation':

> Let me tell you this: as far as prisons are concerned, Horthy's jails were
> far better, even for communists, than Rákosi's prisons. Not only was
> my husband killed, but my little baby was torn from me . . . These crim-

inals have not only murdered László Rajk. They have trampled under-
foot all sentiment and honesty in this country. Murderers should not be
criticized, they should be punished.[75]

The audience applauded, whistled, stamped its feet. A few nights
later, another Petőfi Circle audience – by now expanded to 6000 people,
many standing outside on the street – gathered to discuss press freedom. They ended their meeting chanting, 'Imre, Imre, Imre, Imre.' They
were calling for the ousting of Rákosi – and the return of Imre Nagy.

They got half their wish. In the middle of July, Anastas Mikoyan,
one of Khrushchev's closest confidants, paid an emergency visit to
Budapest. Once again, the Politburo had received from Yuri Andropov, then the Soviet ambassador to Hungary (and General Secretary
of the communist party thirty years later) disturbing reports of enemy
activity in Hungary, of spontaneous discussions, of revolutionary
youth. Mikoyan was sent to fix the problem. In the car on the way
from the airport, he told Rákosi that 'in the given situation' he must
resign on grounds of ill-health. Rákosi did as he was told and flew to
Moscow for 'medical treatment', never to return: he spent the final
fifteen years of his life in the Soviet Union, most of it in distant
Kirghizstan.[76] But Mikoyan did not replace him with Nagy. Instead,
the Politburo chose Rákosi's faithful sidekick, the conservative,
unimaginative and, in the final analysis, incompetent Ernő Gerő.[77]

More than fifty years have now passed since October 1956. Since then,
the events of that month have been described many times, by many
great writers, and there is no space here to summarize all of their work
in detail.[78] Suffice to say that between July and October, Gerő tried
desperately to mollify his countrymen. He rehabilitated fifty Social
Democratic leaders who had been imprisoned. He effected a reconciliation with Tito. He reduced the size of the Hungarian army.

After much agonizing, he also allowed Júlia Rajk to hold a funeral
for her husband. On 6 October – the anniversary of the execution of
thirteen generals who had led the Hungarian revolution of 1848 –
Júlia and her son László stood solemnly, dressed in black, beside
her husband's coffin, waiting for Rajk to be re-buried in Kerepesi
cemetery alongside Hungary's national heroes. Tens of thousands of
mourners were in attendance at what was by all accounts a bizarre

event. 'It was a cold, windy, rainy autumn day,' one remembered. 'The flames of the large silver candelabra darted about in a wild *danse macabre*. Mountains of wreaths lay at the foot of the biers.' Funeral orators praised Rajk – himself a murderous secret police boss, responsible for thousands of deaths and arrests as well as the destruction of Kalot, the other youth groups, and the rest of civil society – and denounced Rajk's killers in the harshest possible terms: 'he was killed by sadistic criminals who had crawled into the sun from the stinking swamp of a "cult of personality"'.[79] Jenő Széll, the party official who had been so doubtful about the communist party's optimistic approach to elections, remembered the funeral as 'ghastly':

> It started pouring with rain – not a cloudburst but enough to get us all thoroughly soaked. And beforehand, what a huge streaming crowd of people with grim faces! . . . People came, acquaintances looked at each other and greeted one another, but they didn't as usual form little groups to gossip . . . Everyone here was looking to see who would be in the leadership from now on.[80]

That evening, a few scattered demonstrations broke out. Some 500 students gathered around a statue of Hungary's first constitutional Prime Minister, who had been executed by the Austrians in 1849. Though these meetings broke up peacefully, the city remained wary: 'The solemn formalities of the funeral had reminded people, instead of making them forget, that *fundamentally* nothing had changed.'[81]

The importance of the Rajk funeral was not immediately understood in Budapest, and it was certainly not understood in Moscow. On the contrary, in the first weeks of October the Kremlin's attention was firmly fixed not on Hungary but on Poland, which was also descending into political turmoil. In June, 100,000 workers had gone on strike in the city of Poznań. Like the East Germans before them, they had begun by demanding better pay and less rigorous work norms, but had rapidly started calling for 'an end to dictatorship' and 'Russians out'. They were dispersed, brutally, by the Polish army: some 400 tanks and 10,000 soldiers fired on the strikers, killing several dozen people, among them a thirteen-year-old boy. Hundreds more were wounded. But Poles didn't blame their compatriots for the violence. The Poznań deployment had been supervised by Marshal Rokossovskii after all, a

Soviet citizen of Polish origin, and the orders to fire were issued by his deputy, also a Soviet citizen. The Chief of the General Staff was at that time a Soviet citizen too, as were seventy-six other senior 'Polish' army officers.[82] Inside the Polish communist party, a vocal group now began to call for the removal of the Soviet officers for good. In October, the Polish United Workers' Party took the unilateral decision not merely to grant full rehabilitation to the de facto leader of that group, Władysław Gomułka, but to make him First Party Secretary.

Alarmed, Khrushchev arrived in Warsaw on 19 October. The visit was unplanned: he intended to prevent Gomułka from taking power. To underline his point, he also ordered Soviet troops based elsewhere in Poland to start marching towards Warsaw immediately. According to several accounts, Gomułka responded with his own threats. He became 'rude', he blamed Soviet officers in the Polish army for creating public anger, and he declared that if put in charge he could easily control the country without Soviet interference. More importantly, he also ordered Interior Ministry troops and other armed groups who were loyal to him, and not to the Soviet-dominated army, to take up strategic positions around Warsaw where they prepared to defend him and his new government. A violent clash pitting Polish troops loyal to Gomułka against Polish troops loyal to Soviet commanders – the latter backed up by the Red Army – suddenly seemed possible.[83]

Khrushchev blinked first. 'Finding a reason for an armed conflict [with Poland] right now would be very easy,' he told colleagues on 24 October, 'but finding a way to put an end to such a conflict later on would be very hard.'[84] He decided reconciliation was the best policy – and eventually agreed to recall Rokossovskii, his deputy and several other Soviet officers. In return, Gomułka promised loyalty to Moscow in matters of foreign policy and swore not to withdraw from the Warsaw Pact.

Khrushchev might well have pushed for more. But he was once again distracted from Poland by events in Budapest, where reports of Gomułka's return to power gave Hungarians hope of reinstating Nagy as well. Rajk's strange funeral had removed any remaining barriers of fear: it was as if Stalinism had been symbolically buried, along with his corpse. All during October, local Petőfi Circles had been forming across the country. Colleges and high schools formed their own democratic governing bodies and debating clubs too. The media reported all of this activity with gusto. One radio station interviewed some high school 'parliamentarians', who said they 'would like to travel and study contemporary Western literature'. They also thought university admissions should be decided by exams, not party connections. Events in Poland were also reported with enthusiasm. When hundreds of thousands turned out in Warsaw to cheer Gomułka, one Hungarian journalist declared that 'the trend of democratisation has the full support of the large masses and, what is more important, the working-class'.[85]

Inspired by this news, 5000 students crammed into a hall at Budapest Technological University on 22 October to vote themselves out of the League of Working Youth, and to form their own organization. From 3 p.m. until midnight they wrote a manifesto, a radical document which eventually became known as the Sixteen Points. Among other things, it called for the withdrawal of Soviet troops from Hungary, free elections, freedom of association, economic reform – and the restoration of 15 March, the 1848 anniversary, as a national holiday.[86] The students also agreed to meet the following day beneath the statue of General József Bem, a Polish commander who had fought with the Hungarians in 1848, and to demonstrate there in favour of their demands and in support of Polish workers.

Twenty-four hours later, there were at least 25,000 people in Bem Square, and thousands more in the streets flowing out of it. They had marched to the Polish general's statue from all over the city, in some cases sent on their way by recitations of a Petőfi verse said to have inspired the revolution of 1848:

> Arise Hungarians, your country calls you.
> Meet this hour, what'er befalls you.
> Shall we free men be or slaves?
> Choose the lot your spirit craves.

As in Poznań the previous June, many were shouting 'Russians go home!' As in Berlin three years earlier, the crowd sacked a Russian bookstore along the way and set its contents alight. One group broke off and headed for the radio station. There they laid siege to the building and demanded, 'We want the radio to belong to the people!' When the station kept playing bland music, they began ramming the building with a radio truck. By nightfall, the crowd had moved on to Hero Square, where a giant bronze statue of Stalin had been erected four years earlier. After a few futile attempts to pull the statue down with ropes, a platoon of workers arrived with heavy machinery – the cranes were borrowed from the city's public transportation department – and metal-burning equipment. They hacked away, the crowd chanted, and the statue began to shake. Finally, at precisely 9.37 p.m., Stalin fell.[87]

The Soviet leadership reacted with dismay, inconsistency and confusion to the events in Budapest, as did the Hungarian regime. Gerő panicked, called Ambassador Andropov and begged for Soviet tanks. Khrushchev sent tanks and then withdrew them. Nagy at first tried to pacify the crowds, initially telling them to go home and let the party elders deal with it. But when Khrushchev changed his mind and sent Red Army troops pouring back over the border, Nagy switched sides, announced Hungary's withdrawal from the Warsaw Pact and called on the United Nations to defend Hungarian neutrality.

The Western powers were equally at sea. The Hungarian service of Radio Free Europe, based in Munich and staffed by angry émigrés, egged on the revolutionaries. But despite his earlier calls for the 'rollback' of communism and the 'liberation' of Eastern Europe, the hawkish American Secretary of State, John Foster Dulles, could do no better than send the Soviet leaders a message: 'we do not see these states [Hungary and Poland] as potential military allies'.[88] At the time, the CIA had but a single agent inside Hungary, and he lost contact with the agency after the second Soviet invasion.[89]

In twelve brief days of euphoria and chaos, nearly every symbol of the communist regime was attacked. Statues were torn down and red stars removed from buildings. The citizens of Sztálinváros, having been coerced into naming their city after Stalin, spontaneously decided to change it back again. Along with about 8000 other political prisoners, Mindszenty was released from the medieval castle where he had been kept in solitary isolation. Young Hungarians took over the national radio and renamed it Radio Free Kossuth, a name which echoed 'Radio Kossuth', the station on which the Hungarian communists had broadcast liberation propaganda during the war. 'For many years our radio has been an instrument of lies ... It lied by night and by day; it lied on all wavelengths,' they declared: 'We who are before the microphone now are new men.'[90]

Across the country, radical workers borrowed an idea from Yugoslavia and began forming 'worker councils', which began to take over factories and expel the management.[91] Instead of fighting the revolutionaries, Hungarian soldiers deserted the army in droves and began distributing weapons to their fellow citizens. One of the first senior officers to defect, Colonel Pál Maléter, was quickly named Nagy's new Defence Minister. The Budapest chief of police, Sándor Kopácsi, also switched sides and joined the revolutionaries. Across the country, mobs lynched secret policemen and broke into secret police archives. Curious crowds broke into Rákosi's villa too, and grew furious when they saw the luxurious furniture and carpets.

The aftermath was equally chaotic and appallingly bloody. General Ivan Serov – the man who had 'pacified' Warsaw and Berlin, and who had since been promoted to the leadership of the KGB – personally supervised the arrests of Maléter and Nagy. The latter had sought asylum in the Yugoslav embassy, was promised safe passage to Belgrade and then betrayed. Both men were eventually executed, not on the orders of Khrushchev but on the command of János Kádár, the Hungarian leader who then ruled the country for the subsequent three decades. Miklós Gimes, the son of the psychiatrist Lili Hajdú, kept up the resistance throughout November, as did many of the factory workers, before he too was arrested and eventually executed. Between December 1956 and the summer of 1961, 341 people were hanged, 26,000 people were put on trial and 22,000 received sentences of five years or more. Tens of thousands more lost their jobs or their homes.[92] Even so, strikes and protests continued across Hungary throughout December and January, especially in the factories. Mindszenty sought refuge in the American embassy, where he remained for fifteen years. Some 200,000 Hungarians fled over the border and became refugees. Faludy, the poet who had been imprisoned in Recsk, was one of them: 'I had a wife and young son. I was afraid that if I stayed I would break, join the Communist party in order to survive and protect my family.'[93]

Across the rest of Eastern Europe and around the world, the Hungarian Revolution helped alter the international perception of the Soviet Union for good, especially in the Western communist parties. After 1956, the French communist party fractured, the Italian communist party broke away from Moscow and the British communist party lost two thirds of its members. Even Jean-Paul Sartre attacked the USSR in November 1956, though he retained a weakness for Marxism long afterwards.[94]

The excellent reporting from Hungary in 1956 helped create this reaction: some of the best journalists of their generation were in Budapest during the revolution, and arguably some of the best war photographers of all time. But the agonizing images were made more powerful by the fact that they had been so unexpected. Until it actually happened, few analysts – even fiercely anti-Soviet analysts – had believed that revolution was possible within the Soviet bloc. Both communists and anti-communists, with a very few exceptions, had assumed that Soviet methods of indoctrination were invincible; that most people believed in the propaganda without question; that the totalitarian educational system really would eliminate dissent; that civic institutions, once destroyed, could not be rebuilt; that history, once rewritten, would be forgotten. In January 1956, a US National Intelligence Estimate had predicted that, over time, dissidence in Eastern Europe would be worn down 'by the gradual increase in the number of Communist-indoctrinated youth'.[95] In a later epilogue to the *Origins of Totalitarianism*, Hannah Arendt wrote that the Hungarian Revolution 'was totally unexpected and took everybody by surprise'. Like the CIA, the KGB, Khrushchev and Dulles, Arendt had come to believe that totalitarian regimes, once they worked their way into the soul of a nation, were very nearly invincible.

They were all wrong. Human beings do not acquire 'totalitarian personalities' with such ease. Even when they seem bewitched by the cult of the leader or of the party, appearances can be deceiving. And even when it seems as if they are in full agreement with the most absurd propaganda – even if they are marching in parades, chanting slogans, singing that the party is always right – the spell can suddenly, unexpectedly, dramatically be broken.

Epilogue

And so it was necessary to teach people not to think and make judgements, to compel them to see the non-existent, and to argue the opposite of what was obvious to everyone ...

Boris Pasternak, Doctor Zhivago

For more than thirty years, right up to the fall of the Berlin Wall in 1989, the communist leaders of Eastern Europe kept asking themselves the same questions they had posed after Stalin's death. Why did the system produce such poor economic results? Why was the propaganda unconvincing? What was the source of continuing dissent, and what was the best way to quash it? Would arrests, repression and terror suffice to keep the communist parties in power? Or would more liberal tactics – a measure of economic freedom or a modicum of free speech – prevent future explosions more effectively? What changes would the Soviet Union accept, and where would the Soviet leadership draw the line?

Different answers were given at different times. After Stalin's death none of the regimes were as cruel as they had been between 1945 and 1953, but even post-Stalinist Eastern Europe could be harsh, arbitrary and formidably repressive. Gomułka's Poland started out with liberal ambitions and popular enthusiasm, but quickly grew sclerotic, conservative and eventually anti-semitic. Kádár began his reign in Hungary with a series of bloody reprisals, but later tried to win legitimacy and popularity by allowing some free enterprise, travel and trade. In the build-up to the Prague Spring in 1968, Czechoslovakia enjoyed a real cultural flowering – writers, directors and playwrights won international acclaim – but after the Soviet invasion, the Czecho-slovak government became one of the most thuggish in the entire bloc. In 1961 East Germany built a wall to keep its citizens in, but in the 1980s the regime quietly started allowing dissidents to leave in exchange for hard currency from the West German government. Both Romania and Yugoslavia tried at different times to carve out individual roles in foreign policy, distancing themselves from the rest of the Soviet bloc, but not necessarily in very meaningful ways.

Though always staying within the framework laid down by the Soviet Union, various Eastern European governments experimented by increasing the role of cooperatives or restraining the church, raising the numbers of secret policemen or allowing more freedom in the arts. Sometimes, the liberal reforms stayed in place: the Polish communists abandoned socialist realism after 1956, for example, and Hungary legalized joint ventures in the 1980s. At other times liberalization ended with violence. At the time of the Prague Spring, the Czechoslovak communist party under the leadership of Alexander Dubček called for evolutionary reform, a decentralized economy and a democratized political system. Soviet tanks rolled into Prague and crushed the reform movement a few months later, and Dubček was removed from power. In August 1980, the Polish communist party legalized the Solidarity trade union, a grassroots movement which eventually contained 10 million workers, students and intellectuals. That experiment ended a year and half later, when the Polish communist party declared martial law, banned Solidarity and put tanks on the street as well.

Over time, the nations of Eastern Europe began to have much less in common. By the 1980s, East Germany had the largest police state, Poland the highest church attendance, Romanians the most dramatic food shortages, Hungarians the highest living standards and Yugoslavia the most relaxed relationship with the West. Yet in one narrow sense they remained very similar: none of the regimes ever seemed to realize that they were unstable by definition. They lurched from crisis to crisis not because they were unable to fine-tune their policies, but because the communist project itself was flawed. By trying to control every aspect of society, the regimes had turned every aspect of society into a potential form of protest. The state had dictated high daily quotas for the workers – and so the East German workers' strike against high daily quotas mushroomed quickly into a protest against the state. The state had dictated what artists could paint or writers could write – and so an artist or writer who painted or wrote something different became a political dissident too. The state had dictated that no one could form independent organizations – and so anybody who founded one, however anodyne, became an opponent of the regime. And when large numbers of people joined an independent organization – when some 10 million Poles joined the Solidarity trade union, for example – the regime's very existence was suddenly at stake.

Communist ideology and Marxist-Leninist economic theory contained the seeds of their own destruction in a different sense too. Eastern European governments' claims to legitimacy were based on promises of future prosperity and high living standards which were supposedly guaranteed by 'scientific' Marxism. All of the banners and posters, the solemn speeches, the newspaper editorials and eventually the television programmes spoke of ever-faster growth. But although there was some growth, it was never as high as the propaganda made it out to be. Living standards never rose as quickly and dramatically as they did in Western Europe either, a fact which could not long be hidden. In 1950, Poland and Spain had very similar GDPs. By 1988, Poland's had risen about two and half times – but Spain's had risen thirteen times.[1] Radio Free Europe, travel and tourism all brought home this gap, which only grew larger as technological change in Western Europe accelerated. Cynicism and disillusion grew along with it, even among those who had originally placed their faith in the system. The smiling communist youth cadres of the 1950s gave way to the sullen, apathetic workers of the 1970s, to the cynical students and intellectuals of the 1980s, to waves of emigration and discontent. The system always had its supporters, of course, particularly after some East European governments began to borrow large sums from Western banks in order to maintain higher levels of consumption. Its beneficiaries went on paying it lip service, and those who had benefited from communist social promotion policies continued to advance through the bureaucracy. But although some East Europeans were later nostalgic for communist ideas and idealism, it is noteworthy that no post-1989 political party has ever tried to restore communist economics.

In the end, the gap between reality and ideology meant that the communist parties wound up spouting meaningless slogans which they themselves knew made no sense. As the philosopher Roger Scruton argues, Marxism became so cocooned in what Orwell once called 'Newspeak' that it could not be refuted: 'facts no longer made contact with the theory, which had risen above the facts on clouds of nonsense, rather like a theological system. The point was not to believe the theory, but to repeat it ritualistically and in such a way that both belief and doubt became irrelevant ... In this way the concept of truth disappeared from the intellectual landscape, and was replaced by that of power.'[2] Once people were unable to distinguish truth from ideological fiction, however, then they were also unable to solve or even describe the worsening social and economic problems of the societies they ruled.

Over time, some political opponents of the communist regimes came to understand these inherent weaknesses of Soviet-style totalitarianism. In his brilliant 1978 essay, 'The Power of the Powerless', the Czech dissident Vaclav Havel called upon his countrymen to take advantage of their rulers' obsession with total control. If the state wanted to monopolize every sphere of human activity, he wrote, then every thinking citizen should work to create alternatives. He called upon his countrymen to preserve the 'independent life of society', which he defined as including 'everything from self-education and thinking about the world, through free creative activity and its communication to others, to the most varied, free, civic attitudes, including instances of independent social self-organization'.[3] He also urged them to discard false and meaningless jargon and to 'live in truth' – to speak and act, in other words, as if the regime did not exist.

In due course, some version of this 'independent life of society' – 'civil society' – began to flourish in many unusual ways. The Czechs formed jazz bands, the Hungarians joined academic discussion clubs, the East Germans created an 'unofficial' peace movement. The Poles organized underground scouting troops and, eventually, independent trade unions. Everywhere, people played rock music, organized poetry readings, set up clandestine businesses, held underground philosophy seminars, sold black market meat and went to church. In a different kind of society, these activities would have been considered apolitical, and even in Eastern Europe they did not necessarily constitute 'opposition', or even passive opposition. But they did pose a fundamental – and unanswerable – challenge to regimes which strove, in Mussolini's words, to be 'all-embracing'.

'You can't make an omelette without breaking eggs.'[4] That grim motto, sometimes incorrectly attributed to Stalin, sums up the world-view of the men and women who built communism and who believed that their high-minded goals justified human sacrifice. But once the omelette finally begins to fall apart – or, more accurately, once it becomes clear that the omelette was never cooked in the first place – how do you put the eggs back together again? How do you privatize hundreds of state companies? How do you re-create religious and social organizations disbanded long ago? How do you get a society made passive by years of dictatorship to become active again? How do you get people to stop using jargon and speak clearly? Though often used as shorthand, the word 'democratization' doesn't really do justice to the changes which took place – unevenly and unsteadily, faster in some places and much slower in others – in post-communist Europe and the former USSR after 1989.

Nor does the word 'democratization' really define the kind of changes which need to take place in other post-revolutionary societies around the world. Many of the twentieth century's worst dictators held power using the methods described in this book, and consciously so. Saddam Hussein's Iraq and Moammar Qadaffi's Libya directly adopted elements of the Soviet system, including a Soviet-style secret police force, with direct Soviet and East German assistance. Chinese, Egyptian, Syrian, Angolan, Cuban and North Korean regimes, among others, have all received Soviet advice and training at different times too.[5] But many didn't need explicit advice in order to imitate the Soviet Union's drive to control economic, social, cultural, legal and educational institutions as well as political opposition. Until 1989, the Soviet Union's dominance of Eastern Europe seemed an excellent model for would-be dictators. But totalitarianism never worked as it was supposed to do in Eastern Europe, and it never worked anywhere else either. None of the Stalinist regimes ever managed to brainwash everybody and thus eliminate all dissent for ever, and neither did Stalin's pupils or Brezhnev's friends in Asia, Africa or Latin America.

Yet such regimes can and did do an enormous amount of damage. In their drive for power, the Bolsheviks, their East European acolytes and their imitators further afield attacked not only their political opponents but also peasants, priests, schoolteachers, traders, journalists, writers, small businessmen, students and artists, along with the institutions such people had built and maintained over centuries. They damaged, undermined and sometimes eliminated churches, newspapers, literary and educational societies, companies and retail shops, stock markets, banks, sports clubs and universities. Their success reveals an unpleasant truth about human nature: if enough people are sufficiently determined, and if they are backed by adequate resources and force, then they can destroy ancient and apparently permanent legal, political, educational and religious institutions, sometimes for good. And if civil society could be so deeply damaged in nations as disparate, as historic and as culturally rich as those of Eastern Europe, then it can be similarly damaged anywhere. If nothing else, the history of postwar Stalinization proves just how fragile 'civilization' can turn out to be.

As a result of this damage, post-communist countries required far more than the bare institutions of 'democracy' – elections, political campaigns and political parties – to become functioning liberal societies again. They also had to create or re-create independent media, private enterprise and a legal system to support it, an educational system free of propaganda and a civil service where promotions are given for talent, not for ideological correctness. The most successful post-communist states are those which managed to preserve some elements of civil society throughout the communist period. This is not an accident.

Here, once again, the history of the Polish Women's League is worth retelling. By 1989 the organization was utterly moribund at the national level. In the early 1990s it more or less collapsed altogether: no one needed a women's group which provided propaganda for a communist party that no longer existed. But in the late 1990s, once again in the city of Łódź, a group of local women decided that some of the functions which the League had originally been designed to perform were still necessary. And so the League regrouped, re-organized and refounded itself – now for the third time – as an independent organization. As in 1945, its leaders identified a set of problems which no one else seemed able to solve, and they set about addressing them. Initially, the League offered free legal clinics for women who could not afford legal advice. Later it branched into assistance for unemployed women, job training, advice and services for single women with children, help for alcoholics and drug addicts. At Christmas, the League began to organize parties for the homeless in Łódź. Its website now carries a straightforward motto: 'If you have a problem, come to us, we'll help you or we'll point you in the right direction.'⁶ It is a much smaller organization, but its character is charitable, just as it was in the past.

In part, the new Women's League succeeded because its leaders, like others in Poland, were so eager to copy West European models. Though they themselves had never worked for a charity or a 'non-profit' organization, the League's leaders certainly knew what these legal entities were. Polish law by then accommodated their existence, and the Polish political class welcomed them, just as they welcomed independent schools, private businesses and political parties. This made Poland different from Russia, where hostility to independent organizations remains strong, even a generation after the collapse of the Soviet Union, and where the legal environment is still not conducive to their formation or their funding. The Russian political elite still considers independent charities, advocacy groups and non-governmental organizations of all kinds suspicious, by definition, and uses both legal and extra-legal means to restrain them.⁷

In Poland the legal framework not only accommodated the exist-ence of independent organization, but also permitted them to raise funds. At first, the Women's League had petitioned the government for money to support their projects, because that was how they had been supported in the past. In an era of economic restructuring, they had only minimal success. But Łódź is a city of textile mills, and textile mills employ women. The Women's League approached the new mill owners and convinced a few of them to help. Donations began to come in, the organization stayed alive. In 2006, seventeen years after the fall of communism, the Łódź Women's League became a registered private charity. As it turned out, the modern Polish Women's League needed not only energetic and patriotic volunteers but also an intact legal system, a functioning economic system and a democratic political system in order to thrive.

Some of the energy and the initiative to start these projects also came from a sharp consciousness of the organization's communist and pre-communist history. One of the new leaders, Janina Miziołek, had spent time as a very small child in one of the shelters set up by the Women's League in train stations. Others who had been active in the League in the communist period sought to retrieve something useful from the organization's wreckage: if they could remove the politics, some of them told me, perhaps they could really do something useful. They remembered what had gone wrong, and they were anxious to fix it.

The women of Łódź were clearly motivated by history, though not by history as it is sometimes used or abused by politicians. They were inspired not by state-sponsored celebrations of past tragedies or national programmes of patriotic re-education, but rather by stories they themselves actually remembered, or stories they knew from someone else who had experienced them. They were motivated by the history of a particular institution in a particular place at a particular time.

What was true in Łódź is true everywhere else in the post-communist and the post-totalitarian world. Before a nation can be rebuilt, its citizens need to understand how it was destroyed in the first place: how its institutions were undermined, how its language was twisted, how its people were manipulated. They need to know particular details, not general theories, and they need to hear individual stories, not generalizations about the masses. They need a better grasp of what motivated their predecessors, to see them as real people and not as black and white caricatures, victims or villains. Only then is it possible, slowly, to rebuild.

List of interviewees

GERMANY

Karl-Heinz Arnold, Egon Bahr, Ernst Benda, Hans-Walter Bendzko, Klaus Blümner, Elfriede Brüning, Stefan Doernberg, Klaus Eichner, Ulrich Fest, Gerhard Finn, Karl Gass, Gisela Gneist, Bernhard Heisig, Herta Kuhrig, Jürgen Laue, Wolfgang Lehmann, Irina Liebmann, Erich Loest, Manfred Meier, Hans Modrow, Alfons Pawlitzki, Gustav Pohl, Klaus Polkehn, Lutz Rackow, Günter Reisch, Werner Rösler, Günter Schabowski, Ulrich Schneider, Gotthold Schramm, Willi Sitte, André Steiner, Hans-Jochen Tschiche, Günter Tschirschwitz.

HUNGARY

János Boór, László Dalos, Ferenc Gergely, Ágnes Heller, György Hidas, Ferenc Hollai, Elek Horváth, Elekné Horváth (Júlia Kollár), Tibor Iványi, Sándor Keresztes, András Kovács, Sándor Ladányi, Tamás Lossonczy, Márta Mészáros, József Nevezi, Ferenc Pataki, Csaba Skultéty, Ferenc Szabó, Pál Szemere, Zsófia Tevan, Áron Tóbiás , Iván Vitányi.

POLAND

Barbara Barańska, Michał Bauer, Szymon Bojko, Halina Bortnowska, Stefan Bratkowski, Wiesław Chrzanowski, Krystyna Czart-Kosacz, Jacek Fedorowicz, Andrzej Garlicki, Stefan Grzeszkiewicz, Józef Hen, Alexander Jackowski, Ksawery Jasieński, Stanisław Juchnowicz, Ludwik Jerzy Kern, Czesław Kiszczak, Tadeusz Konwicki, Janina

Miziołek, Karol Modzelewski, Jerzy Morawski, Eugeniusz Mroczkowski, Krzysztof Pomian, Józef Puciłowski, Antoni Rajkiewicz, Ludwik Rokicki, Marta Stebnicka, Janina Stobniak, Janina Suska-Janakowska, Józef Tejchma, Jerzy Turnau, Leopold Unger, Andrzej Zalewski.

Notes

LIST OF ARCHIVES

1956 Institute	Archives of the 1956 Institute, Budapest.
AAN	Archiwum Akt Nowych – Central Archive of Modern Records, Warsaw
ÁBTL	Állambiztonsági Szolgálatok Történeti Levéltára – Historical Archives of Hungarian State Security (secret police archives), Budapest
AdK ABK	Akademie der Künste Archiv Bildende Kunst – Academy of Arts Visual Arts Archive, Berlin
AUL	Archiv unterdrückter Literatur in der DDR – Archive of Suppressed Literature in the GDR, Berlin
BStU MfSZ	Der Bundesbeauftragte für die Stasi-Unterlagen – The Federal Commission for the State Security Archives of the GDR (Stasi archives), Berlin
CAW	Centralne Archiwum Wojskowe – Central Military Archive, Warsaw
DRA	Deutsche Rundfunkarchiv – German Broadcasting Archive, Potsdam
GARF	Gosudarstvennyi Arkhiv Rossiiskoi Federatsii – The State Archive of the Russian Federation, Moscow
GEOK	Gedenkbibliothek zu Ehren der Opfer des Kommunismus – Memorial Library of the Victims of Communism, Berlin
HIA	Hoover Institution Archives, Stanford, California
IPN	Instytut Pamięci Narodowej – The Institute of National Remembrance (secret police archives), Warsaw
IWM	Imperial War Museum Archives, London
Karta	Archives of the Karta Centre Foundation, Warsaw

MNFA	Magyar Nemzeti Filmarchívum – Hungarian National Film Archive
MOL	Magyar Országos Levéltár – National Archives of Hungary, Budapest
NA	National Archives, Kew, Richmond, UK
NAC	Narodowe Archiwum Cyfrowe – National Digital Archives, Warsaw
OSA	Open Society Archive, Budapest
PIL	Archive of the Institute of Political History, Budapest
RGANI	Rossiiskii Gosudarstvennyi Arkhiv Noveishei Istorii – Russian State Archive of Contemporary History, Moscow
SAPMO-BA	Stiftung Archiv der Parteien und Massenorganisationen der DDR im Bundesarchiv – Foundation for the Archives of the GDR's Parties and Mass Organizations in the Bundesarchiv, Berlin
SNL	Széchenyi National Library, Budapest
TsAMO RF	Tsentral'nyi Arkhiv Ministerstva Oborony Rossiiskoi Federatsii – Central Archive of the Ministry of Defence of the Russian Federation, Podolsk
TVP	Telewizja Polska – Polish Radio Archives, Warsaw

INTRODUCTION

1. Interview with Janina Suska, Łódź, 16 October 2007.
2. Both quotes from Barbara Nowak, 'Serving Women and the State: The League of Women in Communist Poland', dissertation, Ohio State University, 2004.
3. The word was coined by Giovanni Amendola, an opponent of Mussolini, in 1923. But it was adopted enthusiastically by Mussolini himself in 1925, and used frequently by his main theoretician, Giovanni Gentile. For an overview, see Abbott Gleason, *Totalitarianism: The Inner History of the Cold War* (Oxford, 1995), pp. 13–18.
4. Benito Mussolini and Giovanni Gentile, *Fascism: Doctrine and Institutions* (Rome, 1935).
5. For a summary of this entire debate, see Gleason as well as Michael Geyer and Sheila Fitzpatrick's introduction to *Beyond Totalitarianism: Stalinism and Nazism Compared* (Cambridge, 2009).
6. Hannah Arendt, *The Origins of Totalitarianism* (Cleveland and New York, 1958).

7. Carl J. Friedrich and Zbigniew Brzezinski, *Totalitarian Dictatorship and Autocracy* (Cambridge, 1956).

8. http://www.trumanlibrary.org/whistlestop/study_collections/doctrine/large/index.php

9. Gregory Bush, *Campaign Speeches of American Presidential Candidates, 1948–1984* (New York, 1985), p. 42.

10. See Geyer and Fitzpatrick in *Beyond Totalitarianism*.

11. Quoted in Richard Pipes, *Communism: A History* (New York, 2001), pp. 105–7.

12. See Michael Halberstam, *Totalitarianism and the Modern Conception of Politics* (Yale, 2000).

13. Slavoj Žižek, *Did Somebody Say Totalitarianism?: Five Interventions in the (Mis)Use of a Notion* (New York, 2001). Žižek argues that the description of Stalinism as 'totalitarian' is nothing more than an attempt to ensure that the 'liberal democratic hegemony' endures.

14. http://www.huffingtonpost.com/james-peron/rick-santorum-gay-rights_b_1195555.html; http://video.foxbusiness.com/v/1328239165001/the-uss-march-toward-totalitarianism; http://articles.latimes.com/2011/dec/25/business/la-fi-hiltzik-20111225

15. http://fare.tunes.org/liberty/library/toptt.html

16. See William J. Dobson, *The Dictator's Learning Curve* (New York, 2012), for a description of the evolution of contemporary dictatorships.

17. This is Mark Kramer's brilliant and precise definition: 'The term "Eastern Europe" ... is partly geographic and partly political, encompassing eight European countries that were under Communist rule from the 1940s through the end of the 1980s ... The term does not include the Soviet Union itself, even though the western Soviet republics (Lithuania, Latvia, Estonia, Belarus, Ukraine, Moldova, and Russia west of the Urals) constituted the easternmost part of Europe. The term does include some countries in what is more properly called "Central Europe," such as Czechoslovakia, Hungary, Poland, and what in 1949 became known as the German Democratic Republic (or East Germany). The other Communist states in Europe – Albania, Bulgaria, Romania, and Yugoslavia – are also encompassed by the term "Eastern Europe." Countries that were never under Communist rule, such as Greece and Finland, are not regarded as part of "Eastern Europe," even though they might be construed as such from a purely geographic standpoint.' Mark Kramer, 'Stalin, Soviet Policy and the Consolidation of a Communist Bloc in Eastern Europe, 1944–1953', p. 1, paper delivered at the Freeman Spogli International Institute, 30 April 2010.

18. This is also Joseph Rothschild's point in *Return to Diversity: A Political History of East Central Europe since World War II* (New York and Oxford, 2000), especially pp. 75–8.

19. *Pravda*, 21 December 1949.

20. *The Communist Party of the Soviet Union (Bolsheviks) is the Leading and Guiding Force of Soviet Society* (Foreign Languages Publishing House, Moscow, 1951), p. 46.

21. See Hugh Seton-Watson, *The New Imperialism: A Background Book* (London, 1961), p. 81.

22. The classic version of this thesis was formulated by William Appleman Williams in *The Tragedy of American Diplomacy* (New York, 1959). A more recent, more sophisticated version is found, for example, in Wilfred Loth, *Stalin's Unwanted Child: The Soviet Union, the German Question and the Founding of the GDR*, trans. Robert F. Hogg (London, 1998).

23. John Lewis Gaddis, *We Now Know: Rethinking Cold War History* (Oxford, 1997); Kramer, 'Stalin, Soviet Policy and the Consolidation of a Communist Bloc in Eastern Europe, 1944–1953'.

24. T. V. Volokitina et al., eds., *Sovietskii faktor v vostochnoi evrope, 1944–1953*, Vol. 1, pp. 23–48; also Norman Naimark, 'The Sovietization of Eastern Europe, 1944–1953', *The Cambridge History of the Cold War* (Cambridge, 2010).

25. Ivo Banac, ed., *The Diary of Georgi Dimitrov, 1933–1949* (New Haven and London, 2003), p. 14.

26. Tony Judt and Timothy Snyder, *Thinking the Twentieth Century* (London, 2012), p. 190.

27. Tomasz Goban-Klas, *The Orchestration of the Media: The Politics of Mass Communications in Communist Poland and the Aftermath* (Boulder, 1994), p. 54.

28. The communist party of Yugoslavia remained more popular than the others for many years but this was at least partly because it eventually broke away from Soviet influence.

29. One exception, and the standard work for many years, was Zbigniew Brzezinski's *The Soviet Bloc: Unity and Conflict* (New York, 1967).

30. Arendt, *Origins of Totalitarianism*, pp. 480–81.

31. See Timothy Snyder, *Bloodlands* (New York, 2011); Jan Gross, 'War as Revolution', in Norman Naimark and Leonid Gibianskii, eds., *The Establishment of Communist Regimes in Eastern Europe, 1944–1949* (Boulder, 1997); Bradley Abrams, 'The Second World War and the East European Revolution', *East European Politics and Societies*, Vol. 16, No. 3, pp. 623–5.

32. See the work of the Harvard Project on Cold War Studies, as well as the Wilson Center's Cold War International History Project. Good recent surveys which use new archives include John Lewis Gaddis, *The Cold War: A New History* (New York, 2005); Vojtech Mastny, *The Cold War and Soviet Insecurity: The Stalin Years* (Oxford, 1996); Melvyn P. Leffler, *For the Soul of Mankind: The United States, the Soviet Union and the Cold War* (New York, 2007). See also Melvyn P. Leffler and Odd Arne Westad, 'Bibliographical Essay', *Cambridge History of the Cold War*, Vol. One: *Origins* (Cambridge, 2010).

33. Paczkowski and Kersten have written multiple works on the period. In English see Andrzej Paczkowski, *The Spring Will be Ours: Poland and the Poles from Occupation to Freedom* (New York, 2003), and Krystyna Kersten, *The Establishment of Communist Rule in Poland, 1943–1948* (Berkeley, 1991). See also Norman Naimark, *The Russians in Germany: A History of the Soviet Zone of Occupation, 1945–1949* (Cambridge, Mass., 1995); Peter Kenez, *Hungary from the Nazis to the Soviets: The Establishment of the Communist Regime in Hungary, 1944–1948* (New York, 2006); László Borhi, *Hungary in the Cold War, 1945–1956: Between the United States and the Soviet Union* (New York, 2004); Karel Kaplan, *The Short March: The Communist Takeover in Czechoslovakia, 1945–48* (New York, 1987); Bradley Adams, *The Struggle for the Soul of the Czech Nation: Czech Culture and the Rise of Communism* (New York, 2005); Mary Heimann, *Czechoslovakia: The State That Failed* (New Haven, 2009).

34. John Connelly, *Captive University: The Sovietization of East German, Czech, and Polish Higher Education, 1945–1956* (Chapel Hill, 1999); Catherine Epstein, *The Last Revolutionaries: German Communists and Their Century* (Cambridge, Mass., and London, 2003); Marci Shore, *Caviar and Ashes: A Warsaw Generation's Life and Death in Marxism, 1918–1968* (New Haven, 2006); Mária Schmidt, *Battle of Wits*, trans. Ann Major (Budapest, 2007); Martin Mevius, *Agents of Moscow: The Hungarian Communist Party and the Origins of Socialist Patriotism 1941–1953* (Oxford, 2005); Mark Kramer, 'The Early Post-Stalin Succession Struggle and Upheavals in East-Central Europe: Internal–External Linkages in Soviet Policy Making', parts 1–3, *Journal of Cold War Studies*, 1, 1 (Winter 1999), 3–55; 1, 2 (Spring 1999), 3–38; 1, 3 (Fall 1999), 3–66.

35. T. V. Volokitina et al., eds., *Vostochnaya Evropa v dokumentakh rossiskikh arkhivov, 1944–1953* (Novosibirsk, 1997), and T. V. Volokitina et al., eds., *Sovetskii faktor v vostochnoi evrope, 1944–1953* (Moscow, 1999).

1. ZERO HOUR

1. Tamás Lossonczy, *The Vision is Always Changing* (Budapest, 2004), p. 82.
2. William Shirer, *End of a Berlin Diary* (New York, 1947), p. 131.
3. Marcin Zaremba, *Wielka Trwoga: Polska 1944–1947, Ludowa reakeja na kryzys* (Warsaw, 2012), p. 71. Page nos. come from the pre-publication manuscript.
4. Anonymous, *A Woman in Berlin*, trans. Philip Boehm (London, 2006), pp. 64–6.
5. Krisztián Ungváry, *The Siege of Budapest: 100 Days in World War II* (London, 2002), pp. 324–5.
6. Władysław Szpilman, *The Pianist* (London, 1999), p. 183.
7. Bradley Abrams, 'The Second World War and the East European Revolution', *East European Politics and Societies*, Vol. 16, No. 3, pp. 623–5.
8. Heda Kovály, *Under a Cruel Star* (Cambridge, Mass., 1986), p. 39.
9. Anonymous, *Woman in Berlin*, p. 297.
10. Zaremba, *Wielka Trwoga*, p. 71.
11. Ibid., pp. 6–7.
12. Stefan Kisielewski, 'Ci z Warszawy', *Przekroj*, 6/V, 1945.
13. Sándor Márai, *Portraits of a Marriage*, trans. George Szirtes (New York, 2012), p. 272.
14. Arthur Marwick, *War and Social Change in the Twentieth Century* (London, 1974), pp. 98–145.
15. Timothy Snyder, *Bloodlands: Europe between Hitler and Stalin* (New York, 2010), p. 19.
16. Ibid., pp. viii–ix.
17. Wolfgang Schivelbusch, *In a Cold Crater: Cultural and Intellectual Life in Berlin, 1945–1948* (Berkeley, 1998), pp. 8–9.
18. Andrew Roberts, *Masters and Commanders* (London, 2008), pp. 561 and 569.
19. Abrams, 'The Second World War and the East European Revolution', p. 631; also Iván T. Berend and Tamás Csató, *Evolution of the Hungarian Economy, 1848–1998*, Vol. I (Boulder, 2001), p. 253.
20. The most recent calculations of German war dead include 5,318,000 military deaths (Rudiger Overmans, *Deutsche militärische Verluste im Zweiten Weltkrieg* (Munich, 2004), p. 260); the rest are civilians who died of starvation or illness, during deportation and expulsion, or during bombing raids.

21. Janusz Wrobel, 'Bilans Okupacji Niemieckiej w Łodzi 1939–45', *Rok 1945 w Łodzi*, pp. 13–30.

22. A few years ago, my husband received a letter from a German, born in the Baltic region, whose family had been given what is now our Polish country house to inhabit during the war. He enclosed a photograph of his smiling German parents, dressed in jodphurs as if about to go riding, sitting on the front steps of our house, which is situated in what is now central Poland. He remembered the property being very run-down, and noted that his father had worked hard to put it back into working order. He hoped his family was remembered positively by people living in the area. In truth, they are not remembered at all.

23. Jan Gross, 'War as Revolution', in Norman Naimark and Leonid Gibianskii, eds., *The Establishment of Communist Regimes in Eastern Europe, 1944–1949* (Boulder, 1997), p. 23.

24. Krystyna Kersten, *The Establishment of Communist Rule in Poland, 1943–1948* (Berkeley, 1991), p. 165.

25. M. C. Kaser and E. A. Radice, *The Economic History of Eastern Europe, 1919–1975*, Vol. II: *Interwar Policy, the War and Reconstruction* (Oxford, 1986), pp. 466–72.

26. Iván Pető and Sándor Szakács, *A hazai gazdaság négy évtizedének, 1919–1975 története, 1945–1985. I. Az újjáépítés és a tervutasításos irányítás időszaka, 1945–1968* (Budapest, 1985), pp. 17–25.

27. Berend and Csató, *Evolution of the Hungarian Economy*, pp. 254–5.

28. Kaser and Radice, *Economic History of Eastern Europe*, Vol. II, pp. 504–6.

29. Janusz Kalinski and Zbigniew Landau, *Gospodarka Polski w XX wieku*, pp. 159–89.

30. Abrams, 'The Second World War and the East European Revolution', p. 634.

31. Kaser and Radice, *Economic History of Eastern Europe*, Vol. II, pp. 338–9.

32. Ibid., pp. 299–308.

33. Jan Gross, 'The Social Consequences of War: Preliminaries to the Study of the Imposition of Communist Regimes in East Central Europe', *Eastern European Politics and Societies*, Vol. 3, No. 2, Spring 1989, pp. 198–214; Abrams, 'The Second World War and the East European Revolution', pp. 623–64; Kalinski and Landau, *Gospodarka Polski w XX wieku*, pp. 159–89.

34. Abrams, 'The Second World War and the East European Revolution', p. 639

35. Czesław Miłosz, *The Captive Mind*, trans. Jane Zielonko (London, 2001), pp. 26–9.

36. Márai, *Portraits of a Marriage*, p. 272.
37. Zaremba, *Wielka Trwoga*, pp. 221–52.
38. Ibid.
39. Interview with Csaba Skultéty, Budapest, 12 March 2009.
40. Zaremba, *Wielka Trwoga*, p. 87.
41. Ibid., p. 273.
42. Hannah Arendt, *The Origins of Totalitarianism* (New York and Cleveland, 1958), pp. 322–3.
43. Karta, Lucjan Grabowski, II/1412.
44. Interview with Tadeusz Konwicki, Warsaw, 17 September 2009.
45. Hanna Świda-Ziemba, *Urwany Lot: Pokolenie inteligenckiej młodzieży powojennej w świetle listów i pamiętników z lat 1945–1948* (Kraków, 2003), pp. 30–50.
46. Quoted in Anna Bikont and Joanna Szczęsna, *Lawina i Kamienie: Pisarze wobec Komunizmu* (Warsaw, 2006), pp. 69–79.
47. Interview with Hans Modrow, Berlin, 7 December 2006.
48. Miłosz, *The Captive Mind*, pp. 26–9.
49. Martin Gilbert, 'Churchill and Poland', unpublished lecture delivered at the University of Warsaw, 16 February 2010. With thanks to Martin Gilbert.
50. Peter Grose, *Operation Rollback* (New York, 2000), p. 2.
51. Dean Acheson, *Present at the Creation* (New York, 1987), p. 85.
52. Ibid.
53. Gilbert, 'Churchill and Poland'.
54. A good analysis of this can be found in Antoni Z. Kamiński and Bartłomiej Kamiński, 'Road to "People's Poland": Stalin's Conquest Revisited', in *Stalinism Revisited: The Establishment of the Communist Regimes in East-Central Europe and the Dynamics of the Soviet Bloc*, ed. Vladimir Tismaneanu (New York and Budapest, 2009), pp. 205–11; also Roberts, *Masters and Commanders*, pp. 548–58.
55. Winston Churchill, *The Second World War*, Vol. VI: *Triumph and Tragedy* (London, 1985), p. 300.
56. Robert Service, *Comrades* (London, 2007), p. 220.
57. Ibid., p. 222.
58. The original drafts and the final version of Operation Unthinkable can be seen at http://web.archive.org/web/20101116152301/http://www.history.neu.edu/PRO2.
59. Stanisław Mikołajczyk, *The Rape of Poland* (New York, 1948), p. 60.
60. László Borhi, *Hungary in the Cold War, 1945–1956: Between the United States and the Soviet Union* (New York and Budapest, 2004), p. 36.

61. Mikołajczyk, *Rape of Poland*, p. 25.
62. John Earl Haynes, Harvey Klehr and Alexander Vassiliev, *Spies: The Rise and Fall of the KGB* (New Haven, 2009), pp. 20–26.
63. Roberts, *Masters and Commanders*, p. 556.
64. Hubertus Knabe, *17. Juni 1953 – Ein deutscher Aufstand* (Berlin, 2004), pp. 402–6.
65. Csaba Békés, Malcolm Byrne and János Rainer, eds., *The 1956 Revolution: A History in Documents* (Budapest and New York, 2002), p. 209.
66. Borhi, *Hungary in the Cold War*, p. 21.

2. VICTORS

1. Ruth Andreas-Friedrich, *Battleground Berlin: Diaries, 1945–1948* (New York, 1990), p. 36.
2. George Kennan, *Memoirs: 1925–1950* (New York, 1967), p. 74.
3. John Lukacs, *1945: Year Zero* (New York, 1978), p. 256.
4. Interview with Lutz Rackow, Berlin, 1 April 2008.
5. Christel Panzig, *Wir schalten uns ein: Zwischen Luftschutzkeller & Stalinbild, Stadt & Region Wittenberg 1945* (Lutherstadt Wittenberg, 2005), pp. 40–42.
6. Zsófia Tevan, interview, Budapest, 3 June 2009.
7. SNL interview with Jenő Széll, Történeti Interjúk Tára, Országos Széchenyi Könyvtár (Historic Interviews at the National Széchenyi Library), Budapest. Interview conducted by András Hegedüs, Gábor Hanák, Gyula Kozák, Ilona Szabóné Dér on 3 August 1985.
8. Interview with Professor Alexander Jackowski, Warsaw, 15 May 2007.
9. Kennan, *Memoirs*, p. 74.
10. Sándor Márai, *Memoir of Hungary: 1944–1948*, trans. Albert Tezla (Budapest and New York, 2000), pp. 44–6.
11. Lukacs, *1945*, p. 75.
12. Antony Beevor and Luba Vinogradova, eds., *A Writer at War: Vasily Grossman with the Red Army, 1941–1945* (London, 2005), pp. 341–2.
13. TsAMO 372/6570/78, pp. 30–32 (thanks to Antony Beevor).
14. Catherine Merridale, *Ivan's War* (New York, 2006), p. 389.
15. Alexander Nakhimovsky and Alice Nakhimovsky, *Witness to History: The Photographs of Yevgeny Khaldei* (New York, 1997).
16. Krisztián Ungváry, *The Siege of Budapest: 100 Days in World War II* (London, 2002), p. 360.
17. My husband played this game as a child in 1960s Poland.
18. *Czterej pancerni i pies*, episode 13, 1969.

19. Márai, *Memoir*, pp. 44–6.
20. Beevor and Vinogradova, *Writer at War*, p. 326.
21. Piotr Bojarski, 'Czołg strzela do katedry, Julian fotografuje', *Gazeta Wyborcza*, 21 January 2011.
22. Norman Davies and Roger Moorhouse, *Microcosm: A Portrait of a European City* (New York, 2003), p. 408.
23. BStU MfSZ, Sekr. Neiber no. 407, p. 80.
24. Beevor and Vinogradova, *Writer at War*, p. 330.
25. Merridale, *Ivan's War*, p. 381.
26. Alexander Solzhenitsyn, *Prussian Nights*, trans. Robert Conquest, Farrar Straus and Giroux (New York, 1977), pp. 38–9.
27. Lev Kopelev, *To Be Preserved Forever*, trans. Anthony Austin (New York, 1977), p. 56.
28. Ibid., pp. 50–51.
29. Ibid., p. 41.
30. Włodzimierz Borodziej and Hans Lemberg, eds., *Niemcy w Polsce 1945–1950: Wybór Dokumentów*, Vol. III (Warsaw, 2001), pp. 57–61.
31. James Mark, 'Remembering Rape', *Past & Present* 188 (2005), p. 149.
32. Stewart Thomson, in collaboration with Robert Bialek, *The Bialek Affair* (London, 1955), pp. 31–3.
33. See, for example, Antony Beevor, *The Fall of Berlin 1945* (New York, 2002).
34. Milovan Djilas, *Conversations With Stalin* (New York, 1990), p. 95.
35. Beevor, *Fall of Berlin*, p. 169.
36. Margit Földesi, *A megszállók szabadsága* (Budapest, 2002), p. 140.
37. Interview with Hans-Jochen Tschiche, Satuelle, 18 November 2006.
38. 'Über die Russen und über uns', Verlag Kultur und Fortschritt (Berlin, 1949). Originally published in *Neues Deutschland* and *Tägliche Rundschau*, 19 November 1948.
39. Ibid.
40. Varga/Vargas did return to Hungary in 1946, to help the government carry out monetary reform and reintroduce the forint, the Hungarian currency.
41. Friederike Sattler, *Wirtschaftsordnung im Übergang: Politik, Organisation und Funktion der KPD/SED im Land Brandenburg bei der Etablierung der zentralen Planwirtschaft in der SBZ/DDR 1945–52* (Münster, 2002), pp. 88–92.
42. Serhii Plokhii, *Yalta: The Price of Peace* (New York, 2010), pp. 108–13 and 256–62.
43. Sattler, *Wirtschaftsordnung im Übergang*, pp. 94–5.
44. Norman Naimark, *The Russians in Germany: A History of the Soviet Zone of Occupation, 1945–1949* (Cambridge, Mass., 1995), pp. 168–9.

45. Ibid., p. 169.
46. SAPMO-BA, DN/1 38032.
47. Ibid.
48. Volker Koop, *Besetzt: Sowjetische Besatzungspolitik in Deutschland* (Berlin, 2008), pp. 71–7.
49. DRA, 201-00-004/001, p. 62.
50. Naimark, *Russians in Germany*, p. 171.
51. SAPMO-BA, DY 30/IV 2/6.02 49, fiche 3.
52. M. C. Kaser and E. A. Radice, *The Economic History of Eastern Europe, 1919–1975*, Vol. II: *Interwar Policy, the War and Reconstruction* (Oxford, 1986), pp. 530–35.
53. Iván T. Berend and Tamás Csató, *Evolution of the Hungarian Economy, 1848–1998*, Vol. I (Boulder, 2001), pp. 257–8.
54. Földesi, *A megszállók szabadsága*, pp. 81–97.
55. PIL, 174/12/217.
56. CAW, VIII/800/24 (NKWD ZSRR), folder 9.
57. Adam Dziurok and Bogdan Musiał, 'Bratni rabunek'. O demontażach i wywózce sprzętu z terenu Górnego Śląska w 1945 r., in *W objęciach Wielkiego Brata: Sowieci w Polsce 1944–1993*, ed. IPN (Warsaw, 2009), pp. 321–44.
58. He lived in the Polish mountain village of Poronin, where one of only two Lenin statues ever erected in Poland once stood. It was taken down in 1990, but in 2011 the city council decided to put it up again to attract tourists.
59. Richard Pipes, ed., *The Unknown Lenin* (New Haven, 1996), p. 90.
60. Ibid., p. 62.
61. For descriptions of the Marxist mentality, see Robert Conquest, *Reflections on a Ravaged Century* (New York, 1999), pp. 34–6; also François Furet, *The Passing of an Illusion: The Idea of Communism in the Twentieth Century*, trans. Deborah Furet (Chicago, 1999).
62. *What is to be Done* is available at http://www.marxists.org/archive/lenin/works/1901/witbd/.
63. Richard Pipes, *The Russian Revolution* (New York, 1991), p. 608.
64. See Paul Lendvai, *The Hungarians: A Thousand Years of Victory in Defeat* (Princeton, 2004), pp. 369–72; Richard Pipes, *Russia under the Bolshevik Regime, 1919–1924* (New York, 1994), pp. 170–72; István György Tóth, ed., *A Concise History of Hungary* (Budapest, 2005), pp. 487–94.
65. Pipes, *Russia under the Bolshevik Regime*, pp. 182–3.
66. See Victor Serge, *Memoirs of a Revolutionary* (Oxford, 1967), for an account of the Second Congress.

67. Martin Gilbert, 'Churchill and Poland', unpublished lecture delivered at the University of Warsaw, 16 February 2010. With thanks to Martin Gilbert.

68. Adam Zamoyski, *Warsaw 1920: Lenin's Failed Conquest of Europe* (London, 2008), pp. 1–13 and 42.

69. Pipes, *Russia under the Bolshevik Regime*, p. 192.

70. Tim Tzouliadis, *The Forsaken: An American Tragedy in Stalin's Russia* (New York, 2008), p. 55.

3. COMMUNISTS

1. Quoted in Carola Stern, *Ulbricht: A Political Biography*, trans. Abe Farbstein (New York, 1965), p. 203.

2. See Marxists' Internet Archive, http://www.marxists.org/archive/bulganin/1949/12/21.htm, among other sources.

3. Ibid. Unless otherwise noted, the biographical information about Ulbricht comes from Carola Stern's superb biography.

4. Stern, *Ulbricht*, p. 15.

5. Stern, *Ulbricht*, p. 89.

6. Elfriede Brüning, *Und außerdem war es mein Leben* (Berlin, 2004), p. 28.

7. Walter Ulbricht, *On Questions of Socialist Construction in the GDR* (Dresden, 1968).

8. Stern, *Ulbricht*, p. 124.

9. Andrzej Garlicki, *Bolesław Bierut* (Warsaw, 1994), especially pp. 1–20; see also Andrzej Werblan, *Stalinizm w Polsce* (Warsaw 2009), pp. 122–31; Piotr Lipiński, *Bolesław Niejasny* (Warsaw, 2001).

10. *Polska-ZSRR: Struktury Podległości: Dokumenty KC WKP (B) 1944–1949*, pp. 59–61.

11. Interview with Jerzy Morawski, Warsaw, 7 June 2007.

12. Lipiński, *Bolesław Niejasny*, p. 41.

13. Both Alexander Orlov, the Soviet defector, and Józef Światło, the Polish defector, have described Bierut as an NKVD agent, see Garlicki, *Bolesław Bierut*, pp. 16–19, and Lipiński, *Bolesław Niejasny*, p. 40. Władysław Gomułka, Bierut's main rival, told Khrushchev about the 'Nazi agent' rumours as well but Khrushchev waved him away.

14. Mátyás Rákosi, *Visszaemlékezések 1940–1956*, Vol. I (Budapest, 1997), pp. 5–26.

15. Ibid., pp. 26–46.

16. Rákosi is mentioned frequently in the diaries of Georgi Dimitrov. See Ivo Banac, ed., *The Diary of Georgi Dimitrov 1933–1949* (New Haven, 2003).

17. Ibid., pp. 46–83.

18. Ibid., pp. 137–8.

19. Harvey Klehr, John Earl Haynes and Kyrill M. Anderson, *The Soviet World of American Communism* (New Haven and London, 1998), pp. 110–42. The American communist party, for example, maintained its links to the Soviet Union through J. Peters, an activist who was born in Hungary, took part in the 1919 Hungarian communist revolution, played a role in Hungarian politics and later emigrated to America, where he continued to conduct both open and clandestine work in cooperation with the Soviet secret police.

20. Anne Applebaum, 'Now We Know', *The New Republic*, 31 May 2009.

21. Thomas Sgovio, *Dear America* (New York, 1979), p. 99.

22. Banac, ed., *Diary of Georgi Dimitrov*, p. 119.

23. Alexander Dallinn and F. I. Firsov, eds., *Dimitrov and Stalin, 1934–1943: Letters from the Soviet Archives* (New Haven, 2000), pp. 28–31.

24. Markus Wolf and Anne McElvoy, *Man without a Face: The Autobiography of Communism's Greatest Spymaster* (London, 1997), p. 32.

25. Margarete Buber-Neumann, *Under Two Dictators*, trans. Edward Fitzgerald (London, 2008), p. 13.

26. PIL, 867/1/H-168.

27. Banac, ed., *Diary of Georgi Dimitrov*, p. 197.

28. Marci Shore, *Caviar and Ashes: A Warsaw Generation's Life and Death in Marxism, 1918–1968* (New Haven, 2006), pp. 73–4.

29. Ibid., pp. 123–7.

30. Ronald Aronson, *Camus and Sartre: The Story of a Friendship and the Quarrel That Ended It* (Chicago, 2004), p. 150.

31. Banac, ed., *Diary of Georgi Dimitrov*, pp. 118–99.

32. R. C. Raack, 'Stalin's Plans for World War Two Told by a High Comintern Source', *The Historical Journal*, Vol. 38, No. 4 (Dec. 1995), pp. 1031–6.

33. Buber-Neumann, *Under Two Dictators*, p. 175.

34. Piotr Gontarczyk, *Polska Partia Robotnicza: Droga do Władzy, 1941–1944* (Warsaw, 2003), pp. 101–2.

35. HIA, Mieczysław Rakowski Collection; also Gontarczyk, *Polska Partia Robotnicza*.

36. Comintern Archive, British Library, 31/1/1/3-31.

37. Comintern Archive, British Library, 31/2/1/1-10.

38. Ibid.

39. Wolfgang Leonhard, *Child of the Revolution*, trans. C. M. Woodhouse (Chicago, 1958), pp. 191–296.
40. Ibid., p. 224.
41. Ibid., p. 226.
42. HIA, Jakub Berman Collection, Box 1.
43. *Deklaracja Ideowa PZPR: Statut PZPR* (Warsaw, 1950).
44. Ibid.
45. T. V. Volokitina et al., eds., *Sovietskii faktor v vostochnoi evrope, 1944–1953* (Moscow, 1999), Vol. 1, pp. 23–48.
46. Buber-Neumann, *Under Two Dictators*, p. 13.
47. Arthur Koestler, *Arrow in the Blue* (London, 2005), p. 311.
48. Leonhard, *Child of the Revolution*, p. 231.
49. Ibid., pp. 241–51.
50. Catherine Epstein, *The Last Revolutionaries: German Communists and Their Century* (Cambridge, Mass., and London, 2003), pp. 8–9.

4. POLICEMEN

1. Jens Gieseke, *The GDR State Security: Sword and Shield*, trans. Mary Carlene Forszt (Berlin, 2004), p. 7.
2. Andrzej Friszke, *Polska: Losy państwa i narodu, 1939–1989* (Warsaw, 2003), p. 9.
3. *Manifest Lipcowy* (Warsaw, 1974), p. 5.
4. Krystyna Kersten, *The Establishment of Communist Rule in Poland, 1943–1948* (Berkeley, 1991), pp. 77–160.
5. Martin Mevius, *Agents of Moscow: The Hungarian Communist Party and the Origins of Socialist Patriotism 1941–1953* (Oxford, 2005), p. 53.
6. Krisztián Ungváry, 'Magyarország szovjetizálásának kérdései', in *Mítoszok, legendák, tévhitek a 20. századi magyar történelemről*, ed. Ignác Romsics (Budapest, 2002), p. 294.
7. László Borhi, *Hungary in the Cold War, 1945–1956: Between the United States and the Soviet Union* (New York and Budapest, 2004), p. 38.
8. Also sometimes referred to by its Russian acronym (Sovetskaia Voennaia Administratsia v Germanii, or SVAG) or its German acronym (Sowjetische Militäradministration in Deutschland, or SMAD).
9. Dirk Spilker, *The East German Leadership and the Division of Germany: Patriotism and Propaganda 1945–1953* (Oxford, 2006), p. 46.

10. The Polish secret police were later renamed the Służba Bezpieczeństwa, or SB. Their Hungarian colleagues were later named the Államvédelmi Hatóság, or ÁVH. Frequent renamings and reorganizations of the secret police were common in most communist states, as no one was ever pleased with their work.

11. T. V. Volokitina et al., eds., *Vostochnaya Evropa v dokumentakh rossiskikh arkhivov, 1944–1953* (Novosibirsk, 1997), Vol. 1, p. 203.

12. Maciej Korkuć, 'Kujbyszewiacy – Awangarda UB', *Arkana*, number 46–7 (4–5 2002), pp. 75–95.

13. IPN, BU 0447/120, pp. 5–12.

14. IPN, BU 0447/120, pp. 13–15.

15. For the Jewish story, see Allan Levine, *Fugitives of the Forest: The Heroic Story of Jewish Resistance and Survival during the Second World War* (New York, 2008).

16. Korkuć, 'Kujbyszewiacy – Awangarda UB', pp. 75–95.

17. IPN, BU 0447/120, pp. 5–12.

18. Krzysztof Persak and Łukasz Kaminski, eds., *A Handbook of the Communist Security Apparatus in East Central Europe, 1944–1989* (Warsaw, 2005).

19. Konrad Rokicki, 'Aparatu Obraz Własny', in Kazimierz Krajewski and Tomasz Łabuszewski, eds., *'Zwyczajny' Resort: Studia o aparacie bezpieczeństwa 1944–1956* (Warsaw, 2005), p. 26.

20. Sławomir Poleszak et al., eds., *Rok Pierwszy: Powstanie i Działalność aparatu bezpieczeństwá publicznego na Lubelszczyźnie (Lipiec 1944–Czerwiec 1945)* (Warsaw, 2004), pp. 50–55.

21. Rokicki, 'Aparatu Obraz Własny', pp. 13–32.

22. Interview with Czesław Kiszczak, Warsaw, 25 May 2007. See also Witold Bereś and Jerzy Skoczylas, *Generał Kiszczak Mówi ... Prawie Wszytko* (Warsaw, 1991).

23. IPN, 352/7. With thanks to Andrzej Paczkowski and Dariusz Stola.

24. Zsolt Krahulcsán, Rolf Müller and Mária Palasik, *A politikai rendőrség háború utáni megszervezése (1944–1946)*, unpublished manuscript, pp. 3–4.

25. Gábor Baczoni, *Pár(t)viadal – A Magyar Államrendőrség Vidéki Főkapitányságának Politikai Rendészeti osztálya, 1945–1946* (Budapest, 2002), p. 81.

26. Zsolt Krahulcsán and Rolf Müller, eds., *Dokumentumok a magyar politikai rendőrség történetéből 1. A politikai rendészeti osztályok 1945–1946* (Budapest, 2010), pp. 9–63.

27. PIL, 274/11/10/pp. 6–7.

28. PIL, 274/11/11/pp. 1–12.
29. In 2002, the building became the Terror Háza, a museum dedicated to the crimes of both the Nazi and Soviet regimes.
30. Krahulcsán, Müller and Palasik, *A politikai rendőrség háború utáni megszervezése*, pp. 5–6.
31. Sándor M. Kiss, from the introduction to Géza Böszörményi, *Recsk 1950–1953* (Budapest, 2005), p. 10.
32. Vladimir Farkas, *Nincs mentség* (Budapest, 1990), p. 106.
33. Krahulcsán and Müller, eds., *Dokumentumok*, pp. 159–60 and pp. 237–8.
34. Mária Palasik, 'A politikai rendőrség háború utáni megszervezése', in György Gyarmati, ed., *Államvédelem a Rákosi-korszakban* (Budapest, 2000), p. 39; also György Gyarmati, 'Kádár János és a Belügyminisztérium Államvédelmi Hatósága', *A Történeti Hivatal Évkönyve* (Budapest, 1999), pp. 118–20; Magdolna Baráth, 'Gerő Ernő a Belügyminisztérium élén', *A Történeti Hivatal Évkönyve* (Budapest, 1999), p. 159.
35. MOL, XIX-B-/1-/787/1945.
36. Erzsébet Kajári, *A magyar Belügyminisztérium szovjet tanácsadói* (Múltunk, 1999/3), pp. 220–27.
37. Farkas, *Nincs mentség*, p. 128.
38. *Magyar Internacionalisták* (Budapest, 1980); *Magyar tudóslexikon A-tól Zs-ig* (Budapest, 1998), p. 192.
39. PIL, 867/11/g-24/pp. 15–58.
40. Ibid.
41. From conversations with Mária Schmidt, Sándor M. Kiss and Barbara Bank; also Böszörményi, *Recsk*, p. 49.
42. Klaus Eichner and Gotthold Schramm, eds., *Angriff und Abwehr: Die deutschen Geheimdienste nach 1945* (Berlin, 2007); also Roger Engelmann, '"Schild und Schwert" als Exportartikel: Aufbau und Anleitung der ostdeutschen Staatssicherheit durch das KGB und seine Vorläufer (1949–1959)', in Andreas Hilger, Mike Schmeitzner and Ute Schmidt, eds., *Diktaturdurchsetzung. Instrumente und Methoden der kommunistischen Machtsicherung in der SBZ/DDR 1945–1955* (Dresden, 2001), pp. 55–64.
43. Engelmann, '"Schild und Schwert"', pp. 55–64; Norman Naimark, 'To Know Everything and to Report Everything Worth Knowing: Building the East German Police State, 1945–1949', Cold War International History Project Working Paper no. 10, August 1994.
44. BStU MfSZ, HA IX, no. 20603, p. 2.
45. Jens Gieseke, *Die DDR-Staatssicherheit: Schild und Schwert der Partei* (Bonn, 2000), p. 18.

46. Engelmann, '"Schild und Schwert"', pp. 55–64.
47. Interview with Klaus Eichner and Gotthold Schramm, Berlin, 24 June 2008.
48. BStU MfSZ, Sekr. D. Min., no. 1920.
49. Engelmann, '"Schild und Schwert"', pp. 55–64.
50. BStU MfSZ, HA VII, no. 4000, pp. 16–17.
51. Gary Bruce, *The Firm: The Inside Story of the Stasi* (Oxford, 2010), p. 34.
52. Interview with Schramm.
53. Gieseke, *Die DDR-Staatssicherheit*, p. 19.
54. Interview taken from *Das Ministerium für Staatssicherheit*, documentary film, directed by Christian Klemke and Jan Lorenzen, Berlin, 2007.
55. Interview with Schramm.
56. Document in possession of Günter Tschirschwitz.
57. Interview with Günter Tschirschwitz, Berlin, 24 June 2008.
58. Richard Pipes, ed., *The Unknown Lenin* (New Haven, 1996), p. 154.
59. BStU MfSZ, 1486/2, part 1 of 2, p. 11.
60. Amir Weiner, 'Nature, Nurture and Memory in a Socialist Utopia: Delineating the Soviet Socio-Ethnic Body in the Age of Socialism', *The American Historical Review*, Vol. 104, No. 4 (October 1999), p. 1121.
61. IPN, 352/7. With thanks to Andrzej Paczkowski and Dariusz Stola.
62. BStU MfSZ, 1486/2, part 1 of 2.
63. BStU MfSZ, HA XVIII, no. 922, p. 210.
64. Kati Marton, *Enemies of the People: My Family's Journey to America* (New York, 2009), p. 118.
65. BStU MfSZ, HA VII, no. 4000, p. 36.
66. BStU MfSZ, Ff 39/52.
67. BStU MfSZ, Ff 39/52.

5. VIOLENCE

1. Wolfgang Leonhard, *Child of the Revolution*, trans. C. M. Woodhouse (Chicago, 1958), p. 381.
2. This is Timothy Snyder's point in *Sketches from a Secret War* (New Haven and London, 2005), p. 210.
3. See Tony Judt on retribution in *Postwar* (New York, 2005), pp. 41–53.
4. Amir Weiner made this point during a talk at the Hoover Archive Russia Summer Workshop, July 2011.
5. RGANI 89/18/4/pp.1–3; from the collection of the late Alexander Kokurin.

6. T. V. Volokitina et al., eds., *Vostochnaya Evropa v dokumentakh rossiskikh arkhivov, 1944–1953* (Novosibirsk, 1997), Vol. 1, p. 42.

7. Quoted in Mark Kramer, 'Stalin, Soviet Policy and the Consolidation of a Communist Bloc in Eastern Europe, 1944–1953', p. 13, paper delivered at the Freeman Spogli International Institute, 30 April 2010.

8. Krystyna Kersten, *The Establishment of Communist Rule in Poland, 1943–1948* (Berkeley, 1991), p. 286.

9. Andrzej Paczkowski has a good, short English summary of the Home Army's formation in *The Spring Will be Ours: Poland and the Poles from Occupation to Freedom*, trans. Jane Cave (University Park, Pa., 2003), pp. 83–9.

10. Ibid., p. 116.

11. Ibid., p. 118.

12. Apoloniusz Zawilski, *Polskie Fronty 1918–1945*, Vol. 2 (Warsaw, 1997), p. 7.

13. Ibid., pp. 458–66.

14. Ibid., p. 45.

15. Keith Sword, *Deportation and Exile: Poles in the Soviet Union, 1939–1948* (London, 1996), pp. 144–7.

16. CAW, VIII/800/19 (NKWD ZSRR), folder 10, pp. 3 and 6.

17. Ibid., p. 4.

18. CAW, VIII/900/19 (NKWD ZSRR), folder 10, p. 9.

19. CAW, VIII/800/29/1 (NKWD ZSRR), folder 1, pp. 1–2.

20. CAW, VIII/800/19 (NKWD ZSRR), folder 10, pp. 6–10.

21. Nikita Petrov, *Ivan Serov: Pervyi Predsedatel' KGB* (Moscow, 2005), pp. 21–34; also Sword, *Deportation and Exile*, p. 14.

22. CAW, VIII/800/19 (NKWD ZSRR), folder 11, pp. 1–2.

23. Karta, Janusz Zawisza-Hrybacz, II/1730.

24. Karta, Henryk Sawala, II/3315.

25. Stanisław Ciesielski, Wojciech Materski and Andrzej Paczkowski, *Represje Sowieckie wobec Polaków i obywateli polskich* (Warsaw, 2002), p. 27.

26. Zawilski, *Polskie Fronty*, Vol. 2, p. 256.

27. There are many excellent accounts of the Warsaw Uprising. The most recent in English is Norman Davies, *Rising '44: The Battle for Warsaw* (New York, 2004).

28. CAW, VIII/800/29/4 (NKWD ZSRR), p. 197.

29. CAW, VIII/800/19 (NKWD ZSRR), folder 13, p. 33.

30. Ibid., folder 11, pp. 70–80.

31. CAW, VIII/800/13 (NKWD ZSRR), folder 13, p. 33; also folder 12, p. 38.

32. Andrzej Panufnik, *Composing Myself* (London, 1987), p. 131.
33. Interviews with Szymon Bojko, Warsaw, 28 May 2008 and 4 June 2008.
34. Andrzej Friszke, *Opozycja Polityczna w PRL, 1945–1980* (London, 1994), p. 9.
35. The text of the Yalta treaty is available at http://avalon.law.yale.edu/wwii/yalta.asp.
36. Kersten, *Establishment of Communist Rule in Poland*, p. 125.
37. HIA, Jakub Berman Collection, folder 1:6.
38. Kersten, *Establishment of Communist Rule in Poland*, p. 135.
39. Ibid., p. 126.
40. Sławomir Poleszak et al., eds., *Rok Pierwszy: Powstanie i Działalność aparatu bezpieczeństwa publicznego na Lubelszczyźnie (Lipiec 1944–Czerwiec 1945)* (Warsaw, 2004), p. 397.
41. Snyder, *Sketches from a Secret War*, p. 207.
42. Notes on WiN from the introduction to Józefa Huchlowa, Mieczysław Huchla, Romuald Lazarowicz, Zdzisław Wierzbicki and Andrzej Zagórski, eds., *Zrzeszenie 'Wolność i Niezawisłość' w dokumentach*, Vol. One, (Wrocław, 1997).
43. Justyna Wójcik, ed., *Stawiliśmy opór . . . : antykomunistyczne organizacje młodzieżowe w Małopolsce w latach 1944–1956* (Kraków, 2008), pp. 33–4.
44. Poleszak et al., eds., *Rok Pierwszy,* pp. 179–80.
45. CAW, VIII/800/13 (NKWD ZSRR), folder 15, p. 31.
46. Anita Prażmowska, *Civil War in Poland, 1942–1948* (New York, 2004), p. 153.
47. Poleszak et al., eds., *Rok Pierwszy*, pp. 352–83.
48. AAN, Ministerstwo Edukacji Narodowej, 587, pp. 2–3.
49. Karta, Lucjan Grabowski, II/1412.
50. Jakub Nawrocki, 'Do Krwi Ostatnej', *Polska Zbrojna*, No. 8, 20 February 2011, pp. 60–62. Krupa went to prison but was released in 1965. He died in 1972.
51. IPN, Rz 05/36/CD.
52. CAW, VIII/800/19 (NKWD ZSRR), folder 18, p. 13.
53. Interview with Erich Loest, Leipzig, 12 December 2006.
54. For an account of de-Nazification in western Germany, see Frederick Taylor, *Exorcising Hitler: The Occupation and Denazification of Germany* (London, 2011), pp. 260–76.
55. The Potsdam protocol is available at http://avalon.law.yale.edu/20th_century/decade17.asp.

56. Gerhard Finn, *Die politischen Häftlinge der Sowjetzone 1945–1959* (Pfaffenhofen, 1960), pp. 26–31; interview with Wolfgang Lehmann, Berlin, 20 September 2006.

57. GEOK, *Zeitzeugen*, Part One, 'Wir dachten der Krieg ist vorbei', documentary film directed by Dirk Jungnickel, 1996.

58. Interviews with Gisela Gneist, Berlin and Sachsenhausen, 20 September and 4 October 2006.

59. Interviews with Gneist; also Gisela Gneist and Gunther Heydemann, *'Allenfalls kommt man für ein halbes Jahr in ein Umschulungslager'* (Leipzig, 2002).

60. Bogusław Kopka, *Obozy Pracy w Polsce, 1944–1950* (Warsaw, 2002), pp. 147–8.

61. Later changed to Special Camp Number One. See the website of Gedenkstätte und Museum Sachsenhausen, http://www.stiftung-bg.de/gums/en/index.htm.

62. From documents in the collection of the Gedenkstätte und Museum, Sachsenhausen.

63. Jan and Renate Lipinsky, *Die Straße die in den Tod führte – Zur Geschichte des Speziallagers Nr. 5 Ketschendorf/Fürstenwalde* (Leverkusen, 1999), p. 177.

64. Interview with Gneist. She worked as a messenger.

65. Quoting from Soviet documents, Norman Naimark (Naimark, *The Russians in Germany: A History of the Soviet Zone of Occupation, 1945–1949* (Cambridge, Mass., 1995), p. 377) gives a figure of 153,953 arrests and 42,022 deaths. Gneist and Heydemann (*'Allenfalls kommt man für ein halbes Jahr'*, p. 12), using Soviet and German sources, give 157,837 arrests and 43,035 deaths.

66. Interview with Lehmann.

67. Interview with Gneist.

68. Bodo Ritscher, *Spezlager Nr. 2 Buchenwald*, Gedenkstätte Buchenwald (Buchenwald, 1993), pp. 86–90.

69. Ernest Tillich, *Hefte der Kampfgruppe*, brochure published in Berlin, 1945.

70. Ritscher, *Spezlager Nr. 2 Buchenwald*, pp. 86–90.

71. From documents in the collection of the Gedenkstätte und Museum, Sachsenhausen.

72. Interview with Lehmann.

73. Tamás Stark, *Magyar hadifoglyok a szovjetunióban* (Budapest, 2006), p. 36.

74. HIA, George Bien Collection; see also George Z. Bien, *Lost Years*, self-published memoirs.

75. Stark, *Magyar hadifoglyok*, pp. 73–85.

76. Ibid., p. 97.
77. László Karsai, 'The People's Courts and Revolutionary Justice in Hungary, 1945–46', in *The Politics of Retribution in Europe*, eds. István Deák, Jan T. Gross and Tony Judt (Princeton, 2000), pp. 233–48.
78. Margit Földesi, *A megszállók szabadsága* (Budapest, 2002), p. 64.
79. Many thanks to Anita Lackenberger, who took me to Baden to see the former NKVD headquarters.
80. Barbara Bank, 'Az internálás és kitelepítés dokumentumai a történeti levéltárban', in György Gyarmati, ed., *Az átmenet évkönyve, 2003* (Budapest, 2004), pp. 107–30; see also Karsai, 'People's Courts and Revolutionary Justice in Hungary', p. 233.
81. István Szent-Miklósy, *With the Hungarian Independence Movement, 1943–1947: An Eyewitness Account* (New York, 1988), p. 136.
82. Ibid., pp. 138–9.
83. ÁBTL, V-113398/1, pp. 1–20; also Margit Balogh, *A KALOT és a katolikus társadalompolitika 1935–1946* (Budapest, 1998), pp. 184–5.
84. ÁBTL, V-113398/1, pp. 241–60.
85. *Szabad Nép*, 4 May 1946.
86. *Kis Újság*, 3 May and 4 May 1946.
87. Sándor M. Kiss, from the preface to Géza Böszörményi, *Recsk 1950–1953* (Budapest, 2005); also interview with Sándor M. Kiss, Budapest, 27 January 2009.

6. ETHNIC CLEANSING

1. Maria Buczyło, 'Akcja "Wisła": Wypędzić, rozproszyć', *Karta*, No. 49 (2006), pp. 32–63.
2. Archie Brown, *The Rise and Fall of Communism* (London, 2009), p. 113.
3. The Potsdam agreements can be found at http://avalon.law.yale.edu/20th_century/decade17.asp.
4. Stefano Bottoni, 'Reassessing the Communist Takeover of Romania: Violence, Institutional Continuity, Ethnic Conflict Management', paper presented to the workshop 'United Europe, Divided Memory', Vienna, 28–30 November 2008, p. 5.
5. Eagle Glassheim, 'National Mythologies and Ethnic Cleansing: The Expulsion of Czechoslovak Germans in 1945', *Central European History*, 33/4 (2000), p. 470–71.
6. Piotr Semków, 'Martyrologia Polaków z Pomorza Gdańskiego w latach II wojny światowej', *Biuletyn Instytutu Pamięci Narodowej*, Nr 8–9 (2006), pp. 42–9.

7. Gerhard Gruschka, *Zgoda, miejsce zgrozy: Obóz koncentracyjny w Świętochłowicach* (Gliwice, 1998).

8. From *'They rocked my cradle then bundled me out'* – *Ethnic German Fate in Hungary 1939–1948*, exhibition catalogue, Terror Háza (Budapest, 2007).

9. Interview with Herta Kuhrig, Berlin, 21 November 2006. Kuhrig and her family were expelled because Czech police found a photograph of her in the uniform of the Jungmädel, the Nazi youth group for very young girls.

10. Włodzimierz Borodziej and Hans Lemberg, eds., *Niemcy w Polsce 1945–1950: Wybór Dokumentów*, Vol. III (Warsaw, 2001), pp. 25–6.

11. Marion Gräfin Dönhoff, *Namen, die keiner mehr nennt: Ostpreußen – Menschen und Geschichte* (Munich, 1964), pp. 16–18.

12. Glassheim, 'National Mythologies and Ethnic Cleansing', p. 470.

13. Piotr Pykel, 'The Expulsion of the Germans from Czechoslovakia', in Steffen Prauser and Arfon Rees, eds., *The Expulsion of the 'German' Communities from Eastern Europe at the End of the Second World War*, EUI Working Paper HEC No. 2004/1, p. 18.

14. Borodziej and Lemberg, eds., *Niemcy w Polsce*, pp. 33–4.

15. Pykel, 'Expulsion of the Germans from Czechoslovakia', pp. 11–21, and Balász Apor, 'The Expulsion of the German-Speaking Population from Hungary', in Prauser and Rees, eds., *Expulsion of the 'German' Communities from Eastern Europe*, p. 32.

16. László Karsai, 'The People's Courts and Revolutionary Justice in Hungary, 1945–46', in *The Politics of Retribution in Europe*, eds. István Deák, Jan T. Gross and Tony Judt (Princeton, 2000), pp. 246–7.

17. Witold Stankowski, 'Centralny Obóz Pracy w Potulicach w latach 1945–1950', in Alicja Paczoska, ed., *Obóz w Potulicach – Aspekt Trudnego Sąsiedstwa Polsko-Niemieckiego w Okresie Dwóch Totalitarnyzmów* (Bydgoszcz, 2005), pp. 58–9.

18. Helga Hirsch, *Zemsta Ofiar*, trans. Maria Przybyłowska (Warsaw, 1999), p. 78; Stankowski, 'Centralny Obóz Pracy w Potulicach w latach 1945–1950', p. 62.

19. Waldemar Ptak, 'Naczelnicy Centralnego Obozu Pracy w Potulicach w Latach 1945–1950', in Paczoska, ed., *Obóz w Potulicach*, pp. 70–78.

20. See Hirsch, *Zemsta Ofiar*, pp. 14–146; Witold Stankowski, *Obozy i inne miejsca odosobnienia dla niemieckiej ludności cywilnej w Polsce w latach 1945–1950* (Bydgoszcz, 2002), pp. 260–69; also John Sack, *An Eye for an Eye* (New York, 1993), pp. 86–97. This book, deservedly controversial, contains a number of mistakes and exaggerations. But Sack's interviews appear to be authentic.

21. Borodziej and Lemberg, eds., *Niemcy w Polsce*, pp. 131–47.
22. Barbara Bank and Sándor Őze, *A 'német ügy' 1945–1953. A Volksbundtól Tiszalökig* (Budapest and Munich, 2005), pp. 9–34.
23. Timothy Snyder, *Bloodlands* (New York, 2010), pp. 323–4.
24. Pykel, 'Expulsion of the Germans from Czechoslovakia', pp. 11–21.
25. Phillip Ther, 'The Integration of Expellees in Germany and Poland after World War II', *Slavic Review*, Vol. 55, No. 4 (Winter 1996), pp. 787–8.
26. Piotr Szubarczyk and Piotr Semków, 'Erika z Rumii', *Biuletyn Instytutu Pamięci Narodowej*, No. 5 (2004), pp. 49–53.
27. Norman Naimark, *Fires of Hatred: Ethnic Cleansing in Twentieth-Century Europe* (Cambridge, Mass., and London, 2001), pp. 110–11.
28. Ibid.
29. Tibor Zinner, *A magyarországi németek kitelepítése* (Budapest, 2004), pp. 19–28; also Barbara Bank, introduction to *A 'német ügy' 1945–1953*.
30. Bottoni, 'Reassessing the Communist Takeover of Romania', p. 5.
31. Mikołaj Stanisław Kunicki, 'The Polish Crusader: The Life and Politics of Bolesław Piasecki, 1915–1979', Ph.D. dissertation, Stanford University, June 2004, pp. 196–203.
32. Bottoni, 'Reassessing the Communist Takeover of Romania', pp. 18–21.
33. Kálmán Janics, *Czechoslovak Policy and the Hungarian Minority, 1945–1948* (New York, 1982), p. 61.
34. Ibid., p. 105.
35. See Andrzej Krawczyk, 'Czechy: Komunizm Wiecznie Zywy', *Gazeta Wyborcza*, No. 155, 5 July 2007, who argues that the expulsions were a crucial part of the legitimacy of the Czechoslovak communist party.
36. *Przesiedlenia Polaków i Ukraińców, 1944–1946*, Vol. 2, document collection prepared by Archiwum Ministerstwa Wewnetrznych I Administracja RP and Derzahvny Arkhiv Sluzby Bezpeki Ukrainii (Warsaw and Kiev, 2000), p. 41.
37. The best short account of the ethnic cleansing operation in Volhynia is Timothy Snyder's 'The Causes of Ukrainian–Polish Ethnic Cleansing, 1943', *Past and Present*, No. 179 (May 2003), pp. 197–234.
38. Barbara Odnous, 'Lato 1943', *Karta*, No. 46 (2005), p. 121.
39. Waldemar Lotnik, *Nine Lives: Ethnic Conflict in the Polish–Ukrainian Borderlands* (London, 1999), p. 65.
40. *Przesiedlenia Polaków i Ukraińców*, p. 253.
41. Ibid., p. 45.
42. Ibid., pp. 737–41.
43. Ibid., pp. 915–17.

44. Dariusz Stola, 'Forced Migrations in Central European History', *International Migration Review*, Vol. 26, No. 2 (Summer 1992), pp. 324–41.
45. *Przesiedlenia Polaków i Ukraińców*, pp. 49, 743.
46. Eugeniusz Misiło, *Akcja Wisła* (Warsaw, 1993), pp. 16–17.
47. Snyder, *Sketches from a Secret War* (New Haven and London, 2005), p. 210.
48. Misiło, *Akcja Wisła*, pp. 66–9 and 73.
49. Ibid., p. 63.
50. Ibid., p. 25.
51. Buczyło, 'Akcja "Wisła"', p. 34.
52. Snyder, *Bloodlands*, p. 329.
53. Mark Kramer, 'Stalin, Soviet Policy and the Consolidation of a Communist Bloc in Eastern Europe, 1944–1953', p. 21, paper delivered at the Freeman Spogli International Institute, 30 April 2010.
54. Dagmar Kusa, 'Historical Trauma in Ethnic Identity', in Eleonore Breuning, Jill Lewis and Gareth Pritchard, eds., *Power and the People: A Social History of Central European Politics, 1945–1956* (Manchester, 2005), pp. 130–52.
55. Janics, *Czechoslovak Policy and the Hungarian Minority*, p. 219.
56. Bennet Kovrig, 'Partitioned Nation: Hungarian Minorities in Central Europe', in Michael Mandelbaum, ed., *The New European Diasporas* (New York, 2000), pp. 19–81; Stola, 'Forced Migrations in Central European History', pp. 336–7.
57. The IPN documents are available at http://www.ipn.gov.pl/portal/en/2/71/Response_by_the_State_of_Israel_to_the_application_for_the_extradition_of_Salomo.html. In 1998, Polish authorities also tried to extradite Helena Brus, a former Stalinist prosecutor who had signed the arrest warrant for General Emil Fieldorf, one of the most heroic of the Home Army leaders, after which he was subjected to a farcical trial and then executed. Brus had moved to Oxford in 1971. She refused to return to Poland, however, on the grounds that she 'could not receive a fair trial' in the 'the country of Auschwitz and Birkenau'. The British government did not agree to the extradition. See Anne Applebaum, 'The Three Lives of Helena Brus', *Sunday Telegraph*, 6 December 1998.
58. Dariusz Stola, *Kraj Bez Wyjścia? Migracje z Polski 1949–1989*(Warsaw, 2010), pp. 49–53. See also Dariusz Stola, Natlia Aleksiun and Barbara Polak, 'Wszyscy krawcy wyjechali. O Żydach w PRL', *Biuletyn Instytutu Pamięci Narodowej*, No. 11 (2005), pp. 4–25.
59. András Kovács, ed., *Jews and Jewry in Contemporary Hungary: Results of a Sociological Survey*, Institute for Jewish Policy Research, No. 1 (2004), pp. 49–53.

60. Jeffrey Herf, *Divided Memory: The Nazi Past in the Two Germanys* (Cambridge, Mass., 1997), p. 70. Some 21,000 remained in all of Germany, out of the 600,000 who had lived there before the war.
61. Stola, *Kraj Bez Wyjścia?*, p. 50.
62. Marek Chodakiewicz, *After the Holocaust* (New York, 2003), pp. 187–99.
63. Jan Gross, in *Fear: Anti-Semitism in Poland after Auschwitz* (New York, 2006), writes that for racially motivated murders of Jews between 1944 and 1946, 1500 is the 'widely accepted' estimate; Marek Chodakiewicz, at the other end of the historiological spectrum, cites in *After the Holocaust*, pp. 207–16, a lower figure of 400–700. Other scholars go as high as 2500.
64. Chodakiewicz, *After the Holocaust*, p. 172; János Pelle, *Az utolsó vérvádak* (Budapest, 1995), pp. 125–49.
65. This is a very simplified version of events. For more detail, see Gross, *Fear*, pp. 11–129, and Bożena Szaynok, *Pogrom Żydów w Kielcach. 4. VII 1946 r.* (Warsaw, 1992). The remaining disputes about what actually happened are well summarized in Bożena Szaynok, 'Spory o pogrom Kielecki', in Łukasz Kaminski and Jan Żaryn, eds., *Wokoł Pogromu Kieleckiego* (Warsaw, 2006).
66. Shimon Redlich, *Life in Transit: Jews in Postwar Łódź, 1945–1950* (Boston, 2010), p. 82.
67. Robert Győri Szabó, *A kommunizmus és a zsidóság az 1945 utáni Magyarországon* (Budapest, 2009), p. 147.
68. Martin Mevius, *Agents of Moscow: The Hungarian Communist Party and the Origins of Socialist Patriotism 1941–1953* (Oxford, 2005), pp. 94–8.
69. See Szabó, *A kommunizmus és a zsidóság az 1945 utáni Magyarországon*, and János Pelle, *Az utolsó vérvádak* (Budapest, 1995), for two recent accounts. In English, Peter Kenez summarizes the events briefly, in *Hungary from the Nazis to the Soviets: The Establishment of the Communist Regime in Hungary, 1944–1948* (New York, 2006), pp. 160–62.
70. As Chodakiewicz writes in *After the Holocaust*, 'currently available materials have neither confirmed nor denied the possibility that the pogroms were instigated by the secret police' (pp. 171–2).
71. Anita J. Prażmowska, 'The Kielce Pogrom, 1946, and the Emergence of Communist Power in Poland', *Cold War History*, Vol. 2, No. 2 (January 2002), pp. 101–24.
72. Szabó, *A kommunizmus és a zsidóság az 1945 utáni Magyarországon*, p. 147.
73. Gross, *Fear*, p. 39.

74. Heda Kovály, *Under a Cruel Star: A Life in Prague, 1941–1968* (Cambridge, Mass., 1986), p. 47.

75. Raphael Patai, *The Jews of Hungary: History, Culture, Psychology* (Detroit, 1996), p. 627.

76. Stola, Aleksiun and Polak, 'Wszyscy krawcy wyjechali', pp. 11–12. Stola also credits Michael Steinlauf's *Bondage to the Dead: Poland and the Memory of the Holocaust* (Syracuse, 1997) and R. J. Lifton's *The Broken Connection: On Death and the Continuity of Life* (New York, 1979) in his review of Gross's *Fear* in *The English Historical Review*, Vol. CXXII, No. 499 (2007), pp. 1460–63.

77. Described in Anna Cichopek-Gajraj, 'Jews, Poles and Slovaks: A Story of Encounters, 1944–1948', Ph.D. dissertation, University of Michigan, 2008, p. 230.

78. Gross, *Fear*, pp. 130–31.

79. Stola, *Kraj Bez Wyjścia?*, pp. 50–52.

80. Ibid., pp. 53–63.

81. Patai, *Jews of Hungary*, p. 614.

82. Bożena Szaynok, *Poland–Israel 1944–1968: In the Shadow of the Past and of the Soviet Union* (Warsaw, 2012), pp. 110–13; also Szabó, *A kommunizmus és a zsidóság az 1945 utáni Magyarországon*, pp. 75–88.

83. Stola, *Kraj Bez Wyjścia?*, pp. 53–63.

84. Ibid., p. 481.

85. Andrzej Paczkowski, 'Zydzi w UB: Proba weryfikacji stereotyp', in Tomasz Szarota, ed., *Komunizm: Ideologia, System, Ludzi* (Warsaw, 2001).

86. Quoted in Gross, *Fear*, p. 224.

87. HIA, Jakub Berman Collection, folder 1:4.

88. Mevius, *Agents of Moscow*, pp. 94–8.

89. Szabó, *A kommunizmus és a zsidóság az 1945 utáni Magyarországon*, p. 91.

90. Herf, *Divided Memory*, p. 83.

91. Mevius, *Agents of Moscow*, p. 184.

92. Marcin Zaremba, *Komunizm, Legitimizacja, Nacjonalizm* (Warsaw, 2005), p. 140.

93. T. V. Volokitina et al., eds., *Vostochnaya Evropa v dokumentakh rossiskikh arkhivov, 1944–1953* (Novosibirsk, 1997), Vol. 1, pp. 937–43. Gomułka did actually purge many of the remaining Jews from the Polish communist party in 1968, and expelled many of them from the country.

7. YOUTH

1. Wolfgang Leonhard, *Child of the Revolution*, trans. C. M. Woodhouse (Chicago, 1958), p. 408.
2. HIA, Stefan Jędrychowski Collection, Box 4, folder 18.
3. AAN, Ministerstwo Oświaty, 686, pp. 1–2.
4. Robert Service, *Spies and Commissars* (London, 2011) p. 232.
5. Leopold Tyrmand, *Dziennik 1954* (London, 1980), pp. 47–9.
6. Marek Gaszyński, *Fruwa Twoja Marynara* (Warsaw, 2009), pp. 12–14.
7. Tyrmand, *Dziennik 1954*, pp. 47–9.
8. There are some who dislike the notion. The eminent Russia scholar Stephen Kotkin says the expression 'civil society' is 'catnip to scholars, pundits and foreign aid donors ... a vague, seemingly all-purpose collective social actor'. Though in writing about Central Europe he needs to describe the phenomenon anyway, and thus uses another term ('niches') for the same thing. See Anne Applebaum, '1989 and all that', *Slate*, 9 November 2009.
9. V. I. Lenin, quoted in *The Communist Party of the Soviet Union (Bolsheviks) is the Leading and Guiding Force of Soviet Society* (Moscow, 1951), p. 28.
10. Dmitri Likachev, 'Arrest', in Anne Applebaum, ed., *Gulag Voices* (New Haven, 2010), pp. 1–12.
11. Stuart Finkel, *On the Ideological Front: The Russian Intelligentsia and the Making of the Soviet Public Sphere* (New Haven, 2007), pp. 1–13.
12. Ellen Ueberschär, *Junge Gemeinde im Konflikt: Evangelische Jugendarbeit in SBZ und DDR 1945–1961* (Stuttgart, 2003), p. 62.
13. Alan Nothnagle, *Building the East Germany Myth* (Ann Arbor, 1999), pp. 103–4.
14. An excellent account of the Lysenko vs Darwin debate in the USSR can be found in Peter Pringle, *The Murder of Nikolai Vavilov* (New York, 2008).
15. Ulrich Mählert, *Die Freie Deutsche Jugend 1945–1949* (Paderborn, 1995), pp. 22–45.
16. Leonhard, *Child of the Revolution*, pp. 299–300.
17. Mählert, *Freie Deutsche Jugend*, pp. 44–5.
18. Leonhard, *Child of the Revolution*, pp. 318–26.
19. DRA, F201-00-00/0004 (Büro des Intendanten Geschäftsunterlagen, 1945–1950), pp. 284–7.
20. Mählert, *Freie Deutsche Jugend*, pp. 72–3.

21. Stewart Thomson, in collaboration with Robert Bialek, *The Bialek Affair* (London, 1955), pp. 68–9.
22. Interview with Ernst Benda, Berlin, 20 May 2008.
23. Manfred Klein, *Jugend zwischen den Diktaturen: 1945–1956* (Mainz, 1968), pp. 20–35.
24. Thomson and Bialek, *Bialek Affair*, pp. 76–8.
25. Klein, *Jugend zwischen den Diktaturen*, p. 34.
26. SAPMO-BA, DY24/2000, p. 13.
27. Ibid., p. 164.
28. Mählert, *Freie Deutsche Jugend*, pp. 114–17; SAPMO-BA, DY24/2000, pp. 36–41.
29. Klein, *Jugend zwischen den Diktaturen*, p. 67.
30. Ueberschär, *Junge Gemeinde im Konflikt*, p. 65.
31. Klein, *Jugend zwischen den Diktaturen*, pp. 73–4.
32. V. V. Zakharov et al., eds., *SVAG I Religioznie Konfesii Sovetskoi Zoni Okkupatsii Germanii, 1945–1949: Sbornik Dokumentov*, pp. 244–7.
33. Ibid., pp. 248–9.
34. DRA, F201-00-00/0004 (Büro des Intendanten Geschäftsunterlagen, 1945–1950), pp. 284–7.
35. *Szabad Nép*, 19 June 1946.
36. Ibid., 20 June 1946.
37. Ibid., 22 June 1946.
38. Ibid., 23 June 1946.
39. Ferenc Nagy, *Küzdelem a vassfüggöny mögött* (Budapest, 1990), pp. 314–16.
40. Imre Kovács, *Magyarország megszállása* (Budapest, 1990), p. 294; József Mindszenty, *Emlékirataim* (Budapest, 1989), p. 134; Margit Balogh, *A Kalot és a katolikus társadalompolitika 1935–1946* (Budapest, 1998), pp. 198–201.
41. Peter Kenez describes it as 'nationalist' and 'anti-Semitic' in *Hungary from the Nazis to the Soviets: The Establishment of the Communist Regime in Hungary, 1944–1948* (New York, 2006), p. 165.
42. Balogh, *A Kalot és a katolikus társadalompolitika*, p. 166.
43. PIL, 286/31/pp. 7–11.
44. Ibid.
45. Ibid.
46. PIL, 286/31/pp. 13–15.
47. PIL, 286/31/pp. 172.
48. Balogh, *A Kalot és a katolikus társadalompolitika*, p. 167.
49. Ibid., pp. 174–5.

50. Ibid., pp. 180–83.

51. Kenez, *Hungary from the Nazis to the Soviets*, p. 279.

52. *Szabad Nép*: 16 July 1946, p. 3; 18 July 1946, p. 1; 19 July 1946, p. 1; 20 July 1946, p. 3; 24 July 1946, p. 3. See also László Borhi, *Hungary in the Cold War, 1945–1956: Between the United States and the Soviet Union* (New York and Budapest, 2004), pp. 94–5; Kenez, *Hungary from the Nazis to the Soviets*, pp. 279–80.

53. Balogh, *A Kalot és a katolikus társadalompolitika*, pp. 206–9.

54. Henryk St Glass, *Harcerstwo jako czynnik odrodzenia Narodowego* (Warsaw and Plock, 1924), pp. 15–18.

55. Norman Davies, *Rising '44: The Battle for Warsaw* (New York, 2004), pp. 177–8 and 496; also Julian Kwiek, *Związek Harcerstwa Polskiego w latach 1944–1950. Powstanie, rozwój, likwidacja* (Toruń, 1995), pp. 5–6.

56. Karta, Bronisław Mazurek, I/531.

57. M. Kowalik, *Harcerstwo w Stalowej Woli 1938–1981. Zapiski kronikarskie* (Warsaw, 1981).

58. Karta, Janusz Zawisza-Hrybacz, II/1730.

59. Interview with Maria Straszewska, Warsaw, 26 May 2008.

60. Kwiek, *Związek Harcerstwa Polskiego*, pp. 8–12.

61. Ludwik Stanisław Szuba, *Harcerstwo na Pomorzu i Kujawach w latach 1945–1950* (Bydgoszcz, 2006), p. 35.

62. Kwiek, *Związek Harcerstwa Polskiego*, p. 47.

63. Ibid., pp. 66–7.

64. Interview with Julia Tazbirowa, Warsaw, 20 May 2009.

65. K. Persak, *Odrodzenia harcerstwo w 1956 roku* (Warsaw, 1996), pp. 60–62; Kwiek, *Związek Harcerstwa Polskiego*, p. 123.

66. Interview with Straszewska.

67. An 'underground' scouting movement was founded in the late 1950s. It remained in place until 1989.

68. AAN, Ministerstwo Oświaty, 592, pp. 1–4.

69. Jan Żaryn, *Dzieje Kosciola Katolickiego w Polsce, 1944–1989* (Warsaw, 2003), pp. 119–20.

70. Ferenc Pataki, *A Nékosz-legenda* (Budapest, 2005), pp. 179–97.

71. PIL, 302/1/15/ p. 11.

72. Also titled, in English, *The Confrontation* (http://www.imdb.com/title/tt0062995/).

73. Interview with Iván Vitányi, Budapest, 28 January 2006.

74. PIL, 320/1/16/ pp. 162–77.

75. Tibor Huszar, 'From Elites to Nomenklatura: The Evolution and Some Characteristics of Institutionalised Cadre Policy in Hungary (1945–1989)', *Review of Sociology*, 11/2 (2005), pp. 5–73.
76. Pataki, *A Nékosz-legenda*, pp. 173–5, and István Papp, 'A Nékosz legendája és valósága', in *Mítoszok, legendák, tévhitek a 20. századi magyar történelemről* (Budapest, 2005), pp. 309–38.
77. Dini Metro-Roland, 'The Recollections of a Movement: Memory and History of the National Organization of People's Colleges', *Hungarian Studies*, 15/1 (2001), p. 84.
78. Pataki, *A Nékosz-legenda*, p. 259
79. PIL, 302/1/15; also 867/1/H-168.
80. Pataki, *A Nékosz-legenda*, pp. 378–9.
81. Papp, 'A Nékosz legendája és valósága', p. 335.

8. RADIO

1. Interview with Andrzej Zalewski, Warsaw, 15 September 2009.
2. Wolfgang Schivelbusch, *In a Cold Crater: Cultural and Intellectual Life in Berlin, 1945–1948* (Berkeley, 1998), pp. 108–9.
3. DRA, B202-00-00-06/0617.
4. DRA, F201-00-00/0004, pp. 646–50.
5. DRA, F201-00-00/0004, pp. 427–35.
6. Peter Strunk, *Zensur und Zensoren* (Berlin, 1996), pp. 10–18.
7. Markus Wolf and Anne McElvoy, *Man without a Face: The Autobiography of Communism's Greatest Spymaster* (London, 1997), p. 36.
8. Strunk, *Zensur und Zensoren*, pp. 10–18.
9. Schivelbusch, *In a Cold Crater*, pp. 109–10.
10. DRA, F201-00-00/0004, p. 554.
11. Strunk, *Zensur und Zensoren*, p. 111.
12. Conversation with Gunter Holzweißig, Berlin, 1 October 2006; conversation with Ingrid Pietrzynski, DRA Potsdam, 16 October 2006.
13. Michael Geyer, ed., *The Power of Intellectuals in Contemporary Germany* (Chicago, 2001), pp. 252.
14. DRA, 201-00-004/001, pp. 1–132.
15. Ibid., pp. 108–9.
16. DRA, B202-00-071/0027.
17. DRA, B202-00-03/0002.
18. DRA, B202-00-06/40.
19. DRA, F201-00-00/0004, pp. 532, 540 and 600–615.
20. Ibid., p. 583.

21. Ibid., pp. 71–3.
22. N. Timofeeva et al., eds., *Politika SVAG v Oblasti Kulturi, nauki I Obrazovaniya: Tseli, Metody, Rezultaty, 1945–1949 gg, Sbornik Dokumentov*, pp. 124–5.
23. TVP, 85/14 and Stefania Grodzieńska, *Już nic nie muszę* (Lublin, 2000), pp. 34–8.
24. The archives of the underground newspaper *Tygodnik Mazowsze* were stored at the Billigs' apartment after martial law was declared in 1981. *Gazeta Wyborcza*, 6 December 2006, http://wyborcza.pl/1,77023,3777590.html.
25. Grodzieńska, *Już nic nie muszę*, pp. 34–5.
26. TVP, 85/2/2.
27. Order reprinted in *Rzeczpospolita*, 15 August 1944.
28. *Dziennik Ustaw Rzeczpospolitej Polskiej*, No. 10, Lublin, 3 November 1944; Agnieszka Sowa, 'Gadające skrzynki', *Polityka* (37/2521), 17 September 2005, pp. 74–6; interview with Piotr Paszkowski, Warsaw, 21 May 2007.
29. Tomasz Goban-Klas, *The Orchestration of the Media: The Politics of Mass Communications in Communist Poland and the Aftermath* (Boulder, 1994), pp. 53–4.
30. Andrzej Krawczyk, *Pierwsza próba indoktrynacji: Działalność Ministerstwa Informacji i Propagandy w latach 1944–1947*, Dokumenty do dziejow PRL, Vol. 7 (Warsaw, 1994), p. 36.
31. NAC, recording catalogues, www.audiovis.nac.gov.pl; also NAC, Dokumentacja programowa Polskiego Radia, 21.02.1945, 9/8, s. 19.
32. TVP, 85/2/2.
33. TVP, 85/2/1.
34. Władysław Szpilman, *The Pianist* (London, 1999), pp. 7–9.
35. TVP, 85/2/2.
36. Ibid.
37. TVP, 85/6/1.
38. István Vida, 'A demokratikus Magyar Rádió megteremtése és a Magyar Központi Híradó Rt. Megalakulása', in *Tanulmányok a Magyar Rádió történetéből 1925–1945* (Budapest, 1975), pp. 239–86, and Béla Lévai, *A rádió és a televízió krónikája 1945–1978* (Budapest, 1980), p. 11.
39. Peter Kenez, *Hungary from the Nazis to the Soviets: The Establishment of the Communist Regime in Hungary, 1944–1948* (New York, 2006), p. 89.
40. Lévai, *A rádió és a televízió krónikája*, p. 15.
41. Ibid., p. 12; Vida, 'A demokratikus Magyar Rádió', p. 246.

42. Jenő Randé and János Sebestyén, *Azok a rádiós évtizedek* (Budapest, 1995), p. 112.
43. Interview with Áron Tóbiás, Budapest, 21 May 2009.
44. Gyula Schöpflin, *Szélkiáltó* (Budapest, 1985), p. 60.
45. Vida, 'A demokratikus Magyar Rádió', pp. 249–51.
46. Ibid., p. 251.
47. Lévai, *A rádió és a televízió krónikája*, pp. 16–26.
48. László András Palkó, 'A Magyar Rádió és az Államvédelmi Hatóság kapcsolata a Rákosi-korszakban', *Valóság* 2008/01, pp. 69–77.
49. Schöpflin, *Szélkiáltó*, pp. 63–4.
50. Randé and Sebestyén, *Azok a rádiós évtizedek*, pp. 110–12.

9. POLITICS

1. NA RG218 Stack 190 2/15/3 CCS/JCS UD47, Box 15 File 94 (courtesy of Antony Beevor)
2. John Lewis Gaddis, *The Cold War: A New History* (New York, 2005), pp. 5–6.
3. One of those killed was the conductor of the Berlin Philharmonic. See Ruth Andreas-Friedrich, *Battleground Berlin: Diaries, 1945–1948* (New York, 1990), pp. 86–92.
4. Quote in Krystyna Kersten, *The Establishment of Communist Rule in Poland, 1943–1948* (Berkeley, 1991), p. 75.
5. Ivan T. Berend, *Central and Eastern Europe 1944–1993* (Cambridge, 1996), p. 30.
6. Teresa Torańska, *Oni: Stalin's Posh Puppets*, trans. Agnieszka Kołakowska (Warsaw, 2004), p. 484.
7. Hermann Weber, ed., *DDR: Dokumente zur Geschichte der Deutschen Demokratischen Republik 1945–1985* (Munich, 1986), pp. 65–6.
8. Stanisław Mikołajczyk, *The Rape of Poland* (New York, 1948), p. 100.
9. T. V. Volokitina et al., eds., *Sovietskii faktor v vostochnoi evrope, 1944–1953* (Moscow, 1999), Vol. 1, pp. 67–76.
10. Gaddis, *Cold War*, p. 100.
11. T. V. Volokitina et al., eds., *Vostochnaya Evropa v dokumentakh rossiskikh arkhivov, 1944–1953* (Novosibirsk, 1997), Vol. 1, pp. 330–31.
12. R. J. Crampton, *A Concise History of Bulgaria* (Cambridge, 2006), pp. 182–3.
13. Mikołajczyk, *Rape of Poland*, p. 98; also Martin Gilbert, 'Churchill and Poland', unpublished lecture delivered at the University of Warsaw, 16 February 2010. With thanks to Martin Gilbert.

14. Kersten, *Establishment of Communist Rule in Poland*, p. 81.
15. Ibid., p. 113.
16. 'Protocol of Proceedings of Crimea Conference', http://www.fordham.edu/halsall/mod/1945YALTA.html.
17. Mikołajczyk, *Rape of Poland*, p. 127.
18. Ibid., pp. 130–34.
19. Kersten, *Establishment of Communist Rule in Poland*, p. 242.
20. IWM, 'The Struggles for Poland, Programme Six', Roll E.156, interview with Włodzimierz Brus (with thanks to Wanda Kościa).
21. HIA, Stanisław Mikołajczyk Collection, Box 103, folder 3, and Box 104, folder 9.
22. Ibid.
23. Tomasz Goban-Klas, *The Orchestration of the Media: The Politics of Mass Communications in Communist Poland and the Aftermath* (Boulder, 1994), p. 52.
24. HIA, Stanisław Mikołajczyk Collection, Box 104, folders 4 and 5.
25. Kersten, *Establishment of Communist Rule in Poland*, pp. 252–3.
26. Torańska, *Oni*, p. 273.
27. Ibid., p. 274.
28. Kersten, *Establishment of Communist Rule in Poland*, pp. 271–7.
29. IWM interview with Brus.
30. IWM interview with Brus.
31. Andrzej Paczkowski, *Referendum z 30 czerwca 1946: Proba wstępnego bilansu* (Warsaw, 1992), p. 14.
32. Andrzej Krawczyk, *Pierwsza próba indoktrynacji. Działalność Ministerstwa Informacji i Propagandy w latach 1944–1947*, Dokumenty do dziejow PRL, Vol. 7 (Warsaw, 1994), p. 91.
33. Paczkowski, *Referendum z 30 czerwca 1946*, pp. 221–2.
34. Torańska, *Oni*, pp. 274–5.
35. Krawczyk, *Pierwsza próba indoktrynacji*, p. 91.
36. Kersten, *Establishment of Communist Rule in Poland*, p. 320.
37. IWM interview with Brus.
38. Mikołajczyk, *Rape of Poland*, p. 198.
39. Anita Prażmowska, *Poland: A Modern History* (London, 2010), p. 167.
40. Solidarity was initially an underground movement but between August 1980 and December 1981 it was recognized as a legal trade union.
41. Ignác Romsics, *Hungary in the Twentieth Century* (Budapest, 1999), pp. 230–31.
42. Peter Kenez, *Hungary from the Nazis to the Soviets: The Establishment of the Communist Regime in Hungary, 1944–1948* (New York, 2006), p. 96.
43. Volokitina et al., eds., *Vostochnaya Evropa*, Vol. 1, pp. 271–4.

44. Interview with Jenő Széll, Történeti Interjúk Tára, Országos Széchenyi Könyvtár (Historic Interviews at the SNL). Interview conducted by András Hegedüs, Gábor Hanák, Gyula Kozák, Ilona Szabóné Dér on 3 August 1985.
45. Interview with Széll.
46. Ibid.
47. György Gyarmati, '"Itt csak az fog történni, amit a kommunista párt akar!": Adalékok az 1947: évi országgyűlési választások történetéhez', *Társadalmi Szemle*, Vol. 8–9 (Budapest, 1997), pp. 144–61.
48. Volokitina et al., eds., *Vostochnaya Evropa*, Vol. 1, pp. 271–4.
49. Volokitina et al., eds., *Sovietskii faktor*, Vol. 1, pp. 243–4.
50. Ferenc Nagy, *The Struggle behind the Iron Curtain* (New York, 1948), p. 369.
51. Ibid., pp. 405–26.
52. Gyarmati, '"Itt csak az fog történni, amit a kommunista párt akar!"', pp. 144–61.
53. Dezső Sulyok, *Két éjszaka nappal nélkül* (Budapest, 2004), pp. 387–91.
54. Károly Szerencsés, *A kék cédulás hadművelet* (Budapest, 1992), pp. 59–73.
55. Margit Balogh and Kataline S. Nagy, eds., *Asszonysorsok a 20. Században*, conference papers of BME Szociológia és Kommunikáció Tanszék, 2000, pp. 297–309.
56. Dirk Spilker, *The East German Leadership and the Division of Germany: Patriotism and Propaganda 1945–1953* (Oxford, 2006), pp. 53–4.
57. Peter Greider, *The East German Leadership 1946–1973* (Manchester, 1999), pp. 17–25.
58. The full text is at http://www.marxists.org/archive/lenin/works/1918/prrk/index.htm.
59. Gary Bruce, *The Firm: The Inside Story of the Stasi* (Oxford, 2010), pp. 34–6.
60. Wilfried Loth, *Stalin's Unwanted Child: The Soviet Union, the German Question and the Founding of the GDR*, trans. Robert F. Hogg (London, 1998), p. 31.
61. Spilker, *East German Leadership and the Division of Germany*, pp. 47–50.
62. Andreas-Friedrich, *Battleground Berlin*, p. 130.
63. Ibid., p. 125.
64. Ibid., pp. 114–15.
65. Walter Ulbricht, *On Questions of Socialist Construction in the GDR* (Dresden, 1968), pp. 78–90.
66. Stefan Creuzberger, 'The Soviet Military Administration and East

German Elections, Autumn, 1946', *The Australian Journal of Politics and History*, Vol. 45 (1999).

67. Karl-Heinz Hajna, *Die Landtagswahlen 1946 in der SBZ* (Frankfurt am Main, 2000), pp.119–68.
68. Spilker, *East German Leadership and the Division of Germany*, p. 101.
69. Creuzberger, 'Soviet Military Administration and East German Elections'.
70. Interview with Benda.
71. Peter Skyba, 'Jugendpolitik, Jugendopposition und Jugendwiderstand in der SED-Diktatur', in *Jugend und Diktatur. Verfolgung und Widerstand in der SBZ/DDR. Dokumentation des XII. Bautzen-Forums am 4. und 5. Mai 2001* (Leipzig 2001), p. 40.
72. Interview with Ernst Benda, Berlin, 20 May 2008.
73. Sidney S. Alexander, *The Marshall Plan*, National Planning Association Planning Pamphlets nos. 60–61 (February 1948), p. 14.
74. Giuliano Procacci et al., eds., *The Cominform: Minutes of the Three Conferences, 1947/1948/1949* (Milan, 1994), p. 26.
75. Volokitina et al., eds., *Sovietskii faktor*, Vol. 1, p. 459.
76. Geoffrey Roberts, 'Moscow and the Marshall Plan: Politics, Ideology and the Onset of the Cold War, 1947', *Europe–Asia Studies*, Vol. 46, No. 8 (1994), p. 1378; also Volokitina et al., eds., *Sovietskii faktor*, Vol. 1, pp. 462–5.
77. Procacci et al., eds., *Cominform*, pp. 26, 225–51 and 379.
78. Ibid., p. 43.
79. Ibid., p. 129.
80. Kenez, *Hungary from the Nazis to the Soviets*, pp. 277–8.
81. Jenő Randé and János Sebestyén, *Azok a rádiós évtizedek* (Budapest, 1995), pp. 127–9.
82. Ivor Lukes, 'The Czech Road to Communism', in Norman Naimark and Leonid Gibianskii, eds., *The Establishment of Communist Regimes in Eastern Europe, 1944–1949* (Boulder, 1997), p. 259.
83. Ekaterina Nikova, 'Bulgarian Stalinism Revisited', in Vladimir Tismaneau, ed., *Stalinism Revisited* (New York and Budapest, 2009), pp. 290–94.

10. ECONOMICS

1. Giuliano Procacci et al., eds., *The Cominform: Minutes of the Three Conferences, 1947/1948/1949* (Milan, 1994), p. 17.
2. Ingolf Vogeler, 'State Hegemony in Transforming the Rural Landscapes of Eastern Germany: 1945–1994', *Annals of the Association of American Geographers*, Vol. 86, No. 3 (Sept. 1996), pp. 432–3.

3. Jonathan Osmond, 'From *Junker* Estate to Co-operative Farm: East German Agrarian Society 1945–61', in Patrick Major and Jonathan Osmond, eds., *The Workers' and Peasants' State* (Manchester, 2002), pp. 134–7.

4. Gary Bruce, *Resistance with the People* (Oxford, 2003), p. 33.

5. Peter Stachura, *Poland 1918–1945* (London, 2004), pp. 47–9.

6. Nicolas Spulber, 'Eastern Europe: The Changes in Agriculture from Land Reforms to Collectivization', *American Slavic and East European Review*, Vol. 13, No. 3 (Oct. 1954), pp. 393–4.

7. Krystyna Kersten, *The Establishment of Communist Rule in Poland, 1943–1948* (Berkeley, 1991), p. 166.

8. *Polska-ZSRR: Struktury Podlegości* (Warsaw, 1995), pp. 114–15.

9. István Harcsa, Imre Kovách and Iván Szelényi, 'The Hungarian Agricultural "Miracle" and the Limits of Socialist Reforms', in Iván Szelényi, ed., *Privatizing the Land: Rural Political Economy in Post-Communist Societies* (London, 1998), pp. 24–6.

10. Spulber, 'Eastern Europe', pp. 394–8. Also Peter Kenez, *Hungary from the Nazis to the Soviets: The Establishment of the Communist Regime in Hungary, 1944–1948* (New York, 2006), pp. 107–18.

11. Stephen Wegren, *Land Reform in the Former Soviet Union and Eastern Europe* (London, 1998), p. 226.

12. PIL, 867/1/H-168.

13. Mark Pittaway, 'The Politics of Legitimacy and Hungary's Postwar Transition', *Contemporary European History*, Vol. 13, No. 4 (2004), p. 465.

14. Harris L. Coulter, 'The Hungarian Peasantry: 1948–1956', *American Slavic and East European Review*, 18/4 (December 1959), pp. 539–54; also Corey Ross, 'Before the Wall: East Germans, Communist Authority, and the Mass Exodus to the West', *The Historical Journal*, Vol. 45, No. 2 (June 2002), pp. 459–80.

15. Interview with Ulrich Fest, Wittenberg, 16 April 2008.

16. The relative wealth of European economies in the interwar period is difficult to measure because data was not collected in the same way across the continent. A very rough estimate, however, puts GDP per capita at $1841 in Czechoslovakia, $1638 in Hungary and $1241 in Poland in 1937, at a time when the UK was at $3610, France at $2586 and Germany at $2736. For a further comparison, the GDP per capita of Ireland in 1937 was $1836, and for Greece the figure is $1373. See Mark Harrison, 'GDPs of the USSR and Eastern Europe: Towards an Interwar Comparison', *Europe–Asia Studies*, Vol. 46, No. 2 (1994), pp. 243–59.

17. V. I. Lenin, *Left-Wing Communism – An Infantile Disorder* (Chippendale, NSW, 1999), p. 30.

18. SAPMO-BA, DY 30/IV 2/6.02 3, pp. 17–25.

19. Primo Levi, *If This is Man and The Truce* (London, 1988), pp. 220–21.

20. AAN, Ministerstwo Przemysłu i Handlu, 2831.

21. Interview with Fest.

22. Interview with Ulrich Schneider, Wittenberg, 16 April 2008.

23. Anders Åslund, *Private Enterprise in Eastern Europe* (Macmillan, 1985), p. 26.

24. Ibid., pp. 30–31.

25. Ibid., pp. 27–9.

26. Interview with Janina Stobniak, Warsaw, 28 November 2007.

27. Conversation with Krystyna Paszkowska, Chobielin, 31 December 2010.

28. Interview with Stefan Grzeszkiewicz, Warsaw, 12 October 2007.

29. György Polák, 'Csapás' a feketekereskedelemre – A gazdasági rendőrség ténykedése 1945 után', *Korrajz 2002 – a XX. Század Intézet Évkönyve, XX.* Század Intézet (Budapest, 2004), pp. 128–37.

30. Ibid., p. 135.

31. Ibid., pp. 128–37.

32. MOL, XIX-G5 480/1946.2.

33. Gergő Havadi, *Dokumentumok a fővárosi vendéglátók államosításáról 1949–1953* (ArchívNet 2009/2: http://www.archivnet.hu/index.phtml?cikk=313).

34. György Majtényi, 'Őrök a vártán. Uralmi elit Magyarországon az 1950-es, 1960-as években', in Sándor Horváth, ed., *Mindennapok Rákosi és Kádár korában* (Budapest, 2008), pp. 289–316.

35. Margit Földesi, *A megszállók szabadsága* (Budapest, 2002), pp. 108–36.

36. Norman Naimark, *The Russians in Germany: A History of the Soviet Zone of Occupation, 1945–1949* (Cambridge, Mass., 1995), pp. 172–3.

37. Marek Jan Chodakiewicz, John Radziłowski and Dariusz Tolczyk, eds., *Poland's Transformation: A Work in Progress* (Charlottesville, 2003), pp. 157–93.

38. David Crowley, *Warsaw* (London, 2003), p. 28.

39. Padraic Kenney, *Rebuilding Poland: Workers and Communists 1945–1950* (Ithaca, 1997), p. 30.

40. Naimark, *Russians in Germany*, pp. 184–6.

41. Ignác Romsics, *Hungary in the Twentieth Century* (Budapest, 1999), pp. 248–9.

42. Kenney, *Rebuilding Poland*, p. 81.

43. Kersten, *Establishment of Communist Rule in Poland*, p. 251. Łódź, Silesia and Gdańsk would all become important centres for the independent Solidarity trade union in 1980.

44. Gyula Belényi, *Az állam szorításában. Az ipari munkásság társadalmi átalakulása 1945–1965* (Budapest, 2009), pp. 49–51 and 158–9.
45. Henryk Różański, *Śladem Wspomnień i Dokumentów (1943–1948)* (Warsaw, 1987), p. 142.
46. Jochen Laufer, 'From Dismantling to Currency Reform', in Konrad H. Jarausch, ed., *Dictatorship as Experience: Towards a Socio-Cultural History of the GDR* (New York, 1999), pp. 73–90.
47. Tamás Lossonczy, *The Vision is Always Changing* (Budapest, 2004), pp. 98–100.
48. William A. Bomberger and Gail E. Makinen, 'Hungarian Hyperinflation and Stabilization of 1945–1946', *The Journal of Political Economy*, Vol. 91, No. 5 (Oct. 1983), pp. 801–24.
49. Jeffrey Kopstein, *The Politics of Economic Decline in East Germany, 1945–1989* (Chapel Hill, 1997), p. 21.
50. Quoted in Kenney, *Rebuilding Poland*, p. 90.
51. Kopstein, *Politics of Economic Decline in East Germany*, p. 26.
52. AAN, Ministerstwo Przemysłu i Handlu, 2832, p. 1.
53. AAN, Ministerstwo Oświaty, 568, pp. 2–12.
54. AAN, Ministerstwo Oświaty, 568, p. 22; see also http://www.drukarnia-anczyca.com.pl/historia/1945–1957.
55. SAPMO-BA, DC 30/IV 2/6.02 116.
56. SAPMO-BA, DY 30/IV 2/6.02 76.
57. SAPMO-BA, DC 20/12046.
58. BStU MfSZ, Sekretariat d. Ministers (Min.) 387, p. 622.
59. Różański, *Śladem Wspomnień i Dokumentów*, p. 145.
60. Jo Langer, *My Life with a Good Communist* (London, 2011), pp. 17–19.
61. DRA, F201-00-00/0004, pp. 309–10.
62. DRA, B204-02-01/0364.
63. Peter Grothe, *To Win the Minds of Men: The Story of the Communist Propaganda War in East Germany* (Palo Alto, 1958), pp. 141–2.
64. DRA, F201-00-00/0004, pp. 318–31.
65. Bolesław Bierut, *Sześcoletni Plan Odbudowy Warszawy* (Warsaw, 1950).

11. REACTIONARY ENEMIES

1. T. V. Volokitina et al., eds., *Vostochnaya Evropa v dokumentakh rossiskikh arkhivov, 1944–1953* (Novosibirsk, 1997), Vol. 2, pp. 25–8.
2. Ibid.

3. Elena Zubkova, *Russia after the War: Hopes, Illusions and Disappointments, 1945–1957*, trans. Hugh Ragsdale (Armonk, 1998), p. 18; also see Joseph Brodsky, *Less Than One: Selected Essays* (New York, 1986), pp. 26–9.

4. Robert Service, *A History of Twentieth-Century Russia* (London, 1997), p. 299.

5. See Amir Weiner, 'The Empires Pay a Visit: Gulag Returnees, East European Rebellions and Soviet Frontier Politics', *The Journal of Modern History*, Vol. 78, No. 2 (June 2006), pp. 333–76, for a general discussion of this idea.

6. Anne Applebaum, *Gulag: A History of the Soviet Camps* (London, 2003), pp. 414–27.

7. Ivan T. Berend, *Central and Eastern Europe 1944–1993* (Cambridge, 1996), p. 34.

8. See http://www.psywarrior.com/RadioFreeEurope.html for an account of the balloon project.

9. See George Urban, *Radio Free Europe and the Pursuit of Democracy: My War within the Cold War* (New Haven, 1997), for an elegant account of RFE's origins, history and impact.

10. See, for example, recent general histories and textbooks such as John Lewis Gaddis, *The Cold War: A New History* (New York, 2005); Elizabeth Edwards Spalding, *The First Cold Warrior: Harry Truman, Containment, and the Making of Liberal Internationalism* (Louisville, 2006); Martin McCauley, *Origins of the Cold War* (New York, 2008); V. M. Zubok, *A Failed Empire: The Soviet Union in the Cold War from Stalin to Gorbachev* (Chapel Hill, 2008); Jonathan Haslam, *Russia's Cold War* (New Haven and London, 2010).

11. Interview with Czesław Kiszczak, Warsaw, 25 May 2007. Although his father was Polish, his mother was Russian. Rokossovskii's birthplace is disputed: it may or may not have been Warsaw, and his biographers give different accounts. Many thanks to Sir Rodric Braithwaite for discussions of this.

12. Andrzej Żak, 'Tradycje Armii Krakowej w Wojsku Polskim', in Krzysztof Komorowski, ed., *Armia Krajowa: szkice z dziejów Sił Zbrojnych Polskiego Państwa Podziemnego* (Warsaw, 1999); also Halmy Kund, 'János Mecséri: An Army Officer in the Revolution', lecture given at the Terror Háza Múzeum, Budapest, October 2006.

13. For the Marshall Foundation's own account, see http://marshallfoundation. org/documents/MarshallPlanArticleOPT.pdf.

14. David E. Murphy, Sergei A. Kondrashev and George Bailey, *Battleground Berlin: CIA vs. KGB in the Cold War* (New Haven and London, 1997), p. 57.
15. Ibid., pp. 67–9.
16. Ibid., p. 71.
17. V. V. Zakharov, 'Mezhdy vlastyiu i veroi', introductory essay in *SVAG i Religioznaya Konfessii Sovetskoi zoni okkupatsii Germanii 1945–49: Sbornik Dokumentov* (Moscow, 2006), pp. 50–51.
18. DRA, F201-00-00/0006, pp. 11–20.
19. József Gyula Orbán, *Katolikus papok békemozgalma Magyarországon 1950–1956* (Budapest, 2001), p. 94.
20. Helmut David Baer, *The Struggle of Hungarian Lutherans under Communism* (College Station, Texas, 2006), p. 16.
21. Richard Pipes, *Russia under the Bolshevik Regime, 1919–1924* (London, 1994), pp. 346–52.
22. V. V. Zakharov et al., eds., *SVAG i Religioznaya Konfessii*, pp. 228–31.
23. Ellen Ueberschär, *Junge Gemeinde im Konflikt: Evangelische Jugendarbeit in SBZ und DDR 1945–1961* (Stuttgart, 2003), pp. 63–4.
24. Jan Żaryn, *Dzieje Kościoła Katolickiego w Polsce: 1944–1989* (Warsaw, 2003), pp. 64–9.
25. PIL, f.83, KV.
26. József Mindszenty, *Memoirs* (New York, 1974), p. 31.
27. Gábor Kiszely, *ÁVH: Egy terrorszervezet története* (Budapest, 2000), p. 102.
28. Ibid., p. 104.
29. *Ofensywa kleru a nasze zadania*, document reprinted in Jan Żaryn, *Kościół w PRL* (Warsaw, 2004), p. 20.
30. SAPMO-BA, DO 1 11/873 and SAPMO-BA, DY 24 3823.
31. Hermann Wentker, 'Kirchenkampf in der DDR: Der Konflikt um die Junge Gemeinde 1950–1953', *Vierteljahrshefte für Zeitgeschichte* (Jan. 1994), p. 116.
32. SAPMO-BA, DY 24 3665.
33. Interview with Ulrich Fest, Wittenberg, 16 April 2008.
34. Mary Fulbrook, *Anatomy of a Dictatorship: Inside the GDR, 1949–1989* (Oxford, 1995), pp. 91–9.
35. Ueberschär, *Junge Gemeinde im Konflikt*, pp. 192–200.
36. Interview with Fest.
37. Kiszely, *ÁVH*, p. 104.
38. Ibid., pp. 104–7.
39. Orbán, *Katolikus papok békemozgalma Magyarországon*, pp. 56–9.
40. Interview with Sándor Keresztes, Budafok, 12 February 2009.

41. Żaryn, *Dzieje Kościoła Katolickiego w Polsce*, p. 94.
42. Marian S. Mazgaj, *Church and State in Communist Poland: A History, 1944–1989* (New York, 2010), pp. 60–61.
43. Żaryn, *Dzieje Kościoła Katolickiego w Polsce*, pp. 101–2.
44. Ibid., p. 116.
45. Ibid., pp. 120–21.
46. Ibid., p. 126.
47. Csaba Szabó, *Egyházügyi hangulatjelentések* (Budapest, 2000), pp. 125 and 136.
48. Wentker, 'Kirchenkampf in der DDR', p. 116.
49. MOL, 276/65/359.
50. See Wojciech Czuchnowski, *Blizna. Proces Kurii krakowskiej 1953* (Kraków, 2003).
51. See Csaba Szabó, *A Grősz-per előkészítés* (Budapest, 2001).
52. Kiszely, *ÁVH*, pp. 104–5.
53. Mindszenty, *Memoirs*, pp. 1–2.
54. Andrzej Micewski, *Cardinal Wyszyński: A Biography*, trans. William R. Brand and Katzarzyna Mroczowska-Brand (New York, 1984), pp. 1–2.
55. Margit Balogh, *Mindszenty József: 1892–1975* (Budapest, 2002), pp. 60–76.
56. Cardinal Stefan Wyszyński, *A Freedom Within*, trans. Barbara Krzywicki-Herburt and Reverend Walter J. Ziemba (New York, 1982), p. 15.
57. Árpád Pünkösti, 'You are Not Primate Here', *The Hungarian Quarterly*, Vol. XXXVII, No. 144 (Winter 1996).
58. Balogh, *Mindszenty József*, p. 100.
59. Mindszenty, *Memoirs*, p. 76.
60. Ibid., p. 100.
61. Wyszyński, *Freedom Within*, pp. 25–6.
62. Micewski, *Cardinal Wyszyński*, p. 66.
63. Żaryn, *Dzieje Kościoła Katolickiego w Polsce*, pp. 134–56.
64. Micewski, *Cardinal Wyszyński*, p. 20.
65. Mindszenty, *Memoirs*, pp. 197–8.
66. Micewski, *Cardinal Wyszyński*, pp. 53–5.
67. Balogh, *Mindszenty József*, pp. 16–18.
68. Interview with Hans-Jochen Tschiche, Satuelle, 18 November 2006.
69. Keith Armes, 'Chekists in Cassocks', *Demokratisatsiya*, No. 4 (1993), pp. 72–83.
70. OSA, 300/50/6, folder 124.
71. M. Tinz, 'Friedenspriester in der Tschechoslowakei. Im Dienste der Partei', *Digest des Ostens* (1977), p. 42.
72. Orbán, *Katolikus papok békemozgalma Magyarországon*, p. 94.

73. Ibid., pp. 103–4.
74. Ibid., pp. 107–8.
75. Ibid.
76. Jacek Żurek, *Ruch 'Ksiezy Patriotow'* (Warsaw, 2008), pp. 56–9.
77. Orbán, *Katolikus papok békemozgalma Magyarországon*, pp. 188–9.
78. Tadeusz Isakowicz-Zaleski, *Księza Wobec Bezpieki* (Kraków, 2007), p. 44.
79. OSA, 300/50/6, folder 124.
80. Żurek, *Ruch 'Ksiezy Patriotow'*, p. 105.
- 81. Isakowicz-Zaleski, *Księza Wobec Bezpieki*, p. 46.
82. Ibid.
83. Interview with Sándor Ladányi, Budapest, 12 March 2008; see also Ladányi, *A magyar református egyház 1956 tükrében* (Budapest, 2006), and Isakowicz-Zaleski, *Księza Wobec Bezpieki*.

12. INTERNAL ENEMIES

1. Arthur Koestler, *Darkness at Noon* (New York, 2006), p. 244.
2. Csaba Békés, Malcolm Byrne and János Rainer, eds., *The 1956 Hungarian Revolution: A History in Documents* (Budapest and New York, 2002), p. 16.
3. Joel Kotek and Pierre Rigolout, *Le Siècle des camps* (Paris, 2001), pp. 544–8; also Andrzej Paczkowski, 'Poland, the Enemy Nation', in Stéphane Courtois et al., eds., *The Black Book of Communism* (Cambridge, 1999), pp. 363–93.
4. Romulus Rusan, *The Chronology and Geography of Repression in Romania* (Bucharest, 2007), pp. 28–30.
5. Paczkowski, 'Poland, the Enemy Nation', pp. 237–8.
6. György Gyarmati, 'Hungary in the Second Half of the Twentieth Century', in István György Tóth, ed., *A Concise History of Hungary* (Budapest, 2005), pp. 58–581.
7. Rusan, *Chronology and Geography of Repression*, p. 31.
8. Karta, Wacław Beynar, II/542.
9. Karta, Stanisław Szostak, II/2944.
10. Alina Gałan and Zygmunt Mańkowski, eds., *Więzniowie Politcyzni na Zamku Lubelskim* (Lublin, 1996), pp. 20–31.
11. Frank Drauschke, Arseny Roginsky and Anna Kaminsky, eds., *Erschossen in Moskau* (Berlin, 2005).
12. Barbara Bank, 'Az internálás és kitelepítés dokumentumai a történeti levéltárban', in György Gyarmati, ed., *Az átmenet évkönyve, 2003* (Budapest, 2004), pp. 125–30; also Gyarmati, 'Hungary in the Second Half of the Twentieth Century', p. 581.

13. Rusan, *Chronology and Geography of Repression*, pp. 31–2.

14. Kotek and Rigolout, *Le Siècle des camps*, pp. 543–4.

15. Dennis Deletant, *Romania under Communist Rule* (Bucharest, 2006), p. 109.

16. Tzvetan Todorov, *Voices from the Gulag*, trans. Robert Zaretsky (University Park, Pa., 1999), pp. 39–40.

17. Kotek and Rigolout, *Le Siècle des camps*, p. 559.

18. Bank, 'Az internálás és kitelepítés dokumentumai a történeti levéltárban', pp. 107–30.

19. See *Magyar tudóslexikon A-tól Zs-ig* (Budapest, 1998), p. 192; *Magyar Internacionalisták* (Budapest, 1980); Rudolf Garasin, *Vörössipkás lovagok* (Budapest, 1967); Rudolf Garasin, *Zrínyi Katonai Kiadó* (Budapest, 1976).

20. PIL, 867/11/g-24, pp. 15–58.

21. MOL, 276/65184, pp. 133–9.

22. From conversations with Mária Schmidt, Sándor M. Kiss and Barbara Bank; also Géza Böszörményi, *Recsk 1950–1953* (Budapest, 2005), p. 49.

23. Bank, 'Az internálás és kitelepítés dokumentumai a történeti levéltárban', p. 122.

24. From a conversation with Barbara Bank, Recsk, 4 July 2009.

25. Böszörményi, *Recsk*, p. 261.

26. ÁBTL, 3.1.9. V-107373.

27. György Faludy, *My Happy Days in Hell*, trans. Kathleen Szasz (London, 2010), p. 304.

28. *Törvénytelen szocializmus – A Tényfeltáró Bizottság jelentése* (Budapest, 1991), p. 96.

29. Faludy, *My Happy Days in Hell*, p. 371.

30. PIL, 962/2.

31. Fitzroy Maclean, *Eastern Approaches* (London, 1991), pp. 82 and 94.

32. I heard this lecture as a Yale undergraduate, in the autumn of 1982.

33. Mária Schmidt, *Battle of Wits*, trans. Ann Major (Budapest, 2007), p. 171.

34. T. V. Volokitina et al., eds., *Vostochnaya Evropa v dokumentakh rossiskikh arkhivov, 1944–1953* (Novosibirsk, 1997), Vol. 1, pp. 814–29.

35. Ibid., pp. 936–42.

36. Andrzej Paczkowski et al., eds., *Polska w dokumentach z archiwów rosyjskich 1949–1953* (Warsaw, 2000), pp. 82–3.

37. Volokitina et al., eds., *Vostochnaya Evropa*, Vol. 1, pp. 830–58.

38. Igor Lukes, 'The Rudolf Slánský Affair: New Evidence', *Slavic Review*, 58/1 (Spring 1999), pp. 160–66.

39. Ibid., pp. 164–6.

40. Jří Pelikán, ed., *The Czechoslovak Political Trials, 1950–1954: The Suppressed Report of the Dubček Government's Commission of Inquiry, 1968* (Stanford, 1975), pp. 104–9.

41. Igor Lukes, *Rudolf Slánský: His Trials and Trial*, Cold War International History Project (Washington, DC, 2006), p. 52.

42. Zbigniew Błażynski, *Mówi Józef Światło* (Warsaw, 2003), pp. 252–3.

43. Andrzej Werblan, *Stalinizm w Polsce* (Warsaw, 2009), p. 128.

44. George H. Hodos, *Show Trials: Stalinist Purges in Eastern Europe, 1948–1954* (New York, 1987), p. 135.

45. Ibid., p. 28.

46. Schmidt, *Battle of Wits*, p. 108; also Lukes, 'The Rudolf Slánský Affair', pp. 166–9.

47. Schmidt, *Battle of Wits*, pp. 133–5.

48. *Lászlo Rajk and His Accomplices before the People's Court*, publication of the Hungarian state prosecutor's office (Budapest, 1949), pp. 146–63.

49. Béla Szász, *Volunteers for the Gallows* (New York, 1971), p. 123.

50. Karel Kaplan, *Report on the Murder of the General Secretary*, trans. Karel Kovanda (Columbus, 1990), p. 44.

51. Ibid., pp. 152–92; *Lászlo Rajk and His Accomplices*, pp. 146–63; Szász, *Volunteers for the Gallows*, p. 123.

52. Pelikán, ed., *Czechoslovak Political Trials*, p. 81.

53. Konrad Rokicki, 'Aparatu Obraz Własny', in Kazimierz Krajewski and Tomasza Łabuszewski, eds., *'Zwyczajny' Resort: Studia o aparacie bezpieczeństwa 1944–1956* (Warsaw, 2005), p. 112.

54. Tomáš Bouška and Klara Pinerova, *Czechoslovak Political Prisoners* (Prague, 2009), p. 14.

55. Szász, *Volunteers for the Gallows*, pp. 51 and 59.

56. Konrad Rokicki, ed., *Departament X MBP: Wzorce – Struktury – Dzialanie* (Warsaw, 2007), p. 113.

57. Ibid., pp. 110–11.

58. Bouška and Pinerova, *Czechoslovak Political Prisoners*, p. 15.

59. István Rév, 'Indicting Rajk', paper given at the University of Pennsylvania Slavic Department Spring Research Symposium, 18 April 2009: http://ccat.sas.upenn.edu/slavic/events/slavic_symposium/Comrades_Please_Shoot_Me/Rev_Rajk.pdf.

60. The quotes which follow are from a transcript which was in the possession of Mieczysław Rakowski and is now available at HIA, Mieczysław Rakowski Collection.

61. Jo Langer, *My Life with a Good Communist* (London, 2011), p. 30.

62. Michael Scammell, *Koestler: The Literary and Political Odyssey of a Twentieth-Century Skeptic* (New York, 2009), p.413.
63. OSA, 23/1/25.
64. József Mindszenty, *Memoirs* (New York, 1974), p. 100.
65. Szász, *Volunteers for the Gallows*, p. 56.
66. Melissa Feinberg, 'Only an Imperialist Could Think Up Such a Notion', paper given at the University of Pennsylvania Slavic Department Spring Research Symposium, 18 April 2009.
67. Karta, file 'Różności, 1944–56'.
68. *Frage und Antwort*, No. 6 (1950).
69. Karta, file 'Różności, 1944–56'. The Colorado potato beetles can also be seen here: http://www.youtube.com/watch?v=oCYKU9jmBKo.
70. *HALT Amikäfer* (Berlin: Amt für Information der Regierung der DDR, 1950).
71. OSA documentary film collection, *Statarium*, directed by András Sipos, 1989.
72. MOL, 276/65/324, p. 36.
73. Faludy, *My Happy Days in Hell*, p. 254.
74. Ibid., p. 240.
75. Langer, *My Life with a Good Communist*, p. 2.
76. Interview with Attila Pók, Budapest, 13 February 2009.
77. Zsuzsanna Ágnes Berényi, *A szabadkőművesség kézikönyve* (Budapest, 2001), pp. 185–7 and 193; '*Grossaufseher*: A magyar szabadkőművesség története 1945 és 1950 között: módszerek és célkitűzések', *Kelet* (2008/1), pp. 62–76.
78. ÁBTL, O-8511, pp. 1–9.

13. HOMO SOVIETICUS

1. See Gyula Schöpflin, *Szélkiáltó* (Budapest, 1985), p. 62.
2. Alexander Zinoviev, *Homo Sovieticus*, trans. Charles Janson (Boston, 1986).
3. *Partei und Jugend: Dokumente marxistischer-leninistischer Jugendpolitik*, Herausgegeben vom Zentralrat der Freien Deutschen Jugend und des Institut für Marxismus-Leninismus beim Zentralkommitee der SED (Berlin, 1986), p. 326.
4. Ulrich Mählert, *Die Freie Deutsche Jugend 1945–1949* (Paderborn, 1995), p. 34.
5. Heinz-Hermann Krüger and Winfried Marotzki, 'Pädagogik und Erziehungsalltag in der DDR: Zwischen Systemvorgaben und Pluralität', in

Studien zur Erziehungswissenschaft und Bildungsforschung 2 (Opladen, 1994), p. 195.

6. See, for example, Janusz Korczak, *Ghetto Diary* (New Haven, 2003); also http://www.holocaustresearchproject.org/ghettos/korczak.html.

7. A. S. Makarenko, *The Road to Life*, Vol. Two, trans. Ivy and Tatiana Litvinov (Moscow, 1951), p. 206.

8. Leonore Ansorg, *Kinder im Klassenkampf: Die Geschichte der Pionierorganisation von 1948 bis Ende der fünfziger Jahre* (Berlin, 1997), pp. 30–40.

9. Marta Brodala, 'Propaganda dla Najmłodszych w latach 1948–1956', in *Przebudować Człowieka* (Warsaw, 2001), p. 21.

10. Ibid., pp. 58–63.

11. Ibid., p. 57.

12. Alex Wedding, *Die Fahne des Pfeiferhansleins* (Berlin, 1953), pp. 231–2.

13. Radek Sikorski, *Full Circle: A Homecoming to Free Poland* (New York, 1997), p. 37.

14. AAN, Ministerstwo Edukacji Narodowej, 230, pp. 1–7.

15. Rafal Stobiecki, *Historiografia PRL* (Warsaw 2007), p. 73.

16. Siegfried Baske and Martha Engelbert, *Dokumente zur Bildungspolitik in der sowjetischen Besatzungszone* (Berlin, 1966), p. 87.

17. Ibid., pp. 4–8.

18. Frederick Taylor, *Exorcising Hitler: The Occupation and Denazification of Germany* (London, 2011), p. 327.

19. AAN, Ministerstwo Edukacji Narodowej, 598, p. 1.

20. AAN, Ministerstwo Edukacji Narodowej, 587, pp. 4–8.

21. AAN, Ministerstwo Edukacji Narodowej, 592, pp. 21–6.

22. AAN, Ministerstwo Edukacji Narodowej, 588, p. 495.

23. AAN, Ministerstwo Edukacji Narodowej, 241, pp. 5–15.

24. Baske and Engelbert, *Dokumente zur Bildungspolitik*, p. 26.

25. AAN, Ministerstwo Edukacji Narodowej, 238, p. 22.

26. John Connelly, *Captive University: The Sovietization of East German, Czech and Polish Higher Education 1945–1956* (Chapel Hill and London, 2000), p. 97.

27. Ibid., p. 43.

28. Ibid., p. 71.

29. Ibid., p. 135.

30. Ibid., p. 84.

31. Ibid., p. 178.

32. *Partei und Jugend*, p. 345.

33. Andrzej Gawryszewski, *Ludność Polski w XX wieku* (Warsaw, 2005), pp. 328–9.

34. Interview with Eugeniusz Mroczowski, Warsaw, 25 May 2007.

35. Connelly, *Captive University*, p. 228.

36. Ibid., pp. 235 and 252.

37. Bartosz Cichocki and Krzyzstof Józwiak, *Najważniejsze są Kadry: Centralna Szkoła Partyjna PPR/PZPR* (Warsaw, 2006), pp. 68–80.

38. Connelly, *Captive University*, p. 239.

39. Ibid., pp. 246–7.

40. James Mark, 'Discrimination, Opportunity and Middle-Class Success in Early Communist Hungary', *The Historical Journal*, 48/2 (June 2005), p. 506.

41. Interview with Krzysztof Pomian, Warsaw, 2 May 2008.

42. Interview with Erich Loest, Leipzig, 12 December 2006.

43. Conversation with Piotr Paszkowski, Warsaw, 10 May 2012.

44. Błażej Brzostek, *Robotnicy Warszawy* (Warsaw, 2002), pp. 45–7.

45. AAN, Ministerstwo Edukacji Narodowej, 581.

46. Brodala, 'Propaganda dla Najmłodszych w latach', pp. 40–44.

47. MOL, 276/65/156, pp. 63–86.

48. SAPMO-BA, DY 30/J IV 2/2 A 415.

49. Brodala, 'Propaganda dla Najmłodszych w latach', p. 48.

50. 'Frohe Ferientage für alle Kinder', Beschluss des Politbüros vom 30.3.1951, Anlagenummer fünf; SAPMO-BA, DY 30/IV 2/905/130, Bl. 8ff.

51. SAPMO-BA, DY 25/482.

52. PIL, 286/23, pp. 118–30.

53. PIL, 286/18, pp. 214–15.

54. Interview with Pomian.

55. 1956 Institute, File 22.

56. Więsław Kot, 'Wyścigowiec ofiarny', *Wprost*, 43/2007, pp. 86–92; see also Padraic Kenney, *Rebuilding Poland: Workers and Communists 1945–1950* (Ithaca, 1997), p. 247.

57. Sándor Horváth, 'Élmunkások és sztahanovisták', *História* (1998/08).

58. John Rodden, *Repainting the Little Red Schoolhouse: A History of Eastern German Education, 1945–1995* (New York, 2002), p. 58.

59. Ibid., p. 59.

60. MOL, 276/65/156, p. 35.

61. Izabella Main, 'President of Poland or Stalin's Most Faithful Pupil: The Cult of Bolesław Bierut in Stalinist Poland', in Bálasz Apor et al., eds., *The Leader Cult in Communist Dictatorships* (New York, 2004), p. 188.

62. Paul Gregory, *The Political Economy of Stalinism: Evidence from the Soviet Secret Archives* (Cambridge, 2004), pp. 103–9.

63. MOL, 276/65/156, pp. 1–6.

64. DRA, F201-00-00/0002, p. 41.

65. David Priestland, *Stalinism and the Politics of Mobilization: Ideas, Power, and Terror in Inter-War Russia* (New York, 2007), p. 314.

66. Quoted in Mark Pittaway, 'The Reproduction of Hierarchy: Skill, Working-Class Culture, and the State in Early Socialist Hungary', *The Journal of Modern History*, Vol. 74, No. 4 (December 2002), p. 742.

67. Dagmar Semmelmann, '*Man war total entwurzelt und musste erst wieder Wurzeln schlagen*': *Zur Integration von Flüchtlingen und Vertriebenen in der SBZ/DDR aus lebensgeschichtlicher Sicht – dargestellt am Sonderfall Eisenhüttenstadt* (oral history, published on CD, 2005).

68. Pittaway, 'Reproduction of Hierarchy', p. 741.

69. MOL, 276/65/186, pp. 10–135.

70. PIL, 286/18, p. 217.

71. The Hungarian Museum of Ethnography commemorated this exhibition in March 2012, on the sixtieth anniversary: see http://www.neprajz.hu/kiallitasok.php?menu=3&kiallitas_id=121.

72. Main, 'President of Poland or Stalin's Most Faithful Pupil', pp. 179–93.

73. SAPMO-BA, DY 30/J IV 2/2, p. 22.

74. Christian Ostermann, ed., *Uprising in East Germany: The Cold War, the German Question and the First Major Upheaval behind the Iron Curtain* (Budapest and New York, 2001), p. 20.

75. SAPMO-BA, DY 30/IV 2/1/61, pp. 136–57.

76. See, for example, SAPMO-BA, DY 30/IV 2/9.06/173; also DRA, F201-00-00/0003, pp. 129–33.

77. BStU MfSZ, Sekretariat d. Ministers (Min.) 387, pp. 502–5.

78. DRA, B012765756; also Harry Pross, 'On Mann's Political Career', *Journal of Contemporary History*, 2/2 (April 1967), p. 80.

79. Alan Nothnagle, *Building the East Germany Myth* (Ann Arbor, 1999), pp. 63–7.

80. AAN, Ministerstwo Kultury, 274.

81. AAN, Ministerstwo Kultury, 274, 724, 747.

82. AAN, Ministerstwo Kultury, 478.

83. SAPMO-BA, DY 24/2.120, p. 55.

84. SAPMO-BA, DY 24/2.414.

85. SAPMO-BA, DY 25/248.

86. PIL, 286/19, p. 207.

87. Artur Pasko, *Wyścig Pokoju w dokumentach władz partyjnych i państwowych 1948–1989* (Kraków, 2009), pp. 21–30.

88. Magdolna Baráth, ed., *Szovjet nagyköveti iratok Magyarországról 1953–1956* (Budapest, 2002), p. 175.

89. J. C. C., 'The Berlin Youth Festival and Its Role in the Peace Campaign', *The World Today*, 7/7 (July 1951), pp. 306–15.
90. Giles Scott-Smith and Hans Krabbendam, eds., *The Cultural Cold War in Western Europe, 1945–1960* (London, 2003), pp. 172–3.
91. BStU MfSZ, BdL 003465.
92. BStU MfSZ, BdL 000012.
93. BStU MfSZ, BdL 000015.
94. BStU MfSZ, BdL 000012.
95. BStU MfSZ, BdL 15194.
96. J. C. C., 'The Berlin Youth Festival and Its Role in the Peace Campaign', p. 311.
97. Available at http://www.youtube.com/watch?v=0IGa6YcTU8s.
98. Interview with Lothar Grimm, Eistenhüttenstadt, 27 April 2007.
99. Jacek Trznadel, *Hańba Domowa* (Paris, 1986), pp. 22–3.
100. Interview with Hans Modrow, Berlin, 7 December 2006.
101. Interview with Józef Tejchma, Warsaw, 14 June 2007.
102. Quote in Hans Modrow, *Ich wollte ein neues Deutschland* (Munich, 1999), p. 59.

14. SOCIALIST REALISM

1. V. I. Lenin, 'Party Organization and Party Literature', *Novaya Zhizn*, No. 12, 13 November 1905.
2. Andrzej Panufnik, *Composing Myself* (London, 1987), p. 189.
3. It is now the German Finance Ministry.
4. Wolfgang Schivelbusch, *In a Cold Crater: Cultural and Intellectual Life in Berlin, 1945–1948* (Berkeley, 1998), pp. 39–50.
5. Elfriede Brüning, *Und außerdem war es mein Leben* (Berlin, 2004), p. 331.
6. SAPMO-BA, DY 271/213.
7. David Pike, *The Politics of Culture in Soviet-Occupied Germany, 1945–1949* (Stanford, 1992), p. 138.
8. SAPMO-BA, DY 27/2751.
9. SAPMO-BA, DY 27/341; also Schivelbusch, *In a Cold Crater*, p. 80.
10. Quoted in the materials accompanying an exhibition of the work of Herbert Sandberg, 'Mit spitzer Feder', Berlin, Akademie der Künste, May 2008.
11. Schivelbusch, *In a Cold Crater*, p. 82.
12. SAPMO-BA, DY 27/1512
13. Ronald Hayman, *Brecht: A Biography* (New York, 1983), pp. 325–6.

14. Anne Hartmann and Wolfram Eggelin, *Sowjetische Präsenz im kulturellen Leben der SBZ und frühen DDR 1945–1953* (Berlin, 1998), pp. 155–6.
15. György Faludy, *My Happy Days in Hell*, trans. Kathleen Szasz (London, 2010), p. 228.
16. AdK-ABK, *Max Lingner, 1888–1959*, exhibition catalogue published in Berlin, 1988.
17. Günter Feist, Eckhart Gillen and Beatrice Vierneisel, eds., *Kunstdokumentation: 1945–1990, SBZ/DDR* (Berlin, 1996), pp. 104–6.
18. T. V. Volokitina et al., eds., *Vostochnaya Evropa v dokumentakh rossiskikh arkhivov 1944–1953* (Novosibirsk, 1997), Vol. 2, pp. 36–41.
19. Ibid., pp. 41–3.
20. Peter Pachnicke pointed out to me that the 'formalism' debate of the 1940s was a repeat of the 'expressionist' debate which took place in the 1930s. Conversation with Peter Pachnicke, Berlin, 20 April 2008.
21. Laurie S. Koloski, 'Painting Krakow Red: Politics and Culture in Poland, 1945–1950', Ph.D. dissertation, Stanford University, 1998.
22. See Wojciech Włodarcyzk, *Socrealizm: sztuka polska w latach 1950–1954* (Warsaw, 1986), p. 112.
23. Conversation with Petra Uhlmann and Michael Krejsa, Akademie der Künste, Berlin, 5 December 2008.
24. Joy Calico, 'The Trial, the Condemnation, the Cover-Up: Behind the Scenes of Brecht/Dessau's Lucullus Opera(s)', *Cambridge Opera Journal*, 14/3, pp. 313–42. See also Hayman, *Brecht*, pp. 354–5.
25. Günter Feist, 'Das Wandbild im Bahnhof Friedrichstrasse', in Eckhart Gillen and Diether Schmidt, eds., *Zone 5: Kunst in der Viersektorenstadt, 1945–51*, exhibition catalogue (Berlin, 1989), pp. 92–124.
26. Conversation with Uhlmann and Krejsa.
27. Protokoły z posiedzeń Rady Wydziału Malarstwa w ASP w Warszawie, 01. 02. 1950–17. 02. 1954, in the collection of Andrzej Bielawski
28. AAN, Ministerstwo Kultury, 321, 322, 326.
29. Koloski, 'Painting Krakow Red', pp. 200–309.
30. AdK ABK, Otto Nagel collection, III and Arnold Zweig collection, V, folder 5.
31. AdK ABK, Max Lingner collection, IV.A.59.
32. Gerhard Strauß, *Vom Auftrag zum Wandbild* (Berlin, 1953), p. 12.
33. Ibid., pp. 16–20.
34. Ibid., pp. 21–5.
35. AdK ABK, Max Lingner collection, VI.A.124.
36. Günter Feist (with Eckhart Gillen), *Stationen eines Weges: Daten und Zitate zur Kunst und Kunstpolitik der DDR 1945–1998* (Berlin, 1988), p. 24.
37. AdK ABK, Max Lingner collection, exhibition catalogue.

38. Wanda Telakowska, *Twórczość Ludowa w Nowym Wzornictwie* (Warsaw, 1954), p. 5.

39. David Crowley, 'Building the World Anew: Design in Stalinist and Post-Stalinist Poland', *Journal of Design History*, Vol. 7, No. 3 (1994).

40. Lou Taylor, 'The Search for a Polish National Identity, 1945–68', unpublished manuscript in the collection of the Polish National Museum.

41. AAN, Ministerstwo Kultury, 321.

42. Krystyna Czerniewska and Tadeusz Reindl, eds., 'Sztuka dla Życia: Wspomnienia o Wandzie Telakowskiej', in *Biblioteka Wzornictwa*, 10/88, pp. 11–12.

43. Conversations with Anna Frąckiewicz, Curator of Decorative Arts, Polish National Museum, 26 November 2007; Krystyna Czerniewska, 'To Oni Tworzyły Wzornictwa', unpublished manuscript in the collection of the Polish National Museum.

44. These designs form the basis of the Polish National Museum's enormous modern design collection, much of which is in semi-permanent storage.

45. Aleksander Wojciechowski, *O Sztuce Użytkowej i Użytecznej* (Warsaw, 1955), p. 65.

46. Quoted in Piotr Majewski, 'Jak zbudować "Zamek socjalistyczny"', *Zbudować Warsawę Pieknę: O Nowy Krajobraz Stolicy 1944–1956* (Warsaw, 2003), p. 33.

47. Interview with Professor Alexander Jackowski, Warsaw, 15 May 2007.

48. Bolesław Szmidt, ed., *The Polish School of Architecture, 1942–1945* (Liverpool, 1945), pp. 85–95 and 186–8.

49. Majewski, 'Jak zbudować "Zamek socjalistyczny"', p. 36.

50. Bolesław Bierut, *Sześcoletni Plan Odbudowy Warszawy: Refereat Na Konferencji Warszawskiej PZPR w dniu 3 lipca, 1949 g* (Warsaw, 1949), pp. 20–21.

51. Krzysztof Mordinski, 'Marzenia o idealnym mieście – Warszaw socrealistyczna', *Spotkania z Zabytkami*, No. 9, 226, pp. 3–8.

52. The designs were published for public consumption in a heavy, luxurious album: *Sześcioletni Plan Odbudowy Warszawy* (Warsaw, 1950).

53. Anders Åman, *Architecture and Ideology in Eastern Europe during the Stalin Era* (Cambridge, Mass., 1992), p. 49.

54. Waldemar Baraniewski, 'Między opresją a obojętnością. Architektura w polsko-rosyjskich relacjach w XX wieku', http://www.culture.pl/pl/culture/artykuly.

55. Edmund Goldzamt, *William Morris A Geneza Społeczna Architektury Nowoczesnej* (Warsaw, 1967).

56. Teresa Torańska, *Oni: Stalin's Polish Puppets*, trans. Agnieszka Kołakowska (London, 1988), pp. 306–7.

57. Konrad Rokicki, 'Kłopotliwe Dar: Pałac Kultury I Nauki', *Zbudować Warsawę Pieknę: O Nowy Krajobraz Stolicy (1944–1956)* (Warsaw, 2003), pp. 107–15.

58. Bierut, *Sześcoletni Plan*, pp. 20–21.

59. David Crowley, *Warsaw* (London, 2003), p. 54.

60. Conversation with Frąckiewicz.

61. Quoted in Wojciechowski, *O Sztuce Użytkowej i Użytecznej*, p. 71.

62. Ibid., p. 71.

63. Interview with Jackowski.

64. See, for example, http://www.youtube.com/watch?v=KI3jZtruxvA.

65. Mira Liehm and Antonin J. Liehm, *The Most Important Art: East European Film after 1945* (Berkeley, 1977).

66. SNL, Historic Interview Collection, interview with István Szőts, by Sándor Csoóri and Gábor Hanák, 8 December 1988.

67. Gábor Szilágyi, *Tűzkeresztség, A magyar játékfilm története 1945–1953* (Budapest, 1992), p. 219.

68. Vsevelod Pudovkin and Andras Kovács, eds., *Pudovkin a magyar filmről* (Budapest, 1952), pp. 46, 61, 62.

69. SNL interview with Szőts.

70. MNFA, Ke 34/10a.

71. MNFA, Ke 34/7.

72. Szilágyi, *Tűzkeresztség*, pp. 233–6.

73. Ibid., p. 234.

74. Interview with Andrzej Wajda, Warsaw, 14 May 2009.

75. Jan Ciechowicz and Zbigniew Majchrowski, *Od Shakespeare'a Do Szekspira* (Warsaw, 1993), pp. 24–5.

76. *Generation* (1955) was already a post-Stalinist movie, as was *Ashes and Diamonds* (1958). *Mephisto* appeared much later, in 1981, by which time obvious allusions to Stalinist terror did not prevent a film from being made or shown.

77. Wisława Szymborska, 'Ten Dzień', *Życie Literackie*, No. 11/61, 15 March 1953.

78. Interview with Ágnes Heller, Budapest, 2 June 2009.

15. IDEAL CITIES

1. Urszula Ciszek-Frankiewicz, *O Nowej to Hucie: Ballady i Wiersze* (Kraków, 1994).

2. Sándor Horváth, 'Alltag in Sztálinváros', in Christiane Brenner and Peter

Heumos, eds. *Sozialgeschichtliche Kommunismusforschung Tschecho-slowakei, Polen, Ungarn und DDR 1948–1968* (Munich, 2005), p. 512.

3. This section is based on interviews with Júlia Horváth and Elek Horváth, Budapest, 30 June 2009, and Zsófia Tevan, Budapest, 4 June 2009.

4. István Horváth, ed., *Dunaferr: Dunai Vasmu Kronika* (Dunaújváros, 2000), pp. 31–3.

5. Andreas Ludwig, *Eisenhüttendstadt: Wandel einer industriellen Gründ-ungsstadt in fünfzig Jahren* (Potsdam, 2000), pp. 53–4.

6. Interview with Stanisław Juchnowicz, Kraków, 19 June 2007; *Idealnego*, catalogue of the Muzeum Historycznego Miasta Krakowa (Kraków, 2006), p. 26.

7. Tadeusz Golaszewski, *Kronika Nowej Huty* (Kraków, 1955), pp. 34–5; also *Nowa Huta: Architektura I tworcy miasta*, exhibition of the Muz-eum Historycznego Miasta Krakowa, Nowohucki Odział.

8. Interview with Juchnowicz.

9. Herbert Nicolaus and Lutz Schmidt, *Einblicke: 50 Jahre EKO Stahl* (Eisenhüttenstadt, 2000), p. 47.

10. Jenny Richter, Heike Förster and Ulrich Lakemann, *Stalinstadt – Eisen-hüttenstadt: Von der Utopie zur Gegenwart* (Marburg, 1997), pp. 18–22.

11. Interview with Dr Herbert Nicolaus, EKO archivist, Eisenhüttenstadt, 5 March 2007; also Ludwig, *Eisenhüttendstadt*, pp. 28–30; also inter-views with Andreas Ludwig, Berlin, 6 December 2006 and Axel Drieschner, Berlin, 5 March 2007.

12. Golaszewski, *Kronika Nowej Huty*, pp. 29–31.

13. Conversation with Leszek Sibila, Nowa Huta branch of the Historical Museum of the City of Kraków, 19 June 2007, Nowa Huta.

14. Richter et al., *Stalinstadt – Eisenhüttenstadt*, p. 14; also interview with Juchnowicz.

15. Simone Haine, ed., *Reise nach Moskau* (Berlin, 1995), pp. 45–53.

16. Ludwig, *Eisenhüttendstadt*, pp. 44–50.

17. Interview with Juchnowicz.

18. Conversation with Márta Matussné Lendvai, Director of the Intercisa Múzeum, Dunaújváros, 19 May 2009; Sándor Horváth, *A kapu es a hatar: mindenapi Sztálinváros* (Budapest, 2004), pp. 14–16.

19. Dagmar Semmelmann, '*Man war total entwurzelt und musste erst wieder Wurzeln schlagen*': *Zur Integration von Flüchtlingen und Vertrie-benen in der SBZ/DDR aus lebensgeschichtlicher Sicht – dargestellt am Sonderfall Eisenhüttenstadt* (oral history, published on CD, 2005), p. 82.

20. OSA, 206/1/1:3.

21. Sándor Horváth, *A kapu es a hatar*, pp. 35–6.

22. Richter et al., *Stalinstadt – Eisenhüttenstadt*, pp. 32–3.
23. Kurt W. Leucht, *Die erste neue Stadt in der DDR* (Berlin, 1957), pp. 79–83.
24. OSA, 206/1/1:3.
25. Richter et al., *Stalinstadt – Eisenhüttenstadt*, pp. 33–5.
26. Interview with Kollár.
27. Richter et al., *Stalinstadt – Eisenhüttenstadt*, p. 33.
28. Interview with Tevan.
29. Ambrus Borovszky memoirs, Dunaferr company archives.
30. Interview with Juchnowicz.
31. Sándor Horvath, *A kapu es a hatar*, pp. 158–72.
32. Interview with Karl Gass, Kleinmachnow (Berlin), 7 May 2008.
33. Nicolaus and Schmidt, *Einblicke*, pp. 54–5.
34. Tadeusz Konwicki, *Przy Budowie* (Warsaw, 1950).
35. AdK ABK, Oskar Nerlinger Collection, folder 141; also, conversation with Petra Uhlmann and Michael Krejsa, Berlin, 5 December 2008.
36. SAPMO-BA, DY 30/IV 2/9.06/175.
37. AdK ABK, Oskar Nerlinger Collection, folder 79.
38. AdK ABK, Oskar Nerlinger Collection, folders 79, 141.
39. AdK ABK, Oskar Nerlinger Collection, folder 79.
40. Günter Feist (with Eckhart Gillen), *Stationen eines Weges: Daten und Zitate zur Kunst und Kunstpolitik der DDR 1945–1998* (Berlin, 1988), p. 29.
41. AdK ABK, Oskar Nerlinger Collection, folder 103.
42. Sándor Horváth, *A kapu es a hatar*, p. 32.
43. Sándor Horváth, 'Alltag in Sztálinváros', pp. 517–18.
44. Polish census data, numbers rounded.
45. Mark Pittaway, 'Creating and Domesticating Hungary's Socialist Industrial Landscape: From Dunapentele to Sztálinváros, 1950–1958', *Historical Archaeology*, Vol. 39, No. 3, Landscapes of Industrial Labor (2005), p. 84.
46. Interview with József Tejchma, Warsaw, 14 June 2007; also József Tejchma, *Pożegnanie z władzą* (Warsaw, 1997), and József Tejchma, *Z notatnika aktywisty ZMP* (Warsaw, 1954).
47. Ryszard Kapuściński, 'To tez jest prawda o Nowej Hucie', *Sztandar Młodych*, No. 234, 30 September 1955.
48. Sándor Horváth, *A kapu es a hatar*, pp. 40–52.
49. Ibid., pp. 22–4.
50. Nicolaus and Schmidt, *Einblicke*, pp. 56–8.
51. Richter et al., *Stalinstadt – Eisenhüttenstadt*, p. 31.

52. Interview with Tevan.
53. Richter et al., *Stalinstadt – Eisenhüttenstadt*, p. 14.
54. Ferenc Erdős and Zsuzsanna Pongrácz, *Dunaújváros története* (Dunaújváros, 2000), pp. 255–6.
55. Márta Matussné Lendvai, '... a nagy Sztálinról nevezhessük el', *Árgus*, 1995/1, pp. 70–74.
56. Nicolaus and Schmidt, *Einblicke*, pp. 65–71.
57. Leucht, *Die erste neue Stadt in der DDR*, p. 86.
58. Interview with Tevan.
59. Reprinted in the Dutch architectural magazine *Volume*, http://volumeproject.org/volume/2009/00/00/Industrialised+Building+Speech%2C+1954/7783.
60. Ludwig, *Eisenhüttendstadt*, p. 52.
61. Ibid., p. 52.
62. Text at http://hamlet.pro.e-mouse.pl/teksty/?id=p01939&idu=006; translation is my own.

16. RELUCTANT COLLABORATORS

1. Interview with Herta Kuhrig, Berlin, 2006.
2. http://www.youtube.com/watch?v=JVq8_gRXlpg
3. Volker Müller, 'Es ist so viel Blut umsonst geflossen', *Berliner Zeitung*, 26 January 2001, p. 11.
4. Interview with Jerzy Morawski, Warsaw, 7 June 2007.
5. Interview with Colonel Ludwik Rokicki, Warsaw, 25 May 2006.
6. Interview with Jacek Fedorowicz, Warsaw, 25 March 2009.
7. Anna Bikont and Joanna Szczesna, *Lawina i Kamienia: Pisarze wobec Komunizmu* (Warsaw, 2006), pp. 103–12.
8. http://fotoforum.gazeta.pl/72,2,746,68832222,74666403.html. The Picasso Warsaw 'mermaid' now appears on T-shirts and coffee mugs.
9. György Majtényi, 'Örök a vártán. Uralmi elit Magyarországon az 1950-es, 1960-as években', in Sándor Horváth, ed., *Mindennapok Rákosi és Kádár korában* (Budapest, 2008), p. 289.
10. Joel Agee, *Twelve Years: An American Boyhood in East Germany* (Chicago, 2000), p. 125.
11. OSA, 300/50/6, folders 35, 42, 43.
12. BStU MfSZ, 5960/60, p. 130.
13. Jacek Kuroń, *Kuroń: Autobiografia* (Warsaw, 2009) (see http://www.krytykapolityczna.pl/Autobiografia/Awans-spoleczny-i-odbudowa/menu-id-232.html).

14. Interview with Wolfgang Lehmann, Berlin, 20 September 2006.
15. Interview with Michał Bauer, Warsaw, 18 June 2007.
16. Andrzej Panufnik, *Composing Myself* (London, 1987), p. 183.
17. David Pike, *The Politics of Culture in Soviet-Occupied Germany, 1945–1949* (Stanford, 1992), p. 365.
18. Jacek Trznadel, *Hańba Domowa* (Paris, 1986).
19. Panufnik, *Composing Myself*, p. 191.
20. A similar campaign was launched in France. See André Heynal, 'Die ungarische Psychoanalyse unter totalitären Regimen', in Ágnes Berger et al., *Psychoanalyse hinter dem Eisernen Vorhang* (Frankfurt, 2010), pp. 27–49.
21. Pál Hermat, *Freud, Ferenczi és a magyarországi pszichoanalízis* (Budapest, 1994), pp. 393–440.
22. Ferenc Erős, 'Psychoanalysis and Cultural Memory', paper presented at the symposium 'Psychoanlaysis behind the Iron Curtain', Collegium Hungaricum, Berlin, 15–16 November 2008.
23. Hermat, *Freud*, pp. 393–440.
24. Interview with Professor Doctor György Hidas, Budapest, 12 March 2009.
25. Heynal, 'Die ungarische Psychoanalyse'.
26. Conversation with Judit Mészáros, Budapest, 20 April 2009.
27. Interview with Antoni Rajkiewicz, Warsaw, 3 June 2007.
28. From a conversation with Piotr Paszkowski, Warsaw, 22 May 2012.
29. Interview with Fedorowicz.
30. Interview with Karol Modzelewski, Warsaw, 28 April 2009.
31. Interview with Krzysztof Pomian, Warsaw, 2 May 2008.
32. Interview with Morawski.
33. John Connelly, *Captive University: The Sovietization of East German, Czech and Polish Higher Education 1945–1956* (Chapel Hill and London, 2000), pp. 216–17.
34. Interview with Iván Vitányi, Budapest, January 2009.
35. Interview with Elfriede Brüning, Berlin, 28 November and 5 December 2006.
36. Elfriede Brüning, *Und außerdem war es mein Leben* (Berlin, 2004), pp. 342–5.
37. Ibid., p. 398.
38. Elfriede Brüning, *Lästige Zeugen: Tonbandgespräche mit Opfern der Stalinzeit* (Halle, 1990).
39. Leopold Tyrmand, 'Sprawa Piaseckiego', *Świat*, 18 November 1956.
40. Jan Engelgard, *Wielka Gra Bolesława Piaseckiego* (Warsaw, 2008), p. 7.
41. Andrzej Jaszczuk, *Ewolucja Ideowa Bolesława Piaseckiego* (Warsaw, 2005), pp. 27–8 and 56–7.

42. Engelgard, *Wielka Gra Bolesława Piaseckiego*, pp. 66–7.

43. Mikołaj Stanisław Kunicki, 'The Polish Crusader: The Life and Politics of Bolesław Piasecki, 1915–1979', Ph.D. thesis, Stanford University, June 2004, pp. 196–203.

44. Czesław Miłosz, *Zdobycie Władzy* (Olsztyn, 1990), pp. 138–9.

45. Engelgard, *Wielka Gra Bolesława Piaseckiego*, p. 85.

46. Ibid., p. 218.

47. Interview with Janusz Zabłocki, Warsaw, 19 June 2009.

48. Kunicki, 'The Polish Crusader', pp. 241–3.

49. This is certainly the belief of Piasecki's family. Conversation with Ładysław Piasecki, Warsaw, 17 February 2012.

50. Interview with Zabłocki.

51. Interview with Leopold Unger, Brussels, 21 March 2009.

52. Interview with Professor Alexander Jackowski, Warsaw, 15 May 2007.

53. SAPMO-BA, ZPA, NY 421/ 5/53, pp. 263–74

54. Klaus Polkehn, *Das war die Wochenpost: Geschichte und Geschichten einer Zeitung* (Berlin, 1997), p. 7.

55. Interview with Klaus Polkehn, Berlin, 20 October 2006.

17. PASSIVE OPPONENTS

1. György Faludy, *My Happy Days in Hell*, trans. Kathleen Szasz (London, 2010), p. 207.

2. Celina Budzyńska, *Krytyka i Samokrytyka* (Warsaw, 1954), p. 44.

3. *Daily Worker*, 20 November 1950, p. 2; see also Phillip Deery, 'The Dove Flies East: Whitehall, Warsaw and the 1950 World Peace Congress', *Australian Journal of Politics and History* (December 2002).

4. *Sheffield Telegraph*, 19 November 1950; also Deery, 'The Dove Flies East'.

5. AUL, Edeltraude Eckert file.

6. Joanna Kochanowicz, *ZMP w Terenie* (Warsaw, 2000), pp. 85–102.

7. John Rodden, *Repainting the Little Red Schoolhouse: A History of Eastern German Education, 1945–1995* (New York, 2002).

8. Maciej Chłopek, *Bikiniarze. Pierwsza polska subkultura* (Warsaw, 2005), pp. 69–75; Sándor Horváth, 'Hooligans, Spivs and Gangs: Youth Subcultures in the 1960s', in János M. Rainer and György Péteri, eds., *Muddling Through in the Long 1960s: Ideas and Everyday Life in High Politics and the Lower Classes of Communist Hungary*, Trondheim Studies on East European Cultures and Socieites, No. 16, May 2005, pp. 199–223.

9. Chłopek, *Bikiniarze*, p. 101; also Kathy Peiss, *Zoot Suit: The Enigmatic Career of an Extreme Style* (Philadelphia, 2011), p. 179.

10. Leopold Tyrmand, *Dziennik 1954* (London 1980), pp. 138–40.

11. Horváth, 'Hooligans, Spivs and Gangs'.

12. Chłopek, *Bikiniarze*, p. 30.

13. Ibid., pp. 142–3.

14. Jacek Kuroń, *Wiara i wina. Do i od komunizmu* (Wrocław, 1995), p. 54.

15. See Sándor Horváth, 'Myths of the Great Tree Gang: Constructing Urban Spaces and Youth Culture in Socialist Budapest', in Joanna Herbert and Richard Rodger, eds., *Testimony of the City: Identity, Community and Change in a Contemporary Urban World* (Aldershot, 2007), pp. 73–93; also Horváth, 'Hooligans, Spivs and Gangs'.

16. Interview with Krzysztof Pomian, Warsaw, 2 May 2008.

17. Chłopek, *Bikiniarze*, pp. 130–35.

18. Kuroń, *Wiara i wina*, pp. 54–5.

19. Toby Thacker, 'The Fifth Column: Dance Music in the Early German Republic', in Patrick Major and Jonathan Osmond, eds., *The Workers' and Peasants' State* (Manchester, 2002), pp. 227–39.

20. Interview with Erich Loest, Leipzig, 12 December 2006.

21. AdK ABK, Arnold Zweig collection, V.

22. Thacker, 'The Fifth Column', pp. 227–39.

23. Interview with Marta Stebnicka, Kraków, 25 February 2009.

24. For a good, informal analysis of communist humour, see Ben Lewis, *Hammer and Tickle* (London, 2009). A short version is available in 'Hammer and Tickle', *Prospect*, No. 122, 20 May 2006.

25. Lewis, *Hammer and Tickle*, p. 11.

26. The jokes in this section come from various people and sources. I'd like to thank Piotr Paszkowski for compiling them.

27. PIL, 286/23, p. 122.

28. AAN, Ministerstwo Oświaty, 346, p. 16.

29. Milan Kundera, *The Joke* (London, 1992).

30. See Lewis, *Hammer and Tickle*, p. 132.

31. Jenő Randé and János Sebestyén, *Azok a rádiós évtizedek* (Budapest, 1995), pp. 146–8.

32. *Ulenspiegel: Literatur, Kunst, Satire*, Vols. II (1947) and III (1948). A conversation with the art historian Peter Pachnicke underlies this discussion of Herbert Sandberg.

33. SAPMO-BA, DY 30/IV 2.9.06/23.

34. Lewis, *Hammer and Tickle*, p. 11.

35. Interview with Józef Puciłowski, Kraków, 24 March 2009.

36. Interview with Hans-Jochen Tschiche, Satuelle, 18 November 2006.
37. Karta, file 'Różności, 1944–56', 7/IV.
38. Jan Ziółek and Agnieszka Przytuła, *Represje wobec uczestników wydarzeń w Katedrze Lubelskiej w 1949 roku* (Lublin, 1999); see also Agnieszka Przytuła, 'Skazani za wiarę w cud', unpublished manuscript, at http://tnn.pl/pamie.php.
39. Karta, file 'Różności, 1944–56', 7/IV.
40. Rudolf Ilona Sántháné, unpublished manuscript.
41. Interview with Halina Bortnowska, Warsaw, 5 February 2006.
42. Dariusz Stola, *Kraj bez Wyjścia? Migracje z Polski 1949–1989* (Warsaw, 2010), p. 27.
43. William E. Stacy, 'US Army Border Operations in Germany 1945–1983' (HQ US Army, Europe and 7th Army, 2002): http://www.history.army.mil/documents/BorderOps/content.htm.
44. Edith Sheffer, 'On Edge: Building the Border in East and West Germany', *Central European History* 40 (2007), pp. 307–33.
45. Stacy, 'US Army Border Operations in Germany'.
46. Corey Ross, 'Before the Wall: East Germans, Communist Authority and the Mass Exodus to the West', *The Historical Journal*, 45, 2 (2002), p. 459; also Frederick Taylor, *The Berlin Wall* (New York, 2006), p. 77.
47. Interview with Herta Kuhrig, Berlin, 21 November 2006.
48. Ross, 'Before the Wall', pp. 465–77.

18. REVOLUTIONS

1. Bertolt Brecht, *Poems 1913–1956*, eds. John Willett and Ralph Manheim (Methuen, 1976), p. 440.
2. In fact Stalin had died on 5 March, having probably had a stroke early in the morning of 1 March, but his death was not announced to the public until the following day.
3. Mark Allinson, *Politics and Popular Opinion in East Germany 1945–68* (Manchester, 2000), pp. 52–4.
4. See the photographs in the collection of the Open Society Archives, at http://www.osaarchivum.org/galeria/05031953/secto6/index.html.
5. *Life* magazine published all of their photographs, 23 March 1953, pp. 33–5.
6. Amy Knight, *Beria: Stalin's First Lieutenant* (Princeton, 1995), p. 182.
7. Mark Kramer, 'The Early Post-Stalin Succession Struggle and Upheavals in East-Central Europe: Internal–External Linkages in Soviet Policy Making', *Journal of Cold War Studies*, 1, 1 (Winter 1999), pp. 18–21.

8. Kramer, 'Early Post-Stalin Succession Struggle', p. 17; also Christian Ostermann, ed., *Uprising in East Germany: The Cold War, the German Question and the First Major Upheaval behind the Iron Curtain* (Budapest and New York, 2001), pp. 86–90 (many of these documents are also available at http://legacy.wilsoncenter.org).
9. Ostermann, ed., *Uprising in East Germany*, pp. 10–101.
10. Kramer, 'Early Post-Stalin Succession Struggles', p. 17.
11. Ibid., p. 23.
12. Csaba Békés, Malcolm Byrne and János Rainer, eds., *The 1956 Revolution: A History in Documents* (Budapest and New York, 2002), pp. 15–20.
13. Charles Gati, *Failed Illusions: Moscow, Washington, Budapest and the 1956 Hungarian Revolt* (Stanford and Washington, 2006), pp. 32–40.
14. Imre Nagy, *On Communism: In Defense of the New Course* (New York, 1957), p. 176.
15. Kramer, 'Early Post-Stalin Succession Struggles', p. 31.
16. Interview with Lutz Rackow, Berlin, 1 April 2008.
17. Interviews with Erich Loest, Leipzig, 12 December 2006, and Elfriede Brüning, Berlin, 28 November and 5 December 2006.
18. Interview with Egon Bahr, Berlin, 26 October 2006.
19. Rudolf Herrnstadt, *Das Herrnstadt-Dokument: das Politbüro der SED und die Geschichte des 17. Juni 1953* (Hamburg, 1990), p. 85; also Hubertus Knabe, *17 Juni 1953 – Ein deutscher Aufstand* (Berlin, 2004), p. 302.
20. Interview with Loest.
21. Ibid. Also Erich Loest, *Durch die Erde ein Riss: Ein Lebenslauf* (Hamburg, 1981), pp. 196–207; on why the Volkspolizei were absent, see Knabe, *17 Juni 1953*, p. 318.
22. Interview with Karl-Heinz Arnold, Berlin, 3 November 2006.
23. Interview with Hans-Walter Bendzko, Berlin, 2 April 2008.
24. Volker Koop explains the different sources and numbers in *Der 17. Juni 1953 – Legende und Wirklichkeit* (Berlin, 2003).
25. Ibid., p. 343.
26. Knabe, *17 Juni 1953*, p. 83. This is more than joined protests in East Germany in October 1989.
27. Interview with Bahr.
28. SAPMO-BA, DY 30/IV 2/1/121, pp. 35–9.
29. Ostermann, ed., *Uprising in East Germany*, p. 186.
30. Mary Fulbrook, *Anatomy of a Dictatorship: Inside the GDR, 1949–89* (Oxford, 1995), pp. 155–61.

31. Interview with Günter Schabowski, Berlin, 7 December 2006.
32. Ronald Hayman, *Brecht: A Biography* (New York, 1983), p. 367.
33. Interview with Klaus Polkehn, Berlin, 20 October 2006.
34. Interview with Rackow.
35. Kramer, 'Early Post-Stalin Succession Struggles', part 2, p. 5.
36. Ostermann, ed., *Uprising in East Germany*, pp. 186, 270; Koop, *Der 17. Juni 1953*, pp. 333–4. There is no Western evidence for this thesis either: the CIA was just as surprised by the riots as the Russians, and even thought the Russians might have provoked them (Ostermann, ed., *Uprising in East Germany*, pp. 210–12).
37. Kramer, 'Early Post-Stalin Succession Struggles'.
38. Gati, *Failed Illusions*, pp. 54–5
39. SAPMO-BA, DY 30/IV 2/1/120, pp. 2–13.
40. Ibid., pp. 25–8.
41. Ibid.
42. Paweł Machewicz, 'Polish Regime Countermeasures against Radio Free Europe', in A. Ross Johnson and R. Eugene Parta, eds., *Cold War Broadcasting: Impact on the Soviet Union and Eastern Europe* (New York, 2010), pp. 174–5.
43. Andrzej Friszke, *Polska: Losy państwa i narodu, 1939–1989* (Warsaw, 2003). See also Andrzej Paczkowski, *Trzy twarze Józefa Światły: przyczynek do historii komunizmu w Polsce* (Warsaw, 2009).
44. Gati, *Failed Illusions*, pp. 55 and 113–22.
45. Andrzej Krzywicki, *Poststalinowski Karnawał Radości* (Warsaw, 2009), pp. 185–90.
46. *Rzeczpospolita*, 4 December 2007.
47. Krzywicki, *Poststalinowski Karnawał Radości*, p. 231.
48. Jacek Kuroń, *Wiara i wina. Do i od komunizmu* (Wrocław, 1995), p. 56.
49. Interview with Jacek Fedorowicz, Warsaw, 25 March 2009.
50. Krzywicki, *Poststalinowski Karnawał Radości*, p. 231.
51. Interview with Krzysztof Pomian, Warsaw, 2 May 2008.
52. Krzywicki, *Poststalinowski Karnawał Radości*, p. 281.
53. K. Kozniewski, 'Sto Wierszy o Festiwalu', *Sztandar Mlodych*, 9 August 1955.
54. Interview with Fedorowicz.
55. William Griffiths, 'The Petőfi Circle: Forum for Ferment in the Hungarian Thaw', *The Hungarian Quarterly*, 2/1 (January 1962), pp. 15–31.
56. István Eörsi, 'The Petőfi Circle', in *Intellectuele kringen in de twintigst eeuw* (Utrecht, 1995), p. 110.

57. Tamás Aczél and Tibor Meráy, *The Revolt of the Mind* (London, 1960), pp. 274–82; also Békés et al., *The 1956 Revolution*, p. 10.

58. Ibid., pp. 345–6.

59. Aczél and Meráy, *Revolt of the Mind*, p. 45.

60. Ibid., pp. 96–113.

61. Iván Vitány, *Önarckép – elvi keretben* (Celldömölk, 2007), pp. 28–32.

62. András Hegedüs, 'The Petőfi Circle: The Forum of Reform in 1956', *Journal of Communist Studies and Transition Politics*, 113/2, pp. 108–22.

63. Békés et al., *The 1956 Revolution*, p. 10.

64. Aczél and Meráy, *Revolt of the Mind*, pp. 267–8.

65. Eörsi, 'The Petőfi Circle', p. 108.

66. Interview with Karol Modzelewski, Warsaw, 28 April 2009.

67. Ibid.

68. Eörsi, 'The Petőfi Circle', p. 110.

69. Mark Pittaway, 'The Reproduction of Hierarchy: Skill, Working-Class Culture, and the State in Early Socialist Hungary', *The Journal of Modern History*, Vol. 74, No. 4 (December 2002), p. 728.

70. Griffiths, 'The Petőfi Circle', p. 22.

71. The speech is available at http://www.marxists.org/archive/khrushchev/1956/02/24.htm.

72. William Taubman, *Khrushchev: The Man and His Era* (New York, 2003), p. 284.

73. Interview with Colonel Ludwik Rokicki, Warsaw, 25 May 2006.

74. Griffiths, 'The Petőfi Circle', p. 17.

75. Victor Sebestyen, *Twelve Days: Revolution 1956* (London, 2006), pp. 86–7.

76. Much later, Rákosi's ashes were brought back to Hungary and reburied in a Budapest cemetery. But after his tombstone became a favourite target for vandals, they were moved to a grave marked only with his initials. See http://www.mult-kor.hu/cikk.php?id=8036&pIdx=4.

77. Gati, *Failed Illusions*, pp. 137–8.

78. Recent accounts which make good use of archives include Gati, *Failed Illusions*, and Sebestyen, *Twelve Days* (both cited above), as well as Mark Kramer's groundbreaking essay 'The Soviet Union and the 1956 Crises in Hungary and Poland: Reassessments and New Findings', *Journal of Contemporary History*, 33/2 (April 1998), pp. 163–214. The Central European University Press in collaboration with the 1956 Institute has published an excellent document collection, *The 1956 Hungarian Revolution*, edited by Csaba Békés, Malcolm Byrne and János Rainer. Older eyewitness accounts published in English include George Urban, *Nineteen Days: A Broadcaster's Account of the Hungarian Revolution*

(London, 1957); Sándor Kopácsi, *In the Name of the Working Class* (New York, 1987); Endre Márton, *The Forbidden Sky* (New York, 1971); and Tibor Meráy, *Thirteen Days That Shook the Kremlin* (London, 1959).

79. Aczél and Meráy, *Revolt of the Mind*, pp. 437–8.
80. Sebestyen, *Twelve Days*, p. 97.
81. Meráy, *Thirteen Days That Shook the Kremlin*, p. 439.
82. Kramer, 'The Soviet Union and the 1956 Crises', pp. 163–214.
83. Békés et al., *The 1956 Revolution*, p. 223; Kramer, 'The Soviet Union and the 1956 Crises', pp. 169–71.
84. Kramer, 'The Soviet Union and the 1956 Crises', p. 172.
85. Urban, *Nineteen Days*, pp. 12–13.
86. Békés et al., *The 1956 Revolution*, pp. 188–9.
87. Sebestyen, *Twelve Days*, pp. 110–19.
88. Ibid., p. 192.
89. Gati, *Failed Illusions*, pp. 165–7.
90. Sebestyen, *Twelve Days*, p. 208.
91. See Bill Lomax, ed., *Hungarian Workers' Councils in 1956* (New York, 1990).
92. Békés et al., *The 1956 Revolution*, p. 375.
93. Sebestyen, *Twelve Days*, p. 281.
94. Ibid., pp. 299–300.
95. Békés et al., *The 1956 Revolution*, p. 70.

EPILOGUE

1. Henryk Domański, 'The Middle Class in Transition from Communist to Capitalist Society', in Edmund Mokrzycki and Sven Eliæson, eds., *Building Democracy and Civil Society East of the Elbe* (New York, 2006), p. 95.
2. Conversation with Roger Scruton, 6 June 2012; also see Barbara Day, *The Velvet Philosophers* (London, 1999).
3. Vaclav Havel et al., *The Power of the Powerless: Citizens Against the State in Central-Eastern Europe* (London, 1985), p. 39.
4. This saying has long been in use in France, where it is sometimes attributed incorrectly to Robespierre or Napoleon. The Russian equivalent, which Stalin did apparently use, is 'When wood is chopped, woodchips will fly' (*Les rubyat – schepki letyat*). Richard Pipes has observed that this phrase, often used by apologists for communism, is nonsensical: 'Apart from the fact that human beings are not eggs, the trouble is that no omelette has emerged from the slaughter.'

5. See Kanan Makiya, *Republic of Fear* (Berkeley, 1998); John K. Cooley, 'The Libyan Menace', *Foreign Policy*, No. 42 (Spring 1981); Gareth Winrow, *The Foreign Policy of the GDR in Africa* (Cambridge, 1990), p. 140. East Germany also helped create the secret police forces of a number of African communist regimes, including those of Ethiopia, Angola and Mozambique.
6. http://www.lkplodz.pl/
7. See, for example, this analysis of the alterations back and forth to Russian non-governmental organization law: http://www.icnl.org/research/monitor/russia.html.

Select bibliography

A partial list of memoirs, fiction, monographs and other secondary literature used in the writing of *Iron Curtain* follows. Articles, papers and other materials are listed in the reference notes along with specific archival references

Abrams, Bradley, *The Struggle for the Soul of the Nation: Czech Culture and the Rise of Communism* (New York, 2004)

Acheson, Dean, *Present at the Creation* (New York, 1987)

Aczel, Tamás and Tibor Meráy, *The Revolt of the Mind: A Case History of Intellectual Resistance behind the Iron Curtain* (London, 1960)

Agee, Joel, *Twelve Years: An American Boyhood in East Germany* (Chicago, 2000)

Allinson, Mark, *Politics and Popular Opinion in East Germany, 1945–68* (Manchester, 2000)

Åman, Anders, *Architecture and Ideology in Eastern Europe during the Stalin Era*, trans. Roger and Kerstin Tanner (Cambridge, Mass., 1992)

Andreas-Friedrich, Ruth, *Battleground Berlin: Diaries 1945–48*, trans. Anna Boerresen (New York, 1990)

Anonymous, *A Woman in Berlin*, trans. Philip Boehm (London, 2006)

Ansorg, Leonore, *Kinder im Klassenkampf: Die Geschichte der Pionierorganisation von 1948 bis Ende der fünfziger Jahre* (Berlin, 1997)

Apor, Balázs, et al., eds., *The Leader Cult in Communist Dictatorships* (New York, 2004)

Arendt, Hannah, *The Origins of Totalitarianism* (Cleveland and New York, 1958)

Arp, Agnès, *VEB Vaters ehemaliger Betrieb Privatunternehmer in der DDR* (Leipzig, 2005)

Åslund, Anders, *Private Enterprise in Eastern Europe* (Macmillan, 1985)

Baczoni, Gábor, *Pár(t)viadal – A Magyar Államrendőrség Vidéki Főkapitányságának Politikai Rendészeti osztálya, 1945–1946* (Budapest, 2002)

Baer, Helmut David, *The Struggle of Hungarian Lutherans under Communism* (College Station, Texas, 2006)

Bajer, Magdalena, *Blizny po Ukąszeniu* (Warszaw, 2005)

Balogh, Gyöngyi, Vera Gyürey and Pál Honffy, *A magyar játékfilm története a kezdetektől 1990-ig* (Budapest, 2004)

Balogh, Margit, *A KALOT es a katolikus tarsadalompolitika 1935–1946* (Budapest, 1998)

—, *Mindszenty József (1892–1975)* (Budapest, 2002)

Balogh, Margit and Csaba Szabó, *A Grősz per* (Budapest, 2002)

Bank, Barbara and Sándor Őze, *A 'német ügy' 1945–1953. A Volksbundtól Tiszalökig* (Budapest and Munich, 2005)

Barany, Zoltan D., *Soldiers and Politics in Eastern Europe, 1945–1990* (New York, 1993)

Baring, Arnulf, *Uprising in East Germany: June 17, 1953* (London, 1972)

Beevor, Antony, *Berlin: The Downfall, 1945* (London, 2002)

Beevor, Antony and Luba Vinogradova, eds., *A Writer at War: Vasily Grossman with the Red Army, 1941–1945* (London, 2005)

Beke, László, *A Student's Diary: Budapest, October 1–November 1, 1956*, trans. Leon Kossar and Ralph M. Zoltan (New York, 1957)

Belényi, Gyula, *Az állam szorításában. Az ipari munkásság társadalmi átalakulása 1945–1965* (Budapest, 2009)

Berend, Ivan T., *Central and Eastern Europe 1944–1993* (Cambridge, 1996)

Berend, Iván T., and Tamás Csató, *Evolution of the Hungarian Economy, 1848–1948* (Boulder, 2001)

Berényi, Zsuzsanna Ágnes, *A szabadkőművesség kézikönyve* (Budapest, 2001)

Beres, Witold and Jerzy Skoczyłas, *General Kiszczak Mowi ... Prawie Wszytko* (Warsaw, 1991)

Biddiscombe, Alexander P., *Werwolf: The History of the National Socialist Guerrilla Movement, 1944–46* (Toronto, 1998)

Biedrzycka, Anna (ed.), *Nowa Huta – architektura i twórcy miasta idealnego*, exhibition catalogue (Kraków, 2006)

Bierut, Bolesław, *Sześcoletni Plan Odbudowy Warszawy* (Warsaw, 1950)

—, *Sześcoletni Plan Odbudowy Warszawy: Refereat Na Konferencji Warszawskiej PZPR w dniu 3 lipca, 1949 g* (Warsaw, 1949)

Bikont, Anna and Joanna Szczęsna, *Lawina i Kamienie: Pisarze wobec Komunizmu* (Warsaw, 2006)

Błazynski, Zbigniew, *Mówi Józef Światło* (Warsaw, 2003)

Boórm, János, *Arcok és értékek az acélvárosban* (Budapest, 2008)

Borhi, László, *Hungary in the Cold War: 1945–1956* (Budapest and New York, 2004)

Böszörményi, Géza, *Recsk 1950–1953* (Budapest, 2006)

Bouška, Tomáš and Klara Pinerova, *Czechoslovak Political Prisoners* (Prague, 2009)

Breuning, Eleonore, Jill Lewis and Gareth Pritchard, eds., *Power and the People: A Social History of Central European Politics, 1945–1956* (Manchester, 2005)

Brodala, Marta, Anna Lisiecka and Tadeusz Rudzikowski, *Przebudować Człowieka: komunistyczne wysiłki zmiany mentalności* (Warsaw, 2001)

Bruce, Gary, *The Firm: The Inside Story of the Stasi* (Oxford, 2010)

Brüning, Elfriede, *Und außerdem war es mein Leben* (Berlin, 1952)

Brzezinski, Zbigniew, *The Soviet Bloc: Unity and Conflict* (New York, 1967)

Brzezinski, Zbigniew and Carl J. Friedrich, *Totalitarian Dictatorship and Autocracy* (Cambridge, 1956)

Brzostek, Błażej, *Robotnicy Warszawy* (Warsaw, 2002)

Buber-Neumann, Margarete, *Under Two Dictators*, trans. Edward Fitzgerald (London, 2008)

Burger, Ulrich, *Das sagen wir natürlich so nicht!* (Berlin, 1990)

Celina, Budzyńska, *Krytyka i Samokrytyka* (Warsaw, 1954)

Childs, David, *The GDR: Moscow's German Ally* (London, 1988)

Childs, David and Richard Popplewell, *The Stasi: The East German Intelligence and Security Services* (New York, 1996)

Chłopek, Maciej, *Bikiniarze. Pierwsza polska subkultura* (Warsaw, 2005)

Chodakiewicz, Marek, *After the Holocaust* (New York, 2003)

Chodakiewicz, Marek, John Radziłowski and Dariusz Tolczyk, eds., *Poland's Transformation: A Work in Progress* (Charlottesville, 2003)

Cichocki, Bartosz and Krzyzstof Józwiak, *Najważniejsze są Kadry: Centralna Szkoła Partyjna PPR/PZPR* (Warsaw, 2006)

Cichopek-Gajraj, Anna, 'Jews, Poles and Slovaks: A Story of Encounters, 1944–1948', Ph.D. dissertation, University of Michigan, 2008

Colditz, Heinz and Martin Lücke, *Stalinstadt: neues Leben, neue Menschen* (Berlin, 1958)

Connelly, John, *Captive University: The Sovietization of East German, Czech and Polish Higher Education, 1945–1956* (Chapel Hill and London, 2000)

Conquest, Robert, *Reflections on a Ravaged Century* (New York, 1999)

Conze, Werner and Jakob Kaiser, *Politiker zwischen Ost und West, 1945–1949* (Stuttgart, 1969)

Courtois, Stéphane, et al., eds., *The Black Book of Communism* (Cambridge, 1999)

Crampton, R. J., *A Concise History of Bulgaria* (Cambridge, 2006)

Creuzberger, Stefan, *Die Sowjetische Militäradministration in Deutschland (SMAD) 1945–1949* (Melle, 1991)

Crowley, David, *Warsaw* (London, 2003)

Czuchnowski, Wojciech, *Blizna. Proces Kurii krakowskiej 1953* (Kraków, 2003)

Davies, Norman and Roger Moorhouse, *Microcosm: A Portrait of a European City* (New York, 2003)

Davies, Norman, *Rising '44: The Battle for Warsaw* (New York, 2004)

Deák, István, Jan T. Gross and Tony Judt, eds., *The Politics of Retribution in Europe* (Princeton, 2000)

Deakin, Frederick W. and Richard Storry, *The Case of Richard Sorge* (New York, 1966)

Djilas, Milovan, *Conversations With Stalin* (New York, 1990)

Doernberg, Stefan, *Befreiung. Ein Augenzeugbericht* (East Berlin, 1985)

—, *Die Geburt eines neuen Deutschlands 1945–1949* (East Berlin, 1959)

—, *Kurze Geschichte der DDR* (Berlin, 1969)

Dönhoff, Marion Gräfin, *Namen, die keiner mehr nennt: Ostpreußen – Menschen und Geschichte* (Munich, 1964)

Drauschke, Frank, Arseny Roginsky and Anna Kaminsky, *Erschossen in Moskau ...: Die deutschen Opfer des Stalinismus auf dem Moskauer Friedhof Donskoje* (Berlin, 2008)

Eichner, Klaus and Gotthold Schramm, *Angriff und Abwehr: Die deutschen Geheimdienste nach 1945* (Berlin, 2007)

Engelgard, Jan, *Wielka Gra Bolesława Piaseckiego* (Warsaw, 2008)

Epstein, Catherine, *The Last Revolutionaries: German Communists and Their Century* (Cambridge and London, 2003)

Erdős, Ferenc and Zszuanna Pongrácz, *Dunaújváros története* (Dunaújváros, 2000)

Erős, Ferenc, *Pszichoanalízis és kulturális emlékezet* (Budapest, 2010)

Faludy, György, *My Happy Days in Hell* (London, 2010)

Farkas, Vladimir, *Nincs mentség* (Budapest, 1990)

Fedorowicz, Jacek, *Dziełka wybrane* (Chicago, 1989)

—, *Kultura młodych – Teatry studenckie w połowie lat pięćdziesiątych*, maszynopis, s.l., s.a (tekst wygłoszony podczas konferencji naukowej na Uniwersytecie Warszawskim)

Fehér, István, *Az utolsó percben, Magyarország nemzetiségei 1945–1990* (Budapest, 1993)

Feist, Günter (with Eckhart Gillen), *Stationen eines Weges: Daten und Zitate zur Kunst und Kunstpolitik der DDR 1945–1998* (Berlin, 1988)

Feist, Günter, Eckhart Gillen and Beatrice Vierneisel, eds., *Kunstdokumentation: 1945–1990, SBZ/DDR* (Berlin, 1996)

Fidelis, Małgorzata, *The New Proletarians: Women Industrial Workers and the State in Postwar Poland, 1945–57*, Ph.D. dissertation, Stanford University, 2005

Finkel, Stuart, *On the Ideological Front: The Russian Intelligentsia and the Making of the Soviet Public Sphere* (New Haven, 2007)

Finn, Gerhard, *Die politischen Häftlinge der Sowjetzone: 1945–1959* (Pfaffenhofen, 1960)

Fischer, Ruth, *Stalin and German Communism: A Study in the Origins of the State Party* (New Brunswick, 1982)

Fitzpatrick, Sheila and Michael Geyer, *Beyond Totalitarianism: Stalinism and Nazism Compared* (Cambridge, 2008)

Földesi, Margit, *A megszállók szabadsága* (Budapest, 2002)

Frazik, Wojciech, Filip Musiał and Mateusz Szpytma, *Obsada Stanowisk kierowniczych Urzędu Bezpieceństwa i Służby Bezpieczenstwa w Krakowie* (Kraków, 2006)

Friske, Andrzej, *Opozycja Polityczna w PRL, 1945–1980* (London, 1994)

—, *Polska: Losy państwa i narodu, 1939–1945* (Warsaw, 2003)

Fulbrook Mary, *Anatomy of a Dictatorship: Inside the GDR, 1949–1989* (Oxford, 1995)

Furet, François, *The Passing of an Illusion: The Idea of Communism in the Twentieth Century*, trans. Deborah Furet (Chicago, 1999)

Gaddis, John Lewis, *The Cold War: A New History* (New York, 2005)

—, *We Now Know: Rethinking Cold War History* (Oxford, 1997)

Gál, Lajos, ed., *Egységbe ifjúság!* (Budapest, 1973)

Garasin, Rudolf, *Vörössipkás lovagok* (Budapest, 1967)

Garlicki, Andrzej, *Bolesław Bierut* (Warsaw, 1994)

Gaszyński, Marek, *Fruwa Twoja Marynara: lata czterdzieste i pięćdziesiąte – jazz, dancing, rock and roll* (Warsaw, 2006)

Gati, Charles, *Failed Illusions: Moscow, Washington, Budapest and the 1956 Hungarian Revolt* (Stanford and Washington, 2006)

Gawryszewski, Andrzej, *Ludność Polski w XX wieku* (Warsaw, 2005)

Gergely, Ferenc, *A magyar cserkészet története 1910–1948* (Budapest, 1989)

Gergely, Jenő, *A katolikus egyház Magyarországon 1944–1971* (Budapest, 1985)

Germuska, Pál, 'Between Theory and Practice: Planning Socialist Cities in Hungary', in *Urban Machinery: Inside Modern European Cities*, eds. Mikael Hard and Thomas J. Misa (Cambridge, Mass., 2008)

Geyer, Hans-Joachim, *Am Anfang stand das Ende* (Berlin, 1954)

Gieseke, Jens, *Die DDR-Staatssicherheit: Schild und Schwert der Partei* (Bonn, 2000)

—, *The GDR State Security: Sword and Shield*, trans. Mary Carlene Forszt (Berlin, 2004)

Gilbert, Martin, 'Churchill and Poland', unpublished lecture delivered at the University of Warsaw, 16 February 2010

Gillen, Eckhart, *Das Kunstkombinat DDR. Zäsuren einer gescheiterten Kunstpolitik* (Cologne, 2005)

Gillen, Eckhart and Diether Schmidt, *Zone 5: Kunst in der Viersektorenstadt 1945–1951* (Berlin, 1989)

Gleason, Abbott, *Totalitarianism: The Inner History of the Cold War* (Oxford, 1995)

Gneist, Gisela and Gunther Heydemann, *'Allenfalls kommt man für ein halbes Jahr in ein Umschulungslager'* (Leipzig, 2002)

Goban-Klas, Tomasz, *The Orchestration of the Media: The Politics of Mass Communications in Communist Poland and the Aftermath* (Boulder, 1994)

Golaszewski, Tadeusz, *Kronika Nowej Huty* (Kraków, 1955)

Gontarczyk, Piotr, *Polska Partia Robotnicza: Droga do Władzy, 1941–1944* (Warsaw, 2003)

Graczyk, R., *Bo jestem z Wilna . . . z Józefą Hennelową rozmawia Roman Graczyk* (Kraków, 2001)

Gregory, Paul, *The Political Economy of Stalinism: Evidence from the Soviet Secret Archives* (Cambridge, 2004)

Greider, Peter, *The East German Leadership 1946–1973: Conflict and Crisis* (Manchester, 1999)

Grodzieńska, Stefania, *Już nic nie muszę* (Lublin, 2000)

Grose, Peter, *Operation Rollback* (New York, 2000)

Gross, Jan, *Fear: Anti-Semitism in Poland after Auschwitz* (New York, 2006)

Gross, Jan T., *Revolution From Abroad: The Soviet Conquest of Poland's Western Ukraine and Western Belorussia* (Princeton, 1998)

—, 'War as Revolution', in *The Establishment of Communist Regimes in Eastern Europe, 1944–1949*, eds. Norman Naimark and Leonid Gibianskii (Boulder, 1997)

Gruschka, Gerhard, *Zgoda, miejsce zgrozy: Obóz koncentracyjny w Świętochłowicach* (Gliwice, 1998).

Gyarmati, György, *Államvédelem a Rákosi-korszakban* (Budapest, 2000)

—, *Az átmenet évkönyve, 2003* (Budapest, 2004)

Gyarmati, György, ed., *A politika redorsege Magyarorszagon a Rakosi-korszakban* (Pécs, 2002)

György, Péter and Hedvig Turai, eds., *A művészet katonái – Sztálinizmus és kultúra* (Budapest, 1992)

Győri Szabó, Róbert, *A kommunizmus és a zsidóság az 1945 utáni Magyarországon* (Budapest, 2009)

Haine, Simone, ed., *Reise nach Moskau* (Berlin, 1995)

Hajna, Karl-Heinz, *Die Landtagswahlen 1946 in der SBZ* (Frankfurt am Main, 2000)

Halmy Kund, János, *Mecséri: An Army Officer in the Revolution*, lecture, presented at the Terror Háza Múzeum, October 2006

Hantó, Zsuzsa, *Kitiltott családok* (Budapest, 2009)

Harmat, Pál, *Freud, Ferenczi és a magyarországi pszichoanalízis* (Budapest, 1994)

Harrison, Hope, *Driving the Soviets Up the Wall* (Princeton, 2003)

Hartmann, Anne and Wolfram Eggelin, *Sowjetische Präsenz im kulturellen Leben der SBZ und frühen DDR 1945–1953* (Berlin, 1998)

Haslam, Jonathan, *Russia's Cold War* (New Haven and London, 2010)

Hayman, Ronald, *Brecht: A Biography* (New York, 1983)

Haynes, John Earl, Harvey Klehr and Alexander Vassiliev, *Spies: The Rise and Fall of the KGB* (New Haven, 2009)

Herf, Jeffrey, *Divided Memory: The Nazi Past in the Two Germanys* (Cambridge, 1997)

Herrmann, Elisabeth Maria, *Die Presse in der Sowjetischen Besatzungszone Deutschlands* (Bonn, 1957)

Hetényi, Varga Károly, *Papi sorsok a horogkereszt és a vörös csillag árnyékában I.-III* (Abaliget, 1992)

Heym, Stefan, *Schwarzenberg* (Munich, 1988)

Hilger, Andreas, Mike Schmeitzner and Ute Schmidt, eds., *Diktaturdurchsetzung. Instrumente und Methoden der kommunistischen Machtsicherung 1945–1955* (Dresden, 2001)

Hirsch, Helga, *Zemsta Ofiar*, trans. Maria Przybyłowska (Warsaw, 1999)

Hodos, George H., *Show Trials: Stalinist Purges in Eastern Europe 1948–1954* (New York, 1987)

Holm, Hans Axel, *The Other Germans: Report from an East German Town* (New York, 1970)

Holzweißig, Gunter, *DDR-Presse unter Parteikontrolle. Analysen und Berichte des Gesamtdeutschen Instituts*, No. 3 (Bonn, 1991)

Horváth, István, ed., *Dunaferr: Dunai Vasmu Kronika* (Dunaújváros, 2000)

Horváth, Sándor, *A kapu es a hatar: mindenapi Sztálinváros* (Budapest, 2004)

Horváth, Sándor, ed., *Mindennapok Rákosi és Kádár korában* (Budapest, 2008)

Isakowicz-Zaleski, Tadeusz, *Księża Wobec Bezpieki* (Kraków, 2007)

Jackowski, Aleksander, *Na Skróty* (Sejny, 1995)

Jagiełło, Michał, *Próba rozmowy. t. 2.: 'Tygodnik Powszechny' i komunizm 1945–1953* (Warsaw, 2001)

Janics, Kalman, *Czechoslovak Policy and the Hungarian Minority* (New York, 1982)

Jarausch, Konrad H., ed., *Dictatorship as Experience: Towards a Socio-Cultural History of the GDR* (New York, 1999)

Jászberényi, József, *A magyarországi szabadkőművesség története* (Budapest, 2005)

Jaszczuk, Andrzej, *Ewolucja Ideowa Bolesława Piaseckiego* (Warsaw, 2005)

Johnson, A. Ross and R. Eugene Parta, eds., *Cold War Broadcasting: Impact on the Soviet Union and Eastern Europe* (New York, 2010)

Judt, Tony, *Postwar: A History of Europe since 1945* (New York, 2005)

Judt, Tony and Timothy Snyder, *Thinking the Twentieth Century* (London, 2012)

Kalinski, Janusz and Zbigniew Landau, *Gospodarka Polski w XX wieku* (Warsaw, 1998)

Kaminski, Łukasz and Jan Żaryn, eds., *Wokoł Pogromu Kieleckiego* (Warsaw, 2006)

Kant, Hermann, *Die Aula* (Berlin, 1968)

Kaplan, Karel, *Report on the Murder of the General Secretary*, trans. Karel Kovanda (Columbus, 1990)

—, *The Short March: The Communist Takeover in Czechoslovakia* (New York, 1987)

Karau, Gisela, *Stasiprotokolle* (Frankfurt, 1992)

Kardos, László, ed., *'Sej a mi lobogónkat fényes szelek fújják'*, Népi Kollégiumok 1939–49 (Budapest, 1977)

Kaser, M. A and E. A. Radice, *The Economic History of Eastern Europe*, Vol. II: *Interwar Policy, the War and Reconstruction* (Oxford, 1986)

Kecskemeti, Paul, *The Unexpected Revolution* (Stanford, 1981)

Kenez, Peter, *Hungary from the Nazis to the Soviets: The Establishment of the Communist Regime in Hungary, 1944–1948* (Cambridge and New York, 2006)

Kennan, George, *Memoirs: 1920–1950* (New York, 1967)

Kenney, Padraic, *Rebuilding Poland: Workers and Communists 1945–1950* (Ithaca and London, 1997)

Kersten, Krystyna, *The Establishment of Communist Rule in Poland, 1943–1948* (Berkeley, 1991)

Kiszely, Gábor, *ÁVH: Egy terrorszervezet története* (Budapest, 2000)

Klehr, Harvey, John Earl Haynes and Kirill M. Anderson, *The Soviet World of American Communism* (New Haven and London, 1998)

Klein, Manfred, *Jugend zwischen den Diktaturen: 1945–1956* (Mainz, 1968)

Klein, Thomas, *'Für die Einheit und Reinheit der Partei': Die innerparteilichen Kontrollorgane der SED in der Ära Ullbricht* (Cologne, 2002)

Klessmann, Christoph, *The Divided Past: Rewriting Post-War German History* (New York, 2001)

Klimov, Gregory, *The Terror Machine: The Inside Story of the Soviet Administration in Germany*, trans. H. C. Stevens (New York, 1953)

Knabe, Hubertus, *17. Juni 1953 – Ein deutscher Aufstand* (Berlin, 2004)

Knight, Amy, *Beria: Stalin's First Lieutenant* (Princeton, 1995)

Kochanowicz, Joanna, *ZMP w terenie* (Warsaw, 2000)

Kochanowski, Jerzy, et al., eds., *Zbudować Warsawę Pieknę: O Nowy Krajobraz Stolicy (1944–1956)* (Warsaw, 2003)

Koehler, John O., *Stasi: The Untold Story of the East German Secret Police* (Boulder, 1999)

Koestler, Arthur, *Arrow in the Blue* (London, 2005)

—, *Darkness at Noon* (New York, 2006)

Koloski, Laurie S., *Painting Kraków Red: Politics and Culture in Poland, 1945–1950*, Stanford University, Ph.D. dissertation, June 1998

Komorowski, Krzysztof, ed., *Armia Krajowa: szkice z dziejów Sił Zbrojnych Polskiego Państwa Podziemnego* (Warsaw, 1999)

Konrád, György, *A Guest in My Own Country* (New York, 2007)

Konwicki, Tadeusz, *Przy Budowie* (Warsaw, 1950)

Koop, Volker, *Besetzt: Sowjetische Besatzungspolitik in Deutschland* (Berlin, 2008)

—, *Tagebuch der Berliner Blockade. Von Schwarzmarkt und Rollkommandos, Bergbau und Bienenzucht* (Berlin, 1998)

Kopácsi, Sándor, *In the Name of the Working Class* (New York, 1987)

Kopelev, Lev, *To be Preserved Forever*, trans. Anthony Austin (New York, 1977)

Kopka, Bogusław, *Obozy Pracy w Polsce, 1944–1950* (Warsaw, 2002)

Kopstein, Jeffrey, *The Politics of Economic Decline in East Germany, 1945–1989* (Chapel Hill and London, 1997)

Kott, Sandrine, Marcin Kula and Thomas Lindenberger, eds., *Socjalizm w życiu powszednim: dyktatura a społeczeństwo w NRD i PRL* (Warsaw, 2006)

Kovács, Imre, *Magyarország megszállása* (Budapest, 1990)

Kovály, Heda, *Under A Cruel Star* (Cambridge, Mass., 1986)

Krahulcsán, Zsolt, Rolf Müller and Mária Palasik, *A politikai rendőrség háború utáni megszervezése (1944–1946)* (Budapest, 2009)

Krajewski, Kazimierz and Tomasz Łabuszewski, eds., *'Zwyczajny' Resort: Studia o aparacie bezpieczeństwa 1944–1956* (Warsaw, 2005)

Kramer Mark, 'The Early Post-Stalin Succession Struggle and Upheavals in East-Central Europe: Internal–External Linkages in Soviet Policy Making', *Journal of Cold War Studies*, published in three parts, 1/1 (1999), pp. 3–55; 1/2 (1999), pp. 3–38; 1/3 (1999), pp. 3–66

Krawczyk, Andrzej, *Pierwsza próba indoktrynacji. Działalność Ministerstwa Informacji i Propagandy w latach 1944–1947* (Warsaw, 1994)

Krzywicki, Andrzej, *Poststalinowski Karnawał Radości* (Warsaw, 2009)

Kuby, Erich, *Die Russen in Berlin* (Berlin, 1965)

Kula, Martin, ed., *Przebudować Człowieka: komunistyczne wysiłki zmiany mentalności* (Warsaw, 2001)

Kundera, Milan, *The Joke* (London, 1992)

Kunicki, Mikołaj Stanisław, *The Polish Crusader: The Life and Politics of Boleslaw Piasecki, 1915–1979*, Ph.D. dissertation, Stanford University, June 2004

Kuroń, Jacek, *Wiara i wina. Do i od komunizmu* (Wrocław, 1995)

Kuroń, Jacek and Jacek Żakowski, *PRL dla początkujących* (Wrocław, 1996)

Kwiek, Julian, *Związek Harcerstwa Polskiego w latach 1944–1950. Powstanie, rozwój, likwidacja* (Toruń, 1995)

Ladányi, Sándor, *A magyar református egyház 1956 tükrében* (Budapest, 2006)

Landsman, Mark, *Dictatorship and Demand: The Politics of Consumerism in East Germany* (Cambridge, 2005)

Langer, Jo, *Convictions: My Life with a Good Communist* (London, 2011)

László, Péter, *Fehérlaposok – Adalékok a magyar-csehszlovák lakosságcsere egyezményhez* (Szekszárd, 2004)

Latotzky, Alexander, *Kindheit hinter Stacheldraht: Mütter mit Kindern in sowjetischen Speziallagern und DDR-Haft* (Leipzig, 2001)

Laufer, Jochen, *Pax Sovietica. Stalin, die Westmächte und die deutsche Frage 1941–1945* (Cologne, 2009)

Leffler, Melvyn, *For the Soul of Mankind: The United States, the Soviet Union and the Cold War* (New York, 2007)

Leonhard, Wolfgang, *Child of the Revolution* (Chicago, 1958)

—, *Spurensuche, 40 Jahre nach 'Die Revolution entläßt ihre Kinder'* (Cologne, 1994)

Leucht, Kurt W., *Die erste neue Stadt in der DDR* (Berlin, 1957)

Lévai, Béla, *A rádió és a televízió krónikája 1945–1978* (Budapest, 1980)

Levi, Primo, *If This is Man and The Truce* (London, 1988)

Lewis, Ben, *Hammer and Tickle* (London, 2009)

Liebmann, Irina, *Wäre es schön? Es wäre schön! Mein Vater Rudolf Herrnstadt* (Berlin, 2008)

Liebold, Cornelia, Jörg Morré and Gerhard Sälter, eds., *Kassiber aus Bautzen: Heimliche Briefe von Gefängenen aus dem Sovjetischen Speziallager 1945–1950* (Dresden, 2004)

Liehm, Mira and Liehm, Antonin J., *The Most Important Art: East European Film after 1945* (Berkeley, 1977)

Lipiński, Piotr, *Bolesław Niejasny* (Warsaw, 2001)

Lipinsky, Jan and Renate, *Die Straße die in den Tod führte – Zur Geschichte des Speziallagers Nr. 5 Ketschendorf/Fürstenwalde* (Leverkusen, 1999)

Loest, Erich, *Durch die Erde ein Riss: Ein Lebenslauf* (Hamburg, 1981)

Lomax, Bill, ed., *Hungarian Workers' Councils in 1956* (New York, 1990)

Łopuski Jan, *Pozostać sobą w Polsce Ludowej: życie w cieniu podejrzeń* (Rzeszów, 2007)

Lossonczy, Tamás, *The Vision is Always Changing* (Budapest, 2004)

Loth Wilfried, *Die Sowjetunion und die deutsche Frage. Studien zur sowjetischen Deutschlandpolitik* (Göttingen, 2007)

—, *Stalin's Unwanted Child: The Soviet Union, the German Question, and the Founding of the GDR*, trans. Robert F. Hogg (New York, 1998)

Lotnik, Waldemar, *Nine Lives: Ethnic Conflict in the Polish–Ukrainian Borderlands* (London, 1999)

Lubelski, Tadeusz, *Wajda* (Wrocław, 2006)

Ludwig, Andreas, *Eisenhüttenstadt: Wandel einer industriellen Gründungsstadt in fünfzig Jahren* (Potsdam, 2000)

Lukacs, John, *1945: Year Zero* (New York, 1978)

Kiss, Sándor M. and Iván Vitányi, *A magyar diákok szabadságfrontja* (Budapest, 1983)

Maciej, Chłopek, *Bikiniarze. Pierwsza polska subkultura* (Warsaw, 2005)

Mählert, Ulrich, *Die Freie Deutsche Jugend 1945–1949* (Paderborn, 1945)

Mählert, Ulrich and Stephan Ger-Rudiger, *Blaue Hemden, Rote Fahnen: Die Geschichte der Freien Deutschen Jugend* (Opladen, 1996)

Major, Patrick and Jonathan Osmond, *The Workers' and Peasants' State: Communism and Society in East Germany under Ulbricht 1945–71* (Manchester, 2002)

Majtényi, György and Zoltán Szatucsek, *A szabó tűje és a cipész dikicse – Dokumentumok a kisipar és kiskereskedelem államosításának történetéből* (Budapest, 2001)

Makarenko, A. S., *The Road to Life*, Vol. Two, trans. Ivy and Tatiana Litvinov (Moscow, 1951)

Makarewicz, Henryk, and Wiktor Pental, *802 procent normy: pierwsze lata Nowej Huty* (Kraków, 2007)

Márai, Sándor, *Memoir of Hungary: 1944–1948*, trans. Albert Tezla (Budapest, 1996)

—, *Portraits of a Marriage*, trans. George Szirtes (New York, 2012)

Márton, Endre, *The Forbidden Sky* (New York, 1971)

Marton, Kati, *Enemies of the People: My Family's Journey to America* (New York, 2009)

Marwick, Arthur, *War and Social Change in the Twentieth Century* (London, 1974)

Massing, Hede, *This Deception* (New York, 1951)

Mastny, Vojtech, *The Cold War and Soviet Insecurity: The Stalin Years* (Oxford, 1996)

Matussné Lendvai, Márta, *Új város születik* (Dunaújváros, 2001)

Mazgai, Marian S., *Church and State in Communist Poland: A History, 1944–1989* (New York, 2010)

McAdams, James, *Germany Divided: From the Wall to Reunification* (Princeton, 1993)

McCauley, Martin, *Origins of the Cold War* (New York, 2008)

McDougal, Alan, *Youth Politics in East Germany: The Free German Youth Movement, 1946–1968* (Oxford, 2005)

Meráy, Tibor, *Thirteen Days That Shook the Kremlin*, trans. Howard L. Katzander (New York, 1959)

Merridale, Catherine, *Ivan's War* (New York, 2006)

Mevius, Martin, *Agents of Moscow: The Hungarian Communist Party and the Origins of Socialist Patriotism 1941–1953* (Oxford, 2005)

Micewski, Andrzej, *Cardinal Wyszyński: A Biography*, trans. William R. Brand and Katzarzyna Mroczowska-Brand (New York, 1984)

—, *Współrządzić czy nie kłamać. PAX i Znak w Polsce 1945–1976* (Paris, 1978)

Mikołajczyk, Stanisław, *The Rape of Poland* (New York, 1948)

Miłosz, Czesław, *The Captive Mind*, trans. Jane Zielonko (London, 2001)

—, *Zdobycie Władzy* (Olsztyn, 1990)

Mindszenty, József, *Emlékirataim* (Budapest, 1989)

—, *Memoirs* (New York, 1974)

Misiło, Eugeniusz, *Akcja Wisła* (Warsaw, 1993)

Mitrovich, Gregory, *Undermining the Kremlin: America's Strategy to Subvert the Soviet Bloc, 1947–1956* (Ithaca, 2000)

Molnar, Virag Eszter, *Modernity and Memory: The Politics of Architecture in Hungary and East Germany after the Second World War*, Ph.D. dissertation, Princeton University, 2005

Mong, Attila, *János vitéz a Gulagon* (Budapest, 2008)

Murphy, David E., Sergei A. Kondrashev and George Bailey, *Battleground Berlin: CIA vs. KGB in the Cold War* (New Haven and London, 1997)

Nagy, Ferenc, *Küzdelem a vasfüggöny mögött* (Budapest, 1990)

—, *The Struggle behind the Iron Curtain* (New York, 1948)

Nagy, Imre, *On Communism: In Defense of the New Course* (New York, 1957)

576

Naimark, Norman, *The Russians in Germany: A History of the Soviet Zone of Occupation, 1945–1949*, (Cambridge and London, 1995)

—, 'The Sovietization of Eastern Europe, 1944–1953', in *The Cambridge History of the Cold War* (Cambridge, 2010)

Naimark, Norman and Leonid Gibianskii, eds., *The Establishment of Communist Regimes in Eastern Europe, 1944–1949* (Boulder, 1997)

Nakhimovsky, Alexander and Alice Nakhimovsky, *Witness to History: The Photographs of Yevgeny Khaldei* (New York, 1997)

Nałkowska, Zofia, *Dzienniki 1945–1954*, Vol.1 (Warsaw, 2001)

Nawrocki, Zbigniew, *Zamiast Wolności: UB na Rzeszowszczyżnie, 1944–1949* (Rzeszów, 1998)

Nicolaus, Herbert and Lutz Schmidt, *Einblicke: 50 Jahre EKO Stahl* (Eisenhüttenstadt, 2000)

Nothnagle Alan L., *Building the East German Myth: Historical Mythology and Youth Propaganda in the German Democratic Republic, 1945–89* (Ann Arbor, 1999)

Nowak, Barbara, *Serving Women and the State: The League of Women in Communist Poland*, Ph.D. dissertation, Ohio State University, 2004

Oestreicher, Paul, *Whose Agents?: Church and Society in Communist East Germany* (London, 1995)

Orbán, József Gyula, *Katolikus papok békemozgalma Magyarországon 1950–1956* (Budapest, 2001)

Osęka, Piotr, *Rytuały Stalinizmu* (Warsaw, 2007)

Ostermann Christian, *The United States, the East German Uprising of 1953, and the Limits of Rollback*, CWIHP, Working Paper No. 11 (December 1994)

Overmans, Rüdiger, *Deutsche militärische Verluste im Zweiten Weltkrieg* (Munich, 2004)

Paczkowski, Andrzej, *Aparat bezpieczeństwa w latach 1944–56: taktyka, strategia, metody, Czesc I. Lata 1945–1947*, Dokumenty do dziejów PRL (Warsaw, 1994)

—, *Od sfałszowanego zwycięstwa do prawdziwej klęski: szkice do portretu PRL* (Warsaw, 1999)

—, *Referendum z 30 czerwca 1946: Proba wstępnego bilansu* (Warsaw, 1992)

—, *The Spring Will be Ours: Poland and the Poles from Occupation to Freedom* (New York, 2003)

—, *Trzy twarze Józefa Światły – przyczynek do historii komunizmu w Polsce* (Warsaw, 2009)

—, 'Zydzi w UB: Proba weryfikacji stereotyp', in Tomasz Szarota, ed., *Komunizm: Ideologia, System, Ludzi* (Warsaw, 2001)

Palasik, Mária, *A jogállamiság megteremtésének kísérlete és kudarca Magyarországon, 1944–1949* (Budapest, 2000)

Panufnik, Andrzej, *Composing Myself* (London, 1987)

Panzig, Christel, *Wir schalten uns ein: Zwischen Luftschutzkeller & Stalinbild, Stadt & Region Wittenberg 1945* (Lutherstadt Wittenberg, 2005)

Pasko, Artur, *Wyścig Pokoju w dokumentach władz partyjnych i państwowych 1948–1989* (Kraków, 2009)

Patai, Raphael, *The Jews of Hungary: History, Culture, Psychology* (Detroit, 1996)

Pataki, Ferenc, *A Nékosz-legenda* (Budapest, 2005)

Pelikán, Jiří, ed., *The Czechoslovak Political Trials, 1950–54: Suppressed Report of the Dubček Government's Commission of Inquiry, 1968* (Stanford, 1975)

Pelle, János, *Az utolsó vérvádak* (Budapest, 1995)

Persak, Krzysztof, *Odrodzenie harcerstwa w 1956 roku* (Warsaw, 1996)

Persak, Krzysztof and Łukasz Kaminski, eds., *A Handbook of the Communist Security Apparatus in East Central Europe, 1944–1989* (Warsaw, 2005)

Pető, Iván and Sándor Szakács, *A hazai gazdaság négy évtizedének története, 1945–1985. I. Az újjáépítés és a tervutasításos irányítás időszaka. 1945–1968* (Budapest, 1985)

Petrov, Nikita, *Pervyi Predsedatel'KGB: Ivan Serov* (Moscow, 2005)

Pickel, Andreas, *Radical Transitions: The Survival and Revival of Entrepreneurship in the GDR* (Boulder, 1992)

Pike, David, *The Politics of Culture in Soviet-Occupied Germany, 1945–1949* (Stanford, 1992)

Pipes, Richard, *Communism: A History* (New York, 2001)

—, *Russia under the Bolshevik Regime, 1919–1924* (New York, 1994)

—, *The Russian Revolution* (New York, 1991)

Pipes, Richard, ed., *The Unknown Lenin* (New Haven, 1996)

Plokhii, Serhii, *Yalta: The Price of Peace* (New York, 2010)

Pludra, Benno, *Die Jungen von Zelt dreizehn* (Berlin, 1952)

Pöhler, Feliks, *Bonner Berichte aus Mittel- und Ostdeutschland. Der Untergang des privaten Einzelhandels in der Sowjetischen Besatzungszone* (Bonn, 1952)

Poleszak, Sławomir, et al., eds., *Rok Pierwszy: Powstanie i Działalność aparatu bezpieczeństwa publicznego na Lubelszczyźnie (Lipiec 1944–Czerwiec 1945)* (Warsaw, 2004)

Polkehn, Klaus, *Das war die Wochenpost: Geschichte und Geschichten einer Zeitung* (Berlin, 1997)

Prauser, Steffen and Arfon Rees, eds., *The Expulsion of the 'German' Communities from Eastern Europe at the End of the Second World War*, EUI Working Paper HEC No. 2004/1

Prażmowska, Anita, *Civil War in Poland, 1942–1948* (New York, 2004)

—, *Poland: A Modern History* (London, 2010)

Priestland, David, *Stalinism and the Politics of Mobilization: Ideas, Power, and Terror in Inter-War Russia* (New York, 2007)

Pritchard, Gareth, *The Making of the GDR 1945–68* (Manchester, 2000)

Pudovkin, Vsevolod and András Kovács, eds., *Pudovkin a magyar filmről* (Budapest, 1952)

Radványi, János, *Hungary and the Superpowers: The 1956 Revolution and Realpolitik* (Stanford, 1972)

Rákosi, Mátyás, *Visszaemlékezések 1940–1956*, Vols. I and II (Budapest, 1997)

Randé, Jenő and János Sebestyén, *Azok a rádiós évtizedek* (Budapest, 1995)

Redlich, Shimon, *Life in Transit: Jews in Postwar Łódź, 1945–1950* (Boston, 2010)

Richter, Jenny, Heike Förster and Ulrich Lakemann, *Stalinstadt – Eisenhüttenstadt: Von der Utopie zur Gegenwart* (Marburg, 1997)

Ritchie, Alexandra, *Faust's Metropolis: A History of Berlin* (London, 1998)

Ritscher, Bodo, *Spezlager Nr. 2 Buchenwald* (Buchenwald, 1993)

Roberts, Andrew, *Masters and Commanders* (London, 2008)

Rodden, John, *Repainting the Little Red Schoolhouse: A History of Eastern German Education, 1945–1995* (New York, 2002)

Rokicki, Konrad, and Sławomir Stępień, eds., *Wobjęciach Wielkiego Brata: Sowieci w Polsce 1944–1993* (Warsaw, 2009)

Rokicki, Konrad, et al., eds., *Departament X MBP: Wzorce – Struktury – Dzialanie* (Warsaw, 2007)

Romsics, Ignác, *Hungary in the Twentieth Century* (Budapest, 1999)

Romsics, Ignác, ed., *Mítoszok, legendák, tévhitek a 20. századi magyar történelemről* (Budapest, 2002)

Ross, Corey, *Constructing Socialism at the Grass Roots: The Transformation of East Germany, 1945–65* (London, 2000)

Rothschild, Joseph, *Return to Diversity: A Political History of East Central Europe since World War II* (New York and Oxford, 2000)

Różański, Henryk, *Śladem Wspomnień i Dokumentów (1943–1948)* (Warsaw, 1987)

Rusan, Romulus, *The Chronology and Geography of Repression in Romania* (Bucharest, 2007)

Sack, John, *An Eye for an Eye* (New York, 1993)

Salamon, Konrád, *A harmadik út küzdelme* (Budapest, 2002)

Sattler, Friederike, *Wirtschaftsordnung im Übergang: Politik, Organisation und Funktion der KPD/SED im Land Brandenburg bei der Etablierung der Zentralen Planwirtschaft in der SBZ/DDR 1945–52* (Münster, 2002)

Scammell, Michael, *Koestler: The Literary and Political Odyssey of a Twentieth-Century Skeptic* (New York, 2009)

Schivelbusch, Wolfgang, *In a Cold Crater: Cultural and Intellectual Life in Berlin, 1945–1948* (Berkeley, 1998)

Schmidt, Mária, *Battle of Wits*, trans. Ann Major (Budapest, 2007)

Schöpflin, Gyula, *Szélkiáltó* (Budapest, 1985)

Sebestyen, Victor, *Twelve Days: The Story of the 1956 Hungarian Revolution* (New York, 2006)

Service, Robert, *Comrades* (London 2007)

—, *A History of Twentieth-Century Russia* (London, 1997)

—, *Spies and Commissars: Bolshevik Russia and the West* (London, 2011)

Seton-Watson, Hugh, *The New Imperialism: A Background Book* (London, 1961)

Shirer, William, *End of a Berlin Diary* (New York, 1947)

Shore, Marci, *Caviar and Ashes: A Warsaw Generation's Life and Death in Marxism, 1918–1968* (New Haven and London, 2006)

Sikorski, Radek, *Full Circle: A Homecoming to Free Poland* (New York, 1997)

Silberman, Marc, *What Remains: East German Culture and the Postwar Public* (Washington DC, 1997)

Timothy Snyder, *Bloodlands* (New York, 2011)

—, *Sketches from a Secret War* (New Haven and London, 2005)

Solberg, Richard, *God and Caesar in East Germany: The Conflicts of Church and State in East Germany since 1945* (New York, 1961)

Solzhenitsyn, Alexander, *Prussian Nights*, trans. Robert Conquest (New York, 1977)

Sowiński, Paweł, *Kommunistyczne Święto: Obchody 1 Maja w latach 1948–1954* (Warsaw, 2000)

Spalding, Elizabeth Edwards, *The First Cold Warrior: Harry Truman, Containment, and the Making of Liberal Internationalism* (Louisville, 2006)

Spilker, Dirk, *The East German Leadership and the Division of Germany: Patriotism and Propaganda 1945–1953* (Oxford, 2006)

Standeisky, Éva, *Gúzsba kötve – A kulturális elit és a hatalom* (Budapest, 2005)

Stark, Tamás, *Magyar hadifoglyok a Szovjetunióban* (Budapest, 2006)

Stern, Carola, *Ulbricht: A Biography*, trans. Abe Farbstein (New York, 1965)

Stobiecki, Rafał, *Historiografia PRL* (Warsaw, 2007)

Stola, Dariusz, *Kraj Bez Wyjścia?* (Warsaw, 2010)

Strauß, Gerhard, *Vom Auftrag zum Wandbild* (Berlin, 1953)

Strunk, Peter, *Zensur und Zensoren* (Berlin, 1996)

Sulyok, Dezső, *Két éjszaka nappal nélkül* (Budapest, 2004)

Świda-Ziemba, H., *Urwany lot. Pokolenie inteligenckiej młodzieży powojennej w świetle listów i pamiętników z lat 1945–1948* (Kraków, 2003)

Sword, Keith, *Deportation and Exile: Poles in the Soviet Union, 1939–1948* (London, 1996)

Sword, Keith, ed., *The Soviet Takeover of the Polish Eastern Provinces, 1939–41* (New York, 1991)

Szabó, Csaba, ed., *A Grősz-per előkészítése – 1951* (Budapest, 2001)

—, ed., *Egyházügyi hangulatjelentések* (Budapest, 2000)

Szabó, Robert Győri, *A kommunizmus és a zsidóság az 1945 utáni Magyarországon* (Budapest, 2009)

Szász, Béla, *Volunteers for the Gallows* (New York, 1971)

Szaynok, Bożena, *Poland–Israel 1944–1968: In the Shadow of the Past and of the Soviet Union* (Warsaw, 2012)

Szaynok, Bożena, *Pogrom Żydów w Kielcach. 4. VII 1946 r.* (Warsaw, 1992)

Szelényi, Iván, ed., *Privatizing the Land: Rural Political Economy in Post-Communist Societies* (London, 1998)

Szent-Miklósy, István, *With the Hungarian Independence Movement, 1943–1947: An Eyewitness Acccount* (New York, 1988)

Szerencsés, Károly, *A kék cédulás hadművelet* (Budapest, 1992)

Szilágyi, Gábor, *Tűzkeresztség, A magyar játékfilm története 1945–1953* (Budapest, 1992)

Szmidt, Bolesław, ed., *The Polish School of Architecture, 1942–1945* (Liverpool, 1945)

Szpilman, Władysław, *The Pianist* (London, 1999)

Taylor, Frederick, *Exorcising Hitler: The Occupation and Denazification of Germany* (London, 2011)

Tejchma, Józef, *Pożegnanie z władzą* (Warsaw, 1997)

—, *Z notatnika aktywisty ZMP* (Warsaw, 1954)

'They rocked my cradle then bundled me out' – *Ethnic German Fate in Hungary 1939–1948*, exhibition catalogue, Terror Háza Múzeum (Budapest, 2007)

Thomson, Stewart, in collaboration with Robert Bialek, *The Bialek Affair* (London, 1955)

Tillich, Ernest, *Hefte der Kampfgruppe*, brochure published in Berlin, 1945

Tismaneanu, Vladimir, ed., *Stalinism Revisited: The Establishment of the Communist Regimes in East Central Europe and the Dynamics of the Soviet Bloc* (New York and Budapest, 2009)

Tóbiás, Áron, *Kettészelt égbolt. A Magyar Rádió regénye. 1945–1956* (Budapest, 2004)

Todorov, Tzvetan, *Voices from the Gulag*, trans. Robert Zaretsky (University Park, Pa., 1999)

Tomka, Ferenc, *Halálra szántak, mégisélünk. Egyházüldözés 1945–1990 és az ügynökkérdés* (Budapest, 2005)

Torańska, Teresa, *Oni: Stalin's Polish Puppets*, trans. Agnieszka Kolakowska (London, 1987)

Tóth, Ágnes, *Hazatértek. A németországi kitelepítésből visszatért magyarországi németek megpróbáltatásainak emlékezete* (Budapest, 2008)

Toth, István György, ed., *A Concise History of Hungary* (Budapest, 2005)

Trznadel, Jacek, *Hańba Domowa* (Paris, 1986)

Tyrmand, Leopold, *Dziennik 1954* (London, 1980)

Ueberschär, Ellen, *Junge Gemeinde im Konflikt: Evangelische Jugendarbeit in SBZ und DDR 1945–1961* (Stuttgart, 2003)

Ulbricht, Walter, *On Questions of Socialist Construction in the GDR* (Dresden, 1968)

Ungváry, Krisztián, *The Siege of Budapest: 100 Days in World War II* (London, 2002)

Ungváry, Krisztián, ed., *A második világháború* (Budapest, 2005)

Urban, George, *Radio Free Europe and the Pursuit of Democracy: My War within the Cold War* (New Haven, 1997)

Vitány, Iván, *Önarckép – elvi keretben* (Celldömölk, 2007)

Volker, Klaus, *Brecht: A Biography*, trans. John Nowell (New York, 1978)

Volkov, V. K., *Uzlovye problem noveishei istorii stran Tsentralnoi i Ugovostochnoi Evropi* (Moscow, 2000)

Wandycz, Piotr, *The Price of Freedom: A History of East Central Europe from the Middle Ages to the Present* (London and New York, 1992)

Wedding, Alex, *Die Fahne des Pfeiferhansleins* (Berlin, 1953)

Wegren, Stephen, *Land Reform in the Former Soviet Union and Eastern Europe* (London, 1998)

Weitz, Eric D., *Creating German Communism, 1890–1990* (Princeton, 1997)

Werblan, Andrzej, *Stalinizm w Polsce* (Warsaw, 2009)

Werner, Ruth, *Sonya's Report: Fascinating Autobiography of One of Russia's Most Remarkable Secret Agents*, trans. Renate Simpson (London, 1991)

Western Belorussia (Princeton, 1988).

Wierzbicki, Marek, *Związek Młodzieży Polskiej i jego członkowie: studium z dziejów funkcjonowania stalinowskiej organizacji młodzieżowej* (Warsaw, 2006)

Williams, William Appleman, *The Tragedy of American Diplomacy* (New York, 1959)

Wir waren schon halbe Russen: Deportiert und uberlebt im GULAG, memoir collection, Gedenkbibliothek zu Ehren der Opfer des Stalinismus (Berlin, 1997)

Włodarcyzk, Wojciech, *Socrealizm: sztuka polska w latach 1950–1954* (Warsaw, 1986)

Wojciechowski, Aleksander, *O Sztuce Użytkowej i Użytecznej* (Warsaw, 1955)

Wójcik, Justyna, ed., *Stawialismy Opor: Antykomunistyczne organizacje młodzieżowe w Małopolsce w latach 1944–1956* (Kraków, 2008)

Wolf, Markus Wolf and Anne McElvoy, *Man without a Face: The Autobiography of Communism's Greatest Spymaster* (New York, 1999)

Wyszyński, Cardinal Stefan, *A Freedom Within*, trans. Barbara Krzywicki-Herburt and the Reverend Walter J. Ziemba (New York, 1982)

Zamoyski, Adam, *Warsaw 1920: Lenin's Failed Conquest of Europe* (London, 2008)

Zaremba, Marcin, *Komunizm, legitymizacja, nacjonalizm: Nacjonalistyczna legitymizacja wladzy komunistycznej w Polsce* (Warsaw, 2005)

Zaremba, Marcin, *Wielka Trwoga. Polska 1944–1947. Ludowa reakcja na kryzys* (Warsaw, 2012)

Żaryn, Jan, *Dzieje Kościoła Katolickiego w Polsce (1944–1989)* (Warsaw, 2003)

Żelazko, Joanna, ed., *Rok 1945 w Łodzi. Studia i szkice* (Łódź, 2008)

Zinner, Tibor, *A magyarországi németek kitelepítése* (Budapest, 2004)

Ziółek, Jan and Agnieszka Przytuła, *Represje wobec uczestników wydarzeń w Katedrze Lubelskiej w 1949 roku* (Lublin, 1999)

Zubkova, Elena, *Poslevoennoe sovetskoe obshchestvo: Politika i povsednevnost', 1945–1953* (Moscow, 2000)

Zubok, V. M., *A Failed Empire: The Soviet Union in the Cold War from Stalin to Gorbachev* (Chapel Hill, 2008)

Żurek, Jacek, *Ruch 'Ksiezy Patriotow'* (Warsaw, 2008)

SELECTED DOCUMENT COLLECTIONS

The 1956 Revolution: A History in Documents, eds. Csaba Békés, Malcolm Byrne and János Rainer (Budapest and New York, 2002)

A Madisz: 1944–48, ed. Sándor Rákosi (Budapest, 1984)

Armia Radziecka w Polsce 1944–1956: dokumenty i materiały, ed. Mariusz Lesław Krogulski (Warsaw, 2003)

Biuletyny Informacyjne Ministerstwa Bezpieczeństwa Publicznego, 1947, eds. Bernadetta Gronek and Irena Marczak, Vol. 1 (Warsaw, 1993)

Das Herrnstadt Dokument: Das Politburo der SED und die Geschichte des 17. Juni 1953, ed. Nadja Stulz-Herrnstadt (Reinbek bei Hamburg, 1990)

DDR: Dokumente zur Geschichte der Deutschen Demokratischen Republik 1945–1985, ed. Hermann Weber (Munich, 1986)

Diary of Georgii Dimitrov, 1933–1949, ed. Ivo Banac (New Haven and London, 2003)

Dimitrov and Stalin: Letters from the Soviet Archives, 1934–1945, eds. Alexander Dallin and F. I. Firsov, (New Haven and London, 2000)

Documents on Germany, 1944–1945, United States Department of State, Office of the Historian, Bureau of Public Affairs, 1985

Dokumente zur Bildungspolitik in der sowjetischen Besatzungszone, eds. Siegfried Baske and Martha Engelbert (Berlin, 1966)

Dokumentumok a magyar politikai rendőrség történetéből 1. A politikai rendészeti osztályok 1945–1946, eds. Zsolt Krahulcsán and Rolf Müller (Budapest, 2010)

Dokumenty do dziejow PRL, a series published by the Polish Academy of Sciences

http://www.archivnet.hu/index.php

http://www.scribd.com/doc/14152546/Soviet-Archival-Documents-on-Hungary-OctoberNovember-1956-Translated-by-Johanna-Granville

Iratok a magyar–szovjet kapcsolatok történetéhez 1944 október–1948 június – Dokumentumok, ed. István Vida (Budapest, 2005)

László Rajk and His Accomplices before the People's Court, publication of the Hungarian state prosecutor's office (Budapest, 1949)

Megforgatott világmegforgatók – A magyar népi kollégiumi mozgalom ismeretlen dokumentumai, ed. László Svéd (Budapest, 1994)

Moszkvának jelentjük, Titkos dokumentumok 1944–1948, eds. Lajos Izsák and Miklós Kun (Budapest, 1994)

Niemcy w Polsce 1945–1950: Wybór Dokumentów, eds. Włodzimierz Borodziej and Hans Lemberg, Vols. I–IV (Warsaw, 2000–2001)

NKVD i pol'skoe podpol'e, 1944–1945: Po 'Osobym papkam' I. V. Stalina, eds. A. F. Noskova et al. (Moscow, 1994)

Partei und Jugend: Dokumente marxistischer-leninistischer Jugendpolitik, Zentralrat der Freien Deutschen Jugend und des Institut für Marxismus-Leninismus beim Zentralkommitee der SED (Berlin, 1986)

Politika SVAG v Oblasti Kulturi, nauki I Obrazovaniya: Tseli, Metody, Rezultaty, 1945–1949 gg, Sbornik Dokumentov, eds. N. Timofeeva et al.

Polska w dokumentach z archiwów rosyjskich 1949–1953, eds. Andrzej Paczkowski et al. (Warsaw, 2000)

Polska–ZSRR: struktury podległości: dokumenty [KC] WKP(B) 1944–1949, eds. Andrzej Paczkowski et al. (Warsaw, 1995)

Powstanie Warszawskie 1944 w dokumentach archiwów Służb specjalnych, eds. Piotr Mierecki et al., Instytut Pamięci Narodowej (Warsaw, 2007)

Przesiedlenia Polaków i Ukraińców, 1944–1946, Vol. 2, document collection prepared by Archiwum Ministerstwa Wewnetrznych I Administracja RP and Derzahvny Arkhiv Sluzby Bezpeki Ukrainii (Warsaw and Kiev, 2000)

Represje Sowieckie wobec Polaków i obywateli polskich, Ośrodek Karta (Warsaw, 2002)

Soveshania Kominforma, 1947, 1948, 1949: Dokumentii I Materialii, eds. Grant Adibekov et al. (Moscow, 1998); also published as Giuliano Procacci et al., eds., *The Cominform: Minutes of the Sovetskii faktor v Vostochnoi Evrope, 1944–1953: Dokumenty*, 2 vols., Vol. 1: *1944–1948* and Vol. 2: *1949–1953*, eds. T. V. Volokitina et al. (Moscow, 1999 and 2002)

SVAG I Religioznie Konfesii Sovetskoi Zoni Okkupatsii Germanii, 1945–1949: Sbornik Dokumentov, eds. V. V. Zakharov et al.

Szovjet nagyköveti iratok Magyarországról 1953–1956, ed. Magdolna Baráth (Budapest, 2002)

Three Conferences, 1947/1948/1949 (Milan, 1994)

Uniting Germany: Documents and Debates, 1944–1993, eds. Konrad H. Jarausch and Volker Gransow (Providence, 1994)

Uprising in East Germany, ed. Christian Ostermann (New York, 2001)

Vostochnaya Evropa v dokumentakh rossiiskikh arkhivov, 1944–1953, 2 vols., Vol. 1: *1944–1948* and Vol. 2: *1949–1953*, eds. T. V. Volokitina et al. (Novosibirsk, 1997 and 1999)

Zrzeszenie 'Wolnosc i Niezawislosc'w dokumentach, eds. Jozefa Huchlowa et al. (Wrocław, 1997)

SELECTED PERIODICALS

Berliner Zeitung
Biuletyn Instytutu Pamięci Narodowej
Gazeta Ludowa
Gazeta Wyborcza
Irodalmi Újság
Junge Welt
Karta
Kis Újság
Neues Deutschland
Polityka
Polska Zbrojna
Pravda
Przekrój
Rzeczpospolita

Spiegel, Der
Szabad Nép
Sztandar Mlodych
Tageszeitung
Tägliche Rundschau
Trybuna Ludu
Tygodnik Mazowsze
Ulenspiegel: Literatur, Kunst, Satire
Zycie Warszawy

Acknowledgements

Because this book took more than six years to research and write, because it required work in archives across Europe, and because it relies on sources written in a wide range of languages, it would not have been possible without the support, advice and assistance of an extraordinarily generous group of people and institutions. I'd like to thank, first of all, Gary Smith at the American Academy in Berlin and Mária Schmidt of the Terror Háza Múzeum and the Twentieth-Century Institute in Budapest. In Germany and Hungary they were not only my hosts, but also my primary advisers on people, sources and culture. I'd also like to thank the National Endowment for the Humanities; the Scaife Foundation; the Smith Richardson Foundation; Chris DeMuth, formerly of the American Enterprise Institute and now at the Hudson Institute; and Paul Gregory of the Hoover Institution Russia Summer Workshop, as well as Richard Sousa and Maciej Siekierski of the Hoover Institution Archive, the world's best place to study the history of communism. All of them provided generous material support for my work at different times and in different ways.

As noted in the introduction, I was helped in translation, logistics and research by two extraordinary people, Attila Mong in Budapest and Regine Wosnitza in Berlin. Both contributed immeasurably to my understanding of the history of their respective countries, as well as their respective transport systems, weather patterns and cuisine. In addition, I was aided in Warsaw at different times by Piotr Paszkowski, Lukasz Krzyzanowski and Kasia Kazimierczuk. I am extremely grateful to all of my interviewees – 'time witnesses', as they are called in Germany – who are mentioned by name in the List of Interviewees.

Among the many other historians, scholars and friends who offered advice and suggestions, I'd like to thank, in Poland, Andrzej Bielaw-ski, Władysław Bułhak, Anna Dzienkiewicz, Anna Frąckiewicz, Piotr Gontarczyk, Stanisław Juchnowicz, Krzysztof Kornacki, Wanda Kościa, Andrzej Krawczyk, Marcin Kula, Józef Mrożek, Andrzej Paczkowski, Ładysław Piasecki, Leszek Sibila, Teresa Starzec, Dariusz Stola, Andrzej Wajda, Andrzej Żak and Marein Zaremba.

In Hungary, I'd like to thank Margit Balogh, Barbara Bank, Mag-dolna Baráth, Ferenc Erős, Tibor Fabinyi, Pál Germuska, György Gyarmati, Gábor Hanák, Sándor Horváth, Sándor M. Kiss, Szilvia Köbel, Erzsébet Kozma, Sándor Ladányi, Bea Lukács, Judit Mészáros, Adrienne Molnár, Zorán Muhar, Zoltán Ólmosi, Mária Palasik, István Papp, János Pelle, Iván Pető, Attila Pók, János Rainer, István Rév, Csaba Szabó, Éva Szabó Kovács, Ferenc Tomka, Krisztián Ungváry, Balázs Varga and Márta Matussné Lendvai in Dunaújváros. Very special thanks to Tamás Stark and especially Csilla Paréj of the Terror Háza Múzeum.

In Germany, I am especially grateful to Jochen Arntz, Jörg Babe-rowski, Marianne Birthler, Zszusza Breier, Jochen Cerny, Thomas Dahnert, Reiner Eckert, Christoph Eichorn, Roger Engelmann, Eck-hart Gillen, Gisela Gneist, Manfred Götemaker, Frank Herold, Günter Höhne, Gunter Holzweißig, Dirk Jungnickel, Anna Kaminsky, Romy Kleiber, Michael Krejsa, Vera Lemke, Andreas Ludwig, Ulrich Mählert, Marko Martin, Peter Pachnicke, Christel Panzig, Ingrid Pietrzynski, Ulrike Poppe, Martin Sabrow, Helke Sander, Johanna Sänger, Dagmar Semmelmann, André Steiner and Petra Uhlmann.

Finally, I am hugely grateful for help and advice from Norman Naimark, László Borhi, Tomek Prokop , Stefano Bottoni, Hope Har-rison, Timothy Snyder, Mark Kramer, Karel Kaplan, Nikita Petrov, Anita Lackenberger, Lady Camilla Panufnik, Yaroslava Romanova, Sir Martin Gilbert and the late, and very much missed, Alexander Kokurin. For advice as well as superb hospitality, thank you, Antony Beevor, Artemis Cooper and Andrew Solomon. And, of course, this book would not have been possible at all without my superb editors, Stuart Proffitt and Kris Puopolo, and my wonderfully patient agent, Georges Borchardt.

Index

mass education in 320, 331,
335–6, 415–16
Old Town, reconstruction of
372–3
Palace of Culture and Science
323, 371–3, 391–2
and party members' privileges
413–14
political and cultural opponents
439, 442, 444, 485–6
political elections 211, 218
prisons in 294–5
public events and demonstration
in 474–6
Warsaw, battle of (1920, 'The
Miracle on the Vistula')
43–4, 156
Warsaw ghetto 198, 372
Warsaw Life: see Życie Warszawy
Warsaw Pact 485, 487
Warsaw radio stations 199
Warsaw Uprising (August–October
1944) 15, 98, 102–4, 177,
194, 281
Washington 19, 22, 128; *see also*
United States
Wasilewska, Wanda 57
Wasilewski, Eugeniusz 130
Ważyk, Adam 408–9
'Poem for Adults' (poem) 408–9
Wedding, Alex 322–3
Die Fahne des Pfeiferhansleins
322–3
Weekly Post, The: see Wochenpost
Wegener, Paul 355
Wehrmacht (German armed forces,
1935–45) 7–10, 14–15, 25,
111, 116, 127, 187–8, 312
Weigel, Helene 357
Weimar (city) 114, 116, 156,
344–5, 357

Weimar Republic (*also* Weimar
Germany, 1919–33) 188,
228, 359
Weiner, Amir 95
Weispapier, Grigorii 354
Welt, Die (West German newspaper)
189
'Werewolves' (Nazi youth battalions) 111–12, 117, 119
Weryński, Father Henryk 290
West Berlin Radio (Rundfunk im
amerikanischen Sektor, RIAS)
91, 193, 444–6, 466–7, 469–70
West German Federal Intelligence
Service (BND) 414–15
West Germany
involvement in public events 345,
349–50
rearmament of 269
West Mark (later Deutsche Mark)
269–70
see also East Germany; Germany
Western allies (*also* Allies)
entering Eastern Europe 8–9, 12,
38–9, 97, 102–3, 210
ethnic conflict and deportations
125, 133, 136, 141–2
in Germany 16, 23, 36, 164, 270,
358, 457–9
relations with Soviet Union 95,
233, 269–70
and Soviet occupation of Eastern
Europe 22, 36–7, 41, 69–70,
104–5, 112–13, 210
see also American army; British
army
Wetzel, Rudi 434–5
White, Harry Dexter 53
Wielkopolskie 129
Wilno: *see* Vilnius
Winzer, Otto 324